THE GERMANS

IN THE AMERICAN CIVIL WAR

Wilhelm Kaufmann

With a Biographical Directory

Translated by Steven Rowan
and Edited by Don Heinrich Tolzmann
with Werner D. Mueller and Robert E. Ward

JOHN KALLMANN, PUBLISHERS

701 West North St. • Carlisle, PA 17013
1999

THE GERMANS IN THE AMERICAN CIVIL WAR

John Kallmann, Publishers
701 West North Street
Carlisle, PA 17013

Front Cover Illustration: An 1861 Union recruit, engraving from *Unser Land: Geschichte der Vereinigten Staaten,* Vol. II, by Benson Lossing, New York, 1880, illustration opposite p. 1250.

Library of Congress Cataloging-in-Publication Data

Kaufmann, Wilhelm, 1847–1920.
    [Deutschen im amerikanischen Bürgerkriege. English]
    The Germans in the American Civil War : with a biographical directory / Wilhelm Kaufmann : translated by Steven Rowan : and edited by Don Heinrich Tolzmann with Werner D. Meuller and Robert E. Ward.
        p.   cm.
    Includes bibliographical references and index.
    ISBN 0-9650926-7-4 (acid free paper)—ISBN 0-9650926-8-2 (pbk. : acid free paper)
    1. United States—History—Civil War, 1861–1865—Participation, German.   2. German American soldiers—History—19th century.   3. German American soldiers Biography Directories.   4. United States—History—Civil War, 1861–1865 Registers.   I. Title.

E540.G3K213   1999
973.7′4—dc21   99-16642
                                                                                      CIP

Table of Contents

Editors' Introduction

In 1911, Wilhelm Kaufmann's *Die Deutschen im amerikanischen Buergerkrieg (The Germans in the American Civil War)* was published by R. Oldenbourg in Munich. It remains to this day the only major work that focuses exclusively on the Civil War service of America's largest ethnic group. This important historical work was translated with accuracy and precision by Steven Rowan, and then prepared for publication by an editorial team consisting of Werner D. Mueller, Don Heinrich Tolzmann, and Robert E. Ward. It was completed as a contribution to an understanding of the role German-Americans played in the American Civil War.

German-Americans (the German-born and those of German stock) formed one-third of the Union Army in the Civil War, making them a major element in the U.S. military. Nevertheless, a review of the many studies of the Civil War reveals that authors have given scant treatment to the role played by German-Americans. What little has been written on this topic, has been mainly gleaned from regimental histories, reminiscences, diaries, and biographies. References to these works can be found in a selective bibliography following this introduction.

As Kaufmann notes in his Foreword, this work represented his third revision of his history, which had been widely published in two earlier editions in more than eighty German-American newspapers. His earlier editions had also been reviewed by approximately one hundred German-American veterans of the Civil War. On the basis of this review process, Kaufmann had amassed an extensive amount of information, and had revised his text based on first-hand accounts. He also cites all the major German-American historians who had written about the Civil War. Hence, his history is one based on primary and secondary German-language sources materials. In the field of German-American Studies it has long since been considered the standard work on the topic.

Although Kaufmann's book received wide publicity in the German-American press, its untimely appearance on the eve of the First World War, made it an unlikely subject for translation. Also, within a few years, the historical achievements of the German-American element would fall victim to the anti-German sentiment and hysteria that swept the land during and after the war. As a result the teaching of German was banned in twenty-six states, German books and newspapers were burned and destroyed, and German-Americans suffered in numerous ways for no reason other than their German heritage. Although interest in German-American history began to rise in the 1930s, it again subsided with the outbreak of World War II. It has only been since the celebration of the American Bicentennial in 1976 that interest in the German heritage has substantially increased, and that German-American Studies has emerged as an academic field.

Kaufmann's Career

Wilhelm Kaufmann, too, suffered the indignities brought on by those who promoted prejudice and hatred towards all things German. When World War I broke out, he was attending to business interests in Dresden. Although a naturalized American citizen, U.S.

authorities prohibited his return to his adopted country because his daughters were married to Germans and his son had been drafted into the German Army. In addition, federal authorities confiscated Kaufmann's property in Cleveland, Ohio, where he had lived for more than a quarter century. Possibly because of his shocking experience, he suffered a heart attack in Copenhagen. After recuperating, he had to return to Dresden, where he lived out his remaining years in despair. He died there on 18 May 1920, four months after his 73rd birthday.

Born in Muenden, Hannover, Kaufmann was 21 years old when he immigrated to America in 1868. After working at various jobs in St. Louis, he found employment as the editor of local news for a German-American newspaper. He then accepted a position as reporter, and later as local news editor of the *Cincinnati Volksblatt*. Subsequently, he became editor for the *Cincinnati Courier*. During his Cincinnati years, Kaufmann became acquainted with several Forty-Eighters, as the political emigres of the 1848 Revolutions in the German states were known. Among them were Friedrich Hassaurek and Carl Schurz, who provided Kaufmann with information on the Civil War. Before his move to Cleveland, Kaufmann had risen to prominence as a German-American civic leader.

In 1877, he moved to Cleveland, where he bought the failing *Cleveland Anzeiger* and began its reorganization as a publication of the German Press & Plate Company. Within a few years, it became one of Ohio's leading German-American Republican newspapers. To place it on a sound financial basis, he had reduced the staff and had taken over the responsibility of writing feature articles, searching out local news, proofreading, and acting as business manager. Kaufmann's venture soon became quite successful, and within a short period of time, he had won contracts from several German-American newspapers whose editions also began rolling off his presses.

By the mid-1880s, he had become a major political force in Cleveland, known throughout the Midwest as a leading German-American journalist. During the Presidential campaign of Republican candidate Blaine, Kaufmann served the Cleveland district as a member of the state nominating committee. During his years in Cleveland, he developed a close working relationship with Forty-Eighters Jacob Mueller, Louis Ritter, and Heinrich Rochette, who, in 1852, had founded the city's second German newspaper, *Der Waechter am Erie*. It endorsed Frémont in 1856, Lincoln in 1860, and the Emancipation Proclamation in 1862.

In 1889, Kaufmann began efforts to effect a consolidation of his newspaper with the *Waechter am Erie* to form the new *Waechter und Anzeiger*. The consolidation was finalized four years later. Known as one of the major newspapers of Cleveland, the *Waechter und Anzeiger* continued for many years into the 20th century as one of the most influential German-American newspapers of the country.

In 1903, Carl Raid, the editor of the *Waechter und Anzeiger,* published Kaufmann's travel descriptions *(Streifzuege durch Deutschland, Baiern und die Rheinpfalz)* in book-form. A year later, Raid also published Kaufmann's book *Wanderungen durch die Schweiz,* a 156 page paperback that was distributed without charge to public school children in Cleveland. Several years earlier, Kaufmann had begun publishing his history of the Germans in the Civil War. Much of it originally had appeared in serial form in numerous German-American newspapers across the country. This series became the foundation for his book, which, almost nine decades later, is available once again by means of this edition.

Influence of the Forty-Eighters

In a section on the Forty-Eighters, Kaufmann cites Jacob Mueller's book, *Erinnerungen eines Achtundvierzigers,* and throughout his own book, Kaufmann reveals that he shared the values that propelled the Forty-Eighters' strong commitment to the Union cause. Perhaps that is why he opens with his rash statement: "While the native-born Americans and the members of all other immigrant peoples split into two hostile camps, we find Germans only on the side of the Union." However, in later sections of this book, he describes, sometimes apologetically, the role of Germans who fought for the Confederacy. Moreover, his biographical directory contains information on German-American Confederate officers.

Kaufmann recognized that the Forty-Eighters provided ethnic leadership at the national, state, and local levels. It was largely due to their efforts that German-Americans gained national political influence. The result was the creation of a political phenomenon known as "the German vote" that by all accounts, became a pivotally crucial element of Lincoln's narrow victory over Stephen Douglas in 1860. German-American support for the Republican Party remained relatively stable force in the coalition that backed the Union cause throughout the Civil War.

Previously, many Forty-Eighters had flirted with utopian schemes, and by their own accounts were at first "politically immature." However, in 1856, the birth of the new Republican Party led by Frémont provided a focus and an outlet for their reformist zeal that was practical as well as idealistic. Frémont's "free soil" strategy of containing slavery geographically and politically until it withered away was well received by most leaders of the Forty-Eighters. They abhorred the institution of slavery as even more oppressive and hateful than the Metternich-inspired system of censorship, espionage, and persecution they had fought to overcome in Europe.

That Kaufmann shared the Forty-Eighters' strong aversion to slavery is evident throughout his work. To construct a viable backdrop for this theme, he devotes considerable space to the historical development of slavery and the treatment of slaves from the early colonial period to Reconstruction. His inclusion of the article in the appendix on Franz Daniel Pastorius and the Germantown settlers who, in 1688, issued the first protest against slavery in America, reminds the reader that German-Americans were among the first to support human rights.

Frémont and the new Republican Party repudiated nativist hostility towards immigrants, and instead treated them with respect. Hence, in backing the new Republican Party, Forty-Eighters could fight effectively both against nativist insults and for containment of the hated institution of slavery. When Buchanan, the Democratic candidate defeated Frémont in 1856, the Forty-Eighters were spoiling for a fight in the presidential election of 1860. German-American newspapers, including Cleveland's *Waechter am Erie,* founded by Forty-Eighters, trumpeted the cause of "free soil" Republicans. Carl Schurz delivered fiery speeches on behalf of Lincoln from Minnesota to Massachusetts, while his Forty-Eighter friends, such as Jacob Mueller of Cleveland, did the same from Cleveland to the rural outposts of northeastern Ohio.

Although many Forty-Eighters knew Seward, Frémont, and Chase better than they knew the "rail splitter," and many may have preferred one of them to Lincoln, almost all celebrated the victory of Lincoln over Senator Douglas, the Democrat who had promoted the Kansas-Nebraska Bill. They had respected Douglas' sincere attempts to unite his party and find a peaceful solution to the issue of slavery's expansion into western territories. However, most of them disagreed with his plan as it was embodied in the Kansas-Nebraska Act of 1854. They saw its provision on "squatters' sovereignty" and the repeal of the Missouri Compromise as yielding to the "southern barons."

When the Civil War broke out in 1861, Forty-Eighters and their sons of the next generation volunteered in large numbers to fight under President Lincoln for the Union cause. Many attained ranks from Captain to Brigadier-General. Forty-Eighter Carl Schurz served as Brigadier-General of Volunteers, and commanded troops in the Second Battle of Bull Run, Chancellorsville, and Gettysburg.

Forty-Eighter Jacob Mueller in his biographical work, summed up the influence of the Forty-Eighters by observing that "the most precious value which they saved and brought with them was their idealism," reminding his German-American readers that their "compatriots in America have a great past," and a continuing duty "to maintain the freedoms of America . . ."

For the Reader

Kaufmann states in his Foreword that he did not start compiling his biographical directory until a few years before his history was published, and his comments indicate that he laid no claim to completeness when listing the high ranking officers and Medal of Honor recipients. He also points out that he relied on several persons for much of his information. It is, therefore, possible that some inaccuracies with regard to spelling and dates would find their way into the work, and the editors would welcome any corrections, or additions, in this regard.

Editors' Preface

The American Civil War has often been referred to as a defining moment in American history. The role played by the various groups making up the American mosaic of the 1860's certainly represents an important factor in that "defining moment." The purpose of this work is to illuminate the role played by German-Americans by means of this translated edition of a history of the topic by Wilhelm Kaufmann.

Originally published in German in 1911, this work has long since been considered the standard work on the topic. A special value of the work was that its author knew, or corresponded with many German-American Civil War veterans, and that this work had appeared in two previous editions in the German-American press, and had been widely screened and reviewed by German-Americans, many of whom, of course, were veterans of the Civil War. Based on their comments and critiques, Kaufmann polished and re-worked the text for many years.

Finally, he decided to bring his work out in book-form. Kaufmann's history is, hence, a German-American history directly based on extensive use of primary sources, and one which had been widely reviewed by German-Americans. Another special value to the work is that it contains a biographical directory of German-American officers who fought for the North, as well as the South. Hence, this is a work which will be of great value to all those interested in the Civil War, and especially those interested in the role German-Americans played in it.

Author's Foreword

The history of the Germans in the Civil War is territory as yet completely untrod. To be sure, several notable researchers busied themselves with the topic shortly after the war, but none of these plans advanced beyond the first stages. General von Schimmelpfennig died trying, Kapp became hostile to America, and Dilger's carefully gathered materials burned up, and so on. Later the view spread that because of the wide scattering of German soldiers through the entire Union army, only a partial completion of the task was possible, and one would only be able to write a fragment of German war history. But is it proper that the finest individual deeds of our people should fall into oblivion due to this certainly overestimated hindrance?

Should the fact that the German-born Union soldiers (216,000 men) could not be united into great army corps cause us to overlook the other major fact, which is that our people were the most loyal of all to the Union? To give in would mean to renounce telling the most significant period of German-American history. Further, it constitutes quite an imposing portion of German military accomplishments, by which one is often reminded that it was the brothers of the victors of Düppel, Königgrätz, and Sedan who fought on American soil.

No event cut so deeply into the life of the German-American people as the struggle for the Union, and our compatriots never appeared in such harmony as during this great time. This unity granted them an exceptional position. While the native-born Americans and the members of all other immigrant peoples split into two hostile camps, we find Germans *only* on the side of the Union.[1] Among them there were virtually no promoters of secession, just as there had been virtually no German slaveowners. They supplied significantly more soldiers than any other element of the people, more than *twice* their share. Further, the Germans stood in their finest flower in the decade from 1855 to 1865. The German immigrant population was already imposing just as a mass, for in those days it was relatively as strong as in the later apex of immigration. But its strength rested particularly in the education and culture represented in its ranks, in the idealism that then permeated it, in the sense of liberty that prevailed down to the lowest population level. Germans never stood under better leadership than in that time, and it is sure that they were never more capable of bearing the demands placed on their loyalty at any other period of their time in America. Simply to demonstrate this fact would be a worthy undertaking and would be a welcomed contribution to the general history of the German people.

1

But even more important reasons speak for a German portrayal of that time. Among the innumerable English-language histories of the war, works are seldom encountered that give our compatriots their just due, such as Hamlin's fine work on Chancellorsville; but slanders and hateful attacks are often made. The sole rebuttal to this is a narration of the genuine German deeds of war. Further, the history of the war has a great impact on the general cultural history of North America, and the history of immigration will be particularly influenced by it. It will not suffice to cover this important part of American cultural history with some statistical tables, or to judge the development of the American people solely according to the accomplishments of its Anglo-Saxon portion. One is permitted to look forward to the appearance in the near future of a great cultural history on North America that deals with matters in a less one-sided manner than has been the case to date. German Americans should prepare building blocks for this future work, for they alone can prepare the material for the history of the German element of the American people, an element that accounts for little less in number than the Anglo-Saxons.

That has already happened for earlier German-American history. The fine particular narratives by Gustav Körner, Kapp, Rattermann, Seidensticker, more recently the works of Deiler, Mannhardt, Bruncken, Löhr, and particularly the researches of Learned, "the German Yankee," can be welcome building blocks for the later cultural historian. But the more recent cultural history of our people has hardly been touched by research. Whether the present book has succeeded in filling one of those gaps must be passed over for now. I see my mission as consisting essentially of making a previously unopened way to some extent passable, of saving material that can still be reached now but that will be hard to collect even ten years from now. Much remains to be done, and any new researcher will surely be bequeathed a fine area for research.

*　　*　　*

The literature I have used is mentioned at the corresponding places. The contemporary German-American press was less used as a source. It dealt with the events of the war in such a way that it unfortunately had rather little to say about the participation of Germans. Also, in those days the reporting service of the newspapers was still very modest. Rather thorough samples were taken from old volumes, but wading through these dusty folios had to be renounced. Still, my coworkers gathered many newspaper clippings, so that source was often drawn upon. More use was made of the correspondence written by O. von Corwin and "F. A." (surely Fritz Anneke) for the *Augsburger Allgemeine Zeitung*. It is obvious that I used the speeches and writings of our fine compatriot Vocke in Chicago and the book by Rosengarten, *The Germans in the Wars of the United States* (although only for the regimental histories). Quite a sizable German periodical literature, mostly from participants, was also gone through, insofar as it has not disappeared. The unforgettable Schurz left us the best narrative concerning the Germans in the Civil War. It is just too bad that it appears in the setting of his autobiography, which hindered him from being more thorough.

The greater part of the material used here is thanks to my coworkers. Much of it was passed orally, particularly from Generals Osterhaus and Stahel, former Governor Salomon of Wisconsin, and the journalists Louis F. Korth in Portsmouth, Ohio, and Ernst Schierenberg. I am particularly indebted to these true collaborators, whom Gallus Thomann from New York joined at the end with the great treasure of his knowledge and experience. Much material came from the war diaries, printed and hand-written regimental histories, and letters of long-dead participants, as well as scrap-books, mostly filled with newspaper clippings. A series of manuscript commentaries on the war from the estates of German officers was also used.

A directory of such sources would have burdened this book beyond measure. Proof that adequate care has been taken with this material is shown by the fact that this is the *third* reworking of the material. Even at the time of preparation, it became obvious that the material could not be mastered without a host of collaborators. For that reason I wrote a rather thorough sketch on the basis of what I knew at the time, and I sent this work as a printed manuscript to about a hundred former officers of the Civil War, as well as a large number of German-America historians and journalists befriended by me. The echo was positive beyond all expectations. Massive new material flowed in, many errors of the preliminary version were corrected, and a complete reformation of the work proved necessary. This second version was published in the summer of 1908 in more than eighty German-American newspapers, including a number of the most important Western newspapers. The project won many new friends through this publication, and the number of my collaborators gradually grew to over two hundred. What had originally been a rescue mission proved to be very fruitful indeed. Through the phased progress of the project, collaborators gained an overview of the material gathered, and this stimulated them to detailed investigations. Even before the publication of the present third version, many points in dispute could be settled among those men, whom one must see as the best connoisseurs of the material. All of these collaborators are here most heartily thanked.

The actual history of the war will be treated here only in its main contours, and only insofar as it appears necessary in conjunction with the presence of Germans. For that reason much more room is given to the struggles for Missouri than the last great battles between Grant and Lee. Despite that, the course of the war in the main theaters, in Virginia and the West, can be pursued with some precision. Every important battle finds a description here, even if necessarily in the briefest form possible. In the interest of the reader, I held it proper to make some brief references to matters dealt with earlier, because orientation in this war, dragging out over four years, is so extraordinarily difficult. All conflicts in which purely German regiments participated, or in which German leaders played a particular role, are thoroughly described. As far as possible, these descriptions are based on the official reports of the German officers participating, or on their own narratives in the specialized press. This is particularly the case with those battles in which General Sigel participated. On the other hand, actions entirely outside the two major theaters, such as the war at sea, the blockade, the Red River Campaign, the conflict in the Carolinas, the irregular campaigns, and the guerilla war, are excluded as not being in *our* area of obligation.

Placed before the main part of this book is a condensed portrayal of the causes of the war, the historical development of the slavery question and secession, and the significance of immigration in the final victory of the North, as well as a portrayal of the character of Lincoln. In the chapter "The War in General," I have attempted to stress those points that seem most suited to introduce the reader to the milieu of the war.

I am afraid that the biographical portion might seem much too thorough to readers in Germany. In opposition to this, it should be said that to American readers this portion will appear much too limited. These portrayals were once intended only for German America. I have kept them in the book because I wanted to say something at least about the German officers of the 180,000 Germans who fought in mixed regiments. The biographical portion also presents a great deal of material that could not be presented anywhere else. Further, it cannot be uninteresting to learn the American destiny of more than five hundred highly educated Germans. Many an interesting character appears to us in this collection. And we owe whatever small literary monument can still be dedicated here to those German men who risked goods and blood for the preservation of the Union. To be truthful, they received little enough recognition for their fine efforts while they lived.

Wilhelm Kaufmann

I

The Preliminaries

The Causes of the Civil War - Cultural History of the Two Sections - Historical
Development of the Salvery Conflict - Secession - The Consequences of the War -Lincoln

The Causes of the Civil War

The American Civil War was the most severe visitation ever to strike a cultivated people in the modern era. More than half a million human lives were demanded by this self-mutilation, and the costs of the war ran to ten times the cost of the war reparations paid by France to Germany [after the Franco-Prussian War][2]. This sacrifice of money and blood was made by a single people who numbered only 32 million in 1860, including 4.5 million Negroes.

Around the turn of 1861 eleven Southern states declared their withdrawal from the old association and immediately formed a republic of their own under the name of the Confederate States of America. At the same time preparations for war began in the entire region of secession, associated with attacks that would have been seen as open hostilities by any European state. The North showed astonishing moderation toward these efforts, which continued for weeks after President Lincoln took up his new office on 4 March 1861. At the start Lincoln renounced any arming. He even neglected to provide military protection corresponding to its peril for the federal capital of Washington, located precisely on the border between the South and the North. He was still seeking a peaceful resolution with moving zeal long after almost every other had assigned these hopes to the realm of dreams. In its efforts for peace and concession, the North went to the extreme limits of what a self-respecting state could do. The South was the party that went on the attack with full intent, while the North was always the restrained party, ready for compromise and willing to sacrifice.

The question concerning the causes of the Civil War is generally met with the answer, "The cause is to be sought in Negro slavery." That is true, as far as regards the position of the Confederates. Before and during the war, in solemn public declarations, in thousandfold

5

statements of its leading men, in word and deed, the Confederacy demonstrated that this passage of arms was only intended to render Negro slavery perpetual. But this does not mean that the North drew its sword for the *liberation* of the slaves. This view is indeed still widespread in the United States, and it appears necessary to point out that it is fundamentally false, particularly because it contains a severe accusation against the Northern people. It is entirely incorrect that one of the noblest and most progressive peoples on earth would have reached for the most barbaric of means to free itself from slavery, while the retarded peoples of Central and South America eliminated this evil through peaceful means. Two and a half million Northerners did not commit themselves to the battlefield for the ideal of the author of *Uncle Tom's Cabin*. Those patriots did not pass through storms of blood and ruin to loosen slaves' bonds. Rather they fought for the *preservation* of the Union in its total power and size. And to be sure, that is an even more praiseworthy ideal than that of freeing the slaves. President Lincoln was the one who stated the position of the North in the war question most tellingly. When he was asked by Horace Greeley in the middle of the war, in 1862, to decree the abolition of slavery as a necessary measure of war, the president responded:

> I was not elected to abolish slavery, but rather I stand on the foundation of the Constitution, which recognizes slavery. It is my duty to preserve the Union undivided. If the abolition of slavery is necessary to do this, it will be abolished, but if the preservation of the Union requires the continuation of slavery, that is what will happen.

This declaration agrees with a similar one that Lincoln made in the most solemn manner in his inaugural address as President.

*   *   *

One could assert that the war would never have arisen over the issue of slavery as it existed in the South in 1860. The slave question was first called up by things that lay outside the area of the politically effective forces, things which came into combination with the cultural development of North America and *only then* conjured up the perils of war. For that reason, the first battlefields of the war of brothers is not to be sought on the Potomac or the *state* of Missouri, but rather in the *central* course of the great Missouri River, in the virgin *new land* of the northern West.

This undeveloped region was roughly equal in size to half of Europe. This new land was properly the common heritage of all citizens of the Union, whether they wished to work the soil themselves or to have this work done by purchased Negroes. So the slave-owners claimed the right to flood the Northwest with their servants and to *expand* slavery to this new land. The free citizens of the North could not concede to this desire, and this conflict of interest is the *cause of the entire conflict*. Incidentally, slaveowners had already agreed to establish a frontier between *free soil* and the *region of slavery* in 1820. Later, however, from about 1845 on, they no longer wished to recognize this border.

If this new land were later to be partitioned into many free states, it would be difficult to preserve slavery in the old Southern states. This fear was the strongest goad for the pressure to expand slavery. According to the views of the barons, the entire region of the United States should be equally divided into slave and free states.[3] But the climate of the Northwest prevented plantations in that region. The barons refused to recognize this iron law with a determination and stubbornness that so often appear in purely agrarian peoples, and they insisted on their right to form slave states in that northern area and to work alongside white small farmers. That was entirely impossible, however, as the example of the old slave states showed, for the plantation economy with slaves is the irreconcilable enemy of free labor. Small farmers are pitilessly driven out by the presence of slave barons or debased into a proletariat.

Slaveowners are blind to all these things, or they at least say that they are, and in the erection of a border between free soil and slavery they always saw the bad will and self-interest of their Northern brothers, who wished to deny them their common heritage. What they held to be greed and bad will was only the expression of a healthy instinct of the Northern people at the outset, the barely expressed desire to preserve that new land to their descendents as free soil in the interest of the whole of the country. During the long duration of those political struggles this desire grew, being recognized ever more as a necessity, even as a holy duty. In the struggle for Kansas from about 1850 on, we see the North asserting itself with conscious decisiveness for the rights of later generations.

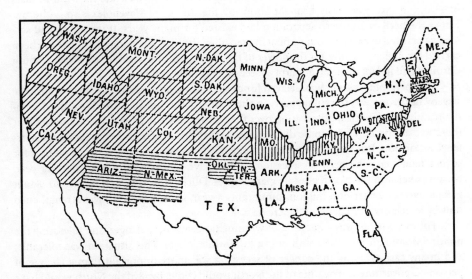

Figure 1. The eastern half of this map shows the region organized as individual states in 1860. The free states of the North and the slave states of the South appear in white. Between the two groups are the border states, in vertical stripes. The western half shows the new lands, essentially unsettled as yet. The hinterland of the North is marked with slanted stripes, and the hinterland of the South in horizontal stripes. The states later erected on this territory are marked here in advance.

The first great blow against the slaveowners came from the farthest West. The barons believed it would be very easy to introduce slavery in California, but the new gold state opted as early as 1849 for free soil, and the free soil movement made steady progress in the regions of Kansas and Nebraska, moving toward statehood. In the free North there arose a powerful new political party, in which the barons thought they saw the sworn enemy of their efforts. Perhaps ten new states would be erected in the next generation in this western region, which would fall into the sphere of influence of the North. The Western hinterland of the Southern states, on the other hand, was then regarded as a desert rather hopeless for development, which would eventually lead to the formation of three states with slavery. The result was that the North would soon have such an increase of power that the continuation of slavery would be seriously threatened in the old Southern states. The leading circles of Southerners saw slavery to be the first and sole condition for the life of their region. They decided to leave the Union in order to protect this institution completely against future attacks.

*   *   *

The demand for withdrawal by the eleven cotton states in 1860 was, by the way, nothing at all new. The specter of secession had haunted the history of the young nation for more than seventy years, since the foundation of the Union. It already appeared in 1787 at the time of discussions on the Constitution, and it raised its head at the creation of every new western state. Until 1860 the North always shrank before this specter, and the compromises of 1820 and 1850 were only brought about by the threats of slaveholders to withdraw. Hence the peril of Southern separation had existed for many years. If the South had seriously persisted in carrying out its plan in 1840, then the division would perhaps have been carried through peacefully, for the power of the two regions was then little different. South Carolina had in fact made an attempt at secession as early as 1830.[4]

The peril of secession was delayed for decades for many reasons, in part because the slaveowner group was the ruling party in the United States until 1860 and practiced a virtually unbroken political domination over the North. This was in part due to the fact that there was always new land to be distributed, so that the slavery area could always experience expansion. It is also not easy for a ruling party to present the necessary excuses for such a fatal step. The peril of secession should have reduced with every passing year, because after 1830 the North grew by giant strides. During the period from 1840 to 1860 it gained over a quarter of a million immigrants a year, while the South was strengthened only by its relatively small natural increase.

For the North it was a question of winning time, avoiding danger, and tolerating the political domination of the South only a little while longer. This situation was tolerable, and in any case avoiding the danger of secession was more important than a change of persons in government. The time of the North would come. By 1870 the North would have had more than a fivefold superiority over the South if it could just have a decade of peaceful development. It is an open question whether the hot blooded aristocrats of the South would have dared the dance then. Probably they would have agreed to the dissolution of slavery, if with gnashing of teeth, particularly if the North had paid about three-quarters of the vast sum of $2.5 billion [to free the slaves]. The North was always ready for such a sacrifice.

The Southerners never showed any understanding for the high cultural value of immigration. They believed that they could leave the "refuse of Europe" to the North with a clear conscience. And because immigrants usually joined the Democratic Party, the political power of slaveowners was at first increased by immigration, for the Northern wing of the Democratic Party never showed anti-slavery tendencies.[5]

* * *

It should be recalled that the Northern people was actually quite indifferent to the slavery question until 1850. To be sure, the tiny party of abolitionists continually agitated against slaveowners, but they gained no ground.[6] The mass of Northerners considered abolitionists to be fanatics who excited themselves quite unnecessarily about a matter that could be placidly left to time. To the North in that period, the region possessed by slavery appeared to be something of a distant, foreign country. The Yankee, pursuing his own business, was little concerned that Negroes were being whipped and sold "down there." And again, in the North virtually nothing concerning slavery was ever *seen*.

Then the slavery question was suddenly brought before the eyes of the Northern people, but only due to the intolerable lust of the slaveowners to dominate. As a result of the Compromise of 1850, the fugitive slave law was decreed, which under high penalties compelled every free man of the North to act as a bailiff for the slaveowners. The Negro, even the Negro long since free, no longer had any asylum in the North. He had to be delivered at once to the South on demand. Through the entirely unnecessary harshness of this law, many Northerners were involved in legal proceedings. The sentiment of compassion was also awakened in the North for the Negroes, hitherto rather generally treated with contempt. The novel of [Harriett] Beecher Stowe that appeared at that time, *Uncle Tom's Cabin,* also had a considerable impact on the change of opinion in the North. It was finally seen that the slavery question also concerned the North. The change of opinion in the North was significantly raised by the efforts of slaveholders to impose slavery on the new Northern territory of Kansas. Because the federal government had a role in this, many of the best and most capable men of the North said, "We cannot tolerate any longer the majority position of the South. We must create a *new political party* that would at least create equality for the North in the administration of federal concerns." Thus the Republican Party was founded in the summer of 1854.

A party arising from such sources, at whose erection awareness of the great political power of the North played a significant role, had to become exclusively a party of Northerners. Its birth certificate signified a great deal more than its rather tame platform. This platform sought only to prevent the future expansion of slavery to the North and to make Kansas and Nebraska into free soil, but not to disturb slavery itself. Still, the founding of the Republican Party marked a turning point from the previous politics of playing for time to overcome the danger of secession gradually. A people that is not organized can easily accept excessive privileges, because millions of shoulders bear the burden; but a *party* must fight in order to live. Hence the Republican Party either had to capitulate or had to take a strong stand for the election of its designated presidential candidate. It did the latter two years after its foundation. In 1856, 1,341,000 Northern citizens voted for the first Republican presidential candidate, Frémont. That was an enormous success, unique in the history of American political parties. To be sure, Frémont's Democratic opponent, the Pennsylvanian Buchanan, was still elected president, and the slaveowners remained in the government until 4 March 1861. But everyone had to say that the future belonged to the Republican Party.

The slaveowners, who had never been opposed by a solid organization of the North, looked on the new party as a declaration of war. They did not want to see that they had contributed considerably to founding this party themselves by imposing the slavery question on the North. In their own opinion, thirty years of abolitionist agitation had called the Republican Party into life. Hence the Republicans were typified by Southerners as abolitionists operating under another name. According to this interpretation, the Republican Party had no other desire than to assault the "hallowed privileges of the South, protected by the Constitution." It was not necessary to tell these hot blooded gentlemen that an assault is the best parade. They at once oriented themselves to attack, and from the autumn of 1856, preparations were under way for the secession that would follow in four years. The word was passed: "Out of the Union as soon as a president is elected from the Republican Party."

The next election took place on 6 November 1860, and Abraham Lincoln, candidate of the Republican Party, was elected president of the United States. This happened only because the old victorious Democratic Party had split into two groups, and because yet a third candidate had appeared. Lincoln won because he was opposed by three other candidates. This splintering of Lincoln's opponents was brought about by the slaveowners in order to elect Lincoln and provide the excuse for rebellion.[7] Lincoln was elected as a minority president, for three-fifths of the eligible citizens had voted against him. South Carolina seceded the day after this election.[8]

Incidentally, slaveowners never made a secret of the fact that they wanted to secede after Lincoln's election. This threat sounds through each of their election speeches and found its echo in every newspaper serving Southern interests. There was no lack of men in the North who were convinced of the seriousness of the threat. But the Republican Party did not want to know anything about it. The strivers and opportunists who rush to any party with a future already had a major influence in the party leadership, and for these people it was simply a matter of offices to be distributed in case of victory. Many idealists also placed themselves on the side of those "practical men." "That is the old specter we have known for seventy years," they said. "It is unworthy for the Republican Party to shrink back. Those threats, too, are entirely baseless, for we do not wish to abolish slavery, and we could not do it even if we wanted to do it."

*   *   *

It would have been in the interest of peace if history knew Lincoln only as one of the many defeated candidates for president. The gain of only four years would perhaps have sufficed to lay the specter of secession to rest, for precisely those years, 1861 to 1865, promised extraordinarily rich, brilliant development for the North.

It was in this time that the seed was cast whose harvest was the astonishing expansion of culture for which the concept of the "land of unlimited possibilities" was coined. Until 1860 the strength of the North still lay largely in a free farmer class. The grand gifts of nature that lay beneath the plowed land, namely iron ore, petroleum, and natural gas; the fortunate distribution of this rich treasury throughout the entire broad North; the possibility that it gave for the development of industry was discovered precisely around this time and began to be developed. The great campaign of development that we call the opening of the American West was in mid-course. The entire energy of the Northern people was involved in the mission of winning ever more new land from the Western wilderness, establishing ever more homesteads, carrying culture ever farther westward across the almost endless prairies which had been the playground of buffalo and Indians for time immemorial. This expansion of the Americans through the West received a sharp spur from auxiliary troops from Europe, the immigrant Germans, whose hunger for land was no less than that of Anglo-Americans.

Around 1860 the foundations had already been laid for a rapid development of industry. The means of transport had dramatically advanced. Sailing ships had just been replaced on the world s seas by the steamer, and great fleets of steamships had long traveled on America's great rivers. The net of railroads already extended beyond the Mississippi, and the construction of the first cross-country route to California was already underway. The first trans-Atlantic cable, planned by the American Field, was about to be laid. In 1861 one could already telegraph from New York to San Francisco, a distance of 7000 kilometers. Today that seems something ordinary, but what this meant in a time that was still in the infancy stage in using steam and electricity! The great cities of the West boomed. St. Louis and Cincinnati already approached 200,000 residents, and in Chicago, where Fort Dearborn recalled the recently ended struggles with the redskins, a city was created that would exceed two million persons in fifty years. Thus in 1860 all preconditions were present for a fabulous development.

What blessings would those four years have given the North if they had been years of peace! All it required was the survival of the old régime. Without the sought-after excuse, without the election of Lincoln, the South could not have rebelled. The ruling party, the cotton barons, would still have been compelled to keep the peace, because under a new president who could not be regarded as the enemy of the slave interests, the mass of the Southern people would not have been able to be enticed into rebellion. The secession could not have been carried out by officers alone; the mass of the people had to be won for it. Whoever considers the hesitation and delay with which the more northerly Southern states, and even Georgia, entered the Confederacy, will not be able to avoid the conviction that without that excuse, without Lincoln the boogeyman, a unanimous decision by the eleven cotton states to associate would have been impossible.

* * *

Justice demands that the point of view of the Southerners concerning secession must be described. What could be said on this in general will be found in the chapter, "Historical Development of the Slavery Question." Here only a few things that influenced the *acute* development of the old struggle will be roughed in:

I. A full measure of envy lay behind the contempt with which the South always treated the immigrants streaming into the North. The North grew so astoundingly rapidly and extensively that even a blind man could see it. The thought could not be suppressed that if Southerners were going to get loose, then they must hurry.

II. A *fata morgana* had blinded the Southerners. They dreamed of a world empire they could construct from a later conquest of Mexico and the small Central American republics along with Venezuela, Colombia, and the Spanish Antilles. The entire Gulf of Mexico, with the weakling states bordering it, would become the domain of the Southern Confederacy. And the importation of slaves from Africa was to be reintroduced.[9]

III. The Confederates entirely expected an alliance with England, for that country relied on the undisturbed exportation of cotton from America. It would have to stop a blockade of Southern ports, and it was believed that this would lead to a war between England and the Union. The fact that these dreams and secret wishes contributed a great deal to the ripening of the decision to secede can be assumed with great certainty. A number of other causes essentially promoted the decision to secede, derived in part from an interpretation of the Constitution or, like the Brown affair, arose from an unfortunate, untimely accident. This part of the manifold causes of the rebellion is particularly important, for it gives the Southern people some justification for the blindness of secession.

IV. The South believed itself to be within its rights when it demanded withdrawal from the Union. It supported itself on the Constitution, which leaves it unclear whether the Union is to be seen as a federal state or a federation of states. Each individual state had possessed sovereign rights before its entry into the Union, and there was no statement in the Constitution that these old rights were lost through entering the Union. The best expert on the Constitution, the German researcher H. von Holst,[10] calls the Constitution "an interweaving of state-federation content with federal-state wrapping." Many of the most significant authorities of America, including Jefferson and Madison, went so far as to concede to individual states of the Union the right to nullify (make invalid within their borders) laws of Congress that appeared to them to be infringing or unjust. Even the withdrawal of the individual state from the federation was recognized as a right in these rulings.

Because the statesmen who represented this standpoint almost all came from the South, this view of the continuing sovereignty of individual states took solid root particularly in the South, but this view also had a strong following in the North. The Democratic Party especially stood for states' rights, and when one recalls that in 1860, 1,280,000 Northerners still voted Democratic against 1,831,000 Northerners voting Republican, it is uncertain whether a majority of the American people saw in the Union a league of states. But it does show that this interpretation of the Constitution was *very* widespread.

V. From the viewpoint of the Southerners, withdrawal from this group of states would take place as peacefully as had the entry, for the remnant of the Union did not possess the constitutional right to compel states desiring to withdraw to remain in the Union.[11] There could thus be no war.[12] If the South had grasped that civil war would be the result of its demand, it would certainly never have carried out its idea of secession, nor would the people of the North ever have elected Lincoln if they knew that this deed would be the pretext for an attempt to secede. No one in the North wanted war, and even in the South the number of hotspurs who believed in the possibility of a war and did not shrink from it in horror was extremely small. They drove toward war without their contemporaries' being really conscious of how that could happen.

VI. A considerable extenuation for judging secession is to be found in the fact that the South was extremely agitated over the coup of the fanatic John Brown in the autumn of 1859.[13] This attempt to free Negro slaves cannot be judged by the impressions it excites today; rather, we must see it in the context of the views of that time of passionate excitement in order to comprehend the effect Brown's assault would have on the South.

The slaveowners, who were even then planning secession, saw Brown as the executor of the will and the secret intent of the Northern people. This entirely groundless suspicion received considerable reinforcement as a result of the taking of sides by many in the North, who made Brown into a martyr. But this taking sides was not a result of Brown's attack on Harpers Ferry; rather it was a result of the worthy appearance of the old Puritan before his judges. The moving drama of his trial caused the misdeeds of the accused to fall entirely into the background. Brown became his judges' accuser, and what he created by doing this found an echo in the hearts of many Northerners who had become opponents of slavery only as a result of the struggles for Kansas. The fact that Brown threw a torch into long-heaped explosives can be conceded without discussion. Without this unfortunate accident it certainly would have been possible to avoid the catastrophe and convince the South that the house built by Washington and his contempories could guarantee all Americans peaceful homes and brotherly cooperation.

Cultural History of the Two Sections

In order to gain a deeper insight into the causes of the Civil War it will be necessary to pursue the entire peculiar development of the South under the impact of slavery.

The two regions of the Union divided roughly by the southern border of Pennsylvania, Ohio and Indiana have taken entirely different paths almost since the first settlement of North America. One might as well assume that Germany and Russia could have been brought under a common administration. The difference between the theoretical regions in such a case could hardly be larger than the actual difference between two halves of the United States.

This situation was not created artificially; rather, it is the result of historical development going back almost a quarter of a millennium. In the North there was a hard-working people without slaves, filled with ideals of progress and liberty, but in the South a white people of the same sort had become work-shy and retarded under the results of slavery. One could even say that they had become slaves of slavery. The Northerner could extend himself to all the areas of culture without restriction, as an independent farmer, in crafts, in trade, in industry, in maritime life, and in the free arts. The rich land and democratic institutions guaranteed to everyone willing to work the broadest area of activity. But in the South, industry existed only in name, large-scale trade was quite insignificant, and crafts were in decay because this branch of activity competed with slave labor. In short, everything in the South was cut to the interests of the plantation, and the general culture of the region rested on imported human working beasts, Africans, treated as things and reduced to articles of commerce.

In the North, compulsory schooling dominated, as well as a free school system that stood open free of charge to everyone desiring learning, even including what is called high schools. In addition there were free trade schools, taking pupils of all ages, and other means of training such as public libraries; there was a broad free press not yet "yellow," and there were extensively frequented expositions of political questions in public lectures. In the South, in contrast, public schools were widely neglected, the number of white illiterates was terrifyingly large, press and pulpit represented only the opinions of the slave barons, and there was a complete lack of other means of training that stood available to the

Northerner. Whoever taught a Negro was tarred and feathered and displayed for public ridicule. Higher institutions of learning, colleges and universities, were available only to the children of the wealthy, for the lower population neither possessed the necessary preparation nor showed any pressure to learn anything. What was taught at the universities was strongly influenced by what was called the Southern viewpoint.

Cotton was also raised in the heads of the new generations; that is, the view was promoted that slavery was an institution created by God and was the desirable foundation of all higher culture. The slaveowner of the South was never aware that slavery created far more evil than advantage. He was of the opinion that there could not be any condition for blacks other than servitude. He had received this institution from a rather long series of forbears, and the slaves were simply family property. And then there arose a secure legal foundation for slavery, its recognition in the Constitution of the United States. A right so extensively and securely possessed over so many years will eventually be seen as a hallowed right by those whom it favors, who are all the more inclined to adhere, the more the objections are raised by those not directly involved. Besides, people practicing agriculture are always the most stubborn and persistent in asserting such privileges.

One very remarkable area of difference between the North and South consisted in the fact that about three-quarters of the Northern people belonged to the middle class, while there was really no middle class at all in the South. Or rather, where it did exist in individual cases, it was completely dependent on plantation owners. In the North of that time a money bag had not yet approached the importance it has today. The number of rich persons was still small in relation to the mass of the middle class, and the proletariat was relatively less numerous. This is because the proletarian element, continually replenished by immigration and other conditions, was ever subject to a desirable absorption into the middle class. This period was the most propitious time ever for the advancement of an ambitious man. He did not even need to be particularly gifted. Whoever was hard-working, knew how to manage, and had an open view for possible developments in his environment in those days had to become prosperous, even if he only used a bit of a peasant's slyness and abstained from speculation. The enormous rise in the value of land in the booming cities hid more gold mines than California, and cheap government land in the northwestern farming states helped many tens of thousands of proletarians to prosperity and a carefree, independent existence.

Conditions were entirely different in the South. There someone who was not endowed could not advance through working the soil, even with the greatest effort. Good land had been bought up by the rich cotton barons. All that was left to the small farmer were the steep mountainsides or the lands exhausted by plantation methods. The land of Southern small farmers did not grow in value. There were no buyers for it. On the free soil of Ohio, the value of farms grew from year to year, but in neighboring Kentucky the value of land remained steady despite better resources of soil and climate, even though Kentucky was only nominally a slave state and the free population exceeded the number of slaves by a factor of four. The situation of the small farmer was even worse in the true cotton states, for he did not possess the opportunity of mobility. Travel conditions were poor, and the way to the far North often more difficult than passage to Europe.

But then again, why should such a farmer emigrate? According to his opinion, things were going well. The astonishing lack of wants on the part of the proletarian farmers of the Carolinas, Georgia, Alabama, and so on made possible an existence almost without labor. They always had extremely cheap whiskey and tobacco; a few pigs that ran about in the woods without any guard provided meat; and the dear sun provided the necessary corn without muscular labor worth the name. So these people without any needs led a sort of proletarian lord's life. Hunting and fishing were free to any white, and they still provided much. Riding animals, whose upkeep cost as good as nothing, were cheap. But such conditions must turn such culturally depressed people into savages. Even in the North, such people, who handled the shotgun and fishing rod more than the plow or ax, were always backward.

The worst of it all was that labor in general was regarded as unworthy of a white in the cotton South. An ambitious man was denigrated as a "white nigger," and large landowners always knew how to promote the unwillingness to work on the part of their poorer racial comrades. Among the small farmers the consciousness was cultivated that they were lords, too, standing high above the Negro, and that even those poor whites who were not able to keep even a house slave, benefitted from slavery. This generalization did not apply to those poor whites who settled under conditions not yet clarified in the mountains of southern Appalachia, where they sank almost to the level of barbarism, shut off from the outside world.[14] Rather, it applied to the small farmers of the South, living next to the plantation owners in the lowlands, or the outlyers of the Appalachians. They also provided most of the officials of the cotton barons: the overseers, the slave drivers, and so on.

The strength of this element of the Southern people cannot be estimated precisely, but it certainly provided half of white Southerners. This people of whole or half-proletarians provided most of the soldiers of the Confederacy. Toward the end of the Civil War, these people came to the realization that they were bleeding for a cause that did not really concern them, that they in fact were fighting for the barons. "It is the rich man's war and the poor man's fight," was murmured often enough around the campfire of a force already considerably reduced, and this mood was expressed by thousands of Confederate deserters. But the majority remained true to their flag and fought to the last cartridge with astonishing persistence. They had become veterans. The mutually endured perils had produced true comrades. Their almost childlike loyalty to their great commander Lee also helped, so that attitudes were created that probably would not have been alien to German armies of *Landsknechten*. But these valiant men had absolutely nothing to win from a triumph of the Confederacy, for their economic position and cultural condition had to remain the same as before. A special state erected on slavery could offer nothing to an insightful, capable citizenry. These poor devils, full citizens of a democratic republic, were never really aware of the degrading aspects of their situation, for they lacked the lights Gutenberg had given the world.

The cotton barons manipulated the stolidity of their poorer racial brothers to assure them political domination in the South. The white proletariat had to vote as the lords prescribed. If what was called the "mean whites" began to get rebellious, the catalog of racial prejudices was brought out and they were threatened with the North, increasingly tired of slavery. The propertyless were flattered with the equality of all whites over against the "nigger." A common noble pride was cultivated, a general contempt for the lowest, and at the same time the hopes of those hungering for land were enlivened by references to the West. Of the political struggles to expand slavery, all the Southern proletariat knew was that a paradise must lie in the West, and entrance to it was being blocked by the evil Northerner. If slavery could only be introduced *everywhere* in the new lands of the West, then every small Southern farmer would find a plantation, because the West had room for everyone. The South could attain this goal, however, only if all the citizens of the South hung closely together. Further, no one could tolerate that the North was cheating the sons of the South of their mutual inheritance. This conjuring of a *fata morgana* probably could have deceived even more sophisticated people than the poor whites of the South. It was only a short step from the feeling of being cheated by his Northern brother to a blind hatred of Yankeeism in general.

What there was in the way of an intellegentsia in the South—the few large merchants and shipbuilders and the numerous preachers, lawyers, physicians, teachers and writers — was always in league with the barons. These men came largely from slaveowning families, and in most cases they were dependent on the sole money men, the plantation owners. Because all members of those circles held a number of domestic slaves, they were also interested in the perpetuation of slavery. It is rare to find opposition to the Southern point of view in those circles. If such an exception did arise, the result was social and economic boycott, which usually meant the same thing as exile. Under such conditions it was relatively easy for the plantation owners to gather to themselves the whole political power of the region and to dominate it permanently. The view that the conflict between South and North consisted of the contrast between an aristocratic and a democratic republic corresponds to the facts.

An agrarian population is always easier to dominate and influence than a people with a considerable metropolitan coloration. In the North around 1860 there was a considerable number of great booming cities, besides a large number of middling towns that had the makings of becoming great cities. In the South, however, there was only a single great city, New Orleans, with 160,000 residents, as well as the middling towns of Richmond and Charleston, both with 40,000 souls, which bore themselves as great cities.[15] But the population of all Southern cities consisted half of slaves. New Orleans, Richmond, and Charleston, as well as Savannah, Mobile and Wilmington, were among the oldest settlements on American soil, but (with the exception of New Orleans) they remained almost untouched by the grandiose development of the first half of the nineteenth century, despite fine harbors. Why was this so? Slavery and slavery again, the curse of the splendid South, so gifted by nature, a curse that through education, custom, and an almost inconceivable short sightedness was seen by its inhabitants as a blessing, the foundation of their higher culture.

The territory of the fifteen slave states (including the four border states) was still considerably larger than the free soil then cultivated in the eighteen Northern states. But much of the area of the South was covered by forests, and other parts consisted of swamp. Texas, the largest state, still hid deserts the size of the Kingdom of Saxony, and the great southern Appalachian Mountains were only slightly explored. There was more than enough land, but the barons sought only to work such land as could bring a rich return without exertion, deforestation, or draining. They knew only exhaustive exploitation, and from this system derived the drive for expansion to the northern West, with its promising prairie soils. But a result of this economic drive is the one-sided nature of Southern views, the formation of a Southern particularism.

The South had truly become a world of its own, much too big for its thinly scattered population, and yet it appeared to be too small for the peculiar, superficial sort of culture that had ensconced itself under the influence of slavery. The plantation owners of the interior South were as good as cut off from the rest of the world, for the distances from cultural centers of other sorts were enormous and many plantation owners led a hermit's life among a majority of Africans and work-shy, retarded whites. The vocation of a slave-owner must eventually have had an anti-cultural, brutalizing effect.

The exclusive concern with politics, a politics that had to fight no contradiction in the South, can hardly be seen as a means of education. And despite the famed princely hospitality practiced at the residences of the barons, of which so many traveling authors tell us, a true culture could hardly have arisen there. Culture requires continual stimulation and competition; its drive is smothered through inbreeding, and only the external forms remain recognizable for a while. The South brought forth only politicians and clever lawyers for its outstanding men, but other than Simms (who is still read) not a single poet, no thinker, no scientist, no artist, and no statesman who ever accomplished anything outside the limits of the Southern viewpoint. The South closed itself off from the culture of the American North out of concern that the "poison" of Northern viewpoints on slavery would be inculcated in books or journals. Postmasters practiced censorship with a brutal force scarcely known in Russia. Suspicious mail was simply destroyed, and the spiritual food of the reading Southerner consisted only of products of Southern origin. They, however, were always in the cotton spirit alone.

* * *

The number of slaveowners was rather small. To be sure, there were 347,525 slave-owners in 1850, but 316,059 owned fewer than ten slaves, including many who owned only one. Then there were 29,733 enterprises with between 10 and 20 slaves. The first group can be seen as the owners of domestic slaves, the second as those who were rising from small farms to plantations. Thus there were only 1733 large enterprises with between 100 and 1000 slaves. These 1733 large slaveowners, with their entourage of lawyers, authors, preachers, teachers, merchants, and other intelligentsia, conjured up the Civil War.

Historical Development of the Slavery Conflict

The cultural work of Europeans on the territory of the current United States begins with the year 1620. To be sure, Englishmen, Spaniards, Frenchmen, and Dutchmen had already been staging experimental settlements for several decades, but it is only around 1620 that the tentative efforts of the first colonists flourished in the form of genuine residency. In this year the Pilgrims landed in Massachusetts, laying the most massive fundament of the Union of today. A few years later the German Minnewit brought real life to the pitiful fishing village of Manhattan (now New York) as governor of New Netherlands. The first women sent from England arrived in 1619 to the Virginian settlers in Jamestown, their transit paid by the planters with tobacco. It is only then that family life, the basic condition of residency, began in Virginia. The originally communal agriculture had only recently been replaced by the transfer of land to individual colonists. Hence the year 1620 may be considered the beginning of the three oldest colonies of Virginia, New Netherlands (New York), and Massachusetts. The two Carolinas, Georgia, Maryland, New Jersey, and Pennsylvania were only settled later.

In the same year, 1620, a Dutch ship brought on land the first twenty Negro slaves at Jamestown, Virginia. Hence slavery was laid in the new land's very cradle. Ten generations of Americans grew up with it, and it lasted 240 years. Slavery thus very much deserves to be called an American institution. Over time it came, in the view of the people, to be naturalized as an established right. But there was also a need for Negro labor. The coastal regions of Carolina and Georgia were honeycombed with giant swamps. Whites who wanted to do field labor there, such as the Protestants from Salzburg, were soon driven away by swamp fever. The colony of Georgia, which was originally organized without slavery, soon had to revoke those rules, for only Negroes were shown to resist the illness. The coastal region could be opened for development only with the labor of blacks. The higher hinterland, where whites certainly could do field work, was not then accessible.

Negro labor existed only in the form of slavery in the seventeenth and eighteenth centuries. In that time the Negro counted as cattle, and nothing was thought unjust in tearing him from the wilds of his homeland in order to make him useful to the cultural efforts of whites in foreign lands. Indeed, some thought they were doing Negroes extracted as slaves a favor through this transfer. The story was that they always did better in foreign countries than in Africa, and that resettlement also brought them Christianity. This view particularly predominated in England, and the Britons of that time were the most zealous slave traders in those days, along with the Portuguese. Queen Anne in particular grew rich on trade in human beings. Thus the introduction of slavery to North America should be seen as nothing at all unusual. It should also be recalled that slavery originally predominated in *all* North American colonies, in New England as well as in Virginia and the Carolinas. New Englanders were still very deeply involved in the slave trade at the start of the nineteenth century, and it took more than a hundred years before the English Quakers began their opposition to the servitude of blacks. The first protest against slavery dates from 1688 and came from the German Quakers in Germantown.[16]

The Constitution. Independence from England was won by the colonies after they unified into a *league of states* under the Articles of Confederation. Each individual state in this league remained sovereign, and the rulings of the general representative body, the Continental Congress, became binding only when every individual state had given its approval. The Continental Congress was little more than an assembly of agents of the individual states (former British colonies). While the war against England was going on, this league of states held together by necessity, although the lack of unifying force, the absence of the means of power to hold to their obligations those "individual sovereigns" who were behind on their payments, had a thoroughly unfortunate impact on the entire conduct of the war.

Washington's greatest accomplishment probably consisted in being continually the master of these difficulties. His qualities of character, which always found a compromise in the fruitless disputes of those years, are to be ranked above his greatness as a commander in the field. But the difficulties grew once peace had come. There was no source of income for the league to balance the enormous debts the war had caused. Congress barely possessed the means to pay for writing materials. The individual states, which had their own war debts, did not want to vote money for the league, and so the interest payments on the war debt were tardy. Foreign lands, particularly defeated England, observed with unveiled mockery the new state entity, which had won freedom but did not possess the strength to fulfill its obligations. It went so far that civil war threatened among the individual members of the league. Fortunately the men who organized and fought the revolution to completion still had adequate influence over the particularist masses of their compatriots to bring them together. The gathering point is the Constitution of the United States.

According to the reliable witness of John Adams, the Constitution was wrung from a resisting people. It was only through this Constitution, passed on 17 September 1787, brought into force on 4 March 1789, that the Americans were strengthened into a nation. In the place of a loose league of states, the goal was a national federal state; but the particularism of the individual states was not completely overcome, and essential concessions were made to the state league view. Despite these failings, the American Constitution is the most important document of modern times. Indeed, one might almost say that modern times only begin with this document. The spirit that lives in it has, on the whole, borne good fruit in the state life of all cultured peoples, first and particularly strongly influencing the French Revolution.

Causes of particularism. The thirteen English colonies in North America arose at different times and under very different conditions and were never administered from England as a unitary daughter country. Each colony possessed a charter of its own and its own laws, and the degree of their autonomy toward the mother country was quite varied. Some colonies were almost entirely independent, while others were strongly influenced by England. Thus each colony went its own way, which naturally led to self-interest and particularism.

The settlements extended along the Atlantic coast from 47° south to 30°, a distance that roughly corresponds to the distance from Berlin to Tripoli in Africa. With such an enormous extension, thin settlement, and the poor means of communication in that time, the relations of the colonies with one another were *very* few. The variety of climate led to various activities of the colonists, and the population was also not of a unified type, although Anglo-Saxons quickly took control all along the entire coast. The Puritanical element dominated exclusively in the North.

In the middle states the Germanic population (Dutch, very many Germans and some Swedes) was for decades as strong as the Anglo-Saxons. Maryland was first settled by English Catholics. In Virginia, both Carolinas and Georgia a mixed population spread in which the English were by far the strongest element, but which also had Romance elements (French Huguenots and remnants of original Spanish settlers) interspersed with Germans (in the Shenandoah Valley as well as in the Carolinas and Georgia).

The Englishman emigrating to the South was distinguished from his Puritan compatriot in New England in many things. Thus we find all the preconditions along this long-stretched coast for the growth of self-interest. The major reason was the isolation of each individual group and the lack of strongly expressed common interests with neighboring colonies. The inclination to particularism not only materially delayed the adoption of the Constitution; obstacles were also erected for later political development. The old specter haunts yet.

Slavery and the Constitution. Around 1787, at the time of consultation for the new constitution, the movement of the times and the situation of the world market were extraordinarily negative for slave interests. In those days the great state of Virginia possessed many more slaves than could be employed. Tobacco planting had dramatically declined due to the exhaustion of soil. The demand of Virginians that importation of slaves be halted, raised as early as 1770, shows that slaves had become redundant on economic grounds even earlier. But the ideas of the Enlightenment of the eighteenth century also advanced in an ever stronger manner.

As early as 1784 Jefferson (a Virginian) moved in the Continental Congress that slavery be banned in all Western areas north of 31°. This would have made the later great slave states of Alabama, Mississippi, and Arkansas, as well as Tennessee, Kentucky, and Missouri, *free* states. Only one vote was lacking to pass this bill, and for that reason alone the law failed. Jefferson wrote on this, "The voice of a single individual would have prevented this abominable crime. Heaven will not always be silent, the friends to the rights of human nature will in the End prevail." That is precisely the language of the man who wrote the immortal lines declaring, "All men are created equal, and they are endowed by their Creator with certain unalienable rights, among which are life, liberty and the pursuit of happiness." Washington was of the same opinion and expressed it clearly enough. Jefferson was also the author of the law that forbade slavery in the new land north of the Ohio River. This region comprehended the later free-soil states of Ohio, Indiana, Illinois, Michigan, and Wisconsin, and parts of Minnesota.

Even in the two Carolinas and Georgia there was trouble with blacks around 1787. East India was rising, producing indigo and rice much more cheaply than the American Southern states. The fine times when the planters could make back the capital invested in a slave within four years were past. But slavery was already the foundation of the entire economic activity in those three states. In the opinion of those planters, ending slavery would mean ruin. More than half their wealth was tied up in slaves. On top of that, what was to be done with the Negroes already there? Still, Jefferson's bills in Congress and the large majorities they received showed which way the wind was blowing. The planters of the three Southern states sought a weapon to protect them from further attacks on slavery, so they demanded that slavery be *recognized in the new constitution.* If that did not happen, they would vote against the constitution. There were even threats by those states of withdrawal.

As a result slavery was recognized in the new constitution under pressure and as the result of an emergency situation.[17] To Washington, Jefferson, Franklin, Adams, and so on, slavery seemed the lesser evil, an evil that was generally believed on its way to extinction from lack of breath. The passage of the Constitution was a necessity of state to which everything else had to yield. And even with this concession to the three Southern states, the Constitution was still adopted by a very narrow majority.[18]

In later years slaveowners always mentioned the fact that Washington, Jefferson, Madison and the other founding fathers were themselves slaveowners. Certainly they were, because they were large landowners in Virginia, and under the existing conditions and the situation of the labor market, only a slaveowner could pursue agriculture. Yet those truly great and farseeing men were fundamentally opponents of slavery. This is shown by their deeds, particularly by Jefferson's precipitous actions. In slavery they saw an evil that must be eliminated and that, in view of contemporary conditions, they presumed would be eliminated. The slaves those patriots owned were mostly received in inheritance from forbears, from a time when slavery was thought of differently than in the period of the American Revolution, which was filled with the ideas of the eighteenth-century Enlightenment. Still, parading the fact that those great men were also slaveowners essentially reinforced the position of the slaveowners of the Cotton Kingdom in a later period.

Cotton becomes King. The Constitution had barely been brought into force when an event took place by which slavery received a significance never before expected. The Yankee Eli Whitney invented what was called the cotton gin in 1793. With the invention of this machine, America was granted an enormous new economy, but with it went a monstrous curse.

Cotton had long been grown in the South, but only the long-staple variety, with only 187,000 pounds exported in 1793. The land was suited essentially for growing short-stapled cotton, whose seeds are so solidly bonded to the fiber that their separation by hand did not pay. Whitney's cotton gin separated seed and fiber mechanically, and in 1795 America was already exporting more than six million pounds of cotton. It proceeded by giant strides. Within a few years after the adoption of the Constitution, the Cotton Kingdom was already a power.

Now there was work for the Negro. Capital invested in human flesh produced more profit than a gold mine. The first impact was a dramatic increase of slave prices.[19] Virginia and Maryland could sell their surplus Negroes to the Southwest at great profit, and those Negroes of the North who had not yet been emancipated were mostly exchanged for gold to the new cotton lands. The high price of the Negro also stimulated the breeding of human cattle, for the ban on importation from Africa was to take effect in 1808. Hence those Southern states that could not plant cotton themselves became producers of Negroes for the Carolinas, Georgia, and the new states of the Southwest. Proud Virginia, the cradle of American freedom, bred Negroes just as the West today produces pigs and cattle for the market.[20] Maryland, and later Kentucky and Tennessee, did the same. Thus those states not producing cotton fell into dependence on the Cotton Kingdom itself.

The human wares produced in the upper South had even a higher market value than those brought from Africa. The Negroes from America possessed a thin layer of culture and were nominally Christian. The ordained servants of the so-called religion of love used this excuse to make their peace with the breeding of Negroes. The Southern clergy always placed slavery under its protection, and they soiled themselves by declaring slavery an institution established by God. There was finally a break between the Methodists and Baptists of the South and North, and Presbyterians and Episcopalians only avoided a split with difficulty.[21] Even the Catholic Church, and not just in the South, was a servant of slavery interests. The most severe opponents to slavery were the Quakers and German Lutherans and Reformed.

* * *

The question of the treatment of slaves by their masters is much disputed and can never be portrayed in an entirely non-partisan manner. Yet the most widely distributed assertions about it are certainly exaggerated. *Uncle Tom's Cabin* is a tendentious novel, and it gives only a distorted image of the plantation economy. Olmsted's penetrating work, *The Cotton Kingdom,* also does not offer a valid image of conditions; the author entered the land of slavery as a stranger and was filled with Northern views. It is certain that Olmsted did not consciously exaggerate, and that the atrocities happened as he portrays them. But these atrocities could not have been the rule.

The Frenchman Ampère, who toured the South long before Olmstead, tells us of a German slaveowner who could not bring himself to use the whip. This planter's slaves thanked him for his mildness with unbounded laziness. Slavery and compulsion to work are inseparable. The slave will do only the slightest bit of work voluntarily. Regular activity was entirely unknown to raw plantation Negroes, and the inculcation of labor over a few generations could not so quickly eliminate the inclination to torpor produced by millennia of savagery and indiscipline. The Negro was whipped the same way horses and cattle were whipped. He was regarded as nothing but livestock. But one should not conclude that Blacks were treated with purposeful cruelty. That would have been against the personal interest of the masters. Every country man knows that a working animal quickly deteriorates if badly handled. That was also true for plantation Negroes. The patriarchal relationship of the slaveowners toward the Negro must have arisen to a wide degree because such a relationship was economically right and necessary. Almost the entire movable capital of the cotton barons was invested in slaves, and the lords would have been raging against their own interests if what Beecher Stowe, Olmsted, and many other authors portray had been the rule.

How else is it to be explained that there was not a single Negro rebellion in the South during the Civil War? All the white men of the South capable of carrying arms were in the field, even men above fifty. But the mass of slaves remained loyal to their masters through all four years of the war. They carried out their field work then as before. They fed the masters who were fighting for the preservation of slavery. To be sure, the stolidity of the mass of Negroes was enormous. Throughout the war they never grasped that the conflict of the whites was essentially about the Negro. Even the hundreds of thousands of Negro soldiers who fought under the Union banner toward the end of the war barely grasped it, although these Negro regiments came mostly from border states. Perhaps all the horror stories that are spread about the treatment of Negroes, and which contain much truth, could be balanced with as many examples of touching dependence of slaves on their masters. How many Negroes adhered to their utterly impoverished former masters after the war and helped them through their hard times of reconstructing the wasted South? Such loyalty was surely not won through inhumane treatment.

The political power of the South. The leaders of the Revolution were mostly Virginians, and Virginia later produced the most presidents. Thus, even during the first decades of the republic, the South received the leadership of the entire Union. With the growing wealth brought by cotton, the South rose. The barons of the South threw themselves virtually exclusively into politics. They had the time and inclination to do so. In those days the drive for education in the socially elevated layers of the population was more intense in the

South than in the North. The sons of slaveowners were sent to colleges and universities. There the training of rhetorical talent in particular was cultivated, and the spellbinders in the Congress came primarily from the South. The slaveowners also observed the practice of reelecting proven senators and representatives, while the deputies of the North were often replaced.

The South concentrated on a single point: slavery. The interests of the North were various and for that reason often collided. Thus the South was always united, and the North usually the opposite of that. And then again the arm of the South often reached far into the North. In those days the North did not yet produce any staple article, but the South massively produced cotton. This staple was used to sustain a dramatically negative balance of trade. Planters were too lazy or too proud to involve themselves in interregional trade. This was taken care of for them by the merchant lords of New York, Boston or Baltimore. Besides, the South, where a luxurious way of life had arisen in the richest families, was the North's best customers. Much Northern capital was invested in cotton plantations. So the merchant lords of the North were in part the paymasters of the South, as well as being purchasers of cotton and purveyors of luxury wares. The traders of Northern harbors came for that reason into a certain relationship of dependence on the South, for they earned a fortune from the money the slave barons minted from the sweat of blacks. This explains why the South could always get enough votes from the representatives of the North to achieve the slaveowners' demands. These Northern representatives who represented slave interests were contemptuously called doughfaces in the South.

The crevice between North and South was already opened during Jefferson's presidency, around 1809. As early as that, the awareness of their own power had grown among cotton planters to such a degree that they began to feel themselves to be the actual masters of the country. It is probable that the same phenomenon would appear in any country undergoing such a hot house development. In the struggle with the interests of the moneybags, idealism usually comes up short, so long as no law stands in the way. But slaveowners could rely on the federal Constitution, and there they had a secure legal foundation which they used to form their local laws in the sense of the slave interest, particularly the police regulations. Such principles were used elsewhere as well. The present-day trust magnates and the beneficiaries of high tariffs only become idealists and tariff reformers once they have retired from business. The great English landlords in Ireland, as well as the exploiters of the *latifundia* economy in Italy, have worked according to formulas very similar to those of the slaveowners of North America.

Nullification. In the resolutions of 1798 and 1799 composed by Jefferson and Madison on the legislation of Kentucky and Virginia, the doctrine of the old rights of individual states was repeated and stated in a particularly coarse manner. Those resolutions gave the individual state the right to nullify any law passed by the federal government, which meant suspending its effect for the individual state. The right of the state to withdraw from the Union was thereby also recognized. On the basis of this doctrine, South Carolina nullified the customs law of Congress in 1832. President Jackson, who was in office at the time, declared that the laws of the United States must be enforced in the entire region of the United States, if necessary through *armed* might. Jackson proceeded to arm against South Carolina. A compromise was found, however, and the customs law was altered to satisfy the rebellious state. In truth, South Carolina came out of the crisis the victor. It certainly would have been better if the knights of principle of that state had felt something of federal power *then*. The nullification of 1832 would have the greatest effect on the secession of 1861.

The view of the persistence of sovereign powers of the individual states toward the Union became, over the course of time, the strongest bulwark of the slave interests. The following passages appear in the significant speech delivered by Jefferson Davis on 10 January 1861, a few days before his resignation:

> All the (rights) not granted to the Union through the Constitution remain with the individual state, and only what the Constitution grants to the federation is its by right. Have the states ever transferred their sovereignty to the federation? Have the states ever obligated themselves never to leave the Union? No, the Constitution is only a contract among independent states, it does not constitute a *national* government.

Jefferson Davis was the pupil of Senator Calhoun of South Carolina, and he in turn stood on the shoulders of Thomas Jefferson, who can be seen as the originator of the idea that the individual state had not lost its old sovereignty through entering the federation. For Jefferson, an enemy of slavery, this matter was simply a question of principle. But with Calhoun this principle advanced to a bulwark of the slave interests, and with Jefferson Davis it became a justification of secession and the establishment of a special state based on slavery. The person who has gone deepest into this connection is von Holst.

The conquest of the West. The region of the coastal colonies was so extensive that it could long have sufficed for the small population of settlers. But the American does not cleave to the soil. His drive for expansion, his daring, and his accomplishments as a pathfinder and pioneer are marvelous. The great procession into the Western hinterlands already began before 1770, a migration of peoples that could probably be designated the most important cultural deed of all times, for it opened up lands that could some day in the distant future contain four hundred million people. By 1870 homesteads reached all the way to the Pacific. The people who accomplished this mission amounted to only 1.25 million whites in 1770.

Slaveowners also contributed to this great work, but the true hero was the land-hungry small farmer of the North. His was a people with little property, of simple manner of life, great valor, and persistence. The men were accompanied by capable women, who were good at the spinning wheel and loom and found satisfaction in an industrious life in the midst of a horde of children. And each settlement soon had a schoolhouse. Many Germans, particularly German Pennsylvanians, were among these settlers, and it might have been German Pennsylvanians who first took up the trek, for their migration to the southwest, toward the Shenandoah Valley, began as early as 1730.

Many a German ruffian could be found among these settlers. Others went savage in the struggle with nature and the redskins, and this conquering campaign, which may be regarded as advancing culture, also produced some very lamentable scenes. The early period of the trek fall together with the wars between the English and French, and the Revolutionary War also took place in this Western territory. Indians were used as auxiliaries by both white belligerents. The red warriors carried on this war in their own way. Torches and tomahawks waved over the white frontier population. But the frontiersman forgot the fact that these atrocities were occasioned by war and turned on the perpetrators, and every offense of the Indians was repaid double through acts of revenge. Thus the entire tragedy of the extermination of the Indians may be derived from the wars of the whites among themselves.

The conquest of the Western hinterland may be seen as the advance of two separate armies, one of which came from the slave states, the other from free soil. The Southern army soon possessed hundreds of thousands of black auxiliaries, was splendidly organized, and almost always enjoyed considerable help from federal power. These columns continued peacefully alongside each other for decades, and it was only after 1850 that the two forces rammed into each other in Kansas. In this race the slaveowners had a considerable head start. They were well capitalized, and many thousands of slaves could be mobilized at a nod. Thus the Southern army rushed by leaps toward the Mississippi, founding the two new Southern states of Alabama and Mississippi, while the Nothern army could only follow step by step. But it brought the new land to a true bloom and settled it much more thoroughly than could happen in the Southern hinterland.

This drive for expansion found its limit at the Mississippi, because before 1803 the area of the United States ended there. Beyond the great river lay the lands of Louisiana territory. The French had ejected the Spaniards there, but they were unable to do anything with the new possession, and Emperor Napoleon, short of cash, offered it to the United States for $15 million. President Jefferson took it up at once, and in 1803 a splendid agricultural country half the size of Europe was incorporated into the United States for a pittance.

The slaveowners triumphed, for they believed that they could now fully satisfy their drive for expansion. The present-day state of Louisiana was devoured at once, and because slavery had ruled there in the Spanish and French periods, the slaveowners felt that the whole region sold by France should be claimed as slave territory. The North did not want to accept that, but they agreed to the reception of Louisiana as a new slave state, and the remnant of Louisiana was recognized as the territory of Missouri. A territory was understood as new land that would be divided into new states after settlement. Until the formation of states, Congress would rule.

One must distinguish between the present-day state of Louisiana and the Greater Louisiana that was bought from the French. This Greater Louisiana encompassed a mass of lands that was almost as extensive as the entire United States before 1803. In the east the Mississippi formed the border of Louisiana. To the northwest the region extended to Canada and across the greater part of the present Rocky Mountain states of Montana, Wyoming, and Colorado. Half of Minnesota also belonged to it, and the nine states of Louisiana, Arkansas, Oklahoma, Missouri, Iowa, Kansas, Nebraska, and North and South Dakota lay entirely within it. The geisers of Yellowstone Park splayed on Louisiana territory, and the Mississippi emptied within it, as well, into the Gulf of Mexico.

No one could measure the unlimited extent of the new acquisition at the time the sale was contracted. The more rapidly pressing South enjoyed the first fruits of it. The harvest the North would enjoy in Greater Louisiana, in the significantly larger and more important northern part of the land obtained, still lay at an unsuspected distance. The slaveowners

Figure 2. Annexation of Greater Louisiana. The Mississippi constitutes the eastern border.

pressed out of their new state of Louisiana into Arkansas at once, toward Missouri. As early as 1817 they had reached the point where Missouri sought admission to the Union as a slave state. But the Ohio River, which had been recognized in 1787 as the frontier between slavery and freedom, emptied into the Mississippi considerably to the south, and if one extended the line of the mouth of the Ohio westward, then the projected state of Missouri was still within the northern zone.

The Missouri Compromise. The struggle over the admission of Missouri to the Union lasted three years. The South gained its will with the help of eighteen Northern doughfaces in the House of Representatives. Missouri was admitted as a slave state, but Maine was admitted at the same time as a free state.[22] It was also stipulated that the border between free soil and slavery would forever be at 36° 30' (the southern border of Missouri).

Forever lasted, as we shall see, barely thirty years. The northern border of Missouri lay at 40° 30', hence almost as far north as New York City. As a result, Missouri is to be seen as a bastion of slavery penetrating the region of freedom. The barons hoped that from this position more conquests could eventually be made in the Northern free-soil regions. The limitation placed between the two cultural regions by Jefferson was broken by the Missouri Compromise. The Compromise is to be seen as the first great political victory of the slaveowners over the free North.

Mexico and Texas. The next assault of the Southerners was directed against the Mexican province of Texas. Delegates of the slaveowners penetrated there, overran the widely scattered, weakling people, and organized a revolution. Texas declared itself independent of Mexico and temporarily organized itself as an independent republic, which restored the slavery Mexico had eliminated in 1829. In 1845 Texas was admitted to the Union as a slave state. Florida had earlier been purchased from Spain, winning a further slave state. In the interests of slavery, war was declared against Mexico in 1847, and the Seminole War in Florida was prosecuted entirely due to slavery. Later, after 1850, the Southerners promoted obtaining or conquering Cuba and other parts of the Antilles, and indeed they sent filibusters to Nicaragua and the coast of Central America in order to prepare revolutions and grab land there. So we see the Southern people grasping the most extreme means at an early point, if needed, to press the expansion of slavery. Through these various undertakings the warlike spirit in the Southern people was kept alive and a not insigificant corps of militarily trained people created.

These campaigns of war and adventure incidentally kept the slaveowners from noticing the great transformations that were taking place in the northern West in the forties and fifties. The army of seekers for new land was considerably increased through immigration. The central states of the West Ohio, Michigan, Indiana and Illinois quickly filled with people. Iowa, Wisconsin and Minnesota were taken over, and in 1850 the frontier line had moved westward to Nebraska and Kansas. It was discovered that the "Great American Desert beyond the Mississippi" still being marked on the maps of the 1840s, did not even exist, but rather that the prairie watered by the Missouri was as fruitful as the region touched by the Ohio River east of the Mississippi.

While the South exhausted a great deal of its strength in adventures, the cultural effort in the northern West took up a continual advance, and it grew with the expansion of immigration from year to year.[23] The new farmer in the West cared little about political things. He had enough to do establishing his farm. But when he discovered through developments in Kansas that slavery would be inserted into his hard-won free soil, he turned to politics with a vengeance. For he was worried about his land. He instinctively felt that his property would have to lose much of its value if a plantation with Negro labor opened next to him. Here is to be sought the key for the astonishing political transformation that took place after the foundation of the Republican Party in 1854.

Kansas. Almost precisely west of Missouri lies Kansas. This region was ripening into a new state shortly before 1850. In keeping with the Missouri Compromise, Kansas was free soil, and slaveowners were not to enter there. But they wanted to do so anyway. Senator Douglas of Illinois discovered the resolution by leaving it to the original settlers of a new state to decide whether that state would have slavery or not.[24] Despite the fact that it broke the legally established frontier of thirty years before, this view was elevated into law through what was called the Compromise of 1850, which brought with it the slave-catching law that has already been mentioned. This new compromise was an even greater political victory of the South over the North than the Compromise of 1820. It was achieved through the unworthy bribing of a number of members of Congress. Even Daniel Webster, the most significant intellectual force America had produced, voted for this pact with crime. It is no marvel that there followed an outbreak of wrath in the North. The sense of humiliation concerning the breaking of agreements with the help of Northern auxiliaries won out over the previous politics of tolerance toward Southern domination aimed at gradually overcoming the peril of secession.

So now there was squatter sovereignty, and now it was for the North to defeat the enslavement of Kansas on the grounds of this new law. The squatters of that new state had to produce a majority for free soil. In order to do that, they must be strengthened by immigrants hostile to slavery. There followed a race between Northerners and Southerners to settle Kansas. The North could only send men to Kansas who would establish residency there. The South, however, believed they would be able to win the necessary votes in Kansas by commanding hordes of pro-slavery men from neighboring Missouri (called border ruffians) to Kansas. These border ruffians always returned to "foreign" Missouri as soon as they had illegally voted in Kansas.

In order to put Kansas under the yoke of slavery, Southerners grasped for the most contemptible means, and the federal government assisted them in the most unworthy manner. One would have to write a book about Kansas to portray its bloody history. The struggle for Kansas was actually the preliminary to the Civil War. There was dreadful arson and murder there for years. John Brown was there, too. It is entirely understandable that he did not just shoot into the air after the border ruffians killed one of his sons and drove a second mad. The Northern view finally prevailed, essentially because the North accomplished the colonization of Kansas better than its opponents, but it was only in 1861 that Kansas was admitted to the Union as a free-soil state. How much those conflicts contributed to the hatred between South and North is immediately clear.

The slaveowners' party achieved *its last victory* in 1857. The Supreme Court decided in the case of the slave Dred Scott that neither Congress nor the individual state had the right to forbid slavery in a new territory. This gave slaveowners far more than they had ever demanded. The value of this decision lay in the new legal principle that the slaveowners received for the secession they were already planning, for they could no longer exploit the territorial advantage of this decision. The Northwest was already strongly settled by Northerners, and slavery could only flourish where it could reign unrestricted. It could not bear simply being tolerated. In addition, it proved to be the case that the number of available Negroes was inadequate to take over further free-soil territory for slavery. The hot blooded masters should have known this earlier, although one might excuse them for not understanding that slavery could not flourish in cooler climates, for they were pitifully backward in economic matters. They were mere cavaliers, regarding themselves as the born lords of the Western world, and they followed exclusively the dictates of their lust for domination.

Douglas. The man who opened the back door to Kansas for the slaveowners was the leader of the Northern wing of the Democratic Party. He wanted to win the favor of the South on the wings of squatter sovereignty, and with it the next presidency in 1860. To be sure, Douglas bore the traits of a demagogue, but he was still honorable enough to put on the brakes when the slaveowners sought to seize control in Kansas by force with the use of Douglas's squatter sovereignty. He protested against the atrocities committed in Kansas. For that reason the barons denigrated him, and when the Northern Democrats unanimously demanded Douglas as candidate for the presidency, the slaveowners presented a second Democratic candidate, Breckinridge. Whether this was done out of hatred for Douglas or as a part of a plan for secession, which could only be realized by Lincoln's election, is obscure. Incidentally, Douglas was the true discoverer of Lincoln. It was only the debates Douglas held with Lincoln in 1858 that made Lincoln's name known in the North. Douglas remained true to the Union and did a great deal in the spring of 1861 to win Democrats for the Union. That should never be forgotten. He died at the very start of the Civil War.

Political parties. The party struggles of that time can only be outlined briefly here. They played an important part in the slavery struggle only after 1854. The Democratic Party dominated the federal government almost without exception. Its chief principle was a stress on the special rights of the individual states. Because the slavocracy based its claims primarily on this principle, they gradually won the upper hand in the Democratic Party. But this party always had a strong Northern wing, essentially a result of the party's liberal views concerning the right of immigrants to vote. For many years the opposition was formed by the Whig Party, whose chief principles were a protective tariff and opposition to state banks. On the slavery question their position was usually weak, and it failed utterly when the crisis broke out. Its chief leader was John Quincy Adams, the sole president with anti-slavery views to serve until the Civil War. Other leaders were Daniel Webster and Henry Clay. The anti-foreigner party of the Know-Nothings (American Party) won considerable ground in the 1850s, a sign of the breakdown within the two old parties.

In 1854 the Republican Party was founded. Everything essential about this party was already mentioned in the first chapter.

The party of abolitionists arose around 1832. Its impact on political organization was entirely insignificant. It was largely a party of agitation, and its program consisted of recklessly combatting slavery and opposing all compromises with slaveowners. It is dubious whether it ever had more than a hundred thousand members, but it encompassed much of the intelligentsia. The fanatical element predominated. These obsessives undoubtedly contributed to stalling any peaceful agreement (such as redeeming the slaves), but they cannot be denied the glory of having been the conscience of the Northern people.

Secession

On 16 October 1859, John Brown attacked the Virginia town of Harpers Ferry at the head of eighteen armed men, seizing the federal arsenal there and announcing that he intended to arm the slaves of Virginia by his own authority. He sent out patrols, had a number of Virginia plantation owners brought in as hostages, and awaited the slaves he expected to stream in in masses to be armed with the weapons in the arsenal. But the slaves did not come. A company of federal troops, remarkably enough under the command of Major Robert E. Lee, later the field commander of the Confederates, stormed the arsenal, leading to the deaths of more than half of Brown s escort, almost all of them relatives of their leader.

The entire country fell to feverish agitation over this coup. It was not seen as the senseless act of a single fanatic; rather its scale was endlessly overestimated. An indescribable rage seized the hotspurs of the South, who had long been preparing for secession. They held Brown to be the executor of the will and the secret intentions of the Northern people, although the pitiful preparation and execution of the attack disproved that adequately.

Bleeding from many wounds, Brown was brought before a Virginia court.[25] He rejected the attempt by his defenders to excuse him as insane. "I am entirely clear and reasonable," he said. "If my plan failed, then it was because God has a better plan for me." With frequent citations from the Bible, he launched a fearsome tirade against the slave-owners. "You people in the South must prepare yourselves for the fact that judgment because of slavery is close at hand. You can hang me, but hundreds of thousands of vindicators will arise from my bones." Through his calm and composure as well as the determination with which he met his accusation, as well as through the bravery with which he went to his death, the man intimidated his judges and all who heard him or read what he said. He wrote to his brother, "I am worth much more if they hang me than for any other purpose." He wrote to his surviving children (he had had produced nineteen), "Pursue with deadly hatred this greatest of all rascalities, slavery!" To a friend, "I am happy to die, for a great cause is advanced through it." Brown was legally hanged on 2 December 1859.

The appearance of Brown before his judges had as great an impact on the North as the deed itself had on the South. The mass of the Northern people saw in Brown a hero, the vanguard of a just cause. Two of America's most important poets, Longfellow and Emerson, spoke on his behalf. On the day of his execution the Legislature of Massachusetts adjourned, there were memorial services in perhaps a thousand Northern churches, and in many assemblies earnest and patriotic men praised the martyr Brown to the jubilation of enthused listeners. They went so far as to compare the hero of the day with Socrates, even with Christ. None of this popular feeling was planned; it broke out entirely on its own, and it raged like a wildfire from Massachusetts to the hamlets of Minnesota. But one could not be enthused for Brown without identifying with his deed. In this context the popular mood was a challenge to the South, a dangerous game with fire, an unthinking heaping up of new incendiary material. But who may command genuine popular opinion in a democratic land? Who may dam it when it seeks to pour out?

Brown became a national hero in the North, and two years later Union troops went into the field with the battle hymn:

John Brown's body lies a-mold'ring in the grave
But his soul goes marching on!

Lincoln's election. The president is not elected by the individual voters; rather, the voters vote for electors of the individual states, who later name the president.[26] The electors are bound by tradition to vote for the presidential candidate of their party. According to this electoral system it can come to pass that a presidential candidate rejected by almost three-fifths of the voters can still become president.

The election took place on 6 November 1860. Four candidates opposed one another: Lincoln, nominated by the Republican Party; Douglas, by the Northern wing of the Democratic Party; Breckinridge, candidate of the Southern Democracy; and Bell, representative of the Constitutional Party, a very mixed association of Whigs, Know-Nothings, and Conservative Southern Democrats. The election had the following results:

	Free States		Slave States	
	A	B	A	B
Lincoln (Rep)	1,831,180	180	26,430 [27]	0
Douglas (Dem.)	1,280,049	3	162,525	9
Breckinridge (Dem.)	279,211	0	570,871	72
Bell (Const. Party)	130,151	0	519,973	39

A is individual votes, and B is electoral votes. The electoral college consisted of 303 votes, with 152 necessary to elect a candidate. Lincoln received 180 votes and was elected, although three-fifths of American voters had voted against him. Among the four candidates, Lincoln and Breckinridge respectively represented the positions of the Republican and the slaveowner parties; Douglas and Bell may be seen as representatives of two moderate groups. Douglas received 1,422,574 votes and Bell 640,124, making 2,082,698 together. From this one may conclude that a majority of the citizens rejected both radical candidates. Lincoln received 1,857,610 votes and Breckinridge about a million.[28] Including South Carolina, 3,082,698 voted for the three candidates against Lincoln, so that Lincoln was in the minority by more than a million votes.[29] The strong vote Breckinridge received in the North was very significant, almost 280,000 votes. This shows how far the arm of secession reached into the North.

The slaveowners, who had only been seeking an excuse for secession, exploited the results of this election to agitate their compatriots, who were far from prepared to secede. "The American people doesn't want Lincoln at all. The anti-Lincoln votes in the North demonstrate that almost half the North is for our cause. This minority president, who wishes to rob us of our property, might be president of the North. But we are leaving." That was the slaveowners' argument against Lincoln the minority president. They were fundamentally incorrect, for Douglas voters in the North did not at all say that they approved of splitting the country, and Lincoln wanted slavery to continue to exist. However, the trick with the concept of a minority president certainly drove many Southerners who were still true to the Union into the camp of the secessionists.

South Carolina starts the process. This state, whose citizens had already rebelled in 1832, was the heart of the entire secession movement. There it was that slavery struck its earliest root and most strongly influenced the whole of the white residents. More than two-thirds of the population of the state consisted of slaves. Immediately after Lincoln's election the secession began, and on 20 December 1860 this state issued its certificate of divorce to the Union. The most stupid rumors were circulated about Lincoln in South Carolina. It was said that the new president would soon free all the slaves and give them suffrage. It was said of Vice President Hamlin that he was himself a mulatto![30]

The Southern Confederacy. There was, however, considerable opposition to be overcome in the other six cotton states. Governor Houston of Texas argued for the Union, and in Georgia the formidable Alexander H. Stephens fought bravely against the secession of his state, but to no avail. In the middle of January 1861, the group of true cotton states South Carolina, Georgia, Alabama, Mississippi, Louisiana, Texas, and Florida had withdrawn from the Union. On 9 February the Southern Confederacy was constituted with Jefferson Davis at its head. In Southern states the decision on secession was left to specially elected bodies called conventions. The people voted on secession only in Tennessee, Texas, and Virginia.[31]

The four hesitant states. One must distinguish three groups among the fifteen slave states, first of all the group I mentioned before, consisting of the seven cotton states; then group II, Virginia, North Carolina, Tennessee, and Arkansas, which only joined much later; and group III, the border states of Missouri, Kentucky, Maryland and Delaware, which did not secede.

Virginia only withdrew from the Union on 17 April, Arkansas on 6 May, North Carolina on 20 May, and Tennessee on 8 June 1861. The hesitation of the second group had an extraordinary influence on the course of the attempts at reconciliation launched by the North. It could be seen that a secession of only the states from group I would not amount to much. It was only the addition of the second group that made the movement threatening.

To be sure, the states of the second group called conventions to consider secession, but in Virginia this body possessed a pro-Union majority. This fact was overvalued in the North, where it was believed that Virginia would remain loyal, and there was little fear of a secession without Virginia. This state was the most populous in the South, and it had been the home state of Washington, the cradle of American liberty. The entire North was proud of the splendid history of Virginia. No one considered that Virginia had become in the meantime a state for breeding Negroes, that thousands of intimate family ties joined Virginians with the cotton land, that John Brown's attempt to free slaves had been directed against the Virginian town of Harpers Ferry, that the state-league interpretation of the Constitution had domesticated itself there, and that the emissaries of the seceded states were doing everything possible to win Virginia. For this state would determine the decision of North Carolina, Tennessee and Arkansas. The pro-Union majority of the Virginia Convention melted away, and after the cannons of Fort Sumter thundered on 13 April, the Virginia Convention voted 88 to 55 to join the powerful state to the Confederacy. The struggle over Fort Sumter clearly decided the matter. The defense of a federal fort by federal troops was seen as compulsion being applied to "sovereign" South Carolina, and the already-shaky loyalty to the Union of the representatives of Virginia collapsed in the face of this "assault" on the hallowed doctrine of states' rights.

The failure of attempts at reconciliation. The North wished to be magnanimous to its erring sisters, wished to build a bridge over which the rebels could return to the bosom of the Union. And it could afford to be magnanimous, for despite many political defeats, the North had emerged from the long struggle over the extension of slavery as the victor, when rightly considered. The North now numbered eighteen states, and with Kansas that was nineteen, with West Virginia twenty. But were there really still fifteen slave states?

How long could the four border states still count as slave states? Their climate assigned them to the North. What still survived there of slavery was little more than domestic slavery. The border states were continually exposed to the influence of the North, and they were also the only Southern states receiving European immigrants. In the near future these four states could be overwhelmed by the cultural tide dominating the North. Hence the actual relationship was twenty free states, eleven slave states, and four border states gravitating ever more toward the North. The North also had a hinterland in which the next generation could establish ten more states (which actually happened), while the slave territory, despite all the favorable laws, had only the still impenetrable Indian Territory and the sandy deserts of Arizona and New Mexico for further expansion. All of the great political victories of the South over the North were mere window-dressing, bills without solid backing. The cultural development the North experienced under the influence of immigration transformed those Southern victories into defeats.

Among the various attempts at reconciliation that were offered in Congress, that of Senator Crittenden (from the border state of Kentucky) proved the most promising. Crittenden proposed a constitutional amendment that would concede all land south of the northern border of Missouri to slavery, and all the land north of there to free soil. But Crittenden also wanted to bar Congress from involving itself further in the slavery question, and he encouraged territorial governments to protect slave property. The final point was basically insignificant, because climate protected the Northern territories better from slavery than laws ever could. But Northern radicals were offended by this proposition, and they spoke about it in Congress for so long that it became too late to pass the Crittenden bill in time. Crittenden invented the following alternative: A proposal should be presented at once to the entire people of the United States as a plebiscite. Given the peaceful and conciliatory mood of the Northern people, such a proposal could certainly be sure of acceptance. Acceptance by the people would not have had force of law, so the ponderous process of amending the Constitution would have to proceed. But such a plebiscite would have had an enormous impact on the *second* group of Southern states, which were still hesitating, and one might hope that after this verdict of the people, Virginia would remain in the federation.

Yet the Constitution knew nothing about a plebiscite. Many members of Congress became stubborn on this matter, and the proposal of a plebiscite was rejected by a narrow majority (20 against 19 in the Senate, 113 against 80 in the House). The Congress did later agree to an amendment to the Constitution based on the Crittenden proposal, but this last gesture of compromise had already been rendered obsolete by the development of affairs in Virginia and could no longer hinder the entry of that state into the Confederacy. The attempts by the North at reconciliation failed essentially due to the lack of time to turn these attempts into deeds through legislative measures. There was no lack of good will to do it. If the people had had an opportunity to compromise, it would certainly have happened.

Buchanan. During the most critical days of the Union, Lincoln had to stand aside and do nothing because the incumbent president steered the storm-beset ship of state until 4 March 1861. Buchanan came from the North, but he had always been an instrument of the slaveowners. He was a mummified old man who prayed every day, "Just no trouble as long as I am in office." He was not a traitor, because such a role demands courage and decisiveness. His first duty should have been to rob the South of the belief that secession could take place peacefully. To do this he would not have had to mobilize the federal army, as the Democratic President Jackson did in 1832 when South Carolina nullified; it would have been enough if President Buchanan had placed the defensive fortifications in Charleston in a state of readiness and referred to the actions of his predecessor Jackson.

Instead, in his New Year's message of December 1860, Mr. Buchanan said, "The agitation of the slavery question in the North is at fault for the dissatisfaction of the South."

After long hesitation, he finally allowed himself to be pressed into sending a single unarmed cargo ship with provisions, munitions, and 200 soldiers to Charleston. When it approached the threatened forts on 9 January 1861, it received fire from the Southern shore batteries and had to go back. Yet Buchanan ignored this hostile act. He also overlooked the fact that South Carolina had occupied two of the three forts, and he left the third fort, Sumter, to its fate. And this president had sworn to uphold the flag of the United States and to defend federal property against attack! If a Jackson had held the place of this dishrag for a mere twenty-four hours, the cotton barons would never have been disabused of the opinion that they could leave the Union without a passage of arms. Buchanan was the strongest promoter of secession, although without willing it.

Compulsion. The question of whether the Union had the right to compel states desiring to depart to remain in the Union was much debated, although the argument of Webster of 1824 had never been adequately answered.[32] A majority of the population of the United States might then have been of the opinion that such compulsion could not be used. On the other hand, only a handful of the completely blinded hotspurs of the South believed that the Union would stand quietly by while it was attacked. As things came together, defense against an attack meant war. The North could not attack, for then no one could predict how Northern Democracy, which constituted half the Northern people together with Northerners of a Southern persuasion, would respond. The South, on the other hand, needed compulsion in order to place its own people in the proper attitude for war. This remarkable situation explains why both parties were still groping for war measures when a state of war already existed. This also explains Lincoln's hesitations from 4 March to the middle of April, which brought him so many rebukes.

Unfortunately there was no lack of derailments of this policy of hesitation. The worst was that of the *New York Tribune,* the leading organ of the Republican Party. On 9 November 1860, three days after Lincoln's election, this paper wrote, "If the cotton states decide to leave the Union, we insist that they should be allowed to depart in peace. The right to secede might be a revolutionary right, but it still exists. If a considerable portion of our Union has decided to leave it, we shall oppose all attempts to compel those states to remain in the Union."

The South could only have interpreted this as encouragement to peaceful secession. Other Republican papers expressed themselves similarly, and very influential Northerners also made this opinion their own.[33] One cannot criticize Southerners for forming their opinions from such concessions in leading Republican circles, "We can rebel with good conscience, the Constitution does not forbid us, and the Northerners themselves say that they cannot compel us to remain in the Union. Thus there shall be no war. First of all, the doughfaces do not want to fight, and secondly they have no permission to do it in the Constitution."

Fort Sumter and war. On 4 March Lincoln was inaugurated president. Thus commences a situation that is surely unique in the history of war. Both parties recognized that they were heading for war despite the fact that they did not want it. Each party was intensely concerned with ascribing to the opponent the odium of the first attack, but neither had an effective army, and each was limited in proceeding by concern for internal conditions.[34] Lincoln could not even arm for war. And at the moment he only disposed of the widely-scattered remnants of the old federal army, which was completely disrupted by the transfer of most of its officers to the enemy. This situation, which was not peace but also not war, could only have lasted a few months, and a reconciliation was not impossible as long as no blood flowed, and as long as the decision of the second group of Southern states still remained open.

Another unfortunate incident—the Brown incident and the Buchanan incident had already taken place—brought the decision. The acute peril of conflict lay precisely there where the South stood armed, in front of the camp of the South Carolinian fire eaters and arch-rebels. Fort Sumter was supposed to defend the harbor of the capital city of Charleston from a foreign enemy. The Union occupied this fort.[35] Major Anderson and sixty artillerymen stood there. The supplies were dwindling. Should Anderson be compelled through hunger to surrender the fort? At first Lincoln and his cabinet pursued a policy headed in that direction. But a storm of indignation was released in the North through this decision. "That is unworthy," it was said, "that is a humiliation before the rebels." Lincoln gave in and sent the cargo ship *Baltic* to Fort Sumter under the protection of three warships to bring provisions to the garrison.

Storms divided the squadron, and only the *Baltic* passed the entrance of Charleston Harbor on the morning of 12 April. The commanders of the South Carolinian troops decided that the *Baltic* should not be allowed to approach the fort. Anderson was ordered to surrender the fort by four negotiators of the rebels on the early morning of 13 April. Anderson replied that he wished to capitulate on 15 April, as his food would reach until then. The negotiators permitted him only one hour's warning. When the Union flag remained displayed over the fort, the bombardment was opened by the South Carolinian beach batteries. This began the Civil War at 4:30 A.M. on 13 April.[36] The bombardment lasted thirty-four hours. Sumter was set to burning, but no member of the garrison was killed. The Union cannons, which gave a strong answer, did not cause any damage. Not a single one of the 7000 South Carolinians participating in the attack fell. Anderson's old-fashioned cannons could not reach far enough. Anderson capitulated on the afternoon of 14 April, when his people were completely exhausted and only three rounds were left. His flag was saluted by the rebels with fifty cannon rounds.

The result of Fort Sumter on the Southern side was Virginia's joining the Confederacy,[37] and the later joining of the three other middle states of the second group. The victory cheers over Fort Sumter overwhelmed the hesitant and the wavering in those states. But that day had an even greater impact on the North. The Northern Democrats stood massively in favor of defending the Union. All fears that had been harbored concerning their opinion now proved pointless. Those friends the South might still have in the North hid out (unfortunately they became all the bolder later), and when Lincoln issued the first declaration of war, far more volunteers enlisted than could at first be placed. It was as if, with the cannons of Sumter, a weight that had long encumbered the Northern people slid away. Once the war had become inevitable, the total people of the North rose in a marvelous manner to defend the indivisibility of the Union.

The Consequences of the War

Even if it had compelled recognition for itself, the Confederacy would not have been able to expect a continuing existence. The pride of the North would never have permanently accepted such a first defeat. There could never have been a lengthy peace between the old Union and a new Confederacy, if only because the North could not leave the mouth of the Mississippi to its opponent. The inevitable result would have been an early second war, for which the steadily growing power of the North, as well as the lessons of the first war, would have been good preparation. The Southern dwarf would probably have been pounded to pieces before it was able to recover from the losses of the first war. An enslaved South as an appendage to the powerfully progressing, great Union would have been possible, and it could have survived for a time, but such a creation could not have been permanent as an autonomous state.

If one wishes convincing proof of the fact that everything the slave barons did to preserve their former economic activity was self-deception and stupidity, this proof is provided by the current amazing development of the South. Now four times the cotton is harvested with free labor as was ever produced in the slavery period.[38] Earlier white Southerners, baron or beggar, eschewed labor. Dire need after the war compelled these work-shy persons into activity, and today the grandchildren of former slaveowners compete with genuine Yankees. This effect can be seen as the sole good thing achieved by this dreadful war. But it would be easy to prove that peaceful development would have achieved the same result, and perhaps even earlier; for the way to healing, to the elimination of the old economy (made possible only by slavery), leading the way along new paths, would then not have required the total ruin of the South.

The war did not solve the race question in the United States; rather it made any compromise in this area significantly more difficult. Difficulties have arisen from the premature granting of suffrage to Negroes, difficulties that have had a disturbing impact on the political development of the entire country. Now only Negroes living in the North are actually able to exercise their right to vote; in cotton country, the seat of the great mass of the blacks, the state legislatures have managed to get around the commands of the current federal Constitution, and the Negro is almost as politically disenfranchised as in the time of slavery. The reason given for this measure is that if the Negroes could vote in the states where they are a majority, they would dominate the whites. This assertion is not entirely without foundation, and public opinion in the North has made its peace with the current conditions in the South as a result of this judgment. Very few white citizens still demand today that Negroes in the South receive their due rights. The views of the North and the South have grown considerably closer on the Negro question, and there is no doubt at all that a large majority of the American people today see the amendments raising Negroes to full citizenship as a mistake, and at best premature. This view dominates despite the fact that, especially in the upper South, the Negro is capable of education and has made quite pleasing progress since emancipation.

It cannot even be asserted that the peril of secession could only be eliminated through war. The redemption of the slaves through a monetary compensation to their owners would at least have created the same situation in the South that we have there now.

And how beneficial the rain of gold would have been for the chances of development of the South. How much more rapidly the Southerners would have been freed from the curse of a one-sided economy, and how much earlier they would have been able to turn to exploiting the many treasures with which their land was so abundantly supplied. A blooming industry has now developed in the South. The old cotton state of Alabama now moves along the path blazed by Pennsylvania, and similar phenomena have occurred in North Carolina, Virginia and Tennessee. And all of this after the South was as good as ruined economically and, after the conclusion of peace, had to endure the terrors of what was called the Reconstruction. With the elimination of slavery, the peril of secession vanished on its own.

The War brought every bit as little good as did slavery. This realization now seems to be general in the American people, which explains the lack of interest shown in the most important event of what is yet the young history of North America. It is almost as if one is dealing with a family tragedy that is no longer spoken of, as the result of a tacit agreement.

Lincoln

Abraham Lincoln, born in 1809 in the slave state of Kentucky, described his joyless youth with a line from Gray's "Elegy," "The short and simple annals of the poor." His father was an unsteady and unindustrious small farmer who had to be taught to write by his wife. His mother, who died early, was said to have possessed extraordinary gifts; at least Lincoln claimed that his intellectual power was inherited from his mother. A loving stepmother took over the boy as hers. At school Lincoln learned only reading and writing. Poverty in his parents' house soon forced the strong young man to follow the plow and fell trees in the forest. Avid to learn, in his few free hours he eagerly devoured anything printed he could get hold of: the Bible, Aesop's Fables, a mathematics textbook, some speeches of heroes of the Revolution. At seventeen he hired on as a boatman on the Mississippi, reaching New Orleans several times. His disgust at slavery was developed on these journeys. While still half a boy, Lincoln achieved considerable respect in his home area, first through the strength of his fists, then through his remarkable talent at telling jokes and adecdotes. He knew how to hold a gaping crowd and win its applause through his native wit. Thus his gift as a speaker developed even in his early youth, and that naturally led him into politics and the profession of a lawyer. His parliamentary activity was restricted to four terms in the state legislature of Illinois and two years in Congress in Washington. He served in the Black Hawk War, but he found no opportunity for distinction.

Lincoln worked at his own advancement with iron determination. The gaps in his legal schooling were quickly filled, and soon he was one of the most sought-after defenders in Illinois. He was regarded as one of the most profound experts on the Constitution and its history. Mathematics also attracted him, for which he had a special gift. His favorite poets were Shakespeare and Burns. He mastered the works of the great Briton as few others ever have. The backwoodsman used Shakespeare to train himself, without any formal schooling, into one of the finest and most thoughtful prose writers in America. Lincoln's two inaugural addresses and the brief but truly moving speech at the Gettysburg battlefield are certainly the best examples of his style. The old classics remained virtually alien to him, and he likewise knew little of European history. His teachers in the political history of North America were primarily Daniel Webster and Henry Clay. Lincoln never fell into the error of fragmentation, by which so many autodidacts fail. The educational means he used were few, but he always returned to them until he had made the material completely his own. Lincoln's career shows us the American self-made man in the best light.

He surprised everyone with his enormous, ungainly body and his ugly, pointed limbs and face. He was six feet, four inches tall, and even his tall friend Schurz only reached to his shoulders. He had extraordinary physical strength and was capable of carrying 600 pounds without trouble. He possessed a remarkable memory for people, and he is supposed to have been on personal speaking terms, using their first names, with half the population of Illinois in those days. He was extraordinarily restrained in personal habits. He rejected the enjoyment of tobacco, which essentially meant tobacco chewing in the backwoods, but he was never a temperance man.

His marriage, which produced four boys, was anything but happy. His wife never understood him, and she was very sorry her husband was no machine for making money. Lincoln was never prosperous, and he actually always lived from hand to mouth.[39] It is little known that Lincoln was a freethinker of the most radical direction into his mature years. It is only in the 1850s that he modified these views under the influence of Theodore Parker, who was a leader of the Unitarians. But from this religion, also known as the Anti-Trinitarians, he drew little more Christianity than its moral teaching. The fact that Lincoln possessed a strong and solid trust in God comes from most of his official writings as well as from his speeches.[40]

In Lincoln's nature, boisterous joyfulness and desire for joking was paired with a melancholy that would overtake him suddenly. He could tell funny stories for hours, many of them quite coarse, and then become deeply serious and taciturn. This turn of mood was always a puzzle to those around him. His biographer Holland was of the opinion that Lincoln consciously took refuge in his jovial nature during the hardest days of his presidency in order to hold at bay the dark thoughts that plagued him. Often his joyfulness was expressed in such a way that strangers thought him to be entirely lacking in dignity.

It was not until 1858 that Lincoln emerged as a great political figure. His debates with Douglas marked the beginning of his fame. In those days Douglas was considered the primary orator and statesman of the Northern Democrats and the presidential candidate of that party. Lincoln, who had fought this Democratic lion so brilliantly, naturally had to appear as one of the presidential candidates of the Republicans of the West.[41] The Republican Convention met in Chicago, in Lincoln's home state. By far the most powerful candidate was Governor Seward of New York, but as a result of a series of fortunate accidents, the convention finally united on the novice Lincoln. This conclusion, which surprised no one so much as Lincoln himself, caused deep sorrow among the Republicans of the East; only much later was it seen that the convention had chosen its best winner in Lincoln. As president, Lincoln named several of his opponents as members of his cabinet. Thus one has the opportunity to observe the accomplishments of these men (Lincoln, Seward, Chase, Bates, Cameron). There can be no doubt that Lincoln was by far the best choice. If the slavery question had to be settled once and for all, then one could not have better trusted the leadership to any Republican then possible than the self-made man from the backwoods of Illinois.

Lincoln's circle of ideas could be called restricted, for it comprehended essentially only one subject, which was the slavery question. The new president possessed no experience in administration, economic questions were alien to him, and it was the same with his knowledge of the foreign relations of the Union. It might have been that had Lincoln's service fallen in quiet times, he would have gone into history as simply a number in the sequence of presidents. But he was the man whom the stormy times demanded, and it was precisely the one-sided nature of Lincoln's political training that was of high value. His qualities of character and his orientation toward the people of the North were perhaps more important still.

A president in the time of rebellion had to possess quite extraordinary gifts. He had to be a burning patriot, possessed by the solid belief that the Union could only fulfill its mission as an indivisible whole. But he also had to be able to be conciliatory to a high degree. Further, he had to be healthy to the core and possess a capacity for work that few persons can have. He also could not belong to the privileged class of Americans. He had to be a true man of the people and be able to work on the people through the power of his personality. And then there could not be the slightest doubt about his personal honor. None of the outstanding Republicans of that time could fill all of these conditions better than Lincoln. His significance lies in the fact that Lincoln was a genuine man of the people, among those leaders of the people of whom history reports, perhaps the one who fulfills that term better than any other.

All of his public addresses speak a powerful pathos, a deep earnestness, and a power of persuasion that arrested and enthused in simple words, but always in a language beautiful and noble. There was nothing artificial in it. The man of the people understands this language, and it satisfied the highly educated through the power of its logic and the originality of its forms of expression. Lincoln enriched the American vocabulary with many turns of phrase that still run in the people's consciousness today, often without their knowing the origin. No one who has ever read the Gettysburg Address can doubt Lincoln's truthfulness and consistency. His words thoroughly corresponded to his actions. Lincoln always kept faith with the lower people, from whom he had come. He drew on a plenitude of power no American before him or after him has ever possessed. But this rare man never showed a trace of arrogance, superciliousness or inaccessibility. Up to his terrible end he remained the same simple man whom the backwoodsmen knew, and even his plain appearance did not clothe him unattractively; in fact it was necessary to his characteristic image.

After the attack on Fort Sumter, far more volunteers presented themselves than could be enlisted. A deep bitterness had seized the Northern people, and the youth rushed in with joy to preserve the Union. In those days one could draw on the whole of a valiant people, and no one had a proper notion of the terrors of this war. Even the first defeat, First Bull Run, did not cool enthusiasm. More than half a million volunteers rallied around the threatened flag in the autumn of 1861. But then came the failures of the Peninsular Campaign, the dreadful defeats of Second Bull Run and Fredericksburg, and the humiliation of Chancellorsville in May 1863). More than a hundred thousand brave men were already rotting in the graves of Virginia. Under such trials, tiredness with the war had to appear in the North. This slackening was natural and has always shown itself in any people relying only on volunteers to make up its army. One must always keep in mind that the North was fighting for a distant ideal, and that it had to carry out a war of attack. Who can blame the young man of 1863 if he was cooler about the troubles of his common fatherland than his bellicose comrades of 1861, or that many said, "There is no point if we haul our hides to market. Besides, what do the Negroes in the South have to do with us? Our great Northern country is under no threat." The Philistine who exists in every person spoke more and more, and often it seemed that this Philistine had prospects of victory in his struggle with the patriot who hides in every American.

In addition to the war exhaustion of the North, which expressed itself in massive desertions, there was something more: the growing disunity of the Northern people. "The war is a failure," echoed Democratic conventions. The true party of war, the Republicans, suffered considerable political defeats, and the sentence mentioned above became the leading slogan at the Democratic national convention of 1864. But even worse than this disunity was the appearance of a secret society that called itself "The Knights of the Golden Circle," which had a very significant leader in Clement Vallandigham of Ohio.

There, these Knights were friends of secession living in the North. They founded secret lodges in the Northwestern states, particularly in Ohio, Indiana, Illinois and Missouri. According to their program, they wished to prepare for a true division of the Union. The middle states and the Northwest were supposed to declare themselves separated from the Eastern states (New England, New York and Pennsylvania) and found its own Western league of states, which would join in close cooperation with the secessionist Southern states. This traitorous plan was a Utopia, to be sure, and even Vallandigham did not think it could be carried out. But the Knights powerfully stoked war-weariness in secret, seducing thousands of Union soldiers to desert, hindering tens of thousands from entering the Northern army, and powerfully aiding secession through espionage and money. Great and respected newspapers in the capitals of the West, such as the *Enquirer* in Cincinnati, the *Times* in Chicago, the *Republican* in St. Louis and the *Sentinel* in Indianapolis, actively supported the agitation of the Knights. Vallandigham was finally arrested, but Lincoln handled him mildly and sent him to the camp of the rebels. Soon Vallandigham got to Canada, and from there he continued his traitorous activities with even greater success, an extraordinary irritant to the Union.

It is in these shifts in the mood of the Northern people—the encroaching exhaustion over the war, the efforts of Democratic leaders to achieve party goals via the misfortune of the Union, the high treason of Vallandigham and his numerous comrades—must be recalled if the significance of Lincoln, the true man of the people as president of the United States is to be sought. You have only to think of a cold party idol such as Seward in Lincoln's place at that time, or the unbending blockhead Chase of Ohio, or the dry lawyer Bates, not to mention the incredibly cracked political wire-puller Cameron of Pennsylvania. Each of these colleagues of Lincoln possessed a strong following at the Republican convention of 1860. Seward's was at first twice the size of Lincoln's, and each of the other candidates would perhaps have been just as electable as Lincoln, for who could measure the power of hidden forces in a deeply troubled people?

The great victory that the North won in this war was the victory over itself and over its own exhaustion with the war, its persistence under the fearful trials of the first three years of war. But the general who led the Northern people in this decisive battle was named Abraham Lincoln. To a great degree it was the power of his folksy personality, his truthfulness and power of persuasion, that overcame the Northern enemy within. A magic from Lincoln passed to the common man of the North, contributing much to creating adequate numbers of recruits.

As president, Lincoln was designated in the Constitution as commander in chief of the armed forces. Lincoln made use of this authority in only a very few cases. Yet his correspondence with the generals showed that Lincoln often had good judgment in military matters. He was a decisive opponent of the Peninsular Campaign. He foresaw the perils McClellan's plan would bring, and he prefered proceeding against Richmond by the land route, with good reasons. It later proved to be the case that Lincoln's war plan of 1862 was far better than McClellan's plan, which was the one actually carried out. Lincoln was offended many times by that general.

The president of the United States actually had to beg the arrogant McClellan for information about war preparations. When Lincoln visited McClellan one evening, he was informed that he should leave because McClellan was already in bed. Lincoln bore this treatment quietly. In fact, he declared, "I will hold General McClellan's horse if he would only give us a victory." It is still unexplained why Lincoln tolerated General Halleck so long as his military adviser. This hanging on to a chief of general staff whose record was an unbroken chain of misapprehensions and subterfuges, is perhaps the weakest point in Lincoln's conduct in office. Another error worthy of censure was his attitude toward his first Secretary of War, Cameron. One might concede to Lincoln that Cameron became Secretary of War for political reasons, but that this gross finagler remained in office until the end of the year is not adequately excused by the answer that Lincoln hesitated to change his cabinet during the first war year.

Lincoln's excessive mildness was entirely beyond propriety. Every condemned person found pardon from him.[42] And Lincoln even had to assert himself against his own cabinet members. The two so-called lions in Lincoln's cabinet, Secretary of State Seward and Secretary of the Treasury Chase, thought the president to be a modestly gifted lucky stiff, and Seward actually attempted to compel Lincoln to renounce his power of government. Seward moved that the slavery question be completely removed from the government program, and that a strong foreign policy be pursued that would instead soon lead to war with Spain and France. Seward appears really to have believed that a foreign war would suspend internal problems, that the seceding states would return to the Union in such a case in order to defend the country against an external enemy. Seward distributed this thoroughly crazy plan in a carefully worked-out state paper, which was only published years later by Lincoln's secretaries Nicolay and Hay. Lincoln, however, treated his rebellious secretary of state magnanimously, permitting the paper to vanish into a secret file and telling Seward that he, the president, would make any alterations of the administration's program when it would seem necessary. Seward took the reprimand calmly, thankful for the president's tolerance, and became from that moment on the true servant of his master. Even the third lion later called to the cabinet, Secretary of War Stanton, brought to his office a very low estimation of Lincoln's ability, but he was just as rapidly disabused and then became one of Lincoln's friends.

Lincoln was distressed that he held his office on the vote of a minority; particularly at the start of his presidency, this counseled him to the most extreme caution. The fact that his election had essentially precipitated the conflict also weighed heavily on him. In addition to that, there was Lincoln's conscientiousness concerning the Constitution. The fear continually plagued him that he would appear to the people as a sort of military dictator, or be forced away from the foundation of the written Constitution, which often enough invited various interpretations, by some necessary measure. All of these things explain what has been called Lincoln's timidity during the first weeks of his administration, in most cases without justification.

Lincoln overcame the most fearsome and lasting of all crises a modern state has endured, with the aid of laws promulgated on the presumption of domestic peace. His entire conduct of office was marked by an unshaking effort to preserve the Constitution and not give up an atom of it. That was his best legacy to the American people. The crisis was overcome without the liberties of the people enduring the slightest permanent damage.

Lincoln was like a man of iron. He possessed an enormous capacity for work and endurance. And yet it is astounding that he did not collapse under the burden that lay on his shoulders. The most important matters, dealing with the existence or non-existence of the Union, had to be decided at once. In addition, not only did a field army have to be created in an instant, but also a host of pro-Union civil officials. Such a turnover of officials normally takes place at the entry of each new president, but one may take his time in peaceful periods. Here, however, it was necessary to act with the highest speed, for traitors in important civil positions could no longer be tolerated. This was known to office hunters, and the pressure was never greater than at that point. A host of self-seeking applicants continually tormented the president, and as many as fifty applicants appeared for many of the most desirable offices.[43]

In a hard time, Lincoln achieved almost superhuman things, endured untold torments, and was uncertain of his life almost every instant. He created a special file for threatening letters, but he did not permit himself to be distracted. All the way to his terrible end, he remained an upright and loyal representative of his people, one of the noblest and most just men known to history.

II

Germans in the Civil War

A Brief Orientation to the Theaters of War

For our purposes the war on the sea and the rivers, the campaigns in the Carolinas, in Louisiana, in Texas and along the Red River, and the privateer and guerilla campaigns remain outside consideration. Only the main theaters of war in East and West will be considered in what follows.

In the East. The eastern theater of war consists only of the state of Virginia, the western part of the state of Maryland (Antietam), and the southern part of Pennsylvania (Gettysburg), hence an area only the size of Southern Germany. The center of this consists of central Virginia, the area between the two capitals of Washington and Richmond, which are 148 miles apart. The Union tried to take Richmond throughout the four years of the war. Six campaigns were undertaken to this purpose. The first of these, in July 1861, already ended on 21 July with the Union defeat at the First Battle of Bull Run. This battle of mobs can be seen as a sort of preliminary, a try-out of the readiness reached at that point.

In the East there followed a pause in the war lasting eight months, which might be seen as preparation for the great struggles of 1862. In March 1862, the Eastern army of the North, the Army of the Potomac, was shipped to what is called the Virginia Peninsula (between the James and York Rivers), so as to attack Richmond from the southeast. This campaign lasted five months, but it only brought success to the Union in the last battle against Lee, at Malvern Hill. It ended with a withdrawal of Union troops under McClellan from the Peninsula on 10 August. At the same time a small-scale war was underway in the interior of Virginia, essentially in the Shenandoah Valley, in which the Confederate commander Stonewall Jackson repeatedly defeated considerably larger Union armies.

August 1862, the third advance of the Union army under Pope, was made against Richmond (from the land side). Pope was severely defeated at Second Bull Run at the end of August.

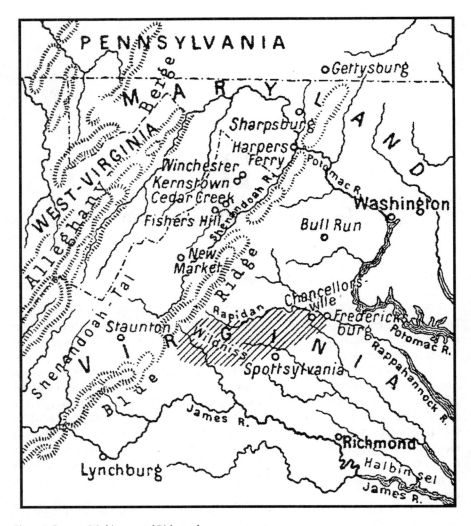

Figure 3. Between Washington and Richmond.

Pope was removed and the Army of the Potomac given once more to McClellan. The Confederates under Lee undertook their first attack on the North. After several successes, the Southern army was forced to retreat at Sharpsburg, on the Antietam River, close to the border of Maryland and Virginia. McClellan pursued the retreating forces in such a negligent manner that he was deposed late in the autumn of 1862.

General Burnside, the new leader of the Army of the Potomac, intended to advance against Richmond again (fourth campaign). But on 13 December he suffered a dreadful defeat against Lee at Fredericksburg.

Burnside passed the command to Hooker. In a fifth advance, the new leader decided to press his enemy, established at Fredericksburg, with his 125,000 men. But he was badly beaten by 61,000 Confederates at Chancellorsville, 1–4 May 1863. This brilliant triumph of Confederate arms raised such expectations of victory in the South that Lee was forced to undertake a second advance into the North. He proceeded to the large Susquehanna River in Pennsylvania with the intention of taking the city of Philadelphia. But the Army of the Potomac, now under General Meade's command, forced Lee to concentrate his army at the great encounter battle of Gettysburg, which ended with the complete defeat of the Confederates. Once more the victorious Meade pursued the enemy in a very cautious manner, and the battles on the Mine Run, in the Virginia Wilderness, proceeded without result.

In the summer of 1864, there was another campaign by the Confederate General Early reaching to the gates of Washington, waged against various Union generals. It was ended by the appearance of Sheridan and the complete dissolution of Early's corps.

May 1864 to the end of April 1865 marked the sixth and last attack on Richmond. General Grant was commander in chief for the Union. He attacked Lee in the Wilderness in order eventually to shatter the chief army of the Confederacy with a series of "hammer blows." There were almost continual battles from 5 May to the middle of June. Through the Battle of Cold Harbor on 3 June, Grant lost more than 60,000 men. He was continually outmaneuvered by his great opponent and driven ever farther east; but in the end Lee had no choice but to protect the Confederate capital behind the ramparts of Richmond. There followed eight months of siege of the double fortification of Richmond and Petersburg.

The decision was brought by the Western field army of the Union, advancing from the south. Having completed a grand march of encirclement and destruction through Georgia and South and North Carolina, it now approached Richmond. The arrival of Sherman's army would have led to a complete enclosure of Richmond. To avoid this and to join up with the Western army of the Confederacy under Johnston, Lee left Richmond at the end of March 1865. But he was forced by Grant's pursuing army into capitulation on 9 April at Appomattox Courthouse. The corps of the German General Weitzel entered Richmond on 3 April. This ended the war, although the last Confederate troops only surrendered on 26 May.

Because all of the North's advancing movements had as their goal the conquest of Richmond, the result was that the great battles took place repeatedly on the same fields. There were two battles on Bull Run, in July 1861, and August 1862. Fredericksburg and Chancellorsville lie only ten miles apart, and another ten miles west we reach the scenes of the mass battles of the Virginia Wilderness in May 1864. Grant led his armies to slaughter at Cold Harbor in June 1864 on the same fields where McClellan confronted Lee in 1862. There were fights time and again at the same strategic points in the Shenandoah Valley for almost four years. What is remarkable is that most of the battlefields of Virginia lay on soil of old German settlement. This is also the case with Gettysburg and Antietam, as well as the Shenandoah Valley. This valley was the sally-port for both armies, both to the north and to the south.

The course of the Potomac was of particular importance. Along it lies Washington, and there the strategically important little town of Harpers Ferry receives the Shenandoah, streaming into it from the south. The Potomac also provided the border between areas of secession and Union. The western border of the Virginia theater of war is roughly the Shenandoah chain of the Allegheny mountains.

In the West. The second principal theater of war, in the West, is larger than half of Europe. The first object of the Union consisted of bringing the two neutral border states of Missouri and Kentucky under its power and creating a secure route by which to march into the heart of the western cotton states. The struggles over Missouri lasted from the start of April 1861 to the middle of March 1862. Germans were especially involved there. Missouri was secured for the Union by Sigel's splendid victory in the battle of Pea Ridge, 7–8 March 1862. Kentucky was easier to overcome, because here the great armies recruited from the free states could advance. But the maintenance of a strong reserve in Kentucky was always overlooked, so that the state remained vulnerable to advances by Confederate forces, particularly irregulars.

The greatest mission of the Western Union forces consisted of bringing the entire course of the Mississippi into their power, thus dividing the three slave states located west of the river (Louisiana, Texas, and Arkansas) from the eastern cotton states. The most difficult part of this mission was accomplished with the taking of Vicksburg by Grant on 3 July 1863. Alongside the battles for the Mississippi and connected with it, there was a campaign in the state of Tennessee, which lasted from March 1862 to November 1863. This war may be seen as a triumph of the North, despite many defeats.

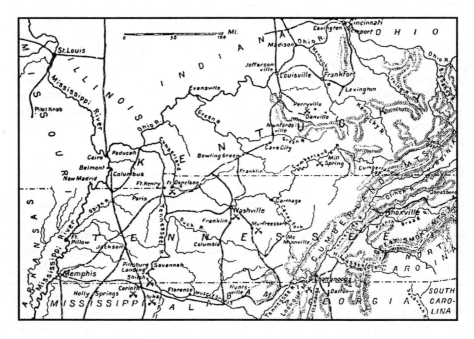

Figure 4. Tennessee and Kentucky.

The campaign began with the first great battle of the Civil War at Shiloh (or Pittsburg Landing, 6–7 April 1862). There followed the struggles for Corinth (two separate undertakings); the great and bloody battles of Perryville, Kentucky, on 7 October and Stones River (or Murfreesboro), Tennessee, 31 December 1862 to 2 January 1863; and the campaign against Chattanooga, which brought the Union the dreadful defeat of Chickamauga on 19–20 September 1863, and the great victory at Lookout Mountain and Missionary Ridge on 23–25 November 1863. Thus Tennessee was conquered, serving in the West in much the same way as Virginia in the East as the chief theater of battles. Still to come was a penetration into Tennessee in the autumn of 1864, by the Confederate General Hood, which was successfully reversed by General Thomas in the battle at Nashville, 15–16 December 1864.

The important Northern field commander Sherman set out from Chattanooga at the start of May 1864 to commence his grand march of conquest into Georgia. In about a hundred battles and skirmishes, all of them Confederate defeats, Sherman levelled the way to the important supply point of Atlanta, Georgia, conquered that city, and then passed right through the middle of Georgia to Savannah, the harbor city of Georgia on the Atlantic. He arrived there on Christmas Day, 1864, then turned toward Richmond through the states of South and North Carolina, with the result already mentioned, which was Lee's withdrawal from Richmond. Sherman's march of encirclement was also a punitive expedition. It took place along a path a thousand English miles long. The route of march was fifty miles wide, and the land lying between those points was ruined by Sherman. This was done in order to prevent the delivery of provisions and war materiel to the rebel army in Richmond.

In order to make a proper evaluation of the success of the Western Union forces, one must consider that these armies not only had to fight off Confederate forces, but also had a latent enemy in the very massiveness of the land to be occupied. Union troops had to assure supply roads of hundreds of miles to their bases in the North, and in the end Sherman renounced all connections and set off on a freebooting expedition. Not a word was heard of Sherman in the North for almost eight weeks, and it was only his victory message from Savannah that announced the success of his bold plan.

The War in General

The Civil War stands unique in history as a thoroughly improvised war. This reason alone is enough to free it completely from European models. Conditions were in almost every case distinct from those operating in Europe. Most of the fighting was in the wilderness. Almost all the strongholds for a land war had to be created. Country roads were in the worst imaginable condition, and the South had few railroads. There was not a settlement at about every hour of march, as was the case with Central European theaters of war; there were no villages at all; and the small towns were widely separated. For months troops saw neither bed nor roof over their heads; it was continual camping in tents or knocked-together huts. The delivery of food was difficult and often failed completely. The forces were also burdened with a huge amount of supplies.

When the struggle began, none of the participants understood anything about waging war in grand style against an equal enemy. The federal army, which then numbered only about 14,000 men (10 regiments of infantry, 5 cavalry and 4 artillery regiments, with an engineering corps) was in fact only a police troop exclusively oriented to fighting the Indians. That led to the division of this army into many tiny detachments. Artillery was mostly in the coastal forts, often hundreds of miles from one another. Since the Mexican War in 1847, which was also not a battle with an equal foe, an American officer would rarely have united more than 500 men under his command. Maneuvers were never done, so that professional officers had only a theoretical training for large-scale war. They were complete laymen in terms of their profession as leaders of larger masses of troops. This explains the failure of so many West Point officers.[1]

The six hundred professional officers divided according to their states of origin and went into the two opposed armies as enemies. The North was able to retain barely more than two hundred of the officers then serving. Still, there was a considerable number of former professional officers who had turned to other ways of life in the meantime. These reported to duty once more, and it is remarkable that the North received its best leaders from precisely this group. Grant, Sherman, Rosecrans, McClellan, Halleck, Hooker, and Sheridan, all of them West Pointers, returned to the Northern army. Most of the soldiers of the Regular Army remained with the North, but these units were so disorganized that they were for that very reason unable to serve as frameworks for the reception of hundreds of thousands of volunteers.

The Civil War was in fact a struggle between two peoples' armies that effectively had to be stamped out of the ground. There were only the barest preparations for training, arming, care, baggage and hospital, replacement, and transport all of the thousands of irreplaceable things an effective great army needs. The arsenals only sufficed for a very small army, and one had to divide many of these supplies with the enemy. Thus everything necessary for the war had to be created new and in the greatest haste, for conditions pressed for a rapid decision. It is no wonder then that much was done wrong, that there were some swindles, that the excess of zeal caused more injury than use, that the influence of politicians was afoot, that millions were wasted in buying bad supplies, or that entirely incapable people smuggled themselves into high positions. Still, marvelous patriotism and self-sacrifice of the people overcame many difficulties, as did their flexibitiy and practical sense.

Each belligerent undervalued the other to an astonishing degree. Northerners believed they could quickly settle the matter with "those few fellows down there," while Southerners held Yankees to be boastful cowards, and the immigrants a mob afraid of a fight. North and South had been one people for over two hundred years, had shared a common destiny, had together led a great war against England, as well as the War of 1812, the Mexican War and innumerable campaigns against the Indians. One would assume that they had come to know each other in that time and would have been able to judge each other correctly, but that was not the case. It turned out that they were total strangers to one another, as if they had been people without common interests. The French in 1870 knew just as little of the Germans as the American South knew of the North. Concerning the views the Northern people had of its Southern brothers, the North had some justification for underestimating its opponent. It was three times larger as a population, and the comparisons were similar in terms of financial strength and resources. But the Southerners vastly outbid their Northern brothers in arrogance, and after their first victories they were completely certain of the outcome.

The war is one of the most interesting and instructive in modern history, and it is surprising that European military has given it so little attention.[2] It took place during a period when we stood on the edge of modern development in military matters. At the outset, the fighting was done with old weapons, and it was only in the summer of 1863 that the breech loader came more into use. For the first time entirely new modes of war were introduced, specifically the massive use of railroads and telegraphs, far more than was the case with the Italian war of 1859. The first armored ships appeared in the spring of 1862, with both belligerents, and at this time a river war in the grand style began on the Mississippi and its tributaries, as well as on the rivers of the East Coast. There were operations by great fleets of armored gunboats with heavy weapons. The North had precisely this weapon to thank for many of its successes in the West. Ericsson built the first *Monitor* in 1862, which excited more attention in its day than the submarine today. Even the air balloon made its first appearance here as a weapon of war, and it is remarkable that Count Zeppelin's interest in airship travel was stimulated by his ascension in a stationary balloon being used in the Western theater of war in America. Count Zeppelin was one of the few German officers to go with the Northern army for the purpose of military studies. An entirely new variety of infantry skirmish eventually developed, and the light trenches the Confederate General Lee first built are now generally respected in military circles.

Thus the war offers much that was new, and it may be said with some justice that it was the first great campaign in which modern technique played a dominant role. On the other hand, we encounter many things that almost recall the Thirty Years War in Germany. The robbing campaigns of the Confederate freebooter Morgan and his comrades led deep into the North, were almost matched by the invasions of the Confederate Generals Bragg and Kirby Smith into Kentucky. Ransoms raised by the Confederate General Early in Maryland and Pennsylvania, where the torch would be thrown into any open town which could not pay the extorter at once. These directly recall the modes of war in the seventeenth century. This also corresponds to the wasting of whole landscapes carried out by the Union General Sheridan, as well as his comrade Sherman in Georgia and South Carolina. The massacre of Negro soldiers and the dreadful suffering of Union prisoners (in Andersonville 13,000 of 40,000 Union prisoners died within eight weeks) are further dark deeds from this dreadful war.

Mobilization in the North. On the day after the battle for Fort Sumter, Lincoln called up 75,000 volunteers for three months in the field, and on 3 May another 42,034 volunteers for three years service. He increased the Regular Army by 23,000 and ships' crews by 18,000 men. On 1 July 1861 there were 186,751 men on the rolls, and there were another 25,600 in the Navy.

The raising of the Northern army had to proceed according to the rules established during the Revolutionary War, which is to say that each of the states remaining true to the Union provided a number of troops in proportion to population. These troops remained connected to the states in question and were regarded as state forces. Only the augmented

Regular Army of the federal government was a national army. This system had very great disadvantages, but although these disadvantages were soon recognized the system was preserved throughout the entire war. The governors of the various states reserved great privileges, and because these gentlemen were not military men, but politicians, they proceeded largely according to the rules of their own profession. Governors named the regimental commanders. Because there were few men with military training, civilians had to be placed in these important offices. It is obvious that this opened the way for patronage. There was also little time to test any applicants. Hence from the very beginning there were many utterly incapable persons in positions of high command. The amount of work it took for the generals to remove these "colonels" can only be suggested here.

The rivalry between states also created problems. Every state sought pride in raising as many regiments as possible. Hence in the course of the war, New York and Pennsylvania raised no fewer than three hundred of them, and Ohio and Massachusetts approached this figure. Instead of providing later replacements for regiments already formed,[3] new regiments were continuously being formed, although many of the old ones had shrunk to two or three companies. The more regiments were created, the more ambitious climbers could be provided with positions as colonels, lieutenant colonels, majors, and adjutants. This was not altered by the fact that many receiving these positions were militia officers. The old militias merely played at being soldiers, and their officers were not differentiated in the least from civilians.

It must have been a true show for the gods as hundreds of colonels, majors and captains, under the command of some old sergeant, sought to learn left face and right face, grips, and the simplest forms of commands. All of Europe laughed its head off over these "officers," being drilled like green recruits. This scornful laughter is understandable, for nations looking back on half a thousand years of military tradition can hardly understand the difficulties a peaceful people must overcome when surprised by the most dreadful of all wars. There was general amazement in Europe that at the start of the war all officers through major were elected. But this method corresponded to the customs of the War of Independence of 1776 and was the only method used here.

The influence of money was supposed to have played a role in the election of company officers, as well, but the stories circulating about this are very much exaggerated. It might be the case that such tricks were pulled in some metropolitan regiments, but this blemish certainly did not mark regiments recruited from the countryside. To be sure, a large number of politicians, adventurers and swindlers reached positions as officers. That could, unfortunately, not be avoided, and it would be found in the case of any non-military people under similar circumstances. Yet many of these incapable officers were removed with little ceremony. There was too much intelligence and too much genuine, fiery patriotism in the Northern army; the capable officers were recognized quickly enough, and the true swindlers soon left or were pushed out. In any case a corps of useful regimental officers was created in the first years of the war, of which many had worked their way up from private. To be sure, the higher leadership continued to leave much to be desired, to the last shot; but that was not due to the officer material, but in part to the political conditions of the country.

In the course of our narrative there will be many negative comments about the West Pointers, the American professional officers. It must always be considered that these gentlemen without doubt had the first claim on positions of leadership. The fact that the alternatives among these officers were often poor is no mystery, for the two or three hundred remaining with the North were virtually untested in their capacity for higher leadership. The most capable of the officer corps of the Regular Army had in fact gone over to the enemy.

The patriotism of the Northern people was not shown simply in the number of volunteers who presented themselves for service. Whoever could not serve offered his means. Rich people organized companies, even whole regiments. The cities, counties, and states provided vast sums. There has never been an accounting of the amount of this sacrifice, but many millions were brought up in this manner. Private charity cared in the finest manner for those who went to battle. Massive hospitals and clinics were established from private resources, and the donations sent to the troops amounted to mountains of goods and often became a burden to military authorities.

The Northern soldier possessed far better schooling and higher intelligence than the private soldier from the Southern people, but many lacked the physical advantages shared by the Southern soldiers. Everywhere the populace of larger cities produced poorer soldier material than the open country, and the regiments formed in the populous East were heavily supplied with residents of larger cities. These people were very demanding, were used to eating a great deal of meat, and had little resistance to the heat and climatic illnesses of the theaters of war. Few sports were then pursued in the North. People had to work hard, and they had little time and less inclination for activities in the open air. There was almost no riding in the eastern North, and only a few knew anything about firearms. Further, the youth was little accustomed to obedience. The free son of the North had difficulty giving in to the necessary discipline, he rebelled easily, and he had reasoning and quarelling in his blood. And now he was supposed to obey officers who understood no more than he and came from the same circles as the private soldier. It was no fun to be an officer over such temperamental soldiers. It was a long time before these problems were somewhat overcome, but these difficulties were never completely put aside, and this "devil of reasoning" always broke out after every defeat.

This is how we should understand desertion, which often reached terrifying scale, particularly after the defeat at Fredericksburg. Deserters should be judged differently from those who abandon European units. Whoever knows what these soldiers were expected to put up with, particularly in terms of marching, care and the arrears of pay; whoever considers that these soldiers were volunteers, feeling themselves still to be free and self-determining citizens of the Union even in uniform, and seeing their position in the army entirely differently from the case in Europe—he will not try to apply the rules of Prussian military penal law to them without further consideration. Desertion was also easy, and the runaway could easily vanish into the thinly-settled land without a trace. The peril a deserter ran was small, for whoever claimed Lincoln's pardon never failed. Many deserted just to enlist in a different regiment. By their flight these men often just wanted to change their position in the army. How many deserters would there be in European armies under similar conditions and without the rigid application of the dreadful punishments for desertion in the face of the enemy? A full 268,000 men deserted the Northern army!

The soldier of the Union army from the West was on average better suited to service than his eastern comrade, for he was more hardened and less demanding. The Western volunteer was more of a country person and many knew about guns, and there were many good riders among them. Perhaps the greater success of the troops recruited in the West was partly attributable to the better soldier material there.

The principal army of the North was always the Army of the Potomac. It fought on the most important theater of war, in Virginia. It always opposed the core troops of the South, under the leadership of the two greatest commanders of the entire war, Lee and Jackson. But the Army of the Potomac was almost entirely recruited from the Union East. It would be unjust to call it of lower quality than the Union army of the West on the whole, but it did contain more elements of lower military qualification than the Western army. Further, the Army of the Potomac always fought under an unlucky star. It suffered tremendously from continual changes in leaders. McDowell commanded it first, then the hesitant McClellan, then the incapable Pope, the equally inept Burnside, the perhaps even worse Hooker, and the careful and lucky Meade. At the end of the war it came under the command of Grant, whose gifts as a commander will probably be judged differently even by Americans once the glory with which success encompassed him is succeeded by a factual evaluation of his actual accomplishments.

The soldier of the North brought with him in any case a good school education, and further, life in America produces particularly alert people. They possess an extraordinary ability to adapt, and experience in practical matters. That makes them particularly suited for pioneer service, especially building bridges, establishing roads, and repairing and extending railroad constructions. They were used to helping themselves in all walks of life, not relying on others. They knew how to use an ax and a spade. Many knew how to handle complex machinery. This ability not only lightened tasks in camp, but also made itself obvious in situations such as the raising or improvisation of new war materiel during Sherman's march through Georgia.

From the beginning of the conflict, the leadership suffered because of the lack of useful general staff as well as good maps. Staffs were not even permitted to leaders at the outset, for they were held not to be a suitable institution for republican America. Hence during the first campaign the highest commander had to concern himself with all the details of the operation in person, and the means for communicating commands were very poor. The lack of general staff maps was even more painful. Never before had there been felt a need for such maps. To the Northern officers the land on which they were to fight was virtually unknown, and they could not rely on guidance from those who knew the places. These locals, usually secessionist, led them where the enemy had placed a trap. During the struggles of 1861 and 1862 the Union leaders continually groped in the dark, and only gradually they obtained knowledge of places and roads in the Wilderness of Virginia where most of the battles took place. The maps that gradually emerged were essentially supplied by *German* officers. Because Union troops did almost entirely without cavalry during the first years of the war, and the cavalry units that did exist quickly deteriorated under their ignorant overloading of mounts, the intelligence service of the North was extremely incomplete. The enormous successes the secessionist General Jackson won with his small but highly mobile and obedient troops against the overwhelming numerical superiority of the Union in the summer of 1862 are understandable in view of the special difficulties under which the Northern army had to fight at the time.

Still, it should always be recalled that Jackson was a rare master of small-scale war and bush war, and that he always had the good luck to be fighting pikers in this area.

The Northern press. The sensationalism of the press was a heavy burden for Northern conduct of the war. Many a military secret was given away, and the best spies of the Confederacy were the involuntary ones who spewed out everything they knew, even things no one should know, in the press of the North. Hence almost all preparations for McClellan's Peninsular Campaign were announced ahead of time. Even the plan for a mine explosion in Petersburg was discussed ahead of time in Northern newspapers. The Confederacy maintained a number of spies in the North who were merely avid readers of newspapers, and they did much for their cause. Many writers in the North thought themselves to be great strategists, and they were extremely fruitful in communicating the most laughable advice to the generals. This was, however, not treated with the disdain it deserved, for the press was a major power in filling positions, and every general placed a high value that his relationship to the "commanding general, the press" remain the best possible.

The suitability of soldiers for service. The investigations of Dr. Gould will counter the view that extraordinarily many young men of 17 and 18 years of age served in the Union army. Of roughly a million soldiers, fewer than 200,000 were under 20 at enlistment, while 450,000 were men between 20 and 25. Many people enlisted who would have been rejected by the French or German armies as unsuited for service. Medical investigations were superficial at the time of the mass enlistments of the first period of the war, and the physicians included many charlatans. This explains the relatively large number taken ill, and those worn out by marching. Screening of soldiers only developed over time. Further, the demands made by generals who were often ignorant dilettantes in these matters were without measure. Many West Point generals were of incredible recklessness. For example, old General Sumner had the German Division wade breast deep in ice-cold streams and then take up night quarters in the open without coats, blankets or tents. The old trooper called that hardening!

Lee's resignation. The oldest general in the federal army by rank was Winfield Scott, the hero of the Mexican War. But he had become a tired, weak, old man in the meantime, entirely incapable of service in the field. Next to him was Colonel Robert E. Lee, an extraordinarily capable officer who belonged to the most respected families in America. Most of the federal officers from Virginia had already resigned their positions. Lee, however, continued at his post in the War Department, and it was assumed that he placed the Union above his home state. Old General Scott was also a Virginian, and he remained loyal to the Union. On 18 April, a few days after Fort Sumter, Lincoln sent his friend Blair to Colonel Lee to offer him the supreme command. Lee later asserted that he had declined, but Blair received the impression that Lee had asked for time to consider. On 17 April 1861, Virginia had joined the secession, on 19 April Lee sent in his resignation and went at once to the camp of the enemy. On 22 April in Richmond he was named chief of general staff of the rebel army, under Johnston.

According to the views which would apply to the Prussian officer corps, Lee would have been treated as a traitor, but the matter was not judged in that way. Lee had the right to choose between his homeland and the Union, and in general he was not rebuked for it. Those who were in the know had no doubts about Virginia's decision two weeks earlier.

Much sentimental nonsense has been written about Lee's supposed struggles of conscience, but there is hardly a doubt that he had long since decided what he would do in the given event. A man in his position, aware of the trust of the president as well as of his old comrade Scott, should at least have surrendered his sword earlier. Lee became the greatest commander of the War of Secession, certainly the only really great commander on both sides. But he was also the first rebel who completely accommodated himself to the new conditions after defeat and began to conciliate and reestablish domestic peace.[4] At the same time as Lee, the Adjutant General of the federal army, Cooper, as well as Commodore Buchanan, commandant of the federal navy yard, passed to the enemy, so that three high military positions lost their holders to the enemy in the hour of greatest peril!

The fleet. The accomplishments of the North at sea were quite extraordinary, even in the first year of the war. Although more than half of the naval officers had opted for the South and about 1200 heavy cannon, to be sure mostly of an antiquated system, had fallen into the hands of the enemy, the blockade of the enemy coastline of 3000 sea miles was energetically undertaken at once. The merchant marine of the North provided a great number of experienced officers, and the leadership immediately commanded respect. Admirals Farragut, Porter, Dahlgren, and Foote have earned a world reputation. As early as December 1862, the Union possessed 137 warships of the high seas, and by the end of the war this power had grown to 671 vessels, including 71 armored ships and about 40 partly protected steamers. The remaining warships were still sailing ships, for in those days the sailing warship was only beginning to vanish. The South sought in vain to compel commerce with the outside world through the use of blockade runners and to practice a sort of sea superiority through raiders, of which the best were built in England and manned by English crews. There were only isolated successes, and one might say the blockade was effectually carried out by the Union fleet in the face of great difficulty.

Through application of power on the sea, the Union successfully confronted certain nations of Europe eager to intervene. The ingenious Swede John Ericsson is particularly to be mentioned in this connection. His Monitors compelled respect not only from the rebels, but also from the English lords.

The armament of the South. The Confederacy immediately called 100,000 men to arms. The troops were at first enlisted for an unspecified time, and somewhat later for the duration of the entire war. This measure proved to be much better than the enlistment for a specific time used in the North. The South soon introduced a general obligation of service for all white men, and toward the end of the war young boys of 16 and old men up to 60 were enlisted. In 1864 there was in Richmond a regiment called the Silver Grays, because all of the soldiers were over 50 years of age.

It often happened that three generations—grandfather, father and son—all stood as comrades in the same unit. Thus the South made a strong claim on its human materiel at an early point, and it established its army more on a national basis than was the case in the North. Further, the South had a very strong support in its slaves. Cotton planting was significantly restricted, and later it virtually ceased, for the cotton could no longer get out of the country due to the blockade. As a result there was a turn to raising corn and cattle. Further, a system was created so that land left behind by soldiers in the field could be worked by slave labor. Slaves could be directed like so many head of cattle. They had no notion that the war had broken out largely because of them. It was only when the Northern army later penetrated deep into the South that this realization began to dawn in black skulls. Negroes were used from the very beginning for actual war purposes by their masters. They served as haulers, servants of officers, cooks, carriers behind the front, helpers in field hospitals and particularly workers in entrenchment. That meant a considerable relief for white fighting Southerners, among whom many a private soldier could keep a black servant of his own.

The estimate that 19 million white Northerners went to war with roughly 6 million white Southerners is not entirely true, because the slaves (about 3.75 million in the 11 seceding states) formed a very important element for strengthening the war power of the South. Almost two million blacks were freed to raise corn and cattle by the cessation of cotton planting. The armies of the Confederacy were fed with the products of this labor. Because the South pursued agriculture almost exclusively, the fighting white people could be relieved all the more easily by slaves and thus use far more men as soldiers than would have been possible in any other land.

Incidentally, the South possessed many other advantages over the North that considerably compensated for the latter's numerical superiority. The advance of the North was seen as an invasion of the South. This made the war for the Confederacy a struggle over house and hearth. The soldier of the North was fighting to preserve the Union, a distant ideal, but the Southerner was fighting an invader and struggling for his own existence. For that reason alone enthusiasm for the war was far stronger in the South than in the North. Also the South had better preparation for service in the field, in the extensive wilderness and woods. The poor people of the South, who provided the great majority of the soldiers, had always looked up to the barons and allowed them to lead. The slave-owners were accustomed to command, and they possessed special talents for service as officers. Hence it was easier to create discipline in the Southern armies. Further, every Southerner grew up with a gun, and he was a born rider. Because the Southern small farmer always did only so much field work and no more, he had always led a sort of care-free life. That created a hardened, healthy people, used to life in the open and to the hot climate. Further, these people were extraordinarily short on wants. Their uniforms often consisted of home-spun civilian clothing, and shoes were almost a luxury article with them. They basically lived on cornmeal and bacon, and if that was short, they could get by with raw corncobs, which were everywhere. The lack of needs of the Southern soldiery, its persistence under difficult conditions, its ability to carry out long marches in the burning sun and to camp in the open without a tent, and its resistance to malaria and other illnesses counted for much, and counterbalanced many of the divisions the populous North was able to send against them. Losses were always modest in the Southern army, but they were terrible for their opponents.

The South started out at once with a splendid cavalry that performed marvelous deeds, first under General Ashby, then under Jeb Stuart, who might be considered the greatest cavalry leader of all times. Both of them fell in battle. The Southern horse is lighter and of nobler blood than the Northern horse, which is usually used as a beast of burden. A cavalry could be rapidly raised without much training, achieving great successes both as an attack force as well as unmounted as infantry. Southern cavalry troops understood well how to spread like a veil around the main army and mislead the enemy. They were the eyes of the Confederate armies, and because the war was fought almost entirely on Southern soil, the local knowledge of the riders was very useful. Further, they always received reliable information from the local population through capable guides.

In contrast, the Confederate artillery was always at a disadvantage. Attempts to create their own foundries usually failed, and they had to rely on the import of cannons. When they were hindered by the blockade, captured cannons had to supply replacements. Confederate generals sought to compensate for this inequality by creating an extremely mobile mounted artillery, rapidly moving close to the enemy and giving fire with small, smoothbore cannons to great effect. The wooded, hilly terrain of Virginia favored this sort of artillery, for the heavy and well-served guns of the North could have little effect there, and there was less need to put down enemy artillery. Southern artillery held somewhat the place now occupied today by machine guns.

Matters in the South were also advantageous so far as officer replacement was concerned, for there were many veterans from the Mexican War. President Jefferson Davis himself had earlier been an officer, and he had functioned as Secretary of War for the Union. He knew many of the professional officers personally, and he was better able to judge their usefulness than Lincoln, who was a total layman in military matters.

One essential disadvantage of the South should not be overlooked: its poor finances. Capital had largely been invested in slaves, and there it was, as dead as if it had been buried in the ground. There was no liquid money. Only in the first period did the gold loans of the Confederates find takers in England and France. What the barons possessed in cash was willingly given to the government, and even the jewelry of the ladies was often given away. But those were only drops compared to the the flood that was needed. Hence the Confederate government created money out of paper, and despite compulsory exchange rates it soon became paper again. Toward the end of the war, a thousand "dollars" were used to pay for a pair of boots. The soldiers had always taken the worthless money as salary, so that they basically served without salary. In fact, the South gave away almost its entire movable wealth for the war. Peace found it a people robbed down to its shirt, with only the treasures bequeathed by nature, which they had owned before without respecting them. When the blindness bestowed on the entire people by slavery at last fell away, after years of sorrow and dreadful "reconstruction," they recovered the ability to see those treasures, and necessity created the strength to seize them.

It cannot be precisely established how many troops the South raised. The estimate of Union General Sherman that the Confederacy on average had 569,000 men under arms, often more, often fewer, seems rather high. There can be no doubt that a people which accomplished something of the sort must have been permeated with the feeling of having justice on its side.

The Impact of Immigration on the Result of the Civil War

The power to throttle the secession was drawn by the Union largely from European immigration. That can be demonstrated as follows.

The results of the first four censuses of the United States, by region, were:

	1790	1800	1810	1820
North	1,968,455	2,684,625	3,758,830	5,132,377
South	1,961,327	2,621,300	3,480,994	4,522,224

Included in this count were 657,047 Negroes in 1790, and 1,524,580 in 1820.

The regions were about equally strong in 1790, but even then there were almost 500,000 more whites in the North than in the South. In 1820 the relationship had shifted so much that, when Negroes are excluded, the North had five million whites in comparison with little over three million whites in the South. Immigration statistics begin in 1820, and we only possess reliable material for from this time on. The last four decades before the Civil War brought five million immigrants to the United States, specifically:

1819–1829	128,502
1830–1839	538,381
1839–1849	1,427,337
1849–1860	2,968,194
In 41 years, in summary	5,062,414

To this should be added the immigrants from the period 1790 to 1819, whose number is probably underestimated at 300,000.

What the South gained from this human torrent was largely lost through the emigration of its own children to the North. In 1860, 607,317 born Southerners lived in the North, but there were only 206,377 native-born Northerners in the South. Other than those expelled from Ireland after 1847, these immigrants represented the best elements. Most of them were in their prime years. The male element predominated, with three men for every two women. The opportunity for work was positive, and cheap new land called for settlement. Under these conditions, the North grew as rapidly as has any state in the history of mankind without the incorporation of conquered people.

In 1860 the United States possessed a total white population of about 27.5 million. This was distributed as follows: the 11 Confederate states possessed barely 6 million of them; the 4 border states, considered Southern but remaining with the Union, had 2.5 million; and the 19 free states of the North (already including Kansas) had 19.25 million whites.

How would the population have grown if the country had renounced immigration from 1790 to 1860? In 1790 the natural increase of the American people amounted to 1.38 percent a year. It can hardly be assumed that this percentage increased in later years.[5] If one figures a natural growth of 1.38 percent a year from 1790, then one obtains the growth due to the excess of births alone, without immigration.

In the following table, created by Friedrich Kapp, on the left is what the white population would have been at the end of each decade if it had increased from only the birth surplus of 1.38 percent per year, and on the right the actual white population in the census for each decade:

1790	3,231,930	the same
1800	3,706,674	4,412,896
1810	4,251,143	6,048,450
1820	4,875,600	8,100,056
1830	5,591,775	10,796,077
1840	6,413,161	14,582,008
1850	7,355,422	19,987,563
1860	8,435,882	27,489,662

According to this table, the natural increase of the white American population from 1790 to 1860 would have been 5,203,952 heads, but in fact increase amounted to 24,257,732. If one subtracts the surplus birth rate of 5,203,952, then one gets an extraordinary increase of 19,053,780 whites. There is no need to prove that this roughly nineteen million surplus in white population is the fruit of immigration. This massive growth in population was largely accomplished by European immigrants from the period 1830 to 1860 (and their descendents). And this period brought forward the men who, together with the sons of earlier European immigrants, or better phrased, Americans of long residence in America, fought for the preservation of the Union.[6]

One should note that there were already 3 million whites in the South in 1820, but only 6 million in 1860, while in the North there was a growth from 5 million in 1820 to 19.25 million in 1860. This is because the South remained reliant almost entirely on the natural increase of its white population from 1820 onward, while the North as a result of immigration could reach an almost threefold superiority over the South by 1860. One searches in vain in Anglo-American war histories for any recognition of this obvious fact. The good star that then guided the destiny of the Union remained true in its hour of greatest peril. The auxiliaries from Europe came at precisely the right time, essentially during the last two decades before the Civil War, in order to help the Union win the decision.

*   *   *

Here a few matters connected with immigration should be reviewed, which will shed even more light on what has been said in the previous sentences.

The total number of immigrants to the United States amounted to 19.5 million persons in the nineteenth century. What a source of power lay in the cost-free reception of such population! How many millions of acres of land have immigrants wrested from the wilderness in the last century? How many cities did they help to found? But most Americans, even immigrants and their children, show no understanding of these continually flowing treasures of ethnic strength and culture. They often received these most valuable of all goods with indifference, even with rejection. Thus even at the very moment when the most worthwhile elements were streaming massively in, that considerable party of xenophobes was formed, the Know-Nothings.

There have been attempts in Germany to estimate the losses that accrued to the Fatherland through the emigration of five million Germans. The uncompensated costs of educating emigrants has been figured. The emigrant realized the capital expended for his education in America. Because emigrants were primarily young people, the sum of education costs expended for them in their homeland was quite considerable. There have also been attempts to estimate the loss of military strength and tax revenues. Schmoller estimated all of these losses at a mere five billion marks, but others estimate it at twice or even three times that amount. Even an approximately correct estimate is impossible. Those evaluators have also never considered what Germany gained as a result of America's rise. The very large German export business with America is primarily driven by emigrated German-Americans, and the astounding development of German shipyards is essentially a result of the emigration business. Germany today is receiving a considerable return on its American investment.

It is more important to estimate the profit to the land of immigration than the losses to the land of emigration. Here, as well, an exact estimate is not possible. But fifty years ago there was a market value for the merchandise called a human being: a grown Negro slave was then worth $1100 on average in 1855. If we should decide, only for purposes of argument, that a white immigrant was worth at least as much, then the immigration of 19.5 million would be worth $21.45 billion. But a white person produced three times the work of a slave, so he should be priced at three times the price of a slave. The white could also figure on a far longer life, so that his work force should be worth considerably more than that of Negroes. Further, if one estimates the higher cultural value of a white person, one could easily set the value at four times higher than the market value of black human merchandise. If anyone wishes to say that immigrant children were worth less than $1100, it should be mentioned that only 22 percent of immigrants were children under 15. Children with the average age of 7.5 years were then capable of earning something after a few summers. Then consider the high education level of some of the immigrants. What was an Ericsson worth to the Union in the summer of 1862? What was a Lieber, a Schurz, a Mergenthaler, or a Carnegie worth?

It is conceded that this evaluation is inadequate, for the full truth will never be known. Further, the purpose is to inform those who only recognize as worthwhile that which is expressed in dollars and cents as to the monetary value of the immigration of the nineteenth century. And because this "Negro estimate" of $21.45 billion will confuse them enough, I leave it to the gentlemen to choose the most eloquent estimate, whether it is $21.45 billion four times that, $85.8 billion, or a figure in between.

No attention has been paid to the cash brought by the immigrants with them, but the average American has a completely false view of this. He contemplates an immigrant with a feeling shifting between contempt and pity; he sees a poor sucker who has been given an act of grace by allowing him to land. Yet the New York immigration officials established in 1870 that every German immigrant then brought with him $150.

According to this, then, Germans alone brought $750 million in the nineteenth century when they emigrated to America. But the Englishmen, Skandinavians, Dutchmen and Bohemians also had considerable means, and many savings also came from Ireland. If one estimates $750 million for the Germans, then the figure of $2.5 billion for the 14.5 million other Europeans would certainly not be too high. That would give us $3.2 billion as a general sum of cash brought by immigrants to America in the nineteenth century.

Finally it should be mentioned what one of the most significant English economists said on the value of European immigrants to America:

One of the imports of the United States, that of adult and trained immigrants, would be in an economical analysis underestimated at £100,000,000 ($500 million) a year.—Thorold Rogers, Lectures in 1888, *Economic Interpretation of History*, p. 407.

The American James Ford Rhodes said on this (vol. 1, p. 355):

The South ignored, or wished to ignore, the fact that able-bodied men with intelligence enough to wish to better their condition are the costliest and most valuable products on earth, and that nothing can more redound to the advantage of a new country than to get men without having been at the cost of rearing them.

*   *   *

To conclude the exposition above, there is a table on German immigration according to decades, and a second table showing the total immigration to the United States in the nineteenth century:

German Immigration

1821–1830	6,761
1831–1840	152,454
1841–1850	434,626
1851–1860	951,667
1861–1870	787,468
1871–1880	718,468
1881–1890	1,452,970
1891–1900	505,152
	5,009,280

Immigration from 1821 to 1890

From	
Germany	5,009,280
Ireland	3,871,253
England, Scotland	3,024,222
Norway, Sweden, Denmark	1,439,060
Canada, Newfoundland	1,049,939
Italy	1,040,459
Austria-Hungary	1,027,195
Russia and Poland	926,902
Other lands	1,726,913
	19,115,221
With the immigrants from 1790 to 1820	300,000
	19,415,221

The German Forty-Eighters in America

One may assume that a half-million Germans emigrated to America merely as a result of the revolutions of 1848–49. But only a small part of this mass is regarded in the United States to be the *true* Forty-Eighters. Only the leaders of this horde are so designated: the academics, artists, technicians, and professional officers among the emigrants, the men who continued the efforts of Young Germany in America in word and writing. How many of them were there? No one knows. [Heinrich] Börnstein speaks of several thousand. Perhaps four thousand would be too few rather than too many. The frontier between the leaders and the led is also hard to draw precisely.

We call the mass simply the *horde* of the Forty-Eighters.[7] This horde consisted of entirely different elements from the other half million who emigrated between 1848 and 1857. They were more highly educated, progressive-thinking people, almost without any element of proletarians. The advancing elements of the South German middle class constituted its core. This "horde," which is given far too little attention, is of great importance. It constituted the echoing background for the deeds of the leaders. There was far more German self-consciousness in it than in the other German immigrants. Many members of the merchant class were there, and most of them possessed a strong drive for further education. It has often been stressed that Germany endured a tremendous loss as a result of the departure of thousands of learned men, and that only a country such as Germany could endure this loss without later showing signs of intellectual impoverishment. But the departure of this horde was an even greater loss for the Fatherland. Think for a moment of the Huguenot immigrants to Germany and the profit they brought, despite the fact that their immigration was much less significant than the transfusion of German popular strength to America.

But let us turn to the Forty-Eighters themselves, the leaders of the horde. What did they see on their first look at America?

The federal government was in the hands of slaveowners, who then stood at the apex of their power. In Kansas the friends of freedom struggled with border ruffians over life and death. There was incredible cheating in that state's elections, and the government favored the swindle. The xenophobic party of the Know-Nothings raged throughout the land. Free citizens were manhandled at free elections in several Northern states if they did not know the Know-Nothing password. The novices saw the doctrine of states' rights as an expression of the same small-state thinking that had laid the groundwork for the German Revolution. In addition there was the narrow-minded Puritanical outlook of the Anglo-Americans, the restriction of personal freedom even of the most harmless personal enjoyment. On top of that there was a church on every fifth street corner, which foreshadowed the worst to many of the novices.

This was not the freedom in which the Forty-Eighters believed, after which they had striven in Germany, for which they had gone into exile, for which their friends rotted in prison, and for which many had fallen under the bullets of executioners. In the eyes of these idealistic dreamers, this was a distorted image of freedom, one which they thought to be almost as bad as the despotism they had fled. They knew nothing of America's history of development, of the compromises of the framers of the Constitution, of the peculiar ways of life of the two parts of the country, of the slavery inherited from English rule. These German enthusiasts could not grasp that King Mob could rule under even the most liberal constitution. They had never engaged in practical politics, and they solidly believed that guaranteed rights would raise human beings to a sort of new nature. Unfortunately our friends understood hardly anything of the English language, the Anglo-Americans did not react to Greek or Latin greetings, and the bits of French brought along proved to be worthless.

The refugees were at first received with philanthropy and pity, being treated as martyrs of freedom, and every possible effort was made to make their way clear, as far as possible.[8]

The Forty-Eighters were appalled by the political conditions they found, and no less by the Americans themselves. The notion that a person could be ready to help and as capable in shirtsleeves with a hat on the head and a chaw of tobacco in the mouth as when observing stiff European ceremonies was inconceivable to them. Despite all their display of democratic convictions, they hid many an aristocratic custom in their hearts; they came from the privileged classes of Germany, and they had experienced the advantages of this position from childhood. It was also alienating to these gentlemen that Europe's artistic efforts were still quite unknown here. Art is a late arrival in all cultures, and a people still involved in the conquest of the West could not develop any artistic understanding. Unfortunately, Barnum was still the hero of the day. All of these externalities and nullities led our novices to the conviction that Americans were still at least half barbarian. The thousand good points of the Yankee—his liberality, which gives without many words; his joy at work; his daring; his practical sense; his genuinely democratic love of freedom; and his patriotism were almost unknown to them then.

In addition, the Forty-Eighters made little effort to learn about Americans, particularly their history and the constitution of the new country. [Friedrich] Hassaurek, who was one of them, stresses that particularly. And why should they have Americanized themselves in that sense? They intended only to stay in the country a short time. The German Revolution was soon to break out again, and then they would throw themselves once more into the struggle in Germany. This dream was fatal for the destiny of many highly gifted and capable men. During this waiting, savings were soon eaten up. More significantly, the Forty-Eighters grew unaccustomed to work, bummed around more than proper, and continually kept their gaze directed to Germany. In the misery of refugee life, even the most capable became ever more embittered. Continuous contact with those sharing such views and sorrows had a negative effect, and the fine years that some individual novices used to accommodate themselves with the country and its demands, under the spur of the energetic impact of a new setting, were allowed to pass uselessly or wasted with flights into cloud-cuckoo-land, which makes us laugh today.

There were too much storm and stress, too much youthful strength and heaven-storming enthusiasm in this crowd. They could not lie still for a minute, and they felt in themselves a mission to reform America profoundly, despite their expectation of a short stay. Further, they had brought with them a recipe, a medicine to make people happy, which they believed would work for all peoples and countries whatsoever. This was the theory of pure democracy hammered out in German study-rooms; trimmed to American needs they were prepared in the form of the following demands: Elimination of the presidency and the bicameral system; elimination of individual state governments; elimination of marriage; education of children by the state alone; elimination of money or at least the introduction of a progressive taxation system, through which it would become impossible for the rich to possess more than a certain amount of property; abolition of inheritance; clothing and feeding of poor children during school years at public expense; naturally also the abolition of slavery; introduction of a system of recall of representatives, etc.

Hassaurek, who was himself one of the most radical, said,

> Things were abolished right and left, and the castles of a new and perfect state were erected in thin air. In heaven our dear God and in hell the devil had no peace. Everyone wanted to go further ahead and offer more than the others. Whoever did not go with the furthest and know how to outbid him was denounced as a reactionary or as a conservative pussyfoot and a coward.

The reforming zeal of the Forty-Eighters peaked in the demand voted at the Wheeling Congress of 1852: "The United States must annex Europe and thus found a 'New Rome' of freedom." All the delegates to this congress (there were only sixteen) voted for this motion. This demand was too mad even for most of the Forty-Eighters; a huge laugh was raised, and the reform zeal began to flag from that time on.

The Anglo-Americans learned virtually nothing about these good deeds bestowed upon them, although there was much reform talk in the English language pamphlets as well as in Esselen's *Atlantis*. The Wheeling idea was dimissed by the Americans with the expression, "Cranks." But when the atheistic tendencies of the Forty-Eighters were openly displayed, Americans took the novices seriously. They saw these efforts to be not only an abuse of the rights of a visitor, but shameless. The answer was a revival of the ailing Know-Nothing Party, and a schism arose among the Germans. The numerous religious elements of the Germans broke contact with those people who wanted to replace the Bible with Feuerbach. The anti-church movement was without doubt a great tactical failure, for it was just a blow in the water. Only a small congregation of freethinkers remain, probably smaller in number and influence than are found in other, smaller lands.

The Forty-Eighters in the refugee period were never particularly united. There was continuous hostility and dispute among them, one group fighting another. Even individual state associations, particularly those of Kentucky and Ohio, lived for long periods in the bitterest feud, repeating the hostilities that had prevailed during the German Revolution.[9] The worst was the struggles between the Greens and the Grays. These lasted for years, and peace between the two groups was only sealed shortly before the outbreak of secession. The Grays were the refugees from what was called the 1830s risings in Germany (Hambach, the Frankfurt putsch, and the like). Some Germans who had emigrated earlier, such as Lieber and Stallo, were also counted as Grays. These early emigrés were idealists, pursuing the same goals as the Forty-Eighters, and suffering for them as the Forty-Eighters had. They had received the Forty-Eighters in a friendly and hospitable manner as brothers. But they could not remain silent about the crazy reforms of the new obsessives, and sought to put on the brakes. Then they really got it. Batteries of filth poured down on the Grays from all sides, and a repellent battle began which was carried out with unnecessary harshness by the Greens. The Grays, too, had a horde behind them, their compatriots who had immigrated before 1848. They were generally well to do, even if they were for the most part rather restricted people. Entirely against the wishes of Körner, Münch, Molitor, and the like, the pride of those who had made it arose and created an ugly weapon for the Gray side. The German who had long been resident in America assumed a position of superiority against the freshly immigrated compatriot. The former servant or peasant boy become rich was glad to play big man in his dealings with the novice, even when the latter was a hundred times superior to him intellectually. This entirely pointless struggle of Germans among themselves was highly lamentable, and it was the Greens who were injured.

The time came, about 1854, when the dream of returning to Germany was given up. Their exile became permanent, and they had to settle in America. But they had missed the best time for that. After the onset of the great financial crisis, it was difficult even for trained workers to find employment. And now there was this mass of German scholars, professors, lawyers, physicians, philologists, artists, officers, and the like. Where were they to be accommodated? What was to be done with these unpractical gentlemen, never educated to work with their hands and still with one foot in Germany? The misery among them was great; they saw that there was at least one reasonable institution in America, the free lunch.[10] Many became cigar makers, others house painters, many tavern keepers or bar waiters, and former officers often enough competed with former high legal officials for positions as house servants.

The lot of heads of families among the Forty-Eighters was particularly sad. Only a few of these gentlemen were able to find positions equal to their knowledge and preparation, so that many professors and pedagogues tortured themselves with private tutoring. The most important virtuoso gave piano lessons for twenty-five cents in the houses of "gaping barbarians," and an artist once celebrated in Munich squandered his energy on Bock beer placards and pill advertisements. Even physicians found it difficult to achieve a tolerable existence, because America then still stood under the sign of charlatanry, and necessity eventually drove many Forty-Eighters into this area of activity. Whoever still had some savings or had received the last positive letter of credit from Germany founded a newspaper, writing it himself, printing it himself, even delivering it to the readers himself. Only the greatest bore up under this distress, for most of these undertakings quickly went under. Out to the country, to the farm, to lead a free life in the forest primeval! But those who did it soon learned that the life of a Wisconsin bush farmer demanded even more severe sacrifice from people of their sort than the holding of some subordinate position in the cities. Most of them came disappointed and impoverished back to the city.

Fortunately the anti-slavery movement was just getting under way when the peril of general obliteration was greatest for the Forty-Eighters. Here a field of useful activity opened for hotheads. They threw themselves into the elections by the hundreds as speakers, literateurs, and agitators. The object was to win compatriots for the new movement, to entice German Democrats into the new Republican Party. Now their rhetorical training, won during the otherwise pointless period of reforms came back into use. They traveled the West in groups of three or four. In every settlement, every little town, German assemblies were held. And the German population came in droves, first of all out of curiosity to see and hear the "moustaches."[11] But interest was quickly aroused.

The speeches of the Germans had an entirely different sound and basic tone from those by English speakers. They were radical, and before all else, they dealt with the heart of the matter, which was slavery. In rallies of English-speaking Republicans, questions of public law were dealt with; the rather meek, carefully claused program of the Republican Party in the matter of slavery was defended; and the speakers offered half-measures and talked around the primary cause. That was not simply boring to the hearers, but actually repellent. The people with its healthy instincts had already determined what the subject was, it had long grown tired of endless niceties and Constitutional tricks. It demanded healthy food, and Germans got that from the moustaches. They tossed away the tame party platform and spoke directly from their guts. The tone very much resembled the one the Forty-Eighters had already developed in Germany. Instead of crowned tyrants, they assaulted uncrowned ones, whose scepter was the slave whip.

The first orator would speak of eternal human rights, the dawning eye of freedom, the principles of Jefferson's Declaration of Independence. Then another would come describing his compatriots and how they had once been half-slaves in Germany, how they could never buy land, how they were held in servitude by the barons, and so on. The third orator would paint the perils of another victory of the slaveowners, how particularly the landed property of German farmers would be endangered if slaveowners could extend their holdings to the Northwest. The final orator had the difficult task of demonstrating to his listeners that the rights of the immigrant would remain protected in the new Republican Party. But the new party was in fact a party of freedom, and Germans would have the greatest influence within it if sleepy Michel did not pass up the opportunity. All of these speeches were saturated with enthusiasm. It was always clear that the orators spoke from inner conviction, that they held the things they presented to be holy and just. And among the listeners, the invisible passenger that every German brought with him made himself known. The old Teutonic hatred against servitude in every form, which had caused the first protest against slavery to come from Germans, can be followed like a scarlet thread throughout the history of American slavery. The celebrations afterwards were nice, too, for many of the old German farmers were even better than the traveling orators. A barrel was opened, and the good old songs of the homeland were sung. While one moustache toasted the German farmer wives, another touched the assembly with a portrayal of his imprisonment in Germany, the third praised the services of the Germans in the conquest of the West, and the fourth nattered on about eternal human rights.

In between there was more singing, and the hours flew. As a result political meetings became German folk festivals, freshened with the breeze from home brought by the orators. And the last part was the most important. If the moustaches returned, and they always returned, the German farmers rushed from great distances with wives and children. The place of festival was surrounded by lines of wagons, an ox was roasted on a spit, and everything was pure joy, song, and conviviality. It could be seen from the participants, who often numbered in the thousands, that they had hungered for long years after the German way of life, for the air of the homeland.

American politicians watched these affairs with amazement, and they streamed to "dutch meetings" in droves. The unusual show appealed to them, as well as the joy and order which reigned there without any police or control, despite the beer. And if these festivals took place on Sunday, then they closed one eye and slid away to Germany in Wisconsin, Ohio, Indiana or somewhere else. "What is going on with the Germans?" they asked one another in distant Boston, the headquarters of the abolitionists. They got translations of the orations and found that they were abolitionist speeches, but more popular and clearer, more penetrating, without any demogogic undertow such as was often found in the declamations of English-speaking opponents of slavery. The Frémont campaign of 1856 brought good fruit from the German switch, and the Lincoln campaign of 1860 brought the victory of the Republican Party.

This is how the German part of the Middle West and Northwest was torn from the Democratic Party and led into the ranks opposing slavery. The leader in this German campaign was Schurz. To be sure he spoke primarily in the cities, and more English than German. But his English speeches were saturated with German liberal views, and they had an effect on his American listeners that was far more infla. ning and convincing than the Anglo-American speakers, who spoke essentially according to the prescriptions of the party platform. His innumerable German comrades, who essentially worked in the "bush" and spoke only German, took their recipe from Schurz. To the *American* ammunition, they added their own impetus and enthusiasm. There were also few pauses in this agitation. They did not want to give good Michel the opportunity to get sleepy again. If there was no political work afoot, the moustaches would make visits to their new friends in the bush. They would be received in a friendly manner, and the relations already established would be preserved in a lively manner. Michel really remained awake.

This electoral work was genuinely a great blessing for the Forty-Eighters. They finally came out of their cliquishness, out of the narrow, closed atmosphere of their too-cultivated refugee comradeship. They were increasingly Americanized, and they finally got to know the Anglo-Americans better. They deepened themselves increasingly in the history and manner of the country, which now was their own homeland, and which they now learned to love. They grew more practical, learning to see and laugh at the silliness of their reform proposals during their time as refugees, although they had nothing to be ashamed about. Everything they had tried to do then arose from profoundly honorable convictions; it was merely the product of a misunderstood situation and of youthful drive to act. They soon felt solid ground under themselves, and eventually their material misery vanished, as well.

The work the Forty-Eighters accomplished during the period from 1855 to 1860 was a fine and great achievement. But they exhausted themselves in that and in their massive participation in the war. What they otherwise did or would have wanted to do is, when closely examined, less their accomplishment than the natural result of the massive advance of Germans into America, specifically of the great ability and higher training that was in the horde they brought with them. The often-heard assertion that the Forty-Eighters created the German-American press would be hard to prove, for example. With the great demand for reading material in those days and the masses of Germans streaming in, it took no particular art to develop a press, and besides, the press in the time before 1848 was not nearly so bad as is asserted. It was only the rural press which was in dreadful shape. The editors before 1848—Rödter, Weber, Walker, Molitor, and Fieser, to name only a few of the gentlemen from the West—probably do not stand behind the most significant journalists from among the Forty-Eighters in terms of their accomplishments. Certainly there were more of the latter, because the number of newspapers grew so dramatically.

Perhaps the fact that so many Forty-Eighters, particularly so many of the best among them, went into journalism, was a hindrance to the intellectual development of these men. Editors in those days always had to translate a great deal, had to deal with dreadful local gossip, had to represent their paper in innumerable German associations, and often had to make speeches and deal with local politics, which is repellent for any serious and scholarly man. In short, they had to fragment and expend themselves, dealing with nullities and plaguing themselves with miseries so that there could be no talk of developing their intellectual forces. With time they were flattened into a sort of intellectual manual laborer. This is probably the reason why Forty-Eighters gave us so few men of *national* reputation.

Who could one name, other than the unique Schurz and perhaps Kapp? Where are the Forty-Eighters whose names have a reputation such as the significant Germans from the pre-1848 period, like Lieber, Stallo, Körner, Grund, the brothers Follen, Engelmann, the great engineers Röbling and Julius Hilgard, the scientist Wizlicenus, Theodor Hilgard, Minnigerode, Münch and Rattermann and many others who would be worth mentioning as well. Can one make a list of Forty-Eighters known outside of German circles who could compete with that of significant Grays? And yet the number of Forty-Eighters was substantially larger, and the time was more propitious for them. For their period of effectiveness fell in the period of the great rise of the American people out of petty-bourgeois and agrarian conditions to a nation aware of its cultural missions.

The basic failure of the Forty-Eighters consisted of the fact that so many of them clung to the Germans and not enough entered into the common life of the American people, contributing too little to tone and content from their rich treasure of knowledge and thought. Many might see the German mania (I use the term hesitantly, since it does not entirely fit) of the Forty-Eighters to be a special advantage for Germans. But the examples of Lieber, Stallo and Schurz already show us that one could be a great American and also be a powerful support to the Germans. Indeed, the intellectual significance of one German recognized by the entire American nation, the national reputation that our best have won has borne deeper regard and possesses more lasting value than the quiet efforts of many gifted and intellectually active men who withdrew to the corner of a German editing office, appeared scattered in Congress, or obtained local fame as physicians, teachers or lawyers, finally becoming German patriarchs of a sort before fading away, without even the next generation of Germans being able to recall them.

So far as Schurz goes, the objection can be made that this refugee from Rastatt, the liberator of Kinkel, was not even an American Forty-Eighter. He went his own way from the first day of his arrival in America, kept himself completely aloof from the reform efforts of his colleagues, buried himself in a small town in Wisconsin, and lived entirely for his studies there. He based himself entirely on the facts and regarded the German Revolution as finished. Schurz might actually be described as the only true emigrant among the crowd of thousands of his comrades. He became an American at once and dedicated to his new country the splendid gifts of his spirit, which he had developed at German universities as well as during his wandering years in London and Paris. His studies in Wisconsin were entirely for America; he felt in himself the strength to do good service to his adopted homeland, but he did not want to emerge until he had thoroughly learned the conditions in America, its history and Constitution, and the English language. When he was so equipped, the times were ready for him. The 22-year-old landed in America in 1852, but only three years later they were speaking in Boston, in New York, in the entire north through Minnesota, about this remarkable German, the great, intelligent orator whose words echoed through the entire country.

It is easy to prove that Schurz never really belonged to the *American* Forty-Eighters from the statements many of the other Forty-Eighters made about him. They often treated Schurz like a renegade, always calling him "Mr." Schurz, or during the war Schurz "the civilian." The manner in which Schurz the politician was unfortunately treated by a large part of the Forty-Eighter press, particularly after he accepted a cabinet post under President Hayes, is among the things that can only be hinted at here. In any case, Schurz's great service on behalf of civil service reform, which he introduced as Secretary of the Interior and whose true originator he was, is more valued by Anglo-Americans than by his compatriots.[12]

Nothing came of the planned German university in America, and only the German teachers' seminary in Milwaukee can be seen as a memorial surviving the period of the activities of the Forty-Eighters. This seminary is still on rather unsure ground, perhaps because it is seen, unjustly, as an institution for instilling radical attitudes, and thus is supported by only a part of the Germans. The Forty-Eighters always advocated German instruction in public schools, as well as the creation and support of German theater. Yet they have never claimed special merit for doing this, simply regarding it as their duty and obligation, as it has always been seen by educated Germans in America.

In recent times there has been complaint that the Forty-Eighters remained critics in the sharpest tones of the reorganization of Germany under Prussian leadership, and that they never showed any understanding for the greatness of Bismarck. In general that is true, but it must be stressed that Schurz and Kapp, and one might say Hecker, took an entirely different position.[13] During the Franco-Prussian War all German-Americans cheered, and Forty-Eighters shed many tears of joy[14] when messages of victory came in from Weissenburg, Metz, Sedan, and Paris. The mood among the old freedom fighters changed, however, after the events at Versailles. The German Revolution of 1848–49 had done more to eliminate German small-statism than it had done to erect a republic. Through the foundation of the German Empire, the situation of the small federal princes appeared more secure than ever, and the new emperor was, after all, the victor of Rastatt.

The Forty-Eighters were also very upset that German Austria had been completely separated from the German Empire. These things were more the cause of that criticism than was self-righteousness or stubbornness. Further, the workaday world in America demanded so much from the capacities of the individual that even intellectually active Germans had trouble keeping up with developments in Germany. The waves from intellectual and political forces in Germany ebb considerably before they reach the prairies of the American West and strike the isolated German, who would love to receive their full force. The educated part of the German-American community has always lacked an intellectual central point from which its scattered compatriots could be supplied with good German literature, or through which a tie could be made to unite all intellectually active German elements. The daily press does not suffice for this purpose, and the various journals that seek that goal, such as Heinzen's *Pionier*, remained restricted to a small circle because of their politics.

To be sure, the hostility of Forty-Eighters to "Prussianized" Germany is not nearly so deep as can be implied from the often very raw and nasty tone clothing its expressions. That mode of expression was a remnant of the broadside literature of the 1848 period, as well as of the later refugee period in America. Whoever knows how the Forty-Eighters stormed against one another in America, and whoever recalls the mode of struggle that unfortunately prevailed during the battle of the Greens and the Grays will find what Forty-Eighters later wrote about Prussianized Germany to be rather mild. That coarseness was more a habit than a point of view. The unfortunate example given by the English press and rostrum during the period of passionate struggle over the slavery question and during the Civil War also deeply influenced the tone of the Germans. In any case, one should not judge the old freedom fighters over things that, properly considered, were only externalities and did not touch the core of their being and effort. The now almost all rest in American soil. Yet each of these graves could be decorated with the touching and true words of Konrad Krez, "And yet I love you, my Fatherland!"

Literature on the Forty-Eighters. Ernest Bruncken, "German Political Refugees in the United States," *Deutschamerikanische Geschichtsblätter,* Chicago (certainly the most penetrating investigation to date). T. S. Baker, "America as the Political Utopia of Young Germany," Learned's *German-American Annals.* Edm. J. James, "The Men of 1848," speech at the Schurz-Feier, Milwaukee, 1906. Friedrich Hassaurek, "Festrede über die deutschen Achtundvierziger," *Deutsche Pionier,* Cincinnati, VII, p. 112. M. von Meysenburg, *Memoiren einer Idealistin.* H. Börnstein, *Memoiren.*[15] C. Schurz, *Erinnerungen.* F. Kapp, *Aus und über Amerika.* Jakob Müller, *Erinnerungen eines Achtundvierzigers.*[16] Julius Fröbel, *Lebenslauf.* Esselen, *Atlantis.* G. Körner, *Das deutsche Element.* Poesche and Goepp, *The New Rome.* K. Heinzen, *Teutscher Radikalismus in Amerika.* H. A. Rattermann, essays in the *Deutscher Pionier,* Cincinnati. In addition there is the German-American press of the time. Francis Lieber, Life and Letters; Hense and Bruncken, "Wisconsins Deutschamerikaner," *Atlantische Studien,* Göttingen, Wiegand, 1853. Herm. J. A. Körner, *Lebenskämpfe in der Alten und Neuen Welt,* Leipzig, E. Keil, 1865. Gustav von Struve, *Diesseits und jenseits des Ozeans.* Julius Göbel, *Das Deutschtum in den Vereinigten Staaten,* Munich, 1904. A. B. Faust, *The German Element in the United States,* Boston and New York, 1909. Hugo Münsterberg, *Die Amerikaner.* Wilhelm Müller, "Der deutsche Protestantismus und die Achtundvierziger," *Deutschamerikanische Geschichtsblätter,* Chicago, 1909.

Participation of Germans in the War

Germans provided more soldiers than any other population group—216,000 native-born Germans, 300,000 Germans of the first generation, 234,000 men of older German ancestry— Criticism of the thesis of Gould—How would it have gone without Germans?

The number of soldiers from Germany in the Union army cannot be precisely established. During the first year of the war, the national origin of volunteers was taken in only a few New York regiments, and there is no basis for attribution for almost all of the first million volunteers. It was only in the second year of the war, when the Provost Marshal's Office was created, that the national origin of new recruits began to be entered in regimental lists. The only official listing of nationality is found for conscripts, and this only began in 1863. Of 343,768 soldiers raised in keeping with the conscription law, 36,740 men, or 10.5 percent, were born in Germany.

Only *one* statistician, Dr. A. B. Gould, took the trouble to gather what could be said about the nationality of soldiers from various sources shortly after the war.[17] We must be thankful to him for this labor, as partial and inadequate as it might be. The difficulties presented to a statistician were extraordinary. The name of one and the same soldier often appears twice or even three or four times in the lists, for the people were recruited for different periods. There were three-month volunteers, those obligated for two years or three years, and those for the duration of the war. Because many of those mustered out later reenlisted, the number of repeated names is very large.[18] The statisticians have concerned themselves with establishing a basic number of soldiers who served for three years from the material as a whole, that is, from the names of those enlisted for three months, for two years, for three years, and so on. But these estimates differ. Gould only gives 2,018,200 white soldiers for three-year service. Pfisterer, however, comes to the basic figure of 2,320,270 men, from which the Negro soldiers, 186,000 men, have to be subtracted, so that according to Pfisterer 134,270 additional white soldiers have to be added to Gould's basic number.[19] Pfisterer's work dates fifteen years later than Gould's, and for that reason he could have used the much more reliable material provided by the Adjutant General in the course of time. The work of this German statistician is seen as the standard and is generally used. The correct basic figure of white soldiers in three-year service would then be 2,018,200 (Gould) plus 134,270 (Pfisterer), altogether 2,152,470 men.

First of all, it should be explained how Gould established the nationality of the soldiers. Of the 2,018,200 men in his basic number, he determined the nationality of 1,205,000 soldiers from the main rolls in Washington and in state capitals, and he determined the nationality of 293,000 of the remaining 813,200 men through a questionnaire to the colonels of the regiments in question. He learned nothing about approximately 510,000 men. The nationality of these men of unknown origin was figured according to the proportion established for the larger figure.[20] All of those not reported in the main rolls belonged to the levies of the first year of the war, and it was precisely among the first volunteers that the Germans were particularly strong.

In the second edition of his work Dr. Gould comes to the following results.[21] *Obligation number,* meaning the number of soldiers each nationality had to produce on the basis of their number according to the census of 1860, is in the first column. The number of soldiers each nationality actually provided according to Gould is in the second column.

	Obligation	number of soldiers
Native-Born Americans	1,660,068	1,523,267
Canadians	22,695	53,532
Englishmen and Scotsmen	38,250	45,508
Irishmen	139,052	144,221
Germans	118,402	176,817
Other foreigners	39,455	48,410
Foreigners, not otherwise described (a plug?)	278	26,445
	2,018,200	2,018,200

Let us look a little more closely at the information displayed above. How can we explain the fact that the Canadians provided 53,532 men when their proportion was only 22,695? Canadians are not resident in the United States in the same sense as Englishmen, Irishmen, or Germans. Men come across the border from Canada seeking work and go home to the north in the winter, but the *obligation* above is figured on the basis of their strength in the *resident* population of the United States. It is because so few Canadians were really resident in the United States that the number of soldiers provided by them appears so extraordinarily large. Why indeed did Canadians throw themselves with such zeal into preserving the Union? This is particularly striking in view of notorious, exaggerated hospitality shown by the Canadian people (and the government of the Dominion) to the enemies of the Union. A headquarters of the secessionists was always located in Canada, and the mail services of the Confederacy with the outside world were maintained throughout the blockade via Canada.

Irishmen only provided 144,221 men with their proportion of 139,520. Their obligation was hence 20,650 men higher than that of the Germans, but their contribution was 32,696 men smaller than the Germans. The Irish element was far stronger in the South than the German, and relatively more Irish than Germans fought with the Confederates. In the West, specifically in Missouri, the Irish stood with the secessionists at the start of the war, but there was a switch later on. The sons of the Green Isle otherwise struck a mighty blow, and the history of the Irish Brigade reads like a book of heroes.

According to Gould, his 176,817 soldiers born in Germany were distributed among the following states:

	Germans (Gould)	Total number of soldiers
Maine	244	54,800
New Hampshire	952	27,800
Vermont	86	26,800
Massachusetts	1,876	105,500
Rhode Island/Conn.	2,919	54,900

	Germans (Gould)	Total number of soldiers
New York	36,680	337,800
New Jersey	7,337	59,300
Pennsylvania	17,208	271,500
Delaware	621	10,000
Maryland	3,107	27,900
Dist. of Columbia	746	12,000
West Virginia	869	23,300
Kentucky	1,943	43,100
Ohio	20,102	259,900
Indiana	7,190	156,400
Illinois	18,140	216,900
Michigan	3,534	72,000
Wisconsin	15,709	79,500
Minnesota	2,715	20,000
Iowa	2,850	56,600
Missouri	30,899	85,400
Kansas	1,090	16,800
	176,817	2,018,200

We now come to the Gould Germans. We call Gould Germans those 176,817 Germans Gould still concedes in his second edition, rather than the 187,858 of his first enumeration. Gould Germans to the number of 176,817 can be compared to the obligation number of 118,402, giving a surplus of 50 percent, an accomplishment found in *no other nationality,* other than the excluded Canadians.

But besides these 176,817 Germans, nearly *40,000 more Germans fought for the Union.* How can that be proved?

Whoever knows Wisconsin, the home of Schurz and one of the principal areas of agitation of German Forty-Eighters, will say at once that the 15,709 Gould German soldiers do not stand in a correct relationship to the 79,260 men the state raised, even if one accepts that a thousand Wisconsin Germans served in Missouri regiments. In Hense and Bruncken's work, *Wisconsins Deutsch-Amerikaner,* it is explained that Gould's estimate of the German soldiers of Wisconsin is at least 1000 men too low. I checked with former Governor Salomon on this situation. Salomon served as war governor of Wisconsin from May 1862 until 1864. He led the business of recruiting and was certainly the best expert of Wisconsin's participation in the war. Governor Salomon responded to my question, "Unfortunately it was not possible for me to do an enumeration of the Wisconsin German contingent. But I have always assumed that at least 20,000 Germans served in Wisconsin regiments, not counting Germans who went to Missouri." If we take only half of Salomon's estimate to be correct, then we would get 2,000 more men from Wisconsin.

Further, one can figure 12,000 Germans from the 134,470 soldiers of Pfisterer's basic number that exceed those of Gould.

The state of Michigan did enumerate according to nationality the soldiers it raised. It is unfortunately the only enumeration of its type taken by the authorities of the states. According to that, Michigan enlisted 4872 German-born soldiers, while according to Gould that state produced 3534 German soldiers. Because Michigan did count its German soldiers, but Gould imputed them on the basis of very thin material, this Michigan result merits much more credit. Hence we have gained 1338 more German soldiers from Michigan.

Gould also did not consider those Union soldiers who came from the rebel states. He only considered the soldiers of the Northern states, the four border states, and West Virginia. But 26,394 men also served what are called the loyal regiments from Tennessee, 7836 from Arkansas, and 3156 men from North Carolina. There is no indication how many Germans served among these roughly 39,000 men, so we can ignore them. Further 1611 served from Alabama, 4432 from Louisiana, 545 from Mississippi, and 1632 from Texas in loyal regiments, not counting the refugees from the German parts of Texas and from Louisiana, so many of whom served in Missouri regiments. There must have been very many Germans among these 7386 men, for Germans made up the strongest single group of local pro-Union people. Yet very little is known about the composition of these loyal regiments from the South. We know only that the 1st Loyal Texas Regiment, 600 men, consisted almost entirely of Germans. Certainly we can claim 1000 men for our people of those 1632 Texans. In addition there are at least 1500 from Louisiana, Alabama, and Mississippi. That would be 2500 more Germans not counted by Gould.

We can also add to the Gould Germans above: 12,000 men from the more correct total of the Pfisterer estimate, 1338 men from Michigan, 2000 men from Wisconsin, 2500 men from Texas, Louisiana, Alabama, and so on, making 17,838 altogether. If it is objected that a part of these Germans is already contained in the Gould Germans, that could only have come from the last three categories (5838) and would only make up a small fraction. Yet this as well would be equalled many times over by the extraordinarily numerous German soldiers who enlisted in the earliest part of the war, who were not registered according to nationality, who must have been treated by Gould as proportionate with other population elements.

Around 1860, immigration consisted essentially of Irishmen, Germans, and Englishmen. The rest of Europe participated only to an insignificant degree, most strongly Switzerland, Holland, Belgium, Luxembourg, and France. The other Latin peoples, as well as the Scandinavians, only arrived in large numbers at a later date, and they hardly counted in 1860. Austria was also weakly represented, but those who migrated from there were all of German nationality. The same is true with the Swiss. Half the Frenchmen were Germans from Alsace.[22]

In most of the countries named, Germans had considerable minorities of their own people. The German emigrants to other lands showed a strong inclination to move later to America, as is shown by the new registration of immigrants according to their mother language in the last fifteen years. During the war, however, arrivals were booked according to their political membership. Hence no small number of Germans did not have German citizenship, but rather they arrived from Holland, Belgium, even from England. Many from Schleswig-Holstein were registered before 1864 as Danes, because as far as the outside world was concerned the seabound land was a Danish province. The remarkably few emigrants from little Luxembourg were also not registered as Germans. The Balts and the Germans coming from Russia were regarded as Russians. Hence the 75,000 foreign soldiers Gould throws together in the last two rubrics of his table include thousands of Germans, and even Gould's Canadians include many a son of a German mother. Germans had strong settlements in the southern-most province of Canada, in Ontario, which lay closest to the United States.

Because the Swiss and Austrians, according to secure figures, together raised 13,000 men of that 75,000, and since at least a further 7000 men must have come from Alsace,[23] Luxembourg and Denmark (Schleswig-Holstein), from Holland, Belgium and so on, we could claim a further 20,000 men for our group, without considering Germans who were booked as Canadians under the Dutch, Belgian or Russian flag.

When I published a forerunner of my work in German-American newspapers in 1908, I had figured the number of German soldiers in the Union army at 216,000 men. This estimate was supported by the first evaluation of the German contingent in Gould, which attributed to the Germans 187,858 men. At the time only the first edition of Gould's work was available to me, but the foregoing considerations entitle me to remain at my earlier estimate of 216,000 soldiers of German origin, even if we take as our starting point Gould's second estimate of 176,817 men.

*   *   *

Dr. Gould has included some explanations for his statistical statements that we shall investigate more closely.

The fact that the immigrants provided far more soldiers than the native Americans moves the statistician to the laudatory remark, "The immigrants took up the undesirable duties of American citizenship as willingly as they did the well-known rights of the same." But Dr. Gould does not seek to explain the superior participation of the immigrants, as will appear soon below. He believes that this stronger participation of immigrants was only apparent, evoked by the confusing fact that so little can be known about the ethnic identity of the first million volunteers. During the first years of the war, the true patriots enlisted in masses, while during the later period this element did not appear so prominently because it had been sucked dry by its earlier enlistment (save for the 125,000 young men who reached military age each year in the last years of the war). Because Gould's material gives only certain information about the nationality of soldiers in the later period of the war, when these soldiers arrived due largely to conscription and bounty, then the true American patriot gets short shrift; according to Gould's view, the nationality statistics are measured according to the results produced by the later conscription and bounty enlistments. Gould actually says, "It should be recognized that the methods used here lead to an underevaluation of the native-born American element, because the relative nationality of the troops recruited during the last years of the war is applied here to the unregistered soldiers who entered at the start of the war."

This presentation by Gould almost seems to be an effort to save the honor of the native-born element. But such a salvation of honor is entirely superfluous, because native-born Americans during those terrible years certainly did as much as any people in the midst of the necessities of war could have done.

The fact that the immigrants could raise more soldiers than the natives had a very simple, natural reason. An immigrating people has many more youthful men than a settled people, burdened with many women and children and much older men, can ever offer. There were only two immigrating female persons for every three immigrants of the masculine sex, and the number of immigrating children made up only 22 percent of the whole horde of immigrants. Older people seldom immigrated, and more than 90 percent of the immigrating men were under forty years of age. These are obvious facts, and the history of the 19.5 million Europeans who emigrated to America in the nineteenth century confirms this precisely. A glance at the statistics of the New York immigration authorities would have taught Dr. Gould why the immigrants could raise so many more soldiers than the native-born.

A quick glance at the statistics of the origin of the volunteers of the first Lincoln levy (figured according to the contingents of the states) would further have shown Dr. Gould that his assertion that the native-born patriots were first to enlist does not conform to the facts in the way Gould would like to display them (reducing the immigrant elements). On 15 April 1861, Lincoln called up 75,000 men for three months of service. What was raised was 91,816 men. Where did they come from? Certainly patriotic New England, where the most abolitionists lived, only raised 11,987 men. But from New York came 12,357, from Pennsylvania 20,175, from Ohio 12,357, from Missouri 10,591. These four states, where Germans were their strongest, produced 57,029, more than half of the men raised.[24] Illinois raised 4820, Indiana 4586, and New Jersey 3123, and the then quite thinly-populated but heavily German states of Wisconsin and Minnesota raised about 1900 men.[25] If the men of the first levy can make a claim on especially patriotic motives, our people does not need to give place, for its accomplishments in that period were larger than those of any other people. The cause for this is particularly to be seen in the agitation of the Forty-Eighters. If any nationality has been slighted in statistics for its military effort because no reliable proof of the national identity of almost the first million volunteers can be had, then it is surely the German, for it was the German nationality which was particularly involved during the first period of the war.

Unfortunately we must consider another error of Dr. Gould, in which he supports himself on the testimony of General Fry, Chief Provost Marshal. In his account (*Provost Marshal Report*, p. 75), Fry says:

It cannot be doubted that a thorough investigation of the facts would prove that desertion is more a crime of immigrants than of the native-born, and that only a small part of those abandoning the flag consisted of Americans. It is also notorious that the Europeans provided the great bulk of bounty jumpers. In the industrial states, particularly Massachusetts, Connecticut, Rhode Island, New York, and New Jersey, the number of deserters is particularly large, and that is not only because these states are sown with cities and towns, but also because these places are overfilled with foreigners. The respectable and diligent portion of this foreign population has certainly provided us with masses of loyal troops, but these were mixed with a large number of adventurers who would be unworthy of any land, who harbor no love for our republic, and serve only because of money.

General Fry, whose report is printed by Gould, appears in his remarks to be concerned primarily with the New England states. Because there are only a few Germans there, this accusation, quite unjustified in any case, strikes our countrymen less than it does the Irish. But the sense which comes from these assertions corresponds to the same nativist arrogance so often aimed against Germans. Wherever things were plundered or demolished, it was supposed to be foreigners; wherever one has to cover the stupidity of officers, such as at Chancellorsville, foreigners have to serve as scapegoats. General Fry should at least have had to prove his assertions from official material on the nationality of the 268,530 deserters[26] and the alleged 125,000 bounty jumpers.[27]

Deserters and bounty jumpers belong together, but most deserters were not bounty jumpers. We will treat them separately.

General Fry must know that most of the deserters acted after the mass murder called the Battle of Fredericksburg. The cause for this is obvious. The soldiers had lost trust in the leadership, specifically in the commanding general, Burnside. A sort of rebellion broke out among his subordinates, and Burnside actually wanted to arrest three of his generals, including his immediate successor Hooker. Desertion was also dreadfully strong after the failed Peninsular Campaign. These things indicate the prevailing mood among the soldiers.

And now the bounty jumpers. Whoever wanted to play this swindle had to be a particularly cool customer. He had to have some knowledge of the law and know the side ways standing open for flight. Above all else, he could not be burdened with a speech defect or the characteristic marks of a particular race, for that would have betrayed him easily if he sought to repeat his swindle. Germans and Irishmen were distinguished at once from the mass of native-born Americans, even before Michel or Pat opened his mouth and betrayed himself with his pronunciation of English. Foreigners were more easily found out in such swindles, and beyond that many of them were lacking what the Americans call smartness, in the sense of boldness.[28] This lack of smartness as well as being a stranger to the country prevented many foreigners from becoming bounty jumpers.

Fry's accusation might suit the Canadians, for they had a special advantage as far as flight was concerned. From years of practice, they knew the side ways leading to Canada. For them it was easy to disappear to Canada from Michigan or New York state and then to reappear in New England as "green" Canadians and take new service with Uncle Sam. Canadians were also not short of smartness, knowlege of the country and linguistic ability.

If, as General Fry asserts, desertion is less a crime of the native-born American than of the immigrants, how does it come about that the number of deserters from the regular federal army is far larger than for any other army in the entire world?[29] And this is unfortunately also true for the American fleet.

*   *   *

German soldiers had an especially high value for the Union army because so many of them were people who had been trained for the military in Germany. Many veteran Germans were scattered about mixed regiments, where they were particularly valuable. They functioned among their green comrades like non-commissioned officers. This influence is strongest in the arm in which the Northern army was greatly superior to the enemy from the beginning, the *artillery*. Even though weapons technology was significantly more developed in the North, there was still a lack of schooled cannoneers. The regular army could only supply a few. There the many veteran artillerymen from Germany provided massive assistance. The many German officers also played a major role in training of recruits. To be sure, not every German officer was a Steuben, but men such as Osterhaus, Willich, Sigel, Steinwehr, Stahel, Hessendeubel, Wangelin, Dilger, Buschbeck, Krzyzanowski, Schimmelpfennig, and others were of incalculable value to the Union army as drillmasters. And many a little ex-lieutenant who had once lost his German epaulettes due to enemies, women, and debts and found his way to the great overseas orphanage for busted German officers helped out and provided his adopted fatherland with significant, if forever hidden, services.

One could write a book of its own about German artillery officers, and another could be dedicated to German engineers in America. Among them were particularly outstanding men, such as Colonel Hassendeubel, who laid out the siege works around Vicksburg and found a soldier's death there; General Weitzel; Colonel Hoffmann of the II Corps; Colonel Flahd; Lieutenant Colonel Ulffers; Colonel von Schrader and the two German-Americans, Haupt and Röbling, Jr.

Three native-born Germans—Hilgard (Villard), Nordhoff and Thomas Nast—worked in leading positions in the Anglo-American press, the first two as war correspondents. Villard's accounts were devoured by millions of readers, and for a long time he was the pipeline from the leadership of the war and the American people. The German Nast was regarded by the rebels as a particularly hateful Northerner. Through his drawings, which always emanated genuine pro-Union sentiment, he served the cause of the North in an invaluable way. How many wavering volunteers were moved to go to war by Nast's pictures in *Harpers Weekly*?

At the outbreak of the war there were almost no general staff maps. Many fatal errors of leaders can be attributed to this lack of maps. Only in the course of time was this lack made up, and the mapmakers were almost all Germans.

The surprisingly strong participation of Germans in the war is particularly due to the fact that German-Americans never had such a splendid leadership as that during the war. In those days there lived the three great German-Americans, Lieber, Stallo and Schurz. They provided a large portion of the intellectual armor for the great struggle. They were assisted by men such as Gustav Körner, Friedrich Münch, and many other chiefs of the pre-1848 immigration. And then there were the Forty-Eighters. Most of these hotheads, even the older among them, went to war at once, and there were never more energetic recruiters and promoters of enthusiasm for war. Many a good Michel who had no notion of taking his hide to market was egged into war by the Forty-Eighters. (See the biographical section.)

According to the 1860 census, 1,276,075 native-born Germans lived in the United States, 72,000 of them in the 11 rebel states, a million in the North and almost 200,000 in the four border states of Missouri, Kentucky, Maryland, and Delaware. In addition came the German immigrants of the period from 1860 to 1864, about 100,000; then the German Austrians, Swiss, and Alsatians, as well as the Germans regarded by the census as Dutchmen, Belgians, Luxembourgeois, Danes, and so on, about 300,000 heads. Hence one could set the immigrant German community subject to recruiting at about 1.6 million heads. During four years this people supplied 216,000 soldiers. That is an accomplishment which exceeds the celebrated efforts of Prussia in 1813. The Prussia of that day, shattered by Napoleon, numbered 4.5 million residents and put 280,000 men into the field in the German War of Liberation.

To be sure the emigrated German people had far more young men than could be found among the same number of Prussians in 1813, and the first war against Napoleon lasted only one year. But in the Prussia of that day there was a standing army of 42,000 men; there was an army organization, although much weakened; the number of officers capable of service from the period before 1806 was significant; and Prussia received some recruits from Germany as a whole. Hence a comparison of the two accomplishments could not be carried out in every point. But the force represented in the accomplishment of the American Germans—216,000 men from 1.6 million persons compared with 280,000 men from 4.5 million Prussians—can be recognized with some restrictions. In any case, the accomplishment of the German-Americans appears to be the greater.

It has been asserted that General Robert E. Lee once said, "Take the Dutch out of the Union army and we could whip the Yankees easily." I have tried in vain to establish whether the great commander really ever said anything of the sort. It is often repeated in war literature written by Englishmen. It was cited by the Berlin correspondent of a great London newspaper on the occasion of Roosevelt's visit to Berlin in the spring of 1910.[30] It is altogether possible that this saying is falsely attributed to the Southern general. Many a flowery word has arisen on the basis of a myth. Yet one can assert that General Lee would not have been exaggerating if he had said it, but in *this* sense: "Without the German element in the North, it would have been easy for us to beat the Yankees." For every third man in the Northern army was of German blood.

The Germans of the South had come largely from the immigration through the middle of the eighteenth century; it was relatively small, and the great stream of later German emigration barely touched the slave South. The North of the United States was the goal for over nine-tenths of all Germans. Hence the Confederate Army consisted essentially of Anglo-Americans, Celts, and Latins, with a touch of Teutons who were completely anglicized by 1860. The Northern army, in contrast, certainly had in its ranks 750,000 men of German origin (immigrant Germans, offspring of Germans in the first generation, and descendents of immigrants of the seventeenth, eighteenth, and early nineteenth centuries).[31]

Truly, if these "Dutch" had been taken from the Northern army, then General Lee would have met with much less trouble. At least the course of the war appears to prove such an assumption adequately. And how would the economic power, particularly the financial strength, of the North have appeared in 1860 if the great migration of Germans to the North had not happened, or if it had taken place as piecemeal as it did with the French, despite the very significant interests they once had to protect in North America? Is it not a remarkable phenomenon that other than the Englishmen who dominate North America, of all the peoples of Europe, only the Germans have sought their way to America so early, so continually and so massively, despite the terrible perils of the crossing in the seventeenth and eighteenth centuries?[32]

The cause of this German emigration did not lie in the call of new land, nor in the lust to wander ascribed to the Germans. If this drive is so much more developed among our compatriots than, for example, the French, how does it happen that Germans now are happy to remain at home although there is still plenty of cheap land in America? The cause of the German emigration through 1860 lay in the miserable conditions of the homeland. Kapp is right when he sees German small-stateism as the most important stimulus to that modern migration of peoples.[33] The pressure on a people once burdened with two hundred sovereigns, religious and political persecutions, continual wars, and the indescribable misery that these brought, launched the mass flight of Germans to America, and an internal land policy too long maintained in its old form caused the powerful stream of peasant emigration that began about 1840. Germany would today be several hundred thousand small peasants richer if it had permitted even a modest redistribution of the latifundia at the right moment. These peasants should also be numbered among the emigration of refugees. They constitute the majority of the 3.5 million Germans who have emigrated since 1860.

* * *

In the preceding review of the participation of our compatriots in the Northern army, only *native-born* Germans were mentioned, but not the sons of immigrant Germans born in America. There is a complete lack of reliable estimates of the participation in the war by the descendents of Germans immigrating before 1830. However, it can be rather precisely determined how many German descendents of the first generation served in the Union army.

One must estimate the results of the census of 1900 on the descendents of German immigrants in its relation to the German population of 1860. (In 1900 this information was included in the census for the first time.) According to this, the German descendents of the first generation provided over 300,000 Union soldiers (estimate of Professor Faust of Cornell University). One should add to this the 216,000 native-born Germans, as well as the soldiers who were the descendents of *earlier* German immigrants. If one figures 750,000 men for all three groups, then one will surely come very close to the truth.[34] General Lee would not have been aware of these facts, just as any understanding of the enormous importance of German immigration to the economic development of the country completely misses Anglo-Americans. They always speak of one mother country, England, and do not suspect how much thanks North America owes to old Germany.

Germany's Sympathy for the Union

Of all the great powers of Europe, Germany alone stood in deepest sympathy for the Union. In England Confederate victories were celebrated with barely-concealed *Schadenfreude*, and privateers were later fitted out for the rebels (the *Alabama* and others). Napoleon III exploited the distress of the Union to carry out his Mexican adventure, in which he at first enticed Spain to cooperate. Even Austrian governmental circles were strongly interested in this situation through Maximilian's relationship with France. Only in Germany did the people as well as the governments stand united on the side of the Union. Frankfurt was the great market for the government bonds of the Union, which were primarily bought by small German savers, less on speculation than because of the cause that stood behind them. Bismarck had been won over to the cause of the Union by the American friends of his youth, Bancroft and Motley. King Wilhelm and Moltke were just as decisively opponents of secession.

In his great address on the occasion of German Day at the World Exposition in Chicago on 15 June 1893, Karl Schurz said:

> We look back to those dark days of the War of the Rebellion, when the Union appeared to shudder on the brink of destruction, when our army suffered defeat after defeat, when our not only enemies and enviers but also our weak-hearted friends in the Old World prophesied the disintegration of the great republic as a certainty, when the credit of our great republic had sunk to its lowest point, when the hopes even of the most courageous began to waver. With happy satisfaction we recall that of all the peoples of the earth, the German people alone never lost its confidence in the ultimate victory of our good cause and the future of America, that it loaned its savings by millions and millions to our hard-pressed republic and gave it new strength in the deadly struggle. That was the friend in need, who stands by his hard-pressed friend with trust, and this trust has been richly repaid, as it deserved.[35] To keep this friendship of peoples between the old and the new fatherland eternally strong is the wish the German-American holds warm in his heart, and which he certainly also finds in the heart of every noble, patriotic native.

Henry D. White, later the ambassador at the Berlin court, spoke at the jubilee celebration of the German Society in New York in October 1884 in a similar manner. He said:

> In the struggle against slavery, the earnestness with which German-American thinkers dedicated themselves to the fight with their pens, and the valor with which German-American warriors participated in deeds of weaponry, remain memorable forever. In those dark and dreadful days of the Civil War, when other European powers had only mockery, biting criticism, and threats for us, it was Germany from whence only words and deeds of sympathy came.

We may also recall a little-known speech of Bismarck. On 4 March 1868, the day on which President Grant took up his new office, Bancroft, the American ambassador in Berlin, had Bismarck, four other statesmen and some of the highest dignitaries of the court as guests at his table. The chancellor rose at the table to give the following address:

> Allow me, gentlemen, to interrupt your conversation for a while to say a few words on the occasion that has brought us together. On this day, on the other side of the ocean, the victorious supreme commander in the service of the United States enters office as your president. This event has a special claim to sympathy in this country, for it was a Prussian king, Frederick II, who was among the first at the birth of the American republic to greet it on its independence. As far as the later relations between the two lands, it gives me the greatest pleasure to establish not only from my personal experience, but also from the

archives the fact that this heartfelt agreement so fortunately inaugurated between Washington and Frederick the Great has never been clouded in the least. Up until now there have never been any difficulties between the two lands; nothing has arisen that could even lead to a dispute. For that reason it is both a pleasure and a duty suited to the occasion to ask you to drink with me in German wine to the health of the President of the United States, General Grant.

Germans in the South

Of the 72,000 Germans in the 11 rebel states, about 20,000 lived scattered across 8 states, so isolated that they were totally defenseless and had to join in the general rising of their neighbors in favor of secession. Only in Tennessee and Arkansas was there opportunity for pro-Union Germans to flee to Northern states, and considerable use was made of that opportunity. The remaining 52,000 lived in Texas, Louisiana, and Virginia. The glorious struggle of the German Texans, who constituted virtually a state within a state, will be portrayed in the following chapter. The Germans of Louisiana mostly resided in the great city of New Orleans, and there they constituted, with a strength of perhaps 15,000 heads, a considerable party among the 80,000 white residents of the city. Very many of them fled to the North at the start of the war. Those who remained behind were bound by their business interests. Their entire property, their position won through many years of painstaking work, was in play. Further, at the onset of the disruption, no one believed that it would expand to such an extent that there would be a four year war to the death. Yet one can say that there were only isolated secessionists among the Germans of New Orleans. This mood of the Germans was well known to the leaders of the rebellion. It was not permitted that the 20th Confederate Regiment of Louisiana become a purely German regiment; Colonel Reichard's six German companies were given four companies of Irishmen to complete the regiment. Many other Germans served in the Washington Artillery of New Orleans, an elite unit. The German Confederate contingent of Louisiana can be estimated at 1500 men, most of them serving under compulsion.

Georgia also raised a German artillery company of about eighty men under Captain Steigen. It was involved in the defense of Fort Pulaski.[36]

Hermann Schuricht's *History of the German Element of Virginia* gives very thorough information about the Germans in Virginia. Special reference must be made to this useful work. Some of Schuricht's most important information can be stressed here. Virginia, the most populous state in the Confederacy, numbered 1,047,299 whites in 1860, including only a few thousand native-born Germans. In contrast, Virginia among all the Confederate states had the largest population of *old* Germans, descendents of the immigration of the eighteenth century. They lived primarily in the Shenandoah Valley and certainly constituted the majority of the population there. It was this strongly anglicized German element that formed the core of the Stonewall Brigade, which won undying fame under General Jackson. Dr. H. Riffner, the president of the Washington and Lee University, who published an extremely sharp protest against slavery in 1847, was also from that stock. Hence even among the old Germans there were brave opponents of slavery.[37] It should also be mentioned in passing that the two Confederate generals, Armistead and Kemper, descended from old Germans. The first fell in the charge at Gettysburg, and Kemper was seriously wounded there.

Schuricht declares (vol. 2, p. 66) that in the first period of the crisis "not a single German Virginian, of American or German birth, was in favor of secession." This assertion is probably not entirely true as far as the old Germans go, but it corresponds to the facts for the small circle of immigrant Germans. Our guide says further, "It can be asserted that all recently immigrated Germans who joined the Confederacy did so with bleeding hearts and under the pressure of compelling circumstances; but whether compelled or not, they fulfilled their duty with unfailing German valor." Schuricht and Melchers, as well as the South Carolinian General Wagener, were opponents of slavery their whole lives long, and they served their states with bleeding hearts. They fought for a peaceful compromise as long as they could, and they were long regarded as abolitionists by their secessionist fellow citizens. One of their friends, the German Union man H. L. Wiegand in Richmond, lingered for months in prison under the suspicion of being a traitor to his home state.

Later, after the war had broken out, the individual was no longer able to abstain from the general movement of things, and these pro-Union Germans had to either leave the country or give military service to the state. Most of them did the latter. There could hardly have been more than a thousand men, including the 110 Jews listed by name by Simon Wolf (*The American Jew as Patriot*), who served in Virginia regiments. Schuricht counts as German Confederate troops 2 companies (160 men) and 2 Home Guard units (also 160 men). The sole official representative of Germany in Virginia was the consul of Bremen, but his protection for Germans not yet naturalized was only respected at the beginning of the war.

In the northwestern part of Virginia that remained loyal, forty counties that later organized as the state of West Virginia, Schuricht says that the German element made up a third of the population, although most of these were old Germans. There were 10,512 immigrant Germans in West Virginia, of which 9612 lived in the capital of Wheeling, a town of 34,500 residents. According to Gould, only 869 Germans enlisted for the Union in West Virginia. But Schuricht declares that this figure is far too low. He says that of the Union troops of the new state, one-third, 12,200 men, were either Germans or descendents of Germans. The first governor of the state, Boreman, was an old German. Of the 44,000 votes given in West Virginia on secession, only 4000 were for secession. To be sure, slavery was almost unknown in the area; like eastern Tennessee, West Virginia is a land of small farmers. Both of these areas proved to be strong bullwarks of pro-Unionists. Schuricht demonstrates thoroughly that the strong old German element of West Virginia was as good as unanimous for remaining in the Union. That immigrant Germans held the same position is shown by the fact that German instruction was introduced in the *public* schools in recognition of the patriotic effort of the Germans for the Union. In the northern Shenandoah Valley, belonging to West Virginia, Union troops always found friends in the strong old German population. It was only beyond the new state boundaries that one found many rebels in the civilian population. Schuricht also remarks that German is taught in every college and university of West Virginia.

The Pro-Union Germans in Texas

A Little Germany in the Wildest West—Sisterdale and Latin Germans—
Olmsted's description—The secession in Texas—The Comanches—Conversion with
the rope—Hundreds of peaceful Germans murdered—The battle on the Nueces River.

Texas presents us with the most splendid, but also the most horrifying example of
German loyalty to the Union. Surrounded by deadly enemies, separated by thousands
of miles from their allies in the North, delivered helplessly to raw force, the Germans of
Texas fought and suffered for their convictions with astonishing tenacity through four
terrible years. Yet in the innumerable histories of the War of Secession, there is virtually
nothing about this struggle, and even the best experts of American military history can
give only a little information. The thorough treatment that this heroic history deserves
can not be undertaken here; I only hope that the history of the Texas Germans will appear
in a study of its own.[38]

* * *

Texas was taken from the Mexicans in 1836 as a result of one of the revolutions
organized by American slaveowners. It organized itself as an independent republic and
entered the Union in 1845 as a slave state. Texas exceeds the area of the German Empire
by more than a third. It is about as large as modern Germany along with Switzerland,
Holland, Belgium and Denmark. The state only had 300,000 white residents, along with
as many Negro slaves, Mexicans, and settled Indians.

Texas took an exceptional position among the Southern states as far as German
immigration is concerned. The state received a relatively intense German immigration
from the powerful streams of the 1840s and 1850s, and in 1860 Texas was one of the most
German states in the Union. A fifth of the white people of Texas were then of German
origin, including 22,000 native-born Germans. The German portion of the huge state lies
in the southwest of Texas, between the Colorado and the San Antonio Rivers. Its center-
point is the charming valley of the Guadalupe near the Comal Mountains. The area is very
well watered, the many river valleys are extraordinarily fertile, and even then the land was
splendidly developed, a blooming garden in the middle of extensive prairies and waste-
lands. In Texas there were among the Germans no Anglicized old Germans, as is the case in
Pennsylvania, New York, and Maryland. The new German element, immigrants and their
descendents, were entirely on their own. The number of native-born Germans was twice
as great as the native-born Irish, English, French, and Spaniards all taken together.

Germans kept to themselves in four purely German counties. They founded three
German towns, Friedrichsburg, New Braunfels and Börne, and in those days they were
a majority of the white population in San Antonio and Austin. In addition to these towns
there were rural communities such as New Ulm that enclosed the towns, villages of High
Hill (once named for Robert Blum), Berlin, Catspring, Millheim, Content, Felsburg, Sisterdale, Kerryville, Ulnau, Concrete, Meyersville, and Hochheim. Batrop, Castroville, Fayetteville, La Grange, and Columbus were also strongly settled by Germans. The entire area was
a Little Germany. The children spoke only German and learned English later, and even
some of the few Negroes in this area spoke German, according to Olmsted. There were

only German churches in this area, and there was from an early time a well-led and influential German press.[39]

The first Germans had already arrived during the Mexican period, at the end of the 1820s, and then from 1842 to 1846 the *Deutscher Adelsverein* brought several thousand Hessians and Nassauers to this area. More than two thousand of these compatriots died dreadfully in the desert that lies between the coast and the German settlements. The strongest German immigration, coming to prepared lands, arrived as a result of the German Revolution. Many very wealthy, even rich Germans were to be found among these refugees, who bought large areas of land and could erect extended plantations. But German money did less service in the establishment of this Little Germany in the heart of Texas than did the capital of a spirit and love of freedom, as well as the hard work and tenacity that these emigrants brought with them from Germany.

The Forty-Eighters made German Texas a citadel of loyalty to the Union, proven true in 1860. They were decided opponents of slavery before they set foot on American soil. What they then saw of slavery in other parts of Texas made them into abolitionists of the type of Garrison and Wendell Philipps. The *Deutsche Zeitung* in San Antonio fought under the leadership of Dr. Douai for the suspension of slavery in Texas in such a manner that the *State Times* in neighboring Austin advised its readers to drown Dr. Douai. A rope or a bullet would be too honorable to eliminate Douai in the eyes of that pro-slavery paper. But the Germans in San Antonio pulled together to defend their countryman, with weapons if need be.[40] Douai had to flee to the North at the end of the 1850s. The newspaper then became colorless, but it still died an honorable death as a Union paper after the outbreak of the Civil War, under Hertzfeld's editorship.

Judge August Richter of San Antonio has written a series of stories on Little Germany in Texas for the Sunday supplement of the *New Yorker Staatszeitung*, the novella, *Ein verfehltes Leben*, which appeared as a prize-winning work in the *Cincinnati Volksblatt*, and an essay in the *Cincinnati Pionier*, vol. 10, p. 57. In the last-mentioned work Siemering concerns himself primarily with the Latin colony in Sisterdale, which may well be seen as the intellectual center of the Germans of Texas.

This settlement lies about fifty miles northwest of San Antonio in a splendid valley watered by the Guadalupe.[41] The landscape recalls Thuringia, and the name comes from the Twin Sisters, two peaks of equal height, the source of two sister streams. Siemering portrays the place as a small paradise. Here settled Ottomar von Behr from Köthen. Eduard Degener, a member of the German preliminary parliament and later a representative of Texas in the United States Congress, soon followed him. He was a very rich man, and his house was the center of the social life in the colony. Prince Paul of Württemberg, brother of the king, was a guest there, and he felt himself quite comfortable in the midst of this circle of German democrats and prince-haters. Julius Dressel, also a very rich refugee from Wiesbaden, became Degener's neighbor. Professor Ernst Kapp, a significant geographer from Westphalia and the uncle of Friedrich Kapp; Dr. Runge from Mecklenburg; Herr von Donopp, a former Prussian officer; Herr von Westphal, brother of the Prussian minister; the former forestry officials Beseler, Küchler, and Brückner and many other highly educated Germans belonged to the circle. Professor Lindheimer, to whom we owe the best description of the flora of Texas, lived alone nearby. Dr. Douai again, and many of the Forty-Eighters from Friedrichsburg, New Braunfels and the farther surroundings often came to Sisterdale, the salon in the middle of German Texas. But the families that gathered for celebrations were not mere elevated spirits or philosophers. During the day they were in the fields, and the women in the kitchen. They were not allowed to avoid any work, for there were neither overseers in Texas to relieve owners of the labor, nor governesses or aides for the housewife. They had to renounce many things of comfort, and mixed with the raw Texas backwoods atmosphere were memories brought from Germany of a past that they might gladly have exchanged for the freedom of their new home.[42]

The landowners of Sisterdale often gathered for scientific lectures, and classical music was also extraordinarily cultivated. Each house possessed a good library of intellectual and cultural works. The young people grew up in the language and outlook of their parents, but teaching in the schools that flourished in Little Germany were always bilingual. The people of Sisterdale placed special emphasis on teaching their children in English, but their everyday language always remained German. In the German population there were no illiterates, so shamefully numerous in the rest of Texas.

The previous account relates to the years immediately before the Civil War. What became of Sisterdale in the fall of 1862? The entire circle had blown apart; the fields lay fallow; the houses were plundered; von Donop was massacred by Indians; and Professor Kapp, Dr. Runge and von Westphal had fled to Germany. Several residents were hiding in the mountains or had gone to the North, while Degener and Dressel lay in a dreadful, filthy prison in San Antonio and stood for months in continual peril of being lynched. The young sons of the Sisterdalers had almost all been murdered in the name of the law. Their bones bleached in the wilderness on the Nueces River. Even the two fine sons of Degener had fallen there. Only later were Degener and his friend Dressel freed from prison, released on bail raised by secessionist citizens of San Antonio; but they had to remain under a form of police supervision in San Antonio and were in peril throughout the entire war of being shot down by any of the many desperados. The cause of these atrocities was the loyalty of those Germans to the Union![43]

* * *

Before the actual portrayal of the sorrows of our compatriots, a peaceful picture may be inserted here, a little idyll, as it has been left us by Frederick Law Olmsted in his wanderings through Texas. Olmsted, an Anglo-American, spent years traveling through the South, and he registered his observations in the great work *The Cotton Kingdom*. His wanderings are a part of that. Olmsted, an important engineer, was the creator of New York's Central Park. The Texas journey of Olmsted falls in the years 1853 to 1854.

Olmsted has rather little good to say about his compatriots, the Anglo-Americans in Texas. He portrays them as allergic to work, for doing things in the fields was the function of a slave. These Texas planters were almost entirely uneducated, their way of life the simplest imaginable. The food repeating itself at every meal consisted of bacon, coffee and cornbread. There was no comfort in the houses, the windows were partly broken in, and dirt and neglect were everywhere.[44]

Olmsted first traveled through the whole east of Texas, coming at last to the southwest, to Little Germany. Among the Anglo-Americans he encountered many prejudices against Germans. The essential basis of these prejudices consisted of the fact that Germans themselves worked in the field, which was humiliating for a white according to the Southern point of view, and the fact that they held no slaves, or very few, and were generally seen as opponents of slavery and loyal to the Union. Olmsted writes:

> The first German settlers we saw lived in little log cabins and had fenced in and worked ten acres around them. The houses were very modest, but they made a very good impression in that everything had been done to decorate them and make them comfortable. It could also be seen even in the winter that they not only harvested the cleared fields, but that the cultivation was of several types. The land was clean and carefully kept and gave a very positive contrast to the fields of the Americans, on which could usually be found standing cornstalks, was choked with tall grass. Everyone, men, women and children, were always busy with something, but they still had time to give the traveler a friendly greeting.

Olmsted came to New Braunfels and stayed in the Guadalupe Hotel of J. Schmitz. He describes what he experienced there (pp. 99–100):

> Never in my life, other than when I have awakened from a dream, have I had such a sudden change of thoughts as I had in that German inn. I did not see any walls of loosely joined boards or brown logs with gaps and holes jammed with mortar or painted with mortar. I did not find four bare walls, such as I had seen a few times at the homes of patriarchal Americans in Texas. Rather, I was physically in Germany. Nothing was lacking. There was nothing too much and nothing too little; I had been set down in one of those marvelous little inns that anyone loves to recall with thanks if he has made a walking tour in the Rhineland. The whole front side of the house was taken up by a long room. The walls were pretty and clean, painted with pleasing stencils. There were lithographic pictures on all sides in glass and frames. In the middle there was a large heavy table of dark oak with a rounded end. Around the walls ran benches. The chairs were of carved oak, and the sofa was covered with flowered chintz. In the corner stood a stove, in the other a small bar of mahogany with bottles and glasses. Tobacco smoke waved through the room. At the great table sat four men with long beards, smoking and telling us a friendly good morning as we entered and lifted our hats.
>
> Immediately the hostess entered the room. She did not understand our English very well, but one of the smokers rose and acted as interpreter. We were to have lunch at once. She took a tablecloth and spread it on the end of the table, and just as we had laid off our coats and warmed our hands a bit at the stove, the woman was back and asking us to take our places. She set before us an entirely splendid soup, then followed two courses of meat—no fried salt pork—two plates of vegetables, salad, fruit preserves, wheat bread, coffee with milk, and also splendid unsalted butter, butter such as I have never found south of the Potomac, where people always say that it is not possible to make good butter in a Southern climate. What is the secret? Hard work, care and cleanliness.
>
> After the meal we spoke for a while with the gentlemen in the inn. They were all trained, educated, well-bred men, friendly, thoughtful, articulate; all born in Germany. They had only lived in Texas for a few years. Some were traveling and

lived in another German settlement. Others had been living in Braunfels for some time. It was so very pleasant for us to meet such people, and they gave us such interesting and satisfying information about the Germans in Texas that we decided to stay here. We went out to look after our horses. A man in a cap and a round jacket was rubbing them. It was the first time anything of the sort had ever happened to them without asking; otherwise I would have had to do it myself or pay a Negro to do it. The best mesquite hay lay in the manger—the first they had to eat in Texas—and it so pleased the animals that they appeared to ask us with their eyes to let them stay the night. But was there still a sleeping room in the inn for us? Guests were already there; we could have slept on the open ground in necessity, and we would have been better off than before. We asked whether there was a place to stay the night. Yes indeed, gladly. Did we wish to see the room in advance? We thought it might be in the henhouse, but that was an error. In the courtyard was a side building, and in there was a small room with blue-painted walls and furniture of oak. We found two beds. Each was to have a bed of his own, so that we would enjoy the luxury of sleeping alone! That had not yet happened to us in Texas. The two windows had curtains, and they were covered outside with an evergreen rosebush. No pane of glass was lacking for the first time since we had been in Texas! There was also a sofa, as well as a secretary, and on it a complete encyclopedia and Kendall's *Santa Fé Expedition*, a statuette of porcelain, flowers in a pot, a brass student lamp, and a well-supplied washing table, and absorbent hand towels were not lacking. How that all appealed to us! The next morning we found that our horses had had a straw bed, also for the first time in Texas!

Olmsted now passed through the German settlements from east to west. His portrayals are always filled with the same enthusiasm concerning the Germans in Texas as on the pages cited. He tells of Sisterdale in the same way we already found in Siemering. And through Olmsted's entire account there runs, like a scarlet thread, the message that all the inhabitants in Texas from Germany were fundamental opponents of slavery, that they rebuked the plans already spiriting about for a division of the South from the North, that they were in general the most loyal adherents of the Union. Olmsted had not encountered a single slaveowner in the West, and while in the entire South there might have been as many as thirty Germans who held slaves, many of them only doing it because they could not find German maids.

Our traveler also found a shadow side of the Texas Germans. Many of them were freethinkers and pursued their veneration of reason to the point of bigotry. They let too much go, in their manner, and they had something raw about them which in fact suited their wild prairies. They also had a personal prickliness, which hindered common and powerful cooperation. That is, to be sure, an old German failing one which did not drown in the Atlantic Ocean. In social and political terms Germans do not take the position to which they are entitled. They extend themselves too little with the Americans. The two peoples know each other only slightly and regard each other with mutual contempt. The Americans have the advantage of having been in the country first. They are used to ruling over slaves and Mexicans, and their language is the dominant one. The have more capital and political influence and are also noisy and full of shameless presumption. Germans, in contrast, keep their peace, go about their own business, and allow themselves to be governed without much complaint. These planters did not like to have Germans in their hire, viewing free workers as competition.

We could cite page after page from this highly interesting book, but we can only pursue cultural history insofar as it is necessary for our better understanding of the struggle of the Germans with the secessionists of Texas.

* * *

Samuel Houston, the victor of the Battle of San Jacinto, which tore Texas from Mexico, was governor of Texas when the secession broke out. He was loyal to the Union and wanted to secure a neutral position for his state.[45] The slaveowners forced him out of office at once. His successor was a rabid secessionist, and Texas joined the secession on 5 February 1861. The people of the state confirmed this decision by 39,415 votes for secession and 13,841 against. The negative votes came mostly from Germans. The secessionists had been arming in secret for months, and at the start of February a mob of about 15,000 men stood ready to fight for secession. Several thousand men went at once to San Antonio, where there were a federal arsenal and a garrison of 1100 men. (The other half of the federal troops still stood on the Indian border.) These troops had been stationed for a long time in Texas to protect the settlers from the wild Comanche Indians, who occasionally advanced from the territories of New Mexico and Arizona. The Mexican border bandits were also a continual threat to the settlers.

The federal troops were commanded by General Twiggs, one of the worst of many secessionists in the officer corps of the day. Twiggs immediately capitulated to the mob on 15 February 1861, delivering to it the arsenal with its weapons and supplies to the value of $1.5 million and obtaining free passage for his soldiers to the North.[46] He himself, along with most of his officers, immediately joined the Confederacy. The capitulation also included the troops stationed on the Indian frontier.[47]

After federal troops had evacuated Texas, the Comanches immediately moved against the unprotected border settlements. Because German Texas essentially formed the cultural border, it was primarily the Germans who bore the consequences of this penetration. Tomahawk and scalping knife raged dreadfully among them.[48] The border people fled, as far as they could, to the urban settlements, particularly to Friedrichsburg, Kerrville, and Börne, the German settlements extending farthest west.[49] It took months before Confederate state troops were able to take over the border protection previously provided by the federal troops, but this protection was always inadequate, and the Germans who left their farms in the West could not dare to return.

The attack of the Comanches was only a preliminary to the period of sorrows descending on the German settlements. After the red devils came the white ones, who were worse because they raged on the basis of the law of the Confederate States. Two of these laws should be mentioned. The law of confiscation, issued by the Confederate Congress on 31 August 1861, decreed the confiscation of all property of pro-Union citizens who refused to swear an oath to the new government, or those of Texas who had already *moved,* leaving their property behind. "Moved" was interpreted to mean that they had fled to the North. That was correct in most cases. Many pro-Union Germans had fled to Missouri in the first period of the war and had enlisted in the Northern army, while others had fled across the Rio Grande border and had reported to the federal consuls in the Mexican cities of Monterrey and Matamoras and had been sent by them by ship to the North. Yet others had escaped through the Texan harbors.[50] It is unknown how many they were, but it is certain that 1000 German Texans stood in Missouri regiments.[51] These refugees had left their families and property behind in Texas in the belief that the old laws would prevail. Through the confiscation law, they were robbed of their property, and their families were surrendered to misery.

As early as 8 August 1861, the Confederate Congress issued the banishment law. Through this, every white male person above the age of 14 who had declared loyalty to the Union and did not wish to issue an oath of allegiance to the secession would be banned from the area of the Confederacy. The courts had the right to ban as public enemies all persons who would not take the oath within forty days. H. H. Bancroft said on this (*Geschichte von Texas*, vol. 2, p. 458):

> Through this law, men who had passed their entire lives in Texas were robbed of their property. It was primarily the German settlers in west Texas who had to suffer under these laws. After the proclamation of a state of siege, the house of every pro-Union person was free [for the taking]. Many of these patriots fled at an early point to the North, but the refugees of later times were pursued and mostly killed.

The local laws of the state of Texas pursued similar goals. In 1863 Governor Lubbock proclaimed on the basis of a state law that every male white person over 16 was regarded as subject to military duty, and that it was forbidden to provide a substitute.

As a result, pro-Union citizens of Texas were placed before the choice of fighting for a hated cause or fleeing the state, leaving behind family and property. Free emigration was banned, and secret flight was frequently equivalent to a death sentence. Texas was surrounded by the sea and other rebel states. Sea travel had ceased as a result of the blockade. Only the way to Mexico was still open, but this way led through the desert, which was beset by Comanches as well as Mexican border bandits. Further, in west Texas there stood strong outposts of the rebel army that pursued refugees but never took prisoners, no matter how many they found. Prisoners were shot or hanged without any trial. The newspapers in those days wrote about the strange fruit "that the trees of Texas carry."[52] Most of the pro-Union people succumbed to compulsion and had themselves enrolled in the Confederate army with the hope of deserting at the first opportunity or being taken prisoner by the enemy, then serving in the Union army. Many carried that out, such as the German soldiers of the 25th Confederate Texas Regiment who were captured by General Osterhaus at Arkansas Post. Germans entered the Union army from other Texas regiments that capitulated there.

Already in the spring of 1861 the persecution of pro-Union people had begun at the hands of a vigilance committee whose seat was in San Antonio and whose head was a prosperous businessman and a leading light of the Methodist Church. The excuse for this secret "people's court" which knew only the rope as a means of punishment, was the many actions of desperados. The Civil War and the imperfect police measures of the new Confederate government stimulated these covert scum to all manner of shameful deeds. But the vigilantes consisted exclusively of secessionists, members of the secret society of the Knights of the Golden Circle. Hence the hundredfold application of these means "to convert Union men to the true faith by way of a halter."

Many Germans could not bring themselves to take an oath of loyalty to the Confederacy, but still they did not want to accept the risk of secret flight. They remained quietly on their farms in the hope that the war would soon end. These people had taken the worst choice.

In the *Official Records,* vol. 15, p. 886 and following, are found a number of documents concerning the mass persecution of Germans beginning in the summer of 1862. The Confederate recruiting officials Flewellen and Bell in Austin demanded soldiers from the Confederate General Magruder to compel recalcitrant Germans into the Confederate army. Magruder answered that all foreigners who did not wish to serve the Confederacy were to be expelled at once from Texas to be placed in the field regiments of other Confederate states. It must, however, be done in such a way that no one was particularly disturbed! The demanded soldiers then came to German Texas to relieve the vigilance committee and "create peace." Their excuse was a rumor that 1500 Germans had hidden in the mountains near Friedrichsburg and were supposedly harrassing secessionist planters from there. All that was true about this rumor was that a number of young Germans who wanted to flee to the North had called a secret meeting of about five hundred persons at Bear Creek and had bound themselves there by oath not to enter the military service of the Confederacy. Of these, a group of sixty-five men organized as a column for escape under the leadership of Fritz Tegner, which group was attacked and scattered on the Nueces River, where more than half of the refugees died (on which more later).

The following information is taken from the book by Williams,[53] as well as from letters of my correspondent Sansom in San Antonio:

In order to drive the supposed 1500 bushwhackers (so they called the German patriots) from the mountains near Friedrichsburg, a strong unit of secessionist troops was sent on 15 July 1862 from San Antonio to Friedrichsburg. A certain Dunn was its leader.[54] He was a provost marshal of the Confederate Army, hence equipped with military police power, and he did not have to take prisoners if he did not want to. It may be assumed that the military commanders in Texas did not know anything more about this lowlife Dunn.

As provost marshal, Dunn issued a proclamation from Friedrichsburg in which the bushwhackers were given three days to come to the Confederate camp and take the oath of loyalty, or they would be treated as traitors. The deadline passed far too quickly, for within three days the demand could not have been made known in the widely spread district, which was in a state of siege starting 21 July. After the end of the grace period Dunn sent out patrols. Our source was involved in only one of them, and this brought in ten Germans from the area of Friedrichsburg. These ten patriots soon hung from trees, supposedly because they had made an attempt to escape.

There then followed, according to Williams, a manhunt for pro-Union Germans throughout the entire summer. Dunn continually sent out patrols, but they needed to take no prisoners. The exception was of one patrol that brought back five men, eight women, and many children. The men were put in prison (later lynched), and the women and children found shelter in Friedrichsburg. The other units never took prisoners, and in drunkenness the participants later bragged of their deeds.

On his way to the Nueces River, Williams came on the area where his comrades had lodged. Everything was wasted there, the fields as well as the houses. All the furniture smashed away by Dunn's means. The number of the murders committed by Dunn's misusing his police power was certainly several hundred. Sansom reported to me that he knew several of Dunn's victims, some of them being companions in fighting Indians in the time before the Civil War.[55]

The rage of the scoundrel Dunn in Friedrichsburg was the occasion for the flight of the sixty-five men (fifty-nine Germans, five Anglo-Americans, one Mexican) which set out from Austin under the leadership of Fritz Tegner at the end of July 1862 to flee to Mexico and go from there to the Union army. There are three different reports on this column: the official report of the Confederate Lieutenant McCrea, which appears in the *Official Records*, vol. 6, p. 49; the report of Sansom, who participated in the expedition as a guest of the Degener family; and the portrayal of the aforementioned Williams, who participated in the assault near Nueces and describes it thoroughly.

A German cad by the name of Burgemann had worked his way into the trust of the German patriots who had organized in the German counties of Gillespie, Kerr and Kendall to flee via Mexico to the North. The company from Gillespie County, those sixty-five men under Fritz Tegner's leadership, started out at the beginning of August 1862. Sansom, who knew the routes through the desert between Little Germany and the Rio Grande, served as scout, but he was under the command of Tegner. Burgemann informed the Confederate authorities, and a fourfold superior force (in which Dunn's murderers were included) pursued the refugees. On 9 August, Tegner had made camp on the Nueces River, a day's march from the river border. This camp was overrun during the night. Tegner did not take Sansom's advice that the troop flee to a neighboring hill more suited to defense, but instead stood and fought. After a brave defense in which nineteen Germans fell, the camp was taken. Nine wounded Germans were shot at once. The other thirty-seven escaped, but of these six were later shot, several starved to death in the wilderness, and only five men, including Sansom, reached Mexico and later entered the 1st Regiment, Loyal Texas. The murder of the wounded was done without the knowledge of the Confederate commander McCrea, who was severely wounded. It was committed by Dunn's people and another company commander named Luk, a New Englander.[56] The corpses rotted unburied for years on the campsite. After the war the bones were buried in a mass grave in Comal. Over it is raised a worthy memorial.

After the murder of the Germans on the Nueces River, there followed the devastation of the so-called Latin settlement on the Guadalupe, already described. But even these atrocities, through which our compatriots were suddenly robbed of most of their previous leaders, did not shake the loyalty of the German Texans to the Union. Then, as before, they stood by the old flag. As hard as it was to flee from the Confederacy in later times, many Germans managed to do it. Sansom alone led three groups—of forty-eight, thirty-six and nine Germans respectively—across the Mexican border, and they all found their way to the Union army. The disappearance of these people and many others was certainly noticed, because every boy over 16 was listed on the secessionist conscription list as liable to service. The families of those who fled often had to suffer in the most bitter manner because their relatives had preserved their loyalty to the Union. The resistance of the Germans against conscription continued until the end of the war.[57] Unfortunately, lynching did not end, either. In April 1865 ten German patriots held in prison at Friedrichsburg on suspicion of loyalty to the Union were taken from their places and hung on the trees in front of the town (Williams, p. 408).

III

German Accomplishments in the Civil War

The First Battle of Bull Run

The reader will now follow us to Washington, in whose immediate vicinity the first battles of the eastern theater of war took place.

There had been a state of war since 13 April, but no one had any idea what a dreadful war it would be. The federal government dreamed of a stroll to Richmond. The Southerners, on the other hand, did not find the energy to use their superior preparation to overrun Washington, although such an action by a few thousand men would probably have succeeded until 15 May. For the first time a certain hesitation could be noted among the rebels, which contrasted sharply with their tenacity and aggressiveness in the next years of the war.

After the surrender of Fort Sumter, the federal capital had been as good as cut off from the North for more than a week. The railroad bridges in Maryland had been destroyed, neither mail nor telegraph functioned, the seat of the federal government was without news from the North, and it was also almost entirely without military protection. Washington then was almost moribund, for most of the residents favoring the rebellion had suddenly left town. Only then did anyone notice how strongly the population of the federal capital had been permeated with enemy sympathizers. Those were anxious days, and there was a continual fear of an attack. But it did not happen. Slowly reinforcements came in, the first forts were laid out, and with that the feeling of security finally returned.

* * *

Emperor Wilhelm II once said, "In the Union the editors of large newspapers count as much as commanding generals in Prussia."[1] That was certainly the case in the first period of the war. Certain editors, particularly Greeley, bellowed like commanding generals. They continually demanded, "On to Richmond!" And yet the young troops could barely handle their weapons!

The South immediately commanded its military units to the north of Virginia. They stood under the supreme command of General Joseph E. Johnston. The larger corps, under

General Beauregard, took up a position behind the Bull Run, and the smaller under Jackson sought to defend the Shenandoah Valley, which offered an easy access to the heart of the South from the north. In response to this disposition of the South, the Union General McDowell also divided the troops available to him through the middle of July. Gathered under McDowell's own command south of Washington were 34,320 men, to advance against Beauregard. There were 18,000 men under Patterson who were to hold Jackson in the Shenandoah Valley and to prevent him from joining with the main Southern army. But Patterson was not up to this mission. On the day before the battle and still on the day of battle, Jackson's 9000 men took the railroad and went from the Shenandoah Valley to Manassas and Bull Run, where Beauregard was to square off with McDowell. Hence the numerical superiority of the North became an inferiority. Patterson's 18,000 men were out of action, 5752 men were to defend Washington, and the 6207 men under Miles formed McDowell's reserve. McDowell hence led 30,000 men fewer into battle than he could have used. In fact only 22,000 Union soldiers fought at Bull Run, including 49 cannons and not a single unit of cavalry! Beauregard, in contrast, had at his disposal 32,072 men and 57 cannons after uniting with Jackson.

If McDowell had attacked a day earlier, Jackson's auxiliaries could not have helped. But the Union general did not know the battlefield and did not even possess reliable maps. So he wasted two days overseeing convenient fording places across the Bull Run.

The battlefield of Bull Run lies twenty-five miles southwest of Washington. Two small towns—Centreville (North), Manassas (South), nine miles apart, with Bull Run in between—were the headquarters of the two armies. The land is very hilly and beset with thick forest with only a few fields. The Bull Run is a wild mountain stream with many shallows and some fords. Only one bridge crosses it, the stone bridge, near where the chief fighting took place and across which the Northerners fled.

Beauregard stood with his army behind the Bull Run, watching all the fords, which compels him to spread his troops wide. McDowell had to cross the river in order to attack. He chose a ford far above Beauregard's position, to take the flank of the enemy. But a very long march was necessary to use this distant ford, and the troops were not yet accustomed to it. This was their first long march. The sun burns very hot in Virginia in July, and the young troops have been under arms since 3 A.M. Soon they were ordered forward. But the troops moved slowly, what with bad roads, heat, and agitation. People left their ranks, plucked huckleberries, and everywhere drank the cold mountain water. Their packs were too heavy, the knapsacks were thrown away, including the vital provisions. Order was soon lost. Whole brigades fell to pieces in the course of the long march, and there were no solid regiments within the first hours of march. The green officers had already lost control of their people.

Hungry and harried, with gaps in their ranks, they encountered the enemy at about 10 A.M. on 21 July. The enemy ran away after a few salvos. Beauregard was not prepared for this flanking movement, and he had to gather his forces, which had been detailed to watching fords. Despite exhaustion, the Northerners attacked valiantly, winning significant terrain. They telegraphed their victory to Washington by 1 P.M. Then, however, the advance stalled. A chain of hills was energetically defended by Jackson. The rebel General Bee grabbed a flag and shouted to his wavering troops, "See, there stands Jackson like a stone wall!" From that dates Jackson's nickname as "Stonewall."

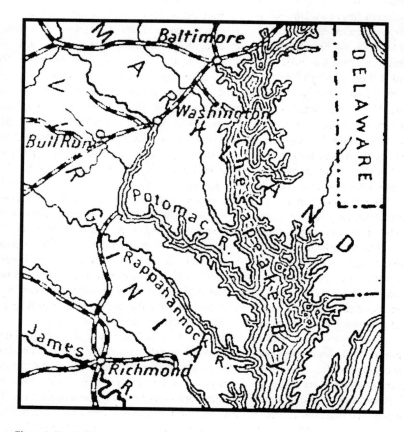

Figure 5. First Bull Run.

The battle came to a standstill. Beauregard and Johnston led masses of new troops in, and McDowell had committed his last man. Often friends were shooting at one another on both sides; so unused to war that they confused friend and foe. There was particularly persistent fighting around the Union batteries of Rickett and Griffin. The cannons were taken three times and lost again. Hence the recruits did not fight badly at all.

Soon after 3 P.M., 1500 rebels under Elzey, just arrived by railroad, emerged from the forest cover in an impetuous attack on the flank of the Northerners. McDowell's exhausted people could not sustain this blow. The regiments hit by the first onset threw down their weapons and ran away. And before it could be described, the larger part of McDowell's army ran. Everyone pressed down on the stone bridge. Some leaders, such as Sherman, later the great commander of the North, rallied forces and organized resistance together with a battalion of experienced federal troops. As a result, those in flight did get across the river, but then the general dissolution continued. Many ran as far as Washington.

Incidentally several units did not participate in this rout. The Michigan Brigade under Colonel Richardson in particular was solid. They stood a bit to the side of the actual battlefield, but they were not infected by the general panic and could cover the retreat in an orderly fashion, a glory later claimed by Blenker with his German Brigade, but which Richardson also deserves.

* * *

The German Brigade under Blenker played an important role on this fatal day. It belonged to Miles's reserve division. It was said that this general was drunk on the day of the battle. In any case, Miles lost his head and ordered his troops to retreat before they had accomplished their mission of receiving retreating troops and defending against pursuit. It appears that Blenker did not heed this order or that, in the general confusion, he did not receive the order. In any case, Blenker did not retreat but actually advanced a bit to where the Cub Run crosses the Centreville Road, which was filled with a great swarm of retreating troops heading for Washington. Here Blenker had his engineers dig trenches, sent part of the 8th Regiment under Stahel out as pickets, and set up his artillery so as to be able to fire if the pursuers gave them an opportunity. Many artillery pieces left behind on the battlefield were also gathered at Blenker's position, so that the position of this brigade was considerable as far as artillery goes, and that it could make an impression on the pursuers.

There was no actual fighting. Blenker's pickets did have a skirmish with the enemy cavalry under Stuart, so that they had a few dead and wounded. Blenker's position won the respect of the enemy, and the pursued forces stopped at this point. Later the battle report of the Southerners declared that regular troops had stood where Blenker stood, and that for that reason they had abstained from further pursuit. Blenker thus had the rare good fortune to be mistaken by the enemy as regulars (the much-respected elite troops of the North). This confusion was what made Blenker the hero of the day, even the savior of Washington, in the eyes of the anxious government and the leading circles.

Incidentally Blenker's Brigade (the German New York 8th, 29th, 39th, 41st Regiments and the 27th Pennsylvania, whose Colonel Einstein stood out by being absent) was also an elite troop, and it would probably have given the enemy as strong a resistance as the regular U. S. infantry, if there had been an attack. The Anglo-Saxon does not stand behind the German in valor, but these German regiments were the best trained in all of McDowell's army, and for that reason they probably would have accomplished more in the battle itself than their comrades.

Blenker remained at his post until 3 A.M. the next day, leaving it on orders. He retreated back to Washington, and he might have believed that his command was the last to leave the field of battle. In any case, Blenker had kept his unit and had disposed his defensive position well. Following him were several hordes of refugees. Blenker had also rescued several flags and a number of cannons. In fact Steinwehr's 28th New York Regiment saved ten or twelve Union cannons that had been left behind in the flight and were being cared for by the enemy. This German brigade received the honor of entering Washington with music and flying flags. Until then the federal capital had seen only the completely demoralized crowds of routed troops returning from the battlefield. Now, however, Blenker appeared. That was a different sight, a fully intact brigade of four thousand men. It is no wonder that the Washingtonians regained hope and came to the conviction that the capital could not be taken by the rebels, as was generally feared. Blenker was the hero of the day, the savior of Washington! That certainly went to the valiant trooper's head, and it was fatal not only for him, but also for the German troops under him.

It has been asserted that the rebels could have taken Washington after their victory. If they had this plan, it failed as a result of Blenker's resistance. But it would still have been impossible to carry through. With their light artillery, the Grays would not have been able to do anything in the face of the fortifications of the capital. Also, the rebel army was very disorganized and barely ready for battle. Many soldiers had gone home at once with the opinion that the war was over. Whole brigades dissolved, and it was several days before new formations were organized. The Gray army was an armed mob, too.

Bull Run can not be seen as anything but a general test of the war readiness achieved by the two armies. Such a battle could not bring the decision of the war, although certainly both Lincoln and Jefferson Davis harbored such a hope. Losses were equal, 1500 dead and wounded on each side, as well as 1400 Northern prisoners. Small spirited Northerners had the word for only a few days after the battle, and then patriotism and self-sacrifice asserted themselves in a splendid way. The volunteers streamed in by the hundreds of thousands, committed now to three years. The president, unwilling to make war, was now carried by a people enthused for war.

Three hundred thousand volunteers were called to arms after the Battle of Bull Run, and soon a second 300,000 men, and the Regular Army was raised to 40,000 men.

Blenker's German Division

The largest purely-German unit—10,000 men from Germany—The miseries of the German officer in exile—Blenker and his large general staff—Complaints against Blenker—Prosperity and fall of a climber.

Between the First Battle of Bull Run in July 1861 and the great struggles on the Virginian Peninsula lay a pause of roughly eight months, which one may call by McClellan's famous words, "All quiet on the Potomac." This period was used by the two opposed armies for their respective preparation for war. There prevailed a sort of armistice on the Eastern theater of war, and fighting continued only in the West during that time. Washington was transformed into a fortress, the strong war fleet of the North was created, and the artillery was prepared for the coming great battles. Yet the training of the young troops for true service in the field did not make any particular progress.

After the first defeat, General McClellan, who had distinguished himself in the small conflicts in West Virginia, took the place of McDowell. McClellan's training camp lay next to Washington, on the other side of the Potomac. The German Division under Blenker also stood there, at Hunters Chapel. The division had developed out of Blenker's brigade. According to Blenker it numbered 12,000 men in January 1862, although 10,000 is the correct number. It actually constituted a small army corps, if one applies the standards later used for a corps. It should be mentioned here that the designation of corps, division, brigade, regiment never gives any guarantee for the effective size of these bodies of troops. There were later corps of 25,000 men and those of only 8000; there were divisions that reached a size of over 10,000 men, and those with hardly 3000 men. Further, there were brigades of nine or ten regiments and those with only three or four. Individual regiments at the start of the war had the strength of Prussian mobile battalions, but they sometimes sank to only 150 members capable of fighting. Blenker's German Division was then perhaps the strongest of the entire Union army. It was composed in the following way:

> First Brigade, General Stahel: 8th New York (Colonel Wutschel), 39th New York (D'Utassy), 45th New York (von Amsberg), 27th Pennsylvania (Buschbeck). Second Brigade, General von Steinwehr: 29th New York (Kozlay), 54th New York (Gellmann), 58th New York (Krzyzanowski), 73rd Pennsylvania (Koltes). Third Brigade, General Heinrich Bohlen: 41st New York (von Gilsa), 68th New York (Kleefisch), 74th Pennsylvania (von Schimmelpfennig), 75th Pennsylvania (Mahler), 4th New York Cavalry (Dickel); artillery batteries (Schirmer, Dilger, Wiedrich and Sturmfels).

Among the men, South Germans prevailed, corresponding to the stronger immigration from the German south then. There were Badener, Bavarian, Rhenish Palatine, and Swabian companies, and even the Low Germans showed the tendency to gather into narrower homeland groups in companies. But most of the companies were made up of Germans, that is, representatives of the German populations. There was always an admixture of Swiss. Many regiments, such as Blenker's and De Kalb, the 8th and 41st New York, consisted almost entirely of German veteran soldiers. They could have added a fourth brigade consisting of the German nos. 7th, 20th, 46th and 103rd New York Regiments, but it did not happen, and these four regiments were given to other divisions. The officers of all of these regiments were Germans, the language of command was German, and even the uniforms recalled the fatherland. There were Prussian and Bavarian uniforms, even Italian in the case of the Garibaldi Regiment.[2] There were even some colored gray, like the uniform of the Confederates. It was only after a considerable number of soldiers fell to friendly fire, with friend confused for foe due to the gray uniform, that the uniform of the regular American army (dark blue blouse, light blue trousers) was generally introduced. The language of command later became English, at least at the regimental level.

The officers of the German Division were mostly emigrated German professional officers. What could be said of these gentlemen! One could fill volumes with their stories. Almost every emigration of an officer from Germany was preceded by a tragedy, and in most cases the sequel in America was little better.

The former officer had a harder time in America than other Germans. He found little help from his own compatriots. He was not trusted, was treated as a martinet and and dealt with according to prejudices that were usually entirely unjustified. His compatriots assumed far too often that the officer looking for a position had taken his departure for less than honorable reasons. And yet most of the emigrated officers were driven overseas, into misery one might add, through no fault of their own. Some were unsuited to the officer's profession, but this became known only after it was too late for the person in question to take another profession in Germany. Others were victims of seduction or frivolity, a wrongly led education, or an eccentric concept of the supposed obligations of a cavalier, victims of usurers who played with the destinies of men. Many former officers had enlisted as privates in the Regular Army. Others had sought work as market helpers and waiters. The noted innkeeper Lindenmüller in New York, a former hero of the barricades in Berlin, employed only waiters who had once shone as guard officers in Berlin and Potsdam. The number of former officers who worked as coach drivers, stable hands, and the like, is very large. Others became tutors, giving instruction in music and languages. Whoever managed to get a position as a teacher or journalist thought he had accomplished something.

When I was gathering material for the biographical part of this book, I learned all too much about the misery of the officer in exile. Often enough, a former lieutenant colonel served as a hired hand with a farmer he had known in Germany from his training of recruits. The subsequent master had come to America as a peasant youth, had settled himself on a bit of cheap new land, and with a business capital consisting of a lack of wants and a habit for hard work had prospered, honorably. The earlier master, however, could not come up with this capital, and he remained a poor devil, finally finding asylum with his ex-recruit, whom he had perhaps mistreated once upon a time in Germany.

When the Civil War broke out, the former officers saw in it salvation, a rare good fortune. But most of them received only disappointment from the war. Half of them were killed, severely wounded, or so damaged in health that they became unemployed. Whoever came out healthy returned to the old misery after the conclusion of peace. After the war there were streetcar lines in New York where the drivers and conductors were almost all former German officers. And many a former colonel was to be found among them. Pensions would only come when the finances of the Union had improved somewhat.

Among the many German former officers one continually meets in America are a considerable number who were only moved to emigrate by the war. Specifically, many Austrian officers were enticed here by the war. But many adventurers and swindlers also reportedly claimed that they were officers without having been, and some swindled their way up to colonel. Naturally each of these officers had the notion of having a field marshal's baton in his knapsack. One did not join a foreign army to remain captain or lieutenant forever.[3] But advancement was slow. Most of the rather green former lieutenants were hard to place in Anglo-American regiments. They lacked a knowledge of the language, nativist prejudice worked against them, and West Pointers thought little of the German officer. Germany had not had a war in fifty years, and at West Point it was regarded as the country of parades and militaristic pedantry.[4] It was obvious that German officers were not suited to handling American volunteers, who remained American citizens even in uniform, were aware of their status, and did not take well to the discipline that a green German officer takes for granted. So the gentlemen essentially had to serve in German or half-German regiments. There we find them in masses, and they could do their best there. But there were too many of them, and each of them wanted to advance quickly. Because that was only possible in one's own regiment at first, there had to be an ugly competition, which worked injury on the entire class.

There were elements in the emigrated German officer corps in those days that one would not find now. Quite a few of the Forty-Eighters had been officers. These included Willich, Weber, von Schimmelpfennig, Osterhaus, Sigel, Stahel, Buschbeck, Salomon, Anneke, and many others. A refugee's life and ten years in America had put them through a hard schooling, and their nature no longer reminded one of German barracks. But these men, still in the prime of life, did have professional training. They, as well as other officers who had emigrated earlier, such as Hassendeubel, von Steinwehr, von Gilsa, and so on, had Americanized themselves enough to serve as leaders of Americans. And so we see this element advancing rather quickly (of the officers of the Baden and Palatine revolutionary army, seven received either the rank or the title of general in the first year of the war), while only a very few of the ex-lieutenants of the later emigration rose. That is too bad. Many a good man never reached a suitable position, no matter how good he was. To mention only one, there is Dilger. He was mustered out as a simple captain, despite the fact that he was probably the best artilleryman in the entire American army.

Incidentally, many German and Austrian officers were invited to emigrate by American officials. In *McClellan's Own Story,* McClellan relates that through his consuls, as well as through agents sent especially to Europe, Secretary of State Seward encouraged the emigration of officers desiring war. McClellan does not say that Seward made any promises to these gentlemen, but one could imagine that the agents were free with such promises. McClellan received a letter from General Klapka, who had distinguished himself as leader of the Hungarian revolutionary army of 1849, which informed him that Klapka had been encouraged to enter the Union army by Seward's agents.[5] Klapka would have loved to come, but he set such shameless conditions that McClellan ran furiously to Lincoln and demanded that he forbid such recruiting efforts by the secretary of state. Klapka demanded a payment of $100,000 in advance, $25,000 salary per year, and his immediate installation as chief of general staff. Later, after Klapka had learned more English, he wanted to take McClellan's place as supreme commander of all armies! It cannot be determined how many German and Austrian officers were recruited for the army by Seward's agents.

McClellan cannot say enough for his two German adjutants, von Radowitz and von Hammerstein, and he was always charmed by Blenker. But his judgment of German officers was otherwise extraordinarily negative. He asserted that German regiments did poorly because so many of their officers were men without character. Both assertions are incorrect. The purely German regiments always numbered among the best of the entire army, and the biographical section of this book will demonstrate the ability of the German officers. But McClellan's portrayal has won such wide distribution that it is necessary once more to reject an entirely groundless assertion. Four purely German New York regiments that fought in McClellan's army the 7th, 20th, 46th and 103rd, which covered themselves with glory and whose colonels (von Schack, Weber, von Rosa and von Egloffstein) were all severely wounded. He says nothing about the extraordinarily capable men he certainly knew, not a word on his German artillerymen heroes: Hexamer, Arndt (who fell at Antietam), von Kusserow, Lepien, and so on. On the other hand he praises Rosecrans as a German, although this capable general was a descendent of Germans and thus was in the same situation as McClellan, born to Irish parents. McClellan's judgment seems to rest entirely on the lying report General Halleck sent him from Missouri. McClellan could have recognized Halleck's report as untrue from his own experience, if he would have bothered to deal with the Germans under his own command.

*   *   *

The striving among the German military described above appeared primarily in the German regiments in the East. The situation was entirely different in the West. Unfortunately efforts to gather German regiments into brigades failed, except for Missouri, where this existed automatically in view of the many German regiments. The fact that many German officers in the East, including the most gifted and capable, were dissatisfied with their positions was natural. How could the American military authorities know which of the many German candidates was the most qualified? They should have marvelled that there were not more mistakes, that more German swindlers, politicos, and crisis hounds did not take all the best positions away from the qualified professional officers. And there was a great deal of selflessness when men such as von Steinwehr, Bohlen, von Schimmelpfennig, Stahel, and the like had to tolerate people such as D'Utassy, Böttcher, Wutschel, and the pseudo-count von Schweinwitz-Crain as colleagues.[6]

*   *   *

The administration had a less fortunate hand in choosing the first German general of the Eastern army. Ludwig Blenker was the chosen one. He had served as a police officer under the Greek King Otto and had later won the reputation of a brave and careful subordinate leader in the German revolutionary army of 1848–49. He was then driven to America, and at the outbreak of the war we find him as the colonel of the 8th New York Regiment. This regiment consisted mostly of veteran German soldiers.

Blenker knew how to awaken the military vanity of his people, "They would show the 'lazy Yankees' how German veterans can drill," and the 8th certainly became an elite regiment, one which even old Wrangel would not have had much complaint about. The regiment came very early to Washington, in the middle of May 1861, and amazed everyone with its strict, genuinely military appearance. Incidentally, this was also the case with the other German regiments. But Blenker presented himself particularly well. He was a fine rider, and he made an outstanding figure on horseback. He paraded down Pennsylvania Avenue in his gold-braided fantasy uniform with his glittering staff. The beauties crowded to the window when Blenker rode by, for colorful cloth often counts for more in a republic than elsewhere, and Blenker quickly had the women on his side. They whispered, "That's the great Blenker, look at him, a splendid fellow." Thus Blenker became the general of the newly formed German Brigade.

Blenker's extraordinary luck at the First Battle of Bull Run has been portrayed already. In addition to this, the supreme general, McClellan, appears particularly to have coddled this German general.[7] Blenker was certainly not a true charlatan, but he was also not the man one would have desired as the first representative of military Germans of that time. What he had learned in the way of military sciences as a police officer of the King of Greece was certainly not significant. And he could hardly have gathered as a subordinate leader in the Baden campaign the technical knowledge a division commander must have. Blenker was a wine merchant during his period as a refugee in America, as well as an innkeeper and finally a vegetable farmer. He had modelled his behavior on that variety of German-American who was spiced with a whiff of the New York Bowery.[8] His Palatine

English was particularly dreadful. When he opened his mouth to give an English speech, educated Germans within earshot were embarrassed, and Anglo-Americans laughed out loud.

Blenker's staff was worth seeing.[9] All German and Austrian officers McClellan could not accommodate at once were attached to Blenker's staff. There the gentlemen lived as decently as possible from hope and the spigot, which often are hard to unite with an enormous thirst. For those so "attached" only received a salary once they were placed in a regiment. Blenker's staff, which once consisted of more than eighty foreign officers, was actually a kind of hiring hall. Blenker was the chief of the hostel for all his staff officers. He could not permit his comrades to starve, and the notion that they should thirst was entirely against Blenker's principles. So Blenker's numerous military family lived spendidly. Batteries of champagne were fired in a fabulous manner. Blenker could not manage a budget, and there was a deficit. Later accounts were drawn up, and then nasty accusations were made against Blenker. It was said that he had embezzled. It is possible that Blenker was not able to keep apart his private moneys and the money given him by Uncle Sam for general army purposes. In any case, Blenker believed that the costs for supporting his unpaid staff officers were to be covered from army funds, because the supreme general kept sending him masses of staff officers.

Blenker also made entirely unnecessary and very costly expenditures, which demonstrated that he loved self-aggrandizement and had become a real show-off. Thus in November 1861 he staged a torchlight parade in honor of McClellan, exceeding in pomp and expense anything ever seen in Washington before. Two thousand of his soldiers participated as torchbearers, and as many paraded under arms in a well-led parade march in column. Blenker himself, followed by fifty-six of his staff officers, rode at the head. All of them were splendidly mounted and appeared in the glittering uniforms of European armies. There were also a dozen military bands. At the end there was an astounding fireworks display costing thousands of dollars. All of Washington was astonished by this show. Even Lincoln, with bared head, watched the parade pass by. The reason for this costly spectacle was Blenker's drive to have himself named as one of the four corps commanders. But he sought this in vain.

Blenker told officials that his troops were unused to the wheat bread received by other soldiers, and that they had to have black bread. So the "Blenkers" were granted money to buy rye, to establish a bakery for black bread, and so on. Blenker also received the privilege to sell beer in his camp at Hunters Chapel. Hunters Chapel naturally became the place of pilgrimage for soldiers of other divisions, and the beer consumption in the German camp soon reminded one of Oktoberfest in Munich. Russell, the noted correspondent of the London *Times*, asserted that Blenker made $6000 a month from his beer privilege. This accusation should not have been directed at Blenker but rather at his quartermaster. Blenker had ordered that any profits should go to the regimental treasuries, but the quartermaster received the money and the regimental treasuries remained empty. There was also serious swindling going on in the bakery for black bread. Blenker's first quartermaster, a certain Dr. Schütte, a former hero of the barricades in Vienna, was discharged dishonorably. Somewhat later the gentleman was able to establish himself as a diamond merchant in New York. I do not believe Blenker himself ever stole anything, although many German contemporaries, particularly Heinzen, made rather naked accusations against him. In any case, there was no proof, and the circumstances speak completely against it. Blenker was highly negligent, and he did not control his subordinates, but that is really all he may be accused of doing. The accusations against him were never investigated. He was also never removed, but rather resigned honorably at his own request. Later his widow was granted a pension of fifty dollars a month. On 31 October 1863 this lucky stiff, once so coddled, died on his farm like a poor devil. It was said that he died as the long-term consequences of a fall from a horse suffered during the dreadful march through the Virginia mountains. In order to bury Blenker decently, his comrades had to take up a collection. He was certainly a climber of the sort best described by the American saying, "He could not stand prosperity." He went to his ruin over grandiosity and display, but he was an honorable fellow anyway.

As the leader of the sole German division, which was then certainly an elite unit, we would have liked to have had a fine, educated German officer. The fact that Blenker received that rank negatively influenced the role that our people were called to play in the Civil War, or that they could claim as a right, in view of their strength and the important military persons they could produce. The West Pointers continually referred to Blenker (whom they rightly regarded as a failure) if another German officer sought to make his claims in the Army of the Potomac.

Blenker never had a successor, although Sigel and Schurz entered the Army of the Potomac after Blenker's departure. But Sigel became a corps commander, and hence had a larger area of activity than Blenker, while Schurz became a division commander. But soon the German Division no longer existed. Schurz merely received units from the old Blenker group. Sigel is to be regarded as the supreme German officer of the Eastern army, but even Sigel never understood how to overawe the West Pointers. For that reason he was unable to put aside and overcome the damage Blenker did to German officers' reputations in the eyes of the authorities. Sigel's position in the Eastern army was made considerably more difficult as a result of Blenker's failure. (More on this in the biographical section on Franz Sigel.)

German Regiments

About 36,000 of the 216,000 German-born soldiers served in purely German regiments or batteries under the leadership of German officers with primarily German as the language of command. The remaining 180,000 men stood in mixed regiments along with Anglo-Americans, Irishmen, and the descendents of Germans, Irish and so on. To be sure, many of these scattered 180,000 were also with their own in the mixed regiments in that they formed purely German companies, and even battalions. But these ethnic units were too few in number to come to account in battle. What those 180,000 soldiers accomplished comes under the heading of the general accomplishments of the Union army.

Even those 36,000 Germans in purely German regiments could not be formed into such large units as to become an army corps or several divisions. The military leadership had to improvise the army, and it organized the available regiments into brigades, divisions, and corps according to the needs of the hour, and could not respect whatever wishes there were to keep German regiments together. When such an association of Germans did take place, it was more often a matter of accident. The German Division, under Blenker, came into being because New York alone had formed ten purely German regiments, and neighboring Pennsylvania four. It was not the intention to form the Germans into a strong division that created this German unit; rather, it created itself as a result of the simultaneous appearance of so many purely German regiments.

In the West, it would have been easy in the first year of the war to create a second division of German troop units of Ohio, Indiana, Illinois, and Wisconsin, but the Germans themselves appear not to have harbored such a wish. Many Germans, especially from the ranks of the Forty-Eighters, believed, "This is an American war, and we will strike as Americans for an American cause. For that reason we will set our narrower identity aside." But regional or national identity plays a large role in war. The Prussian Army owes a great deal to the fact that each of its corps contains the men of a single province. The French have recognized this as well, for they have copied the Prussian Army in these matters. Pride in one's own people is a factor that works positively on the capacity of units. Hence the association of the immigrant element into larger units would probably have been of great use, without one having to worry that it could bring harm in any other way.

For reasons similar to those in the East, a German brigade was formed immediately in Missouri. Reorganized after the discharge of the three-month volunteers, that brigade survived the entire war under the name of the Osterhaus Brigade, commanded by Wangelin.

Another German brigade (with some admixture of non-German elements) was the 2nd Brigade of the 3rd Division, XX Corps under Colonel Laiboldt. It consisted of the purely German 2nd and 15th Missouri Regiments and the half-German 44th and 27th Illinois Regiments as well as the German Missouri artillery under Schüler. It fought with distinction under Sheridan's command at Stones River, Chickamauga, and Chattanooga. Sheridan speaks of the deeds of this brigade with great respect and the highest praise, and one could likewise fill a fat little volume with the heroic deeds of the Osterhaus Brigade.

In general, however, the German contingent of 216,000 men presents an image of dispersal within an army numbering almost 2.5 million men and having almost 1500 infantry regiments alone. If we imagine that the Bavarian, Badener, and Württemberger troops had mostly been distributed to Prussian regiments at the start of the Franco-Prussian War, while perhaps four brigades of these South German troops, each of them only the strength of a mobile Prussian regiment, had been left intact, then we can get an approximate picture of the scattering of troops raised by Germans across the entire Union army.

German farmers and Germans from small towns could never get into German regiments, for outside Missouri and Ohio in the West only a few purely German regiments were formed, and there was little ethnic solidarity among the German rural population. Even in the large cities, where some German regiments were raised, many Germans entered mixed regiments. Captain Bohm in Cleveland, Ohio, has left us a summary of the German soldiers of that city, and this useful effort gives a good notion of the scattering of Germans. In 1860, Cleveland numbered approximately 70,000 residents, a good third of them German. Our compatriots in Cleveland provided almost half of the German 37th Ohio Regiment, a third of the 7th Ohio Regiment, almost all of the purely German

107th Ohio Regiment, and more than 100 men of the 20th Ohio Battery. Besides that, many Germans from Cleveland served in 22 mixed Ohio regiments and many of the cavalry and artillery units of the state, as well as in regiments of the states of Michigan, Missouri, Illinois, Indiana and Pennsylvania; in the regular infantry, cavalry, and artillery; and in the federal fleet.

My esteemed collaborator, Gallus Thomann of New York, has figured that 138 batteries in the Union army were commaded by Germans or the descendents of Germans. Germans also had a strong representation in the fleet, but unfortunately there is no further information. The officer corps of the United States Navy, according to Thomann, shows not fewer than 722 German names, including 28 German-American admirals and 6 commodores.

I now come to the review of the purely German regiments, and here I have to say a word of caution. This chapter has been a problem child. It has been reworked six times, and it is possible that the third reworking was freer of errors than what stands here. I had to give my collaborators a free hand, and these gentlemen were in little agreement among themselves. That is easy to understand. Who can still say, after fifty years, that regiment X was a purely German regiment, or that Y was more Swiss than German? In the same way, some regiments were purely German at the outset of the war, but they later received replacements through Irishmen or Anglo-Americans. The decision was toughest with half-German regiments. For that reason I will carry few regiments as half-German. Originally the list was much longer, and certainly a considerable number of regiments are missing that had a strongly German flavor.

New York raised the following purely German regiments:

7th, Steuben Rifles, Colonel von Schack.
8th, Colonels Blenker, Stahel, Wutschel, and Prince Salm-Salm.
20th, Turner Regiment, Colonel Max Weber.
29th, Astor Rifles, Colonel von Steinwehr.
41st, De Kalb Regiment, Colonel von Gilsa.
45th, mostly Low German, Colonel von Amsberg.
46th, Colonels von Rosa and Gerhard.
52nd, Sigel Rifles, Colonel Freudenberg.
54th, Colonel Gellmann.
103rd, Colonels von Egloffstein, Ringgold, and Heine.

All of these regiments, as well the 58th and 68th (half to three-quarters German), were organized in 1861, the first six already in April and May 1861, in response to Lincoln's first call. Included in these first German troops is what is called the Garibaldi Regiment, 39th New York, only about half of which consisted of Germans and Swiss. Also half German were the Serret Pioneer Regiment, the 119th Regiment, the 1st (Lincoln) Cavalry. Schurz organized the first four companies of this last unit and was being considered as colonel when he was sent as minister to Spain. The 4th Cavalry was also half German. In addition there were the purely German batteries, led by Schirmer, Wiederich (recruited from Buffalo), and von Sturmfels. There was one company of Anglo-Americans in the 103rd Regiment.

The German 52nd Regiment carried 2800 names on its roster, and only 200 men came back. Of 1046 Germans in the De Kalb Regiment, only 180 men were mustered out. At Cross Keys the 8th Regiment lost 220 out of only 600. The destinies of the other German regiments, the 7th, 20th, and 46th, were similar. They suffered dreadfully on the Peninsula and especially at Antietam and Fredericksburg. At Appomattox only three companies of the 103rd Regiment still survived. Not a single one of the almost 300 regiments raised in the state of New York was without a German touch. In April 1861, for example, von Steinwehr's 29th New York Regiment received a battalion of German Turners from Philadelphia that could not be accommodated in any of the German regiments in Pennsylvania.

Pennsylvania raised 17,208 German-born soldiers, according to Gould. But there were also 100,000 descendents of Germans. Among these were the Schalls, eight brothers who all served in the Union army. The only purely German regiments were the 27th, under Colonel Buschbeck, 73rd, under Koltes, 74th, under Schimmelpfennig, and the 75th, under Bohlen, later Mahler. The 75th was equipped by Bohlen at his own expense. The 74th Regiment was from Pittsburgh. The 21st Pennsylvania Regiment was almost entirely German, organized by Colonel Ballier and was later changed into the 98th Pennsylvania. Almost exclusively Pennsylvania Dutch, with an admixture of native born Germans, were the following regiments: 4th, 8th, 9th, 10th, 11th, 14th, 15th, 16th, 48th, 50th, 51st, 56th, 65th, 79th, 88th, 96th, 97th, and 98th as well as the 112th, 113th and 115th artillery units.

New Jersey. Many Germans from New Jersey served in New York and in Pennsylvania. Other than the 3rd Cavalry Regiment, recruited in Hoboken, no purely German regiments were formed in this state. Still, only a few New Jersey infantry regiments lacked German companies. Battery A of the 1st Artillery Regiment, led by Captain Hexamer, was purely German.

Ohio. A third of all members of Ohio regiments are said to have consisted of Germans and their descendents. The German part of Cincinnati resembled a war camp in the spring of 1861, says Rattermann. Eleven Ohio regiments are regarded as German, but only four were really pure German. They were the 9th (Turner) Regiment of Cincinnati, under Colonels McCook and Kämmerling; the 28th, also a Cincinnati regiment, under August Moor; the 37th, under E. Siber and L. von Blessing, from Cleveland, Toledo, Sandusky, and northern Ohio; and the 107th from Cleveland, under Colonel Meyer. The other regiments from Ohio regarded as German were, in most cases, either half German, or three-quarters German. They were the 47th, under Porschner; the 58th, under Brausenwein; the 74th, under A. von Schrader; the 106th, under Tafel; the 108th, under Lindberg; the 165th, under Bohländer. The 7th, consisting of a third Germans, can also be mentioned with this group. There was also the 3rd Cavalry Regiment, under Colonel Zahm, and three German batteries, including that of Dammert from Cincinnati, which was commanded from the second year of the war by Hubert Dilger and won undying fame. Further, there was the 4th Ohio Battery under Captain Louis Hoffmann of Cincinnati, later commanded by Captain Fröhlich. Markgraf's Battery from Cincinnati was half-German, and among the 243 men of the 20th Ohio Independent Battery of Cleveland there were 100 Germans. Ohio provided the German corps commandant Louis Weitzel, the famous cavalry general A. V. Kautz, General August Moor, and the titular brigadier generals von Schrader, von Blessing, and Zahm.

One of the best experts of the history of the war, J. E. McElroy, said of the German 9th Ohio Regiment in the *Record of the Chickamauga National Park Commission,* "No regiment is more justly entitled to the thanks of the patriotic people of Ohio for distin-guished services in support of the Union and the flag than the 9th Regiment." Two purely German Ohio regiments, the 28th (Moor) and 37th (Siber), were also raised early; the former was already organized in June 1861.

Missouri. Missouri raised 31,000 German soldiers, so that every second man in Missouri regiments was a German. Because the German population of the state was not even 90,000, this accomplishment seems extraordinary. The participation of Germans in the war was stronger in Missouri than in any other state. Many Germans might have entered the army because they were safer in the army than if they had stayed on their farms. The hatred of Missouri Confederates for Germans was fearsome. German farmers were shot down without mercy, their fields wasted, and their houses burned, because Germans in the chief city of St. Louis had thwarted the attack of the secessionists at Camp Jackson. Sigel brought over a thousand German refugees from southern Missouri to St. Louis. The bush-war did not cease in Missouri when the state was cleared of rebel armies.[10] The Home Guard of this state, consisting largely of Germans, had to do harder service than the soldiers who entered large-scale battles in the field. Further, Missouri was the great collector of Germans who had fled to the North from the Southern rebel states of Texas, Louisiana, Arkansas and Tennessee. Several thousand of these refugees served in Missouri regiments. Other thousands of Germans came from the neighboring states of Illinois, Indiana, Kentucky, Wisconsin, Iowa, Kansas and so on. Two thousand Germans are supposed to have served in Missouri from Illinois alone. Our source Schierenberg does not hold these figures to be exaggerations. Among the German regiments of the state should be mentioned the 1st (only half-German); 2nd, Colonel Börnstein; 3rd, Sigel; 4th, Schüttner; 5th, Salomon. Those were three-month volunteers. After the completion of their service, the 1st Regiment was changed into an artillery regiment, the 4th was completely dissolved, the 2nd, 3rd and 5th were reorganized for three year service with the addition of more German recruits, the 12th, 15th and 17th were refounded as German regiments. The 15th consisted largely of Swiss, the 17th was a Turner regiment in which a company came from as far away as Philadelphia; further Turner clubs from Cincinnati, Detroit, Milwaukee, Oshkosh, Peoria, Keokuk, Davenport, and Gutenberg in Iowa sent strong detachments to the 17th. The core of it was the St. Louis Turners. The 12th, 15th, and 17th regiments were formed in August, 1861. In addition there were the artillery battalion of Backoff and the batteries under Essig, Mann, *Neustädter, Wölfle* and *Landgräber* (the last called "The Flying Dutchmen"), as well as the German pioneer company founded by Sigel.

In addition, Missouri raised many infantry and cavalry regiments that were half or a third German. Ten thousand Germans volunteered for the longer term of service. Of the German Home Guard regiments, some of which were already organized in May 1861, the organizations commanded by Colonels Almstedt, Kallmann, Fritz, Hundhausen, Stiefel and Wesseling should be mentioned. Missouri regiments which were primarily German were the 39th, Colonel Kutzner; the 40th, under Weidemeyer; the 41st, under von Deutsch; and the 4th Cavalry, under von Helmreich. The first colonels of the three purely German regiments, the 12th, 15th, and 17th, were Osterhaus, Conrad, and Hassendeubel respectively.

Illinois. In Illinois, Friedrich Hecker founded two regiments, the 24th and 82nd. The first was not a purely German unit. Hecker soon resigned from the command of the first, taking to the field as commander of the 82nd, which was purely German. There was a Jewish company in the 82nd, from whose ranks came the later Colonel Edward S. Salomon (no relation to the four Salomon brothers). Their Chicago brethren raised a large fund for this company, and it was the richest in the entire army. The company was added to Hecker's regiment in recognition of Hecker's efforts for the emancipation of Jews. The company, which also contained some Low Germans, would have done honor to the old Maccabees. There was also a Swiss company, under Emil Frey, in the 82nd. The Körner Regiment, the 43rd under Colonel Raith, consisted almost entirely of descendents of Germans of Belleville. The 44th under von Knobelsdorf, later part of the Osterhaus Brigade, was also more than half German. The same was the case with the 9th, under Colonel Mersi, which suffered so terribly at Shiloh, although the regiment received non-German replacements after the battle. The 36th, under Colonel Greusel, the 45th, the 57th and the 58th may still be considered half German, but in the course of the war strong reinforcements of non-German elements were added. The 13th and 16th Illinois Cavalry Regiments were half German, as were the batteries of Stollemann, D'Osband, and Gumbert.

Wisconsin. In Wisconsin, the 9th Regiment was raised by Germans in response to Lincoln's first call, but it later became a mixed regiment as a result of replacements. The 26th Regiment, created by Governor Salomon in 1862, and commanded by Colonels Jacob and Winkler, remained German throughout the war. Its heroic story is similar to those of other German regiments such as the 9th Ohio; the 32nd Indiana; the 3rd, 12th and 17th Missouri; and the 82nd Illinois. One may also functionally regard the 45th Wisconsin as a German regiment. Among the regiments from Wisconsin that were more than half German were the 27th, under Colonel Krez; 34th, under Anneke; the 35th, under Orff; the 20th, under Bertram; the 18th, under Bruck; and the 23rd, under Jüssen. The famous sharpshooter regiment from Wisconsin under Colonel Kaspar Trepp consisted almost entirely of German Swiss. Wisconsin also fielded several half-German cavalry regiments and batteries.

Indiana. Indiana raised the purely German 32nd Regiment under Willich, which won immortal laurels. The 24th Indiana, under Gerber, who fell at Shiloh, was half-German, as was the 136th, recruited from Evansville. The latter distinguished itself on Sherman's march through Georgia. The batteries of Behr from Indianapolis and Klaus from Evansville were entirely German. Most Indiana regiments had a strong German flavor. The Germans Albert Lange and Johann B. Lutz (called Mansfield) stood out in the organization of the units of this state.

Minnesota. In Minnesota, Germans entered the army in large numbers at the start of the war. The 1st, 2nd, 4th, and 6th Regiments were more than a third German. The battery of Münch (later Pfänder) consisted entirely of Turners from New Ulm. One company history is that of Company A of the 1st Minnesota Regiment, which had 47 Germans out of 118 men. Of those, fourteen fell or died of wounds, thirty were wounded, and only three returned from the war whole. The 2nd Minnesota almost always fought at the side of the German 9th Ohio and played a glorious role in the decisive bayonet charge of the 9th at Mill Springs.

Texas. The 1st Loyal Texas Regiment, 600 men, was almost entirely German.

Michigan. Michigan's 4872 German soldiers all served in mixed regiments.

West Virginia. West Virginia raised one German battery.

Kansas. The 1st and 2nd Kansas Regiments consisted half of Germans.

Iowa. The same is true of the 1st Iowa Regiment. The other Iowa Germans, mostly from Schleswig-Holstein, served in mixed regiments.

Nebraska. The 1st Cavalry from Nebraska (Colonel Bäumer) was half-German.

Kentucky. The half-German 5th and 6th Kentucky Regiments both came from Louisville. The 6th Kentucky was regarded as the the state's best. The 2nd Cavalry and Stone's Battery also had many Germans.

All told, there were more half-German regiments than purely German regiments, but it is no longer possible to list them all.

The Saving of St. Louis

The first victory is a German victory—General Grant's evaluation of this success—Germans as bearers and protectors of loyalty to the Union in Missouri—Eight thousand German volunteers and home guards instantly in rank and file—Taking of Camp Jackson by Germans.

The first aggressive advance of the Union took place on 10 May 1861 in St. Louis. This provided the Germans with the occasion for a great independent deed, their most glorious single deed throughout the entire Civil War. They saved the most important city of the West from a coup by the rebel state government of Missouri, compelling the secessionists gathered in Camp Jackson (within the boundaries of the city) to surrender and thereby capturing the weapons robbed from federal arsenals. All of this took place without battle, through the encirclement of the rebel camp. There was no opportunity for deeds of heroism, but the fact that the Union was able to develop a superior force and win a success of such significance without sacrifice must be seen as a great deed. And the Germans deserve the credit for it.

The immediate results of this raid were enormous. The largest arsenal in the West of the Union was located in St. Louis. The volunteers of the bordering Northern states were to be supplied with weapons and supplies from this arsenal. The rebels, who had plenty of soldiers but they were short of weapons, had planned on having these weapons for 30,000 men. During the entire first period of the war, long before the outbreak of the first hostilities, Southerners had taken over most of the arsenals lying in seceding areas.[11] One smaller arsenal located in northwestern Missouri, in Liberty, was taken by the rebels on 20 April, and the troops captured at Camp Jackson were largely supplied with weapons stolen from there.[12]

Thus the saving of the St. Louis Arsenal was a deed of great importance. The rebels would have immediately been able to gather a strong army in St. Louis if the arsenal had fallen to them. But the great significance of that German victory lay in other things. Not only were weapons saved, but St. Louis itself was prevented from becoming an important fortress of secession and a sally port into the free states of the West.

In the book *General Grant Around the World*, dictated by Grant to his biographer J. R. Young, the following passage appears (vol. 2, p. 465):

> The great accomplishments that were done in Missouri at the start of the war have almost been forgotten. If St. Louis had then been captured by the rebels, this would have made a great difference in the conduct of the war. It would have been a fearsome task to reconquer St. Louis, one of the most difficult any commander could have. Instead of a campaign before Vicksburg, there would have had to be a campaign before St. Louis.

This judgment by the conqueror of Vicksburg can hardly be criticized. In addition, there is to be considered the moral impact that the conquest of a great city by the rebels would have had on the bordering Northern states. The war would immediately have been shifted to the North. The important border state of Kentucky would not have been able to preserve its neutrality if the Confederate coup against St. Louis had succeeded. In such a crisis a large part of the population at first stands apart and waits to see how the struggle will develop. But the first great success of one party brings these wavering and shaking persons to a decision. It was only after the victory in the mob battle of First Bull Run that the entire Southern people stood behind secession. It may thus be assumed with certainty that a secessionist success in St. Louis would have acted in the same way on the hundreds of thousands of undecided people in Missouri, Kentucky, and even southern Illinois and Tennessee.

St. Louis then meant for Missouri about what Copenhagen means for Denmark. The city was the heart of the entire state. Without St. Louis, Missouri could never have become a dependent to the cotton states, but with St. Louis, one of the most important of all the border states became enemy country to the Union. All of these factors indicate that the salvation of St. Louis by the Germans must be seen as one of the most significant and wide-ranging of all Union victories during the entire Civil War.

* * *

The border states of Missouri, Kentucky, Maryland, and Delaware lay between the rebel cotton states and the free North. They were slave states, and the great majority of their populations sympathized with the South. In Maryland and Delaware, the secessionist spirit was suffocated by the Northern army sent to protect Washington. But the federal government did not have one man or one dollar to spare for the protection of Missouri and Kentucky. Hence these two Western border states inclined ever more to the Confederacy, for their state governments were in the hands of secessionists. When Lincoln made the call to arms for the first 75,000 volunteers, alloting 4000 to Missouri, Missouri's Governor Jackson responded, "Your requisition is unlawful, unconstitutional and revolutionary, inhuman and diabolical in its purpose, and it cannot be concurred with. Missouri will not provide one man for such an unholy war!"

The countryside population of Missouri had already been in a virtual state of war against the Union for almost eight years. The struggles in and around the neighboring state of Kansas should be recalled. It was to be made into a slave state by auxiliary troops from Missouri. A dreadful guerilla war, man against man, farm against farm, had broken out in Kansas, substantially aided by Missouri border ruffians. In the course of this struggle the people was extensively coarsened. The failure of the slaveowners' coup against Kansas left a severe bitterness behind among their Missourian helpers. At the outbreak of the war the spirit of rebellion was almost as strong in Missouri as in the region of secession. This may be seen from the bloody persecution of the few Missourians who remained true to the Union and who had the courage to stand up for their convictions.

The state numbered around 1.2 million residents in 1860, including only 115,000 slaves. But the non-German parts of the white people—the Anglo-Americans, Irishmen, Frenchmen, and so on—were for the larger part sympathetic to secession, particularly in the rural areas. In the city of St. Louis, with a population of 170,000, there were about 60,000 Germans, Swiss, and Alsatians. These were all loyal to the Union, and the few exceptions could be counted on the fingers. There were also some upstanding, brave friends of the Union among the Anglo-American population. They stepped forward immediately, and as a result of their forthrightness they became the leaders of the Germans. Most important to be mentioned here is Frank P. Blair (a brother of Montgomery Blair, a member of Lincoln's cabinet), as well as [Benjamin] Gratz Brown and Captain [Nathaniel] Lyon, the leader of the regular soldiers protecting the Arsenal. But this element was very small in number. Only 400 Anglo-Americans stood in the 5 regiments, otherwise all German. General Grant, who had long lived in St. Louis and the vicinity, himself speaks of the city as a "rebel nest." There is similar testimony from Grant's brother in arms, the later General W. T. Sherman. In his memoirs Sherman says that the garrison of Camp Jackson consisted for the most part of the sons of the best families of St. Louis. As it happens, both Grant and Sherman were in St. Louis at the outbreak of the war, and both were among the onlookers at the capitulation of Camp Jackson. It should be stressed that the mood among the Anglo-Americans became more pro-Union after the taking of the camp. Only then was the peril in which the city stood was recognized. Under the Union flag, St. Louis could not be dragged suddenly into the confusion of war, and this did not actually happen for the duration of the war. Yet before 10 May, Grant's description of the city as a rebel nest is entirely appropriate.

The causes of that orientation lay essentially in the long years of trading between the city and the cotton states. St. Louis had become large and rich through this relationship. There had been important shipyards there for a long time. Loaded with goods, the steamers passed south along the convenient waterway of the Mississippi, and they returned with a freight of cotton. Hence large-scale trade, railroad and shipping interests, the banks, and the entire English-language press (with the exception of the *Democrat*) on the side of secession. This orientation had extended itself to the Irish element as well, consisting of 30,000 souls.

It was entirely different with the Germans. They stood man for man with the Union. This was essentially a result of the very effective agitation of the many Forty-Eighter refugees, who had been joined by the older German leaders from what was called the Gray immigration of the 1830s.

Incidentally, one might say that the broad mass of St. Louis Germans were then more capable of enthusiasm and less self-seeking than in later times. Our compatriots strongly felt the pulse of a great time. The so-called leading circles of the city had no idea of this mood. The pro-secession merchants did not know what was in the German newspapers, what was said in many of the German mass meetings, what took place in the Turner Halls.

Americans and Germans were much more strangers then than later. The true Anglo-Saxon looked down on the "Dutchman" with much more arrogance than in our days, and the German under the leadership of the Forty-Eighters had reached a less surprising over-appreciation of his own worth.

Even before Lincoln's election of 1860, the Germans of St. Louis had achieved a polit-ical unity such as has unfortunately never again occurred among our compatriots. Karl Schurz, who had begun to attract general attention for his flaming speeches, represented the principles of the Republican Party in a masterful fashion, unleashing the stormy applause of thousands of his German listeners in a great mass meeting. William H. Seward, the presidential candidate defeated by Lincoln, expressed himself as follows in a remarkable speech in St. Louis:

> Everywhere I go in Missouri it has been said to me that the Republican Party
> of this state consists principally of the German population. I am pleased that
> it is so. For wherever the Germans come, it is their mission to create a way for
> freedom. Whoever defends right against injustice is in the right place, wherever
> he might have been born. So let us happily permit Missouri to be Germanized.
> It was the Germanic spirit that won the Magna Carta in England, it was German
> philosophy that has filled the heart of all free men with hope wherever it has
> penetrated, indeed it was only the German genius that has encouraged freedom
> throughout the world So if it is the Germans who are to free Missouri, then let
> them be Germans. Yet I will not say that one has to be born here or there to have
> a heart in his bosom glowing for freedom, but I assert that the German spirit is
> the spirit of tolerance and freedom, and that it fights oppression everywhere,
> whatever mask or disguise it should assume.

It was of particular importance for the efforts of German friends of the Union that the Germans did not just live in a neighborhood of their own in St. Louis, but that Germans also gathered together outside the city borders in fine, flourishing communities. There was a circle of territory around the city, consisting of the counties of Franklin, Gasconade, St. Charles and Warren, that was in touch with the urban Germans and had its own leaders of special ability. Friedrich Münch, widely known under his pen name of Far West; Gert Göbel, whom we have to thank for a splendid book on the first German settlement of Missouri; federal Judge [Arnold] Krekel; the brave wine-maker [George] Husmann—all are particularly to be named here. They were all Grays and were highly respected by the German rural population.

The entire German-born population of Missouri, according to the census of 1860, amounted to 90,000 souls, of which 80,000 lived in St. Louis and environs. There were also many Germans on the other side of the Mississippi. The little town of Belleville, Illinois, was actually a German suburb of St. Louis, and one could describe the place as a small German republic of scholars. (See the biographical section on Belleville.) There lived Hecker, and many other Forty-Eighters had joined the older circle of Belleville German Latins. Nearby was the Swiss colony of Highland. Our compatriots in Illinois stood chiefly under the influence of Gustav Körner, for many years a friend of Lincoln. Franz [Francis]

Hoffmann, the lieutenant governor of Illinois, was also a fine leader. Hence the preconditions for a great German uprising in St. Louis were the best imaginable. The German press of the city was splendidly led by the editors Olshausen, Börnstein, Dänzer, Bernays, and Schierenberg. As early as January 1861, it could be said that being German and being pro-Union were equivalent concepts. The German leaders in the West quickly saw that there would be a passage of arms with the slave barons, and they made all possible preparations to mobilize the friends of the Union for these battles at the right instant.

On 18 April, a day after his rude response to Lincoln's first levy of troops, Governor Jackson opened the state arsenal to the so-called Minute Men (the rebel militia). The flag of secession hung in many streets in St. Louis at the several recruiting stations for the rebel army. Pro-Union citizens, particularly Germans, were mistreated by Jackson's police. Some of them vanished without a trace and were probably lynched.

The outspoken rebel C. F. Jackson had taken office as governor of Missouri on 1 January 1861. A law was immediately passed setting the death penalty for the seizure of a Negro slave. There was also a militia law giving the governor unrestricted disposition of the person, life, and property of all citizens. According to Börnstein's memoirs, there was no money to pay for this new militia which was to serve the secessionist army, so they took the money reserved for education and used it for defense. In St. Louis alone, almost 10,000 children were pushed into the streets. Börnstein relates that the urban police were taken from the city of St. Louis, and a new state police was organized consisting only of rebels. The new governor turned especially against the Germans, suppressing their theater, disorganizing their militia, and closing German places of entertainment with his police force.

Germans had already begun arming at the start of January 1861. At that time were organized three German Turner companies and the Black Rifle (*Schwarze Jäger*) corps, for which the rebel press invented the double-entendre name of Black Guards. At that time the Turner Society of St. Louis had eighty Anglo-American members. These immediately resigned once their German comrades began drilling. The preparations of the Turners and the Black Rifles could not be kept secret. Their drilling place was the Turner Hall, which was always being watched by rebel spies and Jackson's police. But this police force was entirely blind when an attempt to blow this Union fort into the air was made from one of the neighboring houses.

The principal work for German mobilization was done in silence. Trusted persons circulated throughout the German part of the city and established the addresses of compatriots who would enlist as volunteers as soon as Lincoln would call on the people. An artillery battalion, which was to be composed of experienced German cannoneers, was also organized early.

The rebels were amazed when, instead of a few hundred Turners and Black Rifles, *four* German infantry regiments and an artillery unit suddenly appeared on 17 April and began to drill in public. Capable officers were elected, and the Missouri contingent of 4000 men called for by Lincoln was soon exceeded. A fifth German regiment was organized, and a Home Guard of 3000 men was also organized.[13] For the moment, Governor Jackson could do nothing against such a force. For that reason he established a camp in the suburbs and occupied it with three regiments. The garrison was to be doubled as soon as weapons arrived from the governor of Louisiana. In a few days Jackson hoped to be strong enough to advance with superior force against the German regiments and take the arsenal.

Among the volunteers there were 400 Anglo-Americans, all in the 1st Regiment. All the others were Germans, according to Börnstein. The 1st Regiment, mostly Turners, elected Blair as their colonel. The 2nd Regiment elected Börnstein, editor of the *Anzeiger des Westens,* as its colonel. He had been an Austrian officer in his youth, then a journalist, an actor, a barricade fighter in Vienna, an actor and director of the German theater in America, and at the same time an editor, an author of novels, a brewery owner and a tavernkeeper. The 3rd Regiment elected the later outstanding General Franz Sigel, and the 4th Regiment (Black Rifles) Colonel Schüttner. In addition there was somewhat later the 5th Regiment under C. Eberhard Salomon.

The German units still had no weapons. The Union arsenal lay crammed with all manner of military supplies, and the men who were to defend the Union could not get to the weapons. Lincoln had qualms. He was afraid of irritating the rebels in Missouri by opening the arsenal to soldiers who did not have legal standing in the army. They could not be regarded as Missouri militia, for they in fact wanted to fight the rebel government of their home state. Nor did the German volunteers want to be enlisted as regular soldiers in the federal army, since they knew the brutal discipline used in the Regular Army.[14] 22 April Postmaster General Montgomery Blair finally managed to grab the president, figuratively, by the lapels and win from him the opening of the arsenal. This happened only after the German regiments threatened to cross over to Illinois and offer their services to the governor of that state.

On 23 April the German regiments marched to the arsenal, were sworn in by Brigadier General Lyon (until recently a captain), and were armed at once. The German Home Guard units were also armed at once. A part of the remaining weapons of the arsenal were sent to Illinois under Colonel Börnstein's leadership in order to arm the volunteers of that state. Now the St. Louis German volunteers drilled every day with weapons on the grounds of the arsenal, and the German artillery under Major Backoff and Captain Neuhauser could finally work with their guns.

After a few days, St. Louis had two hostile garrisons, the Confederates in Camp Jackson, the pro-Unionists in the arsenal. Governor Jackson tried to send as many men to Camp Jackson as possible, but his people deserted in droves once they learned of the strength of the Germans. General Lyon wanted to move against the camp as soon as possible, but he was hindered by his chief, the peacetime commander in the West, General Harney (probably a secret rebel). Thus days and weeks passed before something happened. On the morning of 9 May, Lyon learned that the weapons from Louisiana had arrived in Camp Jackson. On Blair's advice, Lyon decided to act before Jackson could strengthen himself further. He needed horses for his guns, and he rented them from livery stables. Thus the attack was known in advance, with the result that 500 rebels deserted during the night. This flight from the rebel flag continued until the morning of 10 May, and instead of the 2000 rebels Lyon had expected, there were only 1200 when the attack took place.

The capture of Camp Jackson. At noon on 10 May Lyon set out for the camp with his 200 regulars and the German regiments. They surrounded it, and after half an hour the commandant, General Frost, capitulated. As the rebel flag went down, secessionist onlookers fired on the German troops with revolvers, so that Captain Blandowski and two men of Börnstein's regiment fell.[15] The volunteers then fired without receiving a command, and they killed fifteen "onlookers."

Eleven hundred men and 75 officers were taken prisoner, and the stolen weapons from Liberty were recovered and brought back to the city along with the prisoners. The rebels of St. Louis foamed with rage. Free Americans had been captured by "mercenary Hessians" (as the defenders of the federal flag were called by secessionists newspapers in St. Louis)! The procession of prisoners had to pass through the city to reach the arsenal. The streets were blocked by the rebel mob, and every instant a street battle threatened. Through the restraint of the victors, who turned a deaf ear to all the curses, battle was avoided. Later, when the mobile regiments moved out to purge Missouri and only the Home Guard remained in the city, there were unfortunate bloody street battles.

During the following night the mob attempted a coup on the German newspapers and the *Democrat*, but preparations had been made. When the mob saw the shotguns of the German Turners, it retreated.[16] Of the curses that then rained down on the Germans in the St. Louis rebel press, I will only mention the assertion that "the Germans should never have intervened without being called into an American matter that did not concern them."

Some of the leaders of the St. Louis Germans in those first critical days of the Civil War should be cited. Mention has already been made of Olshausen, Börnstein, Münch, Hecker, Körner and Göbel. To them should be added Sigel, Bernays, Dr. Hammer, Osterhaus, Hertle, Schnacke, Dr. Weigel, Dr. Döhn, Hugo Gollmer, Governor Hoffmann, C. Eberhard Salomon, Judge Krekel, the Engelmanns, the Hilgards, and the Ledergerbers from Belleville. Dänzer remained more in the background. The finest thing about it all was that there were no self-seekers among the German leaders; no one sought to pluck laurels for himself, and all of these brave men were enthused with a selfless spirit of duty. There are few examples in American history of such selfless dedication, such purity of motive, or idealism so paired with intelligence and alertness.

*   *   *

One may seek in vain in the many English-language histories of the war for a proper recognition of this first and most glorious action of Germans in the Civil War. Insofar as the deed is mentioned at all, it takes place in conjunction with hymns of praise for Blair and Lyon alone. Even General Grant, who clearly knew the course of the taking of the camp, said at the end of the passage previously cited:

> We may thank Frank Blair and General Lyon for the saving of St. Louis, primarily Blair. It was necessary to give a decisive blow quickly, and Blair decided to do that. Blair called up *his German regiments,* placed himself under Lyon's command, went to Camp Jackson, threatened to fire if the rebels in the camp would not capitulate, and brought the entire band as prisoners back to St. Louis.

Grant gives Blair all of the glory, and the Germans are treated simply as fellow travelers. Blair called up *his German regiments!* These troops were not Blair's creation, but exclusively the work of German patriots. And to whom did the rebel camp actually capitulate? To Blair's lovely eyes, perhaps? Certainly not, but rather in the face of German bayonets. That was the only way capitulation was forced. Without these German soldiers, Blair would have been nothing.

Blair's work should certainly not be underestimated: in the face of the cowardly and treasonous attitude of the mass of Anglo-Americans of St. Louis, he is praiseworthy in the highest degree. The same is true of Lyon. These two men were the proper leaders of a movement carried by Germans. Blair was Lincoln's representative in Missouri, and Lyon was the only loyal professional officer on the spot. For these reasons, as well as the fact that Germans had formed irregular units and not state militia or federal troops, the Germans renounced the highest leadership and placed themselves under Blair and Lyon. But from this situation the view later developed that Germans were only fellow travelers, while in fact they alone gave the entire action the push to victory. The finest leaves in the laurel crown that was won in St. Louis do not belong to the two leaders, but rather to the German patriots. For they provided not only the troops, but also all the officers other than Blair and Lyon. And it was the Germans who, as Seward admits, lit and preserved enthusiasm for human rights in Missouri, making the preservation of the Union a question of life and death and providing the Union cause with support and backbone. Imagine how much respect would be paid to them if the Irish had done it instead.

General Grant closes his remarks in the following manner:

> The taking of Camp Jackson had a good and a bad effect. Many Union Democrats were offended by it, seeing it as a violation of states' rights. It was asserted that the government had acted too harshly. Further, the fact that the Germans had been used to coerce Americans—free Americans, who stood in their own camp ordered by the governor of the state gave offense. But no truly loyal man to whom the Union was the highest ideal ever disapproved of that act. The taking of the camp saved St. Louis for us, spared us a long and dreadful siege of the city, and was one of the greatest successes of the entire war.

The strong sensitivity about the feelings of the Union Democrats, emprisoned in their doctrine of states' rights, is explained to some extent by the fact that General Grant had once belonged to these circles himself. And when he adds that Union Democrats were offended by the fact that "the Germans had been *used* to coerce Americans," he is obviously only reflecting the mood of those Union Democrats. The naive style of narrative permits us to see that any offense to the Germans is far from his intention.

But if General Grant finds a "bad effect" in the taking of Camp Jackson, this reads almost like a justification of that constitutional howler which asks, in a time of crisis, whether the Union has the right to defend itself when murderers are at its throat. And with all his care about the states' rights people, Grant does not find a single word for the Germans.

Grant was not a man of advanced education, no Motley or Bancroft, Everett, Longfellow, Emerson, Whittier, Parker, Bayard Taylor, not even a Seward, Sumner, or Garfield. One cannot expect from General Grant the kind of evaluation of the German spirit that is found among these and many other great Americans. He only knew the German worker who came to America poor and hungry for land, the German whom one could use, whether as economic fertilizer or for fighting. The notion that it was the German spirit that won Magna Carta was entirely alien to Grant, although Senator Seward had said this a short time before in St. Louis. General Grant speaks the notion, promoted through education and custom and held as something proper, that the native born is a higher nature in comparison to the immigrant. The notion that Germans could show American patriotism that would be realized in deeds equal to those of the heroes of the Revolutionary War is entirely inconceivable to people of such cut. He and millions of his fellows knew only one variety of American, the "Americans of yesterday," as Motley tellingly described native-born Americans. In these matters one is dealing with a morbid tumor of nationalistic feeling.

Things have recently gone better because of the rising status of the German Empire. The astonishing economic development of Germany, the German Army, and the strong fleet have inspired some respect. But even today there is rarely a trace of the cultural power of the German spirit among the broad masses of the American people.[17]

The First Campaign in the State: Boonville and Carthage
Sigel's first retreat action—The departure of the three-month volunteers

After the attack of the secessionists on the city of St. Louis had been frustrated in the manner described, the next task was to occupy the rest of the state as quickly as possible in order to show the power of the Union to the great number of Missourians still wavering in their loyalties, thus overawing them. A fine beginning had already been made through the taking of weapons at Camp Jackson and through the occupation of the St. Louis Arsenal. Confederate troops in Missouri were then still a badly armed mob. It would have been easy to occupy the most important places in the state with 25,000 Union soldiers. These troops already existed in neighboring states; although they were only raw recruits, they would have been good enough as occupying forces.

Local authorities, however, relied on the government in Washington to requisition these troops, and during that time the government had completely lost its head. There was no dispatch of men from Illinois, Kansas, Iowa, or Wisconsin, and the opportunity to take the state of Missouri into federal hands was passed up until the middle of May. A bloody campaign lasting ten months was then necessary to do what could have been done with a little energy during the first weeks of the war, virtually without a struggle. Lincoln himself bears the primary guilt for this neglect, for he could not be moved to any aggressive action. He could not even decide to remove the supposedly loyal General Harney, who then commanded in Missouri and who made so many concessions to the rebels that it differed little from open treason. Only after weeks of hesitation was Harney removed and replaced by Lyon.

The campaign began in the middle of June. Only the five German regiments, the German artillery, and some companies of regular infantry and artillery were available. Lyon went with the larger half of these troops (the 1st and 2nd Infantry Regiments and the regulars) toward pro-Union northwestern Missouri to scatter the bands of forces gathered there by the Confederate General Price. He was able to transport his people up the Missouri on steamboats, and he remained in continual contact with St. Louis. His enemy tried to show some resistence at Boonville, but it was terrified by Captain Neustädter's heavy cannon and fled. The Confederates evacuated the state capital, Jefferson City, and Colonel Börnstein established himself there as military governor of Missouri. The scattered Confederate troops moved to the southwest of the state, but they were not pursued by Lyon, supposedly because he lacked means of transport. Lyon remained inactive for weeks at Boonville, although he had promised his colleague Sigel to press quickly to Springfield, in the center of the state, and meet Sigel there.

The mission Sigel was given was much more difficult. He led the German 3rd and 5th Regiments and the German artillery under Backoff. He was to advance into the rebel southwest of Missouri and scatter the rebels gathered there. But this force under Governor Jackson was about 4000 men strong. Further, the secessionists scattered by Lyon had also retreated to this area, and southern Missouri lay on the marching route of approaching auxiliary troops from Louisiana, Arkansas, and Texas who were to support the Missouri rebels. In addition, the railroad Sigel could use went only as far as Rolla, and that place had to be occupied by Sigel to serve as the base for supplies and replacements. From Rolla to Springfield there ran a long, poor country road of 120 miles. Sigel could only commence his mission from Springfield. The plan could only have been carried out if Lyon had moved rapidly on Springfield and taken over the covering of Sigel's rear, specifically by protecting his supply depot in Rolla. But Lyon remained for a long time in the north of Missouri and trusted his German colleague to pursue an aggressive campaign in a completely isolated position against an enemy with fivefold superior forces.

Sigel did what he was commanded, although he only had 1100 men on continuing his march from Springfield to the southwest.[18] There were few friends of the Union in southwest Missouri, where the population was seven-eighths rebels. Sigel soon ran short of food, for the supplies from Rolla were unreliable. As a result the German troops had to requisition if they were not to starve. This is the basis of accusations later raised against Sigel's "barbarians and robbers," accusations that the Union General Halleck repeated in his official report and swelled into a mighty atrocity of the Germans. By the start of July, Sigel had advanced about fifty miles southwest and stood completely cut off from support in enemy country, facing far greater rebel forces. This situation led to the encounter at Carthage.

Carthage lies on the border of Kansas and the Indian Territory. Sigel's unit consisted of 950 infantry and the crews for 8 cannons. Because he completely lacked cavalry, all scouting had to be done by infantry patrols. That was slow going, and it often led to a scattering of the units. Sigel only knew that the Confederate troops of General Price, 800 men, were seeking to join the 4000 men of Governor Jackson, but he could not establish that the Confederate General McCulloch was also approaching with about 5000 men and was already in his vicinity. Sigel turned first against Price, who fled before him. Sigel then encountered Jackson's troops at Carthage on 5 July. He sent his skirmishers out, had his artillery fire, and told the officers that he wanted to take the heights, occupied by 4000 men. He writes in his official report:

> In this critical moment, Captain Wilkins, leader of one battery, reported that "he had no ammunition and hence could not advance. A part of the troops on the right and left flanks were already fighting with the enemy cavalry. An advance of the whole without the cooperation of all the artillery could have led to defeat. There is no denying that the appearance of the Confederate cavalry at our rear had a moral effect on our troops, although the real peril was not very great. But our supply train was greatly endangered by the enemy riders."

For these reasons, Sigel broke off the skirmish before it had really begun, sent back half of his unit to cover the trains, and placed six companies of infantry and four cannons under Captain Essig behind the Dry Fork stream to hold the enemy. There followed a two-hour exchange with the enemy, who had a fourfold advantage. In the meantime, the cavalry had completely encircled Sigel, but all attempts to take over the supply train were beaten back. Sigel then left the bravely defended position at Dry Fork and pulled back in good order to Springfield, although beset by the enemy for hours more. Sigel lost thirteen dead and thirty-one wounded. According to the enemy's own report, they lost only a few more.

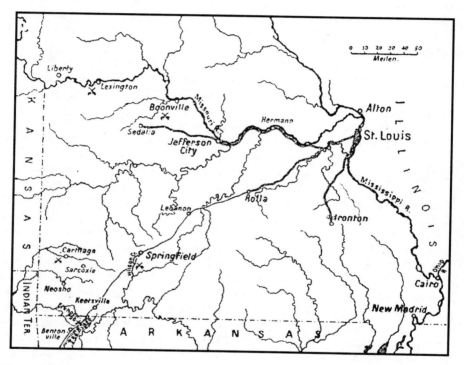

Figure 6. Missouri.

This little skirmish was made by Sigel's friends (although not by Sigel himself) into a great victory. Even Friedrich Kapp, in the introduction to his biography of De Kalb, celebrates Sigel as the victor of Carthage. Sigel obviously did not want to retreat without any attempt at battle, in the presence of superior force, and he certainly intended that his troops should smell powder once and be tested for their solidity. This test went very well, the defense of the position at Dry Forks was splendid, and the retreat was well handled. On the other hand, it makes a less positive impression when one learns that Wilkins' battery[19] had no ammunition when they were supposed to fire. It was also very risky to leave the train three miles behind the front without protection when it was well known that the enemy had a very strong cavalry force. If the train had fallen into the hands of the enemy, then Sigel's unit would have been without the means of support. Sigel also cannot be absolved of blame that he left Conrad's company, ten percent of his men, behind in Neosho in order to protect a few pro-Union citizens there. Magnanimity is certainly worthy of praise, but it seldom goes together with a warrior's rude handiwork.

Conrad heard the cannons from Neosho and was trying to retreat when he was surrounded by 2000 cavalry and had to surrender. These riders were the vanguard of the Confederate General McCulloch, who was coming to the aid of the Missouri rebels with 5000 Louisianans and Texans. Hence on 5 July almost 10,000 Confederates opposed Sigel's 1100 men at close range. If Sigel had known that, he certainly would have retreated to Springfield without a fight. The retreat from Carthage to Springfield was completed without great trouble, and Sigel was safe in Springfield, where reinforcements were arriving and where he finally met Lyon.

* * *

After the first brief campaign in Missouri, most of the German volunteers went home. Their three-month enlistment expired on 20 July. According to the report of Adjutant General Simson, there were more than 10,000 reenlistments. Thus, the massive withdrawal of the first three-month volunteers must have had some entirely special reason. These reasons, according to Schnake, were:

1. Congress had not yet passed the law for three-year service in the middle of July, when the transfer of the three-month volunteers into three-year service was to take place. Several legal experts among the German volunteers asserted that those who enlisted would have no legal standing in the army if they began their longer service before the passage of the law. It later happened that this view was correct. Those German Missourians who joined in July later received their pensions only after long waiting and overcoming many severe difficulties.

2. The three-month people were very poorly supplied by the officials. Sigel reports that each man had a wool blouse, a pair of trousers, a felt hat, a short blanket, and a bread bag. This equipment cost $3.50. There were no overcoats, knapsacks, or leather goods. Ammunition was carried in the bread bags. The soldiers of course did not complain, although their clothing was completely worn out after three months. They knew full well the haste with which their mobilization had taken place, but most certainly they could have been supplied. The care of the soldiers was also extraordinarily sparse. The mess officers were not yet trained, and the principal nutrition was crackers. Often the soldiers just had to go hungry.

3. The German soldiers thought it improper that the whole burden of the war was loaded on the Germans of Missouri. Out of the total force, there were about 5000 Germans and only about 400 Anglo-Americans. Similar proportions reigned in the Home Guard, as well. In July, troops came to Missouri from Kansas and Iowa, and later from Illinois and Indiana, as well. There had been reserves all along to relieve the Germans who had jumped in during the first emergency. But the German soldiers were also upset that President Lincoln, who wrote so many letters about the question of war in Missouri, did not bother to say a single word of praise directly to the Germans. Lincoln only thanked the Germans by speaking to Bernays. A few lines from Lincoln that could have been publicized would have given the soldiers much joy.

4. There were many older men no longer suited for war service. Börnstein and Hecker, who were then over 50 years of age, had set an example for many older Germans. (Hecker

served as a private in Sigel's regiment.) These older people had to leave after the end of their obligation, for they were incapable of serving. Many of the younger soldiers were also fathers of families, for people married younger then. Another very important reason for discharge in those days was the economic situation then in St. Louis. The outbreak of the war had led to a cessation of business, and credit had been completely suspended. The majority of German volunteers consisted of St. Louis businessmen and artisans. They were more or less dependent on credit. The economic existence of many German soldiers was then in question. Is it any wonder that these people said, "We have done enough for the time being"? But the most important fact is that, before the war, there was a great deal of speculation in St. Louis property, particularly by Germans. Whoever was not able to make a payment on the day due would lose his title for land already half paid for. A snap judgment could be obtained by a creditor in a few hours. The creditor obtained the land cheaply, for other buyers would not be present. Börnstein, who was then a rich man, gives a thorough account of how he lost two very valuable lots in this manner during his time of military service.

5. Even the three German Turner Companies of Blair's half-German 1st Regiment went home. Other reasons besides those given above applied here. The Turners did not feel comfortable in the mixed regiment, specifically because Lieutenant Colonel Andrews was a nativist. The companies presented their complaints to General Lyon. Nineteen days before the Battle of Wilson's Creek, they offered to serve longer if Lyon believed a battle would soon be taking place. Lyon, of course, could not respond to that. The Turners then offered to serve for a further four weeks if they could be released from the regiment and be joined to Sigel's 3rd Regiment as a special battalion. Lyon could not approve that, for it would have been against the general regulations of the army. Hence these companies were virtually compelled to resign for legal reasons.

It can be seen from all these matters that it was not exhaustion with the war that caused withdrawal.

The German artillery, a very well-trained unit in which many Turners served, also went home for similar reasons, and that was the worst loss of the first Missouri volunteer force. Sigel, Osterhaus, and many other infantry officers remained in service, although they did not have any position in the Union army after 26 July. The others went home to St. Louis, where the younger among them entered the newly formed German 12th, 15th, and 17th Regiments before the end of August. Only Sigel's 3rd Regiment and Börnstein's 2nd Regiment continued to retain their organization. These matters were of great importance because they help explain the otherwise completely inconceivable failure of Sigel's brigade at Wilson's Creek.

The Defeat of Sigel and Lyon at Wilson's Creek

General John C. Frémont took over command in Missouri on 25 July. At the same time the rebel leaders McCulloch and Price, united since the encounter at Carthage, were advancing on Springfield. Lyon and Sigel had finally met there on 13 July, and Lyon had taken command of both units, about 6500 men. At the beginning of August the rebel army had reached Wilson's Creek, about 12 miles from Springfield, and had made camp there with about 12,500 men. The first large encounter appeared to be coming, if one of the two opponents did not abandon the field to the other. General Lyon described his difficult position to Frémont at the proper time and sought reinforcements, but the new commander did not want to provide them. Frémont believed that what was going on in Springfield was only a bush war which Lyon could carry on as he pleased.

Frémont himself wanted to carry on the war on a grand scale. He wanted to proceed with a strong force down the Mississippi, defeating the rebel forces in detail, and if possible proceed in a single campaign all the way to New Orleans. He believed this plan was so promising that the Washington government would very quickly give him the troops to carry it out. Until these reinforcements arrived, he would retain the troops gathered in northern Missouri and not divide them up for Lyon's bush war. His general staff, consisting to a considerable degree of adventurers (mostly former Hungarian revolutionaries), favored this plan. There was not a single cool military head capable of dealing with the current military situation. Besides, these gentlemen were as much novices in Missouri as Frémont himself. Frémont and his people profoundly underestimated the strength of the opposition, and they highly overestimated the aid to be expected from Washington. Following the dreadful collapse of First Bull Run on 21 July, all available troops were desperately needed in the East, and Lincoln had nothing left for Frémont's grandiose plan.

It was bad enough that Lyon received no reinforcements from Frémont, but his own army, small as it was, suffered yet more losses. The service term of the first three-month volunteers had expired, and several thousand men of Lyon's corps went home for this reason. Lyon also had to give up five companies of regular infantry for the war in Virginia. Thus his unit shrank to about 5400 men by the start of August, despite some reinforcements. And still Frémont did not give Lyon any rules of engagement, leaving it instead to his subordinate to decide whether to retreat or to give battle to an enemy twice his size.

An experienced commander in Lyon's position would certainly have decided to retreat to Rolla. Such a retreat would not have been dishonorable in the least, for it would have meant very little if the secessionists controlled the region between Springfield and Rolla for a while. Springfield was a small town of perhaps 2000 residents at that time, without any great military significance. General Lyon did not have the least bit of cover for his rear. If his 5400 men did not manage to beat the 12,500 rebels on Wilson's Creek, the peril of the complete annihilation of Lyon's unit was very great, for the enemy had at its disposal a strong cavalry and could cut Lyon off from his base of supply at Rolla. Further, little would be gained from a victory, for Lyon had only a few hundred cavalry. Despite this, Lyon decided to attack, not wishing to withdraw before the rebels. At noon on 9 August, Lyon's commands were given. According to them, Sigel was to attack the southern part of the Confederate camp at dawn with 1118 men, while Lyon, with the main force of 4300 men, would attack the northern part of the enemy position. This plan of attack entailed a division of the small army and granted Sigel an entirely separate role in carrying it out.

Lyon's plan of attack could not be called bold; it bordered on the reckless to divide a force that was was already much too small. The Confederates possessed a superiority of double the forces, they were in a good position, and they were rested at the time the attack began, while the Northern troops had to complete a tiring night's march before the battle.

This daring could perhaps have been carried out by war-hardened veterans led by well-trained officers. But seven-eighths of the tiny Northern army consisted of young soldiers who lacked any training for the field and who were commanded by officers as untried as they were. Only the 300 men of the Regular Army as well as the unit of the federal artillery fighting with Lyon, could be regarded as units superior to the Confederates in fighting ability. Sigel's division, which was to advance from the south, was in particularly poor condition and would best have been used by an experienced leader as a reserve. It was certainly a go-for-broke act to use such troops for a dangerous encircling maneuver.

The course of the battle justifies the proposition that the North could perhaps have won the engagement if it had fought as a unit. The first attack of Lyon's division led to a considerable loosening of the Confederate position. But there was no reserve to exploit the advantages realized. If Sigel's troops had been with the main corps and had been used at the right moment to follow up, the enemy center could have been broken. That was the view of Lyon's officers, who conducted themselves beyond reproach during the main battle. Whether this view is correct is unknown. Perhaps Lyon's first attack would have failed even with the assistance of Sigel's troops. But the decision was to be made where Lyon was fighting, and every available man should have been used.

Lyon's officers now assert that Sigel convinced his superior general to this division of forces, and that the battle was lost only because Lyon stood under Sigel's influence. Because this view is the foundation of the later hostilities and persecutions of Sigel by West Point officers, it is of the greatest importance to establish whether Sigel was actually the spiritual father of that plan of division. Adequate proof does not exist. Lyon fell in the battle. He told no one before the battle that he was following Sigel's advice, and he left nothing about it in writing. Only the order of the day, signed by Lyon, survives. However, there are unfortunately very strong indications of Sigel's participation in the unfortunate plan to divide.

On 13 February 1862, Colonel Schofield, who was General Lyon's chief of staff at Wilson's Creek, reported to his commanding general, Halleck (*Official Records*, series 1, vol. 3, p. 60), as follows: "On 7 August the plan of attack was thoroughly discussed between Lyon, the members of his staff, Colonel Sigel, and various officers of the Regular Army. Sigel, who appears to have desired a separate command, favored an attack from two sides. All the others were, as I believe, opposed." This report by Schofield, which also contains a very severe evaluation of Sigel's leadership in battle, was endorsed by the officers Du Bois, Totten, Coryn, Lothrop, Burke, Sokalsky, Wood, and Barnes.[20] This is important because several of these officers were present when Sigel (according to Schofield) first proposed the division of forces on 7 August.

Lyon held a council of war on the evening of 8 August. The officers Steele, Totten, De Bois, Granger and Coryn reported on it (p. 96 of the same volume). These gentlemen say that Lyon spoke in favor of attack, but it was delayed by a day. Then, later in the same report, it says: "In the meantime, Colonel Sigel had a meeting with General Lyon and persuaded him to give (Sigel) a separate command." The complaints against Sigel thus were not raised by chief of staff Schofield alone; rather, nine other officers in high positions confirmed Schofield's assertions.[21]

It is possible that the accusations those officers made against Sigel would have had a different tone if Sigel had been a West Pointer. On the other hand, it should be pointed out that Lyon's division fought splendidly. Lyon lost 22 percent dead and wounded (208 dead, 700 wounded) and only 70 captured from a troop of 4300 men.[22] He lost no cannons and no flags. Of Sigel's 1118 men, only 15 fell, and 20 were wounded, but 230 of Sigel's men were captured. Five of Sigel's six cannons were taken by the enemy, and of the two regimental flags, one was lost.[23] Just this contrast of losses had to produce bitterness. Such a feeling is unjust, however, because the remarkable combination of misfortunes heaped on Sigel's band and the entirely dreadful state of the second division have to be taken into account.

It is human to use these figures as a proof of the extraordinary courage of the first division and the entirely extraordinary failure of the other. But the specific conditions of Sigel's defeat were not known to Lyon's officers, and they had exaggerated the rumors circulating about it in an unworthy manner. Further, it should be recalled that the Western army was still strongly under the influence of the first dreadful defeat of their comrades in the East at First Bull Run, and they were concerned with eradicating the impression of it through a victory in the West. Now a second defeat had taken place, supposedly because a German leader had brought about his plan of division. That hurt, deeply and lastingly. Whoever notes the brave fighting of Lyon's division, whoever wishes to read from the losses of those 4300 men how gloriously these young soldiers fought for victory against a vastly superior force to rescue the honor of their country, can comprehend this mood.

Sigel could not immediately protest this report by his comrades, for the accusation was not printed until years later. But Sigel must have known the content of that report when he wrote his justification for *Century Magazine* in 1880. There Sigel defends himself against other accusations made against his men at the time, namely that they plundered the camp after taking it, that they were scattered by this fact, and so on. But Sigel does not say one word about the most important accusation, merely mentioning in passing that he had a brief conversation with Lyon on the morning of the ninth and then received the command to attack the camp with his brigade from the south. Further, in the same volume of *Battles and Leaders* that contains Sigel's second description, there is an essay by General Wherry, who declares that Sigel had a private meeting with Lyon on the morning of 9 August, and that Sigel persuaded him to allow a separate attack by Sigel's brigade. This statement by Wherry stands alongside Sigel's own justification. It is impossible that Sigel did not see Wherry's assertions. Yet in his third justification (in Sigel's *New York Monthly,* in 1890), the German general does not say a word about Wherry's assertions, although Sigel thoroughly refuted several accusations against himself there. It is also remarkable that Sigel, who expressed himself with the greatest thoroughness on three occasions regarding the battle, its leadership, and its results, never said anything about the propriety of the plan of dividing forces, although it was basically this plan that was to blame for the worst defeat in his entire career.

I tried in 1907 to get information from German circles on the origins of the plan of dividing forces. Unfortunately, at that time, almost all German officers who fought at Wilson's Creek under Sigel had long since been called to the "Grand Army." Only three Germans who could be trusted to have good judgment on the matter were considered.

These were General Osterhaus; former Governor Salomon of Wisconsin (who died in 1908) and whose brother, Eberhard Salomon, led the 5th Missouri Regiment under Sigel at Wilson's Creek; and Ernst Schierenberg (who died in 1909), who was assistant editor of the *Westliche Post* in St. Louis in 1861 and soon afterward an officer in Sigel's division. These three men had been good friends of Sigel through a long life. Osterhaus was Sigel's comrade, and Salomon named the 26th Wisconsin Regiment he created the Sigel Regiment. Schierenberg was the best expert on the military history of Missouri. His position at the *Westliche Post* gave him the opportunity to hear everything which happened in German units. When General Osterhaus was not able to give a precise answer to my questions, he would say, "Turn to Schierenberg, he knows everything!"

I asked those three for their opinion on the accusations against Sigel. Schierenberg responded, "I hold it to be correct that my old friend Sigel should be seen as the originator of the plan for dividing forces. That was also the view of most of my German comrades. Lyon would never have come up with such a maneuver on his own. He had no idea about leading large masses of troops. He was only a charger. But he possessed a very high opinion of Sigel's gifts as a leader. Sigel's extensive reading in military history particularly impressed him, so he surely permitted himself to be persuaded by Sigel into that unfortunate act." Governor Salomon only confirmed that he had heard rumors, but he declined to give his own opinion on it, with the reason that he could not pursue the details of Missouri war history from Wisconsin. General Osterhaus did not deal with the question at all, but rather said that he had fought in Lyon's division at Wilson's Creek and knew nothing of the events that took place in Sigel's division, and that the whole matter lay forty-six years in the past, etc.

* * *

Let us then consider the effective size of Sigel's brigade. It consisted of 912 infantrymen from the 3rd and 5th Missouri Regiments, 85 artillerymen (infantrymen serving as artillerymen) who were to serve 6 cannons, and 121 regular cavalrymen, altogether 1118 men. The state of these troops is described as follows by Sigel in his official report, dated 18 August 1861:

> The period of enlistment for the 5th Regiment had expired before the battle. I had asked each company not to leave us in this critical time, and I took them into service for an additional week. This new obligation ran out on 9 August, the day before the battle. The 3rd Regiment, from which 400 men had already been discharged, consisted for the most part of recruits who had never seen the enemy and were quite inadequately trained. The people serving the guns were infantrymen from the 3rd Regiment and mostly recruits who had only been instructed for a few days. About two-thirds of our officers had departed. Some companies had no officers at all, which was to be regretted, but which was a result of the three-month system.

This narrative corresponds totally to the facts. Sigel's troops had only been enlisted for three months. Sigel's earlier, well-trained artillerymen had all gone home together with their officers. The 3rd Regiment, previously a solid unit, consisted on 10 August of perhaps 200 three-month soldiers and 200 green recruits. The 5th Regiment, 500 men, only served out of an obligation to Sigel. Only Sigel's cavalry was ready for action, but it was too weak to be used in attacks against the strong cavalry units of the enemy. It was used only in the attack on the camp and to cover the flanks on Sharp's Farm as well as on the retreat.

After a tiring night march, such a brigade was supposed to complete an extremely difficult mission. Its completion would have demanded a force easily twice as large of well-disciplined old soldiers and particularly a well-trained artillery with self-confidence and firing discipline. Sigel's artillerymen, only eighty-five men with two officers (Schützebach and Schäfer), were disguised infantrymen who had barely been with the guns for fourteen days and had not even learned to handle the horses yet. They had no idea about positioning and aiming. Above all else they lacked self-confidence. Who could assume that such people would have the necessary cold-bloodedness and firing discipline if they were suddenly to come under cross-fire from two enemy batteries and found an aggressive enemy infantry in front? They had to be ready for such situations in this more-than-daring maneuver. Sigel knew intimately the dreadful condition of his brigade, in any case better than Lyon. He would have been obligated to protest against any command from Lyon to take these troops on a perilous march of encirclement. And if Lyon's division were beaten, Sigel's brigade would have been abandoned to an enemy ten times its size, yet he took this mission without any hesitation.

* * *

The enemy camp at Wilson's Creek stretched along a length of more than seven miles. At about 5:30 A.M., Sigel attacked it from the south at the same time Lyon did on the other end from the north. The attack was a success in that both Sigel and Lyon were able to take parts of the camp, partially trapping the enemy and partially chasing him away. Only the larger central part of the camp remained in the hands of the Confederates. This part supported itself on a wooded ridge, where the main enemy force stood, and which Lyon thought was the location of the camp itself. Between Sigel and Lyon, who were separated by about two miles during the battle, then, lay this ridge. Lyon at once stormed it, while Sigel sought to take a position behind that height. Several roads (see the map) ran from the height down to Sigel's last position at the hill on Sharp's Farm behind Skegg's Branch. If the Confederates were able to hold their high position against Lyon, they could throw a strong force against Sigel as soon as there was a lull in the battle, which usually occurs after the repulse of a large attack.

Until 8:30 A.M., Sigel had only engaged in skirmishes with the enemy, while Lyon had already engaged for several hours in the most intense battle with an enemy three times his size. Lyon was not able to overcome the enemy. Lyon's battle waved back and forth, with some of the attacking troops pressing all the way to the heights, but they were soon thrown back for lack of the support Sigel's troops would have been able to offer if they had been with Lyon.

Before we pass to Sigel's dreadful defeat, it is necessary to establish what Sigel was doing between 6 and 9 A.M., and to determine whether Sigel did not advance too slowly during this time, and why he did not come closer to Lyon's position.

In his first official report, Sigel declared, "According to orders it was the duty of this brigade to attack the enemy in the rear and cut off his retreat, which order I tried to execute." According to that, Sigel had two missions, to attack the enemy in the rear and

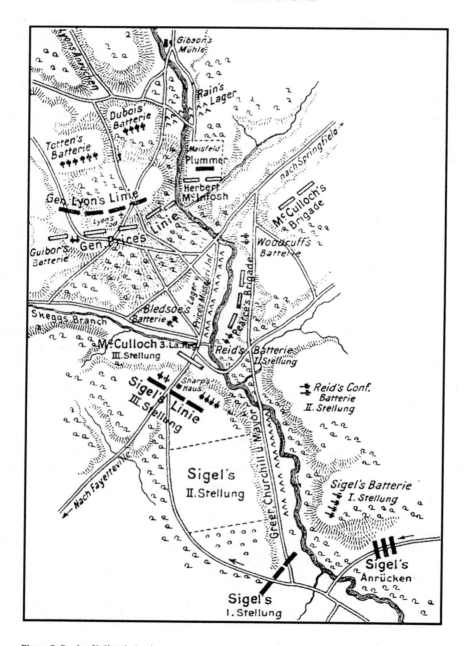

Figure 7. Battle of Wilson's Creek.

to cut off his retreat. Sigel's opponents assert that Sigel paid too much attention to the second part of this mission, and that he was concerned only about catching those enemy driven to him by Lyon. Sigel had time enough to press farther than Sharp's Farm, for during this period the enemy was completely preoccupied with Lyon. Even at 8 A.M. Sigel could have been a mile farther, perhaps at the crossing of Springfield Road and Wilson's Creek. Then he would have been closer to Lyon, and Lyon would have been able to send him reinforcements. Certainly Sigel would have encountered the Pearce Brigade posted along the length of the stream and would have had to fight there, but a lively battle near Lyon would have been better than Sigel's long delays in his first, second and third positions. Critics of Sigel spoke even then of the slowness of the German leader, of which West Pointers would say so much concerning Sigel's later campaigns. It is indeed possible that this criticism has some validity for the early morning of 10 August, a blind charge concerned only with approaching Lyon as closely as possible might have been successful and that Sigel might have been able to advance without any trouble to that crossing, only a mile away from Lyon. But the fact that Sigel did not charge blindly and did not compel a penetration cannot be made into an accusation against him. He first had to consider the enormous problems of carrying off such an undertaking. As a result caution took the lead in his decisions. To be sure, it took only a bit shorter advance to reach the southern end of the enemy camp than Lyon made to reach the northern part of the same camp, and Lyon was already engaged in serious battle at 6 A.M., but the Confederate cavalry was located between the main enemy position and Sigel.

Now we hear Sigel himself on his advance, as related in the *Century* account. Unfortunately Sigel's times are very imprecise. He does not say how long he was in each of the three positions assumed during his advance, or where he was every half hour. Even Sigel's assertions of the precise time of the attack on Sharp's Farm do not entirely agree. Sigel says on his advance (from the *Century* report):[24]

At 6:30 P.M. on 9 August the brigade left the camp near Springfield, followed the Yokermill Road for five miles, and with some difficulty found its way to the south of the enemy's camp. Arrival there was between 11 P.M. and midnight. It was a rainy, dark night. Thus far our movements were unknown to the enemy. At the break of day the advance was continued for 1.5 miles. Our cavalry patrols found forty enemy; they said that there were twenty Confederate regiments from Missouri, Texas, Arkansas, and Louisiana encamped in the nearby valley. From the top of a hill one could look into the enemy camp, and I gave orders to place four guns there, and for the infantry and two more guns and Lieutenant Ferrand's cavalry unit to follow the road down to Wilson's Creek. At this time—5:30 A.M.—gunfire was heard to the northwest. This signalled the encounter of General Lyon's troops with the enemy, and for that reason I ordered the four cannons to open fire on the enemy camp. The enemy, who was at breakfast, was completely surprised. It was only possible for a single cavalryman to escape Lieutenant Farrand's dragoons and report our advance to the Confederate General Price. I told myself to lose no time in coming to the aid of our friends. Wilson's Creek was crossed, and we marched through Dixon's Farm to Terrel

Creek. Because I did not know whether it would be possible to bring along all our guns, I left four cannons on the hilltop with an infantry guard. We marched to the south side of the valley, which runs about 3000 paces north to Sharp's house and is about 1000 paces wide.[25]

While this was taking place, an enemy unit of about 2500 men formed itself not far from the northern end of the valley. I ordered halt for that reason [Sigel's first position – WK], called for the four guns left on the hill, formed our troops to the right of the road, and formed in battle formation between the road and the abandoned enemy camp [Sigel's second position – WK]. Severe cannon fire was opened against the concentrated mass of the enemy cavalry; after twenty minutes, the enemy fled in wild disorder to the north and into the woods. We then turned about, marched toward Sharp's house, and reached the Fayetteville Road, which led north to the battlefield where General Lyon's troops were located. We now held the primary retreat line of the enemy, having marched for fifteen miles without interruption in complete order and discipline, had completed a successful action (the partial capture of the camp); and had had an artillery battle with the Confederate cavalry. The troops were enthused with the best spirits over what they had accomplished. It is absolutely untrue, as a rumor spread after the battle declared, that "Sigel's soldiers occupied themselves with plundering the camp," and that they were scattered and surprised by a returning enemy.

When we had taken our position near Sharp's Farm on the plateau, we opened cannon fire on the enemy left flank, which stood opposite Lyon, and we continued it for thirty minutes. Suddenly the shooting on the enemy's side ceased, and it appeared as though we were firing on Lyon's troops. For that reason I ordered the firing stopped. At the time between nine and ten o'clock—not a single shot was heard, and unarmed enemy units streamed down the road from Skegg's Branch toward us; they were taken captive. In the meantime a part of McCulloch's troops advanced toward our position at Sharp's Farm [Sigel's third position], while Reid's Confederate battery took a position on the hill east of Wilson's Creek opposite our right wing, and was followed by a unit of cavalry.

This narrative of Sigel tells us that he had advanced carefully up to that point, as the situation warranted, but not that he was moving forward too slowly.

As Sigel took up his position on Sharp's Farm, the fighting waged by Lyon declined. Lyon's first attack on the hill held by the enemy's main force had been repulsed, and the attackers had fallen into disorder as a result. A pause was taking place in the battle, which was used by both sides to put their units back into order and make ready for more fighting. The enemy had the advantage of being able to deal with Sigel in good order, and besides the McCulloch Brigade there was also the Pearce Brigade, which had not yet fought. Further, there were the two Confederate batteries, Bledsoe's and Reid's, and very strong cavalry.

Sigel's Defeat. We now come to portray the catastrophe of the Sigel division.

There was not the slightest connection between Sigel and Lyon. Lyon did not know what Sigel was doing, and vice versa. However, Sigel noticed at about 8:15 A.M. that a number of Confederate deserters were running into his position. These were stragglers, cowards who appeared behind all fighting units in those days. Sigel, however, took these stragglers to be the Confederate army, already beaten by Lyon! And when closed masses of troops emerged on the road leading to Sharp's Farm, Sigel thought these were friends pursuing the "defeated." At 8:30 A.M., according to Sigel, those troops were about 700 yards to the right of his position. Let us listen to Sigel's first report on the battle (*Official Records*, series 1, vol. 3, p. 87):

> At about 8:30 the fire, which had continued from Lyon until then without inter-ruption, ceased.[26] At about this time,[27] Adjutant Melchers and several of our pickets reported that Lyon's troops were marching toward us down the road. Colonels Albert and Salomon, commanding the 3rd and 5th Missouri Regiments, forbade their troops to fire on the troops marching toward us, and I myself forbade my artillery to fire. Our people waved their flags as a signal for our approaching comrades. Suddenly we were bombarded by two enemy batteries, one of them [Bledsoe's battery – WK] firing from the Fayetteville Road [left of Sigel], the other [Reid's battery – WK] from the hill [from Sigel's right – WK] where we thought Lyon was pursuing the enemy, while an infantry unit we had hitherto assumed was our own 1st Iowa Regiment[28] approached down the Fayetteville Road [very near Sigel – WK] and attacked our right wing. It is impossible to describe the shock and dreadful confusion that descended after this event. The cry, "They [Lyon's people – WK] are shooting at us," spread like wildfire through our ranks. The artillerymen whom I urged to fire could only be brought to their guns with difficulty, the infantry could barely lower their guns before it was too late. The enemy came within ten paces of the mouths of our cannons, killed the horses, fell on the flanks of the infantry, and forced them into flight. The troops fled into the woods and the side ways, continually pursued and attacked by Arkansas and Texas cavalry. We lost five cannons and the flag of the 3rd Regi-ment, after the first bearer was wounded and the second killed.

Sigel wrote three accounts of his defeat, which vary at not a few points. The report quoted above is dated a week after the battle. The second account appeared a good twenty years later in the *Century Magazine* and stands in the series *Battles and Leaders*. The third, in Sigel's *New York Monthly*, was written even later. Because the matter is so important to us Germans, Sigel's second description is inserted here, as well:

> All of these circumstances—the cessation of fire in Lyon's front, the appearance of deserters from the enemy, the southward movement of Reid's Confederate artillery and the enemy cavalry—caused us to believe that the enemy was in retreat. This supposition was reinforced by Dr. Melcher's report that Lyon's troops were marching up the road, so that we could not fire. However, I remained in doubt about the character of the troops approaching us only a few rods away and did not want to trust my eyes; for that reason I sent Corporal Tod to recon-noiter.[29] He was immediately shot. On that I immediately ordered the infantry and artillery to fire. But it was too late. The cannons fired off only one or two shots, while the infantry did not fire a shot, as if they had been paralyzed. The 3rd Louisiana Regiment, which we had held to be the gray-clad 1st Iowa Regi-ment, charged the plateau, while Bledsoe's battery in front and Reid's battery

from the heights to our right bombarded us with cartridges. As a cautionary measure, I had ordered four of our guns in the battery on the right wing against the troops on the hill and Reid's battery. But after Reid's fire was answered for a few moments, the drivers of three cannons suddenly abandoned their guns and galloped away with their caissons in wild flight, down the Fayetteville Road into the ranks of our infantry, who were thrown into panic, were turned about in disorder and were exposed at the same moment to the fire of the line of attack.

It may be added to this report from other sources that the Sigel's brigade was not only suddenly fired upon by the two batteries and threatened at close range by the Louisiana infantry,[30] but that an Arkansas cavalry regiment serving as infantry was approaching from the left side, and further that several cavalry regiments from Arkansas and Texas were approaching. The conclusion is that Sigel could hardly have maintained his position even if his people had fought energetically. The dismissal that 1000 Germans ran away from 300 Louisiana "Tigers" without firing a shot is hence incorrect. Sigel was attacked by a strongly superior force, even if a part of them were farther away.[31]

The flight of Sigel's troops should not be surprising. They had been forbidden by their officers to fire on the approaching enemy because that force had been thought to be friendly. After the discovery of the error, Sigel's artillery should have been able to beat off the attackers with a couple well-aimed shots into the closely packed formation. But what could be expected of artillerymen who have been with their cannons such a short time? The artillery was the first to flee, bringing disorder to the infantry, and then there was no stopping it. There followed a repetition of the events of First Bull Run.

In that first battle of the Civil War on 21 July, only three weeks before the battle on Wilson's Creek, the panic of the Northern army was caused by a surprise staged by the enemy. The fresh Confederate Elzey Brigade suddenly broke out of a forest cover and fell on the flank of the Union troops. Then everything wearing a blue uniform ran away in wild flight, some 20,000 men. And yet these same soldiers had stood bravely in battle for several hours and had won significant advantages through bold attacks. Untrained recruits often do good service when attacking, but their ability to resist is quite small when they are suddenly surprised. They lack the serenity and solidity that only fundamental field training, as well as trust in their leadership, can give them. That is shown not only by the events at First Bull Run and the performance of Sigel's troops at Wilson's Creek, but by hundreds of examples that can be given from the history of the Civil War.

Lyon's young recruits went on the attack on the enemy positions with great ardor, but after this first advance failed due to a lack of reserves, and the enemy advanced with superior force; only the solid conduct of Lyon's artillery (veteran regular cannoneers) prevented an immediate defeat of his troops. Here the recruits in the infantry found reliable support, which gave them confidence, and those who had been rebuffed were led forward to new courageous charges. But Sigel did not have this support. His improvised artillery left their guns behind, and the cannoneers saved their precious lives on the horses that were supposed to transport the guns. The fact that his artillery was not capable of service was not Sigel's fault; rather, it was the fault of the short service time of the first levy. Sigel had to improvise if he was not to give up completely on that type of weapon.

Still, such poorly trained troops should never be exposed to the hazards of such a maneuver of encirclement, when only two young officers were available to control six guns. The only truly trained artilleryman in the entire unit was Sigel himself. It should also be stressed repeatedly that the misfortune that suddenly broke over Sigel's division was extraordinarily large. Just consider that 1100 men were suddenly exposed to cross-fire from two enemy batteries, that the Lousiana Regiment was already at hand, and that other enemy forces were also coming within firing range. In such critical instants, green recruits cannot be expected to preserve calm and cold bloodedness. They will run away even if they come from the most capable war-making people in the world.

Sigel's losses in the attack on Sharp's Farm were insignificant, despite the fact that the troops were exposed to cross-fire from two enemy batteries as well as the gunfire of the 3rd Louisiana Regiment. Sigel himself says that he had his worst losses while in flight from the second attack later, on the White River. But the total losses of Sigel's entire brigade were in fact quite insignificant.

* * *

Sigel's retreat to Springfield also proceeded with extreme misfortune. The cavalry under Captain Carr formed the vanguard, but they rode so quickly that the harried infantrymen could not keep up. Sigel was able to gather 250 men, while Colonel Salomon gathered 450 men of the 4th Regiment, as well as the last cannon. The two units took different roads. Sigel's people had to cross the White River. There they were attacked by enemy cavalry and completely scattered, because Carr's cavalry had already crossed the river. Sigel escaped capture only because he was thought to be a Confederate. He wore a yellow hat, had thrown a blanket over his shoulder, and looked like a Texas Ranger. He writes this himself. He crossed the river in the company of Lieutenant Schützebach, but he was recognized on the other shore, had to cross a fence, was pursued for five miles and finally arrived in Springfield with great difficulty.

This was later interpreted as if Sigel had left his men behind and had fled alone. Whoever did not know the circumstances of the attack on the refugees at the White River was inclined to believe this distortion. It was of great significance to Sigel's later position in the Army of the Potomac that this lie—that Sigel had only acted to bring himself to safety—had such wide circulation. Nothing so damaged Sigel's reputation as the unfortunate fact that he arrived in Springfield, escorted by one officer, before his beaten troops. Salomon's unit was more fortunate. They arrived in Springfield unmolested. By evening about 700 men of the brigade could be brought to safety with the other refugees.

Lyon's Defeat and Death. The other division was involved in a very severe battle. Lyon had considerable success at first, but he then saw himself compelled to attack the ridge behind Wilson's Creek, where the primary force of the enemy stood in battle order. This attack was made with great commitment by the 1st Missouri, 1st and 2nd Kansas, and 1st Iowa Regiments, a battalion of the German 2nd Missouri Regiment under Osterhaus, and a battalion of regular infantry under Plummer. But the enemy position was very strong and the Confederate superiority in numbers very great. Only the 2nd Kansas Regiment was able to reach the top of the ridge and break through the enemy's position, but it had to withdraw due to a lack of support. There was then extremely bloody hand-to-hand fighting on the side of the ridge. The Confederates, who already regarded themselves as the victors, went over to attack but were thrown back, primarily due to the fire of the Union batteries under Totten, Steele, and Dubois. There was then a pause in the battle used by both sides to gather and order their forces. Then the attack was renewed by one and then the other side, always thrown back. But the Confederates could always bring in fresh troops, while the Union men had invested their last man at the very start.

Lyon worried and looked in the direction from which Sigel was supposed to come. Lyon had been grazed by two bullets at the very start of the battle, but he rode along the firing line and reached the 2nd Kansas Regiment at the moment when their Colonel Mitchell fell from his horse, severely wounded. Lyon called to the Kansans, "I shall lead you now," and set himself at the head of the regiment for another attack. Lyon was shot again immediately, and Major Sturgis had to take over command. Another attack of the Confederates was thrown back by the fire of the Union artillery. Shortly thereafter the enemy received reinforcements. McCulloch approached with the troops that had defeated Sigel, and the secessionists now fired cartridges from the cannons taken from Sigel.[32] The destiny of Lyon's reduced division now seemed sealed. But the regular batteries under Totten and Dubois opened such a devastating fire that even this last attack of the enemy could be repulsed. The Regular infantry was also energetically involved in this last fighting. The charging Confederates came almost to the guns of Totten's Battery. Because they were carrying the Union flag taken from Sigel, Totten did not fire. Fortunately he saw the subterfuge in time, and he fired into the tightly packed mass of the enemy, which had the result of sending the enemy in flight.

The Confederate artillery, which was incidentally very poorly served and which shot poorly, had used up all its ammunition, and for this reason McCulloch gave up the battle. Both sides left the field at almost the same time. Despite that, the Confederates claimed a complete victory. On the evening of 10 August Lyon's troops returned to Springfield, where they learned of the dreadful defeat their comrades had suffered under Sigel. McCulloch and Price estimated the losses of the secessionists at 295 dead and 800 wounded. Lyon's division lost 22 percent in dead and wounded.[33]

Colonel Sigel was elected by the other officers as Lyon's successor, and under Sigel's leadership the retreat on Rolla commenced. The troops were only slightly harassed by the completely exhausted enemy. During the march to Rolla, Sigel was notified by the regular officers that he had to withdraw from command, as he [Sigel] had no official commission as an officer. That was technically correct. Sigel's service as a three-month volunteer had run out, and he had remained with the flag without considering that he should have waited for a new commission from Washington. The seventeenth of August found Sigel in Rolla, where he received his appointment as brigadier general, but he had given command over the troops to Major Sturgis, an officer of the Regular Army, on 13 August.[34]

*   *   *

After the Battle of Wilson's Creek, Frémont immediately decreed a state of martial law in St. Louis, a completely unnecessary measure that greatly harmed a city already heavily burdened.

Lexington. A second very severe defeat was suffered by Union troops as a result of the capitulation of Colonel Mulligan in Lexington; 2140 prisoners, including 400 wounded, 7 guns, an extraordinary amount of supplies, and a treasury of $900,000 fell into the hands of the enemy. Incidentally, Mulligan defended himself in a marvelous manner. He held out for a full week against a considerably superior force, although his troops did not have a drop of water for days. Mulligan could easily have been relieved if the Union war leadership had not been carried out in such an amateur fashion. But the commanding General Frémont believed that Mulligan would be relieved by Generals Pope and Sturgis, and these two gentlemen believed that it was Frémont's duty to help their persecuted comrade. So brave Mulligan was left on his own and in the end, on 26 September 1861, had to strike his colors.

Because Lexington was located on the Missouri River, with good steamboat communications to St. Louis, it is inconceivable that Frémont did not direct a few thousand men to Lexington out of the troops he commanded. One could comfortably reach the place from St. Louis in two days by steamboat!

One fine victory was in fact won during the dreadful period of leadership under Frémont. Frémont's much-mocked bodyguard, consisting mostly of former Hungarian hussars and German-Austrians, combined with a unit of regular dragoons (altogether 300 sabers under the leadership of the Hungarian Zagonyi) to make a heroic attack on the city of Springfield and conquer it. Two thousand rebels were overrun by Zagonyi, but about eighty saddles were empty after the victory.

Frémont and the Germans

Major General John C. Frémont played a remarkable role in the Germans' history of the war. He was long the darling of our compatriots, and as far as the Forty-Eighters were concerned, he was their demigod. Unfortunately, the Germans were enthused for one who was little worthy of their love. Only Frémont's later development, particularly his involvement in undertakings of a quite questionable nature, demonstrated that he was more an adventurer and climber than a man one could imagine the first magistrate of the republic.

Frémont was the first presidential candidate of the young Republican Party in 1856. At that time there was no expectation of victory, and the candidate was merely chosen for his attractiveness. This appeared great, for Frémont had won a national reputation as an explorer, he had no enemies, and he had taken no positions on the great questions of the day. His Southern origin and even his romantic love story, the abduction of the beautiful daughter of Senator Benton, were all interpreted to his benefit. But when the Republican Party entered the campaign in 1860 with expectations of victory, Frémont was ruthlessly pushed aside. Properly so, for he did not have the slightest gift as a statesman.

The man impressed Germans for his significant accomplishments as an explorer. He discovered the source of the Mississippi, and later he was the true pathfinder to California. He had taken four great journeys across the Rocky Mountains, and he discovered the usable passes across them. Even today the Pacific Railroad uses the same path Frémont traced. His scientific companion was the German Karl Preuss, who made the survey of lands and drew the maps. The scientific accomplishments of Frémont's journeys rest almost entirely on the work of Preuss, but Frémont harvested all the fame connected with them as the leader of the expedition.

Frémont had been trained as a professional officer at West Point, and he served for a while as an officer of the Army Corps of Engineers, but then he resigned in order to be able to dedicate himself completely to his career as an explorer. At the outbreak of the Civil War, Lincoln named him a major general and permitted him to choose his own military activity, upon which Frémont decided for the command of the West, with headquarters in St. Louis. He remained in the East for weeks to raise weapons and supplies for 23,000 men, and he only took up his office in St. Louis on 25 July. The Battle of Bull Run had been lost four days before. Great panic had broken out in Washington, and there was neither a man nor a musket left for the West. All troops and all weapons were seized for the defense of Washington. The supplies set aside for Frémont were used by the Army of the Potomac, and not even the money needed by Frémont in St. Louis was granted.

So Frémont came to St. Louis with empty hands. There he supposedly found 23,000 men, but only 15,000 of them were capable of field service. The period of enlistment had expired for the other 8000 or they were still entirely green recruits.

It was soon demonstrated that Frémont was not to be taken seriously as a military man. He surrounded himself with a staff consisting mostly of Hungarian officers, formed a body guard, and occupied himself with preparations for a campaign in the Mississippi Valley for which he lacked all means. Two weeks after Frémont took charge came Lyon's, and Sigel's, defeat at Wilson's Creek and Lyon's death in that battle.

Frémont could easily have given Lyon adequate assistance before that battle, and if he did not wish to do so, he could have recalled his subordinate. The fact that he did neither is certain proof of his military inability, particularly when one considers how Frémont was as indecisive, not to say negligent, in relieving Colonel Mulligan in Lexington. There were certainly grounds for Frémont's later removal for proven military incompetence.

Yet the decisive factor in Frémont's service in Missouri was not those two dreadful defeats (Wilson's Creek on 10 August; Lexington on 20 September), but his proclamation 31 August, according to which the slaves of those Confederates who took arms against the Union were declared free. At first glance that would appear to be a measure justified by the military situation, and it applied only to the area under Frémont's command, hence essentially Missouri. But if the Washington government recognized this proclamation, its impact would be much greater. Lincoln could not regard this as a purely local matter. If the principle expressed there was recognized for Missouri, it had to apply throughout the country. It was, however, even more important that the Washington government should not tolerate any particular general's going over its head and taking a position on the most important political matter, contradicting Lincoln's own declaration. Generals were not to deal with political matters at all.

Lincoln's inaugural address made clear that he, although personally close to the efforts of the abolitionists, would only proceed on the basis of the Constitution and the current pro-slavery laws. He had been forced into war, and he was compelled to put down a rebellion with the force of weapons. He did not see the war as a means of forcefully eliminating slavery, but as a measure necessary for preserving the Union. Throughout the whole of 1861 he held fast to the faith that reconciliation without regard to the immediate resolution of the slavery question was still possible. He knew his opponents in the rebel camp well enough to know that, as soon as the banner of the emancipation of slaves was raised, there would follow a war of annihilation of the opponent.

Lincoln was wrong in thinking that reconciliation, with whatever sacrifices, was still possible; yet seeking a compromise was not reprehensible, even if it was an error. He decided on the proclamation of 22 September 1862 with a heavy heart, declaring the slaves of the seceding states to be free. But this proclamation opened with the statement, "I, Abraham Lincoln, as commander in chief of the Army and the Navy, command as necessary *measures of war*." And the document closed with the words, "and hereto, in that I regard this as an act of justice permitted in military necessity by the Constitution, I appeal to the calm judgment of men and the good grace of Almighty God."

Here we have the position of Lincoln concerning war and slavery. But this position was not that of the radical abolitionists, to whom our German Forty-Eighters belonged. For these people, the liberation of slaves was the first purpose of the war. They had fought and taken their skins to market for this ideal. For months they had bitterly condemned what they called Lincoln's lukewarmness on the slavery question. The Forty-Eighters had long ago become bitterly disappointed by Lincoln. They liked to call him a dishrag, and their prejudice against the Washington government rose steadily the more Missouri was ignored in military matters.

Most of these gentlemen lacked proper understanding of the problems of the government after the Battle of Bull Run. In their opinion, St. Louis, the "Washington of the West," was far more threatened than the federal capital. They had also made marvelous efforts with their own strength to organize the Germans in Missouri for the Union cause, and they had saved St. Louis. But they never received recognition for this great deed. Blair and Lyon and other Anglo-Americans received the fame won by German bayonets. Hence the original enthusiasm of our idealistic compatriots for Lincoln cooled significantly, and if one said that they had grown indifferent to the president, that was the mildest that could be said. The distance from love to hate was not very far with such hot-blooded men, who had not yet completely acclimatized themselves to America and who regarded prevailing American political conditions with an attitude little influenced by a knowledge of the facts.

Frémont's proclamation worked on our German friends as a deed that freed them from a long-borne pressure. They were half mad for joy. Frémont appeared to them as the first man who knew how to give the entire war some meaning. Frémont's right to make such a proclamation caused them no pains, for it was an exceptional situation, and the proclamation appeared to them to be justified by the war situation.

In Washington, Frémont's bomb had an entirely different effect. There it was seen as an attempt by Frémont to promote himself for the presidential election of 1864, and this interpretation is not without reason. Frémont could not be directly defied in Washington, for that would have had too negative an impact on the popular mood in the North. Hence an attempt was made to have Frémont weaken his proclamation. But the general would not agree to this. There were serious sins on both sides in this matter, the worst being on the side of the government in its ill-timed removal of Frémont.

The document removing him was dated 24 October, but it was only carried out on 2 November. The document went along with a special message by Lincoln, according to which Frémont's removal was not to take place if he had given battle or if he was about to give battle. Frémont had gathered an army of 25,000 men and 88 cannons before Springfield, and the enemy stood 12 miles away, on the old battlefield of Wilson's Creek. The reports of the Confederate General McCulloch say that the enemy expected an attack at any moment. Frémont's plan of war had also been worked out in every detail.

According to Lincoln's letter, then, General Hunter, Frémont's designated successor, should not have presented Frémont's dismissal. He did so anyway, appearing at the army on the evening of 2 November, under the false impression that there was no enemy in the area and that a battle was thus impossible. Frémont immediately gave up his office and presented Hunter with his war plan. Hunter immediately ordered the retreat of the proud army, the largest and best that had yet appeared in the West. This retreat certainly rested on higher orders. It was enormously stupid, and its impact was worse than a lost battle. In the West there was the impression that Washington did not want to allow Frémont the glory of a victory, and even that they did not want to permit an army organized by Frémont to win under the leadership of another general. The fact that Frémont was being removed for his previously demonstrated incompetence was really not believed by anyone in the West; rather, it was generally believed that it was Frémont the liberator of slaves who was being punished.

The Germans were the most aroused, and not just in Missouri but in the entire West.[35] Frémont was even criticized for giving up his command. He should have shoved Hunter aside and advanced against the enemy the next day, who would certainly have been defeated. Lincoln certainly would not have dared to punish Frémont for disobedience after a victory, it was asserted in many German circles. The officers in Sigel's division protested against Frémont's dismissal, and German citizens held mass meetings along with many Anglo-Americans in which Lincoln was abused in the most improper manner. The enthusiasm for war among the Germans considerably declined, and it was a long time before people understood that the dispute only benefitted the cause of Jefferson Davis.

Lincoln's later actions had some calming effect. He offered the same man he had just dismissed for military incompetence a new command in the Army of the Potomac, and when Frémont made it a condition that he receive Blenker's German Division, Lincoln made the concession, although McClellan protested mightily against it. Even in his war memoirs, *McClellan's Own Story*, the general repeatedly complained that the "Blenkers" were taken from him and placed in Frémont's corps.

Blenker himself flew into rage when he heard about his transfer. He was said to have broken his saber in front of his soldiers. One continues reading the chapter, "Fate of the German Division" and the narrative of the Battle of Cross Keys, in which the German Division did not have the opportunity to act with full force, partly due to the dreadful leadership of General Frémont. To be sure, McClellan's Peninsular Campaign was also a botched enterprise, and the miseries of the troops fighting on the peninsula were perhaps as great as those the German Division suffered during that march through the snowy mountain wilderness of Virginia; but with McClellan there were opportunities to excel. There the Germans could have demonstrated what well-trained soldiers were in the position to accomplish.

So the Frémont enthusiasm of the Forty-Eighters had a dreadful effect on the destiny of the best and strongest German military unit our people ever produced. The offense of his German friends in the West struck Lincoln deeply. He remained an abolitionist at heart, as much as his official acts might veil this fact. He could easily place himself in the position of the German offended, and he knew that this opposition arose from patriotic and honorable motives.

But let us return to Missouri from this excursus. Hunter was only the temporary successor of Frémont. Soon General Halleck took command. The proud army Frémont had gathered before Springfield no longer went into action. The force was decimated through detachment of units, but more through dreadfully high mortality in virtually unprepared winter quarters, and when they began to try to carry out Frémont's war plan three months after his dismissal, only 11,500 men of the earlier 25,000 men were capable of field service. The enemy who had trembled in the presence of Frémont's army remained in undisturbed possession of southern Missouri, recruited there as it wished, chose its winter quarters, and made all preparations for the new campaign early in the year. This campaign brought the first full victory at Pea Ridge, Arkansas, the hero of which was Franz Sigel.

Sigel's Victory at Pea Ridge

General Halleck arrived in St. Louis as Frémont's successor on 12 November. He named Sigel as commander of the troops gathered in Rolla, but three days later he sent him General Curtis as his superior and commanded Sigel to continue to serve under Curtis. In response, Sigel resigned for the first time. The commissions of the two generals had been issued on the same day, but Halleck decided that a West Point officer had precedence over a volunteer officer. Sigel made his peace with this decision and served under Curtis.

In the middle of February operations resumed with the advance of Curtis's (and Sigel's) division to southwest Missouri, the same area where Sigel had fought in June at Carthage. The Confederates had withdrawn from Springfield to rest for the winter on the border of Missouri, Arkansas, and the Indian Territory. Shortly before the arrival of Curtis's army in that area, a new Confederate commanding general, Van Dorn, arrived, essentially to end the perennial conflicts between the two Confederate generals McCulloch and Price. Hence the rebel army at last had a united leadership when the two opponents met at Pea Ridge at the start of March 1862.

The Northern army numbered 11,500 men, the Southern army 16,200 and some 1000 Indians. The artillery of the Confederates was of little value, but they did possess a very strong cavalry. Further, in case of defeat, the Southern army was assured of reserves and thus not exposed to a pursuit, for Curtis did not want to advance farther from his supply depot. The greatest peril existed for Curtis's Northern army in this advance so far to the south. It stood in the middle of enemy country over 300 miles from St. Louis and almost 200 miles from the Rolla depot, and it did not have any cover. A defeat could easily turn into a catastrophe. On the other hand, Curtis possessed a considerable advantage in his artillery, three-quarters of which consisted of German crews.

Curtis's army was divided into four divisions, commanded by Osterhaus, Asboth, Jefferson C. Davis, and Carr. The first two divisions stood under Sigel, with the troops of Davis and Carr under Curtis. According to Sigel's report, about 5000 of the 11,500 men were Germans. These were almost all in Osterhaus's and Asboth's divisions, as well as in the artillery. Among the regiments Osterhaus and Asboth led, the 2nd, 3rd, 12th, and 17th Missouri were entirely German, and the 15th Missouri consisted only of German Swiss and Germans. Also in Sigel's portion were the 25th, 44th, and 36th Illinois, with a very strong German element, and the rest were mostly sons of immigrant Germans. Davis's and Carr's divisions consisted mostly of Anglo-Americans, although many Germans were in these units, and the entirely German Klaus Battery from Evansville, Indiana, fought on the first day of battle in the Davis Division.

Pea Ridge lies almost immediately on the border of Missouri, within the secessionist state of Arkansas. There the deciding battle for Missouri took place on 6–8 March, and the first *great* victory for the Union was won, essentially by German troops and under the leadership of German officers.

For reasons of supply, Curtis had spread his army out, so that on early morning of 6 March Sigel's units were still in and near Bentonville, ten miles from their comrades. Curtis ordered concentration, and the primary part of Sigel's force retreated on 6 March to Sugar Creek Valley, in front of Pea Ridge, where Curtis was already located. Sigel himself remained near Bentonville with 600 men (parts of the 12th Missouri Regiment under Wangelin, three cannons under Elbert and some squadrons under Nemet) to protect a unit sent out on a raid that was expected back soon. Sigel came into great danger as a result. He had led his main unit on a retreat through the entire night, and he had just lain down to rest in the morning when the vanguard of the Confederates, 3000 men strong, advanced disturbingly close to his camp. The troops were called up in great haste and ordered to retreat from Bentonville to Sugar Creek.

In his battle report, the Confederate General Van Dorn declared that the enemy's retreat was carried out in "an admirable manner." Sigel's troops were completely surrounded by the enemy several times, but he always managed to break through and to keep his troops together. Sigel used the tactics proved at Carthage, having his cannons halt and fire occasionally. Sigel's losses were insignificant, with the 60 dead and 200 wounded of that day coming largely from Asboth's Division, which also had a skirmish that day. Osterhaus, who heard of Sigel's predicament, sent him the 2nd and 15th Missouri and the 25th and 44th Illinois. Sigel's unit was thus rescued and soon united with its comrades in the Sugar Creek Valley.

The enemy army of Van Dorn preserved its old division into two corps. McCulloch led one corps, consisting of the troops from Louisiana, Texas and Arkansas, as well as Indian auxiliaries. The other corps consisted of Missouri Confederates under Price. This was essentially the same army which had won the victory over Lyon and Sigel at Wilson's Creek. Van Dorn believed he could defeat the two corps of Curtis individually, but this was frustrated by Sigel's timely retreat to Sugar Creek. This brook flows immediately through the Elkhorn Pass in the Pea Ridge chain of hills. Curtis had been encamped on the stream for several days and had taken a strongly fortified position there in expectation that the enemy would have no choice but to assault it. But when Sigel arrived on the evening of 6 March, he at once declared that the enemy would never be so stupid as to fight on the battlefield that Curtis had prepared. Sigel referred to the fact that the enemy had a good road available to go around Curtis's fortified camp and seek a position in the area right

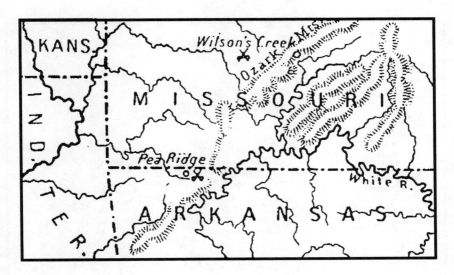

Figure 8. Wilson's Creek and Pea Ridge.

behind Elkhorn Pass, which was honeycombed with many hollows and which could be excellently exploited for either attack or defense. Such a position also had the advantage for the enemy of cutting off the sole line of retreat to Springfield and the North for the Union troops. If the enemy chose this position, then Curtis's fortress would be of no use, for Curtis would be compelled to act as the aggressor. Sigel was immediately shown to have judged the situation correctly. During the night of 6–7 March the enemy's enveloping maneuver, predicted by Sigel, actually took place.

But only one enemy corps, the Missouri Confederates under Price, was able to win the position sought behind Elkhorn Pass. The other part of the enemy army, the stronger corps under McCulloch, had halted in its advance and had only reached a position left of Big Mountain (see the map) about 10 A.M. on 7 March. Hence the two enemy corps were divided by about four miles on the first day of battle. This also required a division of the Union troops, for it was too late to set the entire Union army against one of the two enemy wings. During fighting in such a situation, the Confederate corps not being attacked could have fallen on the rear of the Union troops. For that reason, Curtis had to leave his fortified position on Sugar Creek and oppose the enemy in two distinct encounters. Still, the Union troops had the advantage of interior lines. They were not so widely spread as the enemy and could thus support one another more rapidly.

On 7 March. Carr's Division advanced to take Elkhorn Pass in order to oppose Price's much stronger corps and to hold it for as long as possible. Sigel's two divisions advanced against McCulloch and maintained contact with Davis's division, which operated in the middle. Carr's division had the hardest task. It was a considerable distance from the other Union troops and had to attack an enemy three times its size.

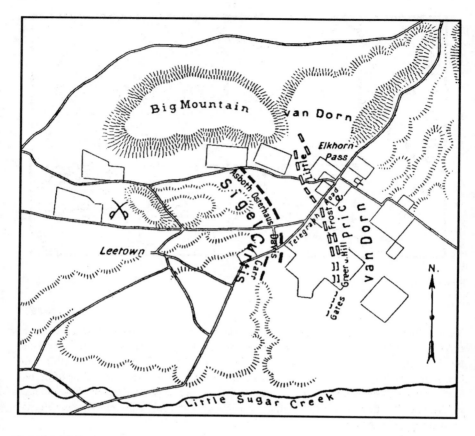

Figure 9. Pea Ridge on 8 March (Left above Leetown is Sigel's battlefield of 7 March).

Let us first pursue this battle on the right wing of the Union troops. Carr was attacked by superior and well-positioned artillery, and after several Union guns were made unusable, the Confederate infantry attacked him. Carr had to withdraw, but he fought with great stubbornness and delayed the enemy. There was bitter fighting over Elkhorn Pass. Finally, Carr was forced out of this position and eventually into the open ground at the foot of the ridge. His losses were severe, his troops had shot all their ammunition, and there was a shortage of ammunition in the artillery. Sigel, who continued to win against McCulloch on the left, noted the bad situation of his colleague Carr at the right moment and sent him Asboth's division to help. Parts of Davis's division were also sent to help Carr. As a result Carr's battered and almost broken division was able to regroup among friends. Price's Confederate corps did not risk pursuing its advantage, for it had suffered much itself, and Price had also learned of the defeat of McCulloch's corps. As a result the battle on this part of the battlefield fell silent about 4 P.M.

Sigel's first victory on 7 March. McCulloch's corps suffered a defeat against Sigel similar to that suffered by Carr's Union division against Price's Confederate corps. Incidentally, Sigel's troops also suffered considerable reverses at the start of the battle. Osterhaus, whose division fought in front, sent forward his cavalry, 150 men, to scout. The troop fell into a trap and was thrown back in great confusion. In the same way, Osterhaus' 12th Missouri and 36th Illinois came into an extremely perilous position when the troops of Davis's division fighting alongside them suddenly broke and withdrew to Leetown, a town located behind the fighting line. This was not due to cowardice; rather Davis's people did not understand how to use their new weapons and were unable to load their new muskets.[36]

As a result the flank of the 12th Regiment, which was shooting with muzzle-loaders, was exposed. Now the 12th and the 36th had to pull back, but only to the border of a neighboring wood. But Hoffmann's battery could not keep pace fast enough, and it remained standing in the open field in front of the line. The rebels immediately attacked the cannons, but they had to withdraw when the 12th gave a withering fire from the cover of the woods.[37] The battery was recovered at once, contact with Davis's division was restored, and the enemy was driven back by a new attack led by Colonel Osterhaus. The two leaders of the Texas troops, General and Colonel McIntosh (father and son), fell in front of the 12th Regiment, and a sharpshooter of the 36th Illinois Regiment killed the corps commander, General McCulloch. The Confederate Colonel Hébert was captured. Through this misfortune the troops of Louisiana and Texas were deeply demoralized and no longer held their position.[38]

The left wing remained victorious all along the line, and Sigel was thus in a position to help the threatened Carr at the right moment. Sigel regarded pursuit of the enemy wing that he had defeated as pointless, for he assumed that the enemy would withdraw the wing that had been victorious against Carr, and that a unification of the two enemy corps who had hitherto fought separately could not be hindered. Thus the battle would revive the next day. And that was what happened. The new position of the unified enemy in the Elkhorn Pass was very favorable. Further, the enemy, who was a third larger, could bear its losses more easily than the Union troops. Hence a very hot day was promised for the morrow, for a considerably weaker army had to expel a stronger enemy from a position which was a natural fortress. If this attack failed, then the Union troops were in a very bad situation, for they would have to retreat to Springfield via difficult detours. The battle situation was such that the Northerners had to fight with their front pointed north. They *had* to take the pass, while the Southerners had several roads available for their retreat.

After Sigel had established that the enemy corps had joined together, he led his tired and hungry troops back to the camp at Sugar Creek for the night so that his people could have a warm camp and cook for themselves. But he took every possible measure of security, precisely investigated the field that would be the area of attack the following day, and sought to protect this area against surprise with a chain of pickets.

Commanding General Curtis regarded the results of the first day quite negatively. The defeat of the right wing was very painful, and Carr's troops were no longer capable of action. The enemy had the advantage of a very strong position and significantly superior forces. On the evening of 7 March Curtis was already speaking of the possibility of surrender in case it was not possible to take Elkhorn Pass. The German officers and General Davis were less concerned, and Sigel and Osterhaus in particular trusted in the strong effect of their well-schooled artillery, if only it could manage to get a good position for attack.

On 8 March. The next morning, Curtis commanded Sigel to advance along the road leading to Elkhorn Pass. Sigel asked for a brief delay in order to await the return of Osterhaus and Captain Assmussen, who had ridden out to find a place better suited for the artillery to support the attack. Soon the two German officers returned and reported that they had found proper places not occupied by the enemy, on the high open field south of Big Mountian. Osterhaus had already posted the 44th Illinois Regiment in such a way that no surprises could be made by the enemy in the meantime. Curtis declared himself in agreement with Sigel's proposals, as well as with the changes in his attack plan made possible by Osterhaus's measures. These changes gave occasion to the rumor that Sigel demanded supreme command and that Curtis agreed. That did not happen, but it might be said that the attack of 8 March went entirely according to Sigel's plan and was carried out from the points chosen by Osterhaus and Assmussen. Curtis had acted rather passively during the main battle on 8 March and left his German officers free to act as they would. Sigel declared that it was a great relief when Curtis agreed to his plan of attack.

In order to leave the enemy in the belief that the main attack on Elkhorn Pass would take place from the Telegraph Road, Davis's division began the attack from this position with strong artillery fire, and both Davis and the remnant of Carr's division moved their infantry in a decoy skirmish. During this time the march of Sigel's two divisions was carried out for the flank attack that was to be the main action according to the new plan. Within a good half-hour this advance had been completed. Now Sigel brought the Hoffmann, Welfle, and Frank batteries together and opened such a heavy fire from the high, open field that, according to the correspondent of the *New York Tribune,* who was there, there had never been such a bombardment on American soil. This artillery fire was all the more effective because the enemy stood under cliffs and behind a stone wall and was often hit by splintered stone.

Sigel at first opened fire at a distance of 800 yards. He soon had his guns advanced 250 yards, and the guns then had a dreadful effect. This attack was extraordinarily daring, but Sigel had not figured on their accuracy in vain. The Confederate batteries were set up to meet a Union attack from Telegraph Road, in keeping with the original attack plan of Curtis, and they were completely surprised by Sigel's flank attack. The Confederates could not find the range of Sigel's considerably higher batteries quickly enough. Sigel had worked tirelessly on the training of his artillery, and most of his artillerymen were from the earlier three-month service, having gone home shortly before the Battle of Wilson's Creek, had returned to service. Sigel was also substantially reinforced by Hoffmann's splendidly trained German battery from Cincinnati. The Klaus's German battery from Evansville, Indiana, also fought with him on 8 March.

Sigel was able to silence several enemy batteries very quickly and open the field to his infantry for attack. Because enemy cannonballs almost all passed over the heads of those attacking, Sigel had very few losses on this bold advance. The infantry of Osterhaus's and Asboth's divisions followed the artillery on foot. The terrain was very propitious for advance, for the lightly rolling plateau across which the attack ran provided much cover for the infantry. Shortly before eleven o'clock Sigel's cannons had beaten down almost all of the enemy artillery, 50 cannons.

The enemy's artillery, under the cover of woods, did not dare go out into the open field in view of the dreadful effect of Sigel's artillery, and their infantry was considerably demoralized over the complete failure of their artillery comrades. Sigel's cannons then tried to purge the woods in front of the enemy artillery, which was successful. The German regiments now had a free path to charge toward the woods, the heights and the pass.

Sigel sent the 36th Illinois Regiment and the three German 2nd, 3rd and 17th Missouri Regiments, against the steep mountainside to the left, where the Confederate General Van Dorn held a strong position. Before these troops reached the top, the Cincinnati German cannoneers under Hoffmann, as well as Sigel's Elbert battery, had placed that top under fire, and the infantry had rather easy work to throw the enemy into Cross Timber Hollow. The 17th Missouri Regiment, German Turners under Major Poten (a former Hanoverian officer), were able to take the enemy from the rear and took many prisoners.

At the same moment as this infantry attack, Osterhaus charged against Elkhorn Pass with the 12th Missouri and the 25th and 44th Illinois Regiments, the 12th leading under Wangelin. They captured Dallas's enemy battery at once, and then they were soon in the pass with their Illinois comrades. The enemy was quickly thrown out, and in half an hour Elkhorn Pass was in Osterhaus's hands. With that the center of the enemy's position was taken.

The success of Sigel on the left wing was seen in time by Curtis, and Davis's and Carr's divisions shifted from decoy skirmishing to genuine attack. The enemy was in full retreat. But there was no cavalry to make the pursuit effective. Osterhaus's and Asboth's divisions did pursue the enemy nine miles to Keetsville, and Bussay's cavalry to Bentonville, but the successes were not great. The victory of the Union troops was complete, and Missouri remained free of invasion by the Confederates for two years after the Battle of Pea Ridge.

The Battle of Pea Ridge is also interesting because about a thousand Indians fought on the side of the Confederates. The redskins only appeared one other time in the Civil War, in their attack on the German town of New Ulm in Minnesota (see appendix no. 8). The Indian Territory lay very close to the battlefield of Pea Ridge. The Confederates had convinced the stolid redskins that the Union government wanted to enslave them, so that a Confederate officer, Pike, was able to lead three Indian regiments into battle at Pea Ridge. But Pike distributed too large a ration of whiskey among the savages. Most of the Indians were said to be very drunk as the battle began. In their intoxication they confused their allies for their common enemies and fired wildly into the Confederate ranks. This is the report of Brown in his book *Four Years in Secessia,* where the report is also made that the Indians mistakenly scalped a number of Confederate wounded. There was supposed to have been a costly skirmish over these atrocities between four companies of one Confederate Arkansas regiment and the Indians. The Indians only came into contact with the Union troops on the first day of battle, with the Germans under Osterhaus and Asboth. Sigel's people captured a number of Indians. Because many dead and even wounded were scalped, Sigel had each Indian flogged with twenty-five strokes on the back, which does not correspond to the usage of war, but which was seen as the proper punishment for scalping.

The German comrades of those scalped did not carry this sentence out with any special mildness. Incidentally, the Confederates were later happy to avoid help from the Indians. These braves were more trouble for their white allies than they were of use. Further, the redskins simply could not stand artillery fire. At the sight of a cannon they would run. It is also significant that the first Negro soldiers appeared on the Union side at Pea Ridge. They were in Asboth's division, but they served primarily as teamsters, porters, and magazine workers.

Our portrayal of the battle rests essentially on Sigel's report in the collection *Battles and Leaders* (Century Press), as well as on Sigel's later portrayal in the *New York Monthly*. A literal translation of Sigel's report would easily confuse the reader, since Sigel had to insert too many details that would have no interest for persons far away and thus only distract. There are also many reports that the author received from his friend Schierenberg and General Osterhaus.

The losses in the Battle of Pea Ridge were 203 dead and 201 captured or missing in the Union army. The Union division commanders Carr and Asboth were wounded. The Confederates gave their losses as 800 to 1000 dead and wounded and 200 to 300 missing. Their actual losses were much higher. The Confederate generals McCulloch and McIntosh fell, Colonel Rivers died of his wounds soon after the battle, and General Price was also wounded.

This battle in Arkansas was Sigel's finest in the entire war. Here he appeared in the best light, not just as a strategist but also as a tactician and an extremely capable leader of troops, an ability the West Pointers consistently denied him. But even here he once again had bad luck, for this one victory of his entire career was won not as the commander in chief, nor in a completely autonomous situation, but as second in command to the West Pointer Curtis. That gentleman officially won the battle, that is, he wrote the the report for the official description of the battle and it was open to him to say about it what suited him.

But who will willingly say that as commander in chief he actually played the second role in an important battle that decided the military situation in the entire Southwest? That out of recognition of the danger and in recognition of his own personal weaknesses, he gave the whole leadership in the battle to a subordinate, a non-West Pointer, and even a German? Even assuming that the battle report of commanding General Curtis were not reedited in the headquarters of General Halleck, it makes sense from the standpoint of the commanding general to give his comrade Sigel only as much glory as was unavoidably necessary. Yet Sigel received even less than that. Whether it was Curtis's or Halleck's hand in play is indifferent. Curtis and Sigel were still good friends shortly after the battle. Even thirty years after the battle, Sigel stressed in the *New York Monthly* that Curtis shook his hand when they met on the battlefield behind Elkhorn Pass after the victory. But General Curtis's account of the battle sounds quite different, and it was only much later that Curtis gave justice to his comrade Sigel.

According to the official account, Sigel's participation in the battle cannot be evaluated. But in the entire West after Pea Ridge, the talk was of Sigel and not of Curtis.

Sigel had himself moved to the Eastern theater of war a few months after the battle. But the cause for that lay less in the recognition denied his accomplishments in the official report than in the continuing intrigues he had to endure from General Halleck.

Sigel and Halleck

In the Frémont chapter, it was already noted that the German officers in Sigel's division publicly protested against Frémont's dismissal in November, 1861. The protest was actually directed against the improper timing of the dismissal. Sigel's division was suffering from the dreadful defeat at Wilson's Creek and longed for an opportunity to eliminate that disgrace. As soon as the opportunity presented itself, when a strong and well-equipped army had gathered to meet the enemy on the same battlefield of Wilson's Creek, Frémont was dismissed and retreat was ordered by the new commander. The rage of Sigel's officers is entirely understandable, and it might also explain why the gentlemen erred in the form of their protest.

Sigel himself did not sign the protest, but the new commander presumed that Sigel was the originator of the document. The protest must have been very uncomfortable for Halleck, because his position in Missouri was a political one. He essentially relied on the Republicans and pro-Union people, and among these the Germans were still the most important element. They were deeply wounded by what they thought to be Lincoln's weakness on the slavery question, and this opinion acted against Halleck, who was seen as Lincoln's representative in Missouri. Almost all the German anti-slavery people joined the protest of Sigel's officers, and this made Halleck's political effectiveness extraordinarily more difficult.

Halleck had come to St. Louis with prejudices against German officers. He was a hard headed man and an intense hater. He had a secret investigation launched of Sigel's acts in the war, and his informants were essentially Sigel's enemies Sturgis and Schofield. This investigation dealt only with Sigel's conduct at Wilson's Creek, and it did not deal with his earlier accomplishments at Camp Jackson and at Carthage. The fact that Sigel came off very poorly in this so-called investigation, of which he did not know, is obvious. He was under a cloud after Wilson's Creek and had not yet found an occasion to cast off the disgrace. On 14 January 1862, Halleck sent a dreadful report on Sigel and the German officers, in which the following passages are found:

> Another real problem lies in the existence and character of many troops that have been organized in Missouri up to now. Some of these corps were not only erected in a completely illegal manner, but are not at all dependable. On the contrary, because they in most cases consist of foreigners, in many cases are commanded by foreign adventurers or perhaps refugees from justice, and influenced by party hacks for political purposes, they form a dangerous element in the army. The Body Guards, Marine Corps, Telegraph Corps, Railroad Guards and Benton Guards have already been mustered out. The Home Guards in Boonville and Jefferson City had to be disarmed by force, and a number of other organizations of these irregular troops were dismissed after a few days. Some of these units formed of foreigners consist of outstanding people, while others are nothing better than barbarians in the field, without discipline or subordination. Wherever they go, they turn all Union people into bitter enemies. The accompanying letter of General Schofield is a beautiful example of what has been said

by others of them. Zealous adherents to the Union from southwest Missouri (including Colonel Phelps, a member of Congress) have asked that it not be tolerated that General Sigel's troops return there, for these troops plunder friend and foe without distinction wherever they go. I will still be compelled to use his (Sigel's) division, because I do not have any other troops to send against the Confederate General Price. As an example of the type of trust one may set in some of these alien adventurers, I will state the fact that has come to me from a very reliable source that a number of alien officers held a meeting, and there they decided that in case the Trent Affair leads to a war with England, they leave our service in a body and go to Canada.[39]

Sigel only learned of this report by Halleck to McClellan many years later, from the publication of the *Official Records.* He could thus not protest at once against these fully ungrounded accusations, but thirty years later Sigel said in his *New York Monthly:*

This accusation [concerning the Trent Affair – WK] was raised by Halleck against men such as Asboth, who was wounded at Pea Ridge and died after the war of a second wound that he received in Florida at the head of his cavalry; against Colonel Hassendeubel, who fell gloriously before Vicksburg; against Colonel Knoderer, who was seriously wounded while bravely fighting at Suffolk, and who died soon afterwards; against Colonel John A. Fiala, the chief of the topographic division under Frémont; against Colonel Meysenberg; against Osterhaus and many others. But Halleck turns these patriots into traitors, these people who defended Missouri against the rebels!

Sigel goes on to say:

As far as Halleck's letter from Schofield goes, it deals particularly with the cavalry battalion of Major Hollan from Warrenton, which did not consist of Germans. And Phelps was then an ardent friend of slavery.

Sigel condemned Halleck's letter all too mildly. It is shameful that Halleck described political refugees from Germany as "refugees from justice," placing them in the same category with criminals who avoided justice through flight. If England had been the victor in the American Revolutionary War, then Washington, Jefferson, Hamilton, Adams, Franklin and the other patriots would perhaps also have had to seek asylum in a neutral country, for it is by no means certain that the British victors would have treated these revolutionaries more mildly than the German governments treated the revolutionaries of 1848–49. The horrors the captured American patriots had to endure on the floating prisons of the English lead one to suppose the opposite.

The goals of the American revolutionaries were the same as those sought by the German Forty-Eighters. Washington and his allies wanted to free America from the rule of England, and the Forty-Eighters fought for a free and united Germany and sought to bring the republican principle to victory. The sole difference between the two groups was the success of the American and the failure of the German revolutionaries. To call the latter "refugees from justice" (because Halleck portrayed Sigel's soldiers as robbers and barbarians, that description has a particularly bitter taste), is an unheard-of insult not simply to the officers and soldiers of Missouri, but also half a million German emigrants who were driven to America by revolution alone. One could not assume that a West Pointer of those days was much conscious of the thanks that the Union owed to this half-million immigrants. But the commanding general in Missouri should have known that the city of St. Louis was saved by the Germans alone, and that those "refugees from justice" played the leading role in that outstanding deed.

Sigel's soldiers were described by Halleck as robbers and barbarians because they took food which the government was not able to supply on time where they found it. Nine-tenths of the population of southern Missouri was rebel. To these people, every Union man was an outlaw, concerning not only his property but also his life. In such conditions and with provocations, were Sigel's soldiers alone supposed to restrict themselves to civilized war conduct, supposed to starve, although the enemy's country could feed them? Halleck's accusation is as illogical as it is infamous. And who was complaining against Sigel's "barbarians"? They were the people who celebrated when the deposed liberator of slaves, Frémont, was replaced by a successor from whom they expected protection for their property, invested in slaves.

Halleck's regret that he had no other troops than Sigel's available for the new campaign against the rebel south of Missouri is silly. What would have happened to Curtis's army at Pea Ridge if Sigel's German troops had not been present?

And then the Trent Affair. If Halleck really learned from "a very reliable source" as he says in that official document, that the German officers desired to go to Canada and serve there under the English against the United States, then that was high treason, and it would have been Halleck's duty to open a court martial and act in the strictest manner against the participants in this supposed assembly of officers. But he did not do that; rather, he denounced his German comrades in a report that he knew would remain secret for a long time and would perhaps never be published. For such official documents were treated in an irregular manner during the war, and hundreds of such reports went into the wastebasket or were burned, probably fortunately. The entire letter shows us the character of the later supreme commander of the Union army, this devious man dominated by prejudices and small thinking, possessed by delusions of grandeur.

* * *

When Halleck took up his office in Missouri, Sigel was ill of dysentery. He was also very upset. Halleck let him know his distrust. Sigel, however, was everything short of a diplomat. Since he was one of the few Union officers who knew the military situation in Missouri in detail, he held it to be his duty to send recommendations to the new commander and to draw up a war plan. This plan was essentially carried out, but Halleck regarded it as presumption that a subordinate whom he regarded as a bungler should dare to deal in such matters. Halleck was also very displeased that Sigel was highly regarded by Lincoln, as well as that Sigel became a major general so early.

Sigel wrote a private letter to his father-in-law Dullon in which he said of Halleck, "He has not acted as a soldier but rather as a picky lawyer toward me [Sigel]." This letter was then unfortunately printed by Dullon in the New Yorker Volkszeitung, translated by the English press from the German text and then passed through the entire press of the land.

Halleck never mentioned the letter to Sigel, but his hostility to Sigel was expressed on every suitable occasion. When Sigel lost the battle of New Market, Virginia, on 15 May 1864, Halleck wrote to General Grant concerning this battle, "Sigel does nothing but run away, and he has never done anything else." And Grant printed this slanderous letter in his memoirs without any commentary, hence giving it a very wide circulation. Sigel opposed Grant when he sought a third presidential term, due to the corruption prevailing under the president. The publication of Halleck's letter on New Market is Grant's receipt for Sigel's political sin.

Incidentally, Halleck treated Grant even worse than he did Sigel in the first period of the war. Despite that, Grant, who was also a strong hater, reconciled with Halleck. It was different with the stubborn Sherman. When Halleck visited Sherman's corps shortly before the end of the war, there was to be a parade before Halleck, but Sherman forbade it and ignored Halleck. Halleck's intrigues against McClellan would also fill a considerable volume, and the capable General Rosecrans owed his fall essentially to Halleck. Yet no American general did so badly as a commander of troops as Halleck during the campaign against Corinth. Among all the blunders of the war, this was Halleck's sole act of leadership and certainly the worst. Despite that, Halleck remained commander of all Union armies for two years, and in the last year of the war he functioned as chief of general staff. His bronze statue stands in New York's Central Park. It is inconcievable that Lincoln maintained this military fraud and arch-plotter through four entire years and always listened to his advice, when the soldiers of the Army of the Potomac regarded Halleck as the evil spirit of the Union cause.

IV

The Civil War in 1862

Donelson and Shiloh
Germans at Rowletts Station and Mill Springs—Grant, Thomas, and Sherman
emerge—Fort Donelson and Shiloh (Pittsburg Landing)—The first great battle of the
Civil War.

(See Figure 4)

It was only in November 1861 that the advance of the Army of the Ohio of General
Buell through Kentucky to the secessionist state of Tennessee could begin, and the first good
news this campaign brought was the fight of parts of the German 32nd Indiana Regiment
at Rowletts Station. Four companies of this regiment, under Lieutenant Colonel von Trebra,
secured the bridge across the Green River for the crossing of the Army of the Ohio. Nearby
stood Colonel Willich with the rest of the regiment.

The enemy believed he could take the bridge in a *coup de main*. He sent General
Hindman with 1100 infantrymen, 250 Texas cavalrymen and 4 cannons against von Trebra's
300 infantrymen, who defended themselves against the five-fold greater force in a splendid
manner. Each attack was beaten off, and when the Texans tried to run down the little force,
the enemy Colonel Terry was shot dead and many saddles emptied. The enemy infantry
could shoot well but not strike, and the Germans did not give an inch. After a battle lasting
an hour and a half in which von Trebra lost eight dead and ten wounded, Willich appeared
with four more companies of his regiment, and the Confederates, who had suffered many
losses, retreated in the face of these reinforcements. The bridge had been saved, and Buell's
army had free passage. Of course, Rowletts Station was only a small skirmish, but among
the hundreds of small skirmishes of the Civil War one would be hard pressed to find one
on the Union side that was fought with such care on the part of the leader and such bravery and coolness on the part of the men.

The main battle for Kentucky, by which this state passed almost completely into the
hands of the Union, took place on 19 January 1862 at Mill Springs. There the German Union
General Schöpf with the 17th and 38th Ohio Regiments opposed the Southern General Zollicoffer, of Swiss ancestry. The battle amounted only to a skirmish among pickets. Zollicoffer

149

was a politician and very popular in his home state of Tennessee, but he knew nothing about leading in war. When General Thomas, later the great Union leader who never lost a battle, learned that Zollicoffer had gone to Mill Springs, across the Cumberland, he advanced toward him and beat his considerably superior enemy after a severe battle.

The battle was decided by a particularly powerful attack of the German 9th Ohio Regiment. The 2nd Minnesota Regiment, which was one-third German, also participated in the attack. These two regiments advanced as if on parade, bayonets lowered, driving all before them. The Southerners fled in a dissolution like that of the Northerners at the First Battle of Bull Run. For that reason the Battle of Mill Springs was called the Western Bull Run by Union soldiers. Zollicoffer was shot. Confederate losses were four times those of the Northern troops. All of eastern Kentucky and the border of Tennessee fell to the power of the Union as a result of this fine victory.[1]

From Mill Springs, Buell's (and Thomas's) campaign entered Tennessee. Now began the large-scale war in Tennessee that filled the years 1862 and 1863, ending with the splendid Union victory of Missionary Ridge and finding its continuation in 1864 in Sherman's world-famous march through Georgia.

*   *   *

The Mississippi streams through the western theater of war almost precisely from north to south. On its right bank lie the slave states of Arkansas, Louisiana, and Texas, on the left bank Tennessee and Mississippi, as well as parts of Louisiana. Hence five of the eleven rebel states stand in direct contact with this river, the "Father of Waters, the most important artery of commerce for this region." The Mississippi is also of the greatest importance for the two border states of Missouri and Kentucky.

Then there are the tributaries. Shortly before entering the main stream the mighty Ohio receives into its course the great rivers of the Tennessee and the Cumberland, coming from the heart of the Confederacy. These tributaries are navigable by steamboat for long stretches. Of the right-bank tributaries, the Missouri comes less into consideration, but the White River, the Arkansas, and the Red River play a considerable role. We are thus dealing with a widely spread system of natural water highways whose military importance is obvious.

Where the Mississippi enters the region of secession, there is also an important political border. The long-extended Northern state of Illinois penetrates here to a point. Kentucky and southern Missouri are separated here by the Mississippi, and the borders of the Northern state of Indiana and of the Confederate states of Tennessee and Arkansas lie very close. The Ohio, which divides Kentucky from Indiana at the end of its course, empties into the Mississippi at the Illinois city of Cairo.

The task of the North consisted of bringing the entire course of the Mississippi into its power, and the Union undertook this mission with meritorious energy. As early as 26 April 1862 the great naval hero Farragut had taken the mouth of the river in a bold assault, and on 28 April the land army of Butler was transported by sea to occupy the country's greatest ocean harbor, New Orleans. Thus was the sole great city of the Confederacy ripped from it, a victory for the North that certainly balanced out several field battles lost in Virginia. The conquest of the middle Mississippi, the stretch from Cairo to Memphis, was undertaken at the same time from the north. Small armored gunboats of shallow draft, armed with heavy

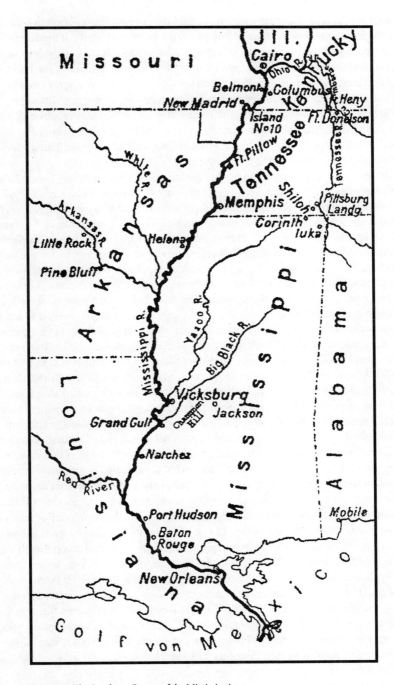

Figure 10. The Southern Course of the Mississippi.

guns were sent against the enemy, who was unable to put anything equivalent against these river ironclads. This demonstrated immediately the great superiority of the North in technical methods and finance. But the North also needed capable men with clear heads and hearts of steel for the river war. The river heroes Porter, Foote, Davis and their brave crews did great things, and the many amateur officers of the land army were given a splendid model.

The Confederacy fully understood the necessity of defending the Mississippi. Strong river fortresses arose along the stretch from Cairo to Memphis. Immediately south of Cairo arose Columbus, called the Gibraltar of the South; opposite, Belmont in southern Missouri; further south New Madrid; then Island No. 10; Fort Pillow and finally Memphis, to mention only the most important bulwarks.

In this process, the South dug itself in far too much. From Bowling Green, Kentucky, over 200 miles east of the Mississippi, there ran a chain of forts, posts and small Confederate trenchworks west to the great river, stretching far into the countryside to Arkansas Post in Arkansas. A second stretch of defenses was south of the first: Fort Henry on the Tennessee River and Fort Donelson on the Cumberland. The Confederates had exhausted themselves building these installations and had considerably scattered their forces, for the fortresses had to hold large garrisons, and huge amounts of supplies were heaped at these exposed points. This materiel was mostly lost, and after the completion of the blockade it was not to be replaced. How much of the fine cash that the rebellion disposed of at the start was built and buried away? Although slaves were largely used for trenchwork, it was precisely this loss of money that counted for so much later. The lost gold dollars never came back.

In conjunction with the Western war, the Confederacy realized too late that its strength would be expressed primarily in the land war, and that all resources had to be saved for that. The middle Mississippi could just as well have been left to the North, if only the Western Confederate land army had been able to strike with a third more force. This would have been possible if the scattered fortification garrisons had been reallocated to the field army. This is because the Confederate soldier was considerably superior to his enemy in 1862. The Southerner was on the average better led, and in battles between poorly trained soldiers enthusiasm and temperament always benefit the unit that is superior in these qualities. The Confederates had a great deal of the *élan* that distinguishes the French, and the Union troops did not yet possess the stubbornness that would later come into play, when a long acquaintance with weapons combined with good discipline. Another hindrance to the effectiveness of Northern forces was the Northern practice of sending out green recruits, not just by the regiment but often by the brigade or even the division, instead of distributing these recruits to regiments already organized. Every Northern body of troops had its undependable elements, and quite often these bad soldiers were the majority. Add to that the lamentable leadership of political generals. It is surprising that 1862 brought the North an unbroken chain of successes and partial successes in the West, and not a single large defeat, while in the East the Union flag was dragged through the dust and hauled from one dreadful defeat to another. The fact that the Confederates in the West had prepared themselves too completely for the defensive is certainly one of the chief sources of their many failures in this theater of war.

*   *   *

Brigadier General Ulysses S. Grant commanded in Cairo when the Union finally felt strong enough in the fall of 1861, to move against the Mississippi and the many Confederate fortifications in Kentucky and Tennessee. He saw the great enemy fortress of Columbus growing in his immediate vicinity. On 7 November 1861 he took ship with 2500 men to Belmont, opposite Columbus on the Mississippi, where he overran a strong Confederate camp and then withdrew before the Confederate General Polk, advancing from Columbus, could catch him. That was Grant's first deed of war, and its boldness quickly earned the completely unknown leader a name.

Forts Henry and Donelson. In the middle of November Halleck became Grant's superior. This outspoken enemy of all boldness had already disciplined Grant for Belmont, but Grant had bigger plans. It is not far from Cairo to Forts Henry and Donelson. Grant learned that these fortresses were rapidly growing. He had received reinforcements and felt strong enough to take those two new river fortresses, on the Tennessee and the Cumberland. On 8 January 1862 he telegraphed to Halleck, "I ask permission to take Fort Henry." Halleck responded, "No." Grant begged through the whole of January for his chief's approval, always with the same no. Then Admirals Foote and Porter joined their comrade Grant and stormed Halleck, assuring him that the gunboats alone could take the two river fortresses and that Grant was only needed as support. Finally, on 30 January, Halleck gave the command to attack, but only for Fort Henry. As early as 2 February, Grant had 17,000 men on the water, going up the Ohio, then south down the Tennessee. On 5 February he was in front of Fort Henry, but he did not have to fight. The gunboats brought the fort under fire, and a few hours later the Union flag waved from the fortress. The garrison had fled to Fort Donelson, which lay only twelve miles away on the Cumberland.

It is unclear whether Grant had received his chief's approval for Donelson. He did not worry about it, set out after the refugees, and on 12 February stood before Fort Donelson. The gunboats had meanwhile steamed down the Tennessee, into the Ohio, then into the mouth of the Cumberland, passing south on that river to Donelson. On 13 February Grant and Foote met near the river fortress on the Cumberland. Once more the little ironclad ships were first to strike, but here it did not go so smoothly as with Fort Henry. Either the people in Donelson shot better, or they had better cannons. Foote was seriously wounded (Porter had already been seriously scalded at Fort Henry by a boiler explosion), several ships were made unfit for service, and Foote had to withdraw to repair his gunboats.

In the meantime Grant had received reinforcements and enclosed the fort from the land side with 27,000 men. There were 17,000 Confederates in the fort (according to Badeau it was 21,123 men) under three generals: Floyd, Pillow and Buckner. This trinity was very unfortunately joined. Floyd was the first, Pillow second and Buckner third in rank. Floyd was a perjured traitor who had collaborated with the rebellion as Secretary of War for Buchanan, Lincoln's predecessor. Pillow was also a great sinner. The sole honorable soldier among these three was Buckner[2]. Floyd and Pillow were terribly worried that in the case of a defeat they would not be treated as prisoners of war but be hanged as traitors. If Grant had had only Buckner to deal with, the strong Fort Donelson certainly would not have fallen so soon. Floyd and Pillow decided on 14 February on a sally of the entire garrison in order to save it (and themselves). Buckner had to obey and go along.

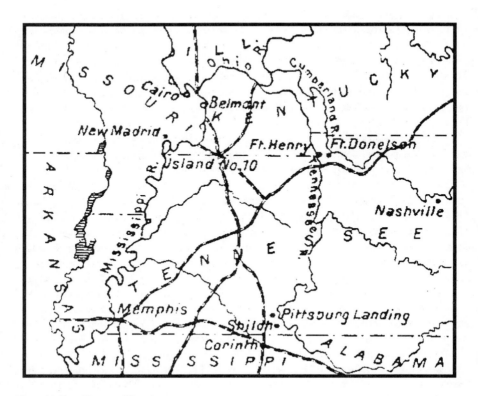

Figure 11. Forts Henry and Donelson.

On the early morning of 15 February, the Confederates advanced from the fortress in three troops. That under Buckner broke through the forces of McClernand opposite him. In fact the way for the withdrawal of the garrison was open for an hour, but Pillow called back his subordinate Buckner and Grant quickly plugged the hole. Grant also saw at once that the garrison was actually trying to decamp, not wage a decoy battle. For that reason he had two of the outer works stormed by Generals Smith and Lewis Wallace while most of the garrison was still outside. Smith and Wallace established themselves 150 yards before the outer works in good positions. At that point, the three generals in the fort decided to capitulate. Floyd and Pillow laid down their commands, and Buckner received the obligation to surrender the fort the next morning. Floyd fled on a steamboat with his Virginia troops up the Cumberland, and Pillow also brought his neck into safety.[3]

It cannot be denied that Grant was extraordinarily blessed by good luck in these operations. Without the anxiety of the Confederate generals, his triumph would not have been half so great. The essential thing about this victory was the speed with which it was completed. In those days Washington hungered for a success. Then appeared this entirely unknown man, this Grant, who took the strongest forts before which the North had long quavered as fast as one, two, three. The name of Grant flew through the entire North. Lincoln immediately appointed him a major general and sent his public thanks.

And Halleck? That gentleman was furious. How could Grant have the shamelessness to win without his permission? In his official report, Halleck praised General Smith for his attack (on Grant's order). The heroes of the fleet were also remembered by the supreme general of the West. But the report does not have a word about Grant. The most pitiful part came three weeks later. On 4 March Halleck telegraphed Grant:

> Surrender the command of the expedition to Major General C. F. Smith and remain at Fort Henry. Why do you not obey my orders and report the strength and position of your unit?
>
> —Halleck

Thus Halleck removed the victor of Fort Donelson. Lincoln and the other great men in Washington, who had celebrated Grant, did not move a hand to undo the injustice. Halleck also denounced Grant to the commanding general, McClellan. Grant defended himself against Halleck in a worthy and restrained manner. He declared that he had followed every one of Halleck's commands, that the "unauthorized" trip he had made to Nashville of which he was accused by his chief was explained by the demonstration that it had been a military necessity. When Halleck abused him again like a schoolboy in a letter of 9 March, Grant demanded his immediate dismissal. Halleck thought better of it, and on 12 March he wrote to Grant that he would receive a new command.

* * *

The results of the victory of Forts Henry and Donelson were seen at once. The Confederates gave up their primary defense position in Kentucky at Bowling Green, and on 27 February they evacuated even their strongest fortress at Columbus on the Mississippi. Now gunboats of the North could begin their victory cruise down the Mississippi, in rapid succession New Madrid, and then the very strong position on Island No. 10 fell, then Fort Pillow was taken, and on 16 June Admiral Davis destroyed the entire Confederate river fleet before Memphis, so that the largest city on the middle Mississippi fell into the Union's hands. The key to all of these successes lay in Fort Donelson.

* * *

The theater of war now moved to southwestern Tennessee. After the defeat of Donelson, the significant Confederate General A. Sidney Johnston gathered an army of 50,000 men in Corinth, Mississippi, near the border of Tennessee, in order to meet the enemy in an open field battle. But first there were many problems to settle in the Confederate camp. There was no harmony between Johnston and his second in command, Beauregard. In addition, public opinion in the South was offended by Johnston, and he was assigned responsibility for the misfortunes up to then. President Jefferson Davis was stormed by the press, by meetings, by petitions and the like to dismiss Johnston. But Davis knew his generals better. He responded to the enraged people, "If Sidney Johnston is not a good general, then we have none." This disharmony contributed to delaying Johnston's attack at a time when the days, even the hours, were precious.

The Northern leaders also wanted to advance aggressively, pursuing the victory of Donelson and destroying the Confederate army gathering at Corinth. For this purpose two Union armies advanced toward southwest Tennessee. Grant's old army, now commanded by Smith, was sent upstream on the Tennessee by steamboats from Fort Henry, and the Army of the Ohio of General Buell advanced overland from Nashville, also toward the area of Corinth. Both divisions were to unite at Savannah on the Tennessee, 80,000 men strong, and confront Johnston on the left bank of the Tennessee.

Smith's army arrived early with its commander, and in the middle of March, reinforced by Sherman's division, part of it was transferred to the left bank. (Savannah lies on the right, eastern, bank of the river.) The river was then in flood stage. It was General Smith who found and established camp on the left bank at Pittsburg Landing, two miles from Shiloh. Smith was already a seriously ill man. He became incapable of service (he died soon afterward), and on 17 March Grant was installed once more in Smith's place. Smith hence only led the force 4–17 March. Whether Smith intended to fortify the new camp near Shiloh cannot be discovered. His successor Grant did nothing in this direction.

Battle at Shiloh (or Pittsburg Landing). This was the first great battle of the Civil War. It is nine miles upstream from Savannah to Pittsburg Landing. Between these two points the steep banks of the Tennessee afford only one other landing place, Crump's Landing. There Lew Wallace's division (6500 men) was unloaded and formed a camp, also unprotected. Grant's main force, 33,000 men, camped about five miles from the Wallace Division between Pittsburg Landing and Shiloh, an isolated church in the woods, in a hilly and hollow-riddled woodland terrain whose two flanks were protected by swampy, low-lying streams. In the rear the camp had the raging Tennessee, without bridges. In the case of a defeat the steamboats could take away 10,000 men at the most to the right bank, according to Grant's own estimate. The western front of this camp, turned toward the enemy, consisted mostly of woodland, penetrated by a few fields and crossed by two poor roads and a railroad. This front opened itself toward the southwest and the city of Corinth, thirty English miles away, where the Confederate army stood. Grant, who was awaiting Buell, well knew that Buell would be delayed by flooded rivers and streams whose bridges had been destroyed by the enemy, but that did not disturb his confidence in the least.[4]

Before we portray the Battle of Shiloh, the march of the Confederate army from Corinth toward the battlefield and Johnston's plan of battle must be briefly reviewed, as well as something about the non-fortification of Grant's position.

Johnston wanted to overrun Grant at Shiloh before Grant could join with the auxiliary troops marching from Nashville (Buell's Army of the Ohio). Johnston marched out of Corinth at noon on 3 April with 40,000 men. He was supposed to be ready to attack at 5 A.M., but the march was considerably delayed. The minor commanders were still entirely inexperienced in leading such operations, and the marching road was often blocked. There were picket skirmishes, 3–5 April, but the Union leader attributed no importance to them, although the Confederate cavalry was accompanied by artillery. In one of these skirmishes a Union major was captured by the Confederates, and this officer said that the camp at Shiloh was still completely unfortified. On the evening of 4 April, Johnston held a council of war. The second in command, General Beauregard, argued that the army should turn about. He said, "Our entire plan supports itself on a surprise attack. It is inconceivable that the enemy cannot have learned of our march. We have already lost an entire day and cannot attack before the sixth of April. The enemy has almost two more days to dig in.

A surprise attack is no longer possible, and we are too weak to fight a strong enemy behind ditches." This argument made a strong impression, but Johnston did not want to listen to it. He insisted on an attack, whether against ditches or not.

None of the higher officers in Grant's camp had any concerns, and their position remained totally unfortified. Grant himself was not with his troops. He had his headquarters in Savannah, nine miles downstream. He had also not named a deputy during his absence. When the attack took place, Grant was in bed in Savannah.

The failure to dig ditches was later defended by Grant, *Century Magazine,* in this way:

> The spade was then little used in the West. I had considered fortifications. The engineer, McPherson, had also made up a line for entrenchments, but according to that the camp would have had to be located closer to the river but would still be too far from the river and the two streams to get enough water, for the streams would have fallen into enemy hands in the case of an attack. Further, the troops needed drill and discipline more than working with spade or ax.

These excuses are discouraging. The simplest breastwork, such as can be put down quickly with felled tree trunks, would have been enough, and the spade would only have been needed where artillery could best be placed. Grant could drill and discipline as much as he wished, but he at least should have secured his area to some degree. The water question was not so important for an army of 30,000 men in a secure position, which would have to be attacked by a force of 40,000. Further, Briar Creek, which would have flowed through a smaller but fortified camp, would have provided enough water for the few hours of a fight from such a position. And how much better would the troops have been able to fight if they had stood together in a small camp and had more contact with one another?[5]

It must be assumed that Grant never considered an attack, that he overestimated the disorder of the enemy army and must have held it to be absolutely incapable of moving on the offensive. The way the camp was organized points to this. Grant's army was encamped as if in time of peace, that is, primarily in keeping with the needs of comfort and without any measures for the possibility of an attack.[6]

In his memoirs, Sherman also defends the non-fortification of the camp (vol. 1, p. 229). He says, "Our untrained soldiers would have become too fearsome through the construction of trenches." A military man who reads this will hardly be able to turn the page without shaking his head. It was precisely because the mass of Grant's units consisted of raw recruits that one had to put up ditches. The people would then have felt more secure and would have fought better. Above all else, however, it is the duty of the officers not to expose his recruits so lightly to the perils of attack. On the same page, Sherman also says, "In a later period of the war we would have been able to make this position untakable even in one night," adding, "but at this time we did not do it, and it may be it is well we did not." With all proper respect to the later great leader through Georgia, one must say, this justification of carelessness is more than thin. What could later be done in one night could certainly have been done then in three weeks!

The following map of the camp shows that the divisions of Sherman and Prentiss were considerably extended forward, so that these recruits had to bear the first impact of the enemy.[7] McClernand's division stood behind Sherman and Prentiss without any contact

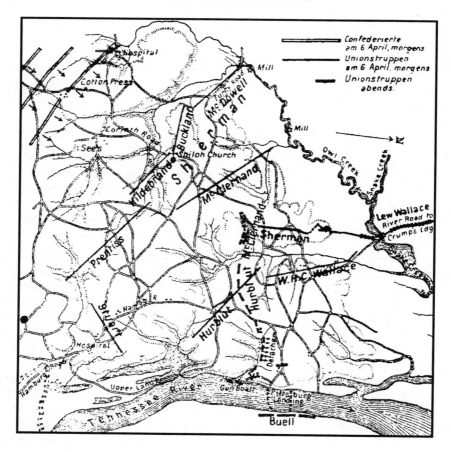

Figure 12. Battle at Shiloh.

with either. W. H. L. Wallace's and Hurlbut's divisions camped even farther back. Each division had its own camp. Of Grant's six division commanders, only Sherman had military training. The other five division commanders, even the two Wallaces, were what was called political generals.[8]

The army was without any general leadership when the attack took place. Grant only arrived via a dispatch boat at 8:30 A.M. when half of his army had already been dispersed. Sherman attempted to advise the other division commanders until Grant arrived, but he could only do so to a limited degree because he had to remain with his own troops and had no general view of the battlefield. Grant was barely capable of service. He had fallen from a horse two days before and was badly injured.[9] The entire battle was led by the division commanders on their own.[10]

Even after Grant's arrival there was no unified operation. The commanding general rode from one division to another giving advice, but there could be no talk of a unified leadership, for the entire battle was an enormous confusion.

We have spoken far more of the lack of order in the Union army than of the leadership in fighting. The latter cannot be portrayed, because the conflict consisted of a mad chain of small battles. Only once that is grasped is it understandable why perhaps a third of the army was transformed into stragglers, seeking protection from the bullets on the banks of the Tennessee or hiding in distant bushes, hollows or wood thickets.[11] Another third was killed, wounded, or taken prisoner. The rest, more than 11,000, found a rather solid position on the northern plateau, close to the Tennessee, under the protection of a strong artillery and the heavy guns of two gunboats.

The attack began at 6 A.M. on 6 April. The Confederates fell on the unprotected camp with a shrill cry. It is probable that most of the people in Sherman's and Prentiss's divisions, the first hit, were still asleep when the pickets, who had been posted only 300 yards forward, came running into the camp. They were followed by the enemy troops, storming with all the élan of the Southerner and with the awareness that the enemy had been completely surprised. What was a green recruit to do when overrun in that way, or a regimental or company leader, just as green? It is no marvel that sleepy, undisciplined soldiers ran away after seeing so many comrades falling or being wounded. Rather, one must be astonished that so much opposition was accomplished. Sherman in particular, who appears for the first time as a leader at Shiloh, accomplished a great deal.[12] Time and again he gathered the remnants of his scattered troops. He changed position eight times, and eight times he recovered, before evening fell. Sherman was always in the thickest rain of bullets. Several horses were shot out from under him, and he was wounded twice, but he held out until the end.

The recruit division of Prentiss also did well after the first surprise. It fell back on W. H. L. Wallace's division and was also supported by Hurlbut's division. Through accident, these continual retreats produced a certain concentration. Sherman and McClernand found themselves together, as did Prentiss, Wallace, and Hurlbut. There was a sort of selection process taking place. The cowards ran away at the beginning, and what was still held together by the leaders from ten o'clock on fought with extremely praiseworthy courage and persistence. These remnants even proved capable of isolated advances, and enemy units were often thrown back from positions already taken. In what was called the Hornet's Nest the remnants of three divisions took their stand from 10 A.M. to 4 P.M., and at about 2:30 P.M. the commanding Confederate General Johnston fell. The man from whose musket that deadly bullet flew should probably be seen as the true victor of Shiloh. Johnston's death was a blow to the Confederacy like Jackson's fall at Chancellorsville the following year.

The defenders of the Hornet's Nest had an entire hour of quiet after Johnston fell. General Beauregard, the next in command, stood far back at headquarters, and he sent forward reserves from there. It was almost 4 P.M. before the attack resumed, but the earlier enthusiasm was not there. To be sure, the remnant of Prentiss's and Wallace's commands were surrounded, and about 2200 men were taken prisoner along with Prentiss. General W. H. L. Wallace fell while bravely fighting, shortly before the surrender. Beauregard was even able to gain a part of the plateau onto which Sherman and McClernand were being pressed. But the attempt to overrun Hurlbut's division and thus win the landing on the Tennessee failed. The Confederates unanimously agree that all of Grant's army would have been annihilated if Johnston had continued in command. But who is to rule on such possibilities?

About 6 P.M., Grant's artillery chief had united thirty-two guns in front of Sherman and McClernand divisions, which were joined by Hurlbut's virtually intact division. A deep slough reaching to the river gave Grant's troops essential protection, for the gunboats could keep that slough safe from attack with their heavy guns. Beauregard was scared away from attempting to attack that last position of the enemy, and he even gave up the part of the plateau that he shared with Grant's troops, thus depriving himself of a good position for the following day. From his first position in the rear, Beauregard had a less positive impression of the success that Johnston had achieved. He saw thousands of secessionist stragglers trying to find safety without their weapons. He presumed from that, that the attacking forces were in the process of breaking up. Then too, the strong artillery of the enemy concerned him, and when the heavy naval guns intervened in the battle, he did not want to accept responsibility for a failure of the last mass attack.[13]

At about the same time, at sundown, L. Wallace's division finally arrived, and Nelson's division of Buell's army also landed.[14] At about 8 P.M. 13,000 fresh troops were gathered under Grant, and during the night another 12,000 men of Buell's army were landed. On the morning of 7 April, Grant was approximately as strong as he had been on the morning of the 6th, and a further 25,000 men from Buell were in the immediate vicinity. On the morning of the 7th, however, the Confederate army numbered barely more than 22,000 men capable of fighting. The battle of the 7th was already decided before it began. Despite this, Beauregard fought from dawn until 3 P.M., when he withdrew to Corinth unmolested. The battle of the 7th does not need to be portrayed here. Grant lost 1437 dead, 5679 wounded, 2934 captured, altogether 10,050 men, primarily on 6 April. Buell lost 263 dead, 1816 wounded, and 83 prisoners. Both of them together lost 12,217 men (according to the revised lists, 13,573 men). The losses of the Confederates amounted to 1728 dead, 8012 wounded, and 959 captured—10,699 men. Grant alone lost 33 percent of the five divisions participating on 6 April. Sherman says in his memoirs that he never saw such terrible fighting as in the first great battle at Shiloh, and Grant says that only the dreadful battles in the Wilderness—May, 1864—could be compared to Shiloh.

The Germans at Shiloh

Only a single purely German infantry regiment, the 32nd Indiana under Willich, participated in the Battle of Shiloh, and only on the second day of the battle, since it belonged to Buell's army, and it arrived on the battlefield early on the morning of 7 April. The German Turner regiment, the 9th Ohio, did not take part in the battle because it was also in Buell's approaching army and was even farther back.

When the 32nd Indiana Regiment climbed the river landing, thousands of stragglers from Grant's army lay there in security. Several of them called out to the 32nd, "Don't go any farther, you'll all be shot dead!" The regiment entered the fighting at once. How it fought is told by General Lew Wallace in his autobiography, as follows:

The enemy charged forward with a shrill war cry. I saw it coming, then I looked back at the woods behind me where the comrades who were to support me had disappeared. Nothing more was to be expected from them. Then, in the last instant, a blue unit flew from the woods into the open field. It was only one regiment, but when the enemy sensed this advance, it stopped and turned around back into the secure cover of the woods. From there it opened strong fire on the newly arrived Union regiment, so that it began to show signs of insecurity. Then an officer rode around the left flank of the regiment and to the front, turning his back to the enemy. I could not hear what he was saying, but I saw that he was ordering a drill sequence even as many in the first rank were falling. The effect was magical. The colonel returned to his post, and the regiment advanced as if on parade, despite the dreadful fire of the enemy, charged the woods from whence the firing came, and occupied it. That was, I believe, the boldest act I saw in the entire war.

And General Sherman reports that Willich's 32nd distinguished itself two further times on the same day in the same manner.

Colonel von Willich declared that his people suffered more from the cross-fire of the Union troops than from enemy bullets. Von Willich was named a brigadier general while still on the battlefield.

The following Germans and German Americans acted as brigade leaders: Colonel Julius Raith (fallen), Colonel Adolph Engelmann [Engelman], Colonel Hildebrand and the Generals Laumann (from Iowa), Wagener (later the hero of Chattanooga) and Ammen. The German-American Ammen led the first reinforcements from Buell's army that arrived on the battlefield. The German Colonel Gustav von Gerber, leader of the half-German 24th Indiana Regiment, fell in the charge on an enemy battery. General Lew Wallace, the poet, said, "No one died more gloriously than Gerber. And yet so many brave men died at Shiloh, and they performed so many glorious deeds." Other than Willich, Gerber and Raith, the German colonels who most distinguished themselves were Engelmann [Engelman], Mersi, and Brausewein.

Colonel Appler of the 53rd Ohio Regiment, in Hildebrand's brigade, was very sharply criticized by General Sherman. This brigade stood entirely isolated on Sherman's extreme left wing. They had to bear the first impact of the enemy, who appeared here with a fivefold superiority as well as with strong artillery. Sherman says that Appler called to his men to save themselves. At that, the entire regiment fled. Lieutenant Colonel Fulton gathered it again, but then Appler reappeared and ordered another retreat. Appler was dismissed. Colonel Hildebrand was particularly praised by Sherman.

Many German batteries fought at Shiloh. The 1st Minnesota Battery particularly distinguished itself, with crews consisting of Turners from New Ulm. The battery only came to the army shortly before the battle. It shot splendidly. In the Hornet's Nest, which plays so large a role in the accounts of the Southern war reports, this battery formed the center. Captain Münch was wounded at the very beginning of the battle. Lieutenant Wilhelm Pfänder, well-known among German-American Turners, took over the command. This battery covered Sherman's retreat to his last defensive position. Incidentally, this German battery of nine cannons fired the first cannon shots on the morning of 6 April. The 5th Ohio Battery, which had claimed this honor, fled before their guns were in position, and the Turner cannnoneers from Minnesota took their position. They held up bravely through the entire day. Their first fire gave Prentiss's completely surprised division time to organize. Several guns were made unusable, but Lieutenant Pfänder fought on in the Hornet's Nest until the rest of Prentiss's division was captured. The battery broke through and finally came to Hurlbut's division, with whom they made the last victorious fight over the landing place. In the evening the battery moved into the strong artillery position Grant had created to protect what was left of his artillery, on the plateau near the Tennessee River. This German battery was the best, along with the Hickenlooper battery from Cincinnati, and made an honorable name for itself.

Sherman also complained of Bähr's German battery from Evansville, Indiana. The first death of the battery was Captain Bähr himself. Then, Sherman says, the battery at once took flight, disturbing the new position of Sherman's shaken infantry, so that Sherman had to take a new defensive line linked to McClernand's left wing. According to the description of Lieutenant Spitz, who followed Bähr (or Behr) in command, it happened this way: Bähr saw a strong enemy unit in front of his battery. When he was about to fire on it, one of Sherman's adjutants forbad it because the "enemy unit" was in truth a scouting unit of the Union army. Immediately the battery was inundated with dreadful fire. Captain Bähr was shot, and the position became untenable. On the evening of the same day, this battery performed a fine deed under the command of Lieutenant Biehler. The battery had only three guns; under the protection of only two companies of infantry, they defended the bridge over Owl Creek for hours, and when Biehler finally had to withdraw, he saved another gun from a unit of his that he had thought he had lost, in the face of great difficulty and peril.

The Mann battery, which had previously fought in Missouri, also distinguished itself under Brotzmann's leadership. Also fighting at Shiloh were the German Welker, Nispel (Schwartz), Markgraf, Dressel, and Timony batteries. The battery of the German-American Hickenlooper from Cincinnati was mentioned for special praise. Brotzmann's battery fought with particular effect against the Confederates who tried to take the landing place on the evening of 6 April but were thrown back by Hurlbut's division. Brotzmann lost so many horses that he eventually was able to bring only three of his guns along. More in the biographical section under Raith.

Battles of Corinth, Perryville and Stones River

Halleck's poor leadership at Corinth—Plunder campaign under Bragg—Indecisive Battle of Perryville—Germans under Sheridan at Stones River.

Immediately after the Battle of Shiloh, Halleck united the forces of Grant, Buell, and Pope, placed himself at the head of 105,000 men, and moved against Corinth, where stood the Confederate army of Beauregard that had been beaten at Shiloh. There are only thirty English miles from Shiloh to Corinth. Halleck needed a full month to move his big army half this distance. He could have overrun the place in a few days and captured the demoralized garrison, but he treated Corinth as if it were Sebastopol. The entire distance from Shiloh to Corinth was winnowed, and Halleck raised new breastworks every two miles.

Beauregard laughed as he gathered reinforcements, reorganized his army, and withdrew with all his supplies on 29 May, seven weeks after Halleck's departure from Shiloh. It would be difficult to find in all of military history a similar example of slowness and excessive caution. But Halleck knew how to mislead the gentlemen in Washington into thinking that he had fought a great victory in Corinth. As a reward for this Lincoln named him *generalissimo* of all the armies of the United States with a seat in Washington.

Before his departure, Halleck dispersed his army. Grant remained in Corinth with 25,000 men, Buell was sent to eastern Tennessee with about 40,000 men, and the rest were used for other expeditions under Sherman, Thomas, and McClernand. In those days the road to Vicksburg was open. The city on the Mississippi, later such an important bullwark, was only weakly fortified, and this could easily have been taken. But Halleck did not consider it. The Confederates immediately made use of Halleck's error. Strong works were erected in Vicksburg, and the available army of Generals Van Dorn and Price came from Missouri to attack Corinth. They won the bloody battle at Iuka on 19 September, but they were defeated by Rosecrans at Corinth, 3–4 October.[15] Grant remained rather inactive throughout the summer and fall of 1862. He was busy with preparations for his campaign against Vicksburg.

Halleck had kept the most important task for the Army of the Ohio under General Buell. It was to beat the strongest Confederate army in eastern Tennessee and take the city of Chattanooga. Halleck had not figured on the supply problems of such an undertaking, however. Buell was actually able to press as far as McMinnville in the wild Cumberland Mountains, and one of his units came up to Chattanooga. But the lack of cavalry to counter Morgan's irregulars, who fell on the rear of the Union troops, made Buell's mission more than he could fulfill. Buell could not maintain his supply lines with distant Louisville in this wild, thinly settled enemy country. His superior forces were of no use to him, for the enemy did not present itself for battle. Yet Buell could not dare go farther south or southeast. Union troops were harassed back and forth, were forced to make hard marches in half-wild areas, and were continually irritated by the swift cavalry of Forrest and Morgan, which had developed the destruction of roads, railroads, and bridges to a true art.

The main Confederate army, which Buell never got to see, now stood under General Bragg, a favorite of Jefferson Davis. He could not be numbered as one of the great military leaders of the Confederacy, but it must be recalled that Bragg appeared upon the scene when the cause of the Confederacy in the West was doing very poorly, when Shiloh and Corinth were taken and the Confederate forces stood in a lamentable state. Bragg had to build from these fragments a new field army that could fight the strong and victorious Union forces.

The Southern people, who could never understand why the Confederate armies continually won in the East and always lost in the West, demanded great deeds of Bragg. It was also extremely painful to the secessionists that the Western war played itself out primarily in Tennessee. Hence public opinion, which was a great power on both sides, demanded an advance into the North. Kentucky must be freed from the Northern invasion and this slave state, that "longed for liberation from the yoke of the Union," incorporated into the Confederacy. This demand also corresponded with the inclinations of General Bragg. He managed to slip past Buell's forces and win a considerable lead in his march to the north before Buell saw through Bragg's plan. Because there was no Union force in Kentucky, the two large Northern cities of Louisville and Cincinnati stood in great danger of being over-run and plundered.[16] Buell set out after his opponent, and through forced marches he managed to locate the enemy on 21 August near Prewitts Knob, Kentucky. The armies lay opposite each other, but neither Buell nor Bragg could decide to attack. Bragg then moved to the northeast to install a secessionist state government in Frankfort, the political capital of Kentucky. This left the road to Louisville open for Buell. He occupied that city and re-inforced himself with several thousand recruits.

The primary purpose of Bragg's raid was thwarted by Buell's arrival in Louisville. To be sure, Bragg had gathered together a mass of war booty, but the thousands of recruits he wanted to enlist in Kentucky did not come. He had to turn back south and was pursued by Buell. On 8 October there was a battle at *Perryville*, Kentucky.

Only half of Buell's army entered the action. Buell's excuse was the severe lack of water then prevailing in Kentucky. Many dray animals died of thirst, and it was not possi-ble to get enough drinking water for the men. The very strong corps under Thomas was prevented by this lack of water from entering the battle in time. Still, Buell's position was very faulty, and several of his subordinate commanders conducted themselves lamentably. Buell only learned of the battle two hours after its start, when McCook's entire corps had already been dispersed. McCook had sent no report. This corps had to absorb the main blow, fighting a force three times its size. The recruits Buell had gathered in Louisville were essentially in the McCook brigades of Jackson and Terrill. Both brigadiers fell while heroically trying to get these unfortunate men—who were barely able to handle their weapons and whose colonels, captains and lieutenants were as green as their men—to stand their ground.

Beside McCook stood Gilbert's corps. The commander was a political general. In *The Army of the Cumberland,* Cist calls Gilbert the worst of all Northern corps commanders. Gilbert awaited orders to assist McCook, but because Buell had no idea that McCook was in danger, he could not give Gilbert any orders. Gilbert's German division commander, General Schöpf, advanced on his own initiative to support his pressed comrade but, gnashing his teeth, was ordered by Gilbert to return to his position. Then Rousseau's divi-sion was destroyed despite brave resistance, and it appeared as if Bragg would eventually roll up the entire Union army. Then Sheridan, whose division consisted largely of Ger-mans, brought the battle to a standstill. This is the first appearance of the man who would later be such an important Union leader. Toward evening Carlin's brigade advanced, and finally General Schöpf was also able to participate. Darkness brought the fighting to an end. Union losses were 4348 men, including 918 dead. The Southerners lost 3400 men. During the night Bragg evacuated the field and went south with his booty. Nothing really came of Buell's pursuit.

After the battle Gilbert was expelled and Buell dismissed. General Rosecrans took over the force, which from then on was called the Army of the Cumberland. Many com-plaints were made against Buell. He was not active, but no one in his position could have prevented Bragg's raid into Kentucky. He was primarily dismissed because he had been disobedient to Halleck. This supreme war lord had ordered Buell immediately after the Battle of Perryville to begin another campaign against Chattanooga. With the means avail-able that would have been impossible for even an ingenious commander, Buell vanished without a sound. But he was the true victor of Shiloh.

* * *

Battle of Stones River (or Murfreesboro). Bragg reorganized his army in late fall, and in December 1862 he advanced to the north a second time. Rosecrans advanced from Nashville toward him, and on the Stones River, near the little town of Murfreesboro, there was a battle on 31 December [1862] and 2 January 1863, one of the bloodiest of the entire war. Bragg's army numbered 46,604 men, while Rosecrans used only 43,400 of his larger army. His losses were 1553 dead, 7245 wounded, and 2800 captured as well as 28 cannons. Bragg lost 10,306 men and 3 guns.

Rosecrans' right wing consisted of McCook's corps, which had already suffered so much at Perryville. According to Rosecrans' plan, McCook was to start a feint early on the morning of 31 December and carry on a restrained skirmish to occupy a part of the Confederate army. At the same time Rosecrans wanted to have his significantly strengthened left wing advance in a real attack in order to decide the issue.

Bragg was pursuing precisely the same plan in reverse. He wanted his right wing to advance cautiously and strike the right enemy flank, McCook's corps, which was extended far to the east. Bragg began an hour earlier than Rosecrans, and his attack on McCook followed before attack movement of Rosecrans' left wing could get under way.

McCook was a very self-willed gentleman. Already at Perryville he had concerned himself little about his chief (then Buell). Rosecrans pointed out to him that the corps had stretched much too far to the right, so that there were gaps between the three divisions. But Rosecrans did not directly order another position, and McCook did not respond to mere wishes. This man was certainly a capable attacker, but he was not the man for the difficult task of an aggressive advance that also had to be restrained.

Johnson, the leader of McCook's wing division, had his headquarters 1.25 miles behind the front. With him was the entire cavalry, which was supposed to be securing the flanks. At the extreme end of the position was posted Willich's brigade, which constituted the wing extended farthest to the right.

Willich was not with his troops when the Confederates hit with dreadful superiority. He had ridden to division headquarters, where he reported to Johnson, "The right wing is waving in the air." When Willich rode away, however, the enemy was not yet in sight. Willich should have sent his adjutant instead of going to headquarters himself, but he must have thought that if he went himself the necessary reinforcements would come sooner. It is untrue, however, that his brigade was not completely in place when the trouble started. [17]

In a few minutes about 450 of Willich's 1600 men lay dead or wounded on the field, and about 500 men had been taken prisoner. Kirk's brigade, standing next to Willich's, lost 473 dead and wounded and 342 captured. Two divisions, Johnson's and Davis's (of McCook's corps) were dispersed in the first shock, and only a few remnants of Davis's division were received in Sheridan's Third Division under McCook. Now the victorious Confederates charged on this division of 4154 men. Sheridan's fearsome artillery and gunfire threw back the gray ranks after the enemy had come within pistol range. But then Sheridan was also attacked to his rear by the enemy, which had already dispersed Johnson's division and now charged to encircle Sheridan in a wide bow.

Sheridan, who was only in contact with Thomas's Negley division, could not maintain his position. He moved to a hill located farther back, cutting through the ranks of his attackers on the march. There Sheridan threw back a second attack, but he had to abandon this position, too, cutting once more through the enemy and taking a third position farther forward. During these difficult fights and marches, Sheridan's division always remained solidly closed, and the guns were hauled along, partly by their crews' bare hands. One battery, whose horses had been shot, remained in the field. Sheridan had to change his position once more, but he kept the main enemy force continually occupied by this, winning Rosecrans time to alter the battle plan completely and move back the forces massed on the left in order to support the remnants of McCook's corps.

Of the 4154 of Sheridan's division, 1633 were killed or wounded and only a few hundred captured. Sheridan's losses consisted of more than 40 percent. Four of his brigadiers were killed: Sill, Roberts, Harrington, and Schäfer. The German Colonel Greusel took Sill's place, and in Schäfer's place the German Colonel Laiboldt became brigade leader.[18] Harrington took the place of the fallen Roberts, but he soon afterward fell himself. The leading officers fell so quickly that it was difficult keeping up with the succession. Fredericksburg is always spoken of as a particularly murderous battle, but for Sheridan's division it was even worse at Stones River, particularly in the German regiments.

After Schäfer's and Greusel's Brigades had used up their ammunition, they met the attacks of the enemy with bayonets. When Sheridan ordered the last retreat, he gave Schäfer and Greusel the order to cover his rear; that is, to ward off further attacks of the enemy with fixed bayonets and empty cartridge bags. These German leaders carried out their mission well, but Schäfer, the brave Forty-Eighter, sacrificed his life. On the left wing the German 9th Ohio fought with grim bravery alongside the half-German 2nd Minnesota Regiment. The German Missouri regiments that were not with Sheridan also fought bravely.

The fighting continued until dark. Rosecrans took a new position during the night and restricted himself to the defensive. On 1 January only skirmishes took place. On 2 January Bragg resumed mass attacks on Rosecrans' solid position, but they were thrown back, and he left the field the following night. Hence, after an initial defeat came a Union victory. Yet Rosecrans' army was so deeply shaken that there could be no thought of pursuit.

In Virginia, 1862

The Fate of the German Division

Before the Quaker cannons—The terror march through the Virginia mountains—Three months on the march—The division loses 4000 men through hunger and illness and to the enemy—Jackson's little war in the Shenandoah Valley—The Battle of Cross Keys.

When McClellan began his Peninsular Campaign in March 1862, he sent two of his corps, under Sumner and Burnside, against the enemy, who was dug in on the Bull Run battlefield. The troops believed that they were supposed to charge the works, but all that was planned was a strategic measure to mask the movements of McClellan's main army. The German Division under Sumner was in the front, and it first came in view of the fearsome trenches near Manassas. Stalking ever nearer, they found the nest empty. The enemy had withdrawn. And the "enormous cannons" of which spies had told such terrible tales were shown to be old smokestacks of locomotives, or tree trunks that had been placed on carts and their ends painted so that they made the impression of giant cannons when viewed from afar. This trick was often used at the start of the war and often had a considerable impact. The soldiers called these things Quaker cannons.

The German Division left its camp at Hunters Chapel on 10 March with very light baggage, planning only to threaten the opposition. Most of the ambulances were left behind in camp, as well as most of the military pharmacy and the entire supply train. They were short of tents and blankets, provisions, and all of the thousand things a belligerent advancing army needs. Thus the division had to bivouac under the most unfavorable circumstances. It rained in streams, and the men did not yet have rubber coats or replacements for worn-out shoes. Despite this more than inadequate supply, the division received an order to march on to Warrenton, about thirty miles. The roads had been transformed into rivers of mud, the many small rivers and brooks of the woods in the area had to be crossed. These waterways had their origins in the high mountains, where snow had begun to melt. Often the men went through ice-cold water up to the breast. The climate of the area is extraordinarily unstable at this time of year. An evening frost can follow a warm day, rain is followed by snow, and a road frozen hard overnight becomes pudding after a few hours of marching. So the division suffered quite extraordinarily on the short march from Manassas to Warrenton. Many became ill, and there were only 6 ambulances for 10,000 men.

In Warrenton, an important crossroads at the foot of the Bull Run Mountains, the division received the order to join with General Frémont, who stood in the southern Potomac valley in northeastern West Virginia. Romney was set as the rendezvous.

In order to reach Romney, the German Division first had to cross the Bull Run Mountains, then scale the high peaks of the Blue Ridge Mountains to reach the valley of the Shenandoah, and then conquer more wild mountains lying between the Shenandoah and the southern Potomac, the hostile North Mountains. Hence three mountain ranges were to be taken, across which only narrow paths usually led. As the bird flies it is a distance of 110 miles. In the zigzag route of the mountain roads, which make a wide swing to the north, it was certainly 200 miles. No one knew the way, no guides could be found, and most of the residents of the area were the bitterest enemies of the Union.

The expected better supplies for the troops never arrived, being sent too late or to the wrong place. Without tents and with very few provisions, many poor soldiers lacking even blankets, Blenker, in keeping with the orders, had to plunge into the wild mountains. His troops were not even carrying good weapons, being still supplied with outmoded Belgian and Austrian guns, heavy, undependable muskets that only worked for very short distances. Only under Frémont, on about 10 May, did the soldiers receive the new, good Enfield muskets. In addition, throughout the entire journey they had to fight off the attacks of bushwhackers, or mounted guerrillas. Whoever became tired and fell behind was lost, whether as a victim of hunger and cold, or of falling into the hands of the bushwhackers who followed the army.

On 4 April, Blenker advanced from Warrenton across the Bull Run Mountains toward Salem. All the horses of the small supply train they had with them had to serve as

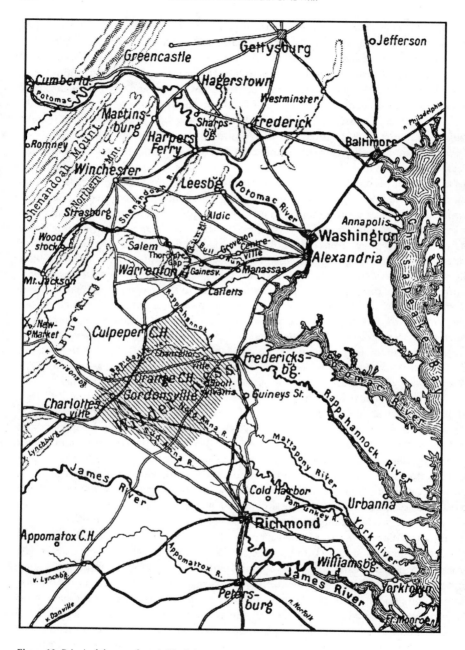

Figure 13. Principal theater of war in Virginia.

dray animals to haul their cannons. It was several days before the last stragglers arrived in Salem, and the march could only be resumed on 10 April. The condition of the division grew worse with every passing day. The provisions brought along were consumed, and it was necessary to forage for the absolutely necessary food. The few farmers available in the thinly settled area were plundered with reckless harshness. After the most dreadful hardship the army attained Paris, a pitiful hamlet still east of the second mountain chain, the Blue Ridge. Here were found some food and unfortunately also a great amount of whisky in a distillery. The men enjoyed the just-distilled alcohol in the most unwise manner. Who could blame the poor devils for wanting to warm themselves? Thus the starved, harassed soldiers suffered the result of excessive alcohol consumption. But the great army supplies they had hoped to find in Paris were not there, although General Rosecrans had ordered them there. The Potomac bridge at Harpers Ferry had been washed away as a result of floods, and the delivery of provisions, coats, blankets and tents was delayed by fourteen days. It was as if everything were conspiring against the division.

Only on 18 April the crossing of the Shenandoah was managed, with great difficulties.[19] It was the end of April before the division could be gathered in Berryville and Winchester. General Rosecrans had been sent by the War Department to seek the Germans, who were thought to be lost. There he held a review on 30 April of the ragged, haggard regiments, and he praised the men to the skies. Rosecrans reported to Washington that the division was without clothing, tents, shoes, ambulances, provisions, or fodder for the horses; was as good as out of ammunition; and had suffered severe losses on the march. More than 2000 men had gone missing during the three weeks; most of them were ill, but many had starved or frozen to death. Rosecrans could not supply the soldiers as would have been desirable, but he gave them rubber coats and tents. The paymaster also arrived, bringing two months' pay. (They were four months behind.)

The division now rested for two weeks at Winchester in the Shenandoah Valley. The troops had covered about half the distance to Romney. Blenker went to Washington to deal with the accusations raised against him. General Stahel led in Blenker's place in the meantime.

* * *

The Allegheny and Appalachian mountains stretch in a long extended chain from northeast to southwest and averaging 3000 feet in height. Between these mountain chains are located broad river valleys, watered by the Shenandoah and the South Branch of the Potomac. Frémont's corps, about 6000 men, whom the German Division was supposed to join, was located in the western river valley, that of the South Potomac. Between it and the Shenandoah Valley lay a raw, wild mountain chain, the North Mountains. This chain was about fifty English miles wide between Winchester and Romney. Frémont's mission consisted of blocking the way of the Confederate General Jackson in case Jackson and his many raiders should move west of the Shenandoah Valley.

About this time, at the start of May 1862, the fighting began between the two opposed armies on the peninsula of Virginia. But Lee had sent his best commander, Stonewall Jackson, with 15,000 men to disturb the 60,000 Union troops who remained in northern Virginia in order to defend Washington. It was from this situation that an extremely interesting campaign developed, with its field of operation chiefly in the Shenandoah Valley. It could best be described as a hunt for Jackson.

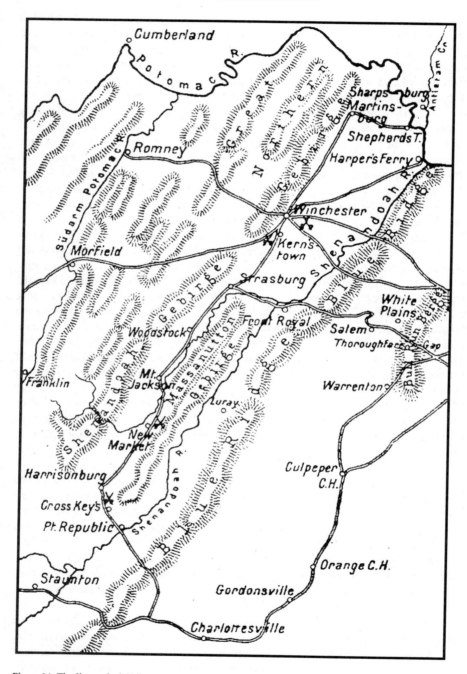

Figure 14. The Shenandoah Valley.

Those 60,000 Union troops were divided into four unequal units under McDowell, Shields, Banks, and Frémont. It was attempted to drive Jackson in such a way that he would be caught between two of these Northern units and would have to surrender. This campaign was managed by Jackson with admirable cleverness and carried out in a splendid manner. Jackson beat his many enemies one after another,[20] collected a huge amount of booty, and rejoined his comrade Lee after all these campaigns and battles to intervene in the great battles on the peninsula and bring them to a decision. Jackson's troops were largely recruited from the Shenandoah Valley, and they intimately knew all the mountain paths. They developed astonishing speed (they were called the Foot Cavalry, or the Virginia Mountain Wolves) and always appeared where the enemy least expected them. The leadership of the four Union corps, on the other hand, was seldom unified. Each of the four generals was more or less on his own, and it is hard to say which was the biggest bungler.

The "terrible" Jackson could very seldom appear with all of his 15,000 men. He had to secure himself and often had only a third of his men ready for action. On 10 May he reached into Colonel Kenly's pocket at Front Royal, taking 700 prisoners and massive war supplies. He next fell on General Banks at Winchester, beat him, and chased him all the way north to the main Potomac River. Then he encountered Shields and withdrew to the south, after a brief fight, in the face of Shields' strong artillery. But Shields followed so slowly that Jackson had nothing to do for a while. During this pause he made a quick "stroll" to the west across the mountains (about thirty-five miles) to obliterate Frémont in the South Potomac valley. He had almost succeeded in doing so when the German Division finally appeared. Jackson had no desire to meet this superior force. So his Mountain Wolves ran back east across the mountains, and he collected the booty he had taken. But we must break off the account of Jackson's deeds here in order to turn our attention back to the German Division.

* * *

The division departed Winchester on 5 May to enter the wilderness of the North Mountains and, after further problems and stresses, finally arrived in Romney. There they were received by Frémont, whose troops stood far to the south in the Potomac valley and were soon to fight with Jackson. The Germans proceeded south in a forced march to aid their comrades. On 16 May they were in Franklin, where they joined Milroy's and Schenk's brigades, which had been pursued by Jackson. Jackson now departed, but another enemy appeared, namely hunger. The supply train had taken the route along the opposite bank of the Potomac. The river was in flood and could not be crossed. The starving soldiers could see the provision wagons standing on the opposite shore, but they could not get to them. There was hunger among the troops 11–21 May.[21] Only then did the river fall, so that they could cross and eat once more.

Jackson was gone, so Frémont's army had to return to the Shenandoah Valley to help hunt precious prey there. Hence once more through those difficult mountains. Thus the German Division was continually on the march from 10 May to 3 June, save for a rest at Winchester. They came 500 miles through wild mountains with poor equipment, often through snow and ice and hot sun, starving and freezing, without having struck a blow. The 10,000 men had dwindled to 6000 when they finally arrived in Strasburg in the

Shenandoah Valley, at the start of June. About this time Jackson moved up the valley with his booty, but had several days' head start. If they were quick, they could still catch him. So after Jackson!

The Germans had good days during this march. At Strasburg they were in old German America,[22] the garden of Virginia, created by the hard work of German peasants. There was Woodstock, where the pastor and general Peter Mühlenberg held his famous last sermon in 1776.[23] There was the former Neumarkt (now New Market), and many another stately German settlement. The land was rich, and the fattest ham, the finest fowl, and the finest milk came by the bucket to the tables of the starved soldiers, although they were also robbed. The Sicilian robber band of the Garibaldi Regiment, the 39th New York, was along with the Germans, and the excesses of these fellows was blamed on the Germans. These robberies cannot be defended. Yet why are the worse deeds of Sherman's bummers in Georgia, and Sheridan's troops in the Shenandoah Valley in 1864 judged so differently?

* * *

Once again a trap had been set for Jackson, who was moving up the valley more slowly than usual because of his many wagons of booty. There was a bridge across the Shenandoah at Port Republic. Jackson had to cross this bridge in order to get to Richmond. The bridge was to be burned, after which it was thought possible to catch Jackson between the two Union corps of Shields and Frémont and capture him. The Shenandoah River consists in its lower course of the North and South Forks. Between the two arms lie the Massanutten Mountains. Shields had the task of proceeding upstream along the South Fork of the Shenandoah, and Frémont proceeded along the North Fork behind Jackson. Shields was to cross the bridge at Port Republic quickly, burn it, and confront Jackson, driving the enemy toward Frémont.

But this trap did not work. Shields was too slow. His vanguard did reach the bridge before Jackson, but it did not destroy the bridge. It occupied the eastern exit of the bridge with two batteries. Jackson saw in time what his opponents intended. He did not want to fight, but rather to bring his booty to safety and take his troop to Lee without any losses, if possible. But Frémont was hot on his back, so that Jackson had to wage several rear-guard actions against Frémont. In these the German artillery Colonel Pilsen particularly distinguished himself, and the important secessionist cavalry leader Ashby fell (brought off his horse by a former Brunswick lieutenant of hussars, Heusinger reports).

Jackson remained concerned about that bridge. He advanced with his booty in double-time and had his subordinate General Ewell stand with 7000 Mountain Wolves at Cross Keys, still a few miles from the bridge, to hold Frémont in check. From this situation developed the Battle of Cross Keys on 8 June, in which the German Division finally received its baptism of fire. The battlefield was old German cultural soil. The battle took place between two German churches, Wetzel's Lutheran Church and the House of Prayer of the United German Brethren. The latter was also called the Friedenskirche ["Peace Church"], or the Union Church. The churches later served as field hospitals.

Frémont believed all of Jackson's army was before him. He divided his 12,000 men into three unequal groups. The right wing was formed by the five weak regiments of Schenck's Ohio brigade. The center was Milroy's West Virginia division (three regiments and the 82nd Ohio, as well as Cluseret's division of perhaps 1000 men).[24] The left wing was the German Division, still about 6000 men. Blenker had returned, but he was completely ignored by Frémont due to the accusations against him. In the vanguard of the Germans stood Stahel's brigade: the 8th, 41st, and 45th New York and the 27th Pennsylvania; then the Bohlen Brigade. The reserve was von Steinwehr's brigade: the 29th and 68th New York, the 27th Pennsylvania, and the 13th New York Battery. This reserve was commanded by Colonel Koltes in the place of von Steinwehr, who was ill. On Frémont's flanks were posted the two half-German cavalry regiments, under Kargel and Dickel. Eight batteries fought in the line, and two stood in reserve. Frémont's chief of general staff was the German Colonel Albert, who had already distinguished himself in the Battle of Pea Ridge.

The fighting was started by Cluseret and the half-German Garibaldi Regiment at about 11 A.M. Milroy also participated in the first attack, but he was thrown back with heavy losses. The Garibaldi Guard did excellently and made gains. The enemy held the defensive at first. Ewell wanted only to fight a delaying action and spare his men as much as possible.

The German Division had the most difficult problem to solve. The main enemy force stood well protected on a spur of the mountain, controlling the road. In front of that position there spread a rising open landscape of meadow and fields, crossed by fences and a brook. An attacker had to cross this open country without protection in order to approach the enemy, who was protected by woods. Stahel's brigade was to take this position. General Stahel sent as skirmishers his 45th under Amsberg forward. He wanted to shake his enemy with artillery fire first, before going on the attack. Before the artillery was completely in position, however, Colonel Wutschel advanced too soon with the 8th New York Regiment, overrunning the protective chain of the 45th. The soldiers of the 8th charged in closed ranks with fixed bayonets, against wooded heights controlled by superior enemy forces. The 8th came within 150 paces of the enemy, where they were met with dreadful close-range fire from four batteries, as well as a hail of rifle fire. In a few seconds almost half of the brave German regiment (220 dead and wounded of 660) lay on the ground. The remnant had to retreat, and they naturally took the 45th with them. The enemy broke out of the woods, and strong masses of infantry pursued the shattered units. The 8th lost its flag, and only with difficulty did General Stahel succeed in saving his decimated half-brigade. The two other regiments of the brigade, the 41st New York and 27th Pennsylvania, advanced to Wutschel's right and achieved something, but they had to withdraw after their comrades' failure.

At this point the Union artillery was in position and could sweep the open fields across which Wutschel's unfortunate advance had gone and on which the enemy infantry was spreading. Dilger's and Buell's batteries, under Schirmer, paid off the enemy with the same coin the 8th had received earlier. At this instant Blenker appeared on the battlefield and took part in Bohlen's attack. This attack was as unsuccessful as well, however, proceeding as it did without the help of artillery (a fact later much lamented by General Bohlen). The fact is that Major Schirmer, as commander of the division artillery, sent back Wiedrich's battery, although it belonged to Bohlen's brigade. Whether Schirmer lost his head or the command for Wiedrich's battery to retreat was an error, is unknown. Incidentally, the entire Schirmer artillery came within a hair of being lost. The enemy had already surrounded it when Colonels von Gilsa and Buschbeck saw the peril and rushed up with the 41st New York and the 27th Pennsylvania to cut Schirmer loose. That was certainly the finest single deed performed by the German Division. Colonel von Gilsa was seriously wounded as a result.

In the German-American newspapers of the time the news was spread that Blenker had been the true hero of Cross Keys. In the instant of greatest need he had brought up his reserves (three regiments under Koltes), which action achieved advantages and was on the way to turning the previous defeat of the left wing into a victory when he was called back by Frémont. To be sure, Blenker did call the reserve brigade forward, but this entire brigade had only one wounded (and eight missing) in the entire battle. It can be seen what that brigade accomplished by the fact that there was only one wounded. The rebels reported three attacks on the left wing: one by Stahel, one by Bohlen, and a third attack. This last was interrupted by the carrying out of Frémont's command for a general retreat of the left wing.

Frémont commanded the retreat because he received a letter from Shields during the battle telling him that only Shields' vanguard had reached Port Republic, but that his main corps had had to make camp due to exhaustion and hunger. So Shields' participation in the battle, which Frémont had only initiated in expectation of his comrade's presence, was not to be. Frémont still believed he had Jackson's entire army before him. After the mishaps, it in fact appeared foolish for Frémont's shaken army to continue to attack a far stronger enemy.

Frémont asserted that his center and right wing had kept their positions, but that is not correct, for Schenck's brigade had to withdraw after Milroy's failed first attack. The fighting diminished in the course of the afternoon. During the night the enemy withdrew to Port Republic, and because Frémont held the battlefield, he could claim victory and receive a telegram of praise from Lincoln.

Colonel Wutschel, who had ordered the premature charge despite the vigorous advice of his officers experienced in war, was dismissed. Incidentally, Wutschel also conducted himself as a coward. He dismounted his horse and ran along in the last ranks. When the dreadful firing came, he fell down on the ground and acted wounded. The other German officers conducted themselves blamelessly. Hubert Dilger stood out, and his battery fired splendidly. General Bohlen also fought like a hero. Frémont officially praised von Gilsa, Buschbeck, and von Amsberg. On the whole, the baptism of fire of the German Division was dissatisfying, essentially due to Wutschel's fault. The losses of the German Division were 482 men, of which Stahel lost 389, Bohlen 73, and Koltes 9 (one wounded and eight missing). Frémont lost on the whole 684 men, of which Milroy lost 159, Schenck 15. and Cluseret 19.

The next morning Frémont followed the retreating enemy. Shortly a thick cloud of smoke was seen ahead. The bridge at Port Republic was finally being burned, but by the enemy after his last man and booty wagon had crossed the river. Jackson, incidentally, also had a sharp skirmish with Shields' vanguard, in which the 5th and 7th Ohio regiments (the latter partly consisting of Cleveland Germans) distinguished themselves.

Jackson had thus achieved his goal once more. Several divisions of Confederates were supplied with the booty he bore away. The Southerners at that time were living largely on stolen provisions, walking in Uncle Sam's shoes, sleeping under U. S. woolen blankets, and often enough dressing in stolen blue uniforms. And a few weeks later Jackson's troops, arriving just in time, decided the great bloody battles between McClellan and Lee at Richmond.

A day after the Battle of Cross Keys, on 9 June, Karl Schurz made his military debut. Schurz arrived with his commission as a general. Frémont immediately made him a division commander. The "general-recruit" Schurz was at first greeted quite coldly by his German comrades, but soon this mood changed, particularly after Schurz proved himself so well at Second Bull Run.

Blenker was called to Washington and laid down his command. Frémont also went, due to his injured pride. He could not stand it that Pope, a younger general, was given the big command in Virginia. The Germans were glad, however, that Frémont went and was replaced on 1 July by Franz Sigel.

McClellan's Peninsular Campaign

The great battles of the Peninsular Campaign must be briefly summarized here, in view of our theme. No large German corps of troops fought in the Peninsular battles, and none of the German leaders achieved any importance there.[25] Our compatriots who fought there were mostly scattered through Anglo-American units, and for that reason these important struggles of the unfortunate year of 1862 interest us only insofar as they are connected with other matters.

The Virginia campaign of 1862 falls into three distinct actions, so intertwined that they can hardly be divided from one another. These actions were: 1. the great campaign on what is called the Virginia Peninsula; 2. Jackson's parallel defensive struggle in the Shenandoah Valley against a Northern auxiliary army under McDowell, who was to protect Washington and support McClellan's advance against Richmond by the land route, and 3. Pope's campaign in central Virginia after the recall of the Union army from the Peninsula, when the newly reorganized army was given to Pope. We turn first of all to the main theater of war on the Peninsula.

On the southern tip of the Peninsula lies Fort Monroe, which was still held by the Union and thus provided a secure landing place for a Northern army transported by ship. It is about seventy-five miles from Fort Monroe to Richmond. In contrast, the distance from Washington to Richmond is twice as great. Hence McClellan was saving half the marching distance against Richmond if his great army could advance from Fort Monroe instead of by the land route from Washington. Further, the two great rivers that embrace the Peninsula, the York and the James, are navigable by large ships far up their courses.[26] Deliveries of reinforcements, provisions and ammunition could be made the comfortable way, by sea, unharassed by the enemy. Gunboats could also be used on both rivers. So McClellan's plan to move the focus of operations to the Peninsula had many advantages.

At first it was overlooked that there could also be disadvantages to this plan, disadvantages which almost completely cancelled out advantages. Only one disadvantage was seen at once: the difficulty of defending Washington adequately when the main army of the North stood on the Peninsula. The consideration of this disadvantage consumed weeks, and this proved to be one of the essential factors of the failure. Such an operation must be carried out as a surprise to the enemy, and it must take place before the heat of the summer. Rapid action was the basic condition of success. But the shipping of troops only began on 17 March. When McClellan arrived at Fort Monroe on 2 April, he found gathered only about 60,000 men with 100 cannons. By 6 April, 100,000 men were loaded. Such a transportation of troops had never before been attempted in America. Even for nations far better prepared, it is no easy matter, as the deployment of the French and English armies to the Crimea showed.

Simultaneous with the advance of the great Union army from Fort Monroe, a force of 60,000 men under McDowell was to advance on Richmond by the land route to assist the Peninsular army before the enemy capital. McClellan had only undertaken his Peninsular Campaign with the presumption of this cooperation. But due to the clever attacks of the enemy General Jackson, as well as the concerns of Washington officials that the capital could not do without protection, McDowell's advance never took place. McClellan remained on his own, and the most important assumptions of his plan failed completely. For this reason it seems unjust to ascribe the failure of the campaign to McClellan alone.

On the other hand, it can be asserted that a Sherman or a Thomas would have exploited the opportunities still offered to McClellan in April quite differently. McClellan was not a man of rapid decision or bold daring. He was an excessively cautious delayer who continually overestimated his opponent and distrusted the strength of his own army. He had been an engineering officer, belonging to the branch that was dedicated essentially to the defensive. He had also participated as an observer in the French general staff in the Crimean War, which was essentially a war of fortresses and a battle over positions. He was almost the only Union officer who had learned anything about war in the grand style, but impressions from the Crimea were most inadequate for carrying out his mission on the Virginian Peninsula.

McClellan also depended heavily on cooperation from the fleet. But it failed him in the first important weeks. The Confederate ram *Merrimac* entered the James River, ran two U. S. Navy ships aground, and caused almost as much terror at sea as the clever Jackson did on land, if only briefly. It was only after the *Monitor* of the ingenious Swede Ericsson appeared on the scene that the enemy ram was checked and, somewhat later, blown up by the enemy. It was May before the U. S. Navy was able to participate in operations to any degree, and then it did not have nearly the effect McClellan had hoped.

In addition, the Peninsula was as good as an unknown country in the North. There was no idea of its extended swamp areas, the extraordinarily rapid rise of the Chickahominy after a rain, or the monstrous heat that set in as early as May. Swamp fever appeared at once among the troops, an illness that would kill far more brave men than would fall in the rain of bullets of the great battles. The Southerners were much more accustomed to such a climate, were more resistant to fever, and possessed the advantage of a good knowledge of the terrain. They gave way slowly before the enemy, being careful to entice him into the great swampy regions on the upper course of the Chickahominy.

McClellan lingered for an extraordinarily long time before Yorktown, only to find that this fortified city had been abandoned by the enemy.[27] During 5–7 May the bloody struggles for Williamsburg took place, ending with the withdrawal of the Southerners. During the first period the rebels fought only rear-guard actions, and it was the middle of

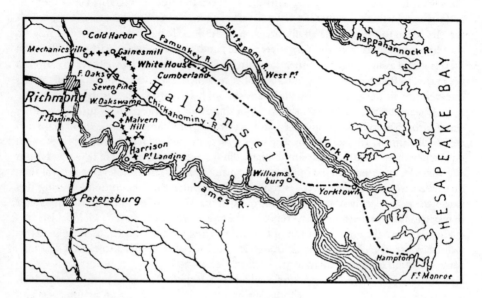

Figure 15. The Peninsula of Virginia.

May when the Union army reached the position of White House and Cumberland Landing on the Pamunkey River, about eighteen miles from Richmond. Losses had been so significant to that point that McClellan, according to his own assertions at the time, was
leading only 80,000 men capable of fighting, although his army had numbered 130,378
men on 30 April, of which 112,392 were regarded as capable of fighting. After considerable
reinforcement, McClellan once more had at his disposal more than 126,000 men with
280 cannons.

One portion of the Northern army, Keyes' corps, stood at the end of May on the
south bank of the Chickahominy near Fair Oaks. The bulk was camped along the northern
bank. When a dreadful storm hit on 30 May, sweeping away many of the bridges across the
river, the Confederate General Joseph E. Johnston (not to be confused with the Confederate General A. Sidney Johnston, fallen at Shiloh) thought he would be able to cut off the
enemy force on the southern bank. There followed the bloody Battle of Seven Pines (or
Fair Oaks) on 31 May. Johnston did not achieve his intended goal because the Union General Sumner traversed the damaged bridge across the Chickahominy and came to aid the
threatened Keyes. Johnston returned to Richmond with a loss of 4000 men. The Northern
army had lost 6000 men. In this battle, Johnston was so badly wounded that he had to

resign his command. General Robert E. Lee became his successor and remained the chief commander of the Southern army until the end of the war.

The Battle of Seven Pines had demonstrated the dangerous nature of McClellan's position along both banks of the troublesome Chickahominy. Because McClellan relied on the York River for his supplies, the necessity grew to keep the area between the Chickahominy and the York strongly occupied in order to secure connections. But this made it impossible for McClellan to concentrate all his forces on one point. He had prepared a plan earlier to shift his supply lines from the York River to the James River, on which Richmond lies. But this took him away from any connection with McDowell, were McDowell ever to carry out his march to Richmond by the land route. Because McClellan still hoped for McDowell's intervention, he temporarily suspended any shift of his base to the James River.

The greater part of June passed with nothing done, in large part because the weather was improper. It rained continuously, and the Union army camped in the flood plain created by the unruly Chickahominy. For weeks the poor soldiers had hardly a dry garment on their bodies. They lived like amphibians. Thousands of victims were taken by typhus and malaria, and more than a quarter of the army was sick. Even a cleverer general than McClellan would have avoided a strong offensive under these conditions. During this pause, the enemy army stood on better ground around Richmond and thus did not suffer so much as the Northern forces. At this time the bold Confederate cavalry General Jeb Stuart rode around the entire position of the Union army with 2000 men, making an extraordinarily useful reconnaissance. Through his bold bit of riding he also caused dramatic demoralization of the Northern army, stuck in the swamps.

At the end of June, General Stonewall Jackson, hitherto occupied in the Shenandoah Valley, approached Richmond with a significantly reinforced body of 30,000 men and joined with Lee, who had 25,000 men.

Now, under the pressure of Jackson's proximity, McClellan decided on the change of positions that he had considered and prepared before: moving his base from the York to the James River. In the North this march made a very negative impression, but his supply from the James was much better than from the York. There were more healthful landing areas, and a position on the James, twenty miles south of Richmond, offered him the advantage of being unable to cross the James and threaten Richmond from the rear in case it should seem desirable. Such a backward swing in the presence of an enemy as McClellan was trying to perform is an extemely dangerous operation, and McClellan deserves credit for having performed his task without very large losses.

As a result of this change in position by McClellan's army, there occurred the Seven Day Battle for Richmond. This fighting began at Mechanicsburg on 26 June, was continued at Gaines's Mill on the 27th, and led to fighting over the following days in the White Oak Swamp near Frayser Farm and Glendale. Even though the victory went to the South in these battles and skirmishes, which were enormously bloody, the stubborn resistance that the Porter's Northern corps showed at Gaines's Mill was very honorable. The Union troops fought with great bravura in these continual battles and won the respect of their opponents. McClellan was able to save his supply train of thousands of wagons, bringing his reserve artillery of 100 cannons and his heavy siege guns through the swamps to establish a good position on the broad plateau of Malvern Hill, directly by the James River.

The battle on 1 July was the last of the seven days of conflict around Richmond. Lee had the strong Union position stormed, but the well-served Union artillery threw back the attack, and the enemy had to return to Richmond with heavy losses. So the last day of battle on the Peninsula was a fine one and a complete success for the Union cause.

On 3 July McClellan took an even better position at Harrison's Point, near Malvern Hill. Lincoln visited him there to establish how justified McClellan's ceaseless demands for reinforcements were. Lincoln found 88,665 men capable of service out of the 158,314 men who had been sent to the Peninsula. A total of 70,000 men were missing! But this does not give all the losses. McClellan had furloughed 32,250 men, including a good 25,000 healthy men. "If we had those furloughed men here, we could at once advance on Richmond," Lincoln said in criticizing his general. Despite this, Lincoln at once sent the units of Burnside and Hunter, stationed in North and South Carolina, to the Peninsula. But McClellan demanded another 50,000 in reinforcements in order to move again against Richmond.

Pope's Campaign in Virginia

Battle on Cedar Mountain—Sigel's supposed slowness—Lee moves between Pope's army and Washington—Severe defeat of the Union at Second Bull Run—Sigel's excellent leadership in this battle—Karl Schurz's baptism of fire.

Just as the situation of Union military leadership on the Peninsula began to improve through McClellan's victory at Malvern Hill, Halleck was called to Washington to take over the supreme leadership of all the armies of the North. McClellan's previous subordinate suddenly became his superior. This was naturally not to the taste of the ambitious Mr. McClellan. He permitted himself the right to criticize this remarkable shift, expressing his astonishment that it was Halleck, the very commander of the completely bungled campaign against Corinth, who had been placed in the highest military office. With that McClellan was finished forever, so far as Halleck was concerned. Because both Lincoln and many influential newspapers were dissatisfied with McClellan, Halleck could also realize his plans to set his opponent aside. These matters, then, are the chief reason for the subsequent suspension of the Peninsular Campaign.

Halleck placed his own protégé, General John Pope, at the head of the troops involved in the earlier failed campaign against Jackson. With McDowell, Shields, Banks, and Sigel, this corps still numbered 49,500 men at the end of July. It was to constitute the core of a new advance against Richmond, by the land route. Assembled on the middle course of the Rappahannock, at Culpeper, it was eventually to be reinforced by the available troops of the Army of the Potomac from the Peninsula. That meant McClellan's replacement by Pope, for the departure of the Army of the Potomac from the Peninsula was ordered at the same time as Pope's appointment.

McClellan remained an important personality. He was very much loved by his troops, and his subordinates remained loyal to him. Pope also relied on McClellan's good will, for it depended on McClellan whether the Army of the Potomac went to Pope's force in droplets or was sent to central Virginia in large units. McClellan held Pope to be a bungler, and not unjustly; but he also saw Pope a partner. But Pope's new dignity went so to the commander's head that, in a florid proclamation he was misled into negative criticism of McClellan's hesitant style of war leadership. Thus the new campaign began with an improper opposition of two Union generals who were supposed to support each other as comrades. The McClellan clique opposed the Pope clique. Incidentally, McClellan did send his troops as rapidly as the circumstances permitted, and his hostility to Pope only was expressed in relatively unimportant things. Pope was and remained throughout the entire summer campaign in Virginia a puppet in Halleck's hand.

* * *

On 1 July, Sigel took over Frémont's previous corps, which from then on was known as the I Corps. On 5 July Sigel wrote to Pope:

> Blenker's division [the German Division—WK] no longer exists. I have placed one of the brigades (Stahel's) in Schenck's division, Bohlen's brigade in Schurz's division, the third of Blenker's former brigades goes into the reserves under Steinwehr. The interests of the service requires this new distribution, for serious differences exist among the brigadier generals, which places their cooperation in question.

This letter, dated so soon after Sigel's taking command, makes the impression of precipitous and unconsidered action, particularly when one considers that Sigel had just arrived and knew his subordinates only superficially. (More on this in the biography of Sigel).

The I Corps (Sigel) was 11,500 men strong and was composed in this manner:

First Division, General Schenck. First Brigade, General Stahel: 27th Pennsylvania, Buschbeck; 8th New York, Hedterich (later Salm-Salm); 41st New York, von Holmstedt (Colonel von Gilsa in Sigel's staff); 45th New York, Wratislaw. Second Brigade, McLean: the 25th, 55th, 73rd, and 75th Ohio; batteries: Wiedrich, New York, and Ohio batteries of Hampton, De Beck, Johnson, and Buell.

Second Division, General von Steinwehr. Consisted during Pope's campaign of the Koltes Brigade alone: 29th New York, Soest; 68th New York, Kleefisch; 73rd Pennsylvania, Mühleck.

Third Division, Schurz. First Brigade, von Schimmelpfennig: 61st Ohio (McGroarty); 74th Pennsylvania, Blessing; 8th West Virginia. Second Brigade, Krzyzanowski: 54th New York, Kowacz; 58th New York, Henkel; 75th Pennsylvania, Mahler. Artillery: Dilger, Heckmann, Dieckmann, Roemer.

Milroy's brigade: 2nd, 3rd, and 5th West Virginia as well as the 82nd Ohio Regiment; Ohio Battery 12, Captain Nöcker.

Cavalry Brigade, Beardsley: 1st Connecticut, Richart; 1st Maryland, Wetschky; 4th New York, Nazer; 9th New York, Knox; 6th Ohio, Lloyd.

* * *

Lee, always well informed, learned at an early point about the intended evacuation of the Peninsula. For that reason he sent Jackson's corps from Richmond to central Virginia to make contact with Pope. On 8 August, Pope received the message that Jackson was advancing against Cedar Mountain, eight miles south of Culpeper. There was no adequate scouting. Pope ordered Sigel and Banks to come to Culpeper at once. The former, who was at Sperryville, had over twenty miles to march, while Banks had only nine miles. Banks' 8000 men entered Culpeper during the night and were sent out alone against Jackson's 25,000 men.[28] Thus developed on 9 August the bloody Battle of Cedar Mountain, in which Banks' troops attacked well and won some success, but then Jackson's superior forces asserted themselves. Banks had to give way after losing a third of his men. Pope had Ricketts' division at hand in Culpeper, but he did not send it to help Banks. Only on the evening of 9 August did Sigel and Ricketts arrive to receive Banks' remnants, and then Jackson withdrew he had only wanted to ascertain Pope's strength. Although Pope praised Sigel in his first reports, the West Point officers soon developed the story that Sigel's later arrival had brought about the failure of Cedar Mountain. Here began the West Pointers' complaints about Sigel's supposed slowness.[29]

*   *   *

After 5 August, when the Army of the Potomac evacuated the Peninsula, Lee could do without Longstreet's corps of 33,000 men in Richmond. He united it with Jackson's, took over command of the army, now 55,000 men strong; and faced his new opponent Pope on the right bank of the Rappahannock. Pope had withdrawn across the river and stood on the left bank, between Kelley's and Freemann's Fords, awaiting the reinforcements McClellan was to send him. Reno and King, with 8000 men of the Peninsular army, joined him, so that the two armies were of equal strength.

The river lay between Lee and Pope. Lee had to strike quickly, if possible before Pope received further reinforcements. But Lee did not want to endure the losses that would come if he made a contested crossing of the Rappahannock. Hence he decided to go around his opponent, reaching his rear, cutting Pope's connection with Washington and if possible separately trapping the troops marching to reinforce Pope. For this purpose Lee moved upstream along the right bank, compelling Pope to follow him on the left bank. Lee had crafted a truly masterful plan.

Northwest of Rappahannock Station lie the Bull Run Mountains. These slide like a curtain toward the east. On the west behind them lies a valley that is excellently suited for a secret march to the northwest. One should look at Orleans, Salem, Thoroughfare Gap, and Gainesville on Figure 16. Thoroughfare Gap is the pass through the Bull Run Mountains. Whoever controlled this pass could reach Gainesville in a half-day march and thus land in the rear of Pope's army. Pope did not occupy that pass. That important sally port from the west to the east lay open to Lee!

Jackson advanced rapidly to Sulphur Springs and Waterloo on Lee's command. Lee remained standing with Longstreet's corps roughly opposite Freemann's Ford. There followed continual artillery duels across the Rappahannock, with small skirmishes. In one of them, at Beverly Ford, the German General Heinrich Bohlen fell.

Pope only learned of the separation of the two enemy corps a couple days later. He believed that Longstreet's corps, under Lee, would cross the river on 22 August at Sulphur Springs, and he gathered his forces in order to attack Longstreet after a large portion of his troops had crossed the Rappahannock. But Lee was not thinking of crossing the river,

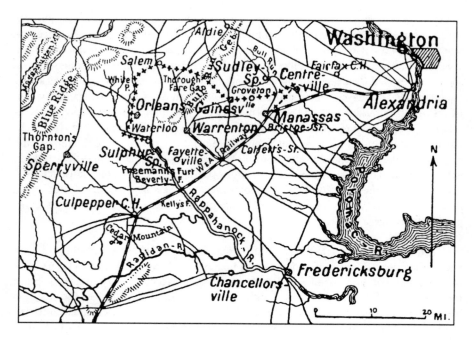

Figure 16. Pope's campaign in central Virginia in the summer of 1862.

restricting himself instead to a feint to hold off the enemy from disturbing Jackson's encircling march. As soon as Jackson had disappeared behind the screen of the Bull Run Mountains, Lee would withdraw along the same path, so that Lee's entire army would slip between Pope's force and Washington. Lee's maneuver led Pope strongly to overexert the Union troops. The troops were moved about on ceaseless, seemingly pointless marches. They lost the little confidence that they still had in their leadership, knowing as well that they opposed the best army of the Confederacy and its most feared leaders.

Pope had committed his cavalry in such a way that the horses could hardly move. His reconnaissance service, always defective, completely failed, while that of the enemy functioned splendidly. The greatest of the Confederate cavalry leaders, Stuart, had long been in Pope's rear before Pope had any idea. During a dreadful storm on the night of 23 August, Stuart fell on Pope s full supply train at Catlett's Station, netting an enormous amount of booty and also finding Pope's dispatch book with the entire correspondence of the enemy general. Stuart had virtually seized Pope's entire general staff and the commanding general himself. Stuart sent the dispatch book to Lee, who found there the disposition of all the reinforcements sent by McClellan to Pope. After destruction of the supplies, Stuart vanished again in order to cover Jackson's flanking movement behind the Bull Run screen.

On 24 August the larger part of Pope's army was directed to Warrenton. There over the next few days McClellan's Heintzelmann and Porter Corps join him, so that Pope had received about 23,000 from the old Army of the Potomac and now disposed of about 65,000 men, rather widely scattered, after subtracting those who had left.

Let us now turn to the Jackson operation. Jackson only left his position opposite Sigel at Waterloo-Sulphur Springs on 25 August, vanished behind the Bull Run Mountains in keeping with Lee's plan. Jackson's retreat was not, of course, hidden from the Union leaders, but they did not think of Thoroughfare Gap; they believed that the Confederates wanted to withdraw to the Shenandoah Valley. At noon Jackson on the 26th reached the unoccupied pass. Ahead of him was the agile Stuart, had already arrived with 500 infantry in Manassas in the evening of 26 August, and who destroyed all telegraph lines between Washington and Pope's army. Pope's second supply station was also located there. Enormous masses of provisions, horse fodder, weapons and munitions were stored. The watch was overpowered by Stuart, and the entire booty fell to the Confederates. On 27 August, Jackson's entire army arrived in Manassas, equipping themselves afresh at the expense of Uncle Sam. The rest of the booty went up in flames. During the prior thirty-six hours Jackson's "Foot Cavalry" had covered over fifty English miles!

* * *

Pope's army in those days was on the march northwards to trap Jackson. The situation on 28 August, immediately before Second Bull Run, offers a picture of boldness bordering on recklessness on the Confederate side, and on the Northern side complete confusion reigned. It was only on the evening of the 27th that Pope learned that Jackson had reached Manassas, and was hence in the Union army's rear. But Pope still did not know that Longstreet and Lee were following their comrade Jackson on the same route, through Thoroughfare Gap. He also did not know that his subordinate McDowell had sent Ricketts' division through the Gap to prevent any more reinforcements for Jackson. Pope believed that, with his superior force, he could get Jackson "easily into the bag" (Pope's turn of phrase in all his commands in those days). In order to do so, he first had to establish where Jackson actually was. But he lacked that information completely. There was almost no scouting, supposedly because Pope's cavalry horses were completely exhausted. Pope was always going where Jackson had already been—first to Manassas, then to Centreville. Thus the entire day of 28 August passed with the pointless charging about of the entire Union army.

Where was Jackson on 28 August? After completing his work of destruction at Manassas, he went to Centreville, some ten miles, but then ten miles west across the stone bridge of Bull Run to Sudley Springs. Here he stood barely eighteen miles from Thoroughfare Gap, through which Longstreet was expected. Here, too, was a retreat line to Aldie, which could be used in case Pope should attack him with superior force before he united with Longstreet. Further, the causeway of an uncompleted railroad at Sudley Springs offered him a strong line of defense. The idea that Jackson wished to accelerate his union with Longstreet as much as possible and would go to join his comrades was so obvious that even a Pope could fall upon it. But Pope must have believed that Jackson would walk directly through the mouth of the "bag" Pope held ready for him.

On the 27th, McDowell's and Sigel's corps stood at Gainesville, hence between Longstreet and Jackson, without this advantageous position being known to Pope. It is only ten miles from Gainesville to Sudley Springs, but Pope did not scout there. Instead he ordered McDowell and Sigel to go on the 28th from Gainesville to Manassas, thus where Jackson had been the day before. While both corps were marching, they received reversal orders for them to go to Centreville instead of Manassas, for Pope had learned in the meantime that Jackson had gone to Centreville.

During the march to Centreville, Sigel's corps and King's division received fire from Jackson's pickets. Sigel had only a light skirmish, but King became involved in a bloody fight. This afternoon encounter on 28 August finally unveiled Jackson's position northwest of Groveton. Sigel and King should have stayed there where they had found the enemy. But King did not do so, instead continuing his march to Centreville as ordered.

It was different with Sigel. He had learned from the afternoon encounter that it made no sense to march on to Centreville. He had scouts go to the northwest and came to the conviction that Jackson was located on the line from Sudley Springs to Groveton, hence directly in front of him. He informed Pope of this, along with the resolution that his corps would bivouac somewhat to the right of the crossing of the two main roads in order to be able to attack the next morning. Pope approved Sigel's disposition. Hence it was Sigel who found Jackson.

*   *   *

The Battle of Groveton, the first day of battle in Second Bull Run, took place on 29 August. It should be mentioned in advance that Longstreet and Lee passed through Thoroughfare Gap with 30,000 men, although only after severe fights with Ricketts' division. Pope had never thought of occupying or defending this pass, and he later did not approve this most reasonable measure of the entire campaign. The vanguard of Longstreet's force arrived in Gainesville by 10 A.M. on the 29th.

On the early morning of the 29th, Pope's army was still widely scattered. Directly before the enemy was only Sigel's corps and Reynolds' division. A third of the main army stood at Centreville, another part at Manassas. Porter's strong corps and Piatt's brigade were marching to Centreville early on the 29th, but on the way they received the (usual) counter-order and were advancing at 9 A.M. toward Gainesville instead (the opposite direction, but, as it turned out, the proper direction). Banks' corps remained on the Kettle Run to watch the supply train.

Sigel Opens the Battle. Pope had ordered the attack to begin at 5 A.M. Sigel moved his troops accordingly. Schurz's division advanced in a northwestern direction, Krzyzanowski's brigade to the left, Schimmelpfennig's brigade right, Koltes' brigade in reserve.[30] Enemy skirmishers were thrown off, and the German regiments advanced to shortly before the enemy position at the railroad causeway. Krzyzanowski found strong resistance in the thick forest behind Buck Hill. Milroy's brigade under Sigel advanced to the left of Krzyzanowski. As early as 8 A.M. it becomes necessary to bring up the 29th New York Regiment from the reserves. Sigel also threw the reserve artillery into the fire. About 10 A.M. the fighting took on a very serious character when Jackson sent up Ewell's division, which hit the dispersed lines of Schurz's division hard. Schurz rapidly regathered his regiments, led them back, and took the strip of woodland in front of the railway. In the meantime the Kearny's Union division had entered to the right of Schurz, and at about noon Hooker's division and Reno's corps appear behind Kearny.

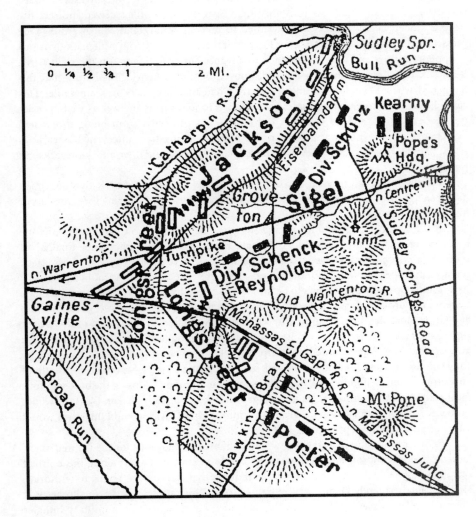

Figure 17. Sigel's fight on the first day of Second Bull Run.

Sigel had asked Kearny through his adjutant to attack at once alongside Schurz. Schurz also believed that Kearny would advance, but that did not happen. (See the detail in the Sigel biography.) Schurz's entire division advanced without any support, with great bravura. Schimmelpfennig's division was not only able to take the railroad by storm, but also advanced beyond that to the Cushing Farm. Jackson led large masses of fresh troops against the threatened Schimmelpfennig, Schurz's exhausted men still held the causeway.

Sigel's left wing (Schenck's division), was to advance along the highway toward Groveton. It encountered less resistance than Schurz, but it still received indirect fire from a hidden enemy battery. Sigel wanted to prevent Schurz and Milroy from being pressed too hard, and for that reason he sent Stahel's brigade (from Schenck's division) to support Milroy and ordered Schenck to advance closer to Schurz on the right wing. Reynolds' division had in the meantime moved behind Schenck. But hardly had this happened when Reynolds saw that Longstreet had marched in from Gainesville. This caused Reynolds to remain in place. Schenck had to join this maneuver as well in order not to be isolated, and so Jackson's right wing was protected from being threatened by Schenck and Reynolds at a very critical moment. Longstreet intervened as early as 11 A.M., holding Schenck and Reynolds in check and preventing their attack on Jackson's right flank.

Finally, only about 1:30 P.M., two of Kearny's brigades relieved Schurz's division, which had been fighting for more than eight hours, and Schurz was able to bring the remnants of his division to a protected position.

If the support of Sigel and specifically of the Schurz Division had come only one hour earlier, victory over Jackson would have been possible. But once Pope finally had more than 25,000 newly-arrived troops at his disposal, there was no energetic mass attack on Jackson. Pope was waiting for the arrival of Porter's corps, but Porter could not come.[31] As a result, Pope permitted hours to be lost. When he finally decided on an attack at 5 P.M., he sent only Grover's division, 1800 men, against Jackson. It was a short, very bloody fight, and Grover lost 500 men. Then Kearny was sent forward, but he also failed in the face of superior forces. More than 25,000 men stood around doing nothing during both of these attacks. Such was Pope's battle leadership. At 6 P.M. there was a third attack, this time by King's division. King hit Longstreet and was sent home bloody. So the entire Battle of Groveton is a series of individual fights. Pope put four of his divisions on the butcher block in one afternoon. A unified mass attack against Jackson, already shaken by Sigel, would probably have thrown Jackson back, and the unification of Jackson and Longstreet would have been delayed if not prevented.

In order to link up in a way that would be most advantageous for the Confederates, Jackson had to concentrate the troops that had been stretched apart along the railroad causeway. Pope saw this movement, and he thought that Jackson was trying to withdraw. Had the enemy merely begun their extremely clever operation in order to slip away at the moment of success and pass up the advantages obtained? Only a military bungler such as Pope could have conceived such a thought. Because he believed that Jackson was withdrawing, he held himself to be the victor. All of his orders for the second day of battle spoke of the pursuit of the beaten enemy! And Pope himself was the one beaten.

Pope had only one completely fresh corps ready for 30 August, Porter's 7500 men. Pope had lost 7000 men on the 29th, besides several thousand stragglers. The enemy, however, was able to commit Longstreet's fresh corps, 30,000 men, on the 30th, and Jackson's veterans were still capable of fighting. Pope's supplies were also giving out. The soldiers were living only on crackers. The artillery horses had not been unharnessed for ten days, and of the 4000 cavalry horses there were hardly 800 still able to carry a rider. Only the strongest of the harassed infantry could still charge.

This situation would have made retreat an obligation for any insightful army commander. And Pope's expectations in case of a retreat were very positive. Centreville, six miles back, was strongly fortified. There Pope could calmly await the enemy. There he would gain Sumner's corps and Franklin's corps, altogether 14,000 men.[32] He could also direct Banks' 5000 men there. Two days later Pope would have been able to unite more than 65,000 men, almost half of them fresh troops, in Centreville. Thus there were a thousand reasons for Pope's retreat on 30 August. But Pope wanted to complete his "victory" of the 29th on the 30th!

After Pope had decided to fight on, one would assume that the attack would be made with his full force. But nothing of the sort took place. Once again it was the testing and probing of the previous day. At noon Porter's corps was commanded to attack. It was to be supported by King's and Reynolds' divisions. But before it could come to blows, Reynolds was so threatened by Longstreet that he was not able to participate in Porter's attack. Porter went toward the railroad fosse, somewhat below the place Schurz had stormed and long held. Now the enemy was there, substantially stronger than on the previous day. Porter only came to attack at 4 P.M., since Pope had permitted him to alter the plan of attack. Porter's assault was supported only by King's division. The enemy was well prepared and greeted the attackers with dreadful artillery and rifle fire.[33] These brave men went forward four times, and they were sent back shattered four times. Only when a third of the attackers lay dead and wounded before the railroad did Porter and King withdraw, received by Schurz's division.

Porter's attack was essentially aimed at Jackson's troops, for Longstreet had advanced his divisions to the southeast in order to grasp Pope's left flank. Porter's retreat was thus Longstreet's signal for advance. One may also say that with Porter's retreat, the Northern army had already lost this rather hopeless battle. After 4:30 P.M. the only task of the Northern army was to prevent the execution of Longstreet's planned encirclement.

*　*　*

It may be seen on Figure 18 that Longstreet had to take Bald Hill if he was to press into Pope's position. As Longstreet's legions hit, only Schenck's division under Sigel (McClean's and Stahel's brigades) stood on Bald Hill. Schenck gave a powerful resistance, and was seriously wounded, and as a result of the dreadful effect of Sigel's artillery, Longstreet's charge was brought to a halt, and some larger units of Confederates had to go back. But new masses of the enemy were always being brought up. McLean's brigade was not able to hold against this enormously superior force, and Stahel's brave brigade was included in its retreat. Yet Schurz saw the peril of his comrades early and rushed up with Koltes' and Krzyzanowski's brigades, then with his last brigade, Schimmelpfennig's. Once again Longstreet advanced in greatly superior numbers, but he made no progress. He could not advance under the cartridge fire of Dilger's battery. The German infantry also covered itself with glory once more here. Yes, they even went over to attack, and Koltes led his brigade against a very irritating enemy battery. The leader was killed by a shell, Major Brückner was severely wounded, and almost a third of Koltes' brigade was wiped out. Sigel, who watched the fight from a neighboring height, saw that Schurz's division was in danger of being cut off, and he ordered retreat. But Longstreet was held up for half an hour by this resistance, and it was basically this time that prevented Longstreet's encirclement from succeeding.

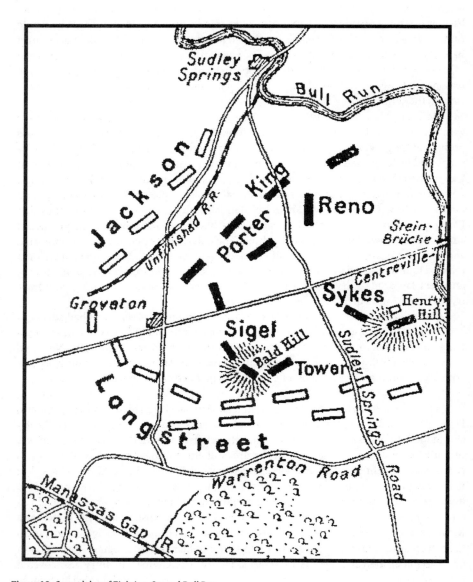

Figure 18. Second day of Fighting, Second Bull Run.

Henry Hill lies to the right of Bald Hill, more toward the highway. There had gathered the remnants of Porter's corps. Ricketts' division also stood there, as well as parts of

Reynolds' division. In order to delay the main attack by Longstreet against Henry Hill, Reynolds' division was sent against the enemy, although it could do little against such a superior force, but it did achieve a delay of the enemy. The defenders of Henry Hill were joined by Schimmelpfennig's brigade under Schurz. Here the most intense fighting developed at sundown. For more than three-quarters of an hour the defenders of Henry Hill held off the most violent attacks of the larger part of Longstreet's corps. In the military histories, the glory is given to regular troops under Sykes, Buchanan and Chapman, but Schimmelpfennig as well as Meade's brigade and Seymour and parts of Reno's corps fought here as bravely as Uncle Sam's regulars. Here I must again mention Dilger, whose artillery arrived with Schimmelpfennig and once more distinguished itself splendidly.

At 8 P.M. Pope ordered a withdrawal to Centreville, so that the battle came to an end. Longstreet's attempt to encircle had failed, and the retreat was orderly. It was covered by Sigel's corps. The stone bridge across Bull Run was destroyed during the night, after 1 A.M., by the 74th Pennsylvania Regiment under Major Blessing, so that Krzyzanowski's German brigade, which was the last to leave the battlefield, had to cross Bull Run through a ford. Dilger's guns, as well as some cannons that Colonel Kenes' "Bucktails" had rescued, were the last to go over the bridge. Until midnight, Dilger's battery stood before the stone bridge to prevent any pursuit. The enemy was so exhausted that it had to permit Pope to withdraw peacefully. After the battle almost all of Dilger's cannons were unusable. The glory of having covered the retreat was later claimed by General Gibbon, but Sigel, Schurz, and Krzyzanowski report unanimously that Schurz's division deserves this honor. Here their commander received his baptism of fire, and he showed himself to be a capable soldier and a brave man.

The days of 29 and 30 August were also days of honor. It was the sole great battle Sigel ever participated in. He proved himself well, but despite that he was never seen as an equal by his West Pointer colleagues. (See the Sigel biography.) Sigel's corps lost 2187 men and 92 officers. Because it could hardly have numbered more than 9000 men, the loss amounted to 25 percent! Koltes' Brigade suffered the most (401), then Krzyzanowski's (372). Stahel lost 169 men, Schimmelpfennig's losses were very heavy but cannot be established. On the second day of the battle, Milroy's brigade of Sigel's corps is never mentioned. It seems that it had been lost. Milroy rode all over the battlefield like a crazy man trying to find his brigade.

*   *   *

What followed this unfortunate battle is quickly told. On 1 September, Jackson made the attempt to place himself between Pope's army and Washington, from which maneuver the extraordinarily bloody Battle of Chantilly arose, in which the Union generals Kearny and Stevens fell. But the Confederates were much too weak to advance on Washington. They had lost over 12,000 men in these struggles. Pope's losses cannot be established precisely, but the entire Pope campaign is said to have cost 30,000 men!

Pope did the wisest thing he ever did during his entire campaign: he resigned. His troops breathed a sigh of relief when they were finally free of this bungler. They cheered their new chief, who was, of course, McClellan.

The Union Victory on the Antietam (Sharpsburg)

Lee's first incursion into the North—Battles for the passes over the South Mountains—Battle on the Antietam—Lee's retreat—General McClellan's removal—
The liberation of the slaves.

After the victories over Pope, popular opinion in the South demanded that Lee enter Maryland. Lee had to give in to this demand, although he did not share the great hopes that were harbored for this campaign. His army was much too weak to threaten Washington, Baltimore, or even Philadelphia seriously. Lee restricted his operations to the western tip of Maryland, and he barely dared go twenty miles beyond the Potomac.

It was the task of the reinstalled General McClellan to oppose this incursion into the Northern states. He had gathered 150,000 men around Washington at the start of September. Of these, Sigel's, Heintzelmann's and Banks' corps, some 60,000 men, remained behind to defend the capital. McClellan set out for Frederick on 7 September with 90,000 men.[34] Lee assumed that his enemy would advance with exquisite slowness, and he was not wrong. Lee once more divided his army. He sent 25,000 men under Jackson to Harpers Ferry and advanced with the remnant, 19,000 men, from Frederick to the valley of the Antietam, a tributary of the Potomac.

In Harpers Ferry stood the later Union General Miles with 12,500 men, in the rear of the rebel army. Jackson was supposed to remove this corps quickly, which was why Lee divided his army.

On 13 September, McClellan entered the town of Frederick, which the enemy had just abandoned. He had a stroke of good luck when a dispatch by Lee to his subordinate D. H. Hill fell into his hands. Lee's entire plan of campaign was laid out in this dispatch of 9 September, which said where each of the units of the Confederate army was to be for the next several days. This dispatch was of enormous value to McClellan. But to draw an advantage, McClellan would have had to act quickly and march immediately against the various parts of Lee's army that were to be in the Antietam valley. Instead, McClellan waited a precious twelve hours before he left.

Between Frederick and the Antietam valley are two mountain ranges, Catoctin and South Mountains. The first mountain offers no problems, and the latter is crossed by the National Road through the 600-foot-high Turner Pass. Six miles south of the Turner Pass lies Crampton Pass. From Frederick to the Turner Pass is fifteen miles, seven of them a quick march on fine roads. McClellan's army was in splendid shape.

The Union army set out on the morning of 14 September in two columns. General Franklin was to take Crampton Pass, with the main army under McClellan taking Turner Pass. As a result of McClellan's slowness, however, Lee was warned. He found time to strengthen the weakly guarded passes, and gave his opponents skirmishes at both passes that ended with Confederate retreats, but gave the Confederates time to bring their baggage and heavy artillery to security.

If McClellan had set out a half-day sooner, he probably could have caught Lee's entire force of 19,000 men, their irreplaceable train and artillery, and perhaps even the supreme commander Lee himself, for McClellan had 90,000 men against Lee's

19,000. Instead, Lee achieved his goal. At about 8 A.M. on 15 September Miles capitulated to Jackson in Harpers Ferry.[35]

* * *

The fighting on Crampton and Turner passes led to the great battle on the Antietam (at Sharpsburg). Lee retreated to Sharpsburg on 15 September. He had only the smaller half of his army with him, for his comrade Jackson was not free at Harpers Ferry until about noon on the 15th. Before him Lee had the enormous army of McClellan, certain of victory. Lee could not fight before Jackson returned. McClellan, on the other hand, could have overrun Lee and crushed him with his tremendous numerical superiority. But Lee depended on the notorious delays of the "Great Hesitator," and he was right!

* * *

Lee's new position at Sharpsburg (or Antietam) supported itself on both sides on turns of the Potomac, so that it was protected from being flanked and had the advantage of being able to receive troops arriving from Harpers Ferry without trouble. In front of it was the little river of Antietam, with its steep banks. The terrain rose from there toward the Potomac, which made possible an advantageous location of Confederate artillery. To have the Potomac at his back was certainly less comfortable, but if Lee did not wish to withdraw to Virginia without a struggle, no other position was available.

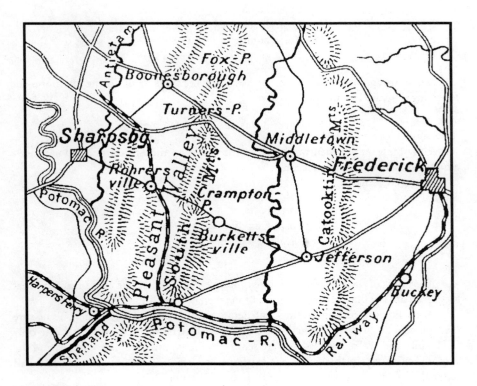

Figure 19. The fight for the passes.

There are ten English miles from the Turner Pass to the Antietam, so that McClellan was already opposite his enemy at noon on the 15th. The Union general had known for hours that Harpers Ferry had fallen, and that Jackson had nothing more to do there and was expected back soon. If he had attacked at once, McClellan would have had a threefold superiority. But he did nothing. He did not even seek fords across the Antietam! Even on the morning of the 16th nothing happened, and it was only in late afternoon that Hooker's corps was sent against Lee's left flank, not as a serious attack but to achieve a position for an attack on the morning of the 17th. McClellan's dispositions were precisely as if he wanted to give his opponent every opportunity to gather his scattered forces. Now let us see how these forces came to Lee.

On the morning of the 17th, Jackson arrived after a 17-hour march and two crossings of the Potomac with about 12,000 men. At noon Walker's division came to Lee. It was only on the morning of the 17th that McLaws' division and finally at 2 P.M. on the day of the battle that A. P. Hill's division arrived. Lee was happy to have all his own together when things were serious, the last coming shortly before the end of the battle. Conditions were such that McClellan was able to figure the arrival of these reinforcements of his enemy rather precisely in advance!

But even after Lee had concentrated all his troops at Sharpsburg, McClellan still disposed of almost double superiority. Here are his own figures on the units:

I	Corps Hooker	14,856 men
XII	Corps Mansfield	10,126
II	Corps Sumner	<u>18,813</u>
	Total	43,795 men

These troops were used on the 17th against Lee's left flank. In the afternoon the following were used against Lee's center:

IX	Corps Burnside	13,819 men

Only these, 57,614 men were used in the Battle on the Antietam, and their losses amounted to more than 20 percent.

In reserve remained:

V	Corps Porter	12,930 men
VI	Corps Franklin	12,300
	Cavalry Division	<u>4,320</u>
	Total	29,550 men

The losses of these 29,550 men were only 2 percent, so that one could easily say that McClellan did not put even 30,000 of his 87,164 men into the fire.

According to Lee's report, the Confederate army numbered 41,500 men. To be sure the Confederates were in the habit of estimating their numbers low. But because only D. H. Hill's and Walker's divisions were sent from Richmond as reinforcements, and the core of Lee's army in the battles against Pope had amounted to 15,000 men and had suffered losses,[36] this number comes quite near to the truth.

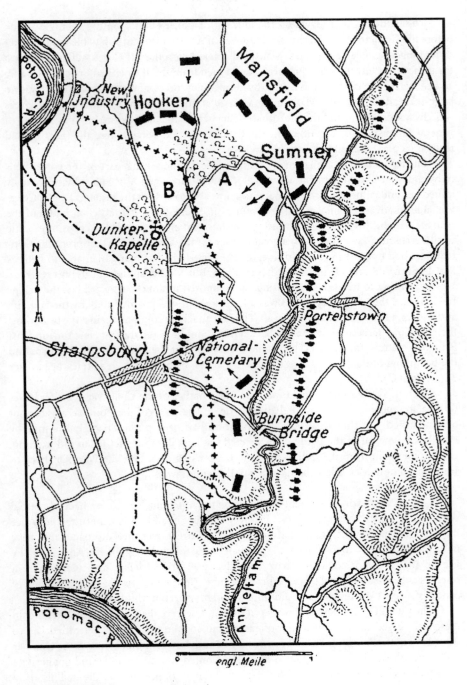

Figure 20. Battle of Sharpsburg (or Antietam).

The battle began at dawn on the 17th with Hooker's attack on the enemy position before the German Dunkard church (Figure 20 at A). After this corps had bled to the point of no longer being able to attack, Mansfield entered with the XII Corps, suffering almost the same fate. Only then did Sumner's 18,000 men from the II Corps enter action (Figure 20 at A). Here as well there was a drop-by-drop use of forces, and here as well there was no large-scale advance of overwhelming masses all at once. Thus the terrain won by charges was always lost again, and the dreadful butchery came to a halt before noon as a result of general exhaustion. The conflict on the Confederate left wing, where the mass battled really took place, was already over by 11 A.M.

Burnside's attack on the enemy center made up the second part of the battle. This only came to full development about 4 P.M., at the time when A. P. Hill's division finally joined Lee and, although tired by marching, was able to absorb the impact. The IX Corps was able to advance as far as the first houses in Sharpsburg. If McClellan had had the courage to send his reserves (almost 25,000 fresh infantry) to aid this corps, the battle would certainly have ended with a great victory for the Union, for at that point the Confederates had not one man left in reserve. They barely had as many men able to fight as McClellan could provide in fresh infantry alone. But McClellan did not use his reserves.

According to his orders, Burnside was supposed to attack at 7 A.M., but the bridge (which since then bears his name) was a hindrance. It was guarded only by the 2nd and 20th Georgia Regiments, 403 rifles in all. The first attacking columns against the bridge lost their way, and the second was beaten back. Only about 1 P.M. did the 51st New York and 51st Pennsylvania take the bridge. Then came the crossing of the bridge by the IX Corps and the beginning of fighting. As a result it was 3:30 P.M. before Burnside's attack began (see Figure 20 at C).[37]

With this attack ended one of the bloodiest battles of the Civil War.[38] Union losses were 12,400 men, including more than 2000 dead. The losses of the Confederates cannot be established, but they were less. Lee's position had been pushed back half a mile by evening. A renewal of the battle was expected the next day, but McClellan did nothing. During the night from the 18th to the 19th, Lee crossed back over the Potomac, back to Virginia, without McClellan's being aware of the withdrawal!

*　*　*

One must ask why Lee fought the Battle on the Antietam. The Union had a threefold superiority, together with the troops before Washington, and on Northern territory Lee did not have the advantages he had in Virginia. A retreat over the Potomac would have moved the battlefield to Virginia, for McClellan had to follow his opponent. Any victory by Lee on the Antietam could not have been decisive, for McClellan had as many fresh reserves as Lee had in actual troops on 17 September. To use such troops for a campaign of conquest against Washington or Baltimore would have been unthinkable.

The pursuit of Lee was so slow that it does not deserve the name of pursuit. Lincoln ceaselessly urged his general to the offensive, but in vain. McClellan permitted Lee to spread out in the Shenandoah Valley as he wished and draw reinforcements. By 20 October Lee's army already had almost 70,000 men. The Confederate commander did not hesitate to display his contempt openly for his eternally hesitant opponent. Lee divided his army again, leaving Jackson's corps in the Shenandoah Valley and proceeding across the

Blue [Ridge] Mountains to Culpeper with two-thirds of his troops. But McClellan did not even trust himself to advance on the isolated Jackson. After seven weeks of patient waiting, Lincoln finally decided to dismiss McClellan. On 7 November, Burnside took McClellan's place.

The Freeing of the Slaves

Immediately after the Battle on the Antietam, Lincoln issued his proclamation to emancipate the slaves. The North was completely surprised by this. Lincoln had even kept his intention to issue this proclamation secret from his own cabinet. [Kaufmann is incorrect here. The matter was long discussed in the cabinet.—Ed.] The proclamation took effect on 1 January 1863.

Dreadful Union Defeat at Fredericksburg

The war leadership was supposed to be different after McClellan's departure. In the place of the previous hesitation, the North would go heartily after the enemy. Thus thought the new man, Burnside, or at least that is how he acted. But he lacked self-confidence. He freely confessed his own incapacity for such a high command before his gathered generals, as we know from Schurz.

Burnside took over command over the Union army gathered at Warrenton on 9 November. At first he wanted to make a feinted attack against Lee's new position at Culpeper, in central Virginia, while throwing his main force against Fredericksburg and then marching rapidly on Richmond. On the 14th the march began toward Fredericksburg and Falmouth, a little town opposite Fredericksburg on the northern shore of the Rappahannock River. Gathering there were: Sumner's Grand Division on 17 November, Hooker on the 18th, and Franklin on the 19th. These three grand divisions numbered 127,574 men.[39] Sigel commanded the fourth grand division, but it followed later, remaining in reserve on the northern bank of the Rappahannock, and it was not used at Fredericksburg.

Nothing came of the feinted attack on Culpeper, for Lee quickly saw through Burnside's maneuver. He threw his 75,000 men in rapid marches toward Fredericksburg in order to meet his enemy there. Now, if Burnside wanted to fight with Lee at all, he would have to fight him in Fredericksburg. The city was very weakly defended when Sumner arrived in Falmouth. Sumner could have taken it with a *coup de main,* along with the important Marye's Heights behind Fredericksburg. But Burnside did not allow Sumner to take such a useful measure!

There were 25 days between 17 November and 13 December. Lee had time to dig in on the heights south of the city and make the natural fortress of Marye's Heights into a man-made fortress. Burnside was forced into this delay because Halleck did not send the pontoons for crossing the Rappahannock in time. This waiting was terrible for the Union troops positioned on the north bank of the river. Winter weather set in, with short days, much fog, and night frosts. For several weeks the troops were able to observe the fortress

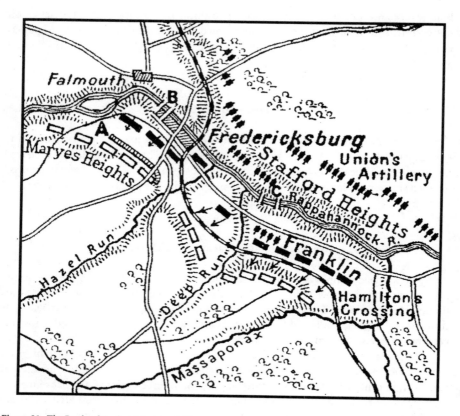

Figure 21. The Battle of Fredericksburg. A. The stone causeway; B. Pontoon bridge for Sumner and Hooker; C. Pontoon bridge for Franklin.

that stood before them, which they one day would have to storm. That is certainly a stern test for the enthusiasm for battle of what was largely a very young army. But no damage could be done to the enemy, because the Union batteries did not reach across the Rappahannock and over the Marye's Heights.

Burnside's undertaking to storm the heights behind Fredericksburg bordered on madness. In order to be able to attack the enemy position, Burnside had to build bridges under fire; lead his forces across the broad, fickle stream; and then storm a fortress with the river at his back. Opposite stood 75,000 Confederates in secured positions waiting for the attack! If the attack failed, and his chances of success were at the most one out of ten, then there was the peril of being thrown into the Rappahannock by the enemy.

Bridges were finally built early on 12 December after the arrival of the pontoons. Then the troops were hastily brought across. The city of Fredericksburg, lying directly on the river, was first secured, at great loss. During the night there was a dreadfully cold bivouac in the streets, with no peace. Fires could not be lit, for enemy cannons could reach the city, which had been abandoned by its residents. Because all preparations for the storm were inadequate, the supplies for soldiers were also wanting. They waited for the fog that preceded dawn, agitated, tired, and hungry.

Sumner was to attack the front of Marye's Heights and be supported by Hooker. On the left wing stood Franklin, 1.5 miles left of Sumner. Franklin was to take the heights at Hamilton's Crossing. But Burnside's commands to Franklin were so imprecise that Franklin did not know whether the commanding general wanted only a strong demonstration on the left wing or a genuine flanking maneuver. Franklin was no man for initiatives; he obeyed orders as he understood them, and if he understood them falsely because they were imprecise, then that was the fault of the commanding general. I cannot irritate the reader with the incongruities between Franklin's conception of Burnside's orders and Burnside's supposed intentions. But the result was that Franklin only committed one of his two corps. Smith's corps remained with weapons by their feet, and afterwards Burnside asserted that Franklin lost the battle because Smith's corps did not enter the action. But Burnside's entire attack on Lee's fortified position was madness. The result of this useless murder called the Battle of Fredericksburg was the following:

Sumner and Hooker advanced from Fredericksburg about 11 A.M. They came to a stone causeway before which a new wall, of corpses of shattered attackers, was forming. New attempts at attack were newly thrown back. This was repeated five or six times. About 8500 dead and wounded lay between the stone fosse and Fredericksburg. Then night fell. It was fortunate, by the way, that the brave soldiers never got across the stone fosse. For on the other side of the fosse they would have been received by a fresh superior force of the enemy and probably ground to nothing. Dead, 1180; wounded, 9028; missing, 2145 (including many dead); altogether 12,353 men lost—that was the result of the dreadful day on the side of the Union troops. Almost 4000 men were lost on Franklin's left wing. Because only half of Franklin's grand division came under fire, these figures show that those who fought there suffered almost as much as those who stormed the center.

Burnside wanted to attack again the next day. He had already issued the orders. It was only with difficulty that he was kept from it as a result of the protests of his subordinates. Later Burnside lamented and cursed in turn. He took on himself the entire responsibility for the attack, saying, "I am the guilty one." Then he put half a dozen of his subordinate generals under arrest and made serious accusations to Lincoln. Later he wanted to attack Lee by another route, but he remained stuck in the mire of the roads, which had become bottomless. A common saying was, "Burnside stuck in the mud." Yet despite all of this, the general does rather well in American military histories. Grant always remained his friend, and Grant's loyalty to old war comrades was without limit.

Of the purely German regiments involved in the Battle of Fredericksburg, the 7th, 20th, 46th, 52nd, and 103rd [New York] were engaged, but they fought in various brigades. The 7th [New York] Regiment (the Steuben Regiment)[40] and the 46th, which was led at Fredericksburg by Colonel Gerhardt, suffered dreadful losses.

V

The War in 1863 and the End of the War

The Humiliation of Chancellorsville

A four-day battle in the Wilderness; 125,000 Union soldiers beaten by 62,000 rebels—
Germans as scapegoats for poor leadership—Justification of our compatriots according to
the findings of Anglo-American investigators—Buschbeck and Schurz at Chancellorsville.

> The German character needs no apology to the student of history for lack of
> martial virtues. Since the days of the Caesars its unquenchable warlike spirit has
> never been denied or questioned.
>
> —Hamlin

The May days of 1863 constituted the low point of the Union cause. There had already
been fighting for two years in Virginia, and the rebels could point to an almost unbroken
campaign of victories: First Bull Run, the unfortunate Peninsular Campaign, the inglorious
campaign against Jackson, the severe defeat of Second Bull Run, the Union half-victory so
poorly exploited on the Antietam, the horrors of Fredericksburg! And now, from 1 to 4 May,
there was added the humiliating defeat at Chancellorsville. The best and strongest army
the Union had ever gathered, 125,000 men, was beat over the head there by a force of 60,000
Confederates. This injured the pride of the Northern people in a way that was almost
beyond bearing. They sought some balsam to overcome the burning sense of humiliation,
and they fell on the extenuation that *the cowardly Germans lost the battle for them!* The
entire Anglo-American press, with the notable exception of the *Chicago Tribune*, eagerly
reached for this excuse to cover up the defeat, and the lies which were spread on the conduct of German soldiers were even more disgraceful than the leadership in that battle.

Military history is full of generals forced into necessary falsehoods, but it would be
hard to find a fable more palpably unbelievable than this accusation against the Germans.
The reason for it rests on the following. The XI Corps, robbed of its reserves and placed in
isolation in thick forest, reduced to 8500 men (including 4600 Germans), was overrun and

dispersed on 2 May by 30,000 Confederates under Stonewall Jackson. It suffered losses of 1500 dead and wounded and 1100 prisoners. The losses in that one-and-a-half hour fight were seldom reached in the Civil War in such a short time. This figure alone shows that those attacked defended themselves well. Cowards give up, but here the number of dead and wounded considerably exceeds that of those captured. Also, this attack was only one episode of a four-day battle. On the next day 120,000 Union soldiers were beaten by less than half as many Confederates. And yet those 4600 Germans in the XI Corps were supposed to have lost the entire four-day battle! This lie by West Pointers would be almost comic if it had not been preserved through the years, despite refutation by honorable Anglo-American historians.

The XI Corps consisted of 11,500 men on 2 May. For the battle, however, Barlow's brigade had been commanded away, so that about 8500 men were subjected to the attack. The corps had basically been the first unit in Pope's summer campaign of 1862, and it was commanded by Sigel until April 1863. For that reason, and because Schurz and von Steinwehr commanded two of the three divisions and many Germans served as commanders of brigades and regiments in the XI Corps, it was regarded by the West Pointers as the German corps or "the foreign contingent." The corps had virtually no cavalry. The artillery consisted of the Dilger, Dieckmann, Wiedrich, Heckermann, and Wheeler batteries and one regular battery.

The infantry was organized as follows. (Immediately after the regimental number is the number of dead and wounded of that regiment.)

First Division, General Devens. Von Gilsa Brigade: 41st New York (30); 45th New York (32); 54th New York (25); 153rd Pennsylvania (46). The brigade numbered a mere 1400 men and had 133 dead and wounded. McLean Brigade: 17th Connecticut (42); 25th Ohio (121); 55th Ohio (96); 75th Ohio (74); 107th Ohio (59). Losses of the brigade, 393 men.

Second Division, von Steinwehr. Buschbeck Brigade: at most 1500 men in the 29th New York (57); 157th New York (87); 27th Pennsylvania (37); 73rd Pennsylvania (74). Loss of the brigade, 225 men. Barlow Brigade, 2950 men, essentially not involved in the battle. It consisted of the 33rd Massachusetts Regiment, Colonel Underwood; 134th New York, Colonel Coster; 136th New York, Wood; and 73rd Ohio, Orlando Smith.

Third Division, Karl Schurz. Schimmelpfennig Brigade: 82nd Illinois (Hecker's regiment, 107 dead and wounded); 68th New York (21); 61st Ohio (60); 157th New York (79); 74th Pennsylvania (22). Krzyzanowski Brigade: 58th New York (11); 119th New York (78); 75th Pennsylvania (8); 26th Wisconsin (Germans from Milwaukee, 158); 82nd Ohio (56). The losses of the Schurz Division, besides 39 from the artillery and staff, were 638 dead and wounded.

Hamlin figured that one must estimate the dead and wounded of the 11th Corps at around 1500 according to later supplements to the lists.

The Sigel biographical section will give the thorough reasons for the resignation of the German corps commander. A few weeks before the battle, the West Pointer General O. O. Howard took Sigel's place at the head of the corps. He was a temperance man and a pious Christian. He was this by conviction, and hypocrisy was alien to him. Pious solders have often been the best. Stonewall Jackson could kneel and pray for hours when he faced a great decision.[1] Jackson's colleague Polk, who also fell in battle, had earlier been a bishop of the Episcopal Church. Lee, as well, was a believing Christian, and he attended the church of the German pastor Minnigerode in Richmond at any opportunity. The same may be said for Jeff Davis. The identical phenomenon among leaders is to be found in the Union army, as well. But we do not find it among the Germans of the XI Corps. A general who knew more about the Bible than about military science was unsympathetic to the Geman portion of the XI Corps, and this mood also dominated among the Anglo-American soldiers of the corps. It is no wonder, as Schurz reports, that not a single cheer came from the ranks of the troops when Howard visited them. Among American volunteers, the personality of the leaders plays a larger role than among the well-disciplined armies of Europe. Generals who are personally unpopular with the soldiers lose much of their effectiveness. Schurz at first wanted to have his whole division moved to another corps when he heard of Howard's appointment, but he remained in place because he feared that Howard's reputation in the corps would be even more shaken by his own withdrawal.

Howard brought two protégés with him into the XI Corps: General Devens became leader of the First Division, and General Barlow commander of a brigade under Steinwehr. Both took the place of well-known officers who had become loved through their military comradeship over more than a year. Division commander Devens is, next to the corps commander Howard and commanding General Hooker, the person most responsible for the misfortune of 2 May.

* * *

First, a brief overview of the war situation in the spring of 1863 should be given.

At the end of January, General Joseph Hooker took Burnside's place as supreme commander of the Army of the Potomac. He was a capable organizer, and he also understood how to revive the good spirits of the troops. The cavalry was raised to 13,000 men, the artillery to 10,000 men. The army was well equipped and according to Lincoln's estimate consisted of 146,000 men, of which only 125,000 took part in the battle.

The enemy armies stood on 26 April in the same positions opposite Fredericksburg that they had taken before the battle on 13 December 1862. Hooker was on the heights on the north shore of the Rappahannock, Lee's 60,681 men in the fortress of Marye's Heights south of Fredericksburg. As in December, the Northern army had to cross the Rappahannock in order to approach its opponent. Hooker wanted to push his opponent out of Marye's Heights by flanking it, so as to force a decisive battle in the open country south of Fredericksburg. For this purpose he divided his army into three groups. The VI Corps, 30,000 men under Sedgwick, was sent across the Rappahannock east of Fredericksburg in order to make Lee believe that another attack on Marye's Heights was intended. The I, II and III Corps first crossed the upper course of the Rappahannock, then crossed the Rapidan via Germanna Ford and gathered at Chancellorsville. The hamlet bearing this name lies ten English miles southwest of Fredericksburg. Hooker's three groups were thus not widely scattered but separated by no more than one day's march. Through this advance, Hooker not only threatened the enemy's flank (through Sedgwick), but also his rear (through V, XI and XII Corps), while I, II and III Corps stood in reserve. As soon as

Hooker advanced to Chancellorsville, he drew to himself the II and III Corps and designated I Corps as the reserve. As a result, on 30 April, Hooker already had the II, III, V, XI and XII Corps with him at Chancellorsville, altogether 80,000 men. The I Corps still stood beyond the Rappahannock and the VI Corps, Sedgwick's, a good day's march east of Hooker. Hooker had sent ahead almost the entire cavalry of 12,000 horses ahead to threaten Lee's lines of retreat. Yet this expedition proved to be a failure.

Hooker convinced himself to an extraordinary degree of the success of this flanking march. He issued a proclamation in which he said, "Lee is now compelled to come out of his entrenchment and give us a battle on a field we have chosen, where certain doom awaits him," and the like. A week later this boaster stood beaten on the opposite shore of the Rappahannock.

Lee's position on 30 April was anything but comfortable. He stood between the fires, with Sedgwick beside him and Hooker's greatly superior forces behind him. Yet the Southern leader still controlled his line of retreat to Richmond. He could give up Marye's Heights and retreat a ways to build a new position of defense. But despite the overwhelming superiority threatening him, Lee wanted to fight here. And his genius as a commander in the field was never demonstrated so splendidly on any other ground. In order to strike, Lee had to fulfill the desires of his opponent by partly evacuating Marye's Heights. On 30 April the two Confederate divisions of Anderson and McLaws moved against Hooker's great army. They took up a fine position at Tabernacle Church and threw up hasty entrenchments there.

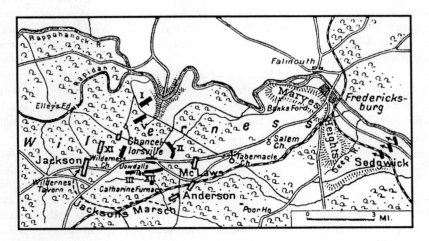

Figure 22. Battlefield of Chancellorsville, situation on 2 May 1863.

From Chancellorsville to Tabernacle is barely three miles. Hooker's II and III Corps had only a brief march and were fresh on 30 April. They could certainly have advanced against Anderson and McLaws on the same day, and units from the other three corps could surely have been spared for immediate attack on the enemy, then numbering only 20,000. But Hooker did nothing at all on 30 April.

It was only at 1 P.M. on 1 May that Hooker entered the open country between Marye's Heights and Tabernacle Church, where the enemy wanted to give decisive battle. About this time, however, not only Anderson and McLaws were at Tabernacle; Lee had brought his entire corps (with the exception of Early's division, which remained in Marye's Heights to observe Sedgwick). The twenty-four hours Hooker allowed to pass without doing anything were splendidly used by the enemy. Considerable entrenchments had risen in the meantime, and behind them stood 50,000 Confederates.

Hooker's 80,000 men probed carefully about this position, there was a small skirmish, and then Hooker ordered a retreat. Several hours later he would bitterly regret this command, and rightly so, for it was the most serious error of all the errors of the Northern leadership contributing to the defeat. The fact that Hooker never attacked the enemy position is understandable. His plan was based on the cooperation of Sedgwick. Sedgwick could not then go into action, and further the I Corps was still not there. Through an attack on the enemy army on 1 May, Hooker would have sacrificed all the advantages of Sedgwick's position in the rear of the enemy.

But Hooker did not need to attack on 1 May. He needed to secure his position against Tabernacle Church. He should not have withdrawn into the Wilderness around Chancellorsville.[2] He had to try to approach Sedgwick as closely as possible, while remaining as near as possible to the open country, where he wanted to fight, where his vastly superior forces would be fully effective, and where his strong artillery could move. The position opposite the enemy at Tabernacle Church that Hooker reached on 1 May was described by General Doubleday as extraordinarily good. There Hooker had Chancellorsville with good road connections at his back, and he could rely on several heights. Above everything else, he was three miles closer to Sedgwick. But Hooker went back into the wilderness, setting up the attack on the 11th Corps.

Jackson's flanking maneuver. Jackson's scouts had located Hooker's position in the wilderness and quickly saw its weakest point, the position of the XI Corps on Hooker's right wing. There the XI was totally isolated and could only defend itself against attack with difficulty, in the thicket. The corps was completely undefended toward the west. But it was from the west that Jackson's peril would come.

Lee and Jackson met at midnight of 1 May to confer. Jackson revealed his plan for flanking the enemy position and overrunning the XI Corps. Lee immediately agreed, and then the two most important commanders of the Confederates said farewell to one another for the last time. Jackson's corps, brought to 30,000 men by detachments, took up the 15-mile march early on the morning of 2 May. Lee remained with the Anderson and McLaws divisions at Tabernacle. Now the Confederate army was divided into three parts. Early's 10,000 men stood at Marye's Heights against Sedgwick's force, Lee stood with 20,000 men opposite Hooker's main force, and Jackson was on a march that would bring him to the rear of the XI Corps shortly after noon.

The relationships of terrain were such that Jackson's advance could be well observed from the Union position. Jackson's strength could even be estimated approximately. It was seen that the enemy carried with him a small train, actually only ambulances and ammunition wagons. At 9:30 A.M. Hooker knew that it was a flanking movement, for at this time he sent the leaders of the XI and XII Corps a warning to this effect.[3] The adjutant bringing this first arrived in the XI Corps at 11:30 A.M. The commander, Howard, was sleeping. Division commander Schurz received the dispatch, woke Howard up, and read it to him. Years later, over his own signature, Howard asserted that he never received this dispatch! The dispatch is found in the papers, and Schurz declares with great thoroughness that he read it to Howard himself and discussed its contents with him.

But even while the adjutant bringing Hooker's warning to the XI and XII Corps was on his way, a complete change of attitude by the Northern leaders concerning the meaning of Jackson's march must have taken place. All of Hooker's measures after 11 A.M. indicate that the Northern commanding general and all his advisors and corps leaders believed that the enemy was in complete retreat. Hooker as well as his generals later declared that they believed from that time on that Jackson was in retreat, not that he was making a flank attack.

In truth, the enemy position at Tabernacle continued to be held by Lee. The enemy had to be very weak in that position after Jackson's withdrawal. In fact, Hooker had four times the force of Lee's 20,000 men at Tabernacle Church. To be sure one does not need to have a certificate from the Prussian General Staff to presume that Hooker's duty was to attack Lee at once. If that had been done, the XI Corps would have been moved out of its isolated position, where it was sitting to no purpose. But Hooker did as much as nothing against Lee. Only the Geary and Williams divisions were directed against the enemy at Tabernacle, and there were skirmishes with some pickets. Lee remained as good as undisturbed.

On the contrary, the following happened:

At noon, General Sickles, leader of the III Corps, asked Hooker for permission to attack the rear guard of the retreating enemy column in order at least to capture their artillery. Sickles marched after Jackson with two divisions at 1 P.M. But these divisions had earlier held the position that maintained a loose connection between the XI Corps and Hooker's headquarters. After their departure, the XI Corps was completely isolated. The result of Sickles' efforts were a few small rear-guard actions and the capture of several hundred men of the Confederate 23rd Georgia Regiment. Jackson was already too far ahead for anyone to injure him in the midday hours. If Sickles' expedition had had some purpose, it would have had to begin at least five hours earlier. Sickles then lingered at Catherine Furnace (see Figure 24) and asked for reinforcements. He was sent Barlow's brigade of the XI Corps. Hence the sole reserve of this entirely isolated corps was detatched! At 4 P.M. Barlow moved toward the Furnace, at exactly the moment when Jackson was preparing his jump on the XI Corps.

The map [Figure 23] shows how the XI Corps was placed. The lead position was held by Devens' division, which stood primarily on the turnpike running through the Wilderness to Chancellorsville. But von Gilsa's two regiments (153rd Pennsylvania and 54th New York) were in the thick, primeval forest. Behind Devens' division stood Schurz's division. This was spread rather widely to the north on Hawkins Farm. Von Steinwehr's division, south of Schurz, was on Doudall's Farm. Buschbeck's brigade was in trenches with their front to the south, while Barlow's strong brigade was north of there in front of the reserve artillery. The position was 1.33 miles long, almost a mile wide and spread out over the three continuous farms of Talley, Hawkins, and Doudall. The corps had cattle and a considerable train with it. Large fields were found only on Hawkins' Farm. At 4 P.M. on 2 May, after the departure of Barlow's brigade, the remnant of the XI Corps was separated from its comrades in the other corps by a gap of 1.5 miles. These 8500 men stood completely isolated, behind the wrong front, in the thick forest.

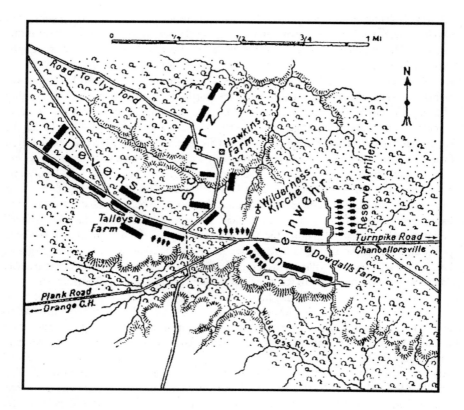

Figure 23. Position of the XI Corps by divisions (Barlow's division had already marched off).

An army of 30,000 men advancing along a very narrow road, sometimes along forest paths, bringing with it over 100 cannons, a strong cavalry, and ambulances, moves very slowly. Hence it was 11 A.M. before Jackson's vanguard appeared before the XI Corps on Luckett Farm. It was 5 P.M. before Jackson was ready to attack. So six hours lay between the arrival of Jackson's vanguard and the attack.

How close the two armies were may be seen by the fact that Jackson could clearly hear the drums of a regimental religious service playing in the enemy camp. During those six hours, the XI Corps could still easily have made ready for an attack; indeed, it had time to carry out the plan Schurz proposed earlier in the day to his corps commander Howard, which was to draw in the right wing, Devens' division, and have the entire corps take up a strongly entrenched position with its front toward the west. This position was to have as its center the little church where the plank road runs into the main road; it would run north and south across the road on Hawkins Farm, and also use the artillery. But the West Pointer Howard, as it later turned out, did not want to hear of the plan of this civilian, Schurz. Howard believed it would be impossible for an enemy to pass through this wilderness. The reasons Howard used against Schurz's plan in the morning might have had some justification, but it was a crime that the position was not changed when the arrival of the enemy in the immediate vicinity had been clearly established. The most inconceivable part of this entire affair is the fact that the commanding general, Hooker, the corps leader, Howard, and the division commander, Devens, did not believe the officers whom they had sent out to reconnoiter.

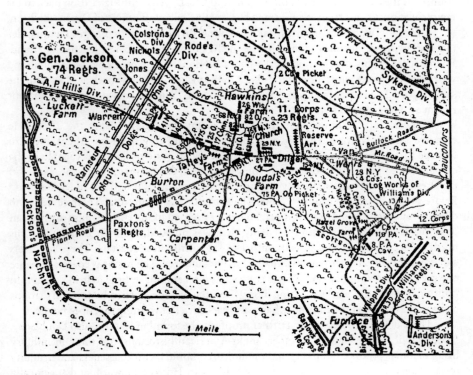

Figure 24. Jackson ready to attack.

Listen to this: Captain Rollins, 55th Ohio Regiment, commander of pickets, sent three messages between 11 A.M. and 4 P.M. announcing Jackson's approach. Colonel Lee brought these messages to Devens personally. Staff surgeon Hubbard of the 17th Connecticut Regiment, was present when Lee made this report to the division commander. Devens' answer, according to Hubbard, was, "You are worried, sir!" Lee brought along a farmer who had seen Jackson's army. Devens did not want to hear anything of this witness, either.

Major Rice of the 153rd Pennsylvania, who had scouted with some companies and had been bombarded by enemy artillery, reported at 2:45 P.M. to his brigadier, von Gilsa, that the enemy had gathered before the Union pickets. Gilsa gave this report to Howard in person, but was repulsed with taunts. When von Gilsa and Rice later reported to the Congressional committee to give testimony, they were not accepted as witnesses.

Major Schleiter of the 74th Pennsylvania Regiment was scouting around 3 P.M. He very clearly heard the commands of Confederate officers. Schleiter reported this to Schurz, who sent him to Howard. Howard, however, was of the opinion that Schleiter should not be concerned!

Colonel Richardson of the 25th Ohio brought four messengers to Devens which confirmed the earlier reports of both Rollins and Lee. Devens sent Richardson back to his regiment at once. This scene is confirmed by Captain Culp, staff officer of Devens' division.

Colonel Friend, officer of the day of Devens' division, reported to his commander that the enemy was forming in mass before the XI Corps. Devens barely listened to Friend. Friend repeated his observation in the corps headquarters, where he was insulted and warned not to cause panic. Friend rode back to the pickets and came back at 2 P.M. with the same report. The response in corps headquarters was, "You are a coward, go back to your regiment! The enemy is in retreat."

General von Schimmelpfennig saw the enemy two hours before the attack. He reported this to Howard. Howard forbade Schimmelpfennig to begin a fight and also forbade further scouting, and sends this brigade leader (one of the most capable in the corps) back to his troops. Schimmelpfennig's adjutant, Captain von Frietzsche, earlier in the Dresden cavalry guards, also saw the enemy, made a report of it, and was rudely rejected.[4] Before 3 P.M. Schurz sent artillery Captain Dilger into the area in front. There could be no doubt about the reliability of this German hero, esteemed in the entire Union army, as an observer. Dilger ran right into the enemy, fled, was pursued, the bullets flying past his head. By accident he came directly into Hooker's army headquarters. There he meets a major of cavalry. Dilger reports what he has encountered. The major is coarse: "You are crazy, go back to your battery!" Dilger got back to his cannons in time to bring them into position, for Jackson was just letting loose. Even the wildlife startled by Jackson's troops come in masses into the camp, deer, hares and rabbits, a last warning that does not lie.

These details should suffice. Further proof is to be found in Hamlin, also Doubleday, Underwood, Dodge, Bates, and other Anglo-American historians. Are there in military history similar proofs of stupidity and prejudice, combined with coarseness and brutality toward conscientious officers such as one finds with Hooker, Howard, and specifically Devens? An explanation must be sought, even the wildest.

Hooker believed solidly that the enemy was in retreat. His corps commander, Couch, the next in command, heard that at noon from Hooker's own mouth. There is in the papers a dispatch from Hooker to Sedgwick in which Hooker says, "The enemy is withdrawing to Gordonsville." Generals Warren and Hancock declared under oath to the Congressional committee that it was generally believed on 2 May that Lee was in retreat. Hooker himself confirmed before that committee his dispatch to Sedgwick to that effect.

The question is posed in vain how this fable of retreat could have come into being, for Lee had made his presence obvious and clear enough at Tabernacle. The originator of this fable was probably General Sickles, who tried to catch Jackson's rear guard as late as 1 P.M. Sickles had the most negative influence on Hooker, but Howard was dominated by the views of his superior general. Devens was the true shield bearer of his corps commander

Howard and believed what he believed. The division commander who recognized the danger, warned continually, and made every possible countermeasure permitted him by Howard, was Karl Schurz. He, along with Buschbeck, must be seen as the hero of 2 May. And yet no one was more savagely cursed by the West Pointers than Schurz.

* * *

At 4 P.M. Barlow's reserve brigade departed. Howard commanded General von Steinwehr to accompany the brigade to oversee its positioning. Howard himself rode a bit with it and only returned to his corps half an hour after the attack began. Steinwehr heard the shooting from around the XI Corps at about 5:30 P.M. and raced back, arriving on the field of battle as part of his Second Brigade, Buschbeck's, already stood in the trenches dug for Barlow's brigade. Von Steinwehr commanded that the the rest of his brigade pull back as well, and he gave Buschbeck autonomous command of the brigade during the battle.

* * *

The attack. About 5:20 P.M., firing began. The pickets returned to their units, and out of the forest rang the shrill war cry of the rebels. The first impact hit Devens' division, which had made no preparation at all to receive the enemy. Guns were stacked and soldiers were dispersed, reading newspapers, playing cards or preparing supper. This division had the worst positioning of all, standing on the public road leading through the thick bush. Only the road itself could be a gathering place, and it was immediately blocked. When the alarm came, the ambulances rushed back along the road, along with many teamsters with supply wagons, musical bands, cattle drovers and other non-combatants. The confusion of the troops can be imagined. Units of troops from all regiments were mixed together trying to organize on the road, but they were scattered by the wagons. Added to that were volleys from the west, and soon from the south. The two cannons standing on the road on the right wing of Devens' division were immediately taken over by enemy. The larger part of Devens' division was as good as defenseless, but the four regiments which were able to get to their weapons in time did fight bravely.

North of the road, in the midst of the woods, stood Brigadier General von Gilsa with his mostly German regiments, the 54th New York and the 153rd Pennsylvania. Gilsa had not obeyed the command of his division commander, Devens, and he had his thousand men together and ready for battle. He greeted the attackers with a volley of fire and brought the Confederate Rodes' division to a standstill. But the second line of attack, the Confederate Colston's division, pressed in behind, and at the same time Gilsa was flanked. He had to retreat. In the woods he encountered the 75th Ohio Regiment, and this fought alongside the remnants of von Gilsa's unit for ten minutes, which were very bloody. The 25th Ohio Regiment also gave some resistance. The other five regiments of Devens' division had to flee, for they could not assemble.

Behind Devens stood Schurz's division. His regiments, the 61st Ohio and the 74th Pennsylvania, were scattered by the rage of the refugees from Devens' units as they attempted to assemble on the road. But many soldiers of those two regiments were able to regroup with Buschbeck's brigade. At noon Schurz had managed to get permission from Howard to set three of his regiments—the 26th Wisconsin, the 58th New York and the 82nd Illinois—with their fronts toward the west. They stood on the north end of Hawkins Farm and were able to prepare themselves well to receive the enemy, who did not turn to them until about 6 P.M. They fought with great bravery and prevented the right flank from being pushed in earlier than it was. The Germans from Milwaukee, the 26th Wisconsin, lost 154 dead and wounded here from 650 men, and later a further 23 men.[5] The regiment fought valiantly and held back an attack by a force ten times its size for twenty minutes. It protected the extreme right flank.

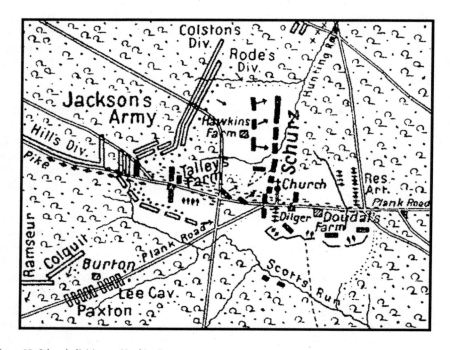

Figure 25. Schurz's division on Hawkins Farm.

General Schurz put his regiments—the 119th, 68th, and 157th New York and the 82nd Ohio, along with parts of the 61st Ohio and 74th Pennsylvania—into order near the road by the Wilderness Church. The 26th Wisconsin, 52nd, and 58th New York and the 82nd Illinois Regiments joined up. Hamlin estimates the number fighting under Schurz at 5000 men (certainly too high). Dilger's and Wiedrich's batteries were there. Here Colonel Peisner, of the 119th New York, fell; Hecker was shot in the hip, and his Major Rollshausen, of the 82nd Illinois, fell. Schurz's troops stood bravely and, according to Hamlin, fired twenty volleys. Then the enemy flanked them from the west and north, and Schurz had to order retreat. Schurz had luck yet again. The Confederate brigades of Ramseur and Colquitt had the order to proceed along the plank road that meets the highway at the Wilderness Church. These brigades were delayed a full hour, probably because they were lost in the Wilderness. It is only as a result of this accident that Schurz was able to show any resistance at all, for their appearance at the right time would have flanked Schurz's division and Buschbeck's brigade from the south a good hour earlier, and Schurz and Buschbeck would have fallen into the trap. But Colquitt's and Ramseur's brigades arrived at the crossroads so late that Buschbeck's Brigade still had time to put up a fine defensive fight.

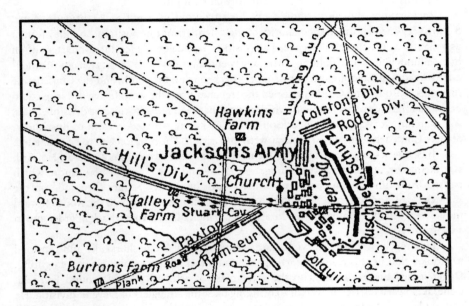

Figure 26. Buschbeck and Schurz in the Trenches.

The artillery also participated in the struggle of Schurz's division. Dilger's and Wiedrich's batteries were for a time able to hold back the advance of the enemy charging out of the woods into the open space in front of the church, and they gave powerful support to the infantry fighting. Dilger's cannons fired over the heads of the 82nd Illinois Regiment. Finally, even the artillery had to retreat. One of Dilger's six guns was lost because the horses had been shot.[6] For the same reason Wiedrich lost two cannons.

Buschbeck's fight. Buschbeck's brigade consisted of 1500 men; the three German regiments of the 29th New York, the 27th and 73rd Pennsylvania, along with the Anglo-American 157th New York. They were able to assemble before the primary blow of the enemy fell. When the enemy appeared, Buschbeck took to the trenches dug for the Barlow Brigade. Schurz's regiments—the 26th Wisconsin; the 82nd Illinois; the 82nd Ohio; and the 119th, 57th, and 58th New York, as well as parts of other units—gathered there, so that the trenches were held by about 3500 men when the fighting started at 6:30 P.M.[7] The entire artillery of the corps had been sent to the rear; only the tireless Dilger had brought up one of his cannons (there was no room to use a large number of cannons) and he directed this cannon himself. His canister fire had a dreadful effect.

The defensive fight Buschbeck and Schurz led here was the finest single deed at Chancellorsville and one of the best in the entire Civil War. Even commanding General Hooker, whose other statements about German soldiers are hard to outdo for falsehood, took off his hat before Buschbeck's brigade. Only corps commander General Warren did not want to recognize this deed. In front of the Congressional committee he declared that the resistance of Buschbeck's brigade was nothing worth mentioning!

Incidentally, this glory should not be attributed to Buschbeck's brigade alone. Schurz's regiments formed the majority of the defenders of this position, and they fought as valiantly as Buschbeck's brigade. The position was defended for three-quarters of an hour, although the actual fighting lasted only twenty minutes. Then, at 7:15 P.M., the Confederate brigades of Colquitt and Ramseur approached from the south, and the Confederate divisions of Rodes and Colston grasped the trenches from the west. In the distance could be seen a forest of enemy bayonets, which meant that even Jackson's reserve division, Hill's, was marching forward. So now Jackson had 20,000 men gathered in front of Buschbeck. Stuart's Confederate mounted artillery went into action. The position had to be evacuated.

Buschbeck's brigade returned to the main road in closed columns. Generals Howard, von Steinwehr, and Schurz went along, and at the end was Dilger's one cannon, which paused from time to time and sent canister into the enemy. Schurz then rode up the Bullock Road, and collected his regiments that had withdrawn through the woods toward the east. Late in the evening there were about 2300 men of his division back in order and in a secure location.

Buschbeck occupied Fairview, somewhat south of Chancellorsville, and reported to Hooker that he was ready to participate in an attack. But there was no more fighting. Dilger joined his five cannon to the great mass of artillery massed around Fairfield. General Howard restricted himself to bringing back the stragglers of Devens' division. He had not led, and he found no opportunity to do so, since the situation was such that each of the subordinates had to decide for himself.

Neither Buschbeck nor Schurz was seriously pursued. The enemy was completely exhausted. It must be recalled that Jackson's men had been on the march for sixteen hours, that they had had time neither to rest nor to cook, and that they also had to advance through the wilderness for two hours and then fight. At 7 P.M. only the reserve division, Hill's, was still intact. Almost all the other Confederate troops had dispersed, and it wasn't until 9 P.M. that Hill's division could reach the front.[8] Jackson was little satisfied with the success of the day. He had hoped to be able to take Chancellorsville during the evening hours and thus break Hooker's main position. He had also suffered heavy losses in his fight with the XI Corps.[9] When he rode out late in the evening to reconnoiter, the second-best man of the Confederacy was severely wounded by his own men in a North Carolina Regiment. In the dark the Confederate pickets mistook the riders for a Union patrol. Jackson died a few days later, an irreplaceable loss for the Confederate cause, a loss that was made manifest two months later at the Battle of Gettysburg.

* * *

The military accomplishment of the XI Corps on 2 May can be summarized as follows. About 6000 of the 8500 men were able to fight. Five regiments of Devens and two of Schurz were dispersed. Yet even from these units part were able to fight, as is the case with two companies of the Irish 61st Ohio Regiment, which protected Dilger through-out the entire fight. The fact that the corps was not able to fight as a unit is explained by the circumstances.

Hence the defensive fighting fell into smaller individual actions: 1. von Gilsa's encounter in the thickets; 2. the resistance of the 25th and 75th Ohio Regiments; 3. the fighting in the northwest of Hawkins Farm; and 4. the fighting of the main part of Schurz's division near the Wilderness Church and of Buschbeck's brigade and the remnant of Schurz's division in the trenches. Each of these individual actions was carried out with great dedication. And among the 6000 men who fought, almost two-thirds were Germans. It was certainly an accident, and the Anglo-Americans would have defended themselves as bravely as the German regiments had they been able to fight.

It must be stressed that not one man from the remaining 116,000 men in Hooker's army came to help the corps. The story told in so many war histories that Berry's division replaced the Germans and halted Jackson's advance is a fable. Berry did advance to help, but when Jackson halted to put his troops in order, about 7:45 P.M., there was still 700 yards of thick original forest between Jackson and Berry. The XI Corps fought entirely alone[10] against the fourfold superior force of the enemy which was under the leadership of the best fighting general of the Confederacy.

* * *

The main battle, 3 May. The main battle took place on Sunday, 3 May. The Union force was gathered about Chancellorsville with the exception of Reynolds' I Corps, Meade's V Corps, and Howard's XI Corps, which remained in reserve except for one division of the V Corps. On 3 May about 46,000 Confederates fought against 50,000 Union troops, for 37,000 of the Union force was not used! The hill of Hazel Grove was conceded by Hooker. This error was probably the main cause for the defeat of 3 May. From there the Northerners' first line, composed of Berry's, Williams' and Geary's divisions, were bombarded with artillery fire. At the same time, the concession of that hill permitted the unification of the previously divided Confederates. Lee knew well how to bring his masses to the most important points, while Hooker always failed to move his masses at the right moment. On 3 May Hooker almost appeared to be fighting for a retreat. Great confusion also reigned concerning the supply of munitions, and the artillery suffered greatly from that.

An enemy cannonball shattered a pillar of the Chancellor House. The pillar fell on Hooker and seriously injured him. The general staff was not present, and General Couch, the oldest corps commander by rank, could not immediately take command. So for a time there was no supreme command at all. When Couch did take over, he hesitated to use the large reserves, for Hooker had always held them back. Somewhat later, Hooker resumed command, although he was both mentally and physically incapacitated. Generals Reynolds and Meade literally begged him to let them lead up fresh troops, and even Howard wanted to put in his XII Corps, but Hooker refused. With the utter exhaustion of the enemy, who had put the last man into the fight, a solid advance using those 37,000 men would certainly have led to success. The fighting troops of the North—the II, III, XII and perhaps a quarter of the V Corps—were driven back to a second, then a strongly entrenched third line, while their comrades of the I, V and XI Corps had to watch the defeat.

Sedgwick's fight. Sedgwick's corps, on which Hooker had placed such great hopes, failed as well.

It was only noon on 3 May when Sedgwick drove Early's division from Marye's Heights, hence at the same time as the main fighting near Chancellorsville. Early fell back and found links to McLaws' and Anderson's Confederate divisions. Sedgwick followed slowly behind; when he finally advanced, he hit the enemy position at Salem Church (figure 22). Lee had separated McLaw's division and a brigade of Anderson's and sent it against Sedgwick. In combination with Early, these troops were almost as strong as Sedgwick himself, whose one division had already gone into bivouac without waiting for a command. Lee's cleverness at sending a part of his troops out of the main battle to act against Sedgwick, who was operating in Lee's rear, must be marvelled at, for Lee certainly knew that Hooker still had a strong reserve at his disposal. Evening was falling, and because Sedwick could not count on the division in bivouac, he gave up for the day any attempt to break through to Hooker.

On 4 May, Early had again occupied Marye's Heights through a clever maneuver. Sedgwick, who stood between Marye's Heights and Salem Church (see figure 22) now found himself between two fires. Hooker did not move at all on 4 May. Sedgwick was left on his own. About 6 A.M. on 4 May Lee, whose troops had rested a bit, went on the attack against Sedgwick. At the same time Early made a sally against Sedgwick from Marye's Heights. Taken in the middle, Sedgwick could only fight a retreat. He succeeded in getting to the two bridges built for this purpose across the Rappahannock, escaping in the night over the river with a loss of 4600 men.

Hooker held a council of war on the evening of 4 May. Of the six corps leaders, Reynolds and Slocum were not present. Meade and Howard advocated continuing the battle, while Sickles and Couch opposed. Hooker then decided for a retreat. Hooker later asserted that Meade and Howard also voted for it! The total losses of the North were certainly 18,000 men, those of the Confederates nearly 13,000.

* * *

Immediately after the retreat began the foundationless accusations against the Germans. Schurz protested in vain. He demanded that his own account of the battle be published, but he received the response that the publication of his report would take place only after Hooker and Howard had sent in their own reports. Hooker never approved an official report. And for that reason Schurz's report, vindicating the Germans, was never published.

Schurz then demanded to be placed before a court martial, for he had been the one most vilified. In response there was the courtly answer, "Not approved, for there lies no accusation against General Schurz." And Lincoln, the just, intimate friend of Schurz? He did not stir himself. Perhaps (one hopes) he thought, "It is better for the Germans to be scapegoats for a time than that the North lose hope in its ability to put down the rebellion." But there is also no statement from Lincoln at any later time to soften the humiliation of the Germans or to shift it onto those genuinely guilty.

In New York an indignant meeting was held of many thousands of people under the leadership of Friedrich Kapp, protesting the unmeasured insult against the Germans.[11] This demonstration was little regarded by non-Germans. But after Chancellorsville the flow of German volunteers into the army stagnated, and the enthusiasm of Germans for the war only returned after Gettysburg.

Great Union Victory at Gettysburg

Lee's second incursion into the North—The battle of encounter at Gettysburg, Pennsylvania—Steinwehr finds an advantageous position—Schurz as the commander of a corps—The mass struggles on Cemetery Ridge—Lee's great assault on 3 July repulsed—The weak pursuit of the enemy by Meade.

After Chancellorsville, the Southern people's certainty of victory rose without measure. That people demanded that the war be brought to the North. Another victory over the Army of the Potomac, but particularly the occupation of a great Northern city such as Philadelphia, would compel the North to peace and recognition of the Confederacy—so it was generally believed in the South. General Lee gave in to the desires of his compatriots only with misgivings. He well recognized the peril of going too far from his base, and the difficulty of maintaining his connections with Richmond, particularly being able to supply his army with munitions. But he held it to be pointless to promote these concerns. He bowed to popular opinion and acted in keeping with it. Longstreet's divisions were added to his, Richmond was virtually stripped of troops, and at the start of June Lee's army numbered 80,000 men.

Two successes of the Confederacy introduced this second sally into the North. In the largest cavalry battle of the Civil War at Brandy Station, 9 June, Pleasonton's Northern squadrons, 9000 horses, were pushed back across the Rappahannock. And soon afterward the Union General Milroy was defeated near Winchester. Through these encounters it was established that Lee's advance would once more be through the Shenandoah Valley.

Until the middle of June, the two main armies had faced one another on the Rappahannock near Fredericksburg. When the Southern army marched away, Hooker's Army of the Potomac naturally had to follow it. Although Hooker had a far shorter distance to cover, he only entered Frederick, Maryland, two days after Lee crossed the Potomac. Lee's army was divided into three corps under Ewell, A. P. Hill, and Longstreet. Ewell, who was now leading Jackson's forces, pressed rapidly ahead. As early as 23 June he occupied the Pennsylvanian town of Chambersburg, and on the 27th he was at the Susquehanna. Just as he was preparing to attack Harrisburg, the political capital of Pennsylvania, he received orders from Lee to retreat to Gettysburg.[12]

Ewell's rapid advance on Harrisburg shows that the Confederates really intended to surprise Philadelphia. Why was Ewell ordered back to Gettysburg?

General Lee had been in the dark for several days concerning the movements of his opponent. The splendid Confederate intelligence service failed precisely in enemy country. Lee had sent Stuart's cavalry, which otherwise went before his army, out on an extended expedition to spread terror in Pennsylvania, destroying the enemy's links with Washington and securing the Wrightsville bridge over the Susquehanna. Stuart was overextended, and his riders with completely exhausted horses did not return to Lee until the evening of the second day of battle in Gettysburg. Thus the Southern field commander only learned very late of the concentration of the Union army at Frederick. If Lee had then continued his advance into Pennsylvania, the Union army would have ended up in his rear, and it could have interrupted his connection with Richmond. Further, Lee's army was widely scattered on the 27th and needed to be gathered in the face of the enemy's march at

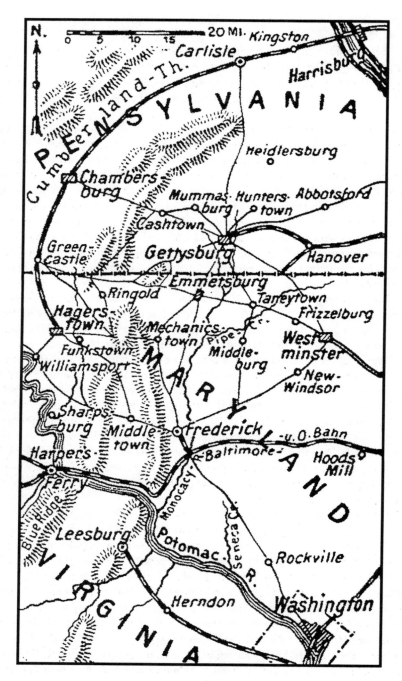

Figure 27. Gettysburg and environs.

Frederick. It was for this reason that Ewell was recalled. The enormous errors of Hooker's leadership at Chancellorsville had made Lee inordinately hopeful. He now had 80,000 men, the Union at the most 100,000 for a field battle. But at Chancellorsville, Lee had defeated a force twice his size with 60,000 men. Hence he believed that he could defeat the enemy anew anywhere, making an advance on Philadelphia much less dangerous. Lee did not go to Gettysburg in order to fight there, but because the excellent road connections made it the chosen place to gather the Confederate force.

* * *

At the same time important changes were being made in the Army of the Potomac. Halleck had long been dissatisfied with Hooker. When Hooker demanded that the 10,000 men in Harpers Ferry be sent to him, Halleck refused this request.[13] At that point, on 28 June, Hooker resigned. The resignation was promptly accepted, and General Meade became commander of the Army of the Potomac. Here was a change of command just before a decisive battle. But because Hooker's reputation had long since been undermined in the Army, the danger of the change was less. Through Meade's designation, climbing was put aside, and all generals willingly placed themselves at Meade's disposal. The new man was certainly no genius. His conduct before, during and particularly after the Battle of Gettysburg was everything but satisfactory. But he was the compromise general available.[14] He issued a modest proclamation and sought the advice of his subordinates. And besides, he had the luck to fall into a defensive position that he had never sought and against which the enemy assault would shatter.

* * *

The 29th and 30th of June were marching days for both armies. Meade, who wanted to fight at Pipe Creek, twenty miles south of Gettysburg, was moving his army north from Frederick, with Buford's Cavalry Division at its head. It entered Gettysburg at sundown on 1 July without any idea that Lee wished to gather there. But Buford was careful and occupied the heights west of Gettysburg, called Seminary Ridge, where the German Lutheran preachers' seminary was located. The I Corps of the Army of the Potomac advanced behind Buford. The XI Corps was within reach. Buford was hardly in position when the lead units of the large enemy army appeared before him. There was an extended fight with Heth's Confederate division. This fight took on a serious character when the Union I Corps appeared in Buford's position. Thus the first day of the Battle of Gettysburg developed as a *battle of encounter* desired by neither of the leaders. Whoever appears first at such an encounter has the advantage of a choice of location, and the fortunes of war threw this grace in the lap of the Northern army.

As early as 10 A.M. the entire I Corps stood under fire next to Buford. One of the first victims was the Union General Reynolds, then the leader of I, XI and III Corps. But the enemy also suffered considerably. Archer's Confederate brigade was captured.

About 12:30 P.M. the XI Corps under Howard arrived. General von Steinwehr, commander of the Second Division, immediately saw the importance of occupying *Cemetery Hill,* directly behind the town, and received permission from Howard to settle in there. This hill became the key to the Union position in the decisive battle of 2 and 3 July. Congress later praised Howard particularly for occupying this significant point, passing over von Steinwehr, who was the true discoverer of this position.[15]

As the oldest officer in rank, Howard took over the command of the I and XI Corps, and Schurz led the XI Corps in the battle.[16] Yet Schurz had only two divisions available, since Steinwehr's division remained behind on Cemetery Hill. The two divisions (under Schimmelpfennig and Barlow) took a position next to the I Corps in the open field north of town. Schurz's troops were very tired from their forced march under the July sun, but they advanced with great enthusiasm. But the enemy columns advanced with a fearsome superiority in force. At about 2 P.M., the Confederates had more than 30,000 men against barely 14,000 men of the I and XI Corps. The I Corps, 8500 men, fought Hill's Confederate corps, while the two divisions under Schurz, 5500 men, stood against Ewell's corps hence against the core of the troops once commanded by Jackson.[17] Two Confederate troops covered the left wing of the XI Corps with shots, and although one of these batteries was soon silenced by Dilger, the losses of the XI were still very heavy.

General Barlow, against Schurz's order, advanced von Gilsa's brigade even further, advancing so far with his entire division that he made it easy for the enemy to flank Schurz's right. Gilsa's brigade was completely isolated by this measure and soon was subjected to the attack of a force five times its size. Gilsa was overrun, and the connection between the two divisions and I Corps was loosened. The fighting of these 14,000 men, who stood in an open field without cover, had early on become pointless, for it was obvious that the superior numbers of the enemy were continually being increased. But Howard delayed ordering a retreat until the enemy had come so close to Schurz's division that the fighters could look into one another's eyes. Regiment stood against regiment in dreadfully close combat. Then finally, at 4 P.M., Schurz received the order to retreat, and at the same time Coster's brigade of Steinwehr's division appeared in front of the town to cover their retreat. Schurz's regiments had to retreat through Gettysburg to reach Cemetery Hill, with the overconfident enemy, certain of victory, on their heels. Many became lost in the streets and were captured.[18]

The remnant of Schurz's two divisions and of the I Corps were gathered on Cemetery Hill. During the evening hours the attack of the enemy was expected any moment. But the enemy did not move, because after all it was no longer commanded by Jackson. If an attack had taken place then, the important hill could have been taken easily. It was only at sundown that the XII Corps arrived and gave support and security to the men defeated in the first day of battle. In his memoirs, Schurz describes how he anxiously expected Ewell's advance out of Gettysburg in those evening hours. But Ewell did not think his soldiers could make the attack because they had been tired by their forced marches.

The defeat of the I and XI Corps on 1 July was a glorious Union success in the sense that the enemy was hindered from making use of the enormous superiority it then had. To be sure, if Stonewall Jackson, seven weeks in the grave, still had his old corps, the storming of Cemetery Hill would certainly have followed. Lee later asserted that he would have won an overwhelming victory at Gettysburg if Jackson had still been with him.

The position of the I and XI Corps before Gettysburg on 1 July was very poor. The troops stood much too far from their base at Gettysburg. This made retreat harder, and several thousand prisoners fell into the hands of the enemy. But no one could know that the *entire* enemy army was nearing Gettysburg, and that an encounter in the open field was entirely hopeless for the Union army. It should also be remarked that a single army corps of the secessionists was more than double the strength of a Union corps.

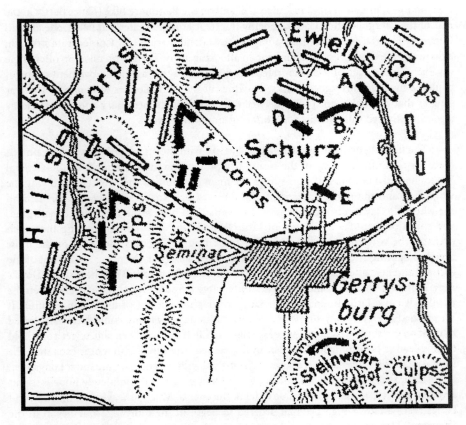

Figure 28. Gettysburg, the first Day. The XI Corps under Schurz; A. Von Gilsa's brigade: B. Ames' brigade;
C. Von Amsberg's brigade; D. Kzrzyzanowski's brigade; E. Coster's brigade of Steinwehr's division, which was to
cover Schurz's retreat. On Cemetery Hill the reserve: the remnant of Steinwehr's division.

* * *

On 2 July. The gathering of the Union army at Gettysburg took place more slowly
than that of the enemy. If Lee's forces had known this, the general attack of the Confederates would have taken place on the morning of 2 July, and it would have been against
Cemetery Hill. Luck was extraordinarily kind to the Union flag in those critical days.

Now a word about the position of the two armies. The Union army hung to its position on Cemetery Hill and its extensions. The land had a great similarity to a fishhook. At
the turn of the hook was the cemetery, occupied by the XI Corps, to the right of that was
Culp's Hill (XII Corps), directly behind the Cemetery was the extension, called Cemetery
Ridge (occupied by the I, II and III Corps and the V and VI Corps, which arrived later, in
reserve). The entire ridge ended with the hillocks Little Round Top and Round Top.

The enemy was posted on the opposing Seminary Ridge, with further extension of its
lines to the south, on Emmitsburg Road, as well as to the north in the town of Gettysburg

itself and west of that in front of Culp's Hill and on the Baltimore Pike (hence partly in the rear of the Union position). So the enemy traced a rather far-extended half-circle around Cemetery Hill. This had the disadvantage of considerably scattering Confederate strength, a disadvantage that is very troubling for an attacking army. The Union position offered the invaluable advantage of a concentrated distribution, so that a quick movement of forces could be made to threatened points. The lines of the Confederates were almost twice as long as that of the Union troops. Between the two heights, Seminary and Cemetery, lay a good, cultivated valley a mile wide, offering almost no cover.

* * *

The fighting on 2 July only began at 3:30 P.M. with the attack of Longstreet's Confederate corps on the left wing of the Union troops. Contrary to command, Union General Sickles had advanced his III Corps from the main position on the heights, occupying the wheatfield and the peach orchard on the Emmitsburg Road.[19] (See Figure 29.) Behind the wheatfield lay a confusion of steep rocks that had been given the name Devil's Den, and south of there lay the height of Little Round Top. This land, including the peach orchard, the wheatfield, Devil's Den and Little Round Top, was the scene of the most dreadful fighting at Gettysburg. Longstreet stormed against it, throwing Sickles out of the orchard and field after brave resistance. Then followed the dreadful butchery of the Devil's Den. This, too, was taken, and Wright's Confederate Brigade even threw itself between the Devil's Den and Little Round Top, breaking through the center of the Union position. If Wright had been strongly supported at this moment, the enemy could have established himself on the southern extensions of Cemetery Hill. If Lee had been able to get a foothold there, Meade's position could have been threatened by entirely different means than the frontal attack on 3 July. Lee was also very dissatisfied with the corps commander Longstreet. Longstreet, who saw the attack on the enemy left wing to be completely hopeless, sent several times to Lee asking to be able to flank the enemy. Much time was lost this way, and Longstreet's attack, which Lee had ordered to begin in the morning, only began in the afternoon. This was extraordinarily advantageous for the defenders at Gettysburg, so often favored by luck.

The advantages of the distribution of the Union troops really functioned in fighting off Longstreet. Meade could always send Sickles fresh troops and keep enough reserves in hand, while half of the Confederates never even got to fight. Lee ordered that Ewell's corps should attack the cemetery at the same time as Longstreet's attack on Sickles. But Ewell only began to attack when Longstreet had already been beaten back. Ewell's attack essentially threatened the XI and XII Corps (Cemetery and Culp's Hill), but the attack came too late. Meade was also able to move significant forces to his right wing, and Ewell was beaten back as well.

In this action several German regiments of the XI Corps particularly distinguished themselves, in particular the German Pole Krzyzanowski and his brigade accomplished great things, but many a compatriot bled there. At the beginning of the battle von Gilsa's German regiments, which stood on the side of Cemetery Hill and received the first impact of superior forces, were broken through and dispersed.[20] The enemy even pressed through all the way to the cannons of Wiedrich's battery, and the crews fought hand to hand, but they were cut loose by the brave 107th Ohio Regiment (Cleveland and Toledo Germans).

The 107th took the flag from a Texas regiment here. The 82nd Illinois and the 26th Wisconsin also fought splendidly here. On 2 and 3 July the German 52nd and 39th New York Regiments particularly distinguished themselves. More on these and other brave deeds of Germans at Gettysburg will be found in the biographical section.

* * *

Evening of 2 July. Meade actually could have congratulated himself. Two heavy attacks had been repulsed. But despite that, the commander had little faith in his position. He only gave into the unanimous opinion of his corps commanders that this was the position destined for a decisive battle, and for that reason had to be held.

And Lee? Would not it be assumed that he would avoid a general assault on this position? Longstreet's fight had cost tremendous sacrifice, and Ewell had suffered much as well. The Union army was now at last together, and its position was a very strong one. Lee, however, was fighting with his front to the south. If he were beaten, retreat would involve great difficulties. In such a case Lee would first have to go around the enemy in order to win the way of retreat to the South. And then the Potomac still lay between him and Virginia!

Lee's confidence in the invincibility of his troops and in the inability of the Union leadership was greater than his awareness of his own peril. His best troops, Pickett's Virginia division, had still not arrived. And besides, Johnson's Confederate division (of Ewell's corps) held an important position before Culp's Hill, hence in the enemy's rear. Wright's Confederate brigade had briefly broken through the center of the Northern army. If Pickett attacked on the east and Johnson on the west of Cemetery Ridge, victory could still be won. Lee permitted himself to be convinced by such arguments. This excessive self-confidence and this excessive undervaluation of the opponent continued even when Johnson's division was beaten on the morning of 3 July by the XII Union Corps and pushed out of its advantageous attack position against Culp's Hill.

Pickett's Confederate division finally arrived. These Virginia veterans were in the best mood for a fight. They demanded to decide the issue. So Lee remained firm in his fatal decision to have them attack the enemy position in the front and, through Ewell, on the right flank (hence against the cemetery). The most intense cannonade of the Civil War introduced this attack. Meade's cannons gave a strong reply at first, but bit by bit they ceased firing in order to convince the enemy that either they were out of munitions or that the Union artillery had been beaten down.

Lee's attack columns had a mile of open country to cross in order to reach the heights, occupied by the opponent. When the attackers came within fatal shooting distance of the Union artillery, more than a hundred cannons threw down an iron hail which mowed them down in masses. But the brave men charged on, and even the fire of the enemy artillery now opening up did not stop them. It was like the charge at Fredericksburg, except that some units of the Confederates managed to reach the plateau and sought to force a decision in hand-to-hand combat. But here there were ten Union soldiers for every Confederate. The Southerners were thrown back, and with that the greatest field battle of the Civil War was decided in favor of the Union.

The losses on the three days of battle were high. The Union army had 2834 dead, 13,709 wounded, 6643 "missing" (mostly prisoners). The Confederates had 2665 dead, 12,509 wounded, 7464 missing. Each of the armies lost more than a fourth of those fighting.[21]

There was no pursuit. It can be said that this was the opportunity to destroy the best field army, the true backbone of the entire Confederacy. But who is to decide how strongly shaken the Union troops were? Meade did have 20,000 fresh troops (French's, Couch's and Smith's divisions) nearby, and the Washington garrison could also have been used. But all moves of that sort were done in a very weak manner, and Lee[22] was fortunate to pass unmolested across the swollen Potomac. The North celebrated two victories, Gettysburg and at the same time Grant's great victory in Vicksburg. But although the South had the worst defeats it ever endured in both the East and the West, its enthusiasm for war did not diminish. Now begins the last period of the war, the fight of the South to the last man and the last cartridge.

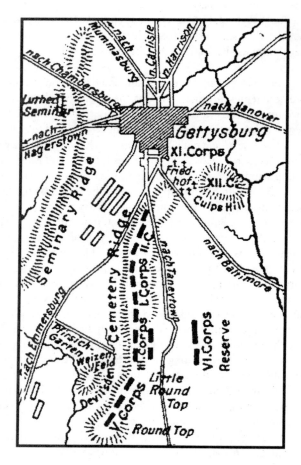

Figure 29. Storm on Cemetery Ridge, 3 July 1863.

* * *

The year of 1863 passed without any further decisions in the Eastern theater of war. In late fall the Army of the Potomac and Lee's army lay opposite each other on the Mine Run. There were hard fights and severe losses on both sides there, but it did not come to a decisive battle.

In the West, 1863

Vicksburg

Sherman's failed attack—Grant's struggle with swamp and water—The fleet steams past Vicksburg—Battle at Champion Hill—Siege and failed assault—Vicksburg capitulates on 3 July 1863. Salomon s victory at Helena. (See Figures 4 and 10.)

Vicksburg, the last great river fortress of the Confederates, was only weakly garrisoned in December 1862. General Pemberton, who commanded in the area, needed every man to defend against Grant, but his position was such that he could quickly fall back to Vicksburg. In the middle of December Sherman was sent forward with 30,000 men to take Vicksburg with a *coup de main* while Grant's task was to occupy Pemberton, preventing him from reinforcing the fortress in time. The plan fell apart. Grant had entrusted an entirely incapable officer, Colonel Murphy, with the guarding of a supply depot in Holly Springs. Murphy could easily have entrenched himself, but he did not do so, and one night Van Dorn's Confederate cavalry rode into the place, overpowered the sleeping garrison of 1000 men, took them and Murphy captive, robbed what of the provisions could be carried and set the rest on fire. Grant was stymied by this. Without provisions he could not proceed against Pemberton. Pemberton, however, threw himself and most of his men at once into Vicksburg. When Sherman, who had not heard of the attack on Holly Springs, tried to attack the Haines and Chickasaw Bluffs that dominate Vicksburg from the north, he found this position well defended.

Incidentally Sherman knew far too little about the difficulties he had to overcome, and because he had to act quickly, he could not find the right place for the attack. He charged directly through water, swamp, and long stretches of quicksand, and his troops were already finished when they reached the trenches. Despite all of this, Blair's brigade of Missourians managed to storm one of the trenches, but General Morgan did not support Blair and so the brave men were thrown back into the swamp. Many drowned, while others were killed by sharpshooters or the artillery. On 29 December Sherman lost 1800 men, of which half were captured. He saw at once the pointlessness of a further attack and withdrew to Arkansas Post. There were severe accusations raised against Sherman in the press, there were disputes among his subordinates, and a bad spirit ruled among his troops after that defeat. The earlier rumor that Sherman was insane came up again. It was only after Grant took up the long struggle for Vicksburg that it was recognized that Sherman had been given an assignment that could not be completed.

Sherman had to pass the supreme command to McClernand (the earlier partner of Lincoln), but he remained a corps commander in the army, which soon stormed Arkansas Post and took 5000 prisoners and 17 cannons. General Osterhaus, who had just been summoned from Missouri, was very honorably involved in this victory. Among the captives were many German Texans pressed into Confederate service, who opted at once for the Union and loyally followed the star-spangled banner. They had waited long enough for the moment when they could do their duty as citizens of the United States. Among the Union forces who beat the Confederates at Prairie Grove and Arkansas Post, pro-Union German Texans found almost as many German compatriots as there were Anglo-American fighters for the Union. We will only mention the German generals and regimental leaders who fought in these battles, which will determine the nationality of the troops they led.

General Osterhaus commanded a division, that is, three brigades, as did Brigadier General Friedrich Salomon and Colonel Adolph Engelmann. Colonel Ritter and Lieutenant Colonel Bertram each commanded a brigade. Among the regimental commanders we find Colonel Charles Salomon of the all-German 9th Wisconsin Regiment; Colonel W. F. Geiger; Lieutenant Colonel R. A. Peter; Colonel Otto Schadt; Colonel Hugo Wangelin, who led the

Osterhaus' old brigade; Colonel F. Hassendeubel; Colonel William Mungen; Major Lotha Lippert; Major Gustav Eberhardt; Major Charles Stephani; Colonel Simon P. Ohr, and finally our unforgettable poet, the Wisconsin colonel, the later General Konrad Krez. Batteries were commanded by the Germans J. W. Rabb, Hermann Borris, Frank Backof, Joseph Foust, Louis Hoffmann, C. Landgräber, and Gustav Stange. Thielemann's cavalry battalion was commanded by cavalry Captain Berthold Marschner. One of these German leaders, Colonel Hassendeubel, should be given special mention as one of the most important engineering officers of the Union army. He later fell before Vicksburg.

* * *

At the end of January 1863, General Grant gathered a large army in the area of Vicksburg. This town had already been made into a great fortress by nature. From twelve miles above Vicksburg until seven miles below it, the left bank of the Mississippi rises to steep heights of 200 to 300 feet. Vicksburg lies high above the river. This entire height was honeycombed with batteries which were placed so high that the heavy guns of the river fleet could not be directed there. Many thousands of Negroes worked for months to strengthen this natural fortification with trenchworks. Further, Vicksburg was extraordinarily well protected through the abundant waters of the area. Spreading out here was an indescribable confusion of old riverbeds of the Mississippi; of tributaries (on the left the Yazoo and Big Black Rivers, on the right but considerably south of Vicksburg, the mighty Red River); innumerable swampy areas; deep bayous; and lakes. This area cannot really be called land, but it is also not water. It is both at the same time, river and swamp, deep old riverbeds continually interchanging with higher-lying areas that are covered with rich plantations. Few steamboats had adequately shallow draft, and they were continually running aground in these perverse waters, which extended for hundreds of miles around.

Grant fought with the Mississippi and the swamps for three months. There, where Vicksburg lies, the great river makes a remarkable bend to the east, creating a sandy peninsula miles long. If this peninsula, 1.5 miles wide, could be cut through, part of the Mississippi would pass through the peninsula and Vicksburg could be avoided—as the engineers believed. Many thousands of soldiers dug for many weeks on this shortcut, living almost like amphibians. They were saturated with fever, and the number of victims was far greater than a great field battle would demand. When the canal was almost ready, there was a flood on the river and the entire work was destroyed. At the same time, Grant tried to create a new waterway through the confusion of lakes, bayous, and swamps that empty in the right bank of the Red River. The waterway would begin 100 miles above Vicksburg and would reach the mouth of the Red River, far to the south. A similar waterway alongside the Mississippi was sought on the left side of the river. The engineers completed marvels in water construction, and the soldiers defied death to wallow in the slimy mud. But the elements were more powerful than man. Vicksburg could not be taken from the water.

On 4 April, Grant decided on a new plan. The troops standing to the north of Vicksburg near Milliken's Bend were to march south along the right bank, work through the swamp area over sixty miles long. They would then be carried across the river to the left bank of the Mississippi, march north and arrive at the rear of Vicksburg. But how were these men to be transported? How were the transport steamers to pass Vicksburg, collect and carry the army to arrive in the south of the town? What would happen if the soldiers, stuck in the swamps of the transition area, had the good fortune to survive the march, but did not find any transports to cross the Mississippi at their landing places? Almost all of Grant's generals opposed this plan. Many declared he was insane and even Sherman, Grant's most loyal squire, protested against the plan's execution. But Grant was not to be moved. He knew he was betting the bank, but that he was for the commitment. It is unfortunately not possible to relate how he managed to convince his superiors in Washington of the chances for success for this plan.

The march through the swamps of the right bank was achieved after overcoming innumerable problems. On 6 April the army corps of McPherson and McClernand were set in motion, and on 29 April they stood in Hard Times (what a fitting name) on the right bank of the river, about thirty miles south of Vicksburg.

On the dark night of 16 April, three transport ships whose decks were crammed with cotton bales to protect them steamed down the river, accompanied by seven gunboats. Porter commanded this fleet. The ships soundlessly slipped down the river under the cover of the cypresses of the right bank. No light was burning. Soon they were before Vicksburg. Then there were flashes on the heights, and a dreadful rain of cannonballs greeted the fleet. They could not halt to return fire. Only speed and good luck could save the fleet. Each of the transport ships hauled a series of barges, for the troops must have provisions. The gunboats lay close to the transports in order to act as cannonball catchers. Only one of the large steamers was so damaged that it drifted rudderless down the river, soon going up in flames, but the gunboats took over the duty of hauling goods and rescued the heavily-loaded barges. The dare succeeded. On 26 April it was repeated, this time five transports with barges passing Vicksburg safely. The entire thing was a worthy companion to Farragut's running of the mouth of the Mississippi. Grant's reckless manner, shown in his later war leadership, won a fine triumph here.

Now there followed the siege of Vicksburg from the land side. Grant, reinforced by Sherman, had to march even farther from Hard Times to find a secure crossing opposite Rodney. Then the Union army passed to the northeast, across Rodney and Bruinsburg, roughly following the course of the Big Black River.[23] This was done with continuous fighting against the Confederate army of Pemberton, 30,000 men now isolated in Vicksburg, and the relief army approaching from the east under the command of General Joseph Johnston.[24] Grant, however, was stronger than both of his opponents, who were operating separately. The attempts by Pemberton and Johnston to catch Grant between them and grind him up failed, partly as a result of Pemberton's military inability. Pemberton's sallies from Vicksburg were carried out with little ability and were never coordinated with Johnston's advances.

Incidentally, Pemberton was disobedient to his superior, Johnston. Johnston saw that Vicksburg could not be held once Grant successfully advanced. He wanted to save the strong garrison of Vicksburg for field battles, and he ordered the evacuation of the place and a unification of Pemberton's 30,000 men with his own before Grant could insert himself between them. But Pemberton did not obey in time.[25] On 16 May, Grant struck against Johnston and against Pemberton's sallying troops at the same time. He chased Pemberton back into his fortress, and after that Johnston could only break off the engagement.

The Battle of Champion's Hill decided the fate of Vicksburg. Johnston alone could not do anything against Grant, and Pemberton suffered such a defeat that he could not dare another sally.[26]

Considerable effort had been expended even before that battle. But those preparations had not advanced nearly well enough when Grant ordered a general attack on Vicksburg on 22 May. This attack appears not to have been adequately prepared.[27] In any case, some units of the attacking columns did reach the enemy walls, but they could not maintain themselves there. The vanguard of Osterhaus's and Hovey's divisions of McClernand's corps came within 400 yards of the enemy's last trenches. McClernand interpreted that as meaning that his troops had taken two of the enemy forts. He reported this to Grant, which misled Grant to order the defeated troops of his other corps to advance in renewed attack. They were smashed back. The dreadful day cost the Union 2500 dead and wounded. The entire struggle over Vicksburg cost more than 10,000 men, not including the thousands who fell victim to illness.

When Grant ordered the attack, he had been inadequately informed about the strength of Joseph Johnston's army approaching in his rear. He still feared for his position between two fires. If Vicksburg could have been taken on 22 May, Grant would have had the opportunity to turn on Johnston at once and annihilate him. Grant said in extenuation, "My troops themselves were of the opinion that they could take Vicksburg then, and if the attack had not taken place they would not have worked with the same zeal in entrenching that they demonstrated after the failure of the attack." One could look for a long time in military history to find a lamer excuse for a failed gamble. Grant never concerned himself with the dominant opinion among his soldiers! Incidentally, in his memoirs Grant regretted having ordered this attack, as he did his attack on Cold Harbor in Virginia in June 1864.

Vicksburg was now completely enclosed. There was no more sign of Johnston, whose intervention Grant had so feared, and on 4 July 1863 Pemberton capitulated to Grant, essentially compelled by hunger. Of the 27,000 captives, only 15,000 men were still capable of service. Grant had to parole the captives, which had the effect that all of those still capable of fighting were immediately placed in the Confederate army.

On 8 July, the last river fortress, Port Hudson, fell, and with it the Mississippi finally ran along its entire course in the hands of the Union.[28]

On 4 July the German General Friedrich [Frederick] Salomon threw back an attack of 12,000 Confederates on Fort Helena in Arkansas in an outstanding manner.[29]

* * *

Immediately after the taking of Vicksburg, Sherman's corps moved against Johnston, beat him and took Jackson, the capital city of Mississippi.

Halleck also found himself among those congratulating Grant. But Halleck did not agree with Grant's plan to keep his large Vicksburg army together and lead it south to Mobile at once. On the contrary, Halleck did exactly what he had done after the taking of Corinth. He dispersed the army along the wide stretch between Arkansas and Chattanooga and sent Grant to support General Banks, operating on the Red River. That campaign had taken a very unfortunate turn. It was an adventurous expedition, in part against the intervention of Napoléon III in Mexico. When your own house is burning, it is no time to send the firemen to put out fires in other countries! The Red River Campaign also sprang from the brain of Halleck. Grant participated very little in it. He was thrown from his horse and lay ill for weeks. By then there occurred the dreadful defeat of Rosecrans at Chickamauga, 18–21 September, giving the war in the West a new turn, and Grant was named Rosecrans' successor.

The Great Battles of Chickamauga, Lookout Mountain and Missionary Ridge

Rosecrans at Chickamauga—Osterhaus on Lookout Mountain—Willich at Missionary Ridge. Steinwehr and Schurz at Wauhatchie. (See Figure 4.)

The enemy forces that had fought the Battle of Stones River at the turn of the year lay opposite one another for nearly six months, until the end of June 1863, in central Tennessee, Rosecrans in Murfreesboro and Bragg entrenched in Shelbyville, blocking his opponent's way to Chattanooga.

Rosecrans would not have been able to advance even without this hindrance. He had to be concerned about his lines of supply to provision his troops. The nimble cavalry hordes of Morgan, Forrest and Van Dorn swarmed about his position, racing through the entire country and destroying bridges and railroads. Rosecrans continually had to repair, and no sooner had he made a stretch of railroad usable again than the freebooters destroyed his painstakingly completed work again. He stood isolated in enemy country and could not move because of his lack of cavalry. His opponent Bragg sent many infantry brigades to his comrades Pemberton and Johnston, then being pressed by Grant in Vicksburg. Bragg did not need his foot troops at all, as long as his cavalry held the Army of the Cumberland in check.[30] Rosecrans telegraphed Washington, "Send me cavalry to fight the freebooters." But he received neither horse nor rider. Halleck, who was able to raise more than 12,000 cavalry for Hooker's completely bungled campaign to Chancellorsville, remained entirely negative to Rosecrans' requests. But Rosecrans had attracted the hatred of the supreme general.[31]

Rosecrans has been much maligned for his "inactivity" in the spring of 1863. But this inactivity was imposed on him. For culpability one must look to Washington.

Battle of Chickamauga. After the Union had brought the entire course of the Mississippi into its hands, the necessity arose to conquer eastern Tennessee and occupy the particularly strategically important town of Chattanooga. This town dominates access to the states of Alabama and Georgia. Chattanooga also guards against interventions from North Carolina. The city is the first station for the encirclement of Richmond from the west. From here Sherman's march through Georgia had its beginning the following year.

After the simultaneous Union victories of Vicksburg and Gettysburg, troops were liberated both in the West and in the Army of the Potomac to be used for the campaign against Chattanooga. A general advance of the Union armies toward eastern Tennessee began in the late summer of 1863. From the Army of the Potomac, 20,000 men under Burnside moved on Knoxville. Hooker[32] was supposed to join Rosecrans at Chattanooga with the XI and XII Corps.[33] But it took a fatally long time for these reinforcements to arrive. The reinforcements sent from Grant's army also arrived much too late. Sherman's corps had to be transported 400 miles by water and then march 400 miles right through

Tennessee, continually harassed by freebooters who broke all of Sherman's lines, destroyed all bridges, and the like.

The Confederates were far faster with their reinforcements. As a result of the slack pursuit by Meade after his victory at Gettysburg, Lee could easily do without a strong army corps in Virginia. So he had 20,000 veterans under Longstreet join Bragg, and these elite troops were the true victors of Chickamauga.

The main federal army against Chattanooga was the Army of the Cumberland under Rosecrans, eventually brought to 60,000 men. On 23 June it advanced from Murfreesboro to the southeast, compelling Bragg to leave his fortified position, and by the end of August the enemy army had been forced toward Chattanooga. Rosecrans now had the choice of following the enemy and besieging the town or going around it on the south, threatening Bragg's rear, enticing his opponent out of the town, and compelling him to a battle in the field. Rosecrans decided for this second plan, although it presented large and incalculable problems.[34] First of all, it was necessary to break through the foothills of the wild Cumberland Mountains, cross the Tennessee River, and then cross the chain of Raccoon and Lookout Mountains and Missionary Ridge in order to reach the valley of the Chickamauga Creek, southeast of Chattanooga. This flanking march is perhaps the boldest and most perilous undertaking of Union troops in the entire war. Rosecrans had to divide his army for this mountain march and have the individual corps advance on their own paths.[35]

Incidentally, Rosecrans cleverly misled his opponent. Bragg expected the enemy to march on Chattanooga by a route to the north, and he did not consider Rosecrans' deviation to the south at all. Further, the German-American General Wagner, who was sent toward Chattanooga with 2800 men, knew how to divide his little unit in such a way that Bragg saw Wagner's troops as the tip of Rosecrans' army. It was only after a considerable time that Bragg recognized the intention of his opponent. Bragg now evacuated Chattanooga (a move that he intended would be temporary) and marched into the western arm of the Chickamauga Creek, in order to catch Rosecrans' corps one by one as they descended the mountains. General Wagner, however, threw himself immediately into the abandoned town. So the star-spangled banner flew once more over Chattanooga. But Wagner could only hold the place with strong help. Bragg has been severely criticized for evacuating the town. He, however, was of the opinion that he would have had to leave two divisions there if he intended to hold it, and he did not wish to do without these two divisions in the coming battle.

Rosecrans managed to bring his army unmolested across the mountains and then into the valley of the Chickamauga. From there he believed he would be able to advance quickly over Rossville to Chattanooga before his enemy had concentrated. He still had to wait several days for McCook's corps, which had gone too far south, to join him. Bragg, however, used this pause to place himself in front of his opponent with 70,000 men and compel him to fight a decisive battle on terrain Bragg had chosen. Thus developed the Battle of Chickamauga, the most dreadful battle in the West, from 18 to 21 September 1863.

The area of the battlefield was very unfavorable for the use of the North's main weapon, artillery. It was a very heavily wooded plain penetrated by only a few cotton fields, from which a few hills rose. Rosecrans was far from finished concentrating his army when the enemy attacked. If Rosecrans had had only one more day, he could have taken the pass he already controlled via Rossville to Chattanooga. Thus the Northern field army had to

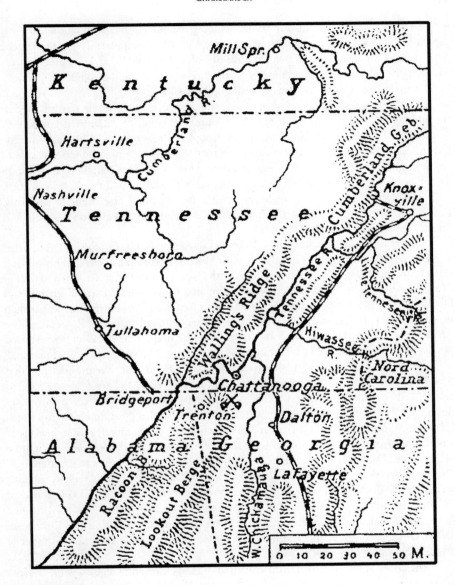

Figure 30. Chickamauga and environs.

force a march through under the most negative conditions. Rosecrans brought at the most 55,000 men into the fire, against 70,000 enemies. The Northern army was also extraordinarily widely spread. Unfortunately a wide gap was opened in this already loose position on the second day of the battle by a change of position of Wood's division, which was actually ordered by Rosecrans out of his misunderstanding the current battle situation. Into this gap pushed the elite troops of Longstreet, throwing back all counterattacks. Despite energetic defense (here the essentially German brigade of Colonel Laibold bled), Longstreet's forces rolled up the Northern army's right wing. Forty guns were lost and thousands of prisoners. What remained sought to save itself in a wild flight to Chattanooga.

Rosecrans was on the right wing at the time of this catastrophe. He was involved in the panic and carried away by it, fearing that his entire army would be annihilated. Longstreet's Confederate Corps stood between the Union troops of Rosecrans and Thomas. With the few thousand demoralized soldiers that Rosecrans still had with him, he was not able to cut through to Thomas. So there remained nothing but to ride for Chattanooga, gathering the refugees there and holding this asylum open in case Thomas also suffered a severe defeat.

Rosecrans should not be made responsible for the loose placement of his army. Rather it was his corps leader McCook, who, as was already said, swung too far south and for that reason arrived too late.[36]

Concerning Rosecrans, it should still be mentioned that he was (improperly) nominated as a Democratic presidential candidate against Lincoln in June 1864, and that his brother was a Catholic bishop. All of that, combined with Halleck's hostility, contributed to the fall of this general, whose deeds of war, when compared to the acts of Pope, Burnside, and Hooker, were genuinely great. Later historians have given Rosecrans much more justice than his contemporaries did. Sheridan, one of his division commanders, said of Rosecrans, "The Army of the Cumberland admired and loved its leader despite the dreadful blame raised against him after the Battle of Chickamauga by the press and the Washington headquarters."

The hero of Chickamauga is General Thomas. Garfield (later the president, at that time Rosecrans' chief of staff) reported to him that the rest of the army was as good as annihilated and that Thomas's 25,000 men would have to cut through a force more than double their own. Thomas gathered his troops together, took a position on the hill called Horseshoe Ridge, and fought there through the whole of 20 September, although a lack of ammunition soon arose. All attacks were thrown back with cold blood, and during the night Thomas was able to begin a heavily harassed retreat via Rossville to Chattanooga. The retreat was protected by Willich's brigade, which was able to capture five enemy cannons on the way. Willich's leadership on this retreat was generally admired. His German 32nd Indiana Regiment covered itself with glory there, as well as in the battle on Horseshoe Ridge. The finest laurels, however, were earned by the German Turner Regiment of Cincinnati, the 9th Ohio. This was the sole regiment that the taciturn Thomas mentioned with special praise in his report of the battle.[37]

The losses of the Northern army consisted of 15,853 men and 60 guns, while the loss of the enemy was certainly something under 12,000. The Confederates celebrated Chickamauga as their most splendid victory in the West. Yet Rosecrans achieved the purpose of his undertaking, which was to hold Chattanooga.

Chattanooga was now besieged by Bragg, and that brought the Northern army into dreadful want, for Bragg was able to isolate the town completely.

There swiftly followed the dismissal of General Rosecrans. His successor was first Thomas, then General Grant, who entered Chattanooga on 23 October. Things got better at once. Reinforcements arrived, the railroad to Nashville was back in operation, and more than a hundred steamers brought provisions, munitions and troops from the North. So Grant came with full hands, and it was not hard for him to create order. His fresh troops of the XI and XII Corps could establish themselves on the left bank of the Tennessee, and from there they could make the provisioning of the suffering Army of the Cumberland in Chattanooga possible. But the enemy did not delay an appearance. In the night of 28 October, Longstreet's Confederate veterans fell on Geary's division encamped near Wauhatchie below Chattanooga. Geary's troops defended themselves bravely, but because they had been surprised on a totally dark night, they were in great danger of being thrown into the Tennessee. The troops of Schurz and Steinwehr, who were camped nearby, rushed to help, and they managed to drive Longstreet off.[38]

As a result of the victory of Wauhatchie, the access roads to Chattanooga became completely open, and the half-starved soldiers of the Thomas Corps could finally be adequately cared for.

An entire month had to pass before Grant could gather enough reinforcements to move against the fortified heights of Chattanooga. During this pause attention was shifted completely to the difficulties of the Union corps of Burnside which had been sent to Knoxville. Knoxville lies seventy-five miles north of Chattanooga at the source of the Tennessee River. Nearby rise the Great Smoky Mountains, the highest part of the Appalachians, reaching 7000 feet. Slavery had never ruled in this part of Tennessee. The country people of that area were on a very low cultural level, but it was freedom loving and pro-Union. They had also suffered much under the conscription laws of the Confederacy, although never to the degree of the pro-Union Germans of Texas.

But the cries of trouble from eastern Tennessee found an easier hearing in Washington. Burnside's expedition essentially derived from Lincoln's soft heart. He wanted to show the old flag to the loyalists in Tennessee and prove to them that the Union had not forgotten them. But in military terms this expedition was stupid. Burnside was too weak to stage an offensive advance on Chattanooga. If the XI and XII Corps of the Army of the Potomac had been added to Burnside's troops at the right time, and above all such a force of about 35,000 men were placed under a capable soldier such as Hancock and located in Knoxville to lend Rosecrans a hand from there, the Battle of Chickamauga probably never would have been fought, and the entire Chattanooga campaign would have had a quicker and better ending. The loyalists of Tennessee also would have been helped far more by this.

At the end of October, Jefferson Davis visited Bragg's headquarters. He saw that the troops had nothing to do for the moment and ordered, over the heads of his generals, that Longstreet's corps march quickly to Knoxville to catch Burnside.[39] When it is recalled that Burnside was sent to Knoxville at Lincoln's desire, and that Longstreet also went there at Jefferson Davis's order, the Knoxville episode is a sort of duel of the two presidents. If Lincoln's advance in this case was stupid, so was the order decreed by Jefferson Davis, and to an even higher degree. This is because the protection of the Confederate positions around Chattanooga had a special need for the core troops of Longstreet, the Old Guard of the Confederacy. Also, as a result of the grouping of the heights to be defended, defensive lines had to be widely extended, and Bragg could not spare a man there. The attacks of Grant's masses on Lookout Mountain and Missionary Ridge would perhaps have had a different result, and the Union would certainly have lost twice as much blood, if Longstreet's soldiers had had to be overcome alongside Bragg's.

The Knoxville episode may be closed at once. After the Battle of Missionary Ridge (to be described hereafter), Sherman went with the XI and XII Corps to Knoxville and arrived just in time to save Burnside from disaster. Longstreet then withdrew across the mountains to Virginia. The march of Sherman's relieving force was certainly the most trying march Northern troops attempted in the whole of the war. (Read the chapter in question in Schurz's memoirs.)[40]

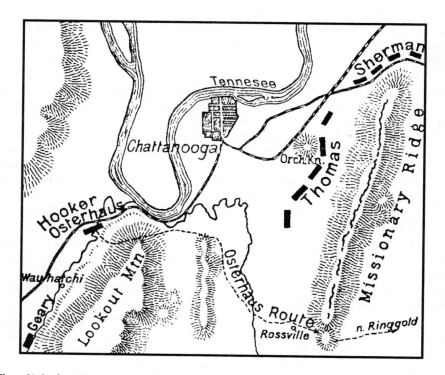

Figure 31. Lookout Mountain and Missionary Ridge.

Lookout Mountain and Missionary Ridge. It was the end of November before Grant felt strong enough to attack enemy positions before Chattanooga. The strongest of these was on a height called Missionary Ridge, which was 500 feet above the floor of the valley, very thickly wooded on top, and cut by deep hollows on the north side. The height is separated from Chattanooga by several miles of broad plain. Between the town and Missionary Ridge lies an extension, Orchard Knob. This was stormed by the Northerners on 23 November. August Willich's nine regiments particularly distinguished themselves there.[41] Orchard Knob served as Grant's headquarters throughout the battle itself.

* * *

As a result of accident, several of the most famous German officers of the Army of the Potomac met with their German comrades of the Western army on the battlefields around Chattanooga. Here we find Schurz, Buschbeck, Steinwehr, Krzyzanowski, and Hecker of the Army of the Potomac, and Osterhaus,[42] Wangelin, Willich, Laibold, Conrad and others of the Western forces. They were working, of course, in different corps, so that the German generals there did not meet together, although they fought alongside one another.

Several of the purely German elite regiments also participated in these glorious battles. The 45th New York under Major Koch; the 26th Wisconsin Regiment under Winkler; Hecker's 82nd Illinois Regiment under Edward Salomon; the 75th Pennsylvania under Colonel Ledig; the 58th New York under Isenbach; the 68th New York under von Steinhausen; Buschbeck's old regiment, the 27th Pennsylvania under Major Riedt; the 37th Ohio under von Blessing; Wiedrich's Battery from Buffalo; and of course Dilger's Battery J, Ohio Light Artillery (which was always there when there was fighting to be done), and Ohio Battery K from Dayton (Captain Nick. Sahm) all fought here together with Osterhaus's old brigade (the 3rd, 12th, and 17th Missouri Regiments, the 2nd and 15th Missouri Regiments of Laibold's primarily German brigade, under Sherman), with Kämmerling's 9th Ohio Regiment, and with Erdelmeyer's 32nd Indiana Regiment and German batteries from Missouri, Ohio, Illinois, and Indiana.

There were also many half-German regiments present in these struggles that cannot be listed. It is probable that the troops that won the splendid victories on Lookout Mountain and Missionary Ridge consisted of one-third Germans and German descendents. Yet here we only find a single purely German brigade, that of Wangelin under Osterhaus, as well as the half-German Laibold's brigade. Schurz commanded more non-German than German regiments, and there was only one purely German regiment, the 27th Pennsylvania, left in Steinwehr's entire division.

There were also only a few German regiments in Willich's large brigade, but the German element was very strong in all of them. Only two of Sheridan's six batteries had a non-German commander.

In the battles around Chattanooga, the troops fighting under German leaders were separated from their old associations. Thus Osterhaus exchanged roles with Schurz and Steinwehr. Osterhaus's division could not cross the Tennessee because the bridge there had been washed away, so Osterhaus was placed in Hooker's corps instead of with his old comrades in arms in Sherman's corps. Likewise Schurz and Steinwehr, previously under Hooker, reported to Sherman. For Osterhaus, this separation was a particularly good stroke of luck, for he gained the opportunity to bring about the finest deed of his career, the storming of Lookout Mountain, while Schurz and Steinwehr were little used.

Lookout Mountain and Missionary Ridge are two extended heights, running parallel and joined by Lookout Valley. Lookout Mountain lies south of Chattanooga adjoining the Tennessee River, and Missionary Ridge turns its face from the east toward the town. Lookout is 2600 feet high, while Missionary Ridge is 800 feet. Lookout had to be taken first, so that the advantage of a concentrated attack on Missionary Ridge could be obtained.

Battle on Lookout Mountain, the Battle Above the Clouds. On the evening of 23 November, General Osterhaus reported to General Hooker and received, in response to his request, the commission to attack Lookout Mountain the next morning. But the swollen Lookout Creek first had to be crossed. The pioneer company of the German 3rd Missouri Regiment under Captain Klostermann put a bridge across the river overnight, to Hooker's amazement, for he was not used to such prompt work. Osterhaus's division crossed this bridge to go on the attack, later followed by the division of the German-American General Grose. Geary's Division from XII Corps had to cross the river in its upper course to take the mountain.

Two distinct attack columns then advanced. Geary's men climbed the mountain several miles to the south, while Osterhaus stormed the heights nearer the town. The plan of attack called for assaulting the enemy from two sides and catching him in the middle. Both units were successful. In any case, there was no particularly strong resistance, for the enemy had to spread his forces in order to meet both Osterhaus and Geary. Longstreet's corps had once stood here, but it was now in Knoxville, and Bragg did not have men enough to hold both his widely separated positions.

The day was dark and rainy. The mountain was ringed with clouds halfway up. As a result, the movements of the attackers were shrouded. Misled about the strength of the enemy by mist and rain, the Confederates did not even make an attempt to hold the easily-defended rocky crown of the mountain, fleeing instead over the other side of the crest down into the Chattanooga valley. Toward evening the stars and stripes were raised over the pinnacle of the mountain.

Grant's headquarters could observe the course of the battle. Thomas's army, stationed before Chattanooga in the battle order, could also see the star-spangled banner high above the clouds that shrouded the main part of the mountain, and its appearance was greeted with a hurrah from 20,000 throats. When the flag went up, one person in Grant's company said, "That is a deed of 'Fighting Joe,'" using the nickname for Hooker. But Grant shook his head at that and said, "I don't think it's 'Fighting Joe,' I think it is Peter Joe," using the nickname for Osterhaus. And Grant was right. Peter Joe is far more the true hero of the Battle Above the Clouds than Hooker the corps commander. But Geary's division also had a full part in the honors of the day. Osterhaus lost 87 dead, 344 wounded, and 66 missing in this battle.

Early the next day the stormers of Lookout were in the opposite valley, that of the Chattanooga stream, with Osterhaus at their head. The bridge over the swollen brook had been destroyed. After an hour and a half, Klostermann had built a new bridge. The pursuers went on, chasing the rear guard of the enemy out of Rossville and getting a start on the second part of their mission, which was to climb Missionary Ridge from the south. Here they encountered only weak enemy troops, since their main force already was sufficiently occupied with Sherman and with Thomas. Osterhaus soon had 2800 captured secessionists in his care. But this accomplishment of the victor of Lookout already belongs to the Battle of Missionary Ridge.

Missionary Ridge. The attack on the north side of these heights by Sherman's corps began at the same moment as the Battle of Lookout Mountain, on 24 November.[43] This was intended to keep the enemy occupied on the north and win a good position for the mass attack of 25 November. But Sherman encountered great problems. A deep hollow on what was called Tunnel Hill, behind which batteries were hidden on the opposite cliffs of the mountain, could not be taken. During an entire day of 24 November there was bitter fighting here.

On the morning of the 25th, Grant sent two divisions, Schurz's and von Steinwehr's, to support Sherman, but of these troops only Buschbeck's brigade, which had served so splendidly at Chancellorsville, actually got to fight. Sherman praised Buschbeck's attack with expressions of enthusiasm. During the entire morning there was fighting over every hollow. Possession of these would have given Sherman the opportunity to reach the rear of the enemy and destroy the important bridge of the Chattanooga and Cleveland Railway across Chickamauga Creek, thus cutting off the sole supply line of the Confederate army. It was soon proved, however, that Missionary Ridge could not be taken from this side.

Bragg's position on the heights was extended over six miles. It was this overextension that was the weakness of an otherwise extraordinarily solid position. Bragg did not have troops enough to apply adequate power at every point of this long line. He had already thrown almost half of his army at Sherman, thus stripping his middle, and the south was conceded, which was where Osterhaus, Geary, and Grose were pressing. A very strong Confederate unit had to remain in front of Sherman, for Bragg was aware of the danger of the destruction of the railroad bridge. Sherman's corps was not directly involved in the taking of Missionary Ridge that now unfolded, but it contributed to the success by relieving Thomas's army. Missionary Ridge was taken by essentially the same troops who had been beaten at Chickamauga under Rosecrans. Their attack came from three sides, with Sherman in the north, Osterhaus and Geary in the south, Thomas in the center.

At 2:30 P.M. the 20,000 men of Thomas's Army of the Cumberland who had been stationed behind Orchard Knob began to advance. Grant had commanded that only the protective chain at the foot of the mountain should be taken, and that the attackers should then await further orders. The attack proceeded with great precision. In the first ranks stood Sheridan's and Wood's divisions, where most of the Germans were found. Old Willich commanded one of Wood's brigades (nine regiments). He passed through an open field in the face of the enemy, who fired with terrible effect from trenches at the approaching masses, but the Union forces did not return fire. The enemy's protective chain at the base of the mountain was overrun. The Union troops were supposed to remain standing there, but they *could not* remain, for the enemy fire was intolerable. Willich's brigade was the most exposed. The old hero did not want to go back, and he is not *supposed* to go forward. "Oh well," he told himself, "they can put me before a court martial, I'm going forward." And a few minutes later Willich's regiments were climbing toward the cliffs, clear of woods but beset by rocks. When soldiers of Wood's and Sheridan's neighboring Brigades see this, they do the same without awaiting a command.[44] Before the commanders of the regiments or brigades could grasp the situation, their men had already advanced far up the hill.

Grant stood on Orchard Knob. His field glass told him that the main attack is under way. He turned to Thomas, asking, "Did you order that?" "Not I," he answered, and then added dryly, "That is certainly a trick of old Willich, or at least it looks very much like one."

Higher and higher the 20,000 came to the crest. Halfway up was the enemy's second line of defense. This was also taken by storm. Now it might be seen from Orchard Knob how Bragg was moving his regiments in masses, fighting Sherman to protect his threatened center. But before this help arrived, the blues were already on top. The defense line at the top of Missionary Ridge was broken in six places. After the battle Sheridan's soldiers disputed with Willich's for the honor of having been first on top.[45] Who pulls his watch out of his pocket at such a moment and establishes the moment of the first breakthrough? But with this non-commanded attack by Thomas' army, the battle was decided. Geary's and Osterhaus's columns soon arrive from the south with their vanguards, and Thomas's army victoriously controlled the middle.

There was still a brief, terrible fight in the woods, then the enemy withdrew over the eastern cliffs of the heights, fully broken.[46] On Sherman's wing the movements of Thomas' troops in the center and the storming of the heights were not even seen. The troops there sensed considerable relief, but they had no idea that Thomas had already done the main work and that Bragg was utterly defeated. It was only in the evening that Sherman learned of his comrades' splendid victory.

Bragg lost 9000 men, including 6100 captured, Grant about 7000 dead and wounded. Bragg could no longer be protected by Jefferson Davis, and he was soon removed. General Joseph E. Johnston took his place.

A pursuit of Bragg by the whole of Grant's army could not take place, because Grant had to send Sherman's corps and Schurz's and von Steinwehr's divisions at once to Knoxville to rescue Burnside from the claws of Longstreet.[47] Because the enemy had to flee southward, it fell primarily to Osterhaus's and Geary's divisions to pursue. Osterhaus was once more in the vanguard. At Ringgold, already across the border in Georgia, he encountered the strong remnant of Bragg's army. He attacked at once, although his artillery was still far behind. He was certainly counting on the cooperation of Geary's division, but it arrived late, and Osterhaus had to rely on his own infantry alone. Wangelin's brigade, which consisted of the four German regiments of the 3rd, 12th, and 17th Missouri and the 44th Ohio, had the honor of the first attack. There developed a terrific fight. Colonel von Wangelin lost an arm; Major Ledergerber was severely wounded; and his brother, Captain Joseph Ledergerber, fell. The brigade suffered terrible losses, and general mourning prevailed in St. Louis and Belleville after this battle.[48] The enemy occupied a pass between two hills, and they could not be expelled from this position by infantry alone. Only when the artillery finally arrived, Landgräber's and Wölfle's riding batteries, could the enemy position be shaken and the enemy beaten.

* * *

Through the victories around Chattanooga, Tennessee was completely conquered. At New Years Day 1864, Union troops dominated the whole of Tennessee and prepared for a march into Georgia. This march would make Sherman's name immortal and was probably the finest deed of the Union in the entire war. Other than Hood's later intervention into Tennessee, thrown back by Thomas, the large-scale war was over in the West with the taking of Chattanooga. Thus Sherman's penetration of Georgia was in fact part of the operations aimed at overcoming Lee's main army of the Confederacy.

The End of the War, 1864–65
Grant's Anaconda Plan

In the spring of 1864, General Grant was named supreme field commander of all the armies of the United States and decorated with the title of lieutenant general, an honor which had only been bestowed on the immortal Washington. At this time the Union had at its disposal 534,000 men, of which more than 100,000 were widely scattered, and about an equal number consisted of very new recruits who would only later be sent to the field armies. Field troops in existence were:

In central Virginia was the Army of the Potomac, 125,000 men, under General Meade. In addition there was the IX Corps under Burnside, 25,000 men. Further there was Sigel's force, initially 24,000 men, in the Shenandoah Valley. Then there was Butler's force, originally 31,000, men on the Peninsula in the immediate vicinity of Richmond. Altogether more than 200,000 men could be used in the Eastern theater of war in Virginia.

In addition there was the large Western army. After Grant's transfer to the East, it stood under Sherman's command at Chattanooga, Tennessee, and numbered 100,000 men capable of being put immediately into the field. An important force, perhaps 57,000 more men, stood in the gulf states under Banks. These were gradually withdrawn and distributed in large part to the Western field army. The same happened with the 28,000 men standing in Missouri and Arkansas.

The Confederacy only had 243,000 men to oppose to these armies, after having made the most extreme exertions to fill the army. Many older men and boys of 16 had already been pressed into service. Almost half of the Confederate troops stood against detached units of the Union army, mostly in the Southwest, or were retained as garrisons. The two largest armies of the Union, under Grant and Sherman, could only be opposed by the 61,000 men under Lee in Virginia and perhaps the same number under Johnston in the West. In addition there were about 15,000 men in the Shenandoah Valley and in Richmond. The scattered corps of the Confederacy were later pulled in and added to the two field armies, which happened on the part of the Union as well.

This last great campaign falls into two parts, of which we will only speak of what relates to the great theaters of war in the East and in the West.

Lieutenant General Grant appeared with a grandiose plan, called the Anaconda Plan. This was the proposition that Lee's army be worn down by repeated battles, called hammer blows by Grant, and Richmond then be taken. For this purpose Grant designated four armies: the Army of the Potomac, with the Burnside Corps, 150,000 men; Sigel's army in the Shenandoah Valley, 24,000 men; Butler's army on the James River, 31,000 men (later 37,000); and Sherman's 100,000 men, who were to make a great flanking march from the far west all the way east to Richmond. All four armies were to go on the attack at the same time, in the first days of May 1864. Of these, only Sherman's army had any really great success.

We will concern ourselves first of all with the mission received by General Franz Sigel, emerged once again from obscurity.

Sigel's Defeat at New Market
(See Figure 14.)

Lincoln was asked by Sigel's influential Forty-Eighter friends to give the German general another command. The president also declared that Sigel's appointment was due partly to his nationality.[49]

Sigel was to keep the Shenandoah Valley free of enemy troop concentrations and hinder the delivery of provisions and munitions from that rich, large district to General Lee, then fighting against Grant's main army in the Wilderness. Numerous passes led out of the Shenandoah Valley across the Blue Ridge Mountains. If the valley remained in enemy hands, then Lee would have a strong base of support there. Sigel's army numbered on paper 32,061 men with 86 cannons, but in fact only 24,000 men were made available. But even before Sigel went into action, General Grant changed the war plan approved for the Shenandoah Valley. He took away most of the troops approved for the expedition and expected Sigel with 7000 men to complete a mission for which 24,000 men had originally been planned, and for which 50,000 men had to be mobilized under Sheridan to accomplish, once Sigel proved unable to do the impossible. Grant commanded that Sigel at once send General Crook with 10,000 men to the far southwest of the valley, and General Averell with 2000 men to another end of the valley. Sigel had to leave behind another 5000 men to defend the Baltimore and Ohio Railroad, so that from the entire army there remained only 7000 men. Hence the 24,000 men were divided into unequal units that stood many days' march from one another. The main part of the train for all 24,000 men remained with Sigel, and supplies from this store had to be sent to the two expeditions of Crook and Averell, almost a hundred miles away. As a result, when Sigel went down the valley from Martinsburg and Winchester, he had to bring with him 200 wagons of provisions. The roads had been turned into mudbaths through the continual rains, the wagons could only move forward slowly, and the troops were tied to the pace of the wagons, so that Sigel's advance was extremely slow. The ability to fight was considerably reduced by the supply train that was taken along.

Sigel set out from Winchester on 1 May, passing through the old German settlements of Kernstown, Middletown, and Strasburg to Woodstock, where he arrived on 10 May. In Strasburg the telegraphic correspondence of the two Confederate generals operating against him, Breckinridge and Imboden, fell into Sigel's hands. These told him that the enemy was well informed of his movements and were trying to meet him with forces that were at least equal. Further the correspondence announced Grant's first defeat against Lee in the Wilderness, as well as the expectation of the Confederates that Sigel would cross one of the passes of the Blue Ridge Mountains to aid Grant.

In order to protect his further advance against surprises, Sigel sent out 500 cavalry on 13 May to secure his right flank and 200 cavalry to protect his left. Both units struck the enemy and were beaten by troops of General Imboden. Sigel could conclude from this only that Imboden stood before him, but he was completely in the dark about Breckinridge's position. A Negro told him that Breckinridge was marching in the same direction as Sigel, up the valley. That could have been true, for it was possible that Breckinridge had turned against Crook. Sigel could not prevent Breckinridge and Imboden from uniting.

Imboden reported that he was in continuous peril from 12 to 15 May of being overrun by Sigel, and that it was only Sigel's great caution and slowness which prevent a duel between the two forces. This assertion is clearly without any justification. Imboden's troop consisted of 1600 cavalry and mounted artillery, a mobile group that could easily avoid Sigel. The skirmish Imboden had on 13 and 14 May against Sigel's vanguard under Moor proves that Imboden was entirely aware of his advantages over Sigel's heavy-footed troops, hindered by their enormous wagon train. On the 14th, Imboden waged an intermittent skirmish, withdrawing slowly in the face of Moor. Imboden could do this for days, withdrawing from Sigel and approaching his comrade Breckinridge. The inevitable battle did not have to be fought in New Market, but could just as well have been fought several days farther south in the valley, as far as the interests of the Confederates were concerned.

These details are necessary because Sigel's many enemies in the Northern officer corps based their criticism on Imboden's unjustified statements and raise against Sigel the accusation that through excessive caution and slowness he passed up the opportunity to render Imboden harmless. The fact that Breckinridge only met Imboden a few hours before the Battle of New Market was then used as a further proof of Sigel's slowness. But all of these accusations are unjustified. Sigel's slow progress was due to his wagon train and the bottomless roads. His measures against attacks were justified, too.

On 13 May Sigel sent his brigadier, Colonel August Moor, with two regiments of infantry and 500 cavalry out for reconnaissance. Moor at once encountered Imboden's vanguard at Mount Jackson and pressed the enemy back across the Shenandoah, occupying the bridge and pursuing him to the vicinity of New Market. Let us now listen to Sigel (*Battles and Leaders*, Century Edition, vol. 6, p. 481):

> This success [of Moor] and the news that Breckinridge was marching up the valley led me to call Moor back on 15 May, at 5 A.M. Moor reported to me at 10 A.M. that he was in a good position. I decided to hold the enemy until the arrival of our main force, and then to take up fighting. I had 5000 men in infantry and artillery and 1000 cavalry. I estimated Breckinridge at 5500 men infantry and and 2000 cavalry. [From this should it be inferred that Sigel learned of the uniting of Breckinridge and Imboden shortly before the battle? —WK] I rode close to New Market with Captain Alexander and Major Meysenburg, and I saw that all the troops could not be put into position before the place. So I ordered Moor slowly to give up his position and take up a new position on the road to Mount Jackson, three-quarters of a mile north.

This change of position was a good measure, to be sure, but it would have been even better if Sigel had moved not three-quarters of a mile but three miles north of New Market and taken a position somewhere by Rude's Hill. Then the positioning could have been made more peacefully and better preparations made, and Sigel's two infantry regiments that did not take part in the battle would have been able to participate. Sigel's troops had to form from a marching column 1.5 miles long. The soldiers had already marched for seven hours on roads covered knee-deep in mud, and it was raining in streams. Under such conditions, collecting and placing troops is a very difficult matter. A position even farther to the north would have given the Northern army at least an hour's more time to get control of such circumstances. Particularly, however, the two Ohio regiments that formed the rear guard with the wagons would have had time to unite with the majority of their comrades. Sigel blames his defeat primarily on the fact that the 28th and 116th Ohio Regiments did not participate.[50]

Sigel's infantry stood under the command of General Sullivan, with the two brigades commanded by Colonels Thoburn and Moor. Sigel's cavalry of about 1000 men was commanded by General Julius Stahel. But General Sullivan did not even take part in the battle. He was with the Ohio demi-brigade at least three miles to the rear.

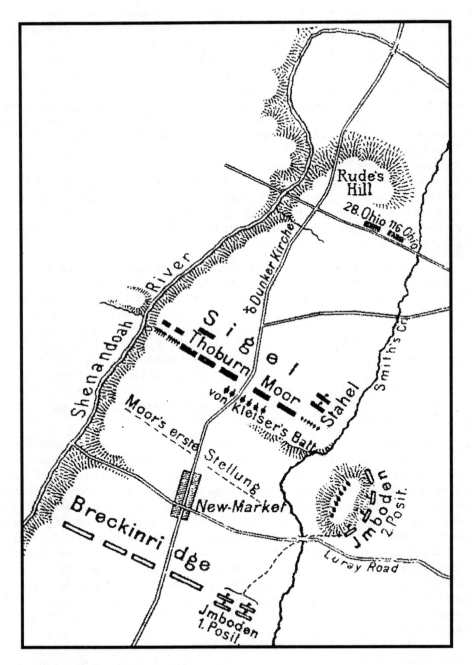

Figure 32. Battle of New Market.

It is clear from Sigel's description that he was surprised. Sigel had not yet finished placing his troops when the attack began. It must be assumed that Sigel had only just ordered the placing of his right wing and center, and it appears very unlikely that Sigel had even inspected his left wing yet. In his battle report, Sigel speaks only of the fighting of the right wing and the center. When portraying the battle on Sigel's left wing one is forced to rely on Imboden's description in *Battles and Leaders,* vol. 4, p. 480. Sigel says virtually nothing about his left wing, yet the fighting started there and it was essentially through the turning of the left wing that the battle was lost. Here is where the two Ohio regiments should have been. In front of Sigel's left wing was a wood that was not occupied by Northern troops, and off to the left of Sigel's left wing stood a very important hill that received no attention. Also overlooked was the hollow running from Smith's Creek directly across Sigel's left wing. This was without a doubt a result of the lack of time, and to that degree one may speak of a surprise of the Northern force. Not only did the left wing lack two of the best regiments, but the land in front offered the enemy, who knew the area precisely, many advantages for attack, and these were excellently exploited.

First of all we want to hear what Sigel has to say about the non-participation of the two Ohio regiments under Sullivan. "At the time I ordered Moor to draw back three-quarters of a mile to our newly chosen main position, I sent two adjutants to General Sullivan with the order for him to bring all his troops forward. When Moor had taken the new position, Captain Prendergast reported to me that all of Sullivan's infantry and artillery had arrived, that their vanguard was within sight, and they were awaiting orders. I assumed that Prendergast's report was based on the truth . . ." (Here follows the description of the placement of the center and right wing which can be seen on the map). "I myself led the placement of the right wing and wanted to see whether all of my troops were in the positions I had ordered, when my attention was diverted by the appearance of the enemy, whose lines appeared on the hill northwest of New Market (opposite our front)."

Here we certainly have a statement by Sigel that the left wing had not even been inspected. Sigel does not even appear to have known that the two regiments were not in line until the battle was well under way. He mentions missing these 1200 men only when describing his retreat, when he halted at the Dunkard Church, three-quarters of a mile behind the battlefield, at about 3 P.M. He says, "Here we noticed dark lines on Rude's Hill. It was our 28th and 116th Ohio regiments that had unfortunately not been with us in the battle." That is all Sigel says about it. He has not a word of criticism against General Sullivan and the two regimental leaders. Nor does he say anything about the reason for the remarkable delay of these regiments, which at 3 P.M., when they were still almost three miles back on Rude's Hill, should at least have been able to reach the Dunkard Church. Someone must bear the responsibility for this inexplicable slowness! How Captain Prendergast came to announce the arrival of these regiments before noon is also never explained. Sigel probably would have pulled back farther if he could have known that he would have to fight without those 1200 men, almost a quarter of his infantry.

* * *

The Confederate force that went against Sigel was an elite troop. Breckinridge's infantry consisted of veterans who had been in the field without interruption for three years; the artillery (only twelve guns against Sigel's twenty-two) was well served; and

Imboden's cavalry was trained to fight as infantry, which is how most of them served in the battle, while Sigel's cavalry only participated on horseback and could hardly participate in the battle at all. Breckinridge and Imboden together had at their disposal about 5000 men, while Sigel only had 5150 of his 6500 men in place. But since Sigel's 1000 cavalry were as good as excluded from the battle, the enemy had the advantage of both better-trained troops and the number of troops brought into use. Almost half of Sigel's infantry consisted of young recruits who had originally been destined for the defense of the Baltimore and Ohio Railroad. The Confederates had every available man in place, including even cadets of the Virginia Military Academy, 225 half-grown boys aged 16 and 17. These boys fought with great spirit, and they suffered severe losses in capturing two enemy guns.

We now come to a portrayal of the battle. First of all we will follow the description of the Confederate General Imboden on the turning of Sigel's left wing.

Imboden rode into the woods that extended to the right of New Market, finding them unoccupied and securing a position by placing pickets. He could see Sigel's left wing from the northern border of this wood. The whole Northern cavalry was set up there in battle order. Imboden now marched to the bridge of Luray Road across Smith's Creek with the 62nd Virginia Cavalry Regiment, serving as infantry; the cadets; and his mounted cavalry; and McClanahan's battery. There he occupied a hill about 100 feet high that lay on the line of Sigel's left wing, without his advance being remarked by the enemy. Suddenly he stood in an excellent position, less than 1000 yards from Sigel's cavalry.

The Confederate battery fired with dreadful effect into the masses of riders and horses, and the surprised enemy, as Imboden said, "did the best that could be done under the circumstances, which was to flee." This ended the participation of the Northern cavalry in the battle.[51] A Northern battery under Ewing, which was located next to the departed cavalry, then exchanged a few shots with Imboden's McClanahan battery, but it soon ceased fire. At this moment Breckinridge's infantry pressed against Sigel's center and right wing.

Imboden goes on to say:

> In front of Sigel's center and left wing stood an enemy battery [von Kleyser's] that gave us extraordinarily much trouble. Breckinridge ordered us to attack this battery, and this mission fell to the 62nd Virginia [Cavalry] Regiment and the cadets. Three hundred yards before the von Kleyser Battery there was a hollow extending from Smith's Creek, which gave our attacking column some cover. But the three minutes it took to go from that hollow to the cannons were dreadful. The cadets were first to the guns, whose crews defended themselves bravely.[52] The cadets lost 8 dead and 46 wounded in this attack; my Virginia regiment of 550 men had 241 dead and wounded; and of its ten captains, 4 fell and 3 were severely wounded. More than half of all of our losses at New Market came from that attack.[53]

It may be seen from this portrayal that Sigel's entire left wing was pushed in. The two infantry regiments placed there helped fight against Breckinridge,[54] while the cavalry was driven away right at the start. No more is said of Ewing's four cannon, which responded to McClanahan's fire at the beginning of the fighting.

We now turn to Sigel's portrayal of the fighting on his right wing and center:

Our pickets fell back, and the fire was opened by our right battery (Snow). I ordered the 34th Massachusetts Regiment to kneel down and to fire sequentially when the enemy approached. There set in a severe half-hour exchange at close range. The enemy was thrown back several times by our fire. The gun smoke was so thick that I had trouble distinguishing friend from foe. The enemy broke forward, this time against our batteries. Lieutenant Chalfant of Carlin's battery rode to me and reported that he could not hold his position. I ordered two companies of the 12th West Virginia Regiment to advance to protect the battery, but despite all threats and urgings these soldiers would not move. I then decided on a counterattack of my entire right wing to rescue the guns. Thoburn's brigade advanced with fixed bayonets in a splendid manner, but it fell into dreadful close-range fire and was thrown back. Before this attack took place, our entire left wing had already been turned and two guns of von Kleyser taken by the enemy, and the enemy had Thoburn's brigade from the flank and rear.[55] After Thoburn's brigade returned from their failed attack, the enemy once more threw himself on our batteries of the right wing, and I saw that these would be lost, for many from the crews and many of the horses of the batteries had fallen. I ordered the batteries to withdraw slowly and by piece. Suddenly Captain Carlin, the chief of our artillery, rushed back, and all of his men followed him with their cannons in great haste. Because some of the horses of two guns had been killed, these two cannons had to be left behind. Now our entire position became untenable, and the infantry withdrew and was pursued for a short stretch. On the retreat we lost one more gun, because its horses could not be brought through a creek. In trying to save this gun, I was almost taken captive. We collected about three-quarters of a mile to the rear, by the Dunkard Church, and soon the troop was in the best order. The enemy did not bother us, and after half an hour our retreat to Rude's Hill was continued and we reunited with Sullivan's two Ohio regiments.

Sigel now goes on to describe how the enemy followed and opened an ineffectual artillery fire on the position on Rude's Hill, and how he [Sigel] resumed the retreat to Mount Jackson after a time. There he wanted to wait for reinforcements, which were under way, as he knew. Sigel's losses at New Market were 93 dead, 552 wounded, and 186 captured. He lost five of his cannons. The enemy gave its losses in dead and wounded at 564.

Sigel heaps extraordinary praise on part of his troops. He says, "No one ever fought better than the 34th Massachusetts, 1st West Virginia and 54th Pennsylvania Regiments (Thoburn's Brigade) at New Market. Their losses were respectively 202, 55, and 132 men. For that reason I have no doubt that the battle would have turned out differently if the two missing Ohio regiments had supported us at the right time."

The fact that a part of his troops were of low quality emerges from one of Sigel's footnotes. He says there:

Through a circumstance that is very difficult for me to relate, I was compelled to remain in my exposed position on the right wing. I wanted to ride to the left wing to see what was happening there. So I rode out of the smoke to a position where I could overlook the battlefield. When I did that, the companies that lay behind the batteries rose up and began following me (that is, they also retreated). I turned about and led the men back to their position and remained with them. Despite the dangerous position, it appeared almost comic to me that a major general commanding a department and an army was compelled to serve as a guard. Then came the attack, and I passed my orders from the right wing. This unpleasant episode hindered me from fulfilling an important duty.—FS.

If General Sigel had not told this strange story himself, one could not have taken it seriously. Those two companies that followed Sigel without orders and then had to be watched by their general were the same cowards who refused to move when ordered to protect the batteries. Such a herd of mutton is entirely worthless for protecting a battery, and if it were necessary to place a guard in order to hold these West Virginians in place, then the commanding general certainly did not have to take over this office, for, as Sigel himself says, he had important duties to fulfill.

Sigel was removed by Grant as early as 19 May and General Hunter put in his place. Sigel then served under Hunter, but he was only concerned with the northern end of the Shenandoah Valley. He had no more battles, but through his very well-executed occupation of Maryland Heights (opposite Harpers Ferry on the Potomac) he held up the Confederate General Early for several days in his later advance on Washington. He compelled Early to go around Sigel's position. In this way Early's overrunning of Washington was probably hindered in as effective a manner as by the Battle of Monocacy against General Wallace, in which Early remained the victor. It was only as a result of that double delay of Early that Grant was able to bring up enough troops in time to defend the capital city.

Through the Wilderness to Cold Harbor

Evaluation of Grant—His defeats in the Wilderness, Spotsylvania and Cold Harbor—Grant slips continually eastwards—He sacrifices a third of his large army.

In large parts of the American Northern people, Grant is regarded as a great field commander, even the savior of the Union. His fame in war brought him the presidency, a result that one can only regret, both in the interests of the country and in General Grant's own interest. A part of his fame must certainly be due to the fact that the Union is seeking to reduce the well-deserved reputation of the Confederate supreme leader. Hence the "conqueror of Lee" is celebrated in the North as the greater of the two. It is certainly wrong to see Grant as Lee's conqueror or as the conqueror of the South. The rebellion was not put down by any individual, and certainly not by the general who suffered only defeats in all of his field battles with Lee, but by the powerful superior force and inexhaustible resources of the North. The South's destiny was already sealed by the simultaneous defeats of Gettysburg and Vicksburg at the start of July 1863. From those days forward the South continued fighting for the honor of fighting, or better said out of pride, and in this it completely bled to death.

General Grant had the remarkable good fortune to be able to act in all his greater operations with powerfully superior force. That was the case at Vicksburg and Missionary

Ridge, in the last hard struggles in the Wilderness, and at Richmond. Where forces were equal, as at Shiloh, Grant failed completely, and the victory of Missionary Ridge was actually accomplished by his subordinates. When Grant's war deeds during the year of 1864 are compared with the contemporary accomplishments of his comrade Sherman, one has to attribute to Sherman the greater glory. For Sherman achieved significantly more through capable maneuvering and sparing his forces than Grant achieved in that period in Virginia. Through his pushing, Grant sacrificed a third of the largest army the Union had raised in the entire war, and yet he was compelled during this entire campaign from the Wilderness to Cold Harbor to retreat in the face of an enemy half as strong.[56] Even his plans for this campaign of hammer blows can hardly be described as intelligent. He expected Sigel with 7000 men to carry out a maneuver for which he had appropriated 24,000 men and for which almost 50,000 men under Sheridan would prove necessary. Further, the fact that he chose the political general Butler to carry out the maneuver before Richmond, despite the fact that the Army of the Potomac had several quite capable and experienced officers who could have carried out the mission much better, is certainly no proof of Grant's gifts as a great field commander.[57]

Despite this, the naming of Grant as commander of the armies of the Union was a proper measure. The position of the leader of the Army of the Potomac, General Meade, had been considerably shaken. Meade's quarrelsome nature had created for him a series of enemies in the circle of high officers. These did not obey him with the necessary good cheer, and Meade was certainly not the man for the powerful offensive that the war situation then demanded. The corps commanders and division commanders of the Army of the Potomac had confidence in Grant, and they obeyed him happily and willingly. A better spirit also entered the army with Grant's naming. He revived trust in the supreme leadership, and this mood continued even after the first severe defeats in the Wilderness. It survived the gross butchery of Cold Harbor. Even the negative influence of Halleck was considerably weakened by Grant taking over command. To be sure, Halleck remained as chief of general staff and Lincoln's military advisor, as before. General Meade also remained in command of the Army of the Potomac, because since the supreme commander was with this army, the result was that all important orders were composed by Grant. All that remained for Meade was to serve as a sort of chief of general staff.

Grant was of the certainly erroneous opinion that the fighting strength of the Army of the Potomac had never been properly exploited. This view dramatically intensified his inclination, corresponding to his whole nature, to be a reckless daredevil.

During the night from 3 to 4 May 1864, he crossed over the Rapidan River from Culpeper via Germanna and Ely Fords and by doing so entered the Wilderness. He believed he could slip past Lee's position with a rapid advance and reach the freer field in the area of Spotsylvania Courthouse without a battle. Nothing could have been more welcome to Lee than his opponent's entering an area in which Confederate troops were at home, and which so well corresponded to their way of fighting. Lee's position lay along the Mine Run to the Rapidan. After the arrival of Longstreet's corps, the confederate commander had at his disposal 62,000 men. These soldiers were the elite of the Southern army, veterans who had fought on many battlefields and almost always won. On figure 33 may be seen the marching route of Grant's army from Culpeper through the Wilderness, via Spotsylvania, and on to Hanover Junction, Hanovertown on the Pamunkey River, and the last battlefield of Cold Harbor, before the fortifications of Richmond.

* * *

Lee threw himself against the marching column of Grant's right flank on the afternoon of 5 May with the intention of breaking through, isolating a large part of Grant's army, and then destroying this part. He did not entirely achieve this aim, essentially because the march of Longstreet's Confederate corps was too long (more than sixty miles). Despite splendid feats of marching, it arrived too late. The fighting cannot be described here; a brief sketch of it would not advance understanding, and an extensive description does not

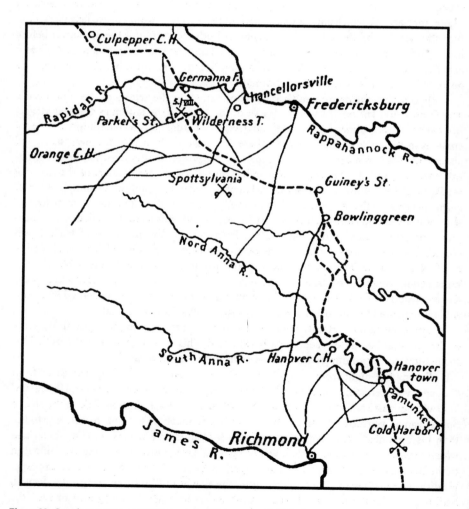

Figure 33. Grant's campaign of 1864 through the Wilderness to Cold Harbor.

correspond to our purpose. It was a dreadful struggle in the bush, a fight in which unified leadership often failed on the Confederate side as well. Grant lost 15,000 men in the three days from 5 to 8 May, while the enemy certainly lost barely half of that, although information on this is unclear. Only infantry could participate in this. Both forces improvised trenches. It was a battle of individual brigades and divisions with one another. The woods caught fire, and many hundreds of wounded fell victim to the flames and terrible smoke of the green wood. Often friend and foe were confused for one another. Whole regiments got lost, were cut off, and found themselves in enemy territory. Yet the troops did not achieve peace; hungry and completely exhausted they were compelled to fight on.

The loss of higher-ranking officers on both sides was considerable in the Wilderness battles and their continuation in Spotsylvania. The Union corps leader Sedgwick was shot to death. The Confederate corps leader Longstreet, like his comrade Jackson a year earlier at Chancellorsville, was so badly wounded by his own soldiers that he had to resign, and the splendid Confederate cavalry commander Jeb Stuart lost his life somewhat later.

Grant moved eastwards on 8 May in order to concentrate at Spotsylvania Courthouse. But Lee had foreseen this movement and received his enemy there in a strong defensive position. Spotsylvania lies somewhat on the edge of the Wilderness, about ten English miles from Parker's Store. Here there are some open fields, but most of the battles that followed were once again battles in the woods, just as in the Wilderness itself. The Northern corps commander Hancock managed to break through the enemy position with a truly heroic attack at the Bloody Angle, and took an entire Confederate division prisoner. But the advantage could not be used, due to the lack of reserves. There was fighting here until 20 May, and Grant once more lost 18,000 men.

There was no compelling reason for Grant to continue the fighting at Spotsylvania. The terrain had few advantages for the attacker, and the experiences in the Wilderness itself would rather have inclined him to find another place to fight. But Grant may have feared that further movement to the southeast would be interpreted as a retreat, and the impression would be created that he had suffered a severe defeat on 5, 6, and 7 May. So he challenged the fortunes of war once more, only to be compelled to move east again after ten further days.

Lee possessed the great advantage of interior lines, which is, his troops had the shortest distance to the points where the they could encounter the enemy. When Grant shifted once more to the east on 20 May, to Guiney's Station, Lee could figure in advance that he would meet his enemy again in a few days at Hanover Junction on the North Anna River, for Grant was bound to the roads leading to Richmond. On 25 May Grant found the entire enemy army at Hanover Junction ready for battle in a secure position. This time the Northern general avoided an attack and continued his march in a southeasterly direction. But he again lost several thousand men probing the strength of the enemy position.

This time Grant went rather far to the left, following the course of the Pamunke River. For the fourth time, the Northern army encountered an entrenched position of the enemy on the little Totopotomoy River, and there developed battles of position that demanded severe sacrifices. On 28 May Grant crossed the Pamunkey. He was only fifteen English miles from Richmond. He had drawn Smith's corps from Butler's Army of the James, thus roughly making up for the losses of the previous eight days. But there was also concern about feeding his troops, for the fleet could not supply him with all he needed from nearby White House, on the navigable York River.

In this position Grant decided to make another attempt to break through the Confederate army. The enemy had moved farther to the right and for the fifth time laid a trap for the Union Army, at Cold Harbor. It is truly marvelous with what rapidity and intelligence the Confederate engineers were repeatedly able to build new trenches. Lee's position was one of extraordinary strength. Grant ordered a mass attack on the position of Cold Harbor for 3 June. This fatal storm could not be adequately prepared because Grant had sent away his extensive heavy artillery in order to be able to advance more rapidly. The Northern troops were also tired from the forced marches and the entrenchment work imposed on them. It was hard to get to the enemy. Lee's left flank was protected by an uncrossable swamp, while his right flank was protected by the Chickahominy and the outrunners of the defenses of Richmond. Thus it was impossible to encircle the enemy, and all that remained was a frontal attack. The Union masses stormed against the parapets with great courage, but the cross-fire of the enemy batteries smashed the attackers to the ground. That attack cost 6000 brave soldiers, and it failed completely. Lee's losses were insignificant.

After this severe defeat, Grant decided to work his way closer to the enemy with spades. There followed terrible days for the troops. The many dead could not be buried. An almost intolerable stench of corpses poisoned the air. There was a cease-fire only on 7 June to bury the dead. Until 13 June Grant persisted in his position, although he must have decided as a result of the failed attack on 13 June to move the operations to the southern bank of the James River, between Richmond and Petersburg. The preparations for the move show this clearly. The soldiers sickened by the thousands of malaria on the same ground on which McClellan had fought two years before. Grant's losses from 28 May to 10 June amounted to more than 13,000 men, while Lee lost barely 4000 in the same time. Lee's total losses since the beginning of the fight with Grant cannot be precisely established, but they could not have run more than about 22,000, while Grant (without the losses due to illness) lost about 50,000 on the battlefields. In addition, the Confederate army had been considerably strengthened though reinforcements, and at the time when Lee moved on Richmond it was back to about 60,000 men.

There was fighting during the march of Grant's army straight across the Peninsula to the position prepared by Butler's army, Bermuda Hundred, south of Richmond. But there were no more real battles. Grant had to be satisfied with forcing his great opponent into the fortress of Richmond. Yet Lee was not really shut up in Richmond, as we shall see.

Butler's failed operation. On 5 May, General Butler disembarked with about 37,000 men at the mouth of the Appomattox River's junction with the James. From there he was to advance on the nearby fortified cities of Richmond and Petersburg. At the time of his arrival there were only 6000 enemy under the leadership of General Beauregard in widely scattered works. But the politician Butler let the right time for attack pass. Beauregard rapidly brought in reinforcements, and by the middle of May he could oppose his enemy with 22,000 men. Butler's attacks were made with little intensity, and Beauregard finally succeeded in fixing his opponent within his fortifications at Bermuda Hundred. The entire advantage achieved by the Butler expedition consisted of preparing a secure position to receive Grant's army and sending Smith's corps, 16,000 men, to support Grant at Cold

Harbor. If a Sheridan or a Hancock had commanded in Butler's place at the start of May, Richmond would probably have fallen then.

The German cavalry General Kautz participated in the Butler operation with 3000 men, and through his clever and successful raids many of the access roads to Richmond were destroyed.

Early's Penetration to Washington

Lee fell back on Richmond after his victory at Cold Harbor because the strength of troops in that city did not permit holding the place when Grant's great army arrived to besiege it. Yet the Southern commander still had more troops in Richmond than he needed to defend it. He also hoped from a powerful offensive to have a positive impression on the increasingly troublesome turn of public opinion in the South. So he sent Early's corps of 17,000 men, soon brought to 20,000 by reinforcements, out of Richmond at the end of June and into the Shenandoah Valley, which was then open. Early at first was only to protect Lynchburg, but he also had an order to advance to the north in case conditions for it were good. Early's adventurous sensibility saw the second part of his mission as the chief purpose of the operation, and thus the *third* invasion of the North by a Confederate army took place. Early believed he could overrun Washington, and he almost succeeded.

Early went rapidly down the Shenandoah Valley. At its exit he encountered three German generals: Sigel had 4000 men, Max Weber had 800, and Stahel with 1500 cavalry, but whose horses were almost exhausted. These weak forces could of course not *defeat* Early, but they did *delay* the enemy for four days. That meant a *great* deal when it is recalled that the reinforcements Grant sent to Washington from Bermuda Hundred only arrived at the very moment when Early was about to attack the federal capital.

Sigel stood at Martinsburg. Early believed he could easily neutralize his small garrison, and he tried to surround him. But Sigel cleverly pulled back on Harpers Ferry after calling in Weber and Stahel. On the heights above the town he took a strong position of defense. Early halted before this position; he did not want to expose himself to Sigel's cannon and felt himself compelled to seek a crossing of the Potomac at Sherpherdstown, behind Harpers Ferry. Through this and through his effort at Martinsburg, Early lost almost four days. Sigel's troops only experienced a skirmish between pickets with Early at Leestown.

Early now had to pass over South Mountain to win the marching route to Washington, although he would have had a shorter route over Harpers Ferry. Lew Wallace, the poet, threw himself at Early on the Monocacy on 9 July. There was an intense, bloody fight, but Early's superior force won out. On 11 July Early's forces stood *within sight of the Capitol.* Only *five* more miles to Washington! It was at that moment that the troops ordered from the Peninsula by Grant arrived. Early, who was far too weak for a successful *coup de main,* was checked by this. But without Early's delays at Martinsburg, Harpers Ferry and on the Monocacy, he could certainly have achieved a temporary success. The encouragement in the South can be imagined if the flag of rebellion had waved over the Capitol in Washington, if only for a few days! There followed a small skirmish before Washington, and Early began his retreat in the night of 12 July.

Pursuit was given in such a stupid manner that Early found the courage to make a second invasion, this time into Pennsylvania. His cavalry general, McCausland, took Chambersburg. When the citizens were unwilling to pay $100,000 in gold at once, arson torches were thrown into the helpless open town.

There followed Sheridan's campaign of devastation through the Shenandoah Valley. Early was beaten by Sheridan at Winchester, Fishers Hill and Cedar Creek, but it was winter before the complete dissolution of the last Confederate field army in Virginia. Then Sheridan came before Petersburg, extended his hand to Grant, and effectively assisted in the final catastrophe.

The Siege of Richmond

Bermuda Hundred is a peninsula formed by a twist of the James River ten miles south of Richmond and six miles north of Petersburg. These two towns formed a connected Confederate fortress whose key was Petersburg, where many railroads and roads from the south come together. Grant and Butler built a new fortress at Bermuda opposite that of the Confederates, protected and provisioned by the Union fleet and James River. It was from this fortified Union position that works were extended, particularly toward Petersburg, which was the chief goal of attack. There were repeated assaults, the most important being the Battle of the Crater, so called because of a crater in the enemy works of Petersburg created by an enormous mine explosion. But all these attacks failed. Grant remained before Richmond for ten months. The position was only taken when the impact of Sherman's victorious march came; when Hood's Western rebel army was annihilated at Nashville; when Sheridan's victory in the Shedandoah Valley had smashed Early's field army; and when the secession, dreadfully injured by all these blows of fate, was breathing its last.

Sherman's Great Flanking March

From Chattanooga to Atlanta—From Atlanta to the Atlantic Ocean—A triumph of the Western Army—Thomas beats Hood at Nashville. Sherman's march through Georgia, South Carolina, and North Carolina—Sherman close to Richmond.

At the same time when Grant was attacking Lee, at the start of May, 1864, Sherman left Chattanooga for Atlanta, Georgia. Between Grant's and Sherman's armies lay 500 miles as the crow flies, so that direct cooperation between them lay in the distant future. Yet the Western theater of war was no longer a thing in its own right. The circle had been drawn much narrower, and the need to provide an equal commander to act against the powerful Sherman certainly hindered the delivery of Confederate reinforcements to Richmond.

According to Sherman's figures, his army numbered 98,797 men and 254 guns. These were divided into the Army of the Cumberland (Thomas, 60,000 men), the Army of the Tennessee (McPherson, 25,000), and the Army of the Ohio (Schofield, 13,500 men). Sherman's opponent Johnston opposed these armies with 60,000 men, and although Johnston received considerable reinforcements, they were mostly of low quality. General Joseph E. Johnston was a formidable field commander. He had been the first chief commander of the South, although he had been compelled to resign in the summer of 1862 due to severe wounds.

The soldier material of Sherman's army was excellent. It consisted of men from the West, and there was a predominance of veterans. These troops had seen their enemy's backs far more often than had their comrades in the Army of the Potomac. On the banners of the Western army were inscribed the glorious days at Fort Donelson, Vicksburg, Nashville, Stones River, Lookout Mountain and Missionary Ridge, and the Western troops could look on their defeats without shame. The army was enthused with the best spirit, the soldiers had confidence in their leader, and the campaign had been excellently prepared.

There was only one German brigade to be found in Sherman's army, that of Wangelin. Its regiments were the 3rd, 12th and 17th Missouri and the 44th Illinois, later joined by the 76th Illinois. Only a small band of the old German leaders accompanied the victorious campaign through Georgia. Willich was severely wounded in the first battle and was incapable of service, Schurz had gone into politics at Lincoln's urging, and von Steinwehr had resigned. Even Hecker only served for a short time longer. But the tireless Osterhaus was still fresh in the saddle. He first commanded a division of the XV Corps, and in Atlanta he took Logan's place as leader of the entire XV Corps. The heroic Buschbeck also took part in this campaign, and Wangelin, now with one arm, left only after the principal battles. Dilger had come to the West with the XI Corps, and now he fought with Sherman's army to the end of the war. Those two German champions, Conrad and Laibold, led brigades. There was added Winkler from Wisconsin, colonel of the brave 26th from Milwaukee. The two Salomons, General Friedrich [Frederick] Salomon and his brother, Colonel Eberhard Salomon, had won laurels west of the Mississippi. Wetzel and Kautz fought under Grant before Richmond; Schimmelpfennig stood before Charleston; Sigel, once again emerged from obscurity, was involved in his thankless mission in the Shenandoah Valley, with Weber and Stahel fighting at his side. But it was only granted to the last of these to distinguish himself and to conclude his active career as a warrior with a glorious deed in the Piedmont.

It has already been emphasized that a third of Sherman's army was probably composed of Germans and the descendents of Germans. That corresponds to the strength of Germans in the West and the continued enthusiasm for the war all the way until the end of the conflict. Still, this cannot be proven, for the old German units had vanished or had been loosened too much. The most Germans were to be found in the XV and XX Corps, the latter being created out of the amalgamation of the earlier XI and XII Corps.

Fighting commenced immediately after the march out of Chattanooga, but Sherman's campaign was run in an entirely different manner from Grant's. He did not seek to overcome his enemy through "hammer blows." He chose, wherever possible, to go around or flank his opponent, and through that means he achieved, step by step, the slow pressing back of Johnston. Johnston was still challenging Sherman to battle at Dalton, but Sherman went around the enemy. Only at Reseca was there intense fighting, which brought each side losses of about 3000 men. Sherman pressed his enemy further back on Adairsville, Kingston, Cassville, and then Allatoona. That was already three-quarters of the way to Atlanta.

The peculiar thing about this war of position, made up of about a hundred large and small skirmishes and battles, was the importance of the railroad for each of the two armies. Sherman depended on the one-way railroad from Chattanooga, and Johnston on the southern end of that same line for his connections with Atlanta. Control of that railroad was of greater importance for Sherman, who stood in enemy country. Moreover, his lines soon became the longer, and because the Confederate cavalry was considerably superior to the Northern, and certainly better led, destruction of the railroad was often a greater concern to Sherman than the enemy attacks on his army. But Sherman had excellent pioneers and engineers with him, As often as the railroad was destroyed, it was as often (and as swiftly) brought back into use. Sherman's rapidity in repair of railroads and bridges often drove Johnston to distraction.[58]

An outrunner of the long chain of the Alleghenies, known as Kennesaw Mountain, lies between Allatoona and Atlanta. Here Johnston had a carefully prepared defensive position, favored by the lay of the land. Sherman, however, swerved to the right, left the railroad and marched in a broad bow toward Dallas. On 27 and 28 May there was severe fighting (in which Osterhaus's division distinguished itself). The battle, which brought each party losses of about 3000 men, remained indecisive. After a few days Johnston returned to his position on the Kennesaw Mountain. Sherman followed him, and there now developed encounters in the days between 3 and 28 June which culminated in Sherman's storming of the Kennesaw Mountain (27 June). Here Sherman experienced the sole defeat of his entire campaign. This was due to his variation from the tactics pursued up until then. His attacking columns were thrown back with a loss of 4000 men (Johnston lost only 650 men). Then Sherman moved his army slowly around Kennesaw Mountain, finally compelling Johnston to evacuate this position as well. Sherman's important success was made possible by the breakthrough of Osterhaus's division at Marietta. Sherman then crossed the Chattahoochee River, and on 16 July he was within view of Atlanta.

Jefferson Davis always underestimated General Johnston and particularly disapproved of his Fabian tactics. Johnston was removed on 18 July and General Hood, a daredevil, took over the command of a Confederate army which, despite heavy losses, had been brought back to 50,000 men. Nothing was more welcome to Sherman than this change of command. Under Johnston's leadership, Sherman would have had to besiege this important town. With Hood as his opponent, a shortened process began. Hood immediately took the offensive, left his trenches, and took up open battle with Sherman on 20, 22 and finally 28 July. These were the bloody and decisive Battles of Peachtree Creek and Atlanta. Hood was defeated and suffered terrible losses, particularly through desertions. He had to evacuate Atlanta. On 3 September Sherman entered this strong bulwark. The town was one of the richest arsenals of the South and contained many important workshops. But even if Hood had evacuated the town, Sherman was not free of the enemy. Indeed, Sherman had to go most of the way back to Chattanooga and battle with Hood continuously. So there were fights through the whole of September and October between Resaca and Atlanta. Finally, Hood cleared the field to restore himself and to prepare for a new campaign to Tennessee.

Thomas beats Hood. Sherman saw through Hood's new plan. He sent three of his veteran corps under Generals Thomas and Schofield to Tennessee to catch Hood there. In November, Hood entered Tennessee, throwing himself first on the weaker Schofield, who was in a secure position in Franklin. Hood was warded off, and Schofield united with Thomas at Nashville. On 16 December came the bloody battle of Nashville (figure 4), which ended with Hood's complete defeat (15,000 lost, mostly captives). With this, Hood was as good as eliminated. Schofield's corps then made a journey of a thousand miles by railroad and ship and concentrated at Goldsboro, North Carolina, 30,000 men strong. They joined up there with Sherman, advancing from the south, at the end of March, 1865.[59]

Sherman's March through Georgia. Through Atlanta, Sherman had lost almost

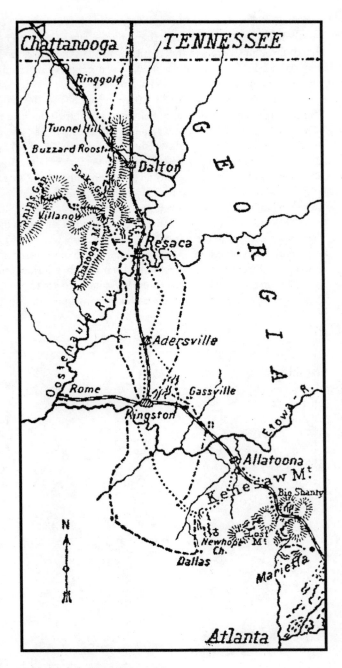

Figure 34. From Chattanooga to Atlanta.

20,000 men. But with reinforcements (despite the detachment of Thomas and Schofield) he still had at his disposal more than 60,000 men when he set out on the world-famous march through Georgia to the Atlantic coast. He knew that the Union Admiral Dahlgren was waiting for him in the waters off Savannah, and that Dahlgren could reequip and reprovision him after the conquest of this town.

This most grandiose of all flanking marches in the modern history of war was Sherman's own conception, although he himself attributes its merit to his superior Grant, who he says was always a brother to him. But Sherman had already drawn up and written about the plan for this expedition the previous year. He also knew the territory from his earlier railroad building in Georgia and knew that the land could feed an army. Jefferson Davis said then that Sherman would suffer the fate of Napoleon, on his march west from Moscow, and that he would find a terrible end in the swamps of eastern Georgia. But Sherman laughed at these declarations.

The greatness and significance of the operation lay less in the preparation of the plan than in the *courage* to carry it out. In fact, the army was never in need. Losses during the long march barely amounted to 1000 men. The soldiers were happy and in a good mood; and during the entire campaign things never went better than during those weeks.

This march through enemy country was immortalized by the beautiful song, "Marching through Georgia." It was not just a military campaign, but also a punitive campaign. The

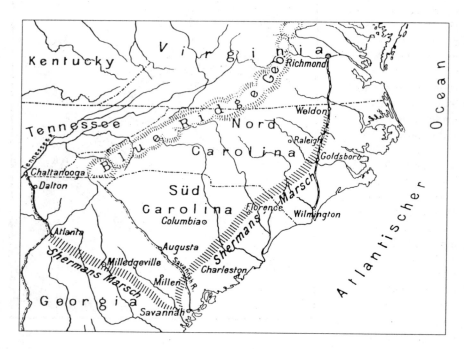

Figure 35. Sherman's great flanking march.

land was supposed to be sucked dry and made incapable of providing the enemy with provisions and war materiel. That is the reason for the 50-mile wide marching order of the campaign. What food was encountered was taken and the means of transportation destroyed. Sherman's bummers (the title was later laughingly adopted by the troops as well) often helped themselves to items of value, but only a few of the soldiers, rendered raw by the long war, participated in these deeds.

Departure from Atlanta took place on 15 November. The four corps advanced along different roads at a distance of thirty to fifty miles. Sherman's arrival at Savannah was on 10 December. On Christmas Day he sent his telegram of victory to Lincoln, "Savannah is taken." Sherman shook hands with Admiral Dahlgren and received new supplies for his troops.

Grant then demanded that Sherman's army be brought to before Richmond by ship, but Sherman was able to point out that a punitive expedition through South and North Carolina would bring him just as surely to the vicinity of Richmond. So Sherman's forces set out to the north at the beginning of January. Theirs was, indeed a punitive expedition. The South was to learn the terror of war and be convinced of the pointlessness of further resistance. Also, the harbors of Wilmington and Charleston (cradle of the secession) now fell into the hands of the North. The means Sherman's bummers used could not always be justified in terms of modern standards for the conduct of war, but extortion practiced by raiding Southern bands must be kept in mind (Morgan's raids, the burning of Chambersburg, and the like).

Johnston, who once more was at the head of a field army, threw himself against Sherman in North Carolina, but after intense fighting he was pressed back. On 23 March 1865 Sherman joined up with Schofield in Goldsboro, North Carolina. By this Sherman's army was brought back to nearly 90,000 men, almost doubly superior to Johnston's deeply demoralized forces. All Confederate efforts to hold up Sherman's advance failed.

Sherman already stood at Raleigh, within reach of Richmond, when General Lee decided to break out of Richmond, going west in the last days of March 1865 to seek to join Johnston's army and then begin a new campaign. While trying to do this, the great leader of the Confederacy was driven into the trap of Appomattox and forced there to lay down his arms.

Appomattox and Peace

Before Richmond, spring of 1865!
General Lee only went to Richmond against his will. The strength of the Confederate army lay in fighting in the field, and Richmond soon became a trap, in view of the inexhaustible resources of the North. For that reason Lee demanded that the place be given up as early as January. He wanted to go out into the open field to give battle to his opponent. Such an outbreak would still have been successful in February, and a unification of Lee with Johnston's Confederate troops at Raleigh would have produced a field army of 90,000 men. But Jefferson Davis did not want to hear of this plan. Davis feared that the surrender of Richmond would drive the Southern people to despair. So Lee had to remain in Richmond.

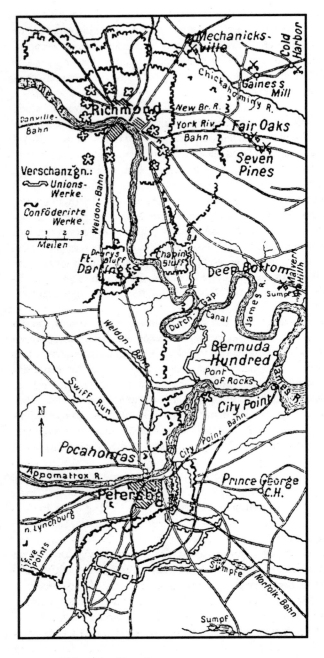

Figure 36. Richmond and Petersburg.

Soon Sheridan's 10,000 Union cavalrymen came from the West, followed by fresh infantry; Sherman's 90,000 men advanced from the south, ever nearer to Richmond, and Grant had 125,000 men on the spot to enclose the city. Obviously this was still not enough to close off Richmond and Petersburg entirely, for the siege of Richmond had been lingering for a long time. On 27 March, Grant shifted two of his corps around Petersburg toward the west. That was the signal for Lee's first attempt to escape. Around this time Petersburg was only weakly garrisoned. Grant attacked it on 1 and 2 April, taking the outer works of Petersburg. On the night of 2 April Lee's main army broke out heading toward Amelia Courthouse. On the morning of 3 April, the German General Weitzel was the first to occupy the abandoned, burning capital city of secession! Finally the star-spangled banner waved over Richmond.

An army breaking out of a fortress has to operate rapidly. The provisions trains cannot keep up the same pace. Lee had foreseen this and had supply stations set up in the surrounding country, but these were taken by Sheridan's cavalry. Lee could perhaps have escaped if "General Hunger" had not entered an alliance with the North. But Lee's veterans had been living on air for several days when they capitulated to Grant and to hunger at Appomattox Courthouse on 9 April (figure 13). There were still 2802 officers and 25,500 men. An equal number had been captured or deserted in the course of the march. On 17 April, Johnston capitulated to Sherman. The final remnants of this admirable army, which fought to the last cartridge, surrendered to Osterhaus deep in the South. That was the end.

Jefferson Davis in flight! He was supposedly captured in woman's clothes.[60] At first it was generally said, "He at least must hang!" He was then held for a long time, and he was finally allowed to go free, as were all the other secessionists except for the German-Swiss Wirz [commandant of Andersonville – SR].

Lincoln's Murder

There was one more victim, now that the war was over, the last victim and the greatest of all! The patriots had streamed into Washington to greet Lincoln. He could not receive all his friends in the White House and promised to appear on the evening of 14 April in Ford's Theater. The actor John Wilkes Booth, a younger brother of the great Shakespearian actor Booth, sneaked behind Lincoln's seat and shot the president. It was at first believed that this shameful deed had been ordered by the heads of the suppressed rebellion, but this was fortunately proven false. Booth was the head of a conspiracy whose members planned simultaneously to murder the president, General Grant, and Secretary of State Seward. Seward was in fact attacked, but he came out of it with his life. Booth was killed in flight, and his companions, including a Mrs. Surratt, were hanged.

Lincoln was mourned not only by the entire North. Many of the rebels who had just been deprived of their weapons saw that they had lost their best friend in Lincoln, the man who had the will and the strength to carry out the reconstruction of the South in a milder and more conciliatory manner. This simple and thoroughly honorable man of the people had compelled respect from most of the leaders of the secession, and from some, including General Lee, he had won admiration. The oft-voiced view that Lincoln died at the right moment for his historical reputation is entirely untrue. Whoever reviews the wild party struggles that developed under Lincoln's successor, Johnson, will have to come to this opinion. At the end of the war, Lincoln possessed an influence that only Washington had exercised before him. If he had been allowed to bring his second term of office to an end in peace, all of the legislative decrees that sought to reconcile the two sections of the country would have borne the stamp of the noble man whose most outstanding characteristic was his love of justice.

Appendix I
Biographical Directory

German Union Officers
Preliminary Remarks

The following list contains about 500 names of outstanding German Union officers of the Civil War, as well as 32 names of Germans from the ranks of civilians who were particularly prominent during the war. Of the officers, 96 fell before the enemy (marked with a †). Yet this list does not comprehend all German staff officers who may be regarded as victims of the war. Many of the remaining died during the war or soon after, as a result of wounds or illnesses from the conflict (including the four German division or brigade commanders von Schimmelpfennig, Krzyzanowski, Blenker and Asboth). In the case of very many of the remaining officers, one will often find the remarks "wounded, severely wounded, often wounded." Yet it could only be established for a part of the officers dealt with here that they were wounded.

Originally the list was only supposed to include those German officers who achieved at least the rank of major, or of battery chief in the artillery. This limitation could not be consistently maintained, however, and so some officers of lower rank are listed of whom something remarkable is known. It may be said that rising to the rank of a staff officer was often not due to merit; many brave and capable Germans remained company officers through the entire war although they would have deserved promotion, and nimble climbers came to high positions without any real merit. Advancement often resembled a lottery.

It should also be remarked that this list does not include anything like all German staff officers. Although about 200 veterans tried to make the list as complete as possible, still many a compatriot who deserves a place here has been forgotten. Unfortunately, the gathering of materials began when more than forty years had passed since the war. Particularly sparse has been information about high officers from the states of Michigan, Maryland, Kentucky, and the New England states, as well as the not insignificant number of German leaders who stood in loyal regiments from the rebel Southern states. Also, rather little also could be said of the relatively many German officers who led Negro regiments.

It should be particularly stressed that our mission could only deal with higher-ranking officers born in Germany, Austria, Switzerland and Alsace. The very numerous group of higher-ranking officers born in America as sons of German immigrants is not mentioned. I would have liked to spend more effort on the great accomplishments of the descendents of Germans than is found in the chapter, "Participation of Germans in the War," but this would demand years of specialized research and a basic insight into the history of the German immigration and its effects. A single person cannot complete such a mission.

The biographies of eight of the nine German-born generals are placed before the other officers. Major General Salomon is found under S with his brothers. It should be mentioned that many questions have been merely summarized in Sigel's biography that were handled in detail in the text. Doing otherwise would have required frequent repetition and a reference to earlier mentions in the text. I held it to be more efficient to portray Sigel's important situations in context.

* .* *

German Field Commanders

OSTERHAUS, Peter Joseph. Major general and corps commander. Born in Koblenz in 1823. In 1911 the 88-year old was still living with one of his married daughters in Duisburg in the Rhineland, still vigorous in body and spirit. He served in Koblenz as a one-year volunteer before becoming a Prussian reserve officer. Due to his participation in the German revolution, he sought refuge in America and resided in Belleville and St. Louis until the War. In April 1861 he enlisted as a private in the German 3rd Missouri regiment,[1] soon becoming its major, later colonel of the German 12th Missouri Regiment, a bigadier general in January 1863, and major general after his battles at Chattanooga in 1863. On 23 September 1864 he received the command of the XV Army Corps, which he led on Sherman's march to Savannah. Osterhaus laid down his sword on 16 January 1866. Hence he had stood under arms for almost five years without interruption. Starting at the lowest rank, he had achieved the highest rank in the volunteer army, fighting with honor in 34 battles and never suffering defeat when in command. He deserves without any doubt the first place among the German officers of the Civil War.[2]

Osterhaus was never able to have any political influence, and unlike Sigel he never enjoyed the support of his countrymen. Every success of his career, so rich in deeds, every military promotion, was the result of his own service, founded on the loyal fulfillment of duty and on the development of his inborn talent as a leader. Because his military training in Prussia was minimal, Osterhaus's career cannot be compared with those of generals who were trained in Germany for an officer's career; rather, he should be compared with other American self-made generals. If one makes this comparison, then one must figure in the special advantage that natives had over immigrants.

If one wished adequately to depict the war deeds of "Peter Joe" (his nickname), one would have to write a history of the greater part of the Western and Southern war. This has already been done, if only in brief strokes, and reference will only be made to that here. Osterhaus began in Missouri in the spring of 1861. He fought along with Lyon's main force at Wilson's Creek. Then came the so-called bush war in Missouri, and the battle of Pea Ridge. Osterhaus rescued the valiantly fighting Sigel on his retreat from Bentonville, and in that decisive battle he led one of the two Sigel divisions in his own right. It was also he who took the position from which Sigel's decisive attack had its beginning. After Sigel's artillery had caused the enemy to waver, Osterhaus stormed the principal position of the enemy at Elkhorn Pass.

Then Osterhaus moved on to the Red River. This was a military side show taking place not on the great Red River on the southeastern end of Arkansas but rather the Little Red River in the north of that state. There half his troops fell ill with malaria. Although shaken by fever himself, Osterhaus forced himself to mount his horse and lead the remnant of his men into battle. Then followed the long siege of Vicksburg and the struggles connected with it. Osterhaus was involved in a most honorable manner in the victory of Arkansas Post, and during the Vicksburg campaign Grant gave him an autonomous command on the Big Black River. There it was his duty to prevent reinforcements and provisions from reaching Vicksburg; this was a painstaking, wearing action involving continual struggle, in which Osterhaus was wounded. Then came the attacks on Vicksburg, in which Grant's army was repulsed. But on 22 May, Osterhaus's division pressed on into the outer works.

While his comrades were able to collect laurels in the universally respected battles of Fort Donelson, Shiloh, Corinth, Perryville, and Murfreesboro, Osterhaus had thankless but extremely difficult missions to resolve. He was involved in continual conflicts without receiving any recognition for his efforts, for the bulk of the public was only interested in the mass struggles and principal battles.

He accompanied Grant on his march south from Vicksburg down the Mississippi, once more a thankless and perilous mission, for he not only had to fight the enemy continuously, but also malaria and yellow fever. As a result Osterhaus was little favored by those fortunes of war that can give leaders opportunity for distinction.

Fortune finally smiled on him in November 1863. He went to Chattanooga with Sherman, but his division was unable to cross the swollen Tennessee, so that Osterhaus was joined to Hooker's corps instead of Sherman's. Then there followed three days of victory that finally brought Osterhaus into the foreground. He was the true hero of the Battle Above the Clouds, lead the vanguard from Lookout Mountain to the south side of Missionary Ridge, where he fought with great glory, then leading the pursuit of the Confederate army beaten at Missionary Ridge by Thomas. He struck the remnant of the fleeing enemy at Ringgold, Alabama.[3] There followed a fearfully bloody battle which was led autonomously by Osterhaus, but the result was the scattering of the enemy and a new laurel for Osterhaus. In the three days of battle before Chattanooga, Osterhaus made far more prisoners than the number of troops he commanded.

Sherman's march through Georgia, which took up the entire year of 1864, found Osterhaus as a division commander in the XV Corps. His troops participated in most of the battles and skirmishes. The division fought with honor at Resaca, Dallas, Pumpkin Vine Creek, and the dreadfully bloody battle on Kennesaw Mountain. It was Osterhaus who broke through at Marietta, rendering Johnston's strong defensive position at Kennesaw Mountain untenable. Osterhaus also had an honorable role in the battle on the Chattahoochee and at

Jonesboro, as well as at the decisive battles of Peachtree Creek and Atlanta. Then followed the many battles connected with holding the position of Atlanta.

One of Osterhaus's brigades, commanded by the brave Corse, born of German parents, victoriously held Allatoona against a force four times its size. On 23 September Major General Osterhaus took command of the XV Corps, leading it through Georgia to Savannah, and his troops participated in the storming of Fort McAllister, which protected Savannah from the land side. It was only after this victory that Sherman was able to send his famous Christmas dispatch to Lincoln, "Savannah is ours." Then Osterhaus became chief of staff of General Canby and fought to the end of the war at Mobile and on the lower Mississippi. Only the most important of Osterhaus's battles and victories can be mentioned here.

After the war Osterhaus was military governor of Mississippi for a time, then American consul in Lyon. During the German-French War he drew the special thanks of the German government for extending the protection of the American flag to Germans in his consular region in a particularly self-sacrificing manner. Osterhaus later served as consul in Mannheim. He only laid down this office in his seventy-seventh year in order to pass the evening of his life in peace.

One of his sons, Hugo Osterhaus, is an admiral in the American Navy. In the spring of 1911, he received the highest position in the fleet, command of the Atlantic squadron. A grandson of the general is also an American naval officer. Another son of our hero was a Prussian major of artillery and went to Southwest Africa, where he fell in the battles at Waterberge. This son had particularly distinguished himself during the international campaign in China.

Osterhaus possessed to a high degree a capacity to conform to American conditions. He made use of this gift without ever denying his German identity. He was only a soldier, not also a "do-gooder," as was so often the case with his Forty-Eighter comrades. Those men so often found fault with American military arrangements and could not see that an improvised people's war by a thoroughly unmilitary nation could not unfold according to the customs and rules of European models. Osterhaus took things the way they were; as they could hardly be different under the given conditions, he sought to conform to them. So we find Osterhaus always at peace with his Anglo-American comrades. There were no irritations, although one must always recall that West Pointers never achieved the significance in the West that they did in the East.

The Western Army was really always a people's army, even as regards the leaders from the Regular Army. Grant, Sherman, Rosecrans. and other generals of the West had long since lost touch with West Point. They had been out of the Regular Army for years, and they presented themselves much more as citizen generals than did the leadership clique that always dominated the Army of the Potomac. Even a true hero such as Thomas always appears in his general's uniform more like a citizen than a West Pointer. Osterhaus, as a German, knew how to get along with Anglo-Americans. All of his superiors spoke of him with only the highest respect, and nativism was only expressed against Osterhaus once (by General O. O. Howard, of course). When Osterhaus was to take Logan's position leading the XV Corps, Howard protested. He thought that such a high command should not be given to an immigrant. Howard apparently had not heard of the immigrant Steuben, to whom Washington gave the post of inspector general of the army.

SIGEL, Franz. Major general and corps commander, born 1824 in Sinsheim, Baden, died 1902 in New York. He resigned as a Baden officer in 1847 as a result of a duel that led to his opponent's death. He studied law in Heidelberg and played a leading role in the revolution in Baden. He fled to America soon after and was a teacher in New York and St. Louis until the Civil War.

In the face of the praise Sigel's compatriots have heaped on him, one would assume that his war deeds were of an entirely extraordinary sort and that they at least, exceeded those of all other German military leaders. Sigel has been honored by two equestrian statues, and his name still lives fifty years later among the German-American people. Almost nothing is heard of any of the other German generals; their names have virtually been erased in the memory of their compatriots, with the exception of an ever-dwindling circle of veterans. That certainly cannot be seen as a just expression of the thanks owed to those with a proper claim. Even if the services of Sigel were such that he deserved honor before all his comrades, this surprising neglect of the others must be felt as unjust. This one-sided honor seems all the less proper when it is seen that Sigel's war deeds have been considerably overvalued, and that at least *one* other German general could claim to be named the *first* German military leader of the Civil War in Sigel's place.

Sigel's accomplishments in war were as follows: participation in the German rising in St. Louis as one of four regimental leaders; retreat action at Carthage, Missouri, on 5 July 1861; severe defeat and complete dissolution of Sigel's brigade at Wilson's Creek, Missouri, 10 August 1861; well-led retreat action at Bentonville, Arkansas, 6 March 1862; splendid victory (under Curtis) at Pea Ridge, Arkansas, 7 to 8 March 1862; two-day great battle at Second Bull Run, 29 and 30 August 1862. Sigel began this last, the sole great battle of his career, with honor, fought on the second day with distinction, and his troops covered the retreat. There was a further defeat of Sigel's division at New Market, Virginia, 15 May 1864. Here, as at Wilson's Creek and Carthage, Sigel commanded autonomously. Further, Sigel saw action in small skirmishes on the Rappahannock. As the leader of a grand division (two army corps) he was unable to participate in any fighting. Through intelligent maneuvering at Harpers Ferry, he delayed Early's advance during the summer of 1864, without its coming to fighting. Sigel stood in the field from April 1861 until February 1863. Then he served a few months in the summer of 1864.

For obvious reasons a comparison of the deeds of German military leaders cannot be made in detail, but each of the German generals has a right to have his total accomplishments during the war considered. If General A fought in almost ten times as many battles as his comrade B, if he more frequently commanded autonomously than B without having a defeat, while the autonomous battles of B were mostly defeats, then it would be hard to designate B as the more accomplished of the two. A comparison of the total war records of only two other German generals with Sigel's war deeds allows us to say that the elevation of Sigel by the German-American people rests on an undeserved prejudice. Here follows just such a comparison of accomplishments:

Sigel: Five actions, including one very great battle in which Sigel participated as a capable corps commander; one medium-sized battle, Pea Ridge, in which Sigel was the second leader and can be considered the real victor; as well as two larger encounters, Wilson's Creek and New Market, which ended in defeat under Sigel's autonomous command; and the retreat actions at Bentonville and Carthage.

Osterhaus: Thirty-four actions, including many great battles and large-scale encounters, as well as many skirmishes and position actions which remain unmentioned. Deeds of special fame were at Pea Ridge (under Sigel); Arkansas Post; battles around Vicksburg, particularly the autonomously led fight on the Big Black River (where he was wounded); Champion's Hill; and the attack on Vicksburg on 22 May; Lookout Mountain and the flanking of Missionary Ridge from the south; the dreadfully bloody encounter of Ringgold, in which Osterhaus led and remained victor over a considerably superior force; Resaca, Dallas, Pumpkin Vine Creek, and the splendidly-done breakthrough of Osterhaus's division at Kennesaw Mountain, and the four large battles around Atlanta. Osterhaus's career as a corps commander from Atlanta to Savannah, autumn of 1864 did not bring any large battle. Osterhaus stood in the field from the first to the last shot of the war.

Willich. Served without interruption from April 1861 to February 1864. He was rendered incapable of service by severe wounds. He was the drillmaster of model German regiments, the 9th Ohio and 32nd Indiana. He saw more than thirty major actions, including the five great battles of Shiloh, Perryville, Stones River, Chickamauga, and Missionary Ridge. The encounter at Orchard Knob was particularly glorious for Willich. Autonomously led victories were at Hoover's Gap and Liberty Gap. Willich unfortunately only became a division commander very late.

The comparison of all the deeds of Osterhaus and Willich with those of Sigel should suffice to counter the erroneous view that Sigel was the *only* significant German field commander of the Civil War.

The one-sided obsession with Sigel on the part of German-Americans not only appears to be an injustice to other and very successful German officers; through it the large and positive role of the German ethnic group in preserving the Union can easily be placed in an unfavorable light. This is because the attempt is made to measure their role essentially in terms of the war deeds of Sigel. Such an interpretation would be easy. Due to the scattering of four-fifths of German soldiers into mixed regiments, their impact cannot be judged from the spirit of German fighting masses; thus special importance is given to German officers standing out from those masses. It would be to little avail if the judgment of the entire German ethnic group rested essentially on Sigel's accomplishments, for we would not receive justice in that way.

For these reasons it is necessary to review the Sigel matter much more thoroughly than would be necessary if we were only dealing with a question of one person. And if our Sigel then appears a bit smaller than he does in his equestrian statues and in the popular view (created with the help of a magnifying glass brought along from Baden), he remains a capable man before whom every German and also every German-American should tip his hat. The basically modest Sigel, who was only occasionally set off balance by the pressing excesses of his friends, would certainly have not objected if his career were evaluated acccording to his military accomplishments.

When Sigel came to Washington in May 1862 to receive a command in the East, the memory of his military glory at Pea Ridge was still green. He had all the Forty-Eighters behind him, as well as the Grays. Specifically, the Gray Körner, one of Lincoln's most intimate friends, acted on Sigel's behalf. The drums were beaten hard in those days for Sigel. But that was not necessary. When Körner's letter of endorsement was presented, and when Schurz, just returned from Spain, spoke with Lincoln alone, everything was already set.

The *Realpolitiker* in the presidential chair knew full well what he owed to the Germans, and when they demanded that Sigel be a corps commander, Lincoln easily said, "All right." It was unnecessary to give the scheming Halleck an opportunity to set off countermines.[4]

The desire of the Germans to have one outstanding general in the armies of the Union, alongside of the masses of German soldiers and officers of lower rank, was natural and thoroughly justified. The selection fell on Sigel, for he was held by his Forty-Eighter colleagues to be a rare military genius. Further, he had obligated his friends to their thanks. He had functioned as the final supreme commander of the Baden revolutionary army, and he had brought the remnants of that force to safety in Switzerland. In this way he had saved hundreds of volunteers from persecution and court martial. Sigel was the sole German military man who brought a legitimate fame as a warrior with him to America.

However, Sigel was always possessed with remarkably bad luck. Right after he had erased the severe setback of Wilson's Creek at Pea Ridge—a fact generally recognized in the West, while it was never adequately recognized in the East by West Pointers he had himself shifted to the Army of the Potomac. He did so in order to avoid his enemy, Halleck. But at almost the same moment Sigel went East, Halleck was moved to Washington as supreme general of all the Union armies. So Sigel jumped out of the frying pan and into the fire. Halleck now really had him in his grasp, and Halleck's power in Washington was immensely greater than it had previously been in Missouri. If Sigel had remained in the West, Halleck could have done little to him, for he could not concern himself so directly with matters in the Western theater of war.[5] Sigel was well known in the West, and after Pea Ridge he enjoyed well-deserved glory. In the West the petty tormentors, who were so numerous in the East, were lacking. He would not have become a corps commander so rapidly there, but what use was such a position if he was not able to keep it in the East? In any case, Sigel would have had an entirely different influence in the West than on the Potomac.

Sigel also departed the Army of the Potomac at the wrong time. He left precisely when the XI Corps had become a respectable troop, when the previous I Corps of only 5000 men was strengthened to more than 12,000 men under the name of the XI Corps. And he left when the dreadful days of Chancellorsville were in preparation. What an opportunity Sigel would have had for distinction on 2 May 1863! For it may be assumed with certainty that Sigel would have put the corps into a good defensive position instead of leaving it undefended, as did his successor Howard. The attack of 2 May did offer every prepared Union leader an opportunity for distinction.[6] Sigel would have been able to earn undying glory on that day, but this "bad-luck bird" resigned too early.[7]

It should be remarked at this point that Sigel chose his worst possible time for his third and last resignation attempt in February 1863. His enemies could say about him, "There he goes because he could not continue to command a grand division (two corps)." Because grand divisions were being dissolved, so that Sigel was only left with the XI Corps, this argument seems believable. But the reasons for Sigel's last resignation were those he gives in his second resignation attempt at the start of October, 1862 (to be discussed later). Sigel should have perservered in the spring of 1863. The best time for his resignation would have been after Second Bull Run, when he could withdraw with fresh laurels. But who can understand the moods of such an irascible man, one who was such an impractical dreamer and idealist as Sigel was? Who could assume that he could recognize the right time for a "good departure"?

* * *

Sigel's overzealous friends never considered that while it was relatively easy for them to get him his new position, it would be difficult for him to survive in his position as a corps commander. The West Point officers of the Army of the Potomac did not look at their new comrade with German eyes. They saw him as an outsider in their circle, a stranger who had taken away a good position from one of their own. These gentlemen had already murmured when the outstanding American politicians Banks and Butler received precedence over West Pointers, but there was no demonstration against them in view of the great respect the two politicians enjoyed.[8] Sigel, however, was the first foreigner to appear as a corps commander. Further, Sigel in particular allowed the West Pointers' position to appear in the most favorable light. The organization of the main Eastern army was such that Lincoln was completely excluded from its internal operations, and all orders, particularly those distributing newly-organized units to the various army corps, were issued by Secretary of War Stanton and General Halleck. These mighty men had the power to prefer some corps and neglect others. The fact that Sigel's corps was not supported was to a large degree the work of Halleck.

The way some of the West Pointer commanders treated their comrade Sigel may be seen from the following episode. During the great battle days of Second Bull Run, Reno's and Kearny's divisions were sent forward to support Sigel's corps, which was fighting at the front. Sigel sent his adjutant[9] to Kearny and asked him to intervene in the fight at the same time as Schurz's division under Sigel. What did the proud West Pointer respond? "Tell your general I don't want any foreign influence with my command." So Sigel did not merely have the highest military officials in Washington against him; he also had the distrust, even the hostility, of his West Point comrades.

Incidentally, any German would have encountered great problems in the same position. The only Germans who could perhaps have survived in such a situation were Schurz and, possibly, von Steinwehr. Schurz's high political position and splendid gifts as a speaker and von Steinwehr's participation in the Mexican War and his military experience, well known to older West Pointers, would have created respect. The fact that Schurz was a novice in military matters would have had little importance, for West Pointers had grown rather used to political generals. In any case, an unwritten page did Schurz less damage than Sigel's written page from Missouri. Schurz, as well as Steinwehr, knew American conditions far better than did Sigel. Both possessed a certain diplomatic talent, as well as the capacity to get along under the given conditions better than the prototypically Teutonic Sigel.

It cannot be disputed that West Point professional officers had first call on superior positions of leadership. This preference was even supported by popular opinion. The fact that they had remained loyal to the Union while the majority of their comrades opted for the country's enemy gave them a right to preference in the eyes of the people. The American professional officers had always felt themselves a caste set apart. In peacetime they were given no respect; but at the outbreak of a war when those gentlemen operated as a club promoting their own class interests, their conduct was seen by the masses of the Northern people as proper. The good citizen of the North also had a very high opinion of the ability of West Pointers. It was only after Fredericksburg and Chancellorsville, when so many professional officers failed but continued in high positions through the officers' clique, that a strong hostility to West Pointers arose.

Incidentally, no other self-respecting nation would have given its troops, recruited from volunteer patriots, to untried foreign officers, so long as there were domestically trained officers available. Further, every former officer of another nationality who volunteers to serve abroad has a certain problem. People look for reasons why this gentleman should have wished to exchange his position in his home army for exile. The fact that such a suspicion could not be extended to the professional officers among the German Forty-Eighters was not noticed in Anglo-American circles. What did the West Pointers know about the Revolution of 1848? One could also draw a very instructive example of the prejudice of Americans against the use of foreign officers in high positions. Think of the problems the great Steuben encountered with his comrades after Washington named him to the office of inspector general of the army. Steuben himself had trouble succeeding, although Washington always supported him. Washington was certainly a different man from the Lincoln, however formidable the latter. And Sigel was certainly no Steuben.

The special problems Sigel encountered on the Potomac, other than the main one of Halleck's hostility, consisted of the following. When Sigel became corps commander, the West Pointers asked, "Who is this stranger from the West? What did he do in the West now to become one of the first officers of the American Guard?"[10] Because Halleck had only recently come to Washington from the West, the questioners thought they could learn everything about Sigel from Halleck. And Halleck was by no means shy with his information. (Incidentally, Halleck also drew on a considerable number of West Pointers who had served with Sigel in the West.) The result of such inquiries was not very positive for Sigel.

When the gentlemen of the Potomac learned that Sigel's brigade had been completely dispersed at Wilson's Creek; that Sigel had lost five of his six cannons, one flag, and a quarter of all of his men as prisoners; that Sigel's troops had run away in wild flight without firing a shot—then Sigel's later victory at Pea Ridge counted for little, particularly because Sigel fought in the latter battle under a West Pointer (Curtis).[11] The rest of Sigel's Missouri record was also portrayed in the worst imaginable manner. At Carthage Sigel had broken off an attack when it had barely begun, and on his retreat from Springfield to Rolla, Sigel had dealt in a thoroughly unmilitary manner, it was said.[12] All of these things were related in terms of dramatic overstatements, but they usually rested on undeniable facts. The hostility toward Sigel was already there, but this mood took on a much more serious form after Sigel's unfortunate debut at Wilson's Creek became known.

Included here is one West Pointer's opinion, by no means the worst that was said about Sigel in these circles. It is the official report of General Schofield to Halleck. What is remarkable about it is that this report was written before Sigel's best deeds at Pea Ridge. But one should consider Schofield's very modest endowments for judging Sigel. This report is important only as an example of the mood, a measure of how Brigadier Sigel appeared to the West Pointers who stood in battle at Wilson's Creek.

To General Halleck,

13 February 1862

My position as staff officer of General Lyon gave me good opportunities to judge the services of General Sigel as an officer, and as a result I know his good and bad characteristics much better than most of those who have undertaken to judge him. General Sigel stands far above the average of American commanders so far as his theoretical training is concerned. He has studied the art of strategy with great care, and he appears to be thoroughly familiar with the campaigns of great military leaders, as far as this relates to their most important strategic measures. He also appears to understand well the duties of a staff officer, but concerning tactics, large- and small-scale logistics (the science of providing time and space for the tactical movement of troops), and discipline, he is very deficient. These lacks are so glaring that it is absolutely impossible for him to win the confidence of American officers and men, and they exclude him from holding any high command in our army. Although I do not condemn General Sigel in the overstated way so many do, for I see in him many fine qualities, I would be neglecting my duties if I did not protest against the naming of a man to a high command of whom I must say that he cannot obtain the trust of the troops he is to command.

—O. M. Schofield, Brigadier General

It was also Sigel's personality, his entire nature and appearance, that made him unsuited for the task of appealing to the West Pointers. Of all the dreamers and idealists of the Forty-Eighter immigration, Sigel was the one whom these descriptive terms fit best. He was the very type of unworldly German scholar who has no eye for his surroundings and simply goes his own way. Absolutely nothing about his appearance and conduct recalled a bluff soldier. He was more like a grumbling German schoolmaster, and on horseback the short, thin man with his eternal corpse-like stiffness made an unheroic impression.[13] The same man who brought hundreds of endangered Unionist refugees to safety from southwest Missouri, and who then ran around for weeks in St. Louis to find work for these poor people, utterly lacked the gift of spreading warmth about himself or winning new friends. Sigel presented himself to strangers, especially non-Germans, in such a way as to make them directly hostile. It was necessary to be a German to know him truly and to value him; but West Pointers saw no point in thawing out this "iceblock," as they called him. In a word, *Sigel was much too German* to be at home as a corps commander in the Army of the Potomac.

Let us hear what his lifelong friend Schurz said about him:

Sigel possessed only a little of the charming forms of manners that disarm hostility and can turn it into comradeship. His conversation seriously lacked sympathetic elements. There was something reserved in his nature, if not positively repellent, which rendered more difficult rather than favored any friendly approach.

In his second request for resignation at the start of October 1862 (Sigel withdrew it when Burnside named him to head one of his four new grand divisions), Sigel gave the reasons he could not remain in the Army of the Potomac. He then stood with a corps reduced to barely 5000 men in a very exposed position in central Virginia. He had the mission in the Shenandoah Valley of preventing Lee's army, pursued in such a slack fashion by McClellan, from using the passes of the Blue Ridge Mountains and entering central Virginia. Sigel's complaints were of the following sort:

> I have been placed under a younger general. My small corps has been weakened even more by the detachment of Milroy's brigade. I have been placed in a position no one can control with the means given. Other than one, all the regiments raised for me in various Northern states have been given to other corps. General Halleck has harassed me personally and in official records in the grossest way. No horses have been issued for my artillery and cavalry. The pay of my soldiers is six months in arrears. Because I can expect no better treatment, and because my soldiers should suffer no longer as a result of hostility directed at me, I wish to resign.

Six governors testified that troops of their states had been specially raised for Sigel's corps, but that these troops had been placed elsewhere.

All of these complaints were entirely justified and corresponded to the facts. These chicaneries all led back to Halleck and to the Secretary of War, who was influenced by Halleck in this matter. But the reasons underlying Halleck's hostility to Sigel were then only partly known to Sigel's friends, and so the attitude developed in the German press that nativism was the primary cause for those persecutions. This opinion then became a hindrance to anyone who saw that Sigel's was precisely the personality least suited to survival in the Army of the Potomac. Sigel would have failed there even if he had had outstanding gifts as a field commander. It was also very difficult to defend Sigel. Wilson's Creek and Sigel's personality both spoke too strongly against him. Incidentally it should be stressed that Sigel was always too much in the hands of his friends, and that these friends often did not conduct his defense very intelligently. Thus they neglected to prevent him from making his final resignation request or prevent him from appearing to resign as a "sorehead," a man who departed because he could no longer command two corps.[14] The loyalty of the Forty-Eighters to Sigel should be honored, but it would have been desirable if more logic had made an appearance, as well.

The Forty-Eighters who then dominated the German-American press were mostly unbending devotees of principle. For them to concede that they had made an error in promoting Sigel for his position was intolerable. They could easily have won their protégé a new command in the West, but they held that to be beneath his dignity. They were of the opinion that the former commander of a grand division could not go on working as a simple division commander, although we find deposed supreme commanders of the Army of the Potomac such as Burnside and Hooker and many others in lower positions in later times. After his resignation, Sigel, in fact, served as the leader of a sort of police troop in Pennsylvania.

The newspaper war on behalf of Sigel continued in the German press even after he resigned. Soon the shameless attacks on German soldiers by West Pointers, such as over

Chancellorsville, appeared to justify Sigel's defenders. They could assert that the inventors of the scapegoat of Chancellorsville were the same people who had pushed Sigel out of the Army of the Potomac. As far as the persons involved were concerned, this was correct; but although the lower sentiments behind both episodes came from the Halleck clique, the causes of the two operations differed dramatically.

When Sigel appeared again as a corps commander in spring 1864, lost the Battle of New Market, and was then immediately relieved by Grant, Sigel's friends saw it as undeserved harshness in view of the fact that so many West Pointers had remained in position after the most dreadful defeats. They did not see that the position of Halleck's West Point gang was extremely strong at that time. This clique permitted members to sin without punishment, while Sigel, back in the Army of the Potomac, carried an official guillotine in his knapsack. It worked automatically in the case of the general's failure. Very little restraint was used in getting rid of such West Pointers as did not belong to Halleck's clique. The accomplished Rosecrans went just as quickly as Sigel, for example, although the confusion in the Battle of Chickamauga was caused not by Rosecrans but by the tardiness of McCook's corps.

Sigel should never have entered the Army of the Potomac a second time, for as long as Halleck and Stanton controlled its inner operations, no positive work could be expected for him. Sigel relied on Grant, the new supreme general of all Union armies. He might have thought that Grant would soon eliminate Halleck's influence, because Halleck had treated Grant even more scandalously in the summer of 1862 than he had Sigel. But Grant, who had been dismissed by Halleck as the victor of Fort Donelson and had been controlled in a totally undignified manner during Halleck's Corinth campaign, had made his peace with his old enemy in 1864 for God knows what reason, and our German bad-luck bird Sigel became the whipping boy of both. Sigel should not have remained glued to the East, but he remained there despite the indominable problems, and he was ground to bits while trying to maintain himself in positions no one could have mastered.

During all four years of the war, Sigel's name continually stood before the German people in America as one persecuted and tormented because of his ethnicity. This eternal justification, this repeated defense of Sigel, this intervention by his friends for him through thick and thin, tied with a systematic silence about his failings, did much to create Sigel's later fame. The tradition of half a century has only increased this fame. Because the Forty-Eighters had so much to do on Sigel, they had no time to commemorate the other German military leaders adequately. As a result, the others have as good as vanished, while Franz Sigel stands cast in bronze high on his horse in both St. Louis and New York. But should we continue to be dominated by such attitudes?

The lovely poem by G. P. Robinson, which was translated into German in New York by Straubenmüller and set to music by Sigel himself, contributed a great deal to Sigel's fame in war. If a closer look is made, however, it appears that the song does not celebrate Sigel so much as it does the German soldier, who wants to fight for the Union under a countryman of his own. With his hit, "I Fights Mit Sigel," Robinson unconsciously struck a tone that echoed the spirit of the ordinary German man. The Germans had a great desire to fight under Sigel, that is, under German leadership, and it was the compatriots' *esprit de corps*, the voice of the blood, that caused such verses to sing.

Schurz gave eloquent expression to this voice in his speech of thanks on his seventieth birthday. There he said, "I can accept this esteem on a public occasion with a clear conscience.

I, as a German-born citizen, have always acted so that the German name in America should never be shamed. That was my honorable intention." The same thought also motivated German soldiers, if perhaps unconsciously. It may be left open whether they clearly saw that by struggling for the preservation of the Union they were also fighting for the honor of the German people, but it is a fact that all purely German regiments were elite troops.

The American military officials would have been acting intelligently if they had paid more attention to ethnic *esprit de corps* among Germans, as well as among Irishmen and Englishmen. Unfortunately, Sigel himself made it harder for German soldiers to gather into a strong military unit. When he took over Frémont's corps, he found in it Blenker's purely German division, which then numbered 6000 men. In one of his first dispatches to his chief, Pope, Sigel reported, "Blenker's division has ceased to exist." Reportedly to allay disputes among brigades, Sigel distributed the three brigades of the German Division to the three divisions of the corps.[15] With this, the largest single German troop unit was destroyed, and later it was never possible to create a purely German corps. In any case, given it was never possible under Sigel's leadership to create a purely German corps for the reasons given. A successor could have accomplished what Sigel failed to do under the circumstances. Somewhat later, the German 82nd Illinois, 26th Wisconsin, and 107th Ohio Regiments joined the XI Corps. These alone would have been a new brigade, and a second could certainly have been found if the Germans had seriously demanded it. But after the elimination of the ethnic division, all efforts proved in vain.

The careers of all other German officers were considerably harmed by the unfortunate position into which Sigel was brought. Blenker's pitiful failure had already had a negative effect on the advancement of German leaders. The Sigel affair raised the prejudices of West Pointers against German officers even more. We particularly see this in the slow advancement of Osterhaus, Willich, von Steinwehr, Buschbeck, and others. Buschbeck, a true hero, never even became a titular major general, and his equally brave comrade von Wangelin also missed this honor. The gifted von Schimmelpfennig remained a divisional commander, and men such as von Gilsa and Krzyzanowski left the army as colonels, precisely the rank at which they had entered it. And the German people in America have virtually forgotten these, as well as so many other important German officers.

SCHURZ, Karl. Major general, born 1829 in Cologne, died May 1906 in New York. When Schurz departed, most German-American newspapers made a brief bow to Schurz the general, while they made a serious effort to do justice to Schurz the statesman. This is due partly to a lack of familiarity with military history, but partly to the continued operation of attitudes developed by German contemporaries during the war about Schurz's military activities. Those contemporaries never gave Schurz his due. For many of his compatriots, Schurz did not become important until long after the Anglo-Americans, particularly the most intelligent and elevated of them, had long since recognized his significance.

Schurz was far in advance of other German revolutionaries when he landed in America at the age of 23. He was carrying with him to America less German ballast than most of his friends. He had expanded his horizons in London and Paris, bringing with him an excellent knowledge of English. In contrast to the other refugees, he had completely finished with Germany as far as politics were concerned. He threw himself into learning the English language, as well as the history and constitution of the Union, and he immediately turned to American politics. He kept far away from the concentration of his German comrades and their fruitless reform attempts, and for that reason many Forty-Eighters regarded him as a climber, indeed as a renegade. There were too many "lions" among the Forty-Eighters, too many unbending knights of principle with their inconquerable inclination to conflict and hair-splitting.

The success of this young man among the Anglo-Americans also played a role. It was only later, when the anti-slavery movement received solid foundation with the founding of the Republican Party, that the liberator of Kinkel was able to impress his old revolutionary comrades from Germany. But the relationship between Schurz and the Forty-Eighters was never actually close. The German refugee element always treated "Schurz the American politician" with a certain coldness, even distrust.

At the start of the war, Schurz wanted to organize a cavalry regiment, but without his seeking it he was sent as minister to Spain. He only returned from this mission, which he never liked, in the spring of 1862, and on his request Lincoln gave him a commission as a brigadier general. Hence he took up the path blazed by the American politicians Banks, Butler, and others to promote their military careers. That alone was contrary to German sensibilities. If Schurz had first organized a regiment, then the promotion of Colonel Schurz to general would have followed within months, for a man with the reputation Schurz then had would not have remained a colonel for long. But because Schurz avoided this detour, he was severely criticized in the German press. The Forty-Eighters were then enthused over Sigel, and they acted only on his behalf. To them, Schurz appeared to be Sigel's rival. How little positive there is in the narratives of the German-American press over Schurz's first appearance in the field! He is consistently called "the civilian" Schurz. He was denied any gift for the military, and he was treated as an intruder who sought to take the place in the sun away from German professional officers.

How little this diminution was justified is shown by Karl Schurz's war record. The shield of Schurz the soldier is as clean as that of the citizen or statesman Schurz. One should refer to the chapters dealing with Second Bull Run, Chancellorsville, Gettysburg, and Missionary Ridge. Schurz stood in the front lines from the spring of 1862, to February 1864. He was moved to the West along with the XI Corps in the autumn of 1863, but his troops only saw action in the encounter of Wauhatchie. During the great Battle of Missionary Ridge, his division was attached to Sherman's corps and stood in reserve during the main conflict. Schurz could not participate in Sherman's March through Georgia because he was detached to Nashville for recruiting duty. He then laid down his sword, in keeping with the desires of Lincoln, who wanted to secure Schurz's political services for his second presidential campaign.

Schurz systematically prepared himself for a military career. When the German Forty-Eighters (and only they) liked to call him "the civilian" Schurz, they should have remembered that Osterhaus had only one year of Prussian military service over Schurz. In fact, the German professional officers who served under Schurz had great respect for him once they saw how well he led his troops in those dreadful eight hours on the morning of 29 August at Second Bull Run. At that time the "recruit and civilian" Schurz had been a soldier and commander only three months! In fact, Schurz (under Sigel) stood alone against Jackson's entire corps. Schurz's troops advanced all the way across the much contested railway causeway to Cushing Farm, and they maintained themselves there despite exhaustion until relieved after long vain expectation, and this small force, barely 3000 men, won advantages that could not be obtained by Pope's whole army a few hours later.

Karl Schurz also shared with Buschbeck the honors of the first day of battle at Chancellorsville. It was Schurz who never gave in to the blindness of his West Point colleagues; Schurz always foresaw an attack by Jackson and took every possible counter-measure his corps commander Howard permitted. Schurz's conduct in the battle days at Gettysburg also deserved the highest praise.

As far as Schurz's "climbing" is concerned, it can only be regretted that he didn't cultivate more of it. Why did he not energetically pursue the command of the XI Corps after Sigel resigned and had recommended Schurz as the most senior ranking of his division commanders?[16] Schurz might have thought that Sigel's support was enough. In addition, he says in his memoirs that only a professional soldier should have such a position. It almost appears that the German concept of "certification for office" was still in Schurz's blood. Schurz had only to send a word to Lincoln, and he would have succeeded Sigel. Schurz had the ear of the president then, as he did at all times when he was in Washington or the vicinity. He only needed to ask to be heard.

Who knows how deeply this would have offended his old German revolutionary comrades, who always accused him of climbing? Whoever can read between the lines will find indications in Schurz's memoirs of the reserve he imposed on himself. And how much he later complained because of his modesty in the spring of 1863. Schurz was obviously disturbed when he considered resigning after Howard's appointment as leader of the XI Corps, but he gave up the decision because he feared to injure the German cause. Not only Sigel, but also Stahel had left the corps, and for that reason alone did Schurz decide to remain in his position as division commander under a Howard.

One may properly evaluate Schurz the soldier on that fatal 2 May, when he continually begged his superior Howard to take defensive measures against an attack; when he composed the best plan to fight Jackson by placing the entire XI Corps in the open field of Hawkins Farm, in a place suited for artillery, then had to satisfy himself with moving three regiments from the wrong to the correct position for defense against the enemy. It is to be regretted all the more that Schurz was too modest to demand the position he deserved.

The fact that Schurz was never a climber shows in his fine letter to Lincoln, in which he declined the planned promotion to major general if his capable comrade Stahel could not also receive this honor.

American Germans can be proud of General Schurz. The ingenious man did fine services for his adopted country as a military leader.

STEINWEHR, Adolf von, born 1822 in Blankenburg on the Harz, died 1877 in Buffalo. He came from an officers' family, studied in Göttingen, and became a Prussian officer and a teacher at the military academy in Potsdam. He came to America in 1847 and served in the Mexican War. He worked in the settlement of Colorado and in the wild Southwest as a mapmaker. He returned to Europe, but soon came back to America to become a Latin farmer. In 1861 he organized the German 29th New York Regiment, becoming its colonel. He then distinguished himself under Blenker at First Bull Run and soon became a brigadier general, participating in the dreadful march of Blenker's division, later serving under Sigel in Pope's campaign, and fighting in the battles of Chancellorsville and Gettysburg in the XI Corps. He then went to Chattanooga and participated in the night battle of Wauhatchie, where his troops threw back the Confederate veterans of Longstreet through a brilliantly executed attack, contributing the most to the Union victory. Later von Steinwehr concerned himself with statistical matters, particularly concerning the strength of the German element in America. He was a significant topographer whose greatest work, a school atlas, is the best and most reliable map book created in America in his lifetime. This atlas was widely distributed and was the means by which von Steinwehr obtained a secure old age.

There is no doubt that von Steinwehr was the most thoroughly trained of all the German officers in the Union army. He also possessed a very precise knowledge of the American military and was much respected by many West Point officers. If it had been a question of knowledge, experience, and military ability when the highest commander for German troops in the East was chosen, von Steinwehr would have had to receive this honor. But in the spring of 1861, there was no time to search among the innumerable applicants. Self-seeking on the part of the climbers was very bad, and German officers were no exception. But von Steinwehr was no climber, and in the great lottery for the highest posts he drew a blank. He had to serve under Blenker, a trooper totally incapable of leading a division and never trained as an officer.

The causes for Steinwehr's relatively late emergence are unclear—whether it was the bitterness of a gifted soldier who had the misfortune of having to serve first under Blenker, then Frémont, then (after several months of service under Sigel, who always valued von Steinwehr) Howard; or whether it was that his inclinations lay more in general staff service than in leading troops. It is remarkable, for example, that Steinwehr's brigade was led at Cross Keys by Colonel Koltes, and that von Steinwehr is so seldom mentioned in the great battle of Second Bull Run. At that time he led one of Sigel's divisions, but it stood in reserve on the first day of the battle, and its regiments were brought forward one by one to strengthen Schurz's division. Nor did von Steinwehr stand out on the second day. His old brigade was led by Koltes, and even after Koltes fell, we do not find von Steinwehr at the head of his own troops. During this battle he was in Sigel's headquarters, and he acted as Sigel's support in leading the fighting.

At Chancellorsville, as well, von Steinwehr did not appear as a fighting general. We do see his capable hand in the preparations for the battle, for he built the trenches into which Buschbeck's brigade fled and then so splendidly defended. But when the attack began, von Steinwehr was escorting Barlow's detached brigade, on the orders of his corps commander, Howard. At the first shots, von Steinwehr rushed to the battlefield and organized a new position for Buschbeck, then left it to Buschbeck to lead the defense and win the glory from it. Von Steinwehr located himself behind Buschbeck's position, but he is not mentioned as a leading officer even by the best portrayer of the battle, Hamlin.

Almost until the Battle of Gettysburg, von Steinwehr did not come to blows on his own. It was in this battle that his military genius shone, and splendidly. It was he who recognized the importance of Cemetery Hill as a point of defense and immediately made use of it (for which Congress voted thanks to his corps commander, Howard). Von Steinwehr effectively defended this hill. Here he received divisions of the XI and I Corps (hardly half of them still capable of fighting) and continued defense on 2 and 3 July. In the

Chattanooga campaign, von Steinwehr had little occasion to intervene. Only Buschbeck's brigade came into combat, fighting several times with great distinction. In the history of the war, Buschbeck's brigade appears more often than the division commander under whom Buschbeck served. Throughout the entire Western campaign, von Steinwehr only earned military glory in the aforementioned night encounter at Wauhatchie. It is much to be regretted that von Steinwehr was not able to work as chief of general staff of the Army of the Potomac. His significant gifts would have had a very different impact in such a position.

WILLICH, August von. Born 1810 in Poznan, died January 1878 in St. Marys, Ohio. Brevet major general and division commander. It is necessary to deny the widely spread story that Willich was of Hohenzollern ancestry. The boy was raised in the Schleiermacher house in Berlin, then attended military academy and pursued a military career in Prussia. In 1841 Willich became a captain of artillery. He dedicated himself to freethinking views, resigned in 1846, and became a carpenter. His family disowned him. This marvelous oddball sought every opportunity to encounter his former colleagues dressed in a worker's blouse, carrying an ax on his shoulder! Then there was Willich's participation in the German Revolution, where he made a name for himself as a leader of volunteers in Baden. He fled to America, to Cincinnati. He became a friend of Stallo, who vainly attempted to dissuade Willich of his communist ideas.[17]

In April 1861 Willich entered the German 9th Ohio Regiment and became its drillmaster. He then organized the German 32nd Indiana Regiment, which took on the excess membership of the 9th Ohio and may be seen as the sister regiment to the 9th. The two regiments were siblings, and there was a good core in both. Willich trained them into splendid fighting regiments, which is how they appeared. Even in their first fights these regiments, advancing in response to Prussian trumpet signals, functioned like veterans. See Mill Creek and Shiloh.

Anglo-American officers were amazed at their discipline. When Willich did field maneuvers with these soldiers in the middle of the war, many Anglo-American officers watched as eager students. At first the Anglo-Americans smiled over the older man, particularly because he spoke a bookish sort of English with a strong German accent. Willich had a complete theoretical grasp of English, but his hard East-Prussian tongue could never master conversational pronunciation. He often used expressions that appeared only in literature and seemed odd to those used to the spare forms of conventional speech. (When such people try to read Shakespeare, they are lost.) But Willich's mockers were soon silenced. Whoever saw our hero in battle was compelled into respect, for the devil rode the old man in battle. He was always in the first ranks, where the bullets whistled the most, and there was where he seemed happiest.

Willich is the real *maréchal avant* of the Civil War. He had never learned fear. If his soldiers showed any inclination to seek in discretion the better part of valor, old Willich rode before the front and commanded, "Shoulder arms," "Unshoulder arms," "Present arms." Then there was a parade march by company as far as the area permitted. This was done several times in the thickest rain of bullets, at Shiloh and Perryville and once again at Chickamauga. We often find descriptions of such episodes by Anglo-American writers in the literature of the war.

Unfortunately, Willich only operated as a subordinate commander, as a brigadier and finally as a division commander. He led in his own right only once, when he took Liberty

Gap and Hoover's Gap, important passes through the Allegheny Mountains. Through Willich's victories in these passes, the advance of Rosecrans' army to Chattanooga was made possible. Willich's soldiers advanced in these struggles as if on parade. All commands were given by trumpet signals. The Anglo-American officers who watched this mode of fighting and its splendid success were amazed. To them it was something entirely new; to be precise, it was Prussian. Willich's German regiments also had a peculiar war cry, a short but loudly intense "Hurra," not the usual long, drawn-out wavering roar, "Hoo-rah-rah-rah."[18]

The old hero was captured by the Confederates when he was trying to return to his troops from headquarters during the Battle of Murfreesboro (or Stones River). His horse was shot dead, and he suddenly found himself surrounded by hundreds of the enemy. He was quickly exchanged, and was at Chickamauga to perform one of the most splendid of his war deeds. Then Missionary Ridge became his finest achievement. Without awaiting a command, he had his nine regiments climb up the heights, bringing along the troops beside them. Along with Sheridan, with whom he shared the honors, he became one of the heroes of this battle, which the commanding general, Grant did not want to fight but which ended with the finest of victories.

Willich fought at the front for three years. In the Battle of Resaca, at the start of Sherman's march through Georgia in May of 1864, he was so badly wounded by an enemy bullet that the old hero was made incapable of further service.

Willich remains one of the most sympathetic figures among the fighters of the Civil War. His most intense worshippers were the Anglo-American officers who served under him. He did have his peculiarities, of which his promotion of communist views was the most suprising. Often he would assemble his 32nd, speaking as a "citizen of Indiana," and he would give them German lectures on communism in camp. Whoever knew him recognized that these views (whose application to practical life in America has only produced failure) came from a great and noble heart. His soldiers came to know his nobility, as well. He shared his last possessions with them, and he starved along with them if necessary.

Among the thousands of German idealists who were driven to America, Willich should be named in the first place. He was the embodiment of selflessness. He was a bachelor, but wherever he appeared children followed him. "All American children are my children," he liked to say. When he died, drawers and chests were found full of candy and nuts for children. He was really a big child his entire life, but also a complete man. His comrade Ferdinand Vogeler held a German oration at his grave in the worthiest manner. A simple memorial in St. Marys, Ohio, decorates the grave of this true German hero.

STAHEL, Julius. A German-Hungarian Austrian officer, he joined the [Hungarian] revolutionary army of Görgey and Guyon. After the victory of the Russians, he fled via Germany to America. He was lieutenant colonel in Blenker's 8th New York Regiment. He was praised by President Lincoln for brave conduct at First Bull Run. In November 1861, Stahel became a brigadier general and leader of the 1st Brigade of Blenker's German Division. He participated in the main attack in the Battle of Cross Keys, which failed due to the stupid leadership of the 8th Regiment by Colonel Wutschel.

Stahel participated in Pope's campaign of 1862 under Sigel and fought with great distinction in Second Bull Run, covering the retreat of Pope's army with Schurz's division. On 29 September Stahel conquered Warrenton and took over a thousand captives. On

27 November he undertook a reconnaissance against Jackson at Ashby Gap, chasing the enemy across the Shenandoah to Sperryville, winning a second victory, and pursuing the enemy. He captured two flags; made considerable booty in provisions, horses, and cattle; and took several hundred captives. In the spring of 1863, Stahel was placed in the branch for which he was best suited, which was cavalry.

Stahel was one of the leaders who reorganized the previously poorly equipped and led cavalry of the Union and finally made it effective. Generals Hooker and Heintzelmann [Heintzelman] declared that Stahel's cavalry regiments were the best they had ever seen. At Lincoln's request these cavalry were used to defend Washington. Stahel was named major general at the same time as Schurz, on 14 March 1863. He served as commander of cavalry under General Reynolds, and at Frederick, Maryland, he had a successful encounter with enemy cavalry under General Young. Until March, 1864, Stahel led the cavalry in General Couch's corps. On 26 April 1864 he was detailed to Sigel's corps, which was advancing in the Shenandoah Valley but which was defeated by Breckinridge at New Market. Stahel did not have any effect on this battle, but he had a great deal in the battles that Sigel's successor, Hunter, had to fight in the Shenandoah Valley. Stahel led the vanguard in this operation. He was attacked by enemy cavalry under Jones on the march to Staunton, but he beat back the enemy and pursued him to Piedmont, where he encountered the strongly entrenched enemy. Stahel held the enemy in check until reinforcements under Hunter could arrive. In the following Battle of Piedmont, Stahel distinguished himself and earned the Medal of Honor. Although severely wounded at the start of the fighting, Stahel still led his squadrons to a splendid attack, broke through the defense lines of the opponents, and shattered them completely. As a result of his wounds he was on leave for a time. Stahel was later entrusted with the organization of recruiting units at Harpers Ferry and Martinsburg. General Stahel briefly worked as a corps commander. He resigned on 8 February 1865. After the war Stahel served as United States consul in Yokohama, and later in the same capacity in Shanghai. He represented the United States in the Far East for about twelve years. Later General Stahel had various successful undertakings in New York. As an elderly man of 85, the old hero makes the impression of someone in his sixties.

WEITZEL, Gottfried [Godfrey]. Major general and corps commander. Born in Winzlen, Rhenish Palatinate, he immigrated as a child, trained as an officer at West Point, and was a lieutenant in the Corps of Engineers of the Regular United States Army. He was chief engineer under Butler in New Orleans, then a brigadier on Banks' unfortunate Red River expedition. Under Grant, Weitzel became division commander in Butler's Army of the James, which lay before Richmond and constituted the right wing of the Army of the Potomac, and finally commander of the XXV (Colored) Army Corps, with which he was the first to enter the conquered rebel town of Richmond. The next day he received President Lincoln. Weitzel's chief significance in the Civil War was in his specialty as an engineer. Weitzel stood out splendidly as a bridge-builder and in laying fortifications, particularly the Union works before Richmond. After the peace he returned to the Regular Army and worked for many more years as an engineer. He died in Philadelphia.

KAUTZ, August V. Titular major general, born in Pforzheim. He emigrated as a child with his parents, who settled in Ripley, Ohio. As an eighteen-year-old he participated in the war against Mexico, and afterwards he became an officer in the United States Army.

Under Doubleday he went into the field with the 3rd Ohio Cavalry Regiment as lieutenant colonel, and he became one of the finest cavalry commanders of the Union, one of those who brought this neglected branch to high significance by 1863. At the end of the war he was commanding the XXIV Army Corps, with which he entered Richmond along with Weitzel on 3 April 1865. Kautz's accomplishments stand out less than those of infantry leaders, for cavalry rarely finds the occasion to attack in masses. Yet our compatriot Kautz had the opportunity as a cavalry commander to make as good a name as the famous Custer, who was incidentally also of German ancestry. General Kautz participated in more than a hundred encounters and battles. After the war Kautz made it to major general in the Regular Army. He died a few years ago in California. He was regarded as one of the most capable soldiers in North America. His brother Albert was an admiral and his third brother a naval captain. The father of these three brothers was the founder of the wine industry in the Ohio Valley in Ripley, Ohio, at the start of the 1830s.

* * *

Other German Officers and Notables of the Civil War Period

ADAMS, Emil. Major in the 9th Illinois Infantry Regiment, served after the war in the Regular Army.

ADOLPHUS, Dr. Philipp. Surgeon in the hospitals of Maryland.

ALBERT, Anselm. Hassendeubel's successor as lieutenant colonel of the 3rd Missouri Regiment, captured at Wilson's Creek as he fled with Sigel. He was exchanged; later colonel in the Battle of Pea Ridge, Arkansas, then chief of staff to General Frémont. He went with Frémont to Virginia in the Shenandoah Valley campaign of 1862 and became the actual leader of Frémont's troops (including the German Division) in the Battle of Cross Keys. When Frémont was replaced by Sigel, Albert withdrew, but he received a later command and was severely wounded and had to resign. He fought in the Hungarian patriotic army under Görgey and led one of the four attacking columns that took Ofen [in the 1848 Revolution – SR].

ALMSTEDT, Henry. Colonel of the 1st Missouri Reserve Regiment, then for three years in the 2nd Missouri Artillery Regiment. Later he became a paymaster in the Regular Army. Almstedt first came from Germany to Washington, where he was recognized as a relative by the Armisteads (a rich planter family in Virginia and Maryland). The president at the time, Polk, had an Armistead for a wife. The transformation of the name Almstedt into Armistead over the course of a century is of interest. On the alteration of German family names in America, see the useful work of Oskar Kuhn in *Americana Germanica*, nos. 3 and 4, 1902.

ALTER, Dr. Henry H. Surgeon in the 52nd Kentucky Regiment.

VON AMSBERG. Colonel of the 45th New York Volunteer Regiment, recruited almost entirely from Low Germans (most of them old soldiers). This regiment belonged to Blenker's German Division and later fought under Sigel and Schurz. Von Amsberg had earlier been a Prussian officer. He fought until the mustering out of the 45th, and later led a brigade.

ANDEL, Kasimir. Officer in the 12th Missouri Regiment. During the Spanish-American War he founded a regiment of Civil War veterans in Belleville.

ANNECKE, Fritz. Colonel of artillery in McClellan's staff, then leader of the 35th Wisconsin Regiment. Last of all he commanded the reserve artillery of the Army of the Tennessee. Annecke could not remain silent about the many inequities of the army. (Old German officers in particular could not quietly watch the often hair-raising failings of the officers placed over them.) As a result of such criticism, which could certainly be contrary to good discipline, Annecke was placed under arrest in 1863 and condemned to discharge. Born 1818 in Dortmund, Annecke had left the Prussian army for similar reasons. Although a Prussian officer himself, he had described duelling as childish. Annecke died after the war as an official of the German Society in Chicago. His wife was the poet Mathilde Franziska Annecke. Schurz was Annecke's adjutant in the Baden campaign. Annecke diligently corresponded for the *Augsburger Allgemeine Zeitung,* and his descriptions of the Battle of Shiloh, as well as of the march of Buell's army from Nashville to Pittsburg Landing, are of particularly great value.

†ARNDT. Major of the 1st Battalion of Light Artillery of New York, a former South German officer and Forty-Eighter who fought in the Baden revolution and fell at Antietam. His battalion, Brickel's artillery, consisted of four batteries, all with German crews under Major Brickel, with Captains Dietrich, Vögelin, Knieriem, and von Kusserow.

ASBOTH, [Alexander S.]. Colonel, former Austrian officer and German-Hungarian, belonged to Frémont's staff in Missouri, was a brigadier in Sigel's Division at Pea Ridge, distinguished himself particularly in that battle and was wounded in the storming of Elkhorn Pass. He later fought in Florida and was wounded several times, quite severely. The American consul in Buenos Aires, he died soon after the war as as a result of his last wounding. He received the rank of a brigadier general.

ASCHMANN, Rudolf. Captain in the Union States Sharpshooter Regiment, known as Berdan's Shooters. He is the author of the excellent book *Eine Schweizer Schützenkompagnie im Nordamerikanischen Kriege* ["A Swiss Rifle Company in the North American War"]. Aschmann lost a leg in the Wilderness Campaign of 1864. Aschmann's company of 106 men included 80 Swiss and 26 Germans. It was the elite sharpshooting troop of the Army of the Potomac and the first to receive repeating rifles. In the course of eighteen battles and encounters, the company was brought down to twelve men.

ASMUSSEN. Colonel, a former Prussian officer who was chief of staff of General O. O. Howard. He went to the Army of the Potomac with Sigel. He distinguished himself in Missouri, particularly in the Battle of Pea Ridge. He resigned after a severe wounding.

AUGUST, Otto. 45th New York, was a major on Howard's staff.

AXT, Dr. Gottfried. Surgeon of the German 20th New York Regiment.

BACHMANN, Dr. J. P. Surgeon in the 4th Kentucky Regiment.

BACKUS, Wilhelm. Served with distinction in Barnett's (Cleveland) Ohio artillery regiment under Groskopf, advancing from sergeant to battery chief.

BACKHOFF, Franz. Major in Sigel's artillery in Missouri. Participant in the military revolution in Rastatt, a Baden Forty-Eighter. He fought with distinction in the German Revolution. In Missouri, Backhoff distinguished himself under Sigel.

†BALBACH. An officer in the Baden general staff. He participated in the Revolution of 1849. Later, in America, he was active in coastal surveying. Major at the start of the war. Fell in one of the first fights.

BALLIER, [John F.]. Colonel of the strongly German 21st Pennsylvania Regiment and of the 98th Pennsylvania Regiment. Antietam campaign. Twice wounded. Ballier had participated in the Mexican War and distinguished himself to such a degree that he advanced from corporal to major. At the end of the Civil War, Ballier was commanding a brigade that particularly distinguished itself in the fighting before Washington in 1864. This was the defense against the attack of the Confederate General Early on Washington. President Lincoln visited the front and named Ballier a brigadier general on the field of battle for his services.

BARTH, George W. Major, 28th Kentucky Infantry Regiment.

BÄTZ, Henry. Major in the 26th Wisconsin Regiment. He was severely wounded at Gettysburg. Although he was ready for service again after recovery, he resigned as a result of the insults against the Germans after the Battle of Chancellorsville.

BÄUMER, Wilhelm. Colonel of the 1st Veteran Cavalry Regiment of Nebraska. From Münster in Westphalia. Distinguished himself in the Indian Wars that ran at the same time as the Civil War. He had Chief Black Kettle hanged despite the fact that 10,000 enemy Redskins were in the area. His regiment was half German.

BECK, Arnold. Major in the German 2nd Missouri Regiment. Led this regiment, in Laibold's brigade, in the Battle of Chickamauga. While attempting to rescue Davis's Union Division, which had been broken by the enemy, his regiment advanced with fixed bayonets, but it came under such murderous fire that almost half the men in the regiment were killed or wounded. It lost its flag after the color bearer and the entire color detachment had been shot down.

BECKER, Adolf. Last colonel of the Frémont Regiment, 46th New York. He enlisted in the regiment in 1861 as a private under Rosa and held all ranks up to regimental commander, going went through all campaigns. He distinguished himself particularly at Antietam and Petersburg.

BECKER, August. Well-known chaplain of the 7th German New York Regiment. An important journalist and poet, died in Cincinnati.

BECKER, Gottfried. Colonel of the purely German 28th Ohio Infantry Regiment, originally commanded by Moors. Led it from 1863 to 1865, primarily in the IX Corps. In the Battle of Antietam, it was the first regiment to cross the Antietam and attacked the strong rebel position on the other side.

BECKER, Karl. From Belleville. He later became the state treasurer of Illinois. Outstanding German. Lost a leg at Pea Ridge in the 12th Missouri Regiment.

†BEHR or BÄHR. Chief of the 6th German Battery of Indiana, fell at Shiloh. See on the Battle of Shiloh.

BELLEVILLE. Nowhere in the United States was enthusiasm for the war greater than in this purely German settlement. Belleville, in St. Clair County, Illinois, lies somewhat southeast of St. Louis; it is actually a German suburb of the large city of St. Louis. There is a highly fruitful, beautiful prairie, marked by some hills. The inspiration for its settlement certainly came from Duden, the Missouri pioneer. The families of Theodor and Eduard Hilgard of Speyer were the first settlers of Belleville in 1832. They were followed by Friedrich Engelmann from Bacharach in the following year. In 1834 came the von Wangelin family from Mecklenburg. The Ledergerbers also were among the pioneers. Their children grew up entirely in the spirit of their parents.

Eventually, around this German core there gathered more and more like-minded people from Germany: writers such as Dr. Gustav Bunsen; Dr. Bechelmann; Neuhoff; the important editor Wilhelm Weber; Decker; Mirus; Abend; Reuss; Schott; Theodor Hilgard from Zweibrücken, a true poet; the great engineer Julius Hilgard, the famed researcher of the Rocky Mountains and one of the premier American scholars. Further there were the physician Trapp; the Tittmann brothers from Dresden; Adolf Wizlicenus, an important scientist; Dr. Wichers; Dr. Georg Engelmann; Ewald von Massow (a friend of Fritz Reuter and like him condemned to death); and so on. With descendents there were about eighty highly educated German families which lived together in the "Latin settlement." This is where the term "Latin farmers in America" originated.

It was a circle such as shall never be found again in America. The year 1848 brought a large reinforcement. This is where Friedrich Hecker came with his friends such as Raith; the later General Osterhaus; Heinrich Hilgard, also known as Villard, the "king" of the Northern Pacific Railway; and many others who settled in Belleville. The Swiss settlement of Highland, founded by Köpfli, lay in neighboring Madison County. Via this neighborhood, the Swiss Emil Frey found access to this circle. Hence Belleville became a little Athens in America, a citadel of German education and liberal sensibility. (Read about it in Gustav Körner, who also belonged to the Belleville circle, and in Rattermann's Cincinnati *Deutscher Pionier*.) Hence it is easy to understand that Belleville became an armed camp with the outbreak of the war, and that the entire German youth of the settlement grabbed for weapons and participated with all their strength in the German uprising in St. Louis. The great German victory in St. Louis would hardly have been so splendid if there had been no help from Illinois. The 43rd Illinois Regiment, organized by Körner, consisted almost exclusively of the German youth of Belleville.

BELITZ, H. F. Colonel of the half-German 45th Wisconsin Regiment.

BENDIX, John E. First colonel of the 7th (Steuben) Regiment of New York, German Turners. Later colonel of the 10th New York Regiment. He was severely wounded at Fredericksburg.

BENECKE, Louis. Major. He organized the purely German Company H of the 18th Missouri and the half-German Company J of the 49th Missouri Regiment. These units fought continually with Confederate bushwhackers. Because the guns provided by the government were not adequate for this sort of warfare, Benecke ordered excellent Spencer carbines for his soldiers at his own expense. For this purpose he sacrificed $4000. Only with these guns could the bushwhackers be put down. Benecke has waited forty years for compensation for the weapons that were lost.

BENTZONI, Charles. Colonel of the 56th Colored Regiment.

BERNAYS, C. L. Journalist in St. Louis. Worked along with Börnstein on the *Anzeiger des Westens*. One of the best pens in German America. Bernays went to Washington to inform Lincoln about the situation of the Germans of Missouri, and it was essentially his doing that the president finally approved the arming of the German regiments.

BERTRAM, [Henry]. Lieutenant colonel of the half-German 20th Wisconsin Regiment, led a brigade in the Arkansas campaign with outstanding valor, distinguished himself at the taking of Mobile. Despite that, he remained a lieutenant colonel serving as a general.

BISCHOF. Lieutenant colonel of the German 15th Missouri Regiment. Died as a result of the exertions of the war.

†BLANDOWSKI, Konstantin. The first German-born officer to fall before the enemy, in the course of the conquest of the rebel Camp Jackson in St. Louis. He died on 25 May 1861. Blandowski had been trained as an officer in Dresden, had served in Algeria under the French, then fought in the Polish Revolution and later in Italy.

BLENKER, Ludwig [Louis]. Born 1812 in Worms, 1863 in Pennsylvania. He served as a police officer under King Otto in Greece. (Otto was a Wittelsbach and was then drawing many Bavarians to Athens.) In 1849 he was a colonel of the revolutionaries in Baden and then in the Palatinate. He conquered Ludwigshafen, occupied Worms, fought the Prussians at Bobenheim and defended Gernsbach (Baden) when fighting was already hopeless. He fled to America. Blenker is the German officer who was most graced by good fortune at the start of the war, but then vanished very quickly from view. He became a brigadier general.

BLESSING, Franz. Colonel. As a major he led the German 74th Pennsylvania Regiment (formerly Schimmelpfennig's) and distinguished himself especially at Second Bull Run. This regiment was one of those that passed across the railway causeway on the first day of battle and took the Cushing Farm.

BLESSING, Ludwig von. Colonel functioning as a general. A former Prussian officer, he became a lieutenant colonel in Colonel Siber's German 37th Ohio Regiment, which was recruited from Cleveland, Sandusky, and Toledo, Ohio. After Siber's resignation he led the regiment. He fought in the West, especially at Vicksburg and Chattanooga, and on the march through Georgia. An outstanding officer, always at the front.

BLÜCHER, F. A. von. Supposedly a relative of the [Prussian] field marshal, a major in the Corps of Engineers of the Rio Grande Department. He built the defensive works of Corpus Christi in Texas.

BLUME, Hans. Lieutenant colonel in Willich's 32nd Indiana Regiment. The last leader of the regiment after Erdelmeyer's resignation in September 1864.

BLUMENBERG, Leopold. Major, 5th Maryland Regiment, fought at Antietam in General Max Weber's brigade, which lost a third of its members in that battle. Blumenberg was seriously wounded there.

BÖCKE, L. Captain, 54th New York,, commanded the sharpshooting company that was the first attacked in the woods at Chancellorsville.

BODEN, Wilhelm. Major, 23rd Kentucky Infantry Regiment.

BÖBEL, Hans. Lieutenant colonel in the 26th Wisconsin Regiment, leading it at Gettysburg until the arrival of Colonel Jacobs. He was severely wounded and lost a leg, after which he had to resign. Böbel was a Forty-Eighter.

†BOHLEN, Heinrich [Henry]. Born 1810 in Bremen. A wealthy merchant in Philadelphia, had a remarkable fondness for the military. He participated in the siege of Antwerp in 1832, visited the Crimean War as an observer, and participated with honor as an officer in the war against Mexico. In 1861 he organized the 75th Pennsylvania Regiment at his own expense, became its colonel, and was already a brigade leader under Blenker in

1861. He fought with honor at Cross Keys, where he led a second assault after Stahel's brigade had been beaten back due to Wutschel's premature advance, but his attack also failed due to the lack of artillery. General Bohlen was shot to death at Freemans Ford on the Rappahannock on 21 August 1862. When the bullet hit him, he was bravely leading his troops in an advance against a superior enemy. Probably because Bohlen was hit in the back, the legend developed that he fell victim to an act of revenge by his own men. This story is probably false. It is most stridently opposed by General Stahel and particularly by those in the 75th. Bohlen was one of the best-loved officers of the entire corps. One of his grandsons is Herr Krupp von Bohlen, the present chief of the House of Friedrich Krupp in Essen.

BORCHERSRODE, Rudolf von. Colonel of the 5th Minnesota Volunteer Regiment, which had a third Germans. The major of this brave regiment, John C. Becht, a Turner from St. Paul, was also a German.

BÖRNSTEIN, H[einrich], [Henry Boernstein]. Colonel of the 2nd Missouri Regiment, a former Austrian officer and a Forty-Eighter. He was one of the chief leaders in the uprising of the Germans of St. Louis. A splendidly gifted man, editor and owner of the *Anzeiger des Westens*. Börnstein participated only in the first fights in Missouri. He was soon sent by Lincoln as consul to Bremen. Börnstein's memoirs are extremely readable.

BOHM, Edward H. Captain in the 7th Ohio Regiment (Cleveland), which was almost a third German. Bohm's special service was the history of almost all the German veterans of the city of Cleveland, which will be mentioned elsewhere.

BORCK, Dr. Surgeon, 46th New York Regiment.

BÖTTINGER, Otto. Major of the German 68th New York Regiment. He was made a prisoner of war and long endured the Confederate prison at Salisbury.

BOURRAY D'IVERNOIS, Gotthilf. Former Austrian officer, later in papal service. Bourray was at first in Blenker's entourage. Schurz mentions him positively at Chancellorsville, where he commanded the 68th New York Regiment in Schimmelpfennig's Brigade. He also led the regiment at Gettysburg. He was, however, an alcoholic and was discharged for that reason.

BRACHT, F. G. Major, 18th Kentucky Infantry Regiment.

†BRAUN, F. Captain. Temporary regimental commander of the 58th New York Regiment, he fell at Chancellorsville when his regiment, together with the Milwaukee Germans of the 26th Wisconsin gave stiff opposition to the attacking columns of Jackson on Hawkins Field.

BRAUN. Captain, an officer of a Wisconsin regiment, wrote a very interesting and important portrayal of the military prison at Andersonville. Braun endured a long stay there as a prisoner. In his writings he defended the Confederate overseer of prisoners, Wirz, who was notoriously hanged as the result of the sentence of a court martial.

VON BRAUSEN. Captain in the German 7th New York Regiment. He took over the leadership of the regiment in the Battle of Fredericksburg after Colonel von Schack took over the brigade.

BRENNHOLTZ. Lieutenant colonel, the half German 50th Pennsylvania Regiment, fought with honor at Fredericksburg.

BRESTEL. Major of the German 7th New York Regiment, leading it in the Battle on the Antietam against an enemy battery, taking it, taking a thousand captives and a Confederate flag. In the course of this, the barely 500 fighting men in the regiment suffered a loss of 22 dead and 42 wounded.

BRICKEL. Major of artillery. One of the best-known artillerymen in the Army of the Potomac. His battery was organized in Buffalo and consisted exclusively of Germans. He fought during the entire war with great distinction. Brickel was a Baden Forty-Eighter.

BRODBECK. German-Swiss colonel of a regiment organized in Dubuque, Iowa. He fought with distinction in several Western battles.

BROTZMANN, E. Lieutenant colonel, earlier captain of Mann's German Missouri battery in General Hurlbut's division. One of the heroes of Shiloh. The battery, whose entire crew was German, always stood in the thick of the fire and held bravely to the last shot. Brotzmann was praised in front of the troops by General Hurlbut. He later distinguished himself at Stones River.

†BRÜCKNER, A. Lieutenant colonel of the 73rd Pennsylvania Regiment in Koltes' brigade. Mortally wounded as leader of this regiment at Second Bull Run.

BRUCKNER, Dr. Karl. Regimental surgeon of the 17th Missouri Regiment.

†BRÜHL, Karl. Captain of Company F of the Benton County Home Guards, Missouri. This company was camped for the night of 19 June 1861 in a barn in Cole Camp near Boonville. During the night rebels under a Union flag came into the camp. Because reinforcements were being expected, the watch was misled by the Union flag. These rebels entered the barn and opened murderous fire on Brühl's sleeping company. Brühl and twenty-five men were killed at once, and many were wounded. The victims of this cowardly assault were mostly Germans fathers of families, farmers from Benton County, Missouri. There developed an intense night skirmish in which the enemy left thirty-one dead behind.

BUCHHOLZ, Alex. German captain of regular cavalry, led a regiment in the Red River campaign.

†VON BUGGENHAGEN. Earlier an officer in the Prussian Garde du Corps Regiment, captain in the German 7th New York (Steuben) Regiment, which he led several times as a deputy. He fell in the storm on Fredericksburg.

BUSCHBECK, Adolf. Prussian officer from Koblenz, teacher in the military academy in Potsdam. He came to Philadelphia in 1853, died in 1881 on a visit to Italy. Lieutenant colonel in the 27th Pennsylvania Regiment, which Buschbeck always led, as his first colonel, Einstein, was a nullity. Buschbeck distinguished himself at First Bull Run, at Cross Keys (in Stahel's brigade), at Second Bull Run and he was the true hero of Chancellorsville. He fought bravely at Gettysburg and Missionary Ridge, where out of the two divisions attached to Sherman, Schurz's and von Steinwehr's, only Buschbeck's brigade got to fight, doing so with great distinction and with Sherman's special praise on Tunnel Hill. Buschbeck participated in Sherman's march through Georgia and had great effect there. Buschbeck won special praise in the bloody Battle of Peachtree Creek on 19 July 1864. Buschbeck threw back the enemy three times at Ezra Church on 28 July. In Georgia the brigade fought in Hooker's XX Corps.

Adolf Buschbeck is one of the most splendid figures of the Civil War and, alongside Willich and Wangelin, one of our primary German fighting generals. He was always at the front, and his war record shows him participating in many decisive battles. His day of greatest glory was in Chancellorsville. (See in the text.)

It is to be regretted that such an outstanding soldier never received the honor he deserved. He certainly had every reason to expect to be a major general.

BUTZ, Kaspar. One of the best poets of German America, born in 1825 in Westphalia, died in 1885 in Des Moines, Iowa. A Forty-Eighter. We owe to him some of the loveliest poetic accomplishments stimulated by the Civil War, including "A Dirge for John Brown" and "To Abraham Lincoln."

CANDIDUS, Wilhelm. Major, 27th Pennsylvania Regiment.

CANTADOR, Lorenz. Colonel, 27th Pennsylvania Regiment. He led it at Chancellorsville and Gettysburg, distinguishing himself in both battles.

†CÄSAR, Hermann. Captain in the 52nd New York Infantry Regiment, regimental adjutant to von Freudenberg, was wounded at Fair Oaks and killed at Chancellorsville.

†The German officers who fell at CHANCELLORSVILLE, as far as known, were: Colonel Elias Peissner, 119th New York, staff; Captain F. A. Dessauer, 45th New York, staff; Major Robert Rother, 68th New York; Captain Jakob Petermann, 74th Pennsylvania; Captain Frank Sauter, 55th Ohio; Captain Karl Pizzola, 26th Wisconsin; Captain Ferd. Bapst, 82nd Illinois; Captain Albert Hoya, 68th New York; Dr. Karl A. Hartmann, 107th Ohio; Captain Heinrich von Schwerin, 119th New York; Lieutenant John Peterson, 107th Ohio; Lieutenant John G. Winkler, 107th Ohio; Colonel Charles Walter, 17th Connecticut; Captain Aug. Schüler, 26th Wisconsin; Lieutenant Colonel L. Hartmann, 29th New York; Captain Lor. Spönemann, 82nd Illinois; Lieutenant Konrad Schonder, 82nd Illinois; Captain Louis Lisky, 45th New York; Captain Chas. Leonhardt, 45th New York; Captain Fred. Braun, 68th New York; Captain John D. Pauling, 68th New York; Captain Jakob Leibfried, 73rd Pennsylvania; Captain August Schneider, 26th Wisconsin; Captain Karl Neukirch, 26th Wisconsin; Captain William Boltz, 73rd Pennsylvania; Lieutenant D. Heiler, 73rd Pennsylvania; Major Oskar von Meusel and Captain Otto Weber of General McLean's staff; Lieutenant Colonel W. Moore, 73rd Pennsylvania; Captain Bernhard Bode and Lieutenant Joseph Grimm of Buschbeck's staff; Captain Jastrow Alexander, assistant adjutant in General Steinwehr's staff altogether thirty-two, of which ten are mentioned individually in other places here.

CLAUSS (Clouse). General, came as a boy from Germany to the United States. In the Civil War he rose to the rank of captain, then entered the Regular Army and became a general. One of the most outstanding military men in America. He also made a name for himself as a teacher of military law, and he was regarded as an expert on American military history. He died in 1908.

COHN, Henry S. He went to war as a drummer of the 5th Kentucky Regiment and returned as a captain. Died in Louisville as leader of the *Anzeiger*.

CONRAD, Joseph. Colonel of the Swiss-German 15th Missouri Regiment, which fought at Pea Ridge in Asboth's brigade. (According to the information of the veteran Kilian in Manhattan, Kansas, the regiment had more Low Germans than Swiss.) Conrad led the regiment in Rosecrans' campaigns of 1863, particularly in the Battle on Stones River, as well as at Chickamauga, where he commanded a brigade that suffered heavy losses trying to protect Davis's division after it was smashed by the enemy; it finally had to give way before superior forces. Conrad distinguished himself in the storm on Missionary Ridge. There

Conrad was one of the first to penetrate the Confederate trenches on the heights. He was shot through the hip, but after a few months he was back with his brigade. In Sherman's campaign of 1864, Conrad led the 3rd Brigade of the 2nd Division in Wood's corps, fighting in the eleven battles through Atlanta before going with Thomas's troops to Tennessee. There his brigade fought with distinction in the last two large battles in the West, at Franklin and Nashville on 15 and 16 December 1864. Conrad led the 3rd Missouri Regiment as lieutenant colonel for the first two years of the war. He became a brigadier general in the Regular Army.

CORWIN, Otto von. Bore the title of a colonel, but he was only an observer of the fighting. A noted Forty-Eighter, one of the most important leaders of the Baden rebellion, for a time commandant of Rastatt. He was condemned to death but pardoned, and he spent many years in prison. He was a writer, a correspondent of the *Augsburger Allgemeine Zeitung* and the *London Times* during the Civil War in 1862. Corwin is very instructive about even the smallest things having to do with camp life, and he is always amusing to read. Corwin developed a plan in 1863 to recruit 20,000 veteran German soldiers in Germany for the Union. He presented the idea to Lincoln, who was charmed, but who let the plan fall after Stanton, the Secretary of War, opposed it. If the plan had been taken up by men such as Schurz, Osterhaus, Sigel, and others, it could perhaps have been carried out. But Corwin, who could be seen to be making money with the plan, was the least suited person to carry it out. Corwin remained in America for several years after the war and was an official in Washington, but then returned to Germany. He was close to the Salm-Salm's, and he either wrote or edited the very readable memoirs of Princess Salm-Salm.

CRÄMER. Colonel of the 17th Missouri (Turner) Regiment. He commanded it in the struggles before Vicksburg.

CRONENBILD. Major in Salomon's German 5th Missouri Regiment. Fought in Sigel's division at Carthage, Wilson's Creek and Pea Ridge.

DALLMEYER, W. K. Colonel of a militia regiment of Gasconade County, Missouri.

DAUM, Philipp. Lieutenant colonel of artillery, former Prussian officer. He was the actual victor in the Battle of Kernstown in May 1862. This victory, which was the sole one Union troops achieved over Jackson in that campaign, was ascribed to General Shields. But Shields was not even present at the battle, although his troops were involved. Irishmen assert that their compatriot Shields was the sole man who could beat Jackson. But the rebels fled before Daum's artillery. There was a continual rivalry between German and Irish regiments throughout the war.

DEGENER, Eduard. Outstanding friend of the German pro-Union people in Texas, co-founder of the German settlement of Sisterdale on the Guadalupe River. He was from Brunswick and emigrated in 1850. His two sons fell in the encounter on the Nueces River. Degener was thrown into prison by the Confederates, but he was released months later on bail. After the war Degener was elected to Congress.

DEGENFELD, Christoph von. Major of the 26th Ohio Infantry Regiment, a Prussian officer. He was severely wounded at Salzburg, Virginia, in October 1864, and died in Sandusky, Ohio, after long suffering. A part of a key Degenfeld was carrying was impaled into his body by the bullet and could not be removed. The 26th Ohio Regiment, organized by Degenfeld, was one of the best in the Western army.

DEITZLER, [George W.]. Colonel of the half-German 1st Kansas Regiment. Colonel Deitzler led a brigade in the fateful Battle of Wilson's Creek, consisting of two Kansas regiments and one Iowa regiment (the same one that wore gray uniforms and had earlier been attached to Sigel's brigade).

DELFOSSE, Jul. N. Major, 12th Kentucky Cavalry Regiment.

†DEMMY, Charles. A post of the Grand Army is named for this brave German captain of the 12th Missouri Regiment. Demmy fell in the storm on Vicksburg.

†DENGLER, Adolf. Outstanding Forty-Eighter. He defended Freiburg im Breisgau against the troops of Baden. Later a Latin farmer in Belleville, Illinois. In April 1861 Dengler organized a company of young Germans from Belleville and led them to St. Louis, where they were attached to Sigel's 3rd Missouri Regiment. An intimate friend of Sigel, Dengler fought at Carthage, Wilson's Creek, and Pea Ridge and became a colonel in the 3rd (German) Missouri Regiment, falling in the great storm on Vicksburg on 22 May 1863.

†DESSAUER. Major in the general staff of the XI Corps. He fell at Chancellorsville, shot from his horse while bringing Gilsa's command for retreat to the 54th New York Regiment.

VON DEUTSCH. Colonel of the half-German 4th Missouri Cavalry Regiment. Its Company M consisted of the former Milwaukee Cavalry, all veteran German soldiers.

DICK, Hermann. Battery chief from Philadelphia. He later became a journalist and local editor of the *Philadelphia Demokrat.*

DIECKMANN, Julius. Major, led the 1st Battalion of the 15th New York Artillery Regiment at Cold Harbor, June 1864.

DIETRICH, Henry. Captain in the 39th New York Regiment (formerly the Garibaldi Regiment). At Gettysburg the regiment numbered only four companies, 307 men. All of them were Germans save a few German Swiss. After the wounding of Major Hildebrandt, Brigadier General Willard functioned nominally as the commander, but each captain led his unit autonomously. On 2 July the 39th recovered the 1st Battery, 5th Regular U. S. Artillery, from the enemy. The regiment lost twenty dead and forty-six wounded in this bayonet charge, hence losing almost a quarter of its numbers within minutes. The state of New York honored this deed by placing a large granite block with an inscription. At its unveiling, Captain Dietrich gave the principal speech in German. This was printed in German in the work *New York in the War.* The 39th Regiment also distinguished itself on 3 July. It stood along with an Ohio and a Minnesota regiment as pickets, ahead of the battle line, as the main enemy attack under Pickett commenced. Pickett was held for a while, which made throwing back his attack much easier, deciding the main battle in favor of the Union. Captain Dietrich was provost marshal in Centreville from 1862 to 1863. He distinguished himself by purging the area of guerillas and bushwhackers. At the young age of 15 he had fought on the barricades in Hesse-Kassel.

†DIETZ. Earlier a captain of engineers in the Confederate army in Texas. He was impressed into service as one of the pro-Union people in Texas. He drew the plans for all the fortifications of Galveston and environs. He was only able to desert in March 1864 and then served under the flag he loved. He fell as a Union officer in the fighting before Petersburg, Virginia.

DILGER, Hubert. Battery commander, earlier an artillery officer in Baden, he came to America to offer his services. So much has already been said in the narrative that there is little left to say. Although recognized as such by Anglo-American historians, this true war hero remained a mere captain in artillery despite his many deeds of glory. After the war, Dilger planned to write a history of the Germans in the Civil War, but a fire robbed him of all his valuable material.

Dilger belonged to Blenker's German Division and first came into the face of the enemy in the Shenandoah Valley in June 1862, at Cross Keys. He led Company J of the 1st Ohio Artillery Regiment as a battery chief. He performed excellent service in Second Bull Run, as well as at Chancellorsville and Gettysburg. He led the sole cannon that came into operation in the defensive fight of Buschbeck's brigade at Chancellorsville. There he escaped from the pursuing enemy as if by a miracle. In late summer, Dilger went with the XI Corps to Chattanooga and was honorably involved in the great battles around that town. He remained in the Western army and went with Sherman through Georgia and both the Carolinas, all the way to Richmond.

Dilger was known all over the entire Northern army and was regarded as one of the finest officers of the Northern forces. He covered himself with glory in every battlefield he entered, particularly in the innumerable fights of Sherman's army. Infantry always went into battle in a better spirit when it knew that Dilger's Battery was also there. The author has received dozens of letters declaring that Dilger was the best artillerist in the entire Northern army. The old hero lived as a farmer in Port Royal, Virginia, which recalled the Black Forest. Dilger took great interest in the author's work, but due to illness he could not participate as a collaborator. He wrote to the author: "My war experiences were so unenjoyable in their results that they swell up in the form of memories that only irritate me, and I can neither lie nor veil them. I now stand on totally neutral ground."

†DISTER, Peter. Lieutenant colonel and temporary leader of the 58th Ohio Regiment. He fell on 28 December 1862 in the storming of the fortifications of Chickasaw Bluffs near Vicksburg, along with Captains Kinser, Deffenbach, Kette and Oderfeld. The regiment was recruited in Dayton and was almost entirely German. He was the first to enter Fort Donelson. Dister, born in Gundersheim near Worms, had been a soldier in Hessia. He fought in the First Battle of Bull Run in the 1st Ohio Regiment, later at Shiloh, and in all fights under Sherman until the first attacks on Vicksburg. A brother of Dister was a captain in the 58th Ohio Regiment.

DOMSCHKE. From Milwaukee. Officer in a Wisconsin regiment. He wrote a book on his war experiences. Compare on the same subject the *Martyria Andersonville* (Boston, 1866), by Augustin Hamlin.

DORRIES, F. Chief of Battery L of the 1st Ohio Artillery Regiment.

DOTZE, August. Lieutenant colonel of the 8th Ohio Cavalry Regiment, fought from 1861 to 1864 in West Virginia, also under Sigel in his second New Market campaign. He was captured and languished in Libby Prison.

DOUAI, Dr. Adolf. Editor of the German *San Antonio Zeitung*. One of the most clever and loyal Union men in Texas, a fruitful author and an outstanding pedagogue.

DÖHN, Dr. From Dresden, a Forty-Eighter refugee. One of the leaders of the German uprising in St. Louis.

DÖPKE, Adolph. Colonel, 45th New York, distinguished himself at Gettysburg, where the regiment took several hundred prisoners. He served until the end of the war. He led the first picket skirmish of the German Division at Annandale, Virginia, in March 1862.

DÖRFFLINGER, Karl. Of Milwaukee, an officer in the 26th Wisconsin Regiment. He lost a leg in the Battle of Chancellorsville. He wrote a history of the German 26th Regiment. An outstanding pedagogue and author in Milwaukee.

†DUYSING. Major. Former Electoral Hessian artillery officer. He gave excellent service in the Army of the Potomac. He died as a result of severe wounds. Buried in Arlington Cemetery.

†EGOLF, Joseph von. Captain in General Carr's staff, fell at Second Bull Run. Earlier a Prussian engineering officer.

VON EGLOFFSTEIN, [Baron Fred W.]. Colonel of the German 103rd New York Regiment. He had been an engineering officer in Germany. Colonel von Egloffstein organized what was called an elite company in the 103rd Regiment whose members consisted entirely of former German officers. The colonel promised these men rapid advancement. They also bore a special decoration on their uniforms. The company cut miles deep into enemy territory in the fighting around New Bern, driving back the enemy pickets and taking 200 prisoners. On this occasion the company was reinforced by volunteers and numbered about 150 men. The colonel was twice wounded on this expedition.

Lieutenant Colonel Kretschmar of the 103rd Regiment conspired against von Egloffstein, and he had to resign, but he was later rehabilitated and was promoted to brevet general. As a result of his wounds, von Egloffstein became incapable of service. His successor was Ringgold from Württemberg, who fell at Suffolk, and then Wilhelm Heine of Leipzig, a well-known writer and artist. Several from his elite company later transferred to the Regular Army or became officers. The 103rd Regiment was supplemented by reinforcements three times, but it suffered so much that only three companies survived at the end of the war. Captain Redlich led this battalion back to New York in 1865. The regiment fought in the IX Corps under Burnside in the New Bern campaign; then on the Antietam; at Fredericksburg; at Suffolk, in the Shenandoah Valley; at the siege of Charleston; and later under Grant at Petersburg and through Appomattox.

VON EINSIEDEL. Saxon officer, led the 41st New York (De Kalb) Regiment at Chancellorsville and Gettysburg.

†VON ENGEL. Major in General Casey's staff. Severely wounded, he jumped out of a window while in a fever. The son of a Saxon lieutenant general, von Engel took part in Frémont's pathfinding expeditions as a topographical engineer.

ENGELMANN [Engelman], Adolf. Brigadier general, born 1825. He emigrated as a child with his famous father to the German Latin settlement in St. Clair County at Belleville, Illinois. He was an officer in the Mexican War and was severely wounded. He went from America to Schleswig-Holstein to fight against the Danes in 1848. Returning to the United States, he became a farmer in his home area. In 1861 he was lieutenant colonel in the 43rd Illinois Regiment, in which the flower of German-American youth of Belleville served. Julius Raith was his colonel. When Raith fell bravely at Shiloh, A. Engelmann became his successor, and soon he was also leader of the brigade. He fought at Vicksburg and in Grant's subsequent campaigns in the West. He particularly distinguished himself in Banks' unfortunate Red River campaign, where he led a brigade under Friedrich [Frederick] Salomon. Gustav Körner wrote of him, "He is his father's son—that says enough."

†ELLWANG, M. Major in the half-German 6th Kentucky Infantry Regiment. Fell at the start of the war.

EPPSTEIN, Joseph. Lieutenant colonel, 5th Missouri Militia.

ERDELMAYER, Franz. The third colonel of the German 32nd Indiana Regiment, he led the regiment from the autumn of 1862 through the rest of the war. Coming from Indianapolis, he had been an officer in Germany. He distinguished himself at Stones River, but particularly at Chickamauga and in the storming of Missionary Ridge, where he was the first to storm the trenches of the Confederates on the heights. The brave old veteran was still living in Indianapolis in 1910.

†ESSIG. Captain, commanded a battery in Sigel's Division during the fighting in Missouri. He had been Sigel's adjutant during the Baden Revolution. General Osterhaus also praises Essig as a capable artilleryman.

THE FIRST VOLUNTEEERS of the Civil War to be put in service by the Union were the German Turner Rifles of Washington. They had already organized in the last days of 1860, immediately after the occupation of Fort Moultrie by South Carolina troops after that site was abandoned by Major Anderson. This company was mustered in during the first days of January 1861 and was reinforced by the Baltimore Turners in April 1861. The Turner Volunteers formed the honor guard and body guard of the new president at Lincoln's inauguration. The company was joined to the 8th Battalion and formed the vanguard of the first march of Union troops into Virginia on 23 May 1861, which opened the Bull Run campaign. Two members of this German Turner Company, Johann Ricks and Martin Ohl, fell on 7 July 1861 as the first victims of the Civil War in open fighting with the enemy. Several militia organizations dispute the honor of having been the first volunteers. It can be remarked that the noted German-American historian L. P. Hennighausen in Baltimore, himself a volunteer from those days, detailed this information at a great veterans' meeting in Washington on 12 April 1886, and that there may be no doubt that German Turners were the first volunteers of the Civil War.

FAHRENHOLTZ, O. W. Coming from one of the German settlements near San Antonio, he entered the Navy as a 16-year-old boy in New Orleans and served through the entire war as a sailor and petty officer. He was wounded several times, remained in the Navy, took an officer's examination, and rose to be a rear admiral, commanding the cruiser *Monocacy* during the Spanish-American War.

FÄHTZ, C. F. M. Lieutenant colonel of the 8th Maryland Regiment, former Austrian officer and a revolutionary in Hungary.

FASTRAM, P. S. Commanded Battery E of the 1st Rhode Island Artillery Regiment.

FIALA, John A. Colonel, chief of the topographical division in Frémont's staff during the Missouri campaign of 1861, he was praised by Sigel as an extraordinarily gifted officer. He had earlier been an officer in south Germany.

FINKELNBERG, Gustav. Adjutant of the 3rd Missouri Reserve Regiment under Colonel Fritz. Later elected several times to Congress from St. Louis. One of the most capable and knowledgeable German congressmen. Currently a federal judge in Missouri. A significant German-American.

FLAD, Henry. Colonel of the Missouri Engineering Regiment. He was one of the most significant engineers in America and during the war distinguished himself particularly as a bridge builder. After the war, Flad became the first assistant to Eads in building the great Mississippi bridge, and he is truly to be seen as the genuine creator of this marvel of technology. Until his death he was the president of the Board of Improvement in St. Louis.

FORSTNER, Siegfried von. Major in the 3rd New Jersey Cavalry Regiment and a topographer, making several reconnaissances under Sumner of the enemy positions at Centreville and Manassas and fixing the results in good maps.

FRANK, John. Chief of Battery G of the 1st New York Artillery Regiment.

FRANK, Paul. Colonel of the 52nd New York, a heroic German regiment that was later led by the brave Colonel Freudenberg. A titular general, he commanded a brigade in Hancock's corps from the Wilderness Campaign until Petersburg and the end of the war.

FREY, Emil. German Swiss, major. After the war he returned to Switzerland and later functioned as Swiss ambassador in Washington and held the office of federal Swiss president. He was still living in Bern in 1910. He organized the Swiss sharpshooters' company in Hecker's 82nd Illinois Regiment. He was an intimate friend of Hecker. He fought with great distinction at Chancellorsville, becoming a major on the field of battle and leading a portion of the regiment at Gettysburg. There, at the withdrawal of the XI Corps, he was captured in the streets of the town and taken to the Libby officers' prison in Richmond. He published his experiences there in the *North American Review*. Mr. Frey provided the author with a translation of this writing. The facts described there were confirmed word for word by Colonel Markbreit (see him). Because the portrayal of prison atrocities is in such disrepute among Southern writers, it should be stressed that two believable witnesses could be presented for what follows.

Major Frey was delivered to Libby on 18 July 1863. He was kept in a room in which there were citizens of Maryland and Pennsylvania who had been taken as hostages by General Lee on his campaign through Pennsylvania. Frey says:

> Some of us still had some hard bread with us, and when we heard that these citizens were suffering from severe hunger, we threw them the rest of our bread. These citizens, who bore the outer marks of respectability, threw themselves on these crumbs with passionate panic, literally slugging one another to possess them. It was painful to see the greed with which those who emerged victorious from this combat gulped the bread they had won.

Major Frey then told the fate of the two officers Sawyer and Flinn, who had been condemned to death as hostages and whose execution was only thwarted because Lincoln threatened to have General Lee's son, who had been captured, shot. Our witness continues:

> Ten months after my imprisonment the fate of Sawyer and Flinn was to strike me. A Northern court martial had condemned to death three Confederate officers, Armsey, Gordon, and Davis. On the orders of Jefferson Davis, three of ours were chosen as hostages for the lives of those condemned, and the lot fell on Major N. Goff, Lieutenant Manning, and me. The commandant of Libby Prison, Major Turner, informed us of the matter and said to us very clearly that if Armsey, Gordon, and Davis were shot, no power on earth could save us from the same fate. We were led to the cellar and locked into a dark cell 9 feet long and

6 1/2 wide. It was 3 May 1864. I was then 25 years old, the eldest of us three. If what we had endured up until then was almost intolerable hunger, then true starvation began. Our daily ration, which we received about noon, consisted of a small piece of cornbread, a piece of rancid bacon and 6 to 7 tablespoons of what are called Negro beans or rice. The entire ration, according to command of the officials, could not weigh more than 14 ounces.

Fortunately whole herds of rats lived in our cellar. Friend Manning proposed to us that we hunt down these beasts and eat them. He constructed the trap, using the half-rotten bacon as bait. When the rat was caught, it was my job to lift the lid carefully so that the rat's head could be seen. In this situation the major was to intervene by beating the rat over the head with a wooden stick until it was dead. The next day the rats would be cleaned and cooked by the Negroes who cleaned our cells in the morning, and we ate them. There has to be powerful hunger in order to overcome the disgust these beasts cause. On 21 May our guard told us that we probably would not be hanged. The Confederate officials did not tell us that President Lincoln had commuted the execution of the three Confederates, and other Southern officers had been designated as hostages for us and put in solitary confinement.

Soon the cell next to us filled with other hostages. Among them were Lieutenants Markbreit and Pavey. We developed as lively an interchange as our increasing weakness permitted. We told one another stories from home, and because the same stories were often repeated, we decided that it would be forbidden to tell the same story more than ten times.

On 18 June we were taken along with some captured Negro soldiers to the military penitentiary in Salisbury, North Carolina. The physician had declared that remaining in the cell any longer, of which a more detailed description the reader has been spared, would unfailingly kill us. In this penitentiary we were with a gang of criminals, never sure of our lives for a moment, until more of our prisoners arrived and we became the majority. A plan to break out was betrayed and all officers taken to Danville, and from there back to Richmond. On 14 January 1865 I was finally exchanged.

In the winter of 1883-84 I met Goff and Markbreit in a soirée of Senator Chandler. I was then Swiss emissary in Washington. Goff had meantime become Secretary of the Navy under President Hayes, and Markbreit represented the United States as resident minister in Bolivia. We could not have dreamed of that in our cells.

FREUDENBERG, C. F. Colonel of the German 52nd New York Regiment which suffered so dreadfully in fighting. Freudenberg was a Forty-Eighter. He was severely wounded twice. After the war he became a captain in the 14th Federal Infantry Regiment and mustered out as a lieutenant colonel in 1877. He participated in a subsequent campaign against the Sioux. Freudenberg participated in the Baden Revolution as a 15-year-old boy.

FRITSCH, F. O. von. Captain in the 68th New York Regiment. Adjutant of General von Schimmelpfennig. Author of the book *A Gallant Captain of the Civil War* (London,

1902). Otto von Fritsch had been an officer of the Saxon Cavalry Guards. After an honorable discharge he went to Mexico to fight for Maximilian, came to the United States in 1862, and soon became Schimmelpfennig's adjutant. He was sent by his general to reconnoiter at Chancellorsville, ran right into the enemy, and reported it, but his report was not believed. In the battle, von Fritsch was severely wounded. His book is certainly the best of the entire literature dealing with the inner operations of the Union army.

FRITSCH, W. A. Medical doctor, Evansville, Indiana. Author of *Die Geschichte des Deutschtums von Indiana* ["The History of the Germans of Indiana"] (New York: Steiger, 1896). This is a very interesting brochure containing reliable information on the participation of the Germans of Indiana in the Civil War. Fritsch served as an officer in the half-German 136th Indiana Regiment, and he was honorably involved in the march through Georgia.

FRITZ, Emil. Captain, commanded the 1st California Cavalry Regiment in the Rio Grande campaign in Texas. He was honorably involved in taking Fort Thorne. He led many severe encounters with the Navajos.

FUCHSHUBER. Chaplain in the 9th Ohio Regiment. His sermons were freethinking lectures. Despite this, he was an excellent advisor to the soldiers, wrote letters for them, and made himself useful in the field hospital.

FUGER, Friedrich. Sergeant-artificer in Battery A, 4th New York Artillery Regiment. He was promoted to lieutenant on the battlefield of Gettysburg and received the Medal of Honor. The citation reads

> This officer, then a sergeant, took over the command of the battery after all the officers had been killed or wounded, and after five cannons had been rendered useless at Pickett's charge against Cemetery Ridge (Gettysburg). Fuger fought with great bravery with the cannons still capable of use, until the battery was pulled back on higher orders.

FUNK, A. Colonel of the reorganized 39th New York, the Garibaldi Regiment. Funk led the regiment, which had been amalgamated with the 37th New York, only after Gettysburg.

†FUSSER. Commandant of the gunboat *Miami,* which sank in battle with the Confederate ironclad *Albemarle.* Fusser and his entire crew died.[19] General Hawkins said of this German naval hero, "He was a rare man, patriotic, loyal, manly, as well as modest, careful and a lover of truth in the highest degree. There never was a braver man than Fusser."

GELLMANN, F. Colonel of the 54th New York Regiment. Distinguished himself several times.

†GERBER, Gustav von. Lieutenant colonel of the 24th Indiana Regiment, fell at Shiloh at the head of a brave band. General Lew Wallace, the poet, in whose corps the 24th fought, said of him, "No one died more gloriously than Gerber. And yet so many brave men died at Shiloh, and so many brave deeds were done."

GERBER. Lieutenant colonel, former Prussian officer, was murdered at the start of the war by a jealous lover who mistook him for another.

GERHARDT, Joseph. Brevet brigadier general, born 1817 in Bonn. Forty-Eighter, escaped at Rastatt and fled via Switzerland to America. At the outbreak of the war he founded the Turner Company in Washington and became its captain. Later colonel of the

46th New York Volunteer Regiment. Served with great distinction and named brevet brigadier at the end of the war.

†GERSON, Otto. Captain in the 54th New York Infantry Regiment, captured at Chancellorsville and shot by the guards in the officers' prison in Macon, Georgia, when he came too near the dead line while grabbing a piece of bread thrown at him. His fate remained unknown into the 1890s and was only discovered through an incidental mention in Hadley's book, *Seven Months a Prisoner.*

†GIESY, Henry H. Major of the 46th Ohio Regiment, was shot while bravely advancing at Dallas, Georgia, in the summer of 1864. Giesy participated in all the campaigns of the XIII Army Corps in which Sherman's original division was involved and fought in all the battles from Pittsburg Landing (Shiloh) to Dallas, Georgia.

GIESECKE, Jul. Captain, opened the skirmish at Pigeon Ranch (Santa Fé Expedition). He was in the 4th United States Infantry.

†GIESLER, Julius. Captain in the 3rd Wisconsin Cavalry Regiment, a former Prussian officer, fought in the West and particularly distinguished himself in tough and bloody fights with the guerillas. He fell shortly before the conclusion of peace, pierced by twelve bullets fired from an ambush near Little Rock, Arkansas, in the middle of March 1865. He came from Westphalia and was an intimate friend of Kapp, Schurz, and Willich.

GILSA, Leopold von. Former Prussian officer. He fought in the army of the patriots in Schleswig-Holstein from 1847 to 1848. He was in America in the early 1850s. As with so many of his comrades, he at first had a hard time. For a long time von Gilsa supported himself in New York through singing performances and as a piano player in the demimonde and polka bars of the New York Bowery. The war freed him from this misery. He became a colonel of the 41st New York (De Kalb) Regiment, which consisted exclusively of veteran German soldiers. He participated in the forced march of the German Division and the Battle of Cross Keys, Virginia, where von Gilsa distinguished himself and was seriously wounded. He then fought with Sigel in Pope's campaign of 1862, was Sigel's chief of staff and particularly distinguished himself at Second Bull Run. In the spring of 1863, he received command of the 1st Brigade of Devens' division in the XI Corps, and he received the full impact of the whole of Jackson's army at Chancellorsville. There he conducted himself well and was able to resist the vastly superior enemy for at least a while. At Gettysburg his brigade suffered heavy losses in the fighting on 1 July. In the Confederate attack on Cemetery Hill on the evening of 2 July, this badly-positioned brigade had to take the full impact of the enemy as it had at Chancellorsville. It was dispersed by superior force, pulled back to the main corps, and then fought on bravely.

Von Gilsa was sent with his brigade to the Carolinas in the autumn of 1863 and fought alongside Schimmelpfennig in the siege of Charleston. The 41st Regiment was the last to be mustered out in 1864. Von Gilsa went back to New York with the remnants of his old regiment, was suitably celebrated there, and in the winter of 1864-65 organized a new regiment, which never got into battle. He was a brave and careful officer, and it is extremely regrettable that he was never promoted to general. Princess Salm-Salm claimed in her memoirs that she was the one who prevented von Gilsa's promotion. (Felix von Salm-Salm was for a while von Gilsa's subordinate, and the two were enemies.) The princess was an intriguer, and it is certainly not impossible that she was the reason this capable German officer left the service after four years of fighting, with the same rank at which he had entered the army. A Grand Army post in New York preserves his name.

Many American military histories, including Doubleday's, report an anecdote about von Gilsa. On the retreat from Chancellorsville, von Gilsa encountered his corps commander, Howard, who was supposed to have admonished von Gilsa to trust in God. In response, von Gilsa roared a selection of barracks curses in German, so that Howard believed that von Gilsa had gone mad.

GLANZ, Charles. Colonel of the mostly Pennsylvania German 153rd Pennsylvania Regiment, which stood on the extreme right at the Battle of Chancellorsville and briefly stood with the 54th New York after the 41st and 45th New York had been dispersed.

GOEBEL, F. Lieutenant colonel of the German 7th New York Regiment.

GOLLMER, Hugo. Speaker of the St. Louis Turner Society, captain in the 1st Missouri Regiment. Even before Lincoln's call in April 1861, Gollmer had organized his Turner Company. He later served as an officer in the 17th Missouri Regiment before entering the topographic service. He designed the first war charts for the Missouri campaign.

GÖBEL, Gert. Leader of the Germans in Franklin County, Missouri. He came as a youth with his father, a professor of mathematics, from Koburg to Missouri. He was a farmer, trapper, and author. His book *Länger als ein Menschenleben in Missouri* ["Longer than a Generation in Missouri"] is one of the most valuable contributions to German-American history.

GÖLZER, August. Lieutenant colonel, 60th Indiana Regiment.

GORDON, William E. Chief of staff for General Osterhaus. Everyone thought this Scot was a German. He had attended school in Württemberg, and he was the drillmaster of the German St. Louis Turner Company, which was already learning the English drill system in January 1861. Gordon was the right hand of General Osterhaus and took part in all his campaigns.

GREBE, Wilhelm. Captain of Company F, 4th Missouri Cavalry. From Hildesheim. He received the Medal of Honor from Congress for his heroic actions in the Battle of Jonesboro, Georgia, 31 August 1864. Grebe waged a duel with his German comrade Hansen, and for that reason they were both discharged by a court martial. Congress suspended that sentence through a special law twenty years later and rehabilitated the brave Grebe.

GREBNER, Konstantin. Wrote the history of the German 9th Ohio Regiment of Cincinnati. The material for this book, published by Rosenthal & Co. of Cincinnati, came essentially from Captain Henry Metzner and Captain Bertsch, officers of the 9th Ohio Regiment.

GREUSEL, Nikolas. German-Alsatian. He came with his parents to America as a child, served with honor as a captain in the 7th Michigan Regiment in the Mexican War, then as a major first with the 7th Illinois Infantry Regiment at the outbreak of the Civil War, later as colonel of the 36th Illinois Regiment. He was honorably discharged due to illness in February 1863.

†GRIMM, Franz. Editor of the *Belleviller Zeitung* and captain in the 43rd Illinois Infantry Regiment. He died a heroic death at Shiloh, pierced by several bullets as he threw his company against attacking rebels.

GROSSKOPF, Edward. Famous artillery leader from Dayton, Ohio. He fought in the 10th Ohio Battery from Shiloh to Milligan Bend; severely wounded several times, he later served as an engineering officer in General Morton's staff; he valiantly led the 20th Ohio Battery in 1863 in the great battles of the West, specifically at Chickamauga and Chattanooga. He finally served as a major in the 9th Colored Artillery Regiment, which Grosskopf led in the Battle of Nashville on 15 and 16 November 1864. He was later inspector general of all military commands in Alabama. He was a former Prussian officer.

GRÜNHUT, Joseph B. Captain of 82nd Illinois (Hecker's regiment), he distinguished himself several times, especially at Chancellorsville, as Frey reports. He capably protected Dilger's batteries with two companies at Gettysburg. He still lives in Peoria, Illinois, and is one of the best-known veterans in the West.

GRUMBACH, Nikolaus. Captain of the half-German 149th New York Infantry Regiment, which was organized in Syracuse. In the defense of Culp's Hill at Gettysburg on 2 July 1863. Grumbach led the regiment after Lieutenant Colonel Randall had fallen. Almost half the regiment was killed and wounded, and the regimental flag received eighty-one bullet holes. Grumbach also commanded the regiment on 3 July. It had already lost 194 men at Chancellorsville.

GUMBART. Battery chief in the 2nd Illinois Artillery Regiment, which fought with honor in most of the battles in the Western theater of war.

GÜLICH, Theodor. Well-known Iowa German, editor of the *Davenport Demokrat*, who did good service as quartermaster of Iowa troops.

HAAS, Max A. F. Captain in the 3rd Missouri Militia Regiment. Later adjutant to Colonel Meumann. He served from the spring of 1861 to November 1864. In 1910 he was living in Mendota, Illinois. He was a zealous co-worker on this biographical section.

HAHN, Michael. Pro-Union German leader in Louisiana, governor of the state in 1864. He worked for the abolition of slavery and was greatly respected by Lincoln. He was later actively attacked by his compatriots in the North during the political struggles over the Reconstruction of the South.

††COUNT VON HAAKE. A capable officer of the 52nd New York Infantry Regiment. He fell alongside his friend, VON STEUBEN, at Todd's Tavern on the Po River, Virginia, in Grant's campaign in 1864. He went with his regiment into the forest against the enemy, where he encountered occasional fire. A severe skirmish soon developed, and enemy artillery lobbed explosive shells into the woods, which soon set the shrubbery ablaze. Count Haake was the last company leader of the 52nd to order withdrawal, which he did in a hollow, throaty voice, for he was still recovering from a neck wound. At the same instant he was struck by an enemy bullet, and he sank to the ground, mortally wounded. Two members of his company, of whom one (our witness) still lives in Chicago, tried to carry the dying man out of the fire across two rifles, but this was hindered by the thick smoke and the exploding shells. They had to leave the dying man lying, and he suffered a dreadful death in the flames.

HAMMER, Dr. Adam. Lieutenant colonel in the 4th Missouri Volunteer Regiment. During most of the war he dedicated himself to leading military hospitals, earning the thanks of thousands of wounded warriors of both armies. Dr. Hammer was one of the most zealous of German patriots to whom the rising in St. Louis and the rescue of Missouri is owed. He was a prominent physician and leading professor at the Missouri Medical College. He later returned to Germany and died in 1878 in Griesbach, in the Black Forest. Hammer was an intimate friend of Hecker and a participant in the German Revolution under him. He fled to America along with Hecker. He had also worked as a military physician in the Swiss *Sonderbund* War. In St. Louis, Hammer founded the first German medical college, the Humboldt Institute, and he led it until the start of the war. Hammer had already organized and armed his students militarily in March 1861. They hid out at night in a neighboring brewery in order to fall on the rear of any rebels seeking to make an attack on the arsenal. These Hammer students were probably the first American volunteers to do actual war service.

VON HAMMERSTEIN. A former Austrian officer, major in McClellan's staff. His general gave him the highest recommendation. If there was difficult and important adjutant work to be done, von Hammerstein or his friend also serving in McClellan's staff, Paul von Radowitz, were sought for it. Later von Hammerstein became colonel of a New York regiment. His fate after the end of the war was a dreadful one. This German officer, once so coddled, was unable to support himself. He enlisted as a private in the regular cavalry in the hope that he would be promoted. "But his habits were against him," McClellan reports, who recalled his old adjutant in later years and memorialized him in his book *McClellan's Own Story*. Von Hammerstein was used to deliver mail in the Wild West. He had to take letters from one fort to another. He fell into a snowstorm, laid down along the way, had both legs frozen, so that they had to be amputated. This misfortune moved his relatives in Austria, and he was taken home and died there.

HARHAUS, Otto. Colonel of the 2nd New York Cavalry Regiment, commanded the 2nd Brigade in Gregg's cavalry division, Pleasonton's corps, and distinguished himself at Gettysburg.

††HARTMANN. Lieutenant colonel of Steinwehr's 29th New York Regiment, fell in the defensive position of Buschbeck's brigade at Chancellorsville (2 May 1863). Alongside Hartmann fell his friend Captain BODE of the same regiment. Bode had once been a Hanoverian officer.

†HARTMANN, Dr. Karl. Staff surgeon of the German 107th Ohio Regiment. He had been active as a physician in Cleveland, Ohio. A Forty-Eighter, true patriot and Union man. In the Battle of Chancellorsville, at the time of Jackson's attack on the badly led and poorly positioned XI Corps, Dr. Hartmann was shot dead. He had drawn his sabre and participating as an officer to aid in positioning his regiment, which was in complete disorder. It is the sole known case where a physician functioned as an officer in a time of great peril. His image in bronze is on the Cleveland Warriors' Memorial.

HARTUNG, Adolf von. Born in Troppau in Saxony, fought with Schimmelpfennig under Kossuth, colonel of the German 74th Pennsylvania Regiment, distinguishing himself in this role at Chancellorsville and Gettysburg. In the taking of Charleston this was the first regiment to enter the town.

HÄRING, Dr. Theodor. Regimental surgeon in the German 9th Wisconsin Regiment. He was also a distinguished surgeon.

†HASSENDEUBEL, Franz. Born in 1827 in Germersheim, Palatinate, emigrated in 1842. He served as an artillery officer in the Mexican War. In 1861 he was a first lieutenant in

Sigel's 3rd Missouri Regiment. Hassendeubel laid out the ten forts through which St. Louis was defended against the rebels. He became a brigadier general in 1863. In the Vicksburg campaign, Hassendeubel was severely wounded while observing the enemy works of Vicksburg, and he died on 17 July 1863. He was one of the most important engineers of the Civil War. The post of the veterans' organization in St. Louis has organized itself as the Hassendeubel Post, Grand Army of the Republic. Thus at least the name of this fine officer shall live on.

HAUPT, Hermann. Colonel functioning as a general, an outstanding engineering officer, chief of transportation in the Army of the Potomac. He distinguished himself particularly in Pope's campaign of 1862. He came from Philadelphia, emigrating from Germany as a child. General Pope, that great bungler, was at first dissatisfied with Haupt and dismissed him. But when support for the army along the line from Alexandria (Virginia) to Culpeper completely collapsed and the soldiers were about to starve, Pope felt compelled to reinstate Haupt. Then everything ran like clockwork. Haupt particularly distinguished himself as a bridge builder.

HAUSEN, Dr. Julius H. von. A Forty-Eighter refugee from Vienna. He was at first a regimental surgeon, then brigade surgeon in the Army of the Potomac. He worked through almost the entire war as a surgeon in the most dedicated manner.

†HAUSCHIELD. Lieutenant in the German 75th Pennsylvania Regiment. He came from Gettysburg. During the battle he visited his old mother, who lived there. He fell a few hours later, as he was throwing his company against the attacking enemy.

HECKER, Friedrich. Colonel, titular brigadier general. The first people's leader in the Baden rebellion, born in 1811, died 1881 in Belleville, Illinois.[20] After the defeat of his volunteers at Kandern, Hecker had to flee to America, but he returned in 1849 to participate once more in the Revolution. Before he could reach his homeland, the catastrophe had already fallen. Hecker then came back to Belleville and became a Latin Farmer. At the outbreak of the Civil War, he first enlisted as a private in the 3rd Missouri Regiment, then organized the German 24th Illinois Regiment, but due to conflict with his officers he resigned and formed a second Hecker Regiment, the 82nd Illinois, which became one of the best regiments in the Western army. He was in Schurz's division on Hawkins Farm and fought bravely there. But a bullet smashed against the large silver snuff box the old hero always carried with him. Hecker only suffered a flesh wound and was ready for service a few months later. He took part in the march to Chattanooga, the encounter at Wauhatchie, and the Battle of Missionary Ridge, then the terrible march to Knoxville. At the beginning of 1864, Hecker resigned because he had been frequently passed over for promotion.

Hecker was one of the most prominent leaders of the German people in America; he was an outstanding orator, able to bring the masses to true enthusiasm. His best achievement was an oration given in St. Louis in February 1871 to celebrate the great German victory over France. In this speech, Hecker completely abandoned his earlier position as a critic of Germany's new development under Prussian leadership. In fiery words, sparked by his love for the German people and his pride for the unique victory of the German army, and particularly the taking of Alsace and Lorraine, Hecker praised the final achievement of a united German state, albeit with a monarchical head.

HEDTERICH, C. B. Colonel of the German 8th New York (Blenker) Regiment, earlier commanded by Stahel and Wutschel, later by Prince Salm-Salm. He led the 8th in Pope's campaign of 1862, and he fought with distinction at Second Bull Run. Hedterich died in New York a few years after the war, in the deepest poverty.

†HEG, Hans C. Colonel of the 15th Wisconsin Regiment, which consisted substantially of Germans and Swedes. In the Battle of Chickamauga, Colonel Heg was severely wounded and died the following day.

HEILAND, Dr. Regimental surgeon of the 20th New York (Turner) Regiment. Through his medical art he saved the lives of many wounded, including General Max Weber.

HEINE, Wilhelm. Brigadier general. A Forty-Eighter from Dresden, where he had worked as a painter and writer, and who had to leave because of his participation in street fighting. He came to America in 1851, took service in the Navy and trained himself as a capable sailor and engineer. In 1861 he entered the Army of the Potomac as an engineering officer, working primarily in the Corps of Engineers. In 1863 he became a colonel, and the next year a brigadier general. He led the German 103rd New York Regiment toward the end of the war. After the war he was American consul general in Paris, then lived in Dresden.

HEINTZ, Karl. Captain under Sigel in General Stahel's staff in the Shenandoah campaign, May 1864.

†VON HELLMERICH. Colonel of the 5th Missouri Cavalry Regiment. A former Prussian officer, von Hellmerich fell through a bridge and was severely wounded on a reconnaissance ride near Atlanta, Georgia. He was then picked up by the Confederates and carried off as a captive. He later managed to escape toward the end of the war and sneaked through to where General Osterhaus stood near Mobile, suffering severely. He was found by his compatriots. They sent a Negro to General Osterhaus and demanded $20,000 in Confederate money for the delivery of the officer. Osterhaus came up with the money, which then had little value, and saved his comrade, but von Hellmerich soon died as a result of his dreadful sufferings in captivity.

HENCKE, Theodor W. von. Famous cavalry officer in the West, captain in the 4th Missouri Cavalry Regiment. Von Hencke returned to Germany in 1870, resumed his position as officer in the same regiment to which he had belonged before his emigration, and he fell in one of the battles before Metz.

HENNE, Robert. Officer in the 12th Missouri Regiment. He had lost an arm in the Schleswig-Holstein rebellion. At the charge on Elkhorn Pass at Pea Ridge under Osterhaus, 8 March 1862, he also lost a leg. He later lived in Davenport, Iowa.

†HENKEL, William. Major of the 58th New York Regiment. He led it on the first day of Second Bull Run and was shot through the breast in Schurz's charge of the railway causeway. He died in a hospital in Washington.

HENNING VON MINDEN. Major in a Minnesota cavalry regiment, a former German officer.

HENNIGHAUSEN, Louis P. One of the most capable researchers of German history in North America. He lived in Richmond, Virginia, shortly before the outbreak of the war and was threatened with prison because he had taught an intelligent young man, who showed no more than a trace of Negro origin, how to read. He then moved to Baltimore and participated in the Turner Rifles of Washington and Baltimore, which were already being militarily drilled in January 1861 at the urging of Mr. Washburn, later the American ambassador to France (1870). These German Turners occupied the railroad station when Lincoln arrived in Washington, and they formed the honor guard at Lincoln's inauguration. Hennighausen served as an officer in the 46th New York (Frémont) Regiment, participating in the Peninsular Campaign and the siege of Fort Pulaski. He lives as a respected lawyer in Baltimore.

He has made great exertions to prove that Lincoln's ancestors came from Germany. It has been proved beyond a doubt that the president's grandfather called himself Linkhorn. The Linkhorn family came from the entirely German Berks County in Pennsylvania and migrated in the middle of the eighteenth century to the German part of the Shenandoah Valley. It was only later that Abraham Linkhorn, the grandfather of the president, moved to Kentucky. Professor Learned, however, is of a different opinion from Hennighausen; according to Learned, the Lincoln family is of English extraction.

HERTZBERG, Dr. Editor of the San Antonio, Texas, *Deutsche Zeitung,* earlier edited by Dr. Douai. Hertzberg restored to the paper, which had become rather colorless after Douai's forced flight from Texas, its earlier pro-Union tone. The newspaper was then suppressed by the Confederates.

HERTZBERG. Battery chief in the 2nd Wisconsin Artillery Regiment.

HEUSINGER, Otto. Officer in the 41st New York Regiment. Later, when he had returned to Germany, he became a lieutenant in the 92nd Brunswick Infantry Regiment. He is the author of *Amerikanische Kriegsbilder* ["American War Pictures"](Leipzig: F. W. Grunow, 1869). The book gossips in a lively manner about life in the camp and on the march. Heusinger was wounded at Chancellorsville. His portrayal of the care of the wounded is particularly interesting.

HEXAMER, W. Artillery chief from New Jersey. He was a Forty-Eighter and a significant leader of Germans in the East. He was an uncle of the president of the German-American National League. He distinguished himself particularly at Antietam. Captain Hexamer thwarted the attack of the Confederates on Hancock's left wing at Antietam, in the course of which he used all his ammunition. His purely German battery suffered large losses in men and horses.

†HILDEBRANDT. Major of the 39th New York Regiment. He was mortally wounded at Gettysburg and died.

HILLGÄRTNER, Dr. Georg. Outstanding journalist. He led the *Anzeiger des Westens* in St. Louis after Börnstein's departure.

HIPP, Karl. Major, 37th Ohio Regiment, an intimate friend of the German General August von Willich, who passed the last years of his life in Hipp's house in St. Mary's, Ohio. Hipp fought with great distinction through the entire war and only resigned in August, 1865. He did brilliant work as a recruiter. He was supposed to have brought more than 200 Germans into the army.

HOFFMANN, Ernst F. Major, chief engineer of the XI Army Corps, formerly a Prussian engineering officer from Breslau. He fought in Schleswig-Holstein, then took his leave. He entered English service and fought in the Crimean War as well as in Africa, then as a staff officer with Garibaldi. He was decorated by the Italian government and received a position as a major in the Italian army. In 1861 he came to America to fight for a rebellion of Negro slaves. Major Hoffmann founded the topographic bureau for both the XI Corps, under Howard, as well as for Thomas's army fighting in Tennessee. After the war Hoffmann accomplished great things in surveying the coasts.

One of his greatest achievements in the war was the rebuilding of the bridge over the Hiwassee River in Tennessee, which had been destroyed by the enemy. This bridge was raised in the course of one dark night, to the amazement of General J. H. Wilson, who was himself one of the most important engineers in the army. Wilson cannot praise Hoffmann's achievements enough. Sherman's troops crossed the bridge the next morning with the intention of relieving Burnside in Knoxville.

Hoffmann's superior, General O. O. Howard, criticized Hoffmann for building this bridge. In his autobiography, Howard says that Hoffmann needed fourteen days to build this bridge, and that Howard's own Vermont soldiers built it in one night. This is an example of the frivolity with which people of Howard's quality write. The eyewitness and technical expert Wilson cannot praise his accomplishment enough, but the corps commander denigrates him for the same deed. Howard mentions the first engineering officer of his corps only three times in his book but his own brother, the insignificant adjutant Howard, thirty-eight times! After the war General Wilson led the government works to regulate the Mississippi, and for that he engaged Major Hoffmann as his first engineer. Hoffmann invented several sensible instruments which made surveying easier that enjoyed considerable recognition among technicians, as Wilson stresses. Wilson further says of Hoffmann, "He was generous, chivalric, unselfish, enterprising, and intelligent; above all loyal to the highest ideals of manhood. His modesty was equal to that of a girl, his courage to that of a palladin. He was ready for every duty, no matter when it came and he was prompt and practical to a degree that no American could surpass."

HÖVET, Dr. From Hannover, regimental surgeon of the German 46th New York Regiment.

HOFFMANN, Franz. Lieutenant governor of Illinois in 1861. He was a brave German patriot, an intimate friend of Gustav Körner. He organized several half-German regiments in Illinois, and he was also outstandingly engaged in the German uprising in Missouri.

HOFMANN, Louis. From Cincinnati. A Forty-Eighter, former Baden artillerist. Chief of Hofmann's battery, which fought so bravely in Missouri and distinguished itself at Pea Ridge and later at Vicksburg. There is a memorial for the battery in Vicksburg.

HOFFMEISTER, Dr. August W. From Fort Madison, Iowa, accomplished regimental surgeon.

HOLMSTEDT, Ernst W. von. Colonel of the 41st New York Regiment, earlier a Saxon officer. He led the regiment in Pope's campaign and in the Second Battle of Bull Run.

HÜBSCHMANN, Dr. Franz. Field surgeon of the 26th Wisconsin Regiment, later a brigade and division surgeon, one of the best medical men of the entire Civil War. He worked in the field hospitals at the great battles of Chancellorsville, Gettysburg, Chickamauga, Chattanooga, Dallas, Kennesaw Mountain, Peachtree Creek, and Atlanta. At Gettysburg he and nine assistants and about five hundred wounded fell into the hands of the Confederates for three days. He died in 1880 in Milwaukee. Hübschmann, born in Saxon-Weimar, had arrived in Milwaukee in 1842, when it was a town of only 5000 residents.

HUNDHAUSEN, Julius. Colonel of the German Reserve Regiment of Gasconade County, Missouri. His brother and brother-in-law served in the same regiment. The latter, a Germanized Scot named Manwaring, was murdered by rebels. His brother, Robert Hundhausen, was colonel of the 4th Missouri Regiment.

ILGES, Guido. Colonel of the 18th United States Infantry Regiment. During the Civil War, Ilges served as captain in the V Army Corps, making all the battles of the Peninsular Campaign and later the great battles of the Army of the Potomac. He joined the Regular Army after the war. One of the most famous officers of the United States Army, he distinguished himself in the Indian Wars. It was he who defeated Chief Gaul in December 1880 and later Sitting Bull himself, taking both chiefs prisoner with 1200 Sioux warriors. Ilges came from Ahrweiler.

IRSCH, Franz. Captain, 45th New York, won Howard's praise at Gettysburg for his personal bravery, received the Cross of the Loyal Legion, languished for a long time as a prisoner in Libby Prison at Richmond, and planned the famous breakout from there along with General Cessnola. He received the Medal of Honor from Congress for his glorious defense of a part of the town of Gettysburg while the XI Corps gathered on Cemetery Hill after being beaten back on the first day.

ISENBACH. Colonel of the 58th New York Regiment, distinguishing himself at Missionary Ridge and Chattanooga.

JACQUIN. A Frenchman, also known by the name of Jackson. In April 1864 he led a cavalry company, consisting of 80 Germans and 20 Frenchmen, from the rebel camp in southern Missouri to the Union camp in St. Louis. The men immediately joined German regiments.

JACOBI, Dr. Abraham. Important staff surgeon. Many, many fighters owe their health and lives to him. One of the most outstanding physicians whatsoever in America. He was a Forty-Eighter, and he is still living in 1910 as a sturdy old man in New York, respected as one of the best men Germany has ever given America.

JACOBS, Wilhelm Heinrich. Colonel of the 26th Wisconsin Regiment. He came from Brunswick, immigrating in 1850, and he died in Milwaukee in 1882. He was wounded at Chancellorsville, but he returned to his regiment on the battlefield at Gettysburg and led it on the last day of battle. The repulsive accusations made by nativists against German soldiers after the Battle of Chancellorsville so disgusted this passionate man that he resigned in November 1864. Jacobs was one of the most respected German citizens of Milwaukee, one of the sort who were particularly proud of their ethnic identity and always powerfully defended the rights of American Germans. He was a banker in Milwaukee and a co-founder of the *Musikverein* [Musical Society]. Jacobs had been an officer of the Home Guard in Germany.

JAHN, Hermann. Captain of artillery. He served in the 8th New York Artillery Regiment. He found a Union battery abandoned in flight on the battlefield of Bull Run and took it over. Colonel Blenker had sixty of his men who had served in artillery in Germany take over the recovered cannons. Jahn became the leader of this battery, which distinguished itself later as the 2nd Light New York Battery under Schirmer's command.

†JÄNSEN. Major, 31st Missouri Regiment, fell in the storm on Chickesaw Bluffs near Vicksburg, 27 December 1862.

JÜSSEN, Edmund. Lieutenant colonel, 23rd Wisconsin Regiment.

KALLMANN, [Hermann]. Colonel of the German 2nd Home Guard Regiment of Missouri. This regiment had the duty of clearing the area around St. Louis of rebel guerilla bands. When Kallmann was returning to St. Louis from one of these marches, the Home Guard men received fire in Seventh Street in St. Louis. Without awaiting orders, the soldiers fired into the houses from which they had been fired upon. Four persons were killed as a result and several severely wounded. Kallmann immediately called a halt and had the firing stopped. But the old cry arose once more against the "German murderers." This was, however, the last street fighting in St. Louis. Friends of the rebels had come to understand that they could not fire on the troops in ambush without penalty.

KÄMMERLING, Gustav. Brigadier general, colonel of the German 9th Ohio Regiment. Born in Rhenish Prussia and formerly a Prussian military man, Kämmerling quickly became the true leader of that heroic regiment because the first colonel, McCook, quickly became a brigadier. Kämmerling died in Tell City, Indiana, in 1902 at the age of 82. His sole son distinguished himself in the Spanish-American War in Dewey's attack on Manila.

KAMPF, C. W. Major, 5th Wisconsin Regiment.

KAPP, Friedrich. Significant German-American, called "the citizen of two worlds" because he returned to Germany and became a member of the German Reichstag. He certainly should be called the premier researcher in the history of German-Americans. He was a member of the German Society of New York, as well as the Immigration Commission. We have Kapp to thank for some of the best works ever created on German immigration to American. He was a true Union man during the war, fighting with his pen and as an orator. He organized the enormous mass demonstration in New York against the shameful slander of the Germans over Chancellorsville. Kapp gave a wonderful oration on that occasion. H. A. Rattermann wrote the best biography of Kapp in the *Deutschamerikanisches Magazin* of Cincinnati.

KAPFF, Eduard. Colonel of the 7th New York Regiment, in which his brother Sixtus Kapff also served as an officer. Both of them were Forty-Eighters from Württemberg.

KÄRCHER, Jakob, lieutenant colonel, 12th Missouri Regiment.

KARGES, Joseph. Colonel of the 2nd New Jersey Cavalry Regiment, a former Prussian officer. He later commanded the 1st Brigade of Grierson's cavalry division. One of the most capable cavalry commanders. After the war he was a professor at Princeton University.

KAUFMANN, Theodor. A Forty-Eighter from Uelzen in Hanover, he died at the age of 86 in New York. Kaufmann served at the beginning of the war as a private and later worked for the Union cause as a speaker and writer, but primarily as an artist. He became the historical painter of the Civil War. His large painting showing Farragut, entitled, "Damn the Torpedoes, Go Ahead, Boys" was distributed by an entrepreneur in thousands of lithographs after the rights were taken from the starving artist for a paltry sum. No buyer was ever found for the original, perhaps because of the broad distribution of the copies. Kaufmann's two great paintings—*Lincoln's Murder*, with many portraits of contemporaries, and the splendidly successful *Sherman Before the Watchfire*—are among the finest artistic creations ever produced on American soil. Kaufmann, who had been trained in Düsseldorf and Munich, also had a long career as a teacher. His most significant student was Thomas Nast, the famous artist for *Harper's Weekly*.

KARBERG, Peter. Colonel, once a sergeant in the German 17th Missouri Regiment. On 18 May 1863, Sherman occupied Walnut Hill in front of Vicksburg. But his army was without provisions. There was a need to notify the fleet of this problem so that the ships could bring supplies. Lieutenant LANGGUT and Sergeant Karberg were selected for this dangerous mission. Both of them crept by night through an unknown wooded wilderness, then swam the treacherous Chickesaw Bayou and hammered together a raft out of old boards, on which they floated down the Yazoo River, which opens into the Mississippi. After about thirty hours they reached the Mississippi and the fleet, in continual peril of drowning or being shot by enemy riflemen. They reported Sherman's need, and a day later their comrades could eat their fill once more. Karberg was later made colonel of a Negro regiment.

KAUFFELD. Captain in a Pennsylvania regiment, served through the entire war. He died in 1895 after having spent nearly thirty years in bed, due to rheumatism, the veteran's disease. The case of Kauffeld is exceptional, but the number of soldiers who took that disease with them to the grave runs into the hundreds of thousands.

KAUTZ, Albert. Admiral, brother of Major General [August] Kautz, served as an officer in the Northern navy. He was trained at the Naval Academy in Annapolis, and he passed his examination in 1858. At the very start of the war, the ship on which Kautz was serving was captured by the enemy. After his exchange, Kautz became flag lieutenant (adjutant) to Admiral Farragut and as such participated in the glorious capture of New Orleans aboard the *Hartford*. He then fought before Vicksburg from 1862 to 1863 and was honorably engaged in many later fights of the navy. In 1898 Kautz became rear admiral of the Navy and commander of the Pacific station. Kautz came to the United States as a boy.

KELLER, Kaspar. Lieutenant colonel of the German 7th New York Regiment.

KELLERSBERG, J. Chief engineer, Red River expedition.

KERLIN, E. H. Major, staff and chief of scouts in the XI Corps.

†KESSLER, Friedrich. Adjutant of General von Wangelin. In the Battle of Ringgold, [Georgia], in November 1863, Kessler saw his childhood friend Captain Henry Kircher lying severely wounded on the firing line. He jumped forward to bring Kircher to safety. As he carried his bleeding friend in his arms, Kessler was shot dead and Kircher added a shattered arm to his already-shattered leg. Kircher was later twice mayor of Belleville. He only died a few years ago. General Osterhaus wrote to the author on Kessler's fine deed, "Kessler's death is an indelible witness to the comradely dedication and military self-sacrifice unto death, a piece of German loyalty."

††VON KIELMANNSEGG and VON KÖRBER. Both former Prussian officers, fell in 1864 in the battles of Grant's Wilderness Campaign. Both served in Kentucky cavalry regiments.

KIELMANNSEGGE, Eugen von. Major in the 4th Missouri Cavalry Regiment, earlier a Prussian officer.

KILIAN, Edward A. K. Served through the entire war in the 1st and 17th Missouri Regiments. He worked as adjutant in the latter. Co-worker in the biographical section.

KITTOE, Dr. E. D. Colonel and staff surgeon, XV Army Corps.

KLAUSS. Battery chief of the 1st Indiana Battery, recruited from Evansville, Indiana, possessing only German crews and using German as the language of command. The battery fought with honor in the Western theater of war.

KLEEFISCH, August. Colonel of the 68th New York Regiment during Pope's campaign and at Second Bull Run.

KLEMM, Johnny. A German drummer boy from Michigan. The little boy, 16 years old, threw away his drum at Chickamauga and fought in the ranks. He shot a high Confederate officer who was trying to take the little Yankee prisoner. After the war, Rosecrans arranged an appointment for him at West Point and Klemm then became an officer in the Regular Army.

KLEYSER, Alfred von. Battery chief in Sigel's, later Hunter's, Army of the Shenandoah, summer of 1864. He particularly distinguished himself in the Battle of Piedmont. In Sigel's unfortunate Battle of New Market in 1864, von Kleyser's Battery stood in the front. It defended itself bravely, but there was no support, and the rebels took two guns. Von Kleyser fought through the entire war. He was a former Prussian officer.

VON KNOBELSDORFF. Colonel of the 44th Illinois Regiment. A former Prussian officer, Knobelsdorff already was commanding a brigade in Asboth's division in 1861 in Missouri.

†KNODERER. Colonel of the 168th Pennsylvania Infantry Regiment, fell in the Battle of Chancellorsville. Knoderer was a former Baden officer.

KOCH, Charles. Colonel of the German 45th New York Regiment.

KOCH, Friedrich. Served in the 7th New York Regiment. Only a German corporal, but a true hero! He saved the flag of the 7th at Second Bull Run.

KOHLER (Coler). Colonel of the 25th Illinois Regiment. Schierenberg reports of him: "I once rode next to Colonel Coler, who told me the following: I am a German, too. Came as a little child to New Orleans with my parents, who died of cholera. An American farmer's wife in southern Illinois took me in and raised me as her own child. So I was completely Americanized, particularly at the college my foster parents later sent me." Coler's story is not unique. Many Germans who immigrated as children had similar fates.

KORTH, Louis F. Entered the Army of the Potomac as a youth of 17 and served through the entire war. He was in Blenker's staff, and later he worked in the topographical division. He was wounded at Cross Keys. Korth has been a true collaborator of the author for many years. He collected materials for many years and has created an invaluable archive for our purposes, which contains rich contributions for a history of Germans in the Civil War. Korth has worked in the German-American press since the end of the war as a correspondent in Portsmouth, Ohio. He is one of our best pens. Mr. Korth's contribution to the biographical part of this book has been outstanding.

†KOLTES, Johann A. Colonel of the 73rd Pennsylvania Regiment. He fell at the head of his troops as a brigade leader on 30 August 1862 at Second Bull Run. While part of Steinwehr's brigade, Koltes participated in the Shenandoah Valley campaign of 1862 and in Pope's subsequent campaign. He led the brigade in von Steinwehr's place at Cross keys as well as at Second Bull Run. He was an extraordinarily brave man who always went before his men. He fell storming a Confederate battery among the first ranks of those attacking. Born in 1827, Koltes came from Trier, emigrating at the age of 17, he took part in the Mexican War and served in the Regular Army. Grand Army Post 228 in Philadelphia bears the name of Koltes.

KÖRNER, Gustav. Judge, [lieutenant] governor of Illinois, author of one of the best books on German-America, *Das deutsche Element 1818 bis 1848* ["The German Element from 1818 to 1848"]. One of the best and most loyal among German-American men of the people. He was a very intimate friend of Lincoln when Lincoln was only a small country lawyer in Illinois. Often in the first difficult days of his administration, Lincoln fled to his friend Körner for advice. Lincoln wanted to give Körner a high military position so that Körner could function even better as a recruiter, but Körner declined. Körner could have been compared with the great German-Americans, if his circle of operation had not been restricted essentially to Illinois, Indiana and Missouri. He emigrated after the Frankfurt Putsch of 1830, in which Körner was involved as a young student.

KÖRPER, Dr. E. A. Staff surgeon of the German 75th [no state given—SR] Regiment.

KOVASZ, Stephan. Major and regimental leader in the 54th New York Regiment. He distinguished himself particularly at Second Bull Run. After colonel Koltes fell, Kovasz took over command of Koltes' brigade. He was a former Austrian officer.

KOZLAY, Eugen Arthur. Colonel of the 54th New York Regiment, The Black Rifles. He had earlier been an Austrian officer. During the Hungarian Revolution he was an adjutant of Kossuth. Kozlay served through the entire war.

KRAUS, Albert. Chaplain of the 12th Missouri Regiment, a Forty-Eighter and a free-thinker. His friends founded a "Free Congregation" so Kraus could bear the title of "Reverend." As a result, this former landed aristocrat became a chaplain. In battle he always stood in the firing line and assisted the wounded.

KRAMER, Adam. Colonel, came as a child to America and enlisted in the Regular Army. He had already served four years in the cavalry when the Civil War broke out. He became captain in the 15th Pennsylvania Cavalry Regiment and fought at Antietam, Murfreesboro, Chickamauga, and the battles around Chattanooga. He then formed a Negro cavalry regiment and returned to the Regular Army after the war. He later distinguished himself in many fights with the Indians.

KRECKEL, Arnold. Outstanding German-American, one of the most important leaders in Missouri in the spring of 1861. He became lieutenant colonel in the 1st Cavalry Battalion of Missouri. In 1864 he presided over the state convention of Missouri, which abolished slavery in that state the adoption of the 15th Amendment to the United States Constitution. Lincoln named Kreckel a federal judge.

KREPPS. Major of cavalry. On 28 August [1862] he charged with his West Virginia cavalry across a burning bridge over the Broad Run, driving the enemy away from the opposite shore. The fire was extinguished and Sigel's and McDowell's corps continued their march to Gainesville without hindrance.

KREZ, Konrad. Colonel of the 27th Wisconsin Regiment, later a brevet brigadier general. He participated in the siege of Vicksburg and campaigns in Arkansas and against Mobile. His significance lies outside the military field. He is the most gifted poet of German America. His splendid song, "An mein Vaterland" ["To my Fatherland"], is without a doubt one of the finest blooms of German poetry. It is said that this song, by a German refugee, made a particularly deep impression on the first German Emperor, and that the oppressor of the South German Revolution loved no other poetry so much as his. The songs created by Krez in America were published in 1875 by E. Steiger of New York. Krez had been condemned to death in Germany.

KRIEGER, E. J. Major, 107th Ohio Regiment.

KRUGHOFF, Louis. Major, born in 1836 in Minden, Westphalia. He entered Captain Coleman's cavalry as a private, rising to the rank of major in the 49th Illinois Infantry Regiment. He distinguished himself in the attack on Fort Donelson, and he was severely wounded several times. He was mustered out in January, 1865.

KRZYZANOWSKI, Wladimir. Colonel. A brave German Pole. He was not named general, as Schurz says, because when Lincoln's nominations were to be confirmed by the senate, none of the senators could pronounce the name of Krzyzanowski (better said, none wanted to pronounce it). "Kriz," as Krzyzanowski was generally known in the army, organized the German 58th Infantry Regiment of New York, in which there were several companies of German Poles. He entered Blenker's German Division, sharing its fate, and during Pope's campaign he became a brigade commander in Schurz's division. Schurz always kept a true friendship with this brave, intelligent and capable officer, and after his death held the funerary oration for his old comrade in arms. "Kriz" was one of the German heroes of Second Bull Run, Chancellorsville and Gettysburg. We later encounter him with Schurz's division in Chattanooga and in Knoxville, Tennessee. He died soon after the war as the result of a disease derived from his four years of exertions.

KÜFFNER, William C. Mustered out as a brevet brigadier general, January 1866. He was born in Rostock, Mecklenburg, and died as editor of the *Belleviller Zeitung*. He came to Texas as a youth, joined the pro-Union people there, and fled to the North after the outbreak of the war. In April 1861, he entered the 9th Illinois Regiment and soon became captain. He participated in campaigns of the Army of the Tennessee. Küffner was wounded four times, severely so at both Shiloh and Corinth. On the whole he participated in 110 battles and skirmishes, and he distinguished himself through great bravery. After his last recovery from a severe wound, he entered the Veterans' Reserve Corps, became colonel of the 149th Illinois Regiment, and served in Prince Salm-Salm's brigade until the end of the war.

KUHN, Johann W. German-Swiss, major in the 9th Illinois Regiment. He was severely wounded at Shiloh. After healing, he became garrison commander of Memphis. He died soon after the war.

KURTZ. Three brothers from the German settlement of Weston, Missouri. One was mortally wounded near Atlanta. The two other brothers, Charles and Andreas, fought for four years in Missouri, essentially against guerillas.

†KURZ, Richard. Captain in the New York De Kalb Regiment. He was mortally wounded at Groveton and died in the hands of the enemy.

VON KUSSEROW. Major of artillery, New York. He distinguished himself particularly on the Antietam. He was praised by McClellan before the troops. He descended from a noted Prussian officers' family.

KUTZNER. Colonel of the 39th Missouri Regiment.

LACKNER, Franz. Lieutenant colonel in the German 26th Wisconsin Regiment, wounded at Gettysburg. He then entered the staff of General Schurz. After the war he was a lawyer in Milwaukee.

LADEMANN, Otto. Captain in Sigel's 3rd Missouri Regiment, commanding this regiment occasionally during the absence of Colonel Wangelin. Lademann took an honorable part in most of the fighting of the German Wangelin's brigade. He was named chief of the 4th Missouri Battery by General Osterhaus in 1864. This battery received crews from the three Missouri regiments, the 3rd, 12th, and 17th, whose time of enlistment had not run out in autumn, 1864.

LAIBOLDT, Bernhard. Colonel of the German 2nd Missouri Regiment, one of the most capable subordinates in Osterhaus's campaigns. He fought in Sheridan's division at Pea Ridge, Perryville, and Stones River with great distinction. Laiboldt commanded a brigade in the Battle of Chickamauga. He was particularly praised there by Sheridan for his bravery. Laiboldt had two occasions for autonomous leadership. Both times he performed his mission in a brilliant manner, and both times against the famous rebel cavalry commander, General Wheeler. In December 1863, Laiboldt led a valuable supply train from Chattanooga to Knoxville. He had with him a few hundred men of the 2nd Missouri He was attacked at the Hiwassee River by Wheeler with 1500 men. Laiboldt beat the enemy and brought the entire train to safety. On 14 August 1864, Laiboldt commanded in Dalton, Georgia, with 480 men of the 2nd Missouri Regiment. The same General Wheeler advanced with more than 3000 men and demanded that Laiboldt surrender. Laiboldt answered, "I have been placed here to hold this post, not to surrender it." When Wheeler wanted to parlay again, he received the answer that Laiboldt would fire on the parlay flag. Then Wheeler attacked. The fighting lasted all night. Laiboldt beat off each attack, and he was reinforced the next morning, whereupon Wheeler withdrew. Laiboldt had been a non-commissioned officer in Germany, but few former German officers earned so fine a name for themselves as Laiboldt. He was known throughout the Western army.

LAMBERT, Louis. Captain of the German 37th Ohio Regiment. He was wounded four times, once lying for more than twenty-four hours on the battlefield of Princeton, West Virginia, taken for dead. Of his regiment, which numbered 1133 men, only 189 men returned after the end of the war.

LANGE, Albert. From Charlottenburg [Berlin], state auditor of Indiana. He deserves much of the fame heaped on Governor Morton of Indiana. He distinguished himself particularly in organizing German soldiers. Lange was a major supporter of the plan to recruit about 20,000 veteran soldiers in Germany for the Union (see Corwin).

LANGGUT, see KARBERG.

LANDGRÄBER, Klemens. Once a Prussian artillery officer, major of the 1st Missouri Artillery Regiment, later artillery chief of Osterhaus's division, XV Corps, on Sherman's march through Georgia. A bold, brave man, one of the best artillerymen of the Western army. He was universally called "the flying Dutchman." Landgräber earned this title on 19 May 1863 while enclosing Vicksburg before the great assault. He managed to reach the heights with his batteries, and he saw that he could take an excellent position if he could advance around the narrow back of the hill. But the enemy had rifle trenches there, and the stretch was also covered by rebel batteries. Landgräber asked his men, "Boys, do you want to gamble with me to get into position through this dangerous way?" Every man said, "If you ride ahead, we shall follow." And the batteries charged off at a gallop. There was no road at all. On one side the hill fell steeply away, on the other side were the rifle trenches of the enemy. The mountain path was barely as wide as the track of the cannons' wheels. But the gamble paid off, despite enemy fire. Landgräber reached the position desired and could send his cannonballs into the enemy's rear. When he later passed by the 30th Iowa Regiment, which had been saved by Landgräber's bold act, the entire regiment cried, "Three cheers and a tiger for the flying Dutchman." Landgräber served through the entire war and fought with particular distinction at Vicksburg, Lookout Mountain, Missionary Ridge, and Ringgold and in the battles of the March through Georgia.

†LEDERGERBER, F. L. A lawyer in St. Louis, born in 1835 as the first sprout of the latin colony in Belleville, an officer in the 12th Missouri Regiment. F. L. Ledergerber was severely wounded at Ringgold, Georgia. His brother, Major Joseph Ledergerber, fell in the same battle. The brothers were grandsons of the pioneer of Belleville, the significant Friedrich Engelmann.

LEDIG, August. Major in the German 75th Pennsylvania Regiment, in which his own son served as captain. After Colonel Mahler fell, Ledig usually led the regiment, particularly in the battles of Gettysburg, Missionary Ridge and Knoxville. Ledig was an extraordinarily capable and brave leader, and he remained in service until peace. His son, Captain Richard Ledig, was severely wounded at Second Bull Run. Both father and son stood in the highest admiration of the 75th.

"LEIBGARDE HOWARDS" [Howard's Body Guard]. The headquarters guard of the XI Corps always consisted of two companies of the Blenker's German 8th New York Regiment. This company served throughout the entire war. Howard had a special medal struck for these men.

†LEICHTFUSS (Lightfoot). Major in the 12th Missouri Regiment. In the storm on Vicksburg on 22 May 1863, he succeeded in climbing Slippery Hill with a part of the German 12th Missouri Regiment, penetrating almost to the enemy bastions. He fell as he was leading his men to storm the enemy works. Most of the troops following him, from the 3rd and 17th Missouri and the 9th Iowa Regiments, remained stuck on the slick sands of the hill, and only a few were able to reach the plateau.

LEIPER, B. J. Lieutenant colonel, 1st Kentucky Regiment.

LEPPIEN, George F. Lieutenant colonel of the 1st Maine Artillery Regiment. He was a former Prussian officer. He first served in a Pennsylvania battery. He later commanded the artillery in the 2nd Division of the I Corps of the Army of the Potomac and distinguished himself at Second Bull Run, Antietam, Fredericksburg, Chancellorsville, and Gettysburg under Meade and Grant. Leppien was one of the most important artillery leaders produced by the war.

†LICHTENSTEIN. Lieutenant colonel of the German 52nd New York Regiment. He fell on the Antietam.

LIEB, Hermann. Titular brigadier general, a German Swiss, he entered the 8th Illinois Infantry Regiment in the middle of April 1861, soon becoming captain, then major. In the winter of 1863, he was colonel of the 9th Negro Regiment. Lieb was severely wounded at Miliken Bend. Lieb later led the 4th United States Regiment, Heavy Artillery, and so distinguished himself that he was named chief of the artillery units in the western district of Mississippi. In January 1865, he led an autonomous expedition against Marion, Arkansas, with his own regiment and the 11th Illinois Cavalry Regiment, surviving two encounters victoriously. After the war, Lieb played a role in politics in Chicago, taking over the leadership of the Chicago *Demokrat* and working as a writer.

LIEBER, Franz. The first and perhaps most significant among the great Germans of America, Lieber, Stallo, and Schurz. He was born in 1800 in Berlin. At the age of 15 he was a volunteer in the Colberg Regiment, in which both his older brothers served. He was severely wounded at Ligny. As a fraternity member during the Prussian Reaction, he was disciplined, and Lieber left for America in 1827. Here he became the apostle of German scholarship. He was a professor of the University of South Carolina and in 1856 at Harvard University. He was intimate friends with Bancroft, Channing, Longfellow, Prescott, Ticknor, and Charles Sumner. The great services of Lieber in constructing American universities in the German spirit can only be sketched here. Lieber was one of the most important scholars of America, perhaps the most important.

His political influence is an uninterrupted struggle against slavery. Lieber was the leader of the few pro-Unionists in South Carolina. He declared to the fire-eaters of that state, "How can you claim the right of slave states to separate from the Union without at the same time incorporating this principle into your new state, the Confederacy? Such a new state would be continuously in danger of falling victim to new revolutions." Lieber did not hesitate to call secession a crime. His bust in the hall of honor of the University of South Carolina was smashed. He was disciplined, and in 1856 he had to flee to the North. Harvard University was happy to receive him, and Lieber became the intellectually most important leader of the anti-slavery party.

One of his sons, Oskar Lieber, remained in South Carolina and fell victim to the blandishments of the slavery party. This promising young man, one of the most important geologists in the United States, entered the Confederate Army and fell in the summer of 1862, near Williamsburg. The old freedom fighter never overcame this pain. Lieber's two other sons both fought in the Union army. One of these was auditor general in the army. He was also highly gifted and helped his father to compose his manual on international law, which was in the hands of every American naval officer during the war to serve as a guide for dealing with representatives of other nations. At General Halleck's request, Lieber wrote *Guerilla Parties, Considered with Reference to the Law and Usages of War*, a work that was also extensively used during the French-German War for the handling of captured *franc-tireurs*. So this German provided many times over the intellectual structure for fighting the secession.

Lieber never lost faith in the ultimate victory of the Union, even during the worst times of the war. When voices rose in the North in favor of a compromise recognizing the Confederacy, it was always Lieber who opposed these war-weary people and demanded the continuation of the fight to the last man and the last cartridge. Lieber was able to experience 1870 and celebrated the resurrection of Germany in fiery poems. King Frederick William IV offered Lieber a professorship in Berlin in 1849, but Lieber remained loyal to his new country to his death. Native-born Americans praised him by saying that he became an American through and through, but on 20 July 1870 Lieber wrote, "My soul is full of the feeling and the thought—Germany!"

LIMBERG, George T. Colonel of the 108th Ohio Regiment, which was three-quarters German and did brave deeds at Murfreesboro. He was captured at Hartsville, Kentucky, along with the 39th Brigade. The regiment later did some good fighting.

LOCKMAN, John T. Lieutenant colonel in the 119th New York Regiment, he particularly distinguished himself at Chancellorsville and was very highly praised by Schurz as a brave soldier and a careful officer. Lockman was one of the speakers at the unveiling of the Sigel Memorial in New York in autumn, 1907.

LÖHR, Dr. Regimental surgeon in the 9th Wisconsin Regiment.

LÜBBERS, John. Colonel of the 26th Iowa Volunteers Regiment. He had earlier been an officer in the German Navy and had fought against Denmark. He emigrated about 1850.

LÜTTWITZ, Adolf von. Formerly an Austrian officer. He served first in the 54th New York Regiment, then on Schurz's staff. He was later commander of the pioneers of Schurz's division. Later he entered English military service and fought in the final Boer War.

LUTZ, John M. Major in the German 107th Ohio Regiment. He functioned as its regimental leader in the Battle of Chancellorsville on 2 May 1863. This regiment stood gathered at the brunt of Jackson's assault. The 107th Ohio was commanded for a time by the later General Edward S. Meyer, whose ancestors were South Germans who had emigrated to northern Ohio around 1820.

LUTZ, John B. (called Mansfield). Commander of the state militia of Indiana. He did great services in raising the contingent of Indiana. He was a delegate at the Republican national convention which nominated Lincoln.

†MAHLER, Franz. Colonel of the 75th Pennsylvania Regiment which was founded by General Bohlen in Philadelphia and which consisted exclusively of Germans. After Bohlen became a brigadier general, Mahler led the division. He had been an officer in Baden and had participated in the Revolution of 1848 to 1849. Mahler was an outstanding drill instructor, and the regiment had primarily him to thank for its excellent training. He belonged to Blenker's German Division, took part in the terror march across the Virginia mountains, and distinguished himself splendidly in the Battle of Cross Keys, and later at Second Bull Run. At Chancellorsville he stood in Schurz's division next to the 26th Wisconsin Regiment. He fought well there, as well. On 1 July 1863, the first day of Gettysburg, Colonel Mahler was shot off his horse as he led the regiment against the enemy. He paid no attention to the wound and remained with his men. Soon thereafter, a second bullet wounded him mortally. He died on 5 July. So the first two leaders of the 75th Pennsylvania, Bohlen and Mahler, fell fighting bravely before the enemy. The regiment later received another excellent leader in Major Ledig, and it fought under him to the end of the war.

MALMROSE, Oskar. Born in Kiel, a lawyer in St. Paul, Minnesota. He was adjutant general of the state of Minnesota from 1861 to 1865 and organized its units, 22,000 men, including a third Germans, Swiss, and Alsatians. Malmrose's services in putting down the Indian rising at New Ulm were especially great. Malmrose was later American consul in Spanish and French harbor towns.

MANN. Battery chief in Missouri. The crew was entirely German. This battery served splendidly, particularly under Sigel, and later also under Osterhaus.

MANNHARDT, Emil. Editor of the *Deutschamerikanische Geschichtsblätter* ["German-American Historical Pages"] in Chicago, which may be seen as a continuation of Rattermann's *Pionier*.

MARKBREIT, Leopold. At the end a colonel. Born in Vienna, half-brother of the Fritz Hassaurek of the Cincinnati *Volksblatt*. Markbreit was elected mayor of Cincinnati in 1907 by a great majority. Dying in 1909, he was one of the last witnesses of the dreadful torments captured Union officers had to endure in Libby Prison in Richmond. He was one of the hostages determined by lot to be shot if the Union government decided to execute three captured rebel officers who had been convicted of espionage. In a cell in the cellar of

Libby, he met his fellow hostage Emil Frey. The dreadful torments the hostages had to endure are described in Frey's article. Markbreit confirmed Frey's account throughout.

MÄRKLIN, Edmund. Forty-Eighter, German-American poet, served in the 35th Wisconsin Regiment. In the Civil War he was active as a surgeon and military pharmacist.

MATTHIES, Karl [Charles] Leopold. Brigadier general from Iowa. He was from Bromberg and had been a Prussian Home Guard officer. He came to Iowa in 1849. Even before the outbreak of the war, he had already organized a company, which Governor Kirkwood of Iowa accepted on 9 January 1861. Thus Matthies was among the first to prepare for war. He was a lieutenant colonel in the 2nd Iowa Regiment at Wilson's Creek, then colonel of this half-German regiment. He was involved in the siege of Corinth and in the Battle at Iuka, where the regiment suffered terribly, losing 217 dead, wounded, and missing of 482 men (including 15 dead or wounded officers). Matthies led a brigade at Iuka and later a division of the XVII Corps. These dreadful exertions made him incapable of action in May 1864. A medallion portrait of Matthies decorates the military memorial in Des Moines, Iowa.

MEDALS OF HONOR for German private soldiers, approved by Congress:

FRITZ FUGER, sergeant, Battery A, United States Artillery. After all the officers of the battery had been killed and five of the guns had been made inoperable, Fuger took charge and continued fighting heroically with the last cannon [Pickett's Charge, 3 July 1863].

IGNAZ GRESSER, 128th Pennsylvania Regiment, born in Baden, who bore wounded comrades out of the thickest rain of bullets to safety at Antietam.

LEOPOLD KARPELES, sergeant, 57th Massachusetts, color bearer, who gathered his fleeing comrades around the flag on 6 May 1864 in the Wilderness, who then stood and threw the enemy back.

JOHN SCHILLER, 158th New York Infantry, who pressed the attack at Chapin's Farm, Virginia, all the way to the ditch of the enemy entrenchment, 1 September 1864.

JAKOB E. SCHWAP, 83rd Pennsylvania Regiment, born in Münden in Hanover, distinguishing himself in the Wilderness, 5 May 1864.

MARTIN WAMBSGAN, born in Migsdorf, Germany, 90th New York Infantry, who saved the regimental flag in October, 1864.

JULIUS LANGBEIN, a German drummer boy, who pulled a wounded officer out of a fire to safety near Camden, North Carolina, April 1862.

BENJAMIN LEVY, who saved the flag after its carrier fell.

CHARLES SCHAMBACH, a Prussian, 11th Pennsylvania Reserves, for capturing a rebel flag, 30 June 1862.

FERD. F. ROHM, born in Esslingen, 16th Pennsylvania Cavalry, for rescuing a wounded officer from a fire at great sacrifice.

KONRAD SCHMIDT, sergeant, 2nd Cavalry Regiment, for saving the wounded Captain Rodenbaugh with great bravery.

This list is unfortunately incomplete.

†MELCHERT, William. Major of the 8th Kansas Infantry Regiment, was stabbed to death next to a captured cannon in the attack on Missionary Ridge.

†MENKE, Gustav. Captain, 9th Pennsylvania Reserve, fell at Second Bull Run. He was a former sergeant of the Bremen Hanseatic [Regiment].

MERSY (or MERCY), [Augustus]. Colonel of the 9th Illinois Regiment, one of the most capable regimental leaders. He fought at Shiloh with great distinction in Colonel Raith's brigade. He was severely wounded there. He led his regiment in all the battles in which it participated. On the march through Georgia Mersy led the 2nd Brigade, 2nd Division, XVI Corps. During the Atlanta Campaign of 1864, Colonel Mersy captured 500 rebels in a stroke of genius. Mersy had been a first lieutenant in Baden. He went over to the revolutionary army and led the 3rd Division of the Baden volunteers.

†METTERNICH, Germain von. Lieutenant colonel of the 46th New York Regiment, met a particularly dreadful death on the island of Tybee near Savannah. An infantryman stumbled and ran a bayonet through his throat. Metternich had been a Forty-Eighter, had fought in Baden under Sigel, and he had once been an Austrian officer of dragoons.

METZENDORFF, Alwin von. Former Prussian officer, lieutenant colonel of the German 75th Pennsylvania Regiment. He was cut off at Chancellorsville with about forty men from his regiment in a skirmish in the woods and fell into captivity.

METZGER, Daniel. Major, Steinwehr's 29th New York Regiment. He led the remnant of the regiment home for its mustering out.

MEYER, Dr. Louis G. Staff surgeon in the 25th Ohio Regiment, later brigade staff surgeon and for a while supreme surgeon of the XI Army Corps. He was from Cleveland, Ohio. He served through the entire war and was one of the best-known surgeons of the Army of the Potomac. In the Battle of Chancellorsville he had himself taken prisoner in order to take better care of the many many wounded among the prisoners.

MEYER, [Edward] Seraphim. Colonel of the entirely German 107th Ohio Regiment recruited from Cleveland, Sandusky, and Toledo. The regiment suffered terribly at Chancellorsville with 220 dead, wounded and missing. It fought splendidly at Gettysburg, where it captured the flag of the 8th Louisiana "Tigers." The losses of the 107th at Gettysburg were 400 out of 550 men!

MEYSENBURG, Theodor August. Born in Cologne, came as a boy to St. Louis. In 1861 he entered Sigel's 3rd Missouri Regiment, soon becoming Sigel's adjutant and advancing rapidly. He was Sigel's right hand at Carthage, Wilson's Creek, Pea Ridge, and Second Bull Run. In October 1862, Meysenburg became adjutant general of the XI Army Corps. As such he was in a leading position at Chancellorsville and Gettysburg, under Howard. He then went to Tennessee with the XI and XII Corps and served General Hooker as chief of staff with the rank of colonel. After Sigel emerged from oblivion once more in 1864, Meysenburg returned to him and again became his chief of staff. As such he participated in the unfortunate Battle of New Market, but he remained loyal to Sigel when he received a small command after that defeat. Meysenburg died in St. Louis, greatly respected.

MEUMANN, Theodor. Colonel of the 3rd Missouri Regiment, an architect and civil engineer. He advanced to leader of Sigel's old regiment on 17 November 1861 after having previously been a major. He was regarded as one of the most capable German officers. The Grand Army of the Republic veterans' organization honored him after his death by naming a post after him. Meumann particularly distinguished himself before Vicksburg. Meumann had served in Prussia and had been a Home Guard officer. He died a few years after the war, as with so many of his comrades, of the consequences of his dreadful exertions.

†VON MEUSEL. Captain of the German 29th New York Regiment, numbered among the missing at the Battle of Chancellorsville. No one ever heard of him again, and he was probably one of the fallen. The number of such people who are listed as missed in battle and are then usually given as captured is very large. It is known that many of the missing were the severely wounded who were taken by the enemy and not mentioned again. In numerous skirmishes in the woods, many poor wounded men remained lying in the thickets. The woods would be set ablaze, and the wounded, lying there helpless, would suffer a dreadful death. There were extensive forest fires at Chancellorsville. Hundreds of wounded were saved by their comrades and by the enemy, but how many remained undiscovered! Von Meusel had previously been a Prussian officer.

†MIHALOTZEY, G. German Hungarian, earlier an Austrian officer, colonel of the 24th Illinois Regiment. Barely recovered from a severe wound received in the Battle on the Chickamauga, he was wounded again so severely on a reconnaissance at Buzzard Roost, Georgia, in February 1864, that he died soon after. He was buried in the National Cemetery in Chattanooga, where 13,000 fallen soldiers rest.

MILLET, Friedrich. German Alsatian, major of a Missouri cavalry regiment.

MINDEL (also MINDIL), Georg [George] W. From Frankfurt am Main, served in the 27th New York Infantry Regiment. Soon he became its colonel, and he was a staff officer to McClellan in the Peninsular Campaign as well as of General Phil. Kearny in the Second Bull Run campaign. He later led a brigade of five regiments in the IX Corps. He also worked in the West under Sherman, during the march through Georgia, as a brigadier. He distinguished himself at Missionary Ridge. He became a brevet major general and rests in the National Cemetery at Arlington. Mindel received two Medals of Honor, the first because he led a regimental attack which broke the enemy center at the Battle of Williamsburg on 5 May 1862, while still serving as an adjutant. The Confederate artillery was silenced through this attack, and those attacking ended up behind the enemy. Mindel received his second decoration on the march through Georgia. General Sherman speaks of this German officer with the highest praise. As with so many others, Mindel died soon after the war of the result of his dreadful exertions.

MITZEL, Alexander von. Lieutenant colonel, 74th Pennsylvania, a former Prussian officer, participating in the Schleswig-Holstein War (1847). Along with Schimmelpfennig he commanded the retreat of the 3rd Division of the 11th Corps at Gettysburg and escaped capture by shooting down his first two attackers, also giving General Schimmelpfennig the opportunity to save himself.

MÖGLING, W. C. Lieutenant colonel, 11th Connecticut Regiment, fought with distinction in the Battle of Cold Harbor, 3 June 1864.

MOOR, August. Brigadier general, born in Leipzig in 1814. At sixteen he participated in the July Revolution in Paris, then he came to America in 1833. He took part in the Seminole War in Florida in 1836 as a lieutenant, and he joined in the Mexican War along with Koseritz and Lehr in 1846 (in Heinrich Bohlen's German militia regiment). Moor advanced to colonel in that war. In May, 1861, he organized the 2nd Cincinnati German Regiment (the 28th Ohio), which particularly distinguished itself at Droop Mountain, Virginia, in November 1863, and which also fought honorably at Piedmont. Moor commanded the vanguard under Sigel in May 1864 which initiated the Battle of New Market, and on the first day he fought alone against Imboden.

MOCHARDT. Engineer, major in Sheridan's staff during his campaign in Tennessee in 1862. He is celebrated by Sheridan as an extraordinarily capable topographer.

MOSKOWSKI, Stanislaus. Chief of Battery A, 1st Pennsylvania Artillery Regiment, which was formed after First Bull Run.

MOSCHZISKER, Dr. Franz A. von. Staff surgeon in the Austrian army, who participated in the rebellion in Hungary. He was an outstanding author, celebrated even by Carlisle [Carlyle]. He came to America in 1853. During the Civil War he was a military surgeon in the major hospitals in Washington.

MÜHLECK, Gustav A. Lieutenant colonel of the 73rd Pennsylvania Regiment. He aprticipated in Pope's campaign and Second Bull Run. A former German officer, he led the regiment after Major Brückner fell.

†McCOOK, Robert. Of Irish heritage, the first colonel of the famous German 9th Ohio Regiment. McCook spoke German and commanded the regiment in German. He was severely wounded at Mill Spring, and he was soon shot dead in the spring of 1862 by bushwhackers. The McCooks were a true family of heroes. They came from Steubenville, Ohio. The father and nine sons entered the army. Three McCooks became generals. Robert McCook was the sole non-German in the Cincinnati Turner Regiment. He was elected colonel on Stallo's advice.

MÜLLER, Karl. Lieutenant colonel in the German 107th Ohio Regiment, lost an arm at Gettysburg.

MÜLLER, Jakob. Cleveland, Ohio. Lieutenant governor of Ohio. He performed great services in organizing German regiments in northern Ohio. He was the author of one of the best works on the Forty Eighters in the United States, *Erinnerungen eines Achtundvierzigers* ["Memories of a Forty-Eighter"]. Well known and honored as a German man of the people in the West. Splendid speaker.

MÜNCH, Friedrich. Theologian from Germany, farmer and vintner in Warren County, Missouri. He was a fruitful, active author, generally known as "Far West." A refugee from the 1830s Movement in Germany, Münch was one of the most loyal and finest of the freedom fighters of 1861. He organized the Germans of his district and sent both his sons into the Union army. One son, a boy of eighteen, died a heroic death at Wilson's Creek. The other son followed the flag until the end of the war.

NAST, Thomas. Famous cartoonist for *Harper's Weekly*. He had a great influence on the patriotism of the Northern people. He was born in 1840 in the Palatinate.

NAZER, F. Lieutenant colonel, led the 4th New York Cavalry Regiment, a German unit once commanded by Dickel, in Pope's campaign of 1862 and at Second Bull Run.

NETTER, Gabriel. Colonel of the 15th Kentucky Cavalry Regiment.

NEUHAUS, Dr. Regimental surgeon in Sigel's corps, was often wounded himself while binding up the wounded, Thus on the Rappahannock at the start of August 1862 he was hit by three bullets, and again at Second Bull Run. He became incapable of service and had to resign. Dr. Neuhaus had been regimental surgeon of the revolutionary troops in Rastatt in 1849.

NEUSTÄDTER, J. Albert. Former Prussian artilleryman, a significant engineer, served as a captain during the entire war. Neustädter was from Trier, fought in Baden in 1848 and was trapped in Rastatt. He fled from this trap along with Karl Schurz. Schurz gives a detailed account of this in his memoirs. Neustädter then became the private secretary of Karl Vogt, emigrated to America in 1851 and functioned under Börnstein as the manager of the *Anzeiger des Westens* in St. Louis. In 1861 he organized a battery, whose chief he became, and went immediately into action in the first battles in Missouri. He fought under Lyon and Frémont, then built Fort Anderson and entered Sherman's staff in the Army of the Cumberland. Neustädter was among the most capable artillerymen of the Western army, participating in most of the battles of the Army of the Cumberland and distinguishing himself often. He was also active as an outstanding writer.

NICODEMUS, William. Adjutant general in the Department of New Mexico, often mentioned during the Red River campaign.

NIX, Jakob. Former South German officer, led the defense of the German Turner town of New Ulm, Minnesota, in its struggle with the Sioux Indians, 23 and 24 August 1862.

NÖCKER, Alfred. Captain of the 12th Independent Ohio Battery. This battery opened the Battle of Cross Keys and Second Bull Run, under Milroy. It, along with Dickel's Battery, covered the retreat. He later fought in the West, particularly in the battles of Franklin and Nashville. Nöcker was twice wounded.

NORDHOFF, Karl. A Westphalian, a significant war correspondent for the great Anglo-American papers of New York.

†ODERFELD. Captain, severely wounded in Sherman's first storming through the Chickasaw Bayou before Vicksburg, December 1862. He died in the hospital.

†OESTERREICH, Georg, also called Hoestrich. Captain in the 46th New York Infantry Regiment (Rosa's Frémont Rifles). He fell at Second Bull Run as he took up the threatened regimental flag.

OLSHAUSEN, Theodor. From Holstein, Editor of the *Westliche Post* in St. Louis. One of the most capable leaders in the German uprising in St. Louis. Olshausen was the most active leader of the rebellion against the Danes in Schleswig-Holstein, The *Westliche Post*, which Olshausen edited until 1865, owes extraordinarily much to this gifted, noble man. After the war, Olshausen longed for home and returned to Germany.

ORFF, H. Colonel of the half-German 35th Wisconsin Regiment.

OTTENDORFER, Oswald. Prominent publicist, editor of the *New Yorker Staatszeitung*. A Forty-Eighter from Vienna, Ottendorfer contributed a great deal to getting German Democrats to become enthused about the Union cause. The *Staatszeitung* was a Democratic Party paper, and during the critical period it served many Forty-Eighters as the target of utterly demeaning assaults. Ottendorfer resigned as presidential elector for New York after the Charleston Convention endorsed the most extreme demands of the slaveowners. Ottendorfer then led his extremely influential paper into the Union camp. Ottendorfer and his wife, the former Mrs. Uhl, placed their great personal wealth at the service of charity, and they left important foundations behind them both in New York and in their old homeland.

OTTO. Colonel, 50th New York Regiment, chief of general staff of Schurz's division at Gettysburg and is praised by Schurz for his apt leadership of the 82nd Illinois and the 45th New York.

PAUL, Gabriel. Led a regiment in the Red River campaign.

PAUL, G. R. General commanded the 3rd Brigade of the 1st Division in Reynolds' I Corps, which threw back the enemy twice in the Battle of Antietam, at the sunken road and at the Piper House. General Paul had both his eyes shot out at the Battle of Gettysburg. Completely blinded, he had to resign. Paul's son also fought as an officer in the Union army, and he was stabbed to death by a drunken comrade in the National Soldiers' Home of Virginia.

†PARCUS. Lieutenant colonel in the German 46th New York Regiment. He was killed before Petersburg by a bomb shortly before the end of the war.

†PEISSNER, Elias. Colonel of the one-third German 119th New York Regiment. He fell at Chancellorsville on 2 May as he was placing his regiment to resist Jackson's attack. He was a professor at Union College in Schenectady, New York, before the war. His appearance was so much like that of King Ludwig I of Bavaria that he was generally regarded as the man's son. Schurz, who knew Peissner intimately and esteemed him, was of the opinion that Peissner really was of Wittelsbach origin. When the great German rally of indignation was held in New York after the Battle of Chancellorsville to protest the accusations raised by West Pointers against German soldiers—that "they were cowards and through their actions lost the Battle of Chancellorsville"—the entire assembly rose at the mention of Peissner's name by Friedrich Kapp in his great oration.

PERCZEL, Nikolaus. Colonel of the 10th Iowa Regiment, a German Hungarian. He led a brigade in the Western campaigns, distinguishing himself at Iuka in September 1863. Perczel could not get along with Anglo-American officers. He complained of the drinking that prevailed among his comrades and particularly among his superiors.

PFÄNDER, Wilhelm. Prominent artillery officer from Minnesota. He fought with distinction at Shiloh (see "The Germans at Shiloh"). He was a noted leader of the Turners in the West.

PFISTERER, Frederick. Captain in the regular United States Infantry, XIV Corps, Army of the Cumberland. He is the author of *Statistical Records of the Armies of the United States* (New York: Scribner's Sons, 1883). The book has appeared in the Scribner series. General W. T. Sherman says that Pfisterer's book is a reliable source. As a statistician, Pfisterer has treated military history with astonishing application and German thoroughness, and his material is so understandibly organized that one may be informed at once on the details of the war. Pfisterer received the Medal of Honor approved by Congress for a heroic ride to the rear of the enemy at Stones River (Murfreesboro). He came to America from Württemberg as a child with his parents.

†VON PILSEN. Colonel of artillery. He was a former Austrian officer, distinguishing himself particularly under Frémont in 1862 in the Shenandoah Valley against Jackson. He was severely wounded on a reconnaissance, and he died as a result.

POMUTZ, George. Lieutenant colonel in the 15th Iowa Regiment.

POSCHNER, Friedrich. Former Prussian officer, a Forty-Eighter, who was the first colonel of the 47th Ohio Regiment.

POTEN, August. Lieutenant colonel of the German 17th Missouri Regiment. He led it at Pea Ridge, and in this battle he stormed an important enemy position. Later he became the colonel of the 5th Missouri Regiment. As such he was honorably involved in the struggles in Tennessee and on the march through Georgia. Colonel Poten was earlier a Hanoverian officer and son of a war minister. He had to struggle to earn his living as a barkeeper in St. Louis after the war.

PRETORIUS, Dr. Emil. Editor of the *Westliche Post*. He bought this paper from Olshausen in 1865. Preetorius brought Schurz to the *Westliche Post* and gave him a partnership in the newspaper. Hence Schurz, who had previously resided in Wisconsin, became a citizen in Missouri and soon a United States senator from Missouri.

PÜCHELSTEIN, Anton von. Major of the 4th New York Cavalry Regiment. He was a former Prussian cavalry officer. He was first on Blenker's staff and became a favorite member of his round table. Von Püchelstein was an extraordinarily keen officer and was always in front. After the war he became the pastor of a German Reformed congregation in Egg Harbor City, New Jersey. Changing mounts from the cavalry to theology is incidentally rather common in America. The author has himself known several former officers who have worked as pastors, and in the most positive manner.

PUTTKAMER, A. von. Outstanding artillery officer, captain of the 11th New York Battery, consisting mostly of Germans. On Jackson's attack at Manassas Junction, Puttkamer lost four guns of his battery, but with the two remaining he rescued Wagner's Brigade from destruction on their retreat. He stood out at Antietam and commanded the artillery of Whipple's division in Sickles' corps, in the battles of Chancellorsville and Gettysburg. He was most highly praised by General Sickles. He belonged to the Pomeranian Mark clan of Puttkamer, which has produced so many outstanding military men and officials.

RADOWITZ, Paul von. Lieutenant colonel in McClellan's staff, earlier an officer of the Prussian Garde du Corps, and a son of the war minister. He distinguished himself several times, particularly on the Antietam.

McClellan speaks of him in *McClellan's Own Story* with actual enthusiasm. When the French-German War broke out, McClellan was on a visit to Berlin. He made the Prussian War Minister aware of von Radowitz, for he believed that Radowitz's experiences in America would be very useful to German war direction. However, the reasons that had led to von Radowitz's departure from the Prussian army prevented his recall from America, although General von Roon made considerable effort to get this prodigal son back into the Prussian army.

After McClellan's dismissal, his staff was dissolved. Its officers lost their positions, which was one of the greatest injustices to take place in the war. One must always recall that the organization of the volunteer army was based on the states, not the federal government. Did von Radowitz, an outstanding officer, become a streetcar driver, like so many of his comrades after the resumption of peace?

†RAITH, Julius. Born in Göppingen, Württemberg, raised in the Belleville Latin settlement, he participated in the Mexican War. In 1861 he was colonel of the 43rd Illinois Regiment, which consisted largely of Belleville Germans. In the first large battle of the Civil War, he commanded a brigade at Shiloh on 6 April 1862. He was severely wounded in one foot. His men wanted to carry him away, but Raith forbade it. He did not want even one man able to fight to leave the battle. But the Union troops were dispersed, and Raith lay for the entire night in the woods. A fire started, and the brave man soon died in it. Next to him fell a nephew, a boy who had just immigrated from Göppingen.

RAPP, Wilhelm. Journalist. He fought bravely for the Union with his pen, in the rebel town of Baltimore. He had to flee from a mob trying to lynch him. He later worked in New York and Baltimore. In 1906 he died in his old age in Chicago.

RASSIEUR, Leo, the sole German to hold the honorary position of supreme commander of the Grand Army of the Republic, the largest veterans' organization. He served in the 1st Reserve Regiment of Missouri, then at the end of the war as a major in a half-German Illinois regiment. He entered the army at the age of 17. Because he had an extraordinary mastery of the English language, almost from boyhood, he was used in April 1861 as a spokesman of Germans in negotiations with the Anglo-American Union men of St. Louis.

RATTERMANN, H. A. Cincinnati. An important and enormously productive German-American historian. He long had the plan to describe the part of the Germans in the Civil War, and he had made important preparatory studies for it. But when the editorship of the *Pionier* was taken from him, he let the plan fall. The closure of this journal, which had risen to high levels under Rattermann's leadership, embittered this capable man. The cause for the change of editorship was petty cliquishness and a complete misunderstanding of the high goals of this editor, who was also an accomplished poet. This was soon followed by the disappearance of the *Pionier*.

REICHENBACH, Dr. H. Capable surgeon with the German troops of Iowa. He was from Davenport, Iowa.

REICHERT, Franz. Battery chief in the 3rd Pennsylvania Artillery Regiment.

REICHHEIM, E. P. Private secretary to Sigel during the first Missouri campaign, later a captain. He fought in many of the battles of the West and often distinguished himself. Captain Reichheim gave his war experiences in a long work which bore the title, *A Yankee Cavalier,* but which unfortunately only survives in manuscript. The portrayals give a good view of the smaller things of the war, life in the field and on the march, and so on.

REMPEL, Ferdinand. Lieutenant colonel of the half-German 58th Ohio Regiment. He led it in the storm on Fort Donelson and pulled down the rebel flag. He had to resign due to wounds.

RETZIUS. Major and final regimental leader of Freudenberg's German 52nd New York Regiment.

REUSS, Dr. P. O. Regimental surgeon of the German 29th New York Regiment. One of the most capable surgeons of the Army of the Potomac. He was best known as an author under the name of Otto Welden. His most significant drama, *Arria,* has been performed many times. Many fine poems, novels and novellas come from his pen. Dr. Reuss went blind in his later years and died in New York. His name as an author has not been forgotten.

REYNOLDS, Major Mrs. [Belle]. The wife of the German Lieutenant Reynolds of the 17th Illinois Regiment. She followed her husband into war and cared for the wounded after the Battle of Shiloh with such dedication that Governor Yates of Illinois issued this brave woman a commission as major as a reward.

RHEINLÄNDER, John. Lieutenant colonel of the 25th Indiana Regiment, who fought through the entire Mexican and Civil Wars to the end. He was severely wounded near Atlanta.

RICHTER, Erhardt. Only a private, but his dreadful fate deserves the greatest sympathy. At the outbreak of the war Richter owned a brewery in the rebel capital of Richmond. As a decided Union man he was boycotted and departed for New York, leaving all his property behind. There he and his two sons, aged seventeen and eighteen, entered the 5th Artillery Regiment. Both sons died heroic deaths. Richter's brewery was burned down by the rebels. When Richmond fell, Richter tried to sell his land in that town. To do so he needed a special permit from the president. Richter went one Sunday to Lincoln. Because a document issued on Sunday had no validity, Lincoln asked him to come another day. Before Richter could again speak with the president, Booth's bullet had eliminated the noble man forever. Richter then turned to General Halleck for a permit, but he was rejected. Richter then lost his mind. He died soon after in the deepest misery.

RIEDT. Major, leader of the German 27th Pennsylvania Regiment, formerly commanded by Buschbeck, at Missionary Ridge.

†RINGGOLD, Benjamin. A Württemberger, the second colonel of the German 103rd [New York] Regiment, falling in the Battle of Suffolk at the head of his troops.

RITTER. Colonel, led a brigade in the Arkansas campaign.

RITTER, Louis. Forty-Eighter of Cleveland, Ohio. He was the author of the history of the German 37th Ohio Regiment found in Whitelaw Reid's work, *Ohio in the War.* Governor Tod of Ohio named Ritter a commissioner for medical care and field hospitals.

ROEMER, Jakob. New York battery chief in Sigel's I Corps in Pope's campaign and at the Second Battle of Bull Run.

ROGGENBUCKE, Oskar. Former Prussian major, a Forty-Eighter. One of the most zealous pro-Union men in Texas. His two sons drowned in the Rio Grande as Union soldiers.

†ROLLSHAUSEN, Ferdinand. Major in Hecker's 82nd Illinois Regiment. He was mortally wounded at Chancellorsville. Captain Frey was Rollhausen's successor as major.

ROMBAUER, Robert J. Colonel, 1st Missouri Reserve Regiment, a German Hungarian who fought under Kossuth.

ROSA, Rudolf von. A Silesian nobleman and Prussian engineering officer, he took his leave in 1848 and joined the Revolution. He fled to America. In 1850 he was in Washington. There he found a position with the coastal survey and was later a civil engineer in New York. In 1862 he organized the 46th German (Frémont) Regiment of New York and became its colonel. In one of the battles on the Peninsula, von Rosa, who was riding at the head of his regiment on attack, was so badly wounded that he became incapable of service. Despite that, he returned to his regiment just before the Battle of Gettysburg and splendidly led his regiment there. He was an impressive, chivalric figure and very calm in battle. He died in New York as an engineer.

ROSENGARTEN, J. C. Author of the oft-cited book *The German Soldier in the Wars of the United States,* dedicated to the memory of the author's brother, who died a heroic death as a major in the 15th Pennsylvania Cavalry Regiment in the Battle of Stones River (Murfreesboro). The brothers were the sons of a German family from Philadelphia. Rosengarten treats in English the part of Germans in all the wars of the Union: the Revolutionary War, border wars, Indian wars, the War of 1812, and the Civil War. This fine book, which appeared in 1882, has been translated into German. The German edition appeared in 1890 with C. Grosse in Kassel. Many of Rosengarten's errors that have been clarified by later research have been corrected here. The book is especially important in its statistical and biographical sections. Unfortunately it does not contain a thorough treatment of the part of the Germans in the Civil War. [Editor's Note: A new, updated edition of this work has been published. See the selective bibliography at the end of this work.]

RÜCKSTUHL, Jakob. Lieutenant colonel, 4th Kentucky Cavalry Regiment.

†RUITINGHAUSEN. Colonel of the 58th Illinois Regiment. He often distinguished himself. His son, serving as a captain in the same regiment, fell at his father's side at Shiloh.

†RUSCH, Nikolas. Major, born in Holstein in 1822. A most capable man of the people in what was then the Far West. He was a state senator in Iowa and sponsor of a law that held the temperance fanatics at bay for twenty years. A splendid orator in both languages, he was lieutenant governor of Iowa. He was immigration agent for Iowa in New York. During the war, Rusch formed a militarily organized corps of woodcutters out of such immigrants as were not fit for military service. These people felled and shipped firewood for the large navy on the Mississippi, but they were trained in such a way that they could protect themselves against guerillas with weapons. The provision of fuel for the gunboats was a deed that could win no glory, but it was of the highest importance, for it kept the fleet capable of fighting. Rusch died in Vicksburg in September 1864. He as well fell on the field of honor.

SAHM, Mich. Battery chief in the 2nd Ohio Artillery Regiment. He was from Dayton, Ohio, where his German crews also originated.

SALOMON. Four brothers from the village of Ströbeck near Magdeburg, where a chessboard hangs from the church tower, and where even children are taught to play chess. They emigrated to Wisconsin in 1848. Three of the brothers stood in the field. Friedrich [Frederick] became a titular major general, C. Eberhard a brigadier. The third brother was a private soldier, and the fourth, Edward was governor of Wisconsin during the war.

SALOMON, Friedrich [Frederick] . The most important of the four brothers, is the conqueror of Helena, Arkansas (see under Vicksburg), as well as Jenkins Ferry, two actions in which Friedrich Salomon operated autonomously and with great honor. General Prentiss, Salomon's superior, later claimed the victory of Helena for himself, but all the Union officers who were involved in the fight witnessed in writing that the defense of the place had been led autonomously by Friedrich Salomon. He was involved in many encounters and battles, but Salomon almost always fought in out-of-the-way theaters of war in the West. It was not granted to him to play a decisive role in the great decisive battles. He died as a federal official in Salt Lake City [in 1897].

SALOMON, C. Eberhard. Colonel of the German 3rd Missouri Regiment and brigadier general, fought at Wilson's Creek and Pea Ridge in Sigel's brigade, at Sarcoxia, Missouri, and Prairie Grove, Arkansas. The latter two encounters were renewed attempts by the Confederates to reconquer Missouri. Salomon very much distinguished himself in this fighting. He also participated in the Red River campaign of 1864, where he fought under his brother Friedrich. His glory days there were in Pine Bluff, Arkansas, and Jenkins Ferry.

SALOMON, Edward. Died in 1908 in Frankfurt am Main, was governor of Wisconsin during the war. He organized the German 26th Wisconsin Regiment. He did not name colonels out of political considerations but for their capacity and experience. He was the sole governor to carry out the conscription law with energy. The Indian War in neighboring Minnesota was restricted to that state due to Governor Salomon's efforts. He was a significant jurist, later working as a lawyer in New York. He was an outstanding German-American.

SALOMON, Edward S. Colonel, titular brigadier general. He was no relation to the Salomon brothers. He organized the Jewish company in Hecker's Regiment, 82nd Illinois. He was lieutenant colonel of that regiment and led the regiment after Hecker was wounded at Chancellorsville. He soon became colonel of the 82nd and led it at Gettysburg. Schurz particularly praised Salomon. He fought in the West from the autumn of 1863 on, at Chattanooga and on Sherman's march through Georgia. At Bentonville in March, 1865, the regiment threw back several enemy attacks, and Salomon received the general's title for this deed. After the war, Salomon became governor of Washington Territory. He was still living in 1910 as a lawyer in San Francisco.

SALM-SALM, Prince Felix. Colonel, later brigadier general. He led the 8th and 68th New York Regiments, and a brigade during the march through Georgia. The Salm-Salms are among the oldest German princely houses, immediate to the Empire. Prince Salm-Salm came to America at the start of the war and was introduced to Lincoln by the Prussian ambassador. When the ambassador mentioned that Salm-Salm was a prince, Lincoln is supposed to have clapped the applicant on the shoulder and said, "Well, we won't hold that against you here." Salm then came to Blenker's staff, the notorious hiring hall for German officers.

It only became possible later for his wife to find a position for him in Blenker's old 8th New York Regiment. Salm-Salm was a brave, careful officer who never found much opportunity to distinguish himself. He became better known as a result of his trip to Mexico, where he became the true friend and companion of the unfortunate Emperor Maximilian and stayed with him until his dreadful end. After the Mexican War, Prince Salm-Salm returned to Prussia and became an officer again. He fell, fighting bravely at the head of his battalion, which he was leading as a major, on 18 August 1870 during the storming of St. Privat by the Prussian Guards.

SALM-SALM, Princess Agnes. Wife of the preceding. She became almost more significant in the Civil War than her husband. In her book *Zehn Jahre aus meinem Leben* ["Ten Years of My Life"], she tells how she made her husband colonel of the 8th New York Regiment, then the 68th Regiment, and finally, by influencing Lincoln, general. She coaxed the governor of New York as well as the president into promoting her husband. American ladies have often worked in such a manner, if we are to believe the author of these memoirs. The Princess, as she was universally called in the army, accompanied her husband to war, was marvelled at as a splendid rider, and experienced innumerable adventures in the field. She was a woman of radiant beauty and charm, with outstanding intellectual gifts and unusual education. She came from a French-Canadian officers' family. Frau von Salm-Salm later followed her husband to Mexico. It was she who obtained from Juárez the postponement of Maximilian's execution. She was also the chief coordinator of the emprisoned emperor's planned escape, which fell through due to the stubbornness of the person to be rescued. After Maximilian's execution, the Salm-Salms returned to Germany. The princess was called to Vienna and Berlin to report to the Emperor of Austria and King Wilhelm [of Prussia] on the details of Maximilian's tragedy. In the War of 1870 the princess headed a Prussian field hospital and performed deeds of genuine heroism in the service of the Red Cross after the Battle of Spicheren.

SCHACK, Georg von. Brigadier general, colonel of the German 7th New York Regiment. He entered the 7th New York as a major and became colonel in February, 1862. The regiment took part in McClellan's Peninsular Campaign and was in the camp at Newport News when the famous duel between the Confederate ironclad *Merrimac* and Ericsson's first *Monitor* took place. The 7th Regiment particularly distinguished itself in the seven-day battle around Richmond, which ended with the Union victory of Malvern Hill. Because of bravery in these battles, von Schack was named brigadier general.

The regiment soon bled at the Battle of Antietam, and on 13 December 1863 it suffered the most dreadful losses in the assault on Fredericksburg. Of twenty-five officers, ten were killed or wounded. Later von Schack reorganized the regiment and joined Grant's campaign of 1864. The regiment particularly distinguished itself at Reams's Station and Hatcher's Run, Virginia. It took part in the siege of Richmond and fought until Lee's surrender at Appomattox Courthouse.

SCHADT. Lieutenant colonel of the 3rd Missouri, later colonel of the 30th Missouri Regiment.

†SCHÄFER VON BERNSTEIN, Karl. Major, 5th Iowa Cavalry Regiment. He fell in an ambush by rebels in northwestern Tennessee. He was on a reconnaissance with 120 riders and had made camp. The camp was overrun in the night by a force twenty times larger. Schäfer was from Darmstadt and had been an officer. His father was the Hessian war minister.

†SCHÄFER, Friedrich. Colonel of the German 2nd Missouri Regiment, later brigadier. He is among the most outstanding among German officers fighting at the front. He had been a policeman in Germany. General Osterhaus, under whose command Schäfer at first stood said that Schäfer was one of the best regimental commanders in the Western army. Schäfer fought at Pea Ridge, Perryville and Vicksburg. In Murfreesboro he commanded a brigade. Going ahead of his troops, Schäfer fell in that battle. General Sheridan speaks highly of him.

SCHENCK, Dr. Konrad, and Dr. Julius C. Schenck. Father and son, both serving as regimental surgeons in the German 37th Ohio Regiment. Both from Cleveland, Ohio.

SHIPWRECK OF THE 75TH PENNSYLVANIA REGIMENT. Hermann Nachtigall of the 75th Pennsylvania Regiment writes to the author about this accident:

> On 15 April the 75th Regiment under Colonel Bohlen was to cross the swollen Shenandoah River at Castleman's Ferry, close to Paris, Virginia. A part of the regiment had already crossed on rafts. A flat-bottomed boat, half burned by the rebels, was brought up and filled with fifty-eight men, including Captain Wyck and Lieutenant Winter. In the middle of the stream, the men could not hold onto the cable stretched across the river. The boat turned over, and with a dreadful cry all its passengers went into the river. All the passengers on the boat drowned.

Nachtigall says nothing about Colonel Bohlen's compelling the people to get into the miserable vehicle against their will. This is claimed by Heusinger, another eyewitness to the accident.

VON SCHILLING. Major, 3rd Pennsylvania Artillery.

VON SCHICKFUSS. Lieutenant colonel, 1st New York Cavalry.

SCHIERENBERG, Ernst. Officer in Osterhaus's 12th Missouri Infantry Regiment. He took part in the war in Missouri but became incapable of service due to physical problems.

He became active at the *Westliche Post* in the spring of 1861, and he was in a position, if not in the leading position, to observe the great German uprising in St. Louis with precision. Many details of our description of the Missouri rising were given by Schierenberg. He also provided many contributions to the biographical part of this book. He died in 1909 in Wiesbaden. He was editor of the *Anzeiger des Westens* along with Dänzer. He was one of our most capable German-American journalists, always a German patriot and one of the best experts on the Western war.

SCHIMMELPFENNIG, Alexander von. Born 1824, died 1865 as a result of the exertions of campaign. One of our best German fighting generals, a brigadier general and division commander. He was a former Prussian officer. He had fought in Schleswig-Holstein and then emigrated to America. He was a colonel of the German 74th Pennsylvania Regiment, recruited in Pittsburgh, one of the elite regiments of the Army of the Potomac. He stood in Blenker's German Division and fought with distinction at Cross Keys, then under Sigel in Pope's campaign of 1862. He distinguished himself particularly at Second Bull Run. His brigade pressed beyond the railroad causeway and threw Jackson's best troops to beyond Cushing's Farm.

He then fought under Schurz at Chancellorsville on Hawkins Farm and in the trenches defended by Buschbeck. The old Prussian officer felt (and correctly so) that his honor was offended after the Battle of Chancellorsville, when West Pointers made the XI Corps the scapegoat for the failures of the higher leadership. With the indignation of a German officer, he wrote a letter to his immediate superior, Schurz, who has published it. On the first day of the Battle of Gettysburg, Schimmelpfennig led a division in the XI Corps, commanded on that day by Schurz. The four fold superior force of the enemy threw the two divisions of the XI Corps standing in the open field back into the streets of the town. Schimmelpfennig was knocked down by a gun butt. He recovered and sought protection in a nearby horse's stall. There he sat for two days, awaiting the conclusion of the struggle. Von Schimmelpfennig then had himself transferred to the Carolinas, for he did not wish to continue serving in the XI Corps. Hence he went into the X Corps, from the frying pan and into the fire, for siege work in the swamps around Charleston brought malaria as the worst enemy. Von Schimmelpfennig then had the honor of being the first to enter the cradle of the secession, Charleston, South Carolina, with his troops. His compatriot, the German secessionist General Johann A. Wagener (see his article), capitulated to him. Schurz learned much from Schimmelpfennig, particularly in the leadership of troops. Von Schimmelpfennig wrote a good book about the Crimean War. He began a second, promising book about the Civil War when illness and a quick death overtook him. German America should preserve an honorable thought for this man, capable but continually persecuted by misfortune and error.

SCHIRMER. Colonel of artillery, New York. He was a former Prussian artillery officer. He fought in the German Division and later under Sigel. One of the most capable artillerymen.

SCHLEN, J. von. Captain, a battery chief in the Army of the Potomac.

SCHLÜMBACH, Fr. von. Cadet in the 5th Württemberg Infantry Regiment. He took service in the Philadelphia Turner battalion, which was amalgamated with the 29th New York Regiment, whose major was his brother. He became a lieutenant, and was wounded and captured at Second Bull Run. He died as a pastor in Cleveland.

VON SCHLÜMBACH. Colonel of German 29th Regiment of New York, originally commanded by Steinwehr.

SCHLUNDT, Fidel. From Immenstadt in the Allgäu, Bavaria. He was a member of the Bavarian representative assembly from 1845 to 1849 and of the Frankfurt Parliament in 1848. He took part in the revolution in Baden and languished for a long time in the fortress at Kempten. At the outbreak of the Civil War he enlisted with four sons. One of them was shot to death in Virginia, and another was severely wounded.

SCHMIDT, Max. Captain, 54th New York Regiment, commanded the skirmish line of Krzyzanowski's brigade at the opening of the Second Battle of Bull Run. He was shot through the shin and lost a leg.

SCHMIDT, Dr. Ernst. Surgeon general of the XVI Army Corps. He died in Chicago. One of the most important German physicians. He was a respected and capable leader of the Germans in Chicago.

SCHNAKE, Friedrich. Noted journalist and poet, fighter in the uprising of the Germans in St. Louis. He wrote a history of that German uprising for Rattermann's *Deutscher Pionier.*

SCHNAKENBURG. Major, later lieutenant colonel in Willich's German 32nd Indiana Regiment, distinguished himself at Shiloh.

SCHNEIDER, Edw. F. Lieutenant colonel in the 8th Kansas Regiment.

SCHNEIDER, Georg. Editor of the *Illinois Staatszeitung* in Chicago at the outbreak of the war. He made a major contribution to the pro-war attitude of the Germans in the West. He was a friend of Lincoln and a member of the convention that nominated Lincoln.

SCHNEPF, E. Lieutenant colonel, 20th New York Regiment.

SCHNITTGER, Gustav. Major of an Iowa regiment. Came from Davenport, Iowa.

SCHÖPF, Alban. Brigadier general, commanded at the start of the war in Kentucky against Zollicofer, but was soon replaced by General Thomas, who outranked him, shortly before the victory of Mill Springs. (See the Battle of Perryville.)

SCHOPP, Phil. Colonel of the 8th West Virginia Regiment, praised by Sigel. He served in General Bohlen's brigade.

SCHRADER, Alexander von. Former Prussian officer, lieutenant colonel, 74th Ohio Regiment, later colonel, titular brigadier general. One of the most capable German engineering officers in the army. He distinguished himself particularly at Corinth, further at Murfreesboro and Chickamauga, and on the march through Georgia. He served through the entire war and transferred to the Regular Army.

SCHUBERT, Emil. Artillery officer of the Army of the Potomac.

SCHULTZ, Fr. Captain of Battery M, 1st Ohio Artillery Regiment. He took part in the campaigns of the Army of the Cumberland, distinguishing himself at Cattlet's Station, where he covered the retreat.

SCHURIG, Karl. Lieutenant colonel of the 18th New York Regiment. He was severely wounded at Second Bull Run by a shot through the breast, and in 1864 he lost an arm in the Wilderness battles.

SCHÜTTNER, Nikolaus. Colonel of the 4th Missouri Volunteer Regiment (Black Rifles). This regiment was the first in the German uprising of St. Louis to prepare for fighting. It began drilling in January 1861.

SCHWAN, Theodor. General in the regular United States Army. From Hanover, he came to the United States as a boy, entered the Regular Army at the age of 16 and participating as a private in the expedition sent against the Mormons. Then came the Civil War. Schwan fought in twenty battles, particularly at Chancellorsville, Gettysburg, in the battles in the Wilderness, Spotsylvania, North Anna, Cold Harbor, Petersburg and others. Congress granted him the Medal of Honor.

After the war he remained an officer of the Regular Army, serving in the many Indian Wars. The redskins gave him the honorable name "The Paleface who never lied." As an Indian agent he was one of the few such officials who learned to understand the savages and treat them humanely and justly. In 1892 Major Schwan was named military attaché to the American embassy in Berlin. His observations of German military institutions were printed and found lively appreciation from German general staff officers. Schwan's greatest military activity came in the Spanish-American War. Here he led a fighting division of 20,000 men in a splendid manner.

†SCHWARTZ, Adolf. Major, 1st Battery, 2nd Illinois Artillery, attacked effectively at Shiloh, but he was killed in that battle by a shell splinter.

SCHWARZWÄLDER. Colonel of the 7th New York Militia Regiment, later a brigadier general.

†SCHWERIN, Heinrich von. Captain of the 119th New York Regiment, was shot through the chest on Hawkins Farm at Chancellorsville and died the next day.

SEIDEL, Charles B. Colonel of the 3rd Ohio Cavalry Regiment. He followed Colonel Zahm in 1863 as supreme commander of this regiment and distinguished himself in the campaigns of Rosecrans, Sherman, and Thomas from Murfreesboro to Atlanta and Nashville.

VON SELDENECK. Artillery captain and leader of the Sigel Battery provided to the 46th New York Regiment. The battery consisted of experienced German artillerymen. They blasted the breach in Fort Pulaski.

SENGES. Colonel of artillery, fought in the Army of the Potomac, distinguishing himself particularly in the bombardment of Fort Pulaski. Colonel Senges had been an artillery captain in the Baden army and went over to the revolutionaries with most of his comrades. Senges sat for a long time in the penitentiary in Freiburg im Breisgau, along with Otto von Corwin.

SERVIÉRE. Major of the German 46th New York Regiment. From a Huguenot family, he had previously been a Prussian officer.

SIBER, Eduard. Colonel of the German 37th Ohio Regiment. One of the best swords Germany gave to America. General Sherman publicly called Siber the best-trained officer of his army. (This statement by Sherman was made to a group of higher officers in Youngstown, Louisiana.) Siber was a captain in the Prussian army and a general staff officer. He took his leave to enter the patriot army of Schleswig-Holstein in 1847, serving with great distinction. After the end of the First Danish War he went to Brazil, where he was an instructor of the army there (as a result of a summons from [Emperor] Dom Pedro). At the outbreak of the Civil War, Siber came to the United States and was at once made colonel of the German 37th Ohio Regiment. He is the one most responsible for the model conduct of this regiment. He was strict in his command, not only to the men but also to his officers. His aging body stood the dreadful exertions of campaign for two years, but after the taking of Vicksburg in 1863 his health compelled him to resign.

SIGEL, Albert. A brother of General Franz Sigel, was colonel of the 5th Regiment of the Missouri State Militia.

†SLEMMER, A. J. Fell in the Battle of Stones River as a lieutenant colonel of a Regular battalion. Through his heroic conduct as a mere lieutenant in the harbor of Pensacola, Florida, in 1861, he had saved that key to the Gulf of Mexico.

SOEST, Klemens. Colonel of the 29th New York Regiment, formerly commanded by von Steinwehr, at Second Bull Run.

SÖLLHEIM, Dr. Konrad. From Cincinnati. He was regimental surgeon in the 9th Ohio Regiment for a year.

SONDERSDORFF. Major in the German 9th Ohio Regiment. He led the regiment several times as a deputy. He fought bravely through the entire war.

SPIEGELHALTER, Dr. From St. Louis, staff surgeon in Osterhaus's 12th Missouri Regiment. An important surgeon. One of those heroes of the war who never take the front of the stage, but who have such a positive effect through their medical art and dedication.

SPRAUL, Karl M. Inspector of infantry in the XI Corps. He was a former Bavarian officer.

STAHL, Wm. A. German battery chief in the Army of the Potomac.

STALLO, Johann Bernhard. A great German-American, born in Sierhausen, Oldenburg, in 1823, and emigrated to Cincinnati in 1839. His comprehensive education was obtained primarily as an autodidact. He was as significant as a jurist as he was a mathematician, physicist, and chemist. His best-known works covered the latter fields. He was a masterful orator in both languages. His German writings were published by Steiger of New York. This treasure of great thoughts and splendid expression on German life in America is unfortunately known to few. Stallo's works on the great questions of the war, particularly on the notorious fugitive slave law, are among the best in this field. Stallo was American ambassador in Rome under Cleveland, remaining in Italy afterwards and closing his industrious life at great age in Florence.

STARKLOFF, Dr. H. M. Regimental surgeon in the 12th Missouri Regiment, an important surgeon in civilian life. He worked through the greater part of the war with great dedication. He was president of the North American Turner League for many years. In all his old freshness at 78 years he commanded the festival that closed German Day in St. Louis in 1908.

†STEINER, F. Captain, 107th Ohio Regiment, was shot through the abdomen at Gettysburg and died on the field.

†STEINHAUSEN, Adolf von. Of Freudenberg's [52nd] New York Regiment, consisting mostly of Germans. He fell at Todd's Tavern, Virginia, in Grant's Wilderness campaign of 1864. Von Steinhausen had earlier been a Prussian officer.

VON STEUBEN. Officer in the 52nd, colonel of the 68th New York Regiment, Chattanooga.

†STÖCKER. Four brothers of this name served in the 9th Ohio Regiment. The first of this regiment to fall was a Stöcker.

STRUVE, Gustav von. Leader of the Baden Revolution. In 1861 he was an officer in Blenker's 8th New York Volunteer Regiment. When Prince Salm-Salm became colonel of the regiment, Struve resigned. "I cannot be the servant of a prince, and I cannot serve under a prince." But because the German prince was simply Colonel Salm in America, Struve's upset was more ridiculed in the army than the old revolutionary would have liked. Struve returned to Germany in 1863. During his military career, he was Blenker's loyal squire. Struve's portrayal from the time of war, *Diesseits und Jenseits des Ozeans* ["This Side and the Other Side of the Ocean"], shows the marks of strong bitterness. He was often hostile to Schurz, whom he pursued with hatred for some reason (envy?).

STUDER, A. G. Major in the 15th Iowa Regiment. He fought at Shiloh and in many of the battles of the West. He was commandant of the garrison in Washington on the evening Lincoln was shot by Booth. He led the first pursuit of the escaped murderer with great energy. Studer was a German Swiss. He later served as consul in Singapore.

STUMBERG, Dr. Henry. Staff surgeon of the German 3rd Missouri Regiment.

SUDBURG. Colonel of a Maryland infantry regiment that consisted to a large degree of Germans. This regiment stood under the worst fire during the Battle of Antietam.

SUHRER, Ferdinand C. Major in the 107th Ohio Regiment. He rose from sergeant as a result of capability and bravery.

SUTTERMEISTER, Arnold. Colonel, a German Swiss. He organized the 11th Indiana Battery in Fort Wayne, Indiana, in the spring of 1861, and led it. He fought in the West, distinguishing himself in Corinth, Chickamauga, and Missionary Ridge. The battery went along on Sherman's March through Georgia and through the Carolinas, fighting honorably in many of the battles of that campaign. Suttermeister commanded the reserve artillery of the 1st Brigade of the 2nd Division in Thomas's army, consisting of Batteries 4, 8, 11, and 21 of Indiana. He was mustered out with the title of a colonel of artillery.

TAFEL, Gustav. Colonel of the 106th Ohio Regiment, deriving from the 9th Ohio Regiment. The 106th distinguished itself at Hartsville, Kentucky, where the entire 39th Brigade was captured due to the incompetence of its commander, Moore. Tafel's regiment was the sole one in the brigade that gave decisive resistance. Tafel later became mayor of Cincinnati.

TASSIN, A. G. Colonel, 35th Indiana Regiment.

THEEL, T. T. Battery chief, Red River campaign, fought with great distinction at Valverde, New Mexico.

THEUNE, Roderich. Adjutant general of General Heinrich Bohlen, originally adjutant of the German 75th Pennsylvania Regiment. Theune lost a leg in the Second Battle of Bull Run. Unable to do field service, he later functioned as provost marshal. He lost his mind due to the stress of war and died soon after the war in a madhouse.

THOMANN, Gallus. Entered the German 103rd Regiment of New York at the age of 16 and served honorably through the entire war. He is one of the best experts of the history of the war. Thomann intended to write a history of the Germans in the Civil War in English, but he soon withdrew from the project when he learned how far this author's preparations had gone. He then became a zealous coworker on the present book, which owes him very much. Mr. Thomann has read and judged many parts of this book in manuscript, and he has been of great use to me through his great knowledge of the literature on the war.

Thomann handles the English language as well as his mother tongue and possesses great gifts as a speaker in both languages, particularly in debate. He is at the present time to be named in the first rank of intellectual leaders of Germans in the United States. He has stood for many years at the head of the office that has issued scientific material to the opponents of compulsion. With his unanswerable arguments he has in fact shown some of the coarsest fanatics of the prohibition movement the way of reason and forced these opponents to recognize his position. Through his influence many of the worst bills have been modified and improved so far as compulsion goes, particularly the excise legislation of the state of New York. This is unfortunately not the place to appreciate Thomann's effectiveness in this field. He has won recognition not only in the United States, but also in Europe, particularly in England and Germany. At the Paris *Exposition du Travail,* Thomann received the gold medal for his history of the brewing industry.

†THOMANN, Max A. Major of the 59th Pennsylvania Regiment, mortally wounded at Chancellorsville.

TRAU, Dr. John Phil. Palatine Forty-Eighter, served as a surgeon in Blenker's Division.

TRAVERS. Major in the German 46th New York Regiment.

TRAUERNICHT, Theodor. [Lieutenant] colonel of the 13th [Colored Infantry] Regiment in [1863,]1864, and 1865.

VON TREBRA. Lieutenant colonel in the 32nd Indiana, leader of this elite regiment after Willich's appointment as brigadier general. Von Trebra commanded a part of the regiment at Rowlett's Station, Kentucky, and with 418 men beat back an enemy five times his size. Lieutenant Sachs and eight men fell, and sixteen men were wounded. The skirmish is thoroughly described in the chapter, "The War in the West, 1862." Von Trebra also distinguished himself at Shiloh, then became colonel of the 32nd. He died of asthma in 1862.

†TREPP, Kaspar. Colonel in the Sparpshooters Regiment, from Splügen, Canton Grisons [Switzerland]. He organized the Swiss sharpshooters company whose heroism has been described by Aschmann. The company soon grew to a regiment, two-thirds Swiss and German, with a splendid war record. Colonel Trepp fell in the Battle of Mine Run.

TÜRCK, Hermann. Officer in the 12th Missouri Regiment. Both his eyes were shot out at the Battle of Pea Ridge. A wealthy Englishwoman fell in love with the blind man, married him, and cared for Türck until his death.

†TYNDALE, Troilus. An officer in the 12th Missouri Regiment. He died as a result of wounds received in the Battle of Pea Ridge. He was one of the Americans who had been completely Germanized by contact with the German Latins in Belleville. Everyone thought Tyndale was a German.

ULFFERS, Hermann. Lieutenant colonel in General Sherman's staff, born in Westpahlia, a civil engineer. He participated in the 1848 Revolution, then fled to America, where he was active mostly as a railroad engineer. He entered the Union army in 1861 as an engineering officer. He participated in the battles of Pea Ridge, Corinth, Perryville and Murfreesboro. Sherman then called Ulffers to his staff. He was captured and ended up in the dreadful Andersonville Prison. His escape from this hell excited general attention. He reached the limits of the Union army clothed in rags, reduced to a skeleton.

D'UTASSY, actually STRASSER. Colonel of the Garibaldi Regiment, 39th New York, which had three German companies and one Swiss. D'Utassy left the regiment in less than honorable circumstances.

VEGESACK, F. von. Colonel, commanded the 3rd Brigade of Howe's division, Reynolds' I Corps at Antietam, where he successfully participated in the fighting.

VIGNOS, August. Major in the 107th Ohio. At Gettysburg he lost an arm, but he remained with his unit anyway and only resigned in 1864 due to wounds received later.

VILLARD, Henry, actually Heinrich Hilgard. Born in Speyer, 1835, died in New York. Villard, called "King of the Northern Pacific Railway," was one of the most significant and influential war correspondents of the English-language newspapers of America.

VOCKE, Wilhelm. Captain in the 24th Illinois Regiment, from Westphalia, emigrated in 1856, a lawyer in Chicago, died in the spring of 1907. Vocke never passed up the opportunity to reject in English speech or writing, the attacks of nativists, particularly by West Pointers, against German soldiers. Excellent works by Vocke are *Der deutsche Soldat im amerikanischen Bürgerkrieg* ["The German Soldier in the American Civil War"], and *The German Soldiers*, better known as *The Schneider Boys*. The latter work makes use of dialect poetry written in the Breitmann style, in which German soldiers are mocked, but which stimulates the laughing muscles by its very language, a dreadful German-English. It has had a great impact on veterans' groups and has often been recited there:

> But Schneider haf urgent peesneess today,
> In Winchester, dwenty miles avay.

Unfortunately, Vocke restricted himself to only a few episodes of German-American war history, essentially those in which he was himself involved.

VÖRSTER, J. D. Captain of the German Pioneer Company organized in St. Louis in May 1861. This was the first pioneer unit of the American volunteer army.

VOSS, Arno. Colonel in the 12th Illinois Cavalry Regiment. Commanded the Union cavalry that escaped Harpers Ferry as the other troops, under Colonel Miles, were capitulating to Jackson. On this ride, Voss also seized an enemy wagon train.

WAGNER, Franz X. Advanced from private to captain of Company D, 9th Illinois Regiment. He served through the entire war, marching with Sherman from Chattanooga to Savannah, and from there through the Carolinas. His war record consists of 110 battles and skirmishes. He was wounded four times. He was an energetic helper in this biographical section.

WAGNER, Georg [George] D. Commanded the 2nd Brigade in Sheridan's division, Army of the Cumberland, which distinguished itself particularly in the storming of Missionary Ridge.

WAGNER, Gustav. Colonel of the 2nd New York Artillery Regiment. He particularly distinguished himself at Fairfax Courthouse on 27 August 1862, during Pope's campaign. The former Prussian artillery officer von Puttkamer fought under him.

WAGNER, Louis. Colonel, 88th Pennsylvania Regiment, titular brigadier general. He came to Philadelphia with his parents in 1849. He was severely wounded at Second Bull Run. Taken by the enemy from the battlefield, he fell into captivity. On being exchanged, he resumed command of the 88th Regiment and fought at Chancellorsville. Then his badly treated wound broke open again, and Wagner was called to be commandant of the military camp in William, Pennsylvania, where he trained colored troops and put 14,000 men into the field in a short time. In 1865 Wagner took over a brigade in the V Army Corps and received the title of general at the age of 27. He was a long-term member of the large Swabian Society of Philadelphia, where there are probably more Swabians and their descendents than in even Stuttgart.

WAGNER, Louis. Colonel of the 1st California Regiment, commanding the 1st Brigade of the Pacific Department.

WAINRIGHT, W. P. Major in the German 29th New York Regiment, became colonel in the 174th New York Regiment.

WALTHER, Geo. H. Colonel of the 35th Wisconsin Regiment.

†WALTHER, Karl. Colonel of the 17th Connecticut Regiment, fell at Chancellorsville, 2 May 1863.

WANGELIN, Hugo von. Brigadier general. He came from a Mecklenburg noble family, was trained in a Prussian military academy, but emigrated with his parents at the age of 16 in 1834. Hugo von Wangelin entered a Missouri regiment in 1861, soon becoming major in Osterhaus's 12th Missouri Regiment and fighting with particular distinction in the storming of Elkhorn Pass (Pea Ridge). Von Wangelin was the true friend and comrade in arms of Osterhaus. He followed Osterhaus in promotions, first as colonel of the 12th Missouri, then as the leader of the old Osterhaus Brigade (3rd, 12th and 17th Missouri and 44th Illinois Regiments). Almost all of the fights Osterhaus had were also waged by Wangelin. The two were inseparable throughout the entire war. Wangelin's brigade distinguished itself at Vicksburg, then Lookout Mountain, Missionary Ridge, and in the bloody Battle of Ringgold, Georgia, where Wangelin lost an arm. The surgeons had to amputate the arm, but when they came with drugs, Wangelin refused them, saying that a soldier could stand a little cutting. He whistled "Yankee Doodle" as the saw went through his bones.

On the march through Georgia, he fought brilliantly. He beat back a severe attack at New Hope Church on 28 May. During the fighting around Atlanta, Wangelin's men discovered the body of General McPherson, commander of the Army of the Tennessee, shot while on a reconnaissance, and captured the rebels who had killed McPherson and taken the general's saber, uniform, and important papers.

Wangelin held Bald Hill in a brilliant manner in this battle. Wangelin was wounded there several times, but he remained with his troops. Unfortunately, all of Wangelin's war deeds cannot be recounted here, but he had a record of more than fifty battles and skirmishes, fought over four years, continuously at the front (his "leaves" were the weeks needed for the healing of his wounds), and among German heroes of the Western army, the name of Wangelin must be mentioned immediately after that of Willich.

WEBER, Max von. Brigadier general. A Forty-Eighter who fought under Mieroslawski and Sigel in the Baden Revolution, a former Baden officer, he ran a well-known hotel in New York that served as headquarters for South German refugees. He aided many poor comrades as a patron. In 1861 he became colonel of the 20th New York (Turner) Regiment and led it until he was named brigadier general.

The regiment was supposed to be joined at the start of the war to Blenker's brigade, but Weber protested against it. He did not want to serve under Blenker, and the regiment was then sent to the Peninsula. Weber was for a time commandant of Fortress Monroe at the tip of the Peninsula, where the landings of the Union troops took place. He distinguished himself in fighting near Norfolk. His greatest military glory came with Antietam. There Weber led the 3rd Brigade of French's 3rd Division in Sumner's corps. Weber held the position near Rulett's house when Sedgwick's left had already folded. He stood there under murderous fire until Kimball's brigade came to his aid. In this dreadful fighting, Weber threw back the enemy several times, retreating only when the Confederates put four more batteries into action against him. Weber was severely wounded in the shoulder and long lay in the field hospital. He participated in Sigel's fighting in the Shenandoah Valley in May 1864, but he only had 800 men and could accomplish little.

WEBER, Dr. Gustav C. A. Surgeon general of Ohio troops. One of the most famed German surgeons in America, a physician and professor of medicine in Cleveland, Ohio, Dr. Weber is originally from Bonn. He did great services for the organization of medicine in the Civil War. The placement of capable surgeons was largely due to him. Dr. Weber worked with great dedication on the battlefield of Shiloh. He was still living on a farm near Cleveland, Ohio, as a robust old man in his eighties.

WEDELL, Karl von. Major, 68th New York Regiment.

†WEHLE, Julius von. Captain in the 66th New York Infantry Regiment, distinguishing himself at Antietam and took command of the regiment at Fredericksburg after the colonel fell. A fatal bullet struck Wehle immediately after that, and Captain Hammel took Wehle's place and was immediately severely wounded, so that the senior lieutenant led the regiment until the end of the battle.

WEIDEMEYER, [Joseph]. Colonel of the half-German 40th Missouri Regiment.

WEIGEL, Eugen. Hecker's adjutant [the 82nd Illinois—SR] at Chancellorsville. He distinguished himself at Gettysburg and Missionary Ridge.

WEINGART, G. Captain, battery chief, Army of the Potomac.

WEISBERG, Alfred. Lieutenant colonel, 9th Wisconsin Regiment.

WEISS. A former Bavarian officer, became colonel of the 20th New York (Turner) Regiment, formerly Weber's, after Weber became a brigadier general. Weiss was a shirker and was dismissed because he stood out in the bloody Peninsular battle of White Oak Swamp through his absence.

†WENTZ, Karl August. From Baden. He emigrated in 1845. He took part in the Mexican War and was promoted for bravery. In the Civil War he was first captain of the German company of the 1st Iowa Regiment, organized in Davenport, Iowa, and later lieutenant colonel of the 7th Iowa Regiment. He fell at the head of his regiment at Belmont, Missouri, on 8 November 1861.

WERTHEIMER, Eduard. Captain in the 54th New York Infantry Regiment, distinguishing himself in the Second Battle of Bull Run in the storming of the railroad causeway by grabbing the flag and swinging it high, he advanced ahead of the columns toward the enemy. The flag was shot to tatters.

WETSCHKY, Karl. Colonel of the 1st Maryland Cavalry Regiment. He took part in most of the fighting of the Army of the Potomac under Pope and later under Hooker. The remnants of his regiment (that is, the few whose horses were still usable) covered the retreat across the stone bridge at Second Bull Run.

WIEDRICH, Michael. Battery chief from Buffalo. His battery, which had almost exclusively German crews, fought in Schurz's division, Army of the Potomac. It took part in the Battle at Cross Keys, all the fighting of Pope's campaign, particularly the Second Battle of Bull Run; and the battles of Chancellorsville, Gettysburg, and Chattanooga.

†WIEBISCHE. Colonel of a New Jersey regiment, fell at Spotsylvania. He was a former Prussian officer.

WILHELM. Lieutenant colonel in the 23rd Pennsylvania Regiment.

WILHELMI, Franz. Major in the German 17th Missouri Regiment, discharged as a colonel. He took part in twenty-three battles. A Baden Forty-Eighter, Wilhelmi particularly distinguished himself in battles against guerillas, as well as in the siege and storming of Vicksburg.

WINKLER, [Frederick] C. Colonel and brevet brigadier. Born in 1838 in Bremen, still living as a robust old man in Milwaukee, a lawyer. He became colonel of the 26th Wisconsin Regiment after Jacob's resignation, and he led the regiment with distinction from the autumn of 1863 to the end of the war. During the fighting on Sherman's march through Georgia, Winkler particularly distinguished himself.

Winkler is the president of the Carl Schurz Memorial Association, which wants to gather a fund of $60,000 the interest from which will pay for a German exchange professor. All German ethnic efforts in America found and find in General Winkler the most zealous supporter.

26TH WISCONSIN REGIMENT. Fallen or died of wounds: 12 officers and 173 men; died of illness, 39; wounded: 18 officers, 295 men; missing, or captured, 4 officers and 74 men. In all, 34 officers and 582 men were made incapable of service, or 52.5 percent of the original force. The entirely German 26th Wisconsin Regiment stands first in Fox's list of the bravest regiments of volunteers.

†WITTICH, W. F. Captain, 83rd Pennsylvania, fell at Second Bull Run in fighting over an enemy cannon. He was an Alsatian who had fought in the Crimean War.

WITZIG, Johann J. Entered the 1st German Turner Regiment in Missouri in April, 1861, which later became the 1st Artillery Regiment of Missouri. He was a German Alsatian.

WÖLFLE. Captain, a famous artillery officer from Missouri who fought gloriously at Pea Ridge, Vicksburg, Chattanooga and in many battles and fights in the West.

WOLF, Friedrich. Captain of the 3rd Missouri Regiment, who took the entire 14th Texas Regiment captive in the attack at Arkansas Post in January 1863. Wolf only had seven men in his company with him. He called to the colonel of the Confederate regiment, "Give up, the fort behind you is taken, and an entire brigade stands behind me." And the colonel surrendered with all his Texans. Wolf and his seven men brought his 300 captives into the camp of the Union troops. These captives were mostly Germans from Texas who had been compelled to serve in the Confederacy. Most of them transferred to the Union army.

WOLFF. Lieutenant colonel in the German 5th Missouri Regiment.

WÖRNER. Major in artillery, from New Jersey. Fought with honor at Antietam.

WRATISLAW, Edward C. Lieutenant colonel of von Amsberg's 45th New York Regiment in Pope's campaign and at Second Bull Run. He had been Mieroslawski's adjutant in the Baden Revolution.

WUTSCHELL. Third colonel of the German 8th New York Infantry Regiment, Wutschell was from Vienna, where he had fought on the barricades. See the Battle at Cross Keys.

YOUNG, Peter F. Captain in the German 107th Ohio Regiment, captured a rebel flag in hand-to-hand fighting at Gettysburg and was severely wounded doing so.

ZAHM, Louis. Colonel of the partly-German 3rd Ohio Cavalry Regiment under Buell and Rosecrans. He was honorably discharged in January 1863. A capable German officer, he received the rank of general.

ZALINSKI, Edmund. Major, discoverer of the pneumatic dynamite torpedo gun. This has not fulfilled the expectations originally placed in it. Zalinski was an outstanding technologist of artillery and produced many inventions.

ZAKRZEWSKI, H. Lieutenant colonel, 2nd Missouri Regiment.

†VON ZEDLITZ. Regimental adjutant, 29th New York Regiment, died of wounds received on 2 May at Chancellorsville during the fighting of Buschbeck's brigade. Von Zedlitz had earlier been a Prussian officer.

ZEPPELIN, Count Ferdinand von. The most important developer of airship travel, came to America in 1863 to observe the war. He made his first flight in the West in one of the tethered balloons used there. His interest in airship travel is supposed to have been stimulated by that experience.

ZIEGLER, Geo. M. Colonel of the 52nd Colored Infantry Regiment.

ZICKERICK, William. Recruited in Sheboygan what was known as the Low German 12th Wisconsin Battery, which distinguished itself in the campaigns of the Army of the Cumberland. He commanded the reserve artillery of the Army of the Cumberland from 1863 to 1865. He helped decide the victory at Champion Hills, [Mississippi]. He died as a preacher of an Evangelical congregation in Oshkosh, Wisconsin.

ZIPPERLEN, Dr. Adolf. Brigade surgeon. He entered the 108th Ohio Regiment, recruited mostly from Cincinnati, as a staff surgeon in June 1862 and served through the entire war. He made campaigns in the West and the march through Georgia. In the victory march in Washington in May 1865, his brigade was part of what was called "Sherman's Bummers." Zipperlen was an outstanding physician and a famous surgeon. He resided in Cincinnati, but he came from Württemberg. He died at almost 90, a beloved author and orator. He was a Forty-Eighter. The story of Zipperlen's emigration was printed in the *Deutscher Pionier* and is one of the best contributions to emigration literature we have.

ZITZER, Dr. Johann. A Forty-Eighter from Freiburg im Breisgau. He was surgeon general of the state of Pennsylvania.

ZOLLINGER, Karl A. From Wiesbaden. Colonel of the 129th Indiana Volunteer Regiment. He fought bravely from the beginning to the end of the war, and he was later mayor of Fort Wayne, Indiana.

†ZOOK, [Samuel K.]. Colonel in the German [57th] New York Regiment. He fell as a general while bravely fighting, at the head of his brigade, at Gettysburg, 2 July 1863.

German Confederates

BACHMANN, W. K. Captain of the German Charleston Artillery, which did outstanding service in Longstreet's corps.

BORCKE, Heros von. The most significant German military man in the Confederate army. He was one of the most outstanding cavalry leaders, and he had been a Prussian officer (Garde-Courasier?), coming to America in 1862 to offer his sword to the secession. In his much-read book, *Zwei Jahre im Sattel und am Feinde* ["Two Years in the Saddle and at the Enemy"], he speaks of his sympathy for the cause of the South.

Von Borcke was a Prussian *Junker* and aristocrat who found the aristocrats of the American South to be brothers in sensibility. He was immediately detailed to the famous cavalry commander Jeb Stuart, becoming his chief of staff and right hand. The two developed an intimate friendship. Von Borcke became more celebrated and recognized *than any German officer of the Union army in the North.* The Confederate Congress passed a motion of special thanks. Twenty years after the war, von Borcke visited America and held a genuine triumphal procession through the South. Reading his book, one is often reminded of Baron Münchhausen, particularly when the author tells of his innumerable rescues from the greatest peril of death. But despite many exaggerations, the book is a worthy contribution to American war history. You feel yourself set into the midst of the noise of battle, and there is an impressive image of life and action in the rebel camp.

Von Borcke was so severely wounded in fighting at Middleburg that he hovered between life and death for months. He became incapable of further service, and in the winter of 1864–65 he undertook a mission of the Confederate government to England. Soon came the collapse of the rebellion, and von Borcke returned to Germany and dedicated himself to portraying his deeds, as well as those of his superior Stuart, who had fallen in May 1864 during Grant's campaign in the Wilderness. Von Borcke was known throughout the Confederate army and esteemed for his bravery and cleverness. His battle saber hangs in the capitol at Richmond.

BUCHHOLZ, E. von. A former Württemberg officer, chief of artillery Governor Wise's brigade of Virginia.

†BÜCHEL, August. Confederate brigadier general. Earlier an officer in Hessen-Darmstadt who entered the French Foreign Legion in 1833, then served under Maria Christina in Spain against the Carlists, was decorated for bravery and made a Spanish knight. Later he served under the Turks, came to Texas in 1845 and fought in the Mexican War. In 1861 he was lieutenant colonel of the 3rd Texas Regiment. He fought on the Rio Grande. At the end of 1861 he was colonel of the 1st Texas Cavalry Regiment, brigadier general in 1863. Büchel fell on 9 April 1864 in the Battle of Pleasant Hill, Louisiana, pierced by seven bullets.

Confederate German companies in CHARLESTON, SOUTH CAROLINA:

German Rifles, Captain J. Small; Palmetto Rifles, Captain A. Melchers;
German Fusiliers, 17th Infantry Regiment (the oldest German militia organization in the United States; originated in the Revolutionary War.)
First Artillery Regiment, Major Johann H. Wagener.
German Hussars, Captain Theodor Cordes, who fell, as did his successor, Captain Fremder.
Marion Rifles, Captain C. B. Sigwald.

EICHHOLZ, W. T. Officer in Major Wilkes' Texas Artillery. He was living in 1910 as a veteran of the press and publisher of the *Deutsche Rundschau* in Cuero, Texas.

ESCHELMANN, B. F. Captain of the 1st Battery of the Confederate Washington Artillery. He was wounded three times.

FRÖBEL, B. W. Major, artillery chief of Hood's division, Lee's army. He was a former Electoral Hessian officer.

GALVESTON, Texas. The largest harbor of the state, it stood completely under the command of the slave barons, and whoever had Unionist attitudes was risking his neck. The Germans residents there were mostly involved in the cotton business, and they distinguished themselves completely from their compatriots in the interior of Texas. A German battalion of 150 men was organized under Lieutenant Colonel Th. Oswald and Major Bruch. A battery also developed whose crews were German Turners from Houston, as well as the Galveston Davis Battery, which consisted mostly of Germans. Two German cavalry companies also were raised.

HENNINGSEN, Karl Friedrich. A Hanoverian, fought for 17 years with the Carlist army in Spain, then in Russia in the Caucasus Wars. He was a revolutionary in Hungary in 1849, then a leader in the filibuster war of Nicaragua in 1850. For the following years he was military advisor to Governor Wise of Virginia.

HOFFMAN. Colonel of a Confederate infantry regiment from Texas in which many pro-Union Germans had to serve.

†KABLER, Nicholas. Major in the 42nd Confederate Virginia Regiment. He was born in Kolberg, and he fell at Cedar Mountain.

KAMPMANN. Colonel of the Confederate army.

VON MASOW. Cavalry officer in Mosby's irregulars. He was severely wounded. He returned to Germany and later became a Prussian officer again. He fought in 1866 [Austro-Prussian War—SR] in the Army of the Main.

†MAUCK, Joseph. Captain in the 10th Virginia Regiment. He fell at Cedar Mountain.

MELCHERS, Franz. Editor of the Charleston *Deutsche Zeitung*, a Confederate officer. He went to war, as did his friend Wagener, "with a bleeding heart."

MEMMINGER, Christoph Georg. From Mergentheim in Württemberg. He immigrated to South Carolina as a child. Rich Americans adopted the parentless boy. Hence he was completely Americanized. There was nothing German left about him when Memminger became the Secretary of the Treasury of the Confederacy, hence a member of Jefferson Davis's cabinet. Körner is of the opinion that Memminger came through this baptism of fire with a clean name and an honorable reputation.

MINNIGERODE, Karl. Doctor of theology and rector of the (Anglican) St. Paul's Episcopal Church in Richmond. He was called the "father confessor of the secession" because Jefferson Davis, General Lee and all the heads of the rebellion belonged to that church. He had been imprisoned for years in Germany because of his participation in the 1830s Revolution. He came from Hesse. He was a splendidly gifted man and the premier pulpit orator in the entire South. He commanded the English language as did few natives. Although personally opposed to slavery, he remained true to the heads of the secession in their misfortune. He frequently visited Jefferson Davis during his imprisonment to give him communion. When Lee gave President Davis the news that Richmond had to be evacuated, Davis was at St. Paul's listening to a sermon of Minnegerode's. Davis rose at once when he received Lee's message and left the church. The other worshippers had the feeling, "This is the end!"

PEPLE, G. A. A Rhinelander, a major in the engineering corps.

†PHINIZA, Jakob. Captain, 8th Georgia Confederate Infantry, fell at Groveton in the attack on Koltes' brigade.

RAINE. Colonel of a Confederate Artillery Regiment which was in part recruited from the Germans of Richmond.

REICHARD, August. Formerly a Hanoverian officer, he was a New Orleans cotton exporter and consul of Prussia. He resigned this position and attempted at the start of the war to unite the German militia companies into a German regiment. It was, however, desired in higher circles that there be no larger German units in the Confederacy; Germans were distrusted due to events in Missouri, and for a while the authorities even hesitated to give them weapons.

Reichard managed to establish a German Battalion consisting of the following companies: Steuben Guards, Captain Kehrwald; Turner Guards, Captain Baehncke; Reichard Rifles, Captain Müller; Florance Guards, Captain Brummerstädt. This German Battalion was organized as the 20th Louisiana Volunteer Regiment by adding four Irish companies. Reichard became its colonel. He particularly distinguished himself in the battles of Shiloh, Murfreesboro, Chickamauga, Atlanta, and Nashville. The losses of his regiment at Shiloh were terrible. The Reichard Rifles shrank from 72 men to 33, and the other companies suffered to such a degree that the 20th Louisiana had to be amalgamated into the 13th Louisiana Regiment. After the war Reichard went to Egypt, taking over a cotton plantation; later he lived in Dresden.

SCHEIBERT, J. Major in the Prussian engineering corps, came to America in autumn, 1862, and accompanied the campaign with General Lee's headquarters. Major Scheibert originally intended only to participate in the war as an observer, but he entered the Confederate army as a captain. He became a comrade in arms of von Borcke, and he participated in the campaigns of Stuart, the cavalry commander. His principal work on the Civil War appeared in 1874 with Mittler & Sohn in Berlin. It is a textbook intended for German officers. The author tries to inform his readers of the military institutions in both camps and particularly to portray the experiences and lessons the Civil War presents.

On the battlefield of Chancellorsville, General Lee said to Major Scheibert, "Give me Prussian discipline and Prussian units for my troops, and you would see entirely different results."

SCHELE DE VER, Maximilian. From Pomerania, a jurist and diplomat, and a Prussian Home Guard officer. He was a professor at Virginia State University in Richmond and a colonel in a Confederate regiment. Toward the end of the war the Confederate government sent him to Germany to build sympathy for the secession. He achieved nothing, for Germany was the loyal and reliable friend of the Union.

SCHLEICHER, Gustav. From Darmstadt, he was a significant German congressman from Texas and a major in the Confederate army. His activity extended primarily to the laying out of fortifications. Schleicher was a decided Union man, but he had to fight for his state. The later President Garfield gave a memorial speech for him in Congress, highly important for the evaluation of German-Americans by Anglo-Americans with great minds.

SCHULTZ, Dr. Surgeon in the Confederate army.

SCHURICHT, Hermann. Confederate officer in Virginia, a German-American historian and a significant pedagogue. In the second volume of his book, *Virginien* ["Virginia"], much is presented on the mood of Germans in the South at the outbreak of the Civil War. Schuricht was pro-Union in his heart, and he followed the rebel flag under compulsion.

SCHWARZMANN, Gustav Adolf. From Stuttgart, a colonel in General Wise's Legion.

STRIEBLING, R. M. Battery chief in Longstreet's corps, a former Brunswick artillery officer.

The TURNERS OF GALVESTON entered Company F of the 2nd Texas Regiment as a group of forty men. Their leader, Captain Müller, fell at Corinth. The following German names are found among those of Texas artillery battery chiefs: Kreuzbauer, Krumbhaar, Heidemann, Welhausen, Reuss and Mechling.

VON ACHTEN DER LETZTE ["The Last of Eight"]. This is the title of an interesting text whose author describes himself as a "former Prussian one-year volunteer." He entered the Confederate Washington Artillery along with seven friends, all young German merchants in New Orleans. The Washington Artillery had a German company and was regarded as the elite artillery of the Confederacy. Only the author of the aforesaid work survived; the other seven all fell in battle.

WAGENER, Johann A. Colonel of the Confederate artillery in Charleston, South Carolina, a unit made up essentially of Germans. He became a brigadier general and later was mayor of Charleston. He was born in 1824 in Bremerhaven, a true German man of the people. He was active as a writer, including poetry. He opposed the separation of his state and was in his heart a Union man, but he could not avoid service. He was commanding in Charleston when this breeding-place of the secession was taken by the German General Schimmelpfennig. One German had to take down the rebel flag and another German raised the Stars and Stripes.

Wagener's best deed was the defense of Fort Walker, which Wagener himself had built in November 1861. Two of his sons, the youngest only 15, fought here under their father. Half the garrison was killed or wounded.

†WALDECK. Colonel of a Texas cavalry regiment. Waldeck led the vanguard of Confederate troops that pressed Sigel so hard on his precipitous retreat from Bentonville in March 1862. He was a son of Count Waldeck, one of the leaders of the German nobles' colony of Texas. Waldeck fell in the Red River campaign of 1864.

The following German captains served in Waul's Texas Legion: Otto Nathusius, Voigt and Wickeland.

†WILDE, Franz. Captain, 19th Georgia Regiment, fell at Chantilly.

WILKE, Hermann. A chief of Confederate artillery.

WIRZ, Dr. Henry. A German Swiss from *Zürich*, the warden of the camp of Union prisoners in Andersonville, Georgia.

Wirz had lived in New Orleans since 1849 as a physician and enjoyed a good reputation. He possessed a good education, and he wrote and spoke several languages fluently. In November, 1865, Wirz was declared guilty of murder by a Union court martial and hanged. In carrying out the police power bestowed on him by the Confederate government, he had supposedly shot three Union prisoners in his custody.

Wirz stalks through American military history, according to the Union point of view, as the greatest monster in human form dishonoring the face of the earth since the days of Judas Iscariot. In all other matters of dispute, former mortal enemies have united on a reasonable concept; but when the name of Wirz is thrown in, the old hatred returns. Most Union veterans who are still alive are so possessed in this matter that any attempt to consider the Wirz case calmly is pointless. Yet it could be demanded that they should cease spitting on the grave of the sole rebel who paid in a shameful death on the gallows for the guilt loaded on him largely through the fault of others.

More than 13,000 Union soldiers died in July and August, 1864 in the prison camp of Andersonville. This horror mocks every description. This is essentially due to an overfilling of the camp. More than 30,000 men were whipped together in an area suited for no more than 12,000 men. The unfortunate men were located in an open field, subject to the rays of an August sun. The Confederate government sent a special deputy, Colonel Chandler, to investigate these conditions, and Chandler's official report confirms all accusations against the administration. But the overfilling was not stopped until three weeks later. Twenty thousand prisoners were then sent to other prisons. At the end of September the number interned amounted to only 8228 men, compared to the high point of 31,693 at the end of August.

The one most guilty is the commandant, Wilder,[21] under whom Wirz worked as overseer. But Wilder died before the end of the war, and the total load of guilt was placed on Wirz. Because only a small number of guards was present, mostly militiamen from Georgia, boys of 15 and 16, it was very hard for Wirz to impose his authority. His defenders say that Wirz only reached for his pistol in self-defense.[22]

Most of the prisoners who died perished due to inadequate food. The Northerners were used to eating meat. Now they were being fed poorly baked cornbread, rice, a little meat and some bacon—food that would have been enough for a Southerner. They had to drink water from a brook infected with the excrement of many thousands. If one says that the Confederacy could not provide better food (which does not jibe with the wealth of this area of Georgia, which Sherman crossed), it should still be said that the Confederacy did not provide what it easily could have, with a good will. Wood was available in plenty, but no barracks were built; the finest drinking water ran outside the fencing, but it was not brought in. The guilt for this is borne by commandant Wilder.

The Union would certainly have been justified in punishing the chief leaders of the rebellion for treason. It did not wish to do so. The angel of reconciliation moved through the reviving land. Even Jefferson Davis was finally released. It was a proud and fine deed, and the federal government soon referred Mexico to its own example in an attempt to save Maximilian, who had been condemned in Mexico.

It is thus surprising that Wirz was distinguished from the other wardens of the Confederacy by being brought to trial. The wardens who exercised their offices in Libby, Belle Isle, Danville, Salisbury, Millen, Charleston, and so on, were left to go free, although many of them were accused of worse direct and personal deeds of atrocity than were attributed to Wirz in his indictment. The prisoners on Belle Isle near Richmond suffered perhaps worse in 1864 and 1865 than did the victims in Andersonville, and we need only recall the accusations of Frey and Markbreit for conditions in Libby (see the Frey biography).

Wirz was the sole foreigner among the wardens. Is it only an accident that he was the only one punished? We should hope. If it is, there should be no special reference to Wirz's being foreign. But this is often done in the contemporary press, and even in one of the best works on the United States, Goldwin Smith's *The United States,* it is said on page 284 that

Wirz was a "foreign mercenary" (a favorite term of abuse among nativists that plays on the business of trading guiltless, hired Hessians). Former Confederates celebrate Wirz as a martyr for their cause. In 1909 a lovely monument was raised in Georgia by those honoring him. The money for this was gathered by ladies. Yet this completely unnecessary honor to a man who was certainly no angel may be seen as a demonstration against the excessive slanders of Wirz.[23]

ZINKEN, Leo von. Son of a Prussian general and earlier a Prussian officer himself, went into the war as a major of the German Battalion of the 20th Louisiana Regiment. He was one of the boldest Confederate officers. At Shiloh three horses were shot out from under him. Two horses were also killed at Chickamauga. His men used to say of him, "No bullet has been cast for him."

Appendix II
Supplemental Articles

1. War Losses

Losses of the North. The adjutant general's office estimated the number of fallen, those dying as a result of wounds and illness at 303,504 Union fighters. Pfisterer enumerates 286,484 such victims of war, including 101,884 fallen and mortally wounded. Fox, a later statistician, enumerates 110,070 fallen and 199,720 Union soldiers dead of illness, not counting those dying in Confederate prisons (about 30,000 men), so that about 340,000 victims died as a result of the war, according to Fox.

A precise figure for the war costs of the North also cannot be set. The expenditures of the states, cities and counties cannot be established. There is also no agreement on income from war taxes. Rhodes estimates the costs of war for the Union at $3.225 billion. The continuing and (astonishingly enough) continually climbing pension burden must be added to that.[1] Through the year 1909 $3.686 billion had already been paid to pensioners of the Civil War. Even if the increase in this expenditure proposed at the time this book was completed is never passed, pensions will surely devour $5 billion before the last widow of a veteran can be stricken from the list. The last so-called Revolutionary widow, with a right to a pension for the war against England vanished about the end of the nineteenth century. Hence the cost of the war and the pension burden will surely end up about $9 billion.

Losses of the South. The Confederacy destroyed all its papers at the time of its collapse. Usable material to estimate losses survives only in the individual states, particularly in North Carolina. According to that, at least 200,000 Confederates lost their lives in the war. This estimate agrees with the data of the *Confederate Handbook.* This source estimates the actual war costs of the Confederacy at $1.5 billion in gold. The question of whether one should include the emancipation of the Negroes, whose monetary value must have been about $2.5 billion, as part of the war losses of the individual states, has been much disputed. Slaveowners had put the larger part of their wealth into blacks, but these values were wiped out by the Emancipation Proclamation. The damage caused by the wasting of the South cannot be estimated. The needy veterans of the Confederate army are provided for by the individual states of the former Confederacy. These payments have been quite modest, but in the course of the years they must have amounted to several hundreds of millions of dollars.

The Civil War demanded at least 500,000 men and a monetary expenditure of about $11 billion for the two parties, even if the emancipation of the slaves without compensation is not placed in the losses column.

2. Impoverished Americans in the Southern Appalachians

Most of the residents of the southern Appalachians (or Alleghenies) were very little culturally advanced beyond the Negroes at the outbreak of the war. Seventy-five percent of them were then illiterate. This people is almost purely Anglo-Saxon and Scottish, with some German descendents. (Several copies of Arndt's *Wahres Christentum* ["True Christianity"] were found in cabins.) At the start of the eighteenth century the rich wildlife attracted many hunters into this mountain wilderness. They made themselves at home in the land and remained there, shut off from the rest of the world. Their descendents quickly descended to the level of barbarism.

The region composed of the states of Virginia, South and North Carolina, Alabama, Tennessee, and Kentucky is larger than the German Reich. The peaks of the Black Mountains and the Great Smoky Mountains rise up to 7000 feet. They are covered with wonderful forests. The whole must be the largest forest complex on earth, except for the tropics. This enormous mountain forest is called "moonshine country" by the people, after the many illegitimate liquor distilleries run there. The first explorer of this region was the German Lederer, who crossed the Appalachians at the end of the seventeenth century and traveled into the southern plains. He has left a good description of his journey in Latin.[2]

It must be marveled at that these moonshiners have not completely deteriorated, despite an excessive consumption of alcohol and tobacco by both sexes. The families are very large, those of twelve to fifteen head being common. The men are shy about working, and the principal burden is placed on the women. The most backward part of the population is in the Kentucky Appalachians, living in the Cumberland Mountains, not all that far from the metropolis of Cincinnati. Until a few years ago, blood feuding prevailed. Families fell into deadly hostility over petty causes. The feud of the Howard family against the Turners in Harlan County, Kentucky, began in 1882 and lasted eight years; twenty-two family members were shot dead. The cause of this was a dispute at a card game between a Howard and a Turner.[3]

In Clay County, Kentucky, the Baker-Howard feud flourished. The widow of a fallen Baker wrote to a captain of militia who wanted the woman to move out of the area, "Captain Brown, I have twelve sons. It shall be the main purpose of my life to raise them to avenge their father. I shall show them every day the wallet soaked with their father's blood and shall tell them who murdered their father!" Thirty-eight members of the Hargiss and Cockrill families fell in Breathitt County, Kentucky, during nine months in 1902. One of the last victims was the lawyer Marcum in Jackson, in Breathitt County. He had gone every day to the courthouse with his little daughter on his arm. This protected him from his enemies' bullets. When he stepped out for the first time alone, a shot rang from a neighboring house, and Marcum fell dead. Two members of the Cockrill gang were sent to the penitentiary for life for this deed.

Twenty-three Tollivers and Martins fell in the feud that broke out in Rowan County in 1884; thirty in the French-Eversole feud in Perry County; the war among the Turners in Bell County—they were all cousins—demanded twenty-six victims. No trials were needed, for all the fighters had fallen. This feud only took place in 1902. In more recent times these feuds have ceased, certainly because of the railroads that now touch the mountains. The new transportation has proven very good at promoting culture. Police protection has also become better, particularly since the murder of Governor Göbel of Kentucky (whose murderer was a moonshiner). Further, many new schools have been raised and new opportunities to work been given to the residents.

At the time of the Civil War, many of these decadent Americans were pro-Union. In the autumn of 1863, in Schurz's division, there was a regiment made up of moonshiners from Alabama, and which was praised by Schurz. (Cf. Schurz's memoirs, which also have much to tell about the social conditions of these people.) One would like to think that the coarsening shown by the many blood feuds came from the war. But feuds had existed there earlier, and the causes established in trials were always minor disputes. It is possible that the inclination to these feuds was brought from Scotland and the clan system prevailing there.

3. Pastorius and the True Beginning of German Immigration

The first protest against slavery, issued by Franz Daniel Pastorius and three of his friends, was unfortunately not addressed to the proper audience. Pastorius was a member of the Pennsylvania legislature around 1688. He should have protested against slavery *there*. But instead he spread his text among the representatives of his faith. The protest was presented only to the monthly, quarterly and annual assemblies, the three instances, of Quaker congregations. The pious brethren allowed the text by their German fellow believer to disappear into their papers, and it was not discovered until almost 200 years later. Pastorius let it go, and although he would live another thirty years, his prolific hand would leave only one little verse relating to slavery. It says, "Möchtest du ein Slav' wohl sein?" ["Do you really wish to be a slave?"] Pastorius' protest lacked precisely the element that would alone have made it worthy, which was *publicity*. The agitation of Quakers against slavery did not begin until eighty years after the protest of Pastorius.[4]

Other than perhaps Schurz, there is no German in America about whom so much is said as Pastorius. The only poetic accomplishment of lasting worth dealing with the enormously important subject of German immigration to America, Whittier's idyllic "The Pennsylvania Pilgrim," deals with Pastorius and his work at Germantown. It would be desirable if Germans showed a bit more interest in those of their compatriots who were contemporaries and forerunners of Pastorius. There are splendid figures among these first Germans in America, men who well deserve to be placed *above* Pastorius.

There are the two Weisers, father and son; the elder Saur, and after that Father Mühlenberg. Then there were the forerunners of Pastorius in New Amsterdam: Minnewit, born in Wesel, the first real governor of New Netherlands in 1626, Augustin Hermann, Stuyvesant's diplomat and a colonizer and pioneer on a grand scale; and Jakob Loyseler (Leisler) from Frankfurt am Main, who fell victim to a judicial murder in 1691, an entirely rare episode noted as such and regretted by the English Parliament. Loyseler may be seen as the first American democrat, a forerunner of the heroes of the American Revolution, a man who first spoke the idea of the cohesion of the American colonies. There should also be thoughts on Johannes Lederer, who explored the Appalachians in 1668; the German Jesuit Father Franz Eusebius Kühn, who appears in southern California in 1670; and many other capable and effective compatriots who are almost entirely forgotten by our times. Many of them deserve more respect than the gentle and reticent closet scholar Pastorius.

Pastorius composed and philosophized in seven languages in Germantown, but he actually never came out from behind his four walls and showed what we seek in men of those days: action and expanded effectiveness. The German society presidents in America, who play the same harp at many (all too many) German Days, and speak in such an edifying manner about Pastorius and his Krefeld linen weavers, should do something with the other German pioneers. Their listeners would certainly thank them for it.

Now the loveliest monument German America has ever produced is to be erected to Pastorius. That is certainly proper, for the monument is less to glorify the efforts of a single pioneer than to mark the cultural deeds of the German element on American soil. Even the choice of place for that monument was correct, for it is Pennsylvania that the German people developed most strongly in their first period of settlement. But it is entirely *false* if this monument is intended to mark the *beginning* of German immigration to North America. The coming of Pastorius in 1682 is only an episode in the history of German immigration, certainly not its beginning. Pastorius and his people did not initiate the great procession of Germans to Pennsylvania.

We know from Rupp, the first historian of Pennsylvania, that until 1720 Germantown had only 200 German residents, and that the masses of Germans came to Pennsylvania after then. Thirty years *before* Pastorius, there were probably more Germans living around Germantown than lived in Germantown at the start of the eighteenth century. They were the Pomeranians, who came with the Swedes in 1650 to the Delaware. The German immigration did not begin in 1682, but in 1620, with the advent of all European culture on the territory of the United States.[5]

Only most recently has light begun to be shed on the history of the earliest German immigration. On this, see particularly the cultivated essay by Otto Löhr in the Sunday supplement of the *New Yorker Zeitung;* Kapp's *Geschichte der Deutschen von New York* ["History of the Germans of New York"] has almost nothing about it. *The Documentary History of the State of New York,* as well as Broadhead's works, contain a great deal about it. I have found thorough accounts that establish with certainty that at least every third Hollander to go to New Amsterdam between 1611 and 1664 was a German. This can be concluded, as well, from the large number of Germans who held high office in the earliest period under the Dutch. Löhr's researches, which appear to rest on Dutch sources, permit us to suppose that the number of Germans among the Dutch was even greater. Perhaps more than half the Dutchmen in New Netherlands were Germans, besides the fact that Hollanders and Low Germans were then one people, and the political distinction between them was only then being drawn. If a son born in America asks his German father when the first Germans came to America, the answer should be, "The Germans came into the country at the time of the Mayflower Pilgrims." The boy will understand it, and it is historically correct. But it is false to set 1682, the landing of Pastorius, as the beginning of German immigration. [Editors Note: Since the publication of this work, it has been established that the first German settlers in America were at Jamestown, Virginia, where they arrived in October 1608. See: Don Heinrich Tolzmann, ed. *The First Germans in America*. (Bowie, MD: Heritage Books, Inc. 1992).][6]

4. The Massacre of Gnadenhütten

The most dreadful deed of the frontiersmen was the murder of ninety-six Christian Indians—men, women and children—at Gnadenhütten in eastern Ohio in 1782. These were Indians converted by German Herrnhuter. Their three villages lay on the path used by the red allies of the English, between the Great Lakes and the Ohio. These settlements were often used by wild Indians, who compelled hospitality from the Christian Indians. The white frontiersmen saw this as support for the wild Indians, and a punitive expedition was sent against Gnadenhütten. Under the leadership of a monster named Williamson, the villages were surrounded. The leader declared to the Christian Indians that they would all be beaten to death the next morning; during the night the victims could prepare themselves for death. The dreadful plan was carried out. Only two boys escaped, and the other ninety-six were slaughtered in the most despicable manner. (For a more extensive account, see descriptions of the missionary Heckewälder.)[7]

5. The New South Without Slavery

The following data come from official sources: the number of illiterates has dropped from 29.7 percent to 23.4 percent from 1890 to 1900. The newspapers of this region have increased in number by roughly 50 percent in the same period. In a period of twenty years, the number of farms in Virginia has doubled. There were 44,078 miles of railways in the South in 1890, and it was 67,129 miles in 1905. The capital invested in industry has doubled in ten years. Bank deposits have risen by a factor of three. From 1900 to 1905, the annual wages of industrial workers in the South have risen from $218 million to $313 million. The value of industrial goods has risen from $1.229 billion to $1.766 billion. The iron production of Alabama, Virginia and Tennessee has doubled in three years.

The best proof of the self-delusion of the secessionists is offered by the rise in cotton production without slaves. With free labor, 11,400,000 bales were harvested in 1906, 13,575,000 bales in 1907, and 11,582,000 bales in 1908, each of 500 pounds. In one of the best cotton years with slave labor, 1859, the South achieved only 4,800,000 bales at 400 pounds each. If the rise in the weight of a bale is taken into account, the South produces more than three times with free labor what it did with slaves. In the slavery period, cotton seeds were thrown away. Now this by-product produces oil and other materials with an annual value of $100 million to $125 million. According to the census of 1860, the South then processed only 178,000 bales in spinneries. In 1908 Southern mills worked 2,235,000 bales of cotton, and Northern mills 2,017,000 at 500 pounds each. Both of the regions together in 1908 spun more cotton than was produced even in a good year, 1859, with slave labor. More than a third of the present mass harvest is transformed into cotton textiles, whose annual worth is set at $1.5 billion. The value of the current mass harvest with by-products is estimated at about $1 billion per year, more than $700 million in excess of the annual production under slavery!

6. The Old Germans in the Shenandoah Valley

When the German soldiers under Schurz and von Steinwehr camped on Cemetery Hill of Gettysburg, they were resting on the graves of their compatriots, some of whom had already slumbered in the earth for almost 150 years. As with all of southern Pennsylvania, Gettysburg (formerly called Götzburg) is a settlement of Germans, whose mass emigration to America began in 1709. Seminary Ridge in Gettysburg, on which Lee's army stood, takes its name from a Lutheran seminary in which German pastors are still educated.

The Pennsylvania Germans began at a very early point to migrate to the south.[8] Already around 1725 we find them very numerous in western Maryland. At the time of the revolution against England, this area was as German as Pennsylvania. Frederick, Maryland, was once an entirely German town. The same applies to Sharpsburg on the Antietam, where the first invasion of the Confederates into the North was beaten back.

A primeval Indian path ran from Götzburg to the Potomac, right through western Maryland. This path became the migration road of the German Pennsylvanians on their way to the south. Robert Harper, who gave Harpers Ferry its name, was a German Pennsylvanian. At a very early date, Germans also advanced across the Potomac to the south, and they were the first settlers in the splendid Shenandoah Valley. Justus Heid was the first pioneer beyond the Potomac. Around 1732 he went with his sons, four sons-in-law, and some friends, altogether sixteen families, to what is today Winchester, where the first large settlement was established. The land was then without a ruler. Heid's treaty with the Indians was later disputed, and his legal title to the land he took into possession was later opposed. Washington had long been president when the tedious "Joist Hide" land case was finally decided.

Many other Pennsylvania German migrants followed in Heid's tracks, and there arose in rapid succession the flourishing German communities of Harpers Ferry, Martinsburg, Schäfterstadt (today Shepherdstown), Stephansstadt (Stephansburg), Winchester (once called Friedrichsstadt), Kernstown, Stauferstadt (now Strasburg), and Müllerstadt (now Woodstock). Keiseltown in Rockingham County was originally named Kieselstadt.

Neumarkt, now New Market, where Sigel suffered his defeat in May 1864 is also an old German settlement, and when the German Division received its baptism of fire on Pentecost Sunday, 1862, at Cross Keys, the wounded found asylum in two German churches located on the battlefield.

The entire Shenandoah Valley was already settled by Germans in the eighteenth century. Kercheval, the earliest historian of Virginia, reports that the Lutheran Synod of Virginia had nearly a hundred churches at the end of the eighteenth century. (In America, Lutheran and German are the same thing.) One must consider that these churches were mostly little log cabins, and that Maryland Lutherans were part of the Virginia Synod. But the German Reformed Church, the Herrnhuter, and the various baptist sects, particularly the Dunkards, had many congregations in that area.[9]

7. The Sioux before New Ulm

The great rebellion of the Sioux or Dakota Indians that took place in August 1862 is to be regarded as associated with the Civil War. These warlike and gruesome redskins exploited the time in which all men capable of fighting in the German settlement of New Ulm, Minnesota, and environs were in the field fighting for the Union, and they fell on undefended settlers. On 24 August the Indians besieged the town of New Ulm. In a large cellar where many of the women and children took refuge, there was a large powder keg to be exploded if the Indians conquered the town. Forty men fell defending the town. Two hundred seventy houses were burned down, and only thirty remained standing.[10]

Colonel Jakob Nix, a former South German officer, led the defense. Reinforcements arrived in the moment of greatest need, and the Redskins departed before they could take the remnant of the town which had been spared from the fire.[11] Hence most residents were saved. On the whole, 700 men, women and children were said to have been killed. Most of the victims were Germans and Swedes. Many were dreadfully tortured to death. Later, thirty-eight leading Indian conspirators were hanged. The Sioux were then transplanted to the Black Hills in Dakota. There, as well, there were bloody fights with them. In the summer of 1876, General Custer and 250 men were surrounded by the Sioux, under Sitting Bull, and the entire force massacred. Not a single soldier escaped. General Custer had been one of the most outstanding cavalry commanders of the Union army. He was of German descent. His father still wrote the name as Kuster.[12]

The settlement of New Ulm was established by German Turners from Cincinnati and Chicago and numbered 1200 members. Now New Ulm is one of the most beautiful and flourishing towns of Minnesota, with an almost purely German population. Concerning the attack of the Sioux, see A. Berghold's account in the eighth and ninth years of the Cincinnati *Pionier,* as well as the *Chronik von Neu-Ulm,* published by the New Ulm *Post.*[13]

It should be remarked in passing that many Germans appeared as leaders in the early struggles against the Indians, particularly in Kentucky and Virginia. More on this may be found in Theodore Roosevelt's noted work, *The Winning of the West,* which unfortunately reaches only to the end of the eighteenth century. In volume 2, page 298, there is mention of the famous German scalp hunter Ludwig Wetzel. The Germans Kaspar Mansker

(Mansco) and Steiner also made feared names for themselves as Indian slayers. Many Stoners descend from Steiner, and those Stoners played a role in the Civil War. Roosevelt, in volume 4, p. 25, quotes a remark of the secretary of state of Kentucky around 1790, as follows:

> For every twelve families of any one immigrant nation, nine German, seven Scottish and four Irish prosper. German women work as hard as their husbands, even in the fields, and both sexes of this nation are equally thrifty. Through this these hard-working settlers rapidly prosper, but they only win influence and leadership in the settlements after they have conformed themselves in language and customs to their American neighbors. The Scots are also thrifty and hard working, and soon one can not distinguish them from natives. The brave, strong Irish are too fond of whisky and trials, and they reach too quickly for their rifle, which means their ruin.

8. The 9th Ohio Regiment at Chickamauga

The 9th went into battle with about 500 men, and only half of them came back. Eleven officers and 237 men lay dead or wounded on the field. Under Kämmerling's leadership, the regiment stormed a battery that the regular artillery had lost, and they took the guns back. (Burnham's battery, then commanded by Lieutenant Günter.) This recovery of these cannons is regarded as one of the finest deeds of the entire war. The monument that was raised to Burnham's battery is actually a monument to the 9th. As the regiment was returning from this attack, the other regiments of the brigade were in the greatest peril of being dispersed by the enemy. Once more the 9th advanced and turned the defeat of their brigade into a victory. This heroic regiment achieved other brave deeds on Horseshoe Hill, where the monument to the 9th stands. The 9th Ohio Regiment had the highest rate of loss of all of the regiments fighting at Chickamauga, but also the most splendid record.[14]

9. Sigel, Schurz, Stahel and Lincoln

After Sigel decided to resign, he wrote a letter to the president on 23 January 1863 in which he recommended Schurz as his successor in command of the XI Corps, and also recommended that a corps of reserve cavalry be created, and that the command of this corps be given to General Stahel.[15] On the reverse of Sigel's letter, Lincoln wrote the following answer on 26 January:

> I believe that an increase in cavalry would be expedient, but I have not promised that I would raise a corps at once in order to conform with the desires of a single officer if it did not appear proper to the government. Concerning General Schurz and General Stahel, I have attempted to be just to all of them, but it always seems to get worse. If General Sigel would say clearly and without condition what he wants concerning the command of the forces placed under him,

I would attempt to do it; but if he has plans which depend on me raising new forces, then he is asking something which is beyond my strength.

26 January 1863   A. Lincoln

Lincoln appears to have understood Sigel's request concerning General Stahel as meaning that a special corps of cavalry be created essentially to make a proper area of activity for Stahel. Lincoln's perception is not all that unjustified, particularly when one considers that the Army of the Potomac was then being reorganized under Hooker, and that Lincoln was being stormed from all sides by such requests. What Sigel saw as the fulfillment of a duty to his two comrades appears to Lincoln to be just another one of hundreds of similar attempts addressed to him. Further, one can hardly overlook a sense of irritation on the part of the president.

Despite that, Lincoln wrote a second letter to Sigel on 5 February, which read as follows:

To Major General Sigel
General Schurz is of the opinion that I was a little cross with you in my last letter. If that appeared so, then I ask your forgiveness. If I do get up a bit of temper, I do not have enough time to be so for long. I would now like to make no new dispositions on the matter under discussion, but it would correspond to my wishes if General Hooker can and desires to give General Stahel a large cavalry command. You may show General Hooker this letter. Most humbly yours,
                                                                                      A. Lincoln

This second Lincoln letter shows that the president was not hostile to Sigel's recommendations. General Stahel actually did receive a large cavalry command. It could hardly be called a corps, although there were smaller cavalry corps. But in this way Stahel received independence, and he could apply his long experience in that branch and create the best cavalry organizations in the Army of the Potomac. Schurz came out of this with empty hands. To judge from their exchange, Sigel's and Lincoln's differences concerned only Stahel, and it could be assumed that Lincoln would have concurred with Sigel's desires concerning Schurz's promotion. But Lincoln had left Hooker a free hand in choosing a new corps commander, and Hooker ignored Schurz's claim. Schurz was the senior divisional commander in the XI Corps. Hooker named a West Pointer, General O. O. Howard, as leader of the corps. Incidentally, Schurz probably would have received the command if he had energetically presented his demand with Lincoln.

10. The Treatment of War Prisoners

Lack of clarity still prevails on both sides concerning the treatment of war prisoners. The Confederacy left virtually no reliable statistics. Union statistics speak of 196,713 Union prisoners in Confederate hands and 227,570 Confederate prisoners in Union prisons. Mortality is supposed to have been 15.3 percent (30,212 dead) among Northern prisoners in the South and 11.7 percent (26,774 dead) among Confederate inmates of Northern prisons. According to other reports which cannot be checked, more than

40,000 Union prisoners died in the South (assertion of the *National Tribune*, an organ of Union veterans).

The statistics above on deaths in both camps are almost the only effort at a non-partisan evaluation of the treatment of prisoners. If only 15.3 percent of the Union prisoners died in Confederate prisons, while 11.7 percent of the Confederate prisoners died as guests of the North, then the treatment Union prisoners received could not have been so much harsher and more gruesome as one would conclude from the accusations against Confederate wardens. This is because a part of the difference in mortality in the two camps would have been equalized by the far better resources the North had for housing Southern prisoners.

In the North these guests could usually be housed in barracks, but in the South most of the prisoners camped on open ground. The North had food in superfluity, and there was never any lack of medicine, while the South was always badly supplied with the latter. Further, the hatred of the Northerners against the enemy was never so strong as that of the Confederates against the Northerners. It was only the Southerners who saw the good spirit which donated support, even for the country's enemy.

Even the climate of the North was more propitious. It is always easier to protect against the cold than against the blazing sun of the South. Further, Northern prisoners on average spent longer times in prison than their opponents, while the mass of Southern prisoners only arrrived toward the end of the war. At that time war-weariness among the Confederates was strong, and thousands let themselves be caught during the last weeks. This explains why the number of Confederate prisoners in the statistics above is so large, although the Southern army at the end of the war was barely a third the size of the Northern host.

The truth on the treatment of the prisoners in both camps will never be established, but there is hope that most reports are strongly exaggerated. This must be hoped, for it would be dreadful if only half of what is said were true.

During the first war years, prisoners were regularly exchanged. That ceased when the North formed so many Negro regiments. The black troops were never recognized by the Confederates as regular soldiers of the North. The Southerners asserted that uniformed Negroes were escaped slaves and thus treated them as the personal property of those to whom they had earlier belonged. Whole masses of captured Negro soldiers were massacred by the Confederates (e.g., Fort Pillow), but most were led back into slavery. The Union could not tolerate a differential treatment of their White and Black soldiers by the enemy, and since the South did not want to exchange captured Negroes, exchanges also ceased for White soldiers. During the last part of the war, prisoners often remained for long periods with the enemy. Incidentally, from the very start of the war the South used tens of thousands of Negroes for war purposes, particularly digging trenches. For this reason alone the North had a right to form Negro regiments, and 185,000 Negroes fought for the Union.

Toward the end of the war the Confederates wanted to revive exchanges, but then reason of state came into operation in the North, saying, "Why should we strengthen a rebellion which is in the process of collapsing by delivering to them a hundred thousand or more prisoners of war who would go into service at once and fight against us? No, peace can only be secured by the complete defeat of the enemy. Our unfortunate brethren going to their ruin in Southern prisons are dying for their country, too. Even more of them would die on the battlefield if we were to exchange them now."

Selected Reference Works and Readings

1. Bibliographies

Eicher, David J. *The Civil War in Books: An Analytical Bibliography.* (Urbana: University of Illinois Press, 1997).

Krewson, Margrit B. *Immigrants from the German-speaking Countries of Europe: A Selective Bibliography of Reference Works.* (Washington, D.C.: Library of Congress, 1991).

McPherson, James M. *The American Civil War: A Handbook of Literature and Research.* (Westport, Conn.: Greenwood Press, 1996).

Nevins, Allan. *Civil War Books: A Critical Bibliography.* (Baton Rouge: Louisiana State University Press, 1967–69).

Tolzmann, Don Heinrich. *Catalog of the German-Americana Collection,* University of Cincinnati. (Muenchen: K.G. Saur, 1990).

Tolzmann, Don Heinrich. *German-Americana: A Bibliography.* (Metuchen, NJ: Scarecrow Press, 1975).

2. General History

Adams, Willi Paul. *The German-Americans: An Ethnic Experience.* Translated and Adapted by LaVern J. Rippley and Eberhard Reichmann. (Indianapolis: Max Kade German-American Center, Indiana University-Purdue University at Indianapolis, 1993).

Faust, Albert B. *The German Element in the United States* (New York: The Steuben Society of America, 1927).

Luebke, Frederick. *Germans in the New World: Essays in the History of Immigration.* (Urbana: University of Illinois Press, 1990).

Moltmann, Guenter, ed. *Germans to America: 300 Years of Immigration, 1683–1983.* (Stuttgart: Institute for Cultural Relations, 1983).

Rippley, LaVern J. *The German-Americans.* (Lanham, MD: University Press of America, 1984).

Tolzmann, Don Heinrich, ed., *German Achievements in America: Rudolf Cronau's Survey History.* (Bowie, MD: Heritage Books, Inc., 1995).

Trommler, Frank and Joseph McVeigh, eds., *America and the Germans: An Assessment of a Three-Hundred-Year History.* (Philadelphia: University of Pennsylvania Press, 1985).

3. The Forty-Eighters

Brancaforte, Charlotte L., ed., *The German Forty-Eighters in the United States.* (New York: Peter Lang, 1989).

Mueller, Jacob. *Erinnerungen eines Achtundvierzigers. Skizzen aus der Sturm- und Drang Periode der Fuenfziger Jahre.* (Cleveland: Rud. Schmidt Printing Co., 1896). This was translated by Steven Rowan for the Western Reserve Historical Society under a grant from Werner D. Mueller and published as: *Jacob Mueller, Memoirs of A Forty-Eighter.* Sketches from the German-American Period of Storm and Stress of the 1850s. (Cleveland: Western Reserve Historical Society, 1996).

Mueller, Werner D. and Duncan Gardiner, *To Cleveland and Away: Of Muellers, Reids, and Others.* (Novelty, OH: Privately Printed, 1993).

Tolzmann, Don Heinrich. *The German-American Forty-Eighters, 1848–1998.* (Indianapolis: Max Kade German-American Center, Indiana University-Purdue University at Indianapolis, 1998).

Wittke, Carl. *Refugees of Revolution: The German Forty-Eighters in America.* (Philadelphia: University of Pennsylvania Press, 1952).

4. The German-American Press

Arndt, Karl J.R. and May E. Olson, *The German Language Press of the Americas.* 3 vols., (Muenchen: K.G. Saur, 1973–80).

Cazden, Robert E. *A Social History of the German Book Trade in America to the Civil War.* (Columbia, S.C.: Camden House, 1984).

Geitz, Henry, ed., *The German-American Press.* (Madison: Max Kade Institute for German-American Studies at the University of Wisconsin, 1992).

Rowan, Steven, ed. and translator, *Germans for a Free Missouri.* (Columbia, MO: University of Missouri Press, 1983).

Tolzmann, Don Heinrich, ed., *German-American Literature.* (Metuchen, NJ: Scarecrow Press, 1977).

Wittke, Carl. *The German-Language Press in America.* (Lexington: University of Kentucky Press, 1957).

5. Special Studies on the Civil War Period

Buell, Clarence C. and Johnson, Robert U., *Battles and Leaders of the Civil War.* (Carlisle, PA: John Kallmann, Publishers, 1991 Reprint of the *Century Edition of 1887–88).*

Phisterer, Frederick, *Statistical Record of the Armies of the United States.* (Carlisle, PA: John Kallmann, Publishers, 1996 *Reprint of the 1883 Edition).*

Tolzmann, Don Heinrich, ed., *Abraham Lincoln's Ancestry: German or English? M.D. Learned's Investigatory History, With an Appendix on Daniel Boone.* (Bowie, MD: Heritage Books, Inc., 1992).

Tolzmann, Don Heinrich, ed., *The German-American Soldier in the Wars of the United States:* J.G. Rosengarten's History. (Bowie, MD: Heritage Books, Inc., 1996).

Table of Maps

Notes

Chapter One, pp. 5–42

{1} [Despite what he says here, the author does supply the biographies of several German officers under Confederate service at the end of his biographical section.–Ed.]

{2} On war losses, see pp. 337–8.

{3} The designation "baron" for a slaveholder already appears at the start of the nineteenth century.

{4} See pp. 23–4 concerning nullification.

{5} Through 1854, German immigrants also usually voted Democratic, because the Democratic Party sought to restrict the civil rights of immigrants less than did the Whigs and Know-Nothings.

{6} See pp. 17–29, "Historical Development of the Slavery Conflict," where political parties are discussed.

{7} Colonel Mosby, the last surviving leader of the secession, declared in *Leslie's Weekly*, 6 April 1911, that Breckinridge was only made a candidate in order to elect Lincoln by splitting the Democratic Party.

{8} The *official* declaration of withdrawal would only follow weeks later.

{9} To be sure, the constitution of the Southern Confederacy did set these demands aside and renew the ban on slave importation that had originated with the Union, out of consideration of the opinion of England.

{10} [Hermann Eduard von Holst (1841–1904) published extensively on the history of the American political thought and institutions, and his *The Constitutional and Political History of the United States,* translated by John J. Lalor, was published in Chicago 1876–92 in 8 vols.–Ed.]

{11} The Union then consisted of thirty-three states. The eleven cotton states rebelled. The four northern slave states declared themselves neutral, although the majority of their citizens sympathized with secession. Thus eleven states opposed eighteen, if one excludes the four border states. But if one counts the groups of states according to their membership in the slavery group, then the relationship was fifteen states against eighteen.

{12} For one, Jefferson Davis, president of the Confederacy, never believed in a peaceful division. At least that is what he said in his memoirs. But the masses of his region were of an entirely different opinion.

{13} See the chapter on secession.

{14} See Appendix II, pp. 338–9.

{15} The two great cities of Baltimore, Maryland, and St. Louis, Missouri, lay in slave territory, but they had a thoroughly Northern development. Washington, also a Southern city, was exceptional in being a city of officials.

{16} See Appendix II, pp. 339–41.

{17} Although the expression "slave" or "slavery" does not appear in the Constitution, the paraphrases for it are so transparent that there can be no doubt. The passages in question are to be found in article II, paragraph 2, part 3, and article I, paragraph 9, part 1.

{18} Only three states approved the new constitution unanimously. The vote in the legislature of Pennsylvania was 46 for to 32 against. Massachusetts approved with 187 for and 168 against, Virginia with 89 against 79, New York with 30 against 26, Rhode Island with

34 against 32, North Carolina with 193 against 75. The Constitution was *not* presented to a direct vote of the people. The strong negative vote of the states shows the great difficulties met in ratifying the Constitution.

{19} Kapp says that the monetary value of slaves amounted to only $10 million in 1790. In 1820 it was already $2 billion. That is an error. A more proper value in 1820 would be $500 million.

{20} This breeding of slaves in the North inevitably led to the division of Negro families. The blacks were sold to the cotton lands when they grew up. The number of black women was extraordinarily large in Virginia. They became breeding machines. A respected lady in Baltimore paid for her luxuries by selling the children of eight Negro women who were that lady's slaves. White people were occasionally sold into slavery. This was the case with the child immigrant Salome Müller, born in Langensulzbach in Alsace. (On her see J. Hanno Deiler.) Slavery had a dreadful impact on the morals of the South. President Madison's sister wrote, "We Southern ladies are complimented with the name of wives, but we are only the mistresses of seraglios." It was often said that the noblest blood of Virginia flowed in the veins of slaves. In the decade 1850–60, mulattos grew from 348,895 to 518,360. The worst was the fate of quadroons and octaroons, who had up to three-quarters white blood, but still were counted as Negroes. Most of them were sold to white lechers as mistresses.

{21} The way that strict religious circles of the South thought about slavery is shown us by an entry in the *Religious Herald* in Richmond. One planter declared there that with God's help he wished to spend the rest of his life as a missionary. At the same time he was offering forty slaves for sale, mostly young and good-looking, whose number and value would rapidly grow.

{22} That corresponded to the earlier practice of always admitting new states in pairs, one slave and one free. So Vermont was admitted along with Kentucky, Ohio with Tennessee, Indiana with Louisiana, and Illinois with Mississippi.

{23} German immigrants perhaps supplied more strength than any other European element. Young Wisconsin was almost a German state, and considerable parts of Iowa and Minnesota were the same. In those days a third of Ohio was of German blood, and in Illinois and Indiana there were extensive pure German settlements. German immigration in those days consisted essentially of peasants, many with property. They rushed in masses to the West, while the Irish immigrants remained mostly in the East, on the coast.

{24} This was called "squatter sovereignty." Squatters were people who had seized a piece of new land without any legal title.

{25} Much blood was on Brown's hands, including innocent blood, but even his opponents conceded that his was a heroic nature. He was a figure such as was often produced in the Peasants' War and Reformation in Germany, the Huguenot Wars, and the English and French Revolutions. He could hardly have been rational when he carried out his last deed. His earlier undertakings were marked by careful preparation and a fundamental weighing of the chances for success.

{26} For the election of electors each state constitutes a unit. If, for example, state X had 100,000 votes for Lincoln and 99,999 votes for Douglas, then the Lincoln electors for X are chosen. This system explains why Douglas, with 1,280,049 Northern votes, received only 3 Northern electoral votes, but with only 162,525 votes in the South he received 9 electoral votes.

{27} Almost all the Lincoln votes from slave states came from the Germans in Missouri.

{28} In South Carolina the legislature elected the presidential electors, so that the popular vote was not expressed, but it should be assumed for Breckinridge.

{29} Lincoln often confessed to Schurz that he owed his election essentially to the Germans of the Northwest. There the Germans had usually voted Democratic. Essentially, due to the influence of the slavery-hating Forty-Eighter refugees, an astounding transfer of Germans to the Republican Party had taken place by 1856. The number of German votes for Lincoln in the West is estimated at more than 300,000. But many American-born sons of German immigrants also participated. Even the splitting of the Democratic Party would not have elected Lincoln if the German switch in the West had not been so massive. The convention that elected Lincoln included twenty German delegates, and there were twelve German natives among the Lincoln electors. It was very exceptional for Germans to be chosen for such honorific offices.

{30} In South Carolina it was indeed the entire white people that rebelled. There was unanimity over it, and it did not bother these people to leave the old association. The German Memminger actually said, "Secession is a necessity, even if it is not our wish." But few agreed with his conditional statement. The people did not have the least doubt about their right "to be autonomous." They regarded the Union as a sort of business partnership: when one partner is tired of the association, he withdraws from it. This view also corresponds to the disposition which the South Carolinian "partner" had to the federal property located in the state. The soil belongs to South Carolina, and the federal buildings (forts, post offices, customs houses, etc.) to the United States. "Those buildings should be appraised, we will pay for them and take them over, so then we are quit." It must be stressed that this was the honest conviction of those citizens, a result of their concept of states' rights.

{31} Result in Tennessee: 104,913 votes for joining the Confederacy, 47,238 against. Most of the negative votes (32,923) came from eastern Tennessee, whose population consisted primarily of the poor and very deteriorated. Virginia voted without the forty counties of what is today West Virginia. These were mostly true to the Union. The vote in Virginia, however, was held so late as to be insignificant. The vote for secession was 129,950, with 20,373 votes against.

{32} At that time Webster said, "Secession makes sense as a revolutionary right. I can understand it as a right proclaimed in the midst of the uproar of a rebellion of citizens, carried at the head of armies. But as a political right recognized in the Constitution, it appears to me to be an absurdity, for it presumes resistance against the government under the authority of the government itself, and it presumes the dissolution of the government without wishing to injure that government's principles; it presumes injury to law without making it a crime, perjury without responsibility, complete overthrow of the government without it being a revolution."

{33} Among them was Henry Ward Beecher, the most outstanding orator in the country and brother of the author of *Uncle Tom's Cabin*.

{34} The new Confederacy was similarly limited as well. At the time it could only command a ready army of at most 12,000 South Carolinian volunteers. These were, however, fixed within their state and could not pass to the north without entering North Carolinian territory. North Carolina had not yet joined the Confederacy. The hallowed principle of states' rights could not be touched. This would have offended the second group of Southern states, but especially also the border state of Maryland, whose entry was then strongly expected by Jefferson Davis.

{35} The three forts in Charleston harbor, Sumter, Moultrie and Pinckney, were for coastal defense. Originally only Moultrie was defended, but because it could be raked by cannon fire from the beach, commandant Major Anderson moved with his few artillerists to the better-situated Fort Sumter. Buchanan fumed with rage when he heard of Anderson's action. But he did not have the courage to order Anderson to return to Moultrie. Moultrie and Pinckney were then occupied by the rebels. The fact that Anderson only had the men for one of three forts was due to the traitorous measures of the then Secretary of War Floyd. The garrison lacked ammunition and particularly food.

{36} The negotiators were operating on their own. They never forwarded to President Davis Anderson's response that he wanted to capitulate on 15 April. It may be assumed that Davis would have forbidden any bombardment if Anderson's response had been made known to him at the proper time, for Davis rightly saw the enormous value to the Union side of this *attack* by the South.

{37} The northwestern part of Virginia (forty counties) remained loyal to the Union, however. It was later divided from Virginia and entered the Northern states as the new state of West Virginia.

{38} See Appendix II, pp. 341-2.

{39} [In fact, Lincoln left a personal estate amounting to several tens of thousands of dollars.–Ed.]

{40} The thorough literature on Lincoln's religious views is found in Rhodes, vol. 2, p. 236.

{41} Lincoln, however, was by no means the first choice of all Western Republicans. Wisconsin, under the leadership of Schurz, was unanimously for Seward; the powerful Western state of Ohio had its own candidates in Chase and Wade; and in Indiana, as well, the majority of the Republicans were originally against Lincoln.

{42} A few examples here. At the start of the War, desertion was to be stemmed by carrying out a large number of executions. But Lincoln wrote on the margin of the judgment, "Unfortunately, there are already too many widows in this country. I do not want to increase their number. Let the poor fellows go!" A young soldier who had fallen asleep at his post in the face of the enemy was to be shot. Lincoln suspended the sentence for the reason: "This seventeen-year old farm boy had marched the entire day. He is used to going to bed early. The fact that he fell asleep was not his fault." There are hundreds of such pardons. When a secessionist who had killed a young Union officer in cold blood was to be hanged, Lincoln fought long with himself before he would confirm the sentence with his signature.

{43} Lincoln did not even find rest in the bosom of his family. One of his worst tormentors was his wife. She remained at the educational level of a former Kentucky country girl [More recent research contradicts this dismissive attitude toward Mrs. Lincoln's origins, education and basic intelligence–Ed.]. She was extraordinarily vain and accessible to the grossest flattery. She wanted to play a political role, and Villard says that Mrs. Lincoln even intervened in filling cabinet posts. Adventurers seeking positions flattered their way to her, won promises from her, and she then sought to fulfill them with her husband (without success). Some even said Mrs. Lincoln had secessionist sympathies, but these rumors are certainly untrue. This story had its origin in the Southern roots of the lady as well as the fact that two step-brothers of Mrs. Lincoln were serving in the rebel army. After the murder of her husband, Mrs. Lincoln did not want to vacate the White House, and energetic efforts were needed in order to get the new President Johnson his rights.

Chapter Two, pp. 43–91

{1} The cadet school of the United States is located at West Point on the Hudson.

{2} The cause for this might be that a European has a hard time understanding American works of history about the war. They assume a very thorough knowledge of geography, as well as a complete familiarity with American conditions. And then there is this multitude of names of commanders on both sides, often sounding alike, this continual shifting of army corps, divisions and brigades, and the frequent changes of command. Understanding is also made more difficult by the fact that most of the historians are concerned with cramming in as much detail as possible, so that the reader is continually led away from the main concern. The objectivity of the narrative is also often suspect. Every historian has his own favorite among the commanders, and the praising is often repellent. Capable and reliable generals are torn down, cheats and fools praised beyond measure. There is still no critical narrative of the war by a professional writer.

{3} This did in fact happen, particularly in Wisconsin and New York, but in most states it was an exception.

{4} Lee was opposed to slavery. This is obvious in his letters from the 1850s.

{5} An American family in 1790 numbered 5.8 heads in 1790, and in 1900 it was only 4.6. In the earlier period there were 2.8 children per family on average, in 1900 only 1.5 (hence Roosevelt's wailing over the Americans' empty cradles). In comparison it might be said that the natural rate of growth in 1860 was 1.25 percent in England, 1.23 percent in Holland, 1.17 percent in Prussia, 1.08 percent in Saxony, 0.44 percent in France. In the German Empire the birth surplus for the census year 1905 was 1.46 percent. In 1885, where immigration from Germany was very strong, the rate of growth of the population in the Empire was only 0.70 percent.

{6} The important American historian Motley, a friend of the young Bismarck, says, "We are Americans; but yesterday we were Europeans — Netherlanders, Saxons, Normans, Swabians, Celts."

{7} Not only the volunteer troops and the revolutionaries who appeared before the public were part of the Forty-Eighters, but also their fellows in spirit, a people of several million. The emigrant horde of the Forty-Eighters came from this people. From 1840 to 1860, 1,386,329 Germans emigrated to America, of which a bare 400,000 did so during the first seven years of the 1840s and the last three years of the 1850s. The rest, around a million, came during the refugee period 1848–57, whose high-water mark was 1854 with 215,000 German immigrants. Afterwards the refugee flood ebbed at the end of 1856. During the three years 1852–54, 503,000 Germans came to America; before and after this refugee period only about 40,000 a year came on average. Hence one is justified in saying that half of the Germans drawn to America from 1848 to 1857 were driven there by the results of the revolution — half a million Forty-Eighters, including both the leaders and their horde.

{8} That benefitted Kossuth and his followers more than the Germans. Germans were far less practiced in dramatic and diplomatic arts, and they could also not deliver flaming speeches in English.

{9} "The saddest and most genuinely intolerable for me to hear is how everyone accuses the other of treason, robbery, cowardice ... Brentano accuses Struve; Struve Brentano." From Hecker's farewell letter to the German people, written in Le Havre.

{10} Rösler von Öls, former member of the Frankfurt Parliament, was asked by friends whether he was ashamed to be leading a newspaper supporting the Whig Party. Rösler gave the sad answer, "You obviously don't know how painful it is to be hungry."

{11} The moustache was the uniform of the novices. In the struggle with the Grays, the Greens were usually called "moustaches," and the Grays received the nickname of "old slouchers" ("*alte Hunker*").

{12} "It is safe to say that if he (Schurz) or a man like him could have remained in that place (as Secretary of the Interior) it would have not been necessary to send a United States senator to the penitentiary for stealing timber lands" (Professor Edmund J. James at the Schurz Festival in Milwaukee, 1906).

That is entirely correct — Schurz did not seek a cabinet post for the reasons average American politicians are accustomed to in such cases. He accepted the nomination because he had a mission to accomplish. He wanted to make civil service reform a reality. He wanted to prove that his theories of reform of official service could be carried out if good will existed at the top. And he succeeded in doing this. He did not ask whether it was pleasing to so many of this Forty-Eighter colleagues that he accepted office under President Hayes. And besides, Schurz had supported the election of this president, and the decision of the electoral commission was as definitive for him as it was for every other citizen. The opportunity to serve in the cabinet would probably never return, and he would have neglected what he regarded as an important obligation if he had not accepted that office.

{13} Of the leading German-Americans of the immigration before 1848, Lieber, Stallo, Münch, and even Körner took a thoroughly friendly position on the new German Empire.

{14} After the declaration of war in 1870, Kaspar Butz sang:

> If wishes could be bullets, if lightning and thunder
> Of anger of the long-exiled, now, on the day of decision,
> How would the thunder roll powerfully across the ocean
> A salvo for Germany and its brave army!
> Forgotten is everything, forgotten every want,
> Forgotten every sentence, even if of death!
> For you, oh Mother earth, you land of splendor,
> Even your distant sons stand with you in the fray!

The poem ended with the following call to Bismarck:

> You who now leads the fate of the Fatherland,
> Stand fast, do not waver for an instant!
> See how sharply Clio looks upon you,
> And do not be a second Metternich to the German people!

{15} [The portion of Heinrich Börnstein's memoirs dealing with America is published as Henry Boernstein, *The Memoirs of a Nobody: The Missouri Memoirs of an Austrian*

Radical, 1849–1866, tr. and ed. Steven Rowan (St. Louis: Missouri Historical Society; Detroit: Wayne State University Press, 1997).–Ed.]

{16} [Jacob Mueller, *Memories of a Forty-Eighter:* Sketches from the *German-American Period of Storm and Stress in the 1850s,* tr. and ed. Steven Rowan (Cleveland: Western Reserve Historical Society, 1996).–Ed.]

{17} Dr. A. B. Gould, *Investigations in the Military and Anthropological Statistics of American Soldiers* (New York, 1869). This work essentially deals with the medical system of the army, and the estimate of nationalities by Gould is only an introduction to his main work.

{18} Adjutant General Simpson declares that of the German soldiers recruited by the state of Missouri, about 10,000 men were enumerated as reenlistments. Gould, who cites this declaration by Simpson, is of the opinion that Simpson included those descendents of Germans in Missouri who had not been de-Germanized.

{19} Frederick Pfisterer, *Statistical Record of the Armies of the United States* (New York: Charles Scribner's Sons, 1883). Pfisterer was a German. His figures are used in all the more recent histories of the war.

{20} This estimate would have been more certain if Gould had done without the information of the colonels on those 293,000 men. For what could those officers still know about the nationality of their people after seven or eight years? They would have decided for American nationality in all dubious cases, for in such evaluations the party with the largest numbers always benefits.

{21} In the first edition, which appeared three years earlier, Gould gives the obligation of the Germans as 128,102, but the number of soldiers given by Germans at 187,858. In the second edition he reduces the obligation of the Germans by 9,700 heads, and the number of German soldiers by 11,041 men. This is the sole correction Gould made in his reprint, and all the other numbers of ethnic groups agree precisely. What is surprising about this is that Gould appears to have misfigured twice concerning the Germans, in the obligation as well as in the number of soldiers, a very remarkable accident. Still, it seems proper to use Gould's second estimate for the number of German soldiers.

{22} Immigration from France fell by half after 1871 [The annexation of Alsace and Lorraine.–Ed.].

{23} It should be stressed that Alsatians in the United States have always adhered to the Germans, specifically to Palatines and Badeners. They belong to German associations and congregations, speak their peculiar "Dütsch," and almost always declare themselves to be Germans. Even in the war this comradeship emerged, particularly in the Western German regiments. This shows once more that blood is thicker than water.

{24} Missouri takes an exceptional position among them.

{25} Among the first troops that arrived to protect Washington were Germans. Two German Turner companies from Baltimore and Washington formed the escort at Lincoln's inauguration on 4 March. Among the very first regiments responding to Lincoln's call and in part standing in the field as early as the end of May 1861 were the following purely German regiments from New York: 7th, 8th, 20th, 29th, 41st, and the half-German 39th Regiment. In addition, there were 400 artillerymen and cavalry, altogether 6000 Germans from the state of New York; from Pennsylvania came the German Regiments 27th, 73rd, 74th, 75th and units of artillery, and so on, 4000 Germans. More than half of the roughly 20,000 Pennsylvanians answering the call were of German ancestry. Ohio immediately fielded the purely-German 9th Regiment, 1068 men, but 400 more Germans enlisted in this regiment, which then joined the 32nd Regiment, organized somewhat later. The two Ohio German regiments, the 28th and 37th, were also formed during the first levy and were ready to march at the start of July and August 1861, respectively. Hence three purely German regiments from Ohio. In Wisconsin, the 9th German Regiment was ready at once. In Missouri, 4000 Germans were already organized when Lincoln's call appeared. In addition there was the almost entirely German Missouri Home Guard. One may accept that 18,000 men of the roughly 92,000 of Lincoln's first levy formed in purely German regiments. But in all the Western states, especially in Ohio, Indiana and Illinois, there were half-German regiments in the first levy. In Indiana the 1st, in Kansas the 1st and 2nd regiments were half-German; these regiments were formed in May 1861 and were already fighting on 10 August at Wilson's Creek. And how many Germans might have stood in the mixed regiments of the first levy! According to a very conservative estimate, at least every fourth man in the first levy was German-born. The participation of our people in the troops that were called up for the First Battle of Bull Run was similarly strong. Almost all purely German regiments were already formed in 1861. See the chapter on "The German Regiments."

{26} On deserters, see "The War in General." According to Pfisterer the number of deserters was around 200,000.

{27} Bounty jumpers were replacement swindlers, people who enlisted as replacements for conscripts capable of paying bounty, and who deserted as quickly as possible, taking new bounties and entering other regiments in order to repeat the swindle soon afterwards.

{28} The penitentiary prisoner in Albany who confessed to having committed bounty jumping more than thirty times was to be sure no German, and no Irishman either.

{29} According to the official report of Secretary of War and later President Taft, in 1906 no fewer than 6258 men, or 7.4 percent of the total of the Regular Army deserted. Nine out of ten of these deserters were native-born Americans, according to the same report.

{30} *Berliner Tageblatt*, 13 May 1910.

{31} Professor A. B. Faust, *The German Element in the United States*, part 2, pp. 1–27, gives a thorough investigation of the elements of the population of the United States according to the census report of 1900. Faust relies essentially on the greater work of the famous German statistician Böckh. This scholar tested in no. 4 of the journal *Deutsche Erde*, 1903, the calculations that Emil Mannhardt published in the Chicago *Deutsche Geschichtsblätter* (1903, no. 3). Mannhardt had calculated the number of residents of the United States descended from Germans at 25 million. Böckh, however, reduced Mannhardt's figure to roughly 18 million. On the basis of Böckh's method, Faust comes to the following result:

The totality of the whites in the United States in 1900: 66,990,000.

These fall into the following groups:

Germanic Element	18,400,000
English Element	20,400,000
Irish and Scottish Element	13,900,000
Scandinavians, Slavs, Latins, etc.	14,290,000
Total white population	66,990,000

It should be stressed that the Dutch are included in the 18,400,000 residents of German origin, which is entirely proper, not only because the Dutch are a pure Low German people, but also because so extraordinarily many Germans who today would be citizens of the German Empire were found among the Dutch emigrants of the seventeenth and eighteenth centuries, and were seen as Dutchmen on their immigration to America.

{32} During the seventeenth and eighteenth centuries, at least a fifth of all German emigrants died during the crossing, usually of hunger or what was called ship fever. This misery lasted in a weakened form even during the first half of the nineteenth century, and it ended only with the introduction of steamers, especially with the founding of North German Lloyd and the Hamburg Packet Company.

{33} Friedrich Kapp, *Aus und über Amerika;* also *On Immigration,* a publication in English of which Kapp published a part separately in German. Further, Kapp's *Geschichte der deutschen Einwanderung nach New York.*

{34} Among the many outstanding generals of the Union army who came from the descendants of Germans are particularly to be named Rosecrans, Heintzelmann, Hartranft and Custer. The descendants of the German immigrants of the seventeenth and eighteenth centuries and the first third of the nineteenth century produced at least a hundred thousand men in Pennsylvania alone.

{35} Through high interest payments of 7 percent, and significant increase in value. Perhaps this is the sole example in history where German idealism was richly rewarded in gold.

{36} Among the besieging troops was the 46th German New York Regiment under Colonel von Rosa. On quiet evenings the Forty-Sixers used to sing German folksongs from the nearby island of Tybee. Those songs were answered with the same notes from the German Georgians in the fort. The commander of the fort took it to be a dangerous signal and banned the singing. (Information of L. P. Henninghaus in Baltimore [46th Regiment] to the author.)

{37} The most courageous and effective fighter of slavery in the South was Franz Lieber (see his biography). He held a flaming oration in the main lecture hall of the University of South Carolina in 1855, while preparations for the rebellion were already underway, against what was called the "American institution," leading to his expulsion from the South. In 1822 a gathering of German Lutheran preachers publicly protested in Tennessee against slavery, in an extremely severe tone. The deeds of these German men deserve to be praised more than the over-celebrated protest of Pastorius (1688), whose text was simply passed around among some spiritual brethren and only became known almost two hundred years later.

{38} My esteemed colleague, Mr. Hanno Deiler, had undertaken to edit contemporary German sources on the subject, but he was called away by death before he could carry out his plan. I then asked Mr. John E. McElroy in Washington, who edits the organ of American veterans, *The National Tribune,* and who is certainly the leading expert on the history of the Civil War, for material for this purpose. He responded that he himself was lacking the necessary documentation. He writes, "It seems to me, that it is a story that some one should make years of study of and write a book. — The story of the Germans of Texas is one of great pathos, heroism, and sacrifice and someone should rise up and tell it adequately, which I could not. Yours in F. C. & L. John E. McElroy." Is there not one of the many wealthy German-Americans who will set a prize for such a work of love?

{39} Olmsted estimated the German Texans, both immigrants and their descendents, at 50,000 souls as early as 1852. This estimate rests on detailed reports from every German settlement.

{40} Olmsted, *Wanderungen durch Texas,* 3d German edition, Leipzig, 1874, p. 265. Olmsted incidentally was of the opinion that Douai's struggle against slavery was of a rather tame nature. Douai might have acted with some care in his English-language articles, and Olmsted was only able to read those essays. Restraint is certainly not cowardice when friendly colleagues are publicly threatening one with drowning. The views of the editor were expressed in much more energetic terms in the German part of Douai's paper, and it took a great deal of courage to criticize slavery at all in English.

{41} San Antonio is one of the oldest settlements of Europeans in America, founded by the Spanish around 1650. The city had degenerated into a miserable Mexican nest when the first Germans came there in 1842. In 1860, San Antonio was the largest city in Texas, a cultural deed achieved essentially by Germans.

{42} Olmsted, p. 260: "I have already mentioned how marvelously many Germans have been able to preserve their intellectual liveliness, their scientific sense and their refined taste, feeling satisfied and happy in Texas, even though they must earn only a modest livelihood through exhausting labor. We find many strange contradictions in the current situation of these educated men in the backwoods. A man in a cotton shirt with a long beard encountered me and recited a passage from Tacitus; in one hand he held a long pipe, in the other a butcher knife. In his very simple room a Madonna hangs on the wall, I drink coffee from a cup of Meissen porcelain, under me instead of a chair is a barrel, and I listen to a Beethoven sonata being played on a grand piano. The settler tells me, 'My wife made these trousers, and my stockings were grown in that cotton field.' He has a gun that cost him a couple hundred dollars, and on the bookshelf sit old classics next to sweet potatoes." This portrayal is particularly apt for the less prosperous among the Latin Germans of Texas, but it also agrees in many matters for the landowners of Sisterdale.

{43} Reference is made to the portrayal by Friedrich Kapp in *Aus und über Amerika.* It might be mentioned in passing that the German fraternity brother Kapp, accidentally encountered as a farmer in west Texas, was later pressed into the military service of the secession and died for a cause he hated. Kapp had encountered a hut in Texas and entered it to find his own picture on the wall. Later the resident of the hut appeared. The story Kapp ties to this encounter is one of his most successful small portrayals and gives us perhaps the best view of the milieu of the German Latins of Texas. Incidentally, Kapp was Olmsted's companion on his journey through Texas.

{44} For several decades, Texas was a sort of asylum for criminals. In the North there was a special designation for persons who had escaped the police: "G. T. T." (gone to Texas). Olmsted cites the remarks from 1831 of a certain Mr. Deewes, who writes, "It would charm you if you could hear how the people in this new land greet one another. It is not at all unusual for us to ask a man why he fled the United States. They are rarely offended by this question; most of them name the crime they had committed. If they deny they had done anything, then they are regarded with suspicion." The Southerners who came to Texas to take the land from the Mexicans were also no angels. The American small farmer, whose heroic deeds are described elsewhere, went to the Northwest. Other than the Germans, few real pioneers came to Texas. The slave barons came from the South with their rope-trains of blacks. The non-German part of the state was the wildest West. It was a long time before the solid part of the population got the upper hand. Still in the years 1865–1868, 470 whites and 429 Negroes died violent deaths, usually through the rope or the bullet. The fact that the whites of Texas had so many desperadoes, criminals, professional gamblers, and smugglers among them partly explains the dreadful persecution of the pro-Union Germans.

{45} The story that the Germans of Texas offered 2000 men to Governor Houston to fight the Texas secessionists was denied by Houston himself. Despite that, this story was believed because the loyalty to the Union of the Germans was generally known. In his book, *Texas on the Eve of Rebellion* (Cincinnati, 1864), Charles Anderson says that the Union people of Texas went massively over to secession after the Battle of Bull Run. In the fall of 1861, Anderson could count on his fingers the number of Union people who were not Germans.

{46} Twiggs was expelled from the federal army with a rebuke by Secretary of War Dix. He did not go very far in the Confederate Army. He was disrespected even in the South.

{47} The very strong German militia company of San Antonio refused to surrender their federal flag or to give an oath of allegiance to the Confederacy. The company was then dissolved and most members fled to the North to fight for the Union.

{48} How many Germans were murdered by the Comanches during this interregnum cannot be established. Williams in his book, *With the Border Ruffians* (New York, 1907), provides a few details. These are so dreadful that we hope that the reporter is exaggerating. Williams found the corpse of a young German farmer whose body was covered with stab wounds. The Comanches had slowly tortured the unfortunate man to death.

{49} The wild men took many children of the Germans. At the end of the 1870s federal troops at Fort Sill encountered a very light-skinned Comanche. He was the son of the farmer, G. Fischer from Friedrichsburg. This young German had passed thirteen years in the wilds, had taken on their language and habits, and was regarded as the tribe's best shot. He had completely forgotten his German mother language except for a few fragments. He slowly accustomed himself to his new setting.

{50} The later General Küffner, one of the most valiant German officers (he was wounded four times) fled from Texas to the North. The later German Admiral Fahrenholt also was one of the pro-Union Germans from Texas.

{51} Union General Butler, then commanding in New Orleans, organized the first loyal pro-Union cavalry regiment from Texas from the refugees arriving in that harbor. The regiment consisted almost entirely of German Texans. German Texans also made up most of those serving in loyal Texan troop units organized later.

{52} *The San Antonio Herald* wrote in those days of the pro-Union Germans (cited in Lossing, p. 336), "Their bones are bleaching on the soil of every county from Red River to Rio Grande, and in the counties of Wide and Denton (German counties) their bodies are suspended by scores from the 'Black Jacks.'"

{53} R. H. Williams, a member of Dunn's company of the Texas Rangers, describes the atrocity thoroughly in the book appearing in 1907 with E. P. Dutton & Co., *With the Border Ruffians*. I would gladly have used a more reliable source than the report of a man who belonged to Dunn's gang. But the evil deeds were done in secret, at a time when there was neither a press that registered such things nor judges who concerned themselves with it. Incidentally, Williams' report is confirmed by J. W. Sansom in San Antonio, with whom I have corresponded. Sansom must be regarded as reliable, for Degener chose him as an experienced and knowledgeable trapper to accompany the expedition of the Germans that found such a dreadful end on the Nueces River. Incidentally, Williams' account and that of Sansom are confirmed by Lossing, *History of the Civil War,* vol. 2, p. 537.

{54} In some reports he is named Duff.

{55} Olmsted stresses that Texas Germans provided the majority of the Rangers who assisted federal troops in fighting the Indians in the 1850s.

{56} A third company leader named Lilley boasted that he had killed several of the wounded Germans with his own hands. He had emptied several revolvers (Lossing, vol. 2, p. 537). Williams says that he pulled out one German who had been thrown into the campfire by his comrades. When Williams returned to bring water to the unfortunate, the man was already dead.

{57} *Official Records,* vol. 15, gives a thorough report of the protest of the Germans in the so-called Beigel Settlement and of the battles with the Germans of Medina County in 1863 and 1864.

Chapter Three, pp. 92–148

{1} Some of these "generals of the press" contributed to the outbreak of the Spanish-American War through spreading the false story that the federal battleship Maine was sunk by a Spanish sea mine. Later it developed that the *Maine* sank as a result of an explosion in the ammunition magazine.

{2} The Garibaldi Regiment, 39th New York Infantry, was described in this manner by McClellan: "The colonel was a certain d'Utassy from Hungary. His real name was Strasser. He had been a rider in Franconi's Circus. The soldiers came from every possible army: Zouaves from Algeria, Foreign Legionnaires, Zephirs, Cossacks, Garibaldians, English deserters, Sepoys, Turkos, Croats, Swiss, beer-swillers from Bavaria, strong fellows from North Germany, and surely also Chinese, Eskimos and warriors from the army of the Grand Duchess of Gerolstein."

So much for McClellan. In fact this Garibaldi Regiment had three German companies and one Swiss. They were good. The other six companies were colorfully mixed, and the two companies of Sicilians were a genuine gang of robbers and murderers. The regiment at first bore the Bersaglieri uniform with a round hat and green feather. Sigel removed the Garibaldi Regiment in July 1862. It was captured with the other troops under Miles at Harpers Ferry, but paroled. The regiment was later reorganized, the scum were run out, and a very good regiment was created which distinguished itself at Chancellorsville and particularly at Gettysburg. There stands a fine monument to the regiment on the battlefield at Gettysburg.

{3} Blenker, the old democrat, had a surprising preference for noble officers. His entourage crawled with counts and barons, and there was even a German prince, Salm-Salm. Blenker's "noble officers' club" was extensively mocked in contemporary papers. Forty-Eighters in particular were offended, and hostility arose between the officers from the circles of the former German revolutionaries and Blenker's noble society.

{4} In Germany itself, even in Prussia, there was no awareness of the country's own military strength. The military importance of Germany has since grown surprisingly quickly. How many knew Moltke before 1866, even though he had already directed the victorious campaigns against Düppel and Alsen in 1864 from Berlin? When Moltke was called by his king to be chief of general staff of the Prussian army, many old Prussian "gaiter buttons" grumbled about the astonishing elevation of this entirely unknown man.

{5} Klapka entered the Prussian army in 1866 as a major general and organized a Hungarian legion, which was to participate in Prussia's war against Austria, but he did not see action.

{6} This so-called count was a former convict from Austria. He came to Washington with falsified recommendations of Archduke Maximilian and a falsified letter of credit; found a niche with the Austrian and Prussian ambassadors, as well as with Schurz; was immediately made a colonel; and swindled in the most shameless manner. He cheated the ambassadors out of large sums. He then probably fled to the camp of the rebellion. Another Austrian "count" who called himself Estvan appeared first in the secessionist capital of Richmond, swindling the government there, then fled to Washington and had himself celebrated as a patriot of the Union. The pavement became too hot for him there, too, and he went to Europe to write a book on the American conflict concocted of total lies. Washington at the time was a gathering place for bands of swindlers gathered from all lands. Many of them impressed those there with false papers and a confident appearance. This business deeply damaged the reputation of the foreign-born, but particularly the many German officers, and it probably influenced McClellan's judgment.

{7} McClellan describes in his memoirs a visit to Hunters Chapel in the autumn of 1861 in the following manner: "As soon as we had come into view of Blenker's camp, Blenker had the officer's call sounded, and soon the 'polyglot collection' was together. There were glittering uniforms, and the colors of these were as varied as those of the rainbow. Blenker, in his dazzling uniform coat with purple lining, received us in the midst of his officers in the most formal manner and with studied courtliness. Because he was a very handsome man of martial appearance, and because he had so many men about him who looked and acted the same, the impression the whole made was very effective and made the greatest contrast with the simple and matter-of-fact manner my visits with other divisions passed. After a few minutes, Blenker would command, '*Ordinanz Nummero Eins*,' and then massive amounts of champagne were served, the band played, and often songs were sung. Blenker's division was of quite a special type. So far as pomp, military show, and such, it exceeded all other divisions. The division was particularly outstanding in drill, and in demonstrating military nature the division was also outstanding, for all the officers and perhaps all the soldiers had been trained in Europe. I always regretted the fact that this division was taken away from me and placed in Frémont's corps rather than mine. The officers and men were very fond of me. I would have been able to control them as no other, and they would have done outstanding services if they had been left in Sumner's corps."

So far McClellan. The fact that he wanted to take the division with him to the Peninsula appears in many of his letters and dispatches that survive in the archives. McClellan literally begged for this division to be entrusted to him. But the War Department remained unbending. The administration wanted to reconcile with Frémont, who had been fired a short time earlier in Missouri. Because Frémont insisted that German troops should fight under him, this was approved.

{8} The Bowery was the low down entertainment area of New York.

{9} A further sight worth seeing in the German division was its chaplains. Every regiment had its chaplain, although the spiritual needs of Blenker's soldiers was certainly not greater than those of Wallenstein's mercenaries. It was the fashion among a considerable part of the German-American community to be in contempt of religion. This was also a result of the great influence of the Forty-Eighter refugees. Because positions for chaplains were in the budget, Blenker had one for each of his regiments. Blenker was easy-going in his standards for a chaplain. The chief requirement was that the gentlemen were an ornament to the drinking table. Hence one of his "Christian chaplains" was a Jew, another had never been sober, and a third had won this comfortable position by praising Blenker in innumerable poems as one of the greatest heroes in history. The others were mostly German journalists who sought the comfortable slot in order to write for their newspapers, and out of this thankfulness they saw to it that the fame of Blenker would never fade.

{10} I thank Ernst Schierenberg, one of the best experts on Missouri war history, for these items of information.

{11} The Union arsenal in San Antonio, Texas, was plundered as early as February 1861.

{12} The rebels had already made an attempt to take the St. Louis Arsenal on 20 April, but on their march there they had to pass through the German section of town. They were blocked there by a mob of thousands of people which called to them, "The Black Rifles are coming!" The rebels turned about at once and gave up their plans for the time being. The Confederate encampment at Camp Jackson was then erected to attack the St. Louis Arsenal with greater force.

{13} The colonels of the St. Louis Home Guard were: 1st Regiment, H. Almstedt; 2nd Regiment, Herm. Kallmann; 3rd Regiment, John McNeil (Lieutenant Colonel Fritz); 4th Regiment, Colonel Gratz Brown; 5th Regiment, Charles G. Stiefel. McNeil and Gratz Brown were pro-Union Anglo-Americans friendly to Germans. But the men of the 3rd and 4th Home Guard regiments were also Germans. Hence St. Louis was defended on 23 April by approximately 8000 armed Germans.

In the interior of the state, German farmers also organized Home Guard units. Their leaders: in Gasconade County, Lieutenant Colonel Jul. Hundhausen and Major Dallmeyer; in Coopers County, Major J. Eppstein; in St. Charles, Colonel A. Krekel; for the Pacific Battalion, Major W. C. Inks; in Benton County, Colonel H. Imhauser; at Moniteau, Major F. Potthoff; at Cape Girardeau, Major G. H. Cramer; in Maries County, Colonel Franz Wilhelmi. Besides the five German volunteer regiments of St. Louis, a strong German pioneer unit was organized under Captains Vörster, Gerster and Krausnick.

{14} For disciplinary infractions in the regular federal army the punishment was to be hanged by the thumbs with an old syrup barrel, its bottom poked out, placed over the body in order to bring a plague of flies on the unfortunate soldier. (Schnacke's report on abuse of soldiers in the Regular Army, *Pionier*, vol. 11.)

{15} This [Polish] German captain was the first officer of the Union army to fall.

{16} Incidentally, the police chief worked very bravely for the preservation of order, although his men were secessionists.

{17} The narrative above of the German rising in St. Louis used the following sources: Friedrich Schnake's essays in the Cincinnati *Pionier*, vols. 11 and 12; excerpts from Krüer's *Deutsche in Missouri*; Börnstein's memoirs; Sigel's *New York Monthly*; writings of Friedrich

Münch and Gert Göbel, and articles of the German press of the time. Further, there was much orally-transmitted material, for which I thank Ernst Schierenberg, General Osterhaus, and others.

{18} The German 4th Regiment under Schüttner remained in St. Louis as a reserve. Parts of Sigel's Brigade were left behind in Rolla, Springfield, and other places to protect the marching route.

{19} Wilkins, whose fault this neglect was, disappears from that day on from the history of the war.

{20} Reference is made here to Schofield's evaluation of Sigel's characteristics as a commander, to be found in the biographical section under "Franz Sigel."

{21} The commanding general, McClellan, sent the reports of the officers at Wilson's Creek on 12 February 1862 to the Secretary of War, directing his attention to the role Sigel supposedly played in the battle. McClellan recommended that Sigel not be promoted until the matter had been substantially clarified. There was never a court martial over Sigel. The investigation Halleck later carried on was secret.

{22} Sigel himself gives the losses as follows: 26 dead, 31 wounded, and over 200 taken captive.

{23} Lyon's division at Wilson's Creek incidentally consisted of about one-third Germans. The 1st Iowa and 1st and 2nd Kansas were half German, the Osterhaus battalion of the 2nd Missouri Regiment was entirely German, Lyon's personal guard consisted of thirty German butchers from St. Louis, the pioneer company was entirely German, and many Germans also served in the Regular Army unit.

{24} The war essays in *Century Magazine* later appeared in four volumes as a special work under the title, *Battles and Leaders.*

{25} The valley described here is shown on the map by Sigel's first, second, and third positions. It extends in a bow extended to the west roughly from Sigel's first position to Sharp's Farm.

{26} According to Sigel's calculations of time, which are contradictory. It must have been at least 9 A.M. or even later.

{27} It was probably about 9:15 A.M.

{28} The 1st Iowa Regiment had belonged to Sigel's brigade until the day before the battle, and only then was it taken over by Lyon. It wore gray uniforms. It must be asked how Sigel's people could have mistaken their comrades from such close range. The troops marching up were units of the Confederate 3rd Louisiana Regiment, only 300 men strong. When Sergeant Tod was shot, according to the account of the Confederate Captain Vigilini (page 117 of the same volume of the *Official Records*), these troops stood only thirty to forty yards from Sigel's cannons and could recognize the "Dutch faces" of their enemies.

{29} If there were reconnaissance to be done, Sigel's cavalry was available. They were more than a hundred experienced soldiers of the regular army. To entrust a single man with such a mission is certainly a measure that would at least trouble those in military circles. When poor Tod encountered the enemy, he fell into the very fate his name indicated [Tod = death –Ed.]. The sending of a single man speaks little for Sigel's assertion that he was in doubt about the character of the approaching troops. The Confederate report says that Tod responded to the question of the Confederate General McCulloch as to whose troops were before him by saying, "Those are Sigel's people!" But at the same moment, Tod raised his musket against the general, and then Tod was shot dead by a Sergeant Gentles. The "confusion" of the troops is almost beyond explanation. The day was rather clear, and it had long since ceased raining. The Count of Paris writes that the 3rd Louisiana Regiment was carrying a United States flag. But Sigel does not say a word about it (in any of his three accounts), although the carrying of the Union flag by the enemy would have freed him of much blame. The Confederates also did not mention any flag bearer, who usually plays a great role in their accounts of battles. Only part of the 3rd Louisiana Regiment was involved, because the larger part still stood before Lyon. The Confederates did make use of Sigel's captured flag in the later course of the battle. Incidentally, Lyon's troops also mistook Confederates for Sigel's soldiers and held their fire for that reason. The confusion of foe for friend was thus not Sigel's mistake alone, if the confusion reported by Schofield, Sturgis, and others is more excusable, for these officers expected Sigel to come from that direction, were misled by the flag, and also said that Sigel's people were uniformed similarly to the Confederates. This is incorrect. Sigel's troops wore blue blouses, but they then were torn and shredded due to the dreadful supply situation the soldiers had to endure.

{30} J. H. Browne, correspondent of the *New York Tribune,* says in his book *Four Years in Secessia,* p. 47, that Sigel only became aware of his mistake about the 3rd Louisiana Regiment when the enemy was a mere thirty yards away.

{31} The Confederate Reid Battery continued to fire when the Louisianans were already in the midst of Sigel's cannons. Two Confederates were killed there by friendly fire.

{32} Sigel denied that the secessionists fired using the cannons taken from him, but the secessionists certainly know better than Sigel in this matter.

{33} The greatest losses were suffered by the German Turner Company J of the 1st Kansas Regiment. Of the 101 men of the company, 32 were killed or wounded. Company J consisted entirely of members of the Turner Society of Leavenworth, Kansas.

{34} Schofield and Sturgis asserted that Sigel's retreat from Springfield to Rolla, which was portrayed in some newspapers as having been carried out in a masterful manner, was a dreadful affair. It was only for that reason that the other officers took Sigel's command away. The assertion that Sigel's commission had expired was only an excuse. Sigel had always used his own people, who had performed so poorly, as the vanguard, and the soldiers who had done the bleeding were given the hard service of rear guard alone. They never got to camp as a result of Sigel's slowness, etc. Those gentlemen also criticize Sigel's magnanimity to pro-Union people from southern Missouri who had fled to the Union camp. Sigel took these refugees to Rolla with him. His opponents were of the opinion that this caused the retreat of the troops great peril and trouble. All of these accusations sound rather hateful. Confederate reports are less critical of Sigel. Specifically, Pollard praised Sigel's energetically managed artillery fire, which took place before the rout at Sharp's Farm.

{35} On 15 November Corwin writes to the *Augsburger Allgemeine Zeitung,* "The demonstrations of rage against Lincoln which appeared particularly in the demonstrations of the Germans in Chicago border on frenzy."

{36} Davis's Division had just been supplied with sevenshooters. The soldiers thought they would be able to perform miracles with these guns, which permitted seven shots to be fired in rapid succession. But the gun jammed after its first shot, and there was no time to clean them. Soldiers who cannot shoot will run away when the enemy fires on them from a hundred paces away. The troops did not have the least experience with their sevenshooters at the moment when they were supposed to use them, one of many examples of the amateur way the war was conducted.

{37} Information provided by General Osterhaus to the author.

{38} Many Confederate leaders conceived of loyalty to officers much like chivalric duty in antiquity. But in those days bare weapons decided the matter. McCulloch and his brave comrades believed they could only activate the undisciplined masses by committing their own persons. The effect was the opposite. Troops left without leaders became demoralized. The brave actions of the Union General Lyon at Wilson's Creek had similar results.

{39} The Trent Affair: two emissaries of the Confederate government, Mason and Slidell, were on the English mail ship *Trent* at the start of November, 1861. It was on the high seas when it was stopped by a U. S. Navy ship, and the two rebels were captured and taken back to the United States. The English raised protests against that sort of sea policing exercise, although England had always acted similarly in earlier cases. England at once armed against the United States, and for a time it appeared that war was inevitable. Such a war would have taken place primarily in Canada, besides on the high seas. The conflict was settled just at the right time when the Washington government returned the two prisoners to England. The despicable part of Halleck's intimation is that the "foreign officers in a high position" (which could only be the higher officers of Sigel's division) supposedly had the intention of going over to the new national enemy and fighting "in a body" on the English side against the United States.

Chapter Four, pp. 149–197

{1} The colonel of the 9th, Robert McCook, the only non-German in the entire regiment, was severely wounded at Mill Springs and later, when he returned to his regiment barely recovered, was murdered in southeastern Tennessee by bushwhackers. Robert McCook was a brother of the corps commander Alexander McCook, who led at Perryville, Stones River, and Chickamauga. Colonel McCook always commanded the 9th in the German language. The regiment exacted bloody revenge for the murder of their leader.

{2} Descendent of Germans from Virginia. His father still wrote the name as Buchner.

{3} The concern of these two was without reason, incidentally. Grant could not have hanged the traitor Floyd without Lincoln's agreement, and Lincoln could never bring himself to sign a death sentence.

{4} On 4 April, two days before the attack at Shiloh, Grant telegraphed Nelson, the leader of Buell's lead division. Nelson was not to rush, because until 8 April Grant had no transportation means at hand to move Nelson's division across the Tennessee. Fortunately, Nelson did not listen to this advice but followed Buell's advice to reach the Tennessee as rapidly as possible.

{5} The value that the simplest wall would have had for the defenders was experienced by Prentiss's division when it came on an old defile whose walls gave them protection. This defile then became the chief support of what was called the Hornet's Nest, a position on which the attackers pounded their heads for hours, and in front of which the Confederate commanding General Johnston was killed.

{6} In Greeley's *The American Conflict*, vol. 2, p. 59, the camp is described in this fashion: "The five divisions were thrown out in a semicircle southward of Pittsburg Landing, with a front like a Methodist camp meeting, straggling from Lick creek on the south or left, to Snake creek on the north and right, a distance of three or four miles."

{7} Sherman's soldiers were all grass-green recruits. Sherman says that they first received weapons in Paducah, and Sherman reached Paducah on 14 February. The Prentiss Division had only been organized three weeks before the battle and consisted of only recruits. The soldiers who had fought at Fort Donelson all stood in the other divisions.

{8} Two commanders of Grant divisions bore the name Wallace. W. H. C. Wallace commanded one of the divisions fighting on 6 April. He fell in the battle. Lewis Wallace, the author of the novel *Ben Hur*, translated into all world languages, led the reserve division of the Army of the Tennessee located at Crump's Landing. Grant has little good to say of Lew Wallace. Lew Wallace had the order to come to Grant on the River Road, the nearest road. Lew Wallace, however, took a road leading far to the west. He asserted that the order sounded as if he were to move to protect the right flank of Sherman's first position. Wallace only arrived on the evening of the 6th, after the first battle was finished. Grant says ironically, "It appears that Lewis W. marched so far west in order to arrive in the rear or the flank of the enemy to do a heroic deed for the fame of his division and the advantage of his country."

{9} It is often asserted that Grant fell from his horse while drunk. That is certainly a lie. Grant certainly was a strong drinker in his youth, but he had overcome this passion and never gave reason for complaint in this matter as general or president. This fact was emphasized in 1908 by the presidential candidate, Taft. But Grant was also never a hypocrite, and he never turned down a good whiskey at the right time. Concerning Grant, an anecdote is told: A delegation of apostles of temperence demanded of Lincoln shortly after the Battle of Shiloh the dismissal of Grant the "drunk." Lincoln responded, "Could you gentlemen tell me what brand of whiskey General Grant prefers? I would like to send a barrel of this whiskey to each of my other generals."

{10} Sherman had to fall back on McClernand's division and then continued the battle united with it. McClernand permitted himself to be led by Sherman although he outranked Sherman. In later times, McClernand, who had once been an associate of Lincoln, became troublesome and intrigued against both Sherman and Grant. He was only dismissed after his dreadful failure at Vicksburg.

{11} These stragglers should be less severely judged than is usual. The recruits could barely handle their weapons. Thousands of them hung on the steep banks of the Tennessee the next morning. General Buell estimated the number of stragglers he found on the banks on Monday morning at more than 10,000 men.

{12} Sherman's brigade stood far back at the mob battle of First Bull Run and only came into action when the great flight had begun.

{13} Remarkably enough, the Confederate troops who had advanced for the last attack were little effected by the shots of the naval cannons. The shells exploded farther back, where Beauregard's headquarters were located, and there they caused terror enough.

{14} Nelson's division had already arrived in Savannah on the evening of the 5th. At 7 A.M. it was supposed to march along the right bank to opposite Pittsburg Landing, 9 miles, and then be put across the stream. But Nelson only got underway at 1:30 P.M. and only came into position after the battle. Due to the negligence of Wallace and Nelson, Grant was deprived of 13,000 men for the first day of the battle.

{15} The battles took place in part within the outer works of Corinth. These works, as well as the entire new fortifications of Corinth, were designed by the German engineer Colonel von Schrader, a former Hanoverian officer. In military histories, the credit for this is usually given to Grant and Rosecrans.

{16} Already in this second year of war poor finances and often hunger compelled the Southerners to use the methods once applied in the Thirty Years War. Not only was the army of the opponent the enemy, but the Northern people were also treated as enemies. The mounted irregular troops of the South were freebooters, robbers in grand style. The regular Confederate army learned from them, and in Kentucky Bragg acted in a manner similar to his irregular comrade Morgan elsewhere.

{17} As Willich was galloping back from Johnson's headquarters, there began an attack that was a complete overrun. Willich's tiny brigade was hit by a force five times its size and immediately dispersed. Willich's horse was killed, and the old hero was surrounded by a hundred rebels and was captured, but he was soon exchanged. Whether matters would have been different if Willich had been with his troops is unknown, for the other five brigades of the McCook's two divisions (Johnson's and Davis's) were dispersed as quickly. If Willich deserves blame for being absent, then his division commander, Johnson, deserves it even more for being posted so far in the rear.

{18} Schäfer's second brigade received the purely German 2nd and 15th Missouri and the almost entirely German-American 44th and the half-German 73rd Illinois Regiment. The four Illinois regiments, the 22nd, 27th (in the end under Major W. A. Schmidt), 42nd, and 51st were a third German. The 24th Wisconsin was more than half German, and the 21st Michigan, 88th and 36th Illinois Regiments had a large German element. The proportion was similar in Sheridan's artillery.

{19} The 75th Pennsylvania Regiment suffered a dreadful accident on 16 April while being ferried across. An old ferry boat was to bring the men to the opposite shore. Three officers and sixty-eight men were sent on the boat, which was probably overloaded. General Bohlen was leading the operation. At the middle of the river the men could no longer hold the cable against the strong stream. The boat sank, and forty-one men (other sources say all seventy-one men) drowned. It was said that General Bohlen was later shot by comrades of the drowned men. It is more likely that Bohlen fell to an enemy's bullet.

{20} Other than the skirmish at Kernstown. There the terrible Jackson was forced to withdraw essentially due to the artillery of the German Colonel Philipp Daum.

{21} From Heusinger's diary: "13 May: Today received a quarter cracker, that is all. 14 May: a quarter cracker, no meat, no salt, we are living on herbs and a sort of leaf which tastes like lettuce. It is raining without interruption, all building of bridges pointless, we can see our train and must starve to death. 15 May: Ate nothing today. We catch a wild rabbit and eat it raw. 16 May: The vermin are getting an upper hand, a half cracker received. 17 May: The men are becoming restless, but what use is a rebellion? Frémont can do nothing about it. It is raining day and night; a half cracker. 18 May: Today nothing received. 19 May: Half a cracker." Crackers are the field bread of the American soldier, also called hardtack. They are baked of wheat flour (many also mixed with bean meal) 6 inches long, 3.5 inches wide, half an inch thick, which keeps for a very long time and is quite nutritious. After the war Heusinger became an officer again in Germany, in the 92nd Regiment. In his *Amerikanische Kriegsbilder,* he often shows himself not to have been well informed, but the story above is confirmed by many others, such as Clemens Häntzschel (74th Pennsylvania Regiment), who later served as a professor in the Lutheran Church Missouri Synod.

{22} See Appendix II, pp.342–3.

{23} Peter Mühlenberg, a son of the Lutheran patriarch Heinrich Melchior Mühlenberg, was an intimate friend of Washington. At the outbreak of the Revolutionary War he took off his priestly robe and stood before his astounded congregation in the uniform of a colonel in the revolutionary army. He called to them, "Now I have given my last sermon. I am going to war, and whoever of you is a real man will come with me." And almost all the men in the congregation went to war with their former pastor.

{24} Cluseret was shot in 1871 in Paris as one of the leaders of the Commune.

{25} The five purely German regiments that participated in this campaign — the 7th, 20th, 46th, 52nd and 103rd New York, stood in different brigades. Several of these regiments were sent first to South Carolina and were only later sent to the Peninsula. The regiments that suffered the most in this campaign were the 52nd, 46th, and 20th.

{26} All of the rivers opening in Chesapeake Bay — the Potomac, the Rappahanock, the York and the James — have extraordinarily large, deep mouths that penetrate like fjords for miles into the interior.

{27} The last great battle of the Revolutionary War also took place near Yorktown under George Washington. There, in the fall of 1781, Germans fought against one another under three different flags. They stood as American patriots under Steuben and Mühlenberg, and as Frenchmen under Rochambeau (including the strong purely German regiment Deux-Ponts [Zweibrücken] and the Electoral Trier Grenadier Battalion), while in the fortress there were mercenary Hessians and Ansbachers under the English flag. In an attack on one of the two redoubts, both friend and foe were being commanded in German, and a quarter of the fighters on both sides were Germans. Neithard von Gneisenau was captured at Yorktown as an Ansbacher officer.

{28} On the march by Sigel's corps to support Banks, Schurz says: "On 8 August we left Sperryville in the afternoon and then marched through the entire night. Even this was very hot, but the day following was dreadfully close. The thermometer was high into the nineties (Fahrenheit), not a cloud in the sky, no movement of air. Dust enclosed the marching columns in thick clouds. Because we were going against the enemy, I gave command that the ranks be kept as close as possible, so that the stragglers could not leave so easily. But as the sun rose higher and the heat became intolerable, discipline loosened. The soldiers, burdened with knapsack, coat, gun and ammunition, were bathed in sweat, dragging themselves along. Where a brook or a spring were encountered, the men fell in masses on it to soak themselves. Hundreds threw away knapsacks and coats. Many remained lying by the road, exhausted. Between 4 and 5 we heard the cannons from Cedar Mountain. Two miles further and we encountered refugees from Banks' beaten army, which told us terrifying stories of a bloodbath and told us that Banks' corps was in complete dispersal." Schurz then reports that Jackson was withdrawing just as Sigel's troops placed themselves in battle order.

From this report by Schurz it may be seen that Sigel's troops could have had only a little impact if they had been led into battle after that dreadful march. Further, an attack on Jackson was not that pressing that Pope had to pass up using rested troops to do it. Pope's entire disposition for battle at Cedar Mountain show us a leader who has neither the slightest idea of scouting nor any measure of what he can trust his troops to be able to do.

The widely spread assumption that Banks attacked prematurely out of a desire for glory is contradicted by Pope's orders. Banks was not so desirous to cross swords with Jackson, but he had to do it. Pope sent Banks his own chief of staff, and he pressed for immediate attack.

{29} Sigel in fact left himself open to attack by asking which road he was to march on from Sperryville to Culpeper, when there was in fact only one road, the turnpike between the two places. To be sure another road led from Sperryville direct to Cedar Mountain, but Sigel was ordered by Pope to Culpeper. Sigel lost six hours in his request for clarification. If Sigel had arrived six hours earlier, that would have meant a considerable relief to Banks' corps, but Sigel's soldiers would not have been able to use much strength in battle after a march such as Schurz described. But Sigel's earlier arrival would perhaps have worked as a demonstration to Jackson. From the time of this episode on, the Sigel corps was always accused of slowness. To be sure Sigel started his march at Second Bull Run quite late, so that Sigel's marching order was confused by the corps following on the same road. Sigel also took along his entire train, 200 wagons, although the troops were only authorized to take along ammunition wagons. Sigel was accused of a third delay in the march to Fredericksburg, but without any reason. Sigel incidentally explained his request for further instructions by the fact that his brigadier, Milroy, arrived at a crossroads and did not know which road to take. Only then did he (Sigel) inquire which road to take. The bulk of the Sigel troops arived in Culpeper at 2 P.M., and the Battle of Cedar Mountain only began at 4 P.M.

{30} This brigade was assigned to Schurz's division for the battle. General von Steinwehr was not leading any troops. He was in the corps headquarters as Sigel's advisor and aide.

{31} Porter was accused of disobedience to Pope. The capable general was dismissed and only rehabilitated years later by another military court. Porter could not come to support Sigel because the Longstreet's Confederate corps had begun to insert itself between Porter and Sigel during the battle. Porter could not have cut through, for Longstreet, three times superior, would have fallen on his flanks in the case of such an attempt. So Porter remained in place. By doing so he prevented Longstreet's corps from intervening further in the battle against Jackson's corps, restricting Longstreet's efforts against Schenck's and Reynolds' divisions. Many volumes have been filled with the later dispute between Pope and Porter. This brief note will suffice for our purposes.

{32} These two had just arrived from the Peninsula without their artillery. McClellan wanted to retain these 14,000 men in Alexandria, using them to defend Washington in case of Pope's complete defeat. But McClellan would not have needed this plan if Pope had fallen back on fortified Centreville. That position offered the capital adequate defense.

{33} Sigel says that before Porter's charge he asked commanding General Pope to shift the attack to a more favorable location indicated by Sigel. Porter later came under cross-fire from enemy cannons. Pope rudely rejected Sigel.

{34} See the map of the environs of Gettysburg.

{35} There 11,500 prisoners, more than 70 guns, and massive supplies fell into Jackson's hands. The prisoners were paroled. The defender of this important position was the same

Colonel Miles who had done so badly as leader of the Union rear guard at First Bull Run. When Jackson approached, Miles evacuated Maryland Heights, although this position commanding Harpers Ferry would have been easy to hold. Miles raised the white flag shortly before 8 A.M. on the 15th. The Confederates did not see it at first and continued to fire. One of their shells killed Miles after the surrender had been concluded.

{36} Report of Confederate General D. H. Hill on the state of individual regiments before the Battle at Sharpsburg: 80th Virginia, 120 men; 56th Virginia, 80 men; 8th Virginia, 34 men; Hampton's Legion, 77 men; 17th South Carolina, 59 men. In Maryland Lee's army lost many deserters, pro-Union men pressed into service by the rebellion. In Virginia deserting the Confederates was almost impossible, because deserters were almost always caught and punished with grisly harshness. But in Maryland the deserters could reach safety easily. Lee only gathered 300 recruits in Maryland.

{37} That storming of the bridge has been blown up into an enormous heroic deed. Burnside became McClellan's successor largely as a result of the entirely undeserved glory he gained from it, and then he became the "butcher of Fredericksburg." Yet the Antietam could have been crossed on foot, if they had only searched for fords earlier! A ford was discovered only in the midst of firing, and Rodman's division and Ewing's brigade (IX Corps) crossed the river in this manner 300 yards from the bridge. In this way, the bridge could have been taken by encirclement if that ford had been sought earlier. (The storming cost 500 men!)

{38} German artillery particularly distinguished itself at Antietam. Major Arndt was killed. The artillery leader von Kusserow was praised before all. The Hexamer and von Putkamer batteries performed splendidly. General Max Weber was severely wounded at the head of his brigade. Of the German infantry he commanded, the 20th New York Regiment (German Turners) distinguished itself. For details see General Weber's biography.

{39} Burnside united several corps into what was called a grand division of about 40,000 men, a formation which later vanished.

{40} This regiment suffered a loss of 68 dead and 150 severely wounded in the storming. Of the twenty-eight officers, eleven fell. Almost all other officers were wounded. The Steuben Regiment also had two cannons, under the command of Captain R. Borini. This German regiment was mustered in as early as 23 April 1861, and it was the first New York regiment ready to march.

Chapter Five, pp. 198–255

{1} Jackson's black servant was an authority on the seriousness of the situation among the Confederates. When this Negro said, "My master has prayed much today," the men in the army knew that a great battle was in prospect.

{2} The Virginia Wilderness arose where the first iron works in America were built, where the flourishing community of Germanna once lay. The founder was Governor Spotswood. In 1716 he began working there. He brought in exclusively Germans. Masses of wood were needed for the ore digs, and then broad stretches of primitive forest were cleared for fields. The colony later decayed because people were enticed away by better land. German was still preached in the "Hopeful Church" in Germanna until 1810, but the last inhabitants left soon after that. The location has now vanished. The deforested district was soon covered with a thick second growth of dwarf oaks, dwarf pine and fir brushwood. Chancellorsville still lies in this wilderness. The dreadful battles of the Grant campaign of 1864 took place in the southwestern part of this Wilderness.

{3} The dispatch has the following text: To Generals Slocum and Howard: the commanding general informs you that the positioning of your corps was made only with regard for a frontal attack. For the case that the enemy should throw himself on your flank, you should investigate the terrain and consider the position you should take in such a case, so that you are prepared for any case of enemy advance. The general advises that you have strong reserves at hand to deal with every possibility. The right flank of your position does not appear to be strong enough. No entrenchments worth the name have been dug, and you also appear to be lacking troops, and those which are there are not placed in an efficient position. We have good reason to believe that the enemy is advancing toward our right flank. Send out your pickets as far as possible so that timely notice may be received on enemy advance. J. H. Allen, Brigadier General and aide-de-camp (of Hooker).

{4} It may be seen from these reports how well barracks cursing flourishes even in American (West Point) soil.

{5} From the regimental history of the 26th Wisconsin Regiment by Lieutenant Dörflinger, who lost a leg here.

{6} Dilger's horse was shot, he did not want to surrender, and he escaped the enemy only by a miracle when his faithful servant brought him a fresh horse.

{7} According to Hamlin's estimate, 4500 men were supposed to have stood in these trenches. I believe this estimate is too high, for the trenches were made for 3000 men, and the losses in Schurz' division had been very high. The right figure is certainly 3500 men.

{8} Each of Jackson's three divisions was 10,000 men strong, while most Union divisions only numbered about 4000 men.

{9} The lists of losses of the Confederates is compiled for all the days of battle. But division commander Rodes says that a considerable portion of his losses fell on the *first* day. His comrade Colston says the same. On 2 May the 12th Alabama Regiment lost seventy-six dead and wounded, the 10th Virginia Regiment fifty men. General Doles, whose brigade was in the first ranks, said, "We lost many dead and wounded there. Included were two colonels, two majors, and seven captains." These fell in a single secessionist brigade. From these partial reports of losses one may conclude that the general losses of Jackson in the fight with the XI Corps must have been very considerable, probably larger than is the case with the Union troops.

{10} A counterpart to Jackson's attack on the XI Corps is the attack the Confederate General Early made early in the morning of 19 October 1864 with 11,000 men and 43 guns at Cedar Creek in the Shenandoah Valley against three Union corps (the VI, VIII and XIX), about 30,000 men. The Union position was strongly fortified. Besides, a dispatch of the Confederate General Longstreet to Early had been captured on 16 October that spoke of an attack to happen. Despite this, Early managed to throw the three corps into complete disarray, taking 1200 captives and capturing 24 cannons! General Sheridan, who commanded the Union force, was in Winchester on 19 October on a return from Washington. At Winchester he encountered refugees of his army, spurred his horse (Sheridan's Ride), and reached the battlefield at noon. Then he gathered his demoralized troops and beat Early. With that, the humiliation of 30,000 men being overrun and beaten by 11,000 Confederates was erased and there was no need for scapegoats. But the 8500 men overrun by 30,000 rebels on 2 May 1863 defended themselves no differently than those three Union corps on 19 October 1864. And the XI Corps did not stand in deep trenches as did their comrades on Cedar Creek, which also had a threefold superiority to their enemy, while those 8500 men had a fourfold inferiority to their enemy. Despite that the battle of 19 October 1864 was also exploited against the Germans. A song in Pennsylvania Dutch dialect entitled "Schneider's Retreat" describes the flight of a German soldier who runs from Cedar Creek to Winchester to find safety. This song insulting the Germans was a hit at gatherings of Union veterans because of its supposedly humorous composition.

{11} It is repellent to review these accusations. The soldiers of the other corps (particularly the III under Sickles) mocked their unfortunate comrades of the XI. Commanding General Hooker wanted to dissolve the corps, and he was only prevented from doing so for political reasons. Many years later he still said that the Germans had run like a herd of bison. Hooker reported to Lincoln immediately after the battle that he would have won if the XI Corps had not left him in the lurch. Corps commander Howard, who was the most guilty after Hooker, confessed in the council of war on 4 May that his corps had "performed badly." The press raged against the Germans in a shameful manner. Some papers demanded that the survivors of the corps should be shot dead! Horace Greeley was of the opinion that the corps should be "decimated." In his war history, The American Conflict, appearing in 1877, Greeley said that the Schurz Division had already withdrawn ("perhaps fled is the apter word") before the enemy was in sight. Only later were there Anglo-American historians who rejected the accusations against the Germans and named the truly guilty: Hooker, Howard and Devens. So Doubleday (Scribner's collection), Bates, Dodge, Underwood, and best and most thoroughly Augustus C. Hamlin, former medical inspector of the XI Corps and a nephew of Vice President Hamlin of Maine. These writings, particularly Hamlin's work appearing in 1896, on which Schurz most relies, are used here, along with many private relations of veterans to the author.

{12} Gettysburg, once Götzburg, is an old German settlement. Even today German Lutherans have a preachers' seminary there. The remarkable phenomenon that most of the decisive battles in the East took place in old German settlement regions is repeated here, as well.

{13} As in the previous year, before the Battle on the Antietam, there were once again 10,000 men at Harpers Ferry. Halleck could not sleep peacefully unless he had 10,000 men at Harpers Ferry. Unfortunately his desire to occupy this strategically important place did not correspond to his ability to make use of that force. Those 10,000 men were always lacking from the Union army and never served any purpose.

{14} Incidentally, Lee's judgment of Meade was extraordinarily positive. To Lee, Meade took first place among his opponents, not excluding even Grant. In the Army of the Potomac, however, Meade became so unpopular that Grant had trouble with the other generals. Meade's dismissal was often considered, but the "victor of Gettysburg" was able to survive.

{15} Yet significant historical researchers, particularly the Count of Paris, later adequately recognized von Steinwehr's services in discovering the defensive position of Gettysburg.

{16} Howard refused to give over command over the two corps to General Hancock, who had been sent for this purpose to the battlefield by Meade. And General Slocum, leader of the 12th Corps, refused to accept the command to advance from Howard, because he disputed Howard's right to command.

{17} It is remarkable that the regiments of Blenker's former German Division always had to fight Jackson's troops, who were among the best in the Confederate army — first in the Shenandoah Valley, then under Sigel at Second Bull Run, then at Chancellorsville, and now once more at Gettysburg.

{18} Here Emil Frey was captured and then taken to Libby Prison, where he was placed as a hostage in the "rathole." General von Schimmelpfennig escaped capture as if through a miracle. He pulled the blouse of a fallen soldier over his general's uniform in order not to be recognized. During the retreat Schimmelpfennig received a gunbutt blow on his head. He was taken for dead, but Schimmelpfennig recovered and crept into a horsestall. There he sat starving and sick through the night of 3 to 4 July. Only once the enemy evacuated the city did the starving man reemerge.

{19} Sickles argued that this was necessary in order to deprive the enemy of a good artillery position, for the peach orchard lay rather high.

{20} Von Gilsa's brigade also received the first impact of superior forces at Chancellorsville.

{21} Pfisterer figured the losses of the Confederates at 31,621 men and asserted that only 70,000 Southern soldiers fought at Gettysburg. According to that, Lee's losses were more than a third of his men.

{22} Lee submitted his resignation to President Jefferson Davis on 8 August. It was rejected and the entire matter was treated as a state secret.

{23} During these days Grant was without telegraphic connections with Washington. Both Deming and Badeau stress how good Grant felt to be freed of Halleck's control for a brief time.

{24} This Joseph E. Johnston is not to be confused with the Confederate General A. Sidney Johnston who fell at Shiloh on 6 March 1862. Joseph Johnston was the first supreme general of the Confederacy, hence Lee's predecessor. Joseph Johnston was severely wounded in one of the seven-day battles around Richmond against McClellan, and Lee took his place. Joseph Johnston was only capable of service a year later. The strongest Confederate field army in the West in 1863 was being led by Bragg, the protégé of Jefferson Davis. We only encounter Joseph Johnston again in 1864, as the very capable opponent of Sherman on his campaign from Chattanooga to Atlanta. In the meantime, Joseph Johnston had commands of lesser importance.

{25} Pemberton was shot to death as a traitor by a secessionist hothead shortly after the capitulation of Vicksburg. Pemberton was certainly no traitor, but he was unsuited for his important position. In excuse it may be said on his behalf that he was too convinced of the impregnability of his fortress and hoped to gain glory and honor by defending it.

{26} In the many battles connected with winning the area east of Vicksburg, the German General Osterhaus particularly distinguished himself. Grant called him from Missouri in January 1863. Osterhaus was a division commander in the corps of the political general McClernand, a vain officer continually intriguing against Grant. McClernand always got on well with Lincoln, who had been a friend of his youth. McClernand was a practiced talker, and he convinced himself that he was the furnisher of brains to Grant's army. Yet he committed one stupidity after another. It was a hard task for Osterhaus to serve under such a chief and yet stand out. This German general distinguished himself particularly in the struggles along the Big Black River, where he was wounded.

{27} Colonel von Wangelin of the 12th Missouri Regiment describes this dreadful attack. Osterhaus's old Brigade, the 3rd, 12th and 17th Missouri Regiments, were with the 9th, 25th, and 31st Iowa Regiments. Wangelin criticizes the inadequate preparations for this attack. The troops had to march three miles up and down hills before they were in position. Then they had to take three positions where they were exposed to enemy fire without protection. Wangelin was of the opinion that all of these distances could have been covered at night without any loss, and that the main attack on the fortifications could have taken place at dawn. Success would have been entirely different if the men were not faced with passing through three blockades, particularly without giving the enemy the chance to count every man being used to attack them in broad daylight. As a result the enemy was able to prepare carefully, while it would have been surprised in the early morning and been attacked by completely fresh troops. The 12th Missouri Regiment went out with 350 men, of which 113 were killed or wounded. Only the 9th Iowa Regiment had heavier losses. In the attack on Vicksburg the German 37th Ohio Regiment particularly distinguished itself and suffered particularly heavy losses.

{28} This conquest formed part of the Red River Campaign, which does not lie in our area of concern.

{29} In the English-language history of the war, General Prentiss is given as the victor of Helena. Prentiss (a prisoner at Shiloh, but later exchanged) was an old friend of Lincoln. He was Salomon's superior. During the battle for Helena, Prentiss sat far from the gunfire on a gunboat on the Mississippi and watched from afar as Salomon threw back the enemy in a heroic combat. (Confederate losses were 1200 dead and wounded, Salomon's losses 143 dead and wounded.) When the enemy had been chased away, Prentiss reported and reclaimed the victory as his own. All the officers who participated in the battle signed a statement that declared that Salomon (who had also built the fort) had led the battle autonomously. But Grant did not permit this statement to reach Lincoln. Grant harbored an old hatred for the Salomon brothers. Before the Civil War, Grant (then an entirely unknown man) ran for county surveyor in St. Louis. Eberhard Salomon, brother of Friedrich, was his opponent and was elected. Grant never got over being defeated by a German. In his dictated memoirs, the ex-president still speaks of that political defeat from his youth. Perhaps Grant confused the victor of Helena with Eberhard Salomon and for that reason allowed the protest of Friedrich Salomon's officers to end up in the waste basket.

{30} Vicksburg could have been taken much earlier and with many fewer victims if the strong and able army of Rosecrans had been able to participate, even if it had only hindered Johnston and Pemberton from getting reinforcements from Bragg. The main part of Johnston's army sent to relieve Vicksburg consisted of troops taken from Bragg's army. But so long as Rosecrans had no cavalry, he could not move against Bragg or Johnston, because his supply lines were continually disrupted and interrupted by the enemy cavalry. Thus Halleck's arbitrary withholding of every reinforcement of cavalry for Rosecrans considerably delayed the operation against Vicksburg and compelled Rosecrans to inaction.

{31} On 1 March 1863 the position of a major general in the regular army had become free. At once Halleck wrote similar letters to Grant and to Rosecrans in which he offered each of them that position as a reward to the first who would win a decisive victory. That sounds almost like rewards offered to a schoolboy for bringing home good grades. Grant laid the letter aside in his papers and did not answer it. Rosecrans, however, wrote to Halleck on 6 March that he felt deeply offended as an officer and a citizen by such an offer of positions of honor. "Is there among us one general who was fighting for his personal advantage and not for the honor of his country? Such an officer would only attract to himself the contempt of all men of honor." This letter probably counted more for the later dismissal of Rosecrans than did the defeat of Chickamauga. (See the letter in Cist, *Army of the Cumberland*, p. 150.)

{32} Hooker was the cause of the humiliation of Chancellorsville, and Burnside had sent thousands of blue youth to the slaughter. Halleck sent two of his least capable high officers to the West.

{33} Certainly it would have been better to send the whole of Grant's army to Chattanooga after the conquest of Vicksburg, but Halleck's demonstration campaign on the Red River, in the distant Southwest, also claimed a part of Grant's powers. Here one could object that the campaign planned by Grant against Mobile would also have wasted these and other forces. But the pursuit of the Grant project would have hindered a large part of the Confederate army from helping at Chickamauga and Chattanooga.

{34} Rosecrans thought (certainly correctly) that the problems of a siege would be even greater. West of Chattanooga lay Walling's Ridge, an unpopulated and entirely wild mountain of stone that was entirely unpassable for provision trains. He did not dare to submit his 60,000 men to the danger of being starved to death between a hostile fortification and that mountain.

{35} It was on this march that the brigade of the German General Willich distinguished itself splendidly by conquering Liberty Pass and Hoover's Pass in the South Appalachians. The advance of the 32nd Indiana Regiment, directed by Prussian trumpet signals, stimulated the general amazement of Anglo-American officers.

{36} This is the same Alexander McDowell McCook (brother of the first colonel of the German 9th Ohio Regiment) who brought Rosecrans into such a bad position in the Battle of Stones River and who sent no report to Buell, then his superior, about the attack on McCook's Corps by Bragg at the Battle of Perryville, so that Buell was unable to send McCook reinforcements. McCook was dismissed after the Battle of Chickamauga.

{37} See Appendix II, p. 344.

{38} The von Steinwehr Division especially distinguished itself in this fight. On this Deming, Grant's biographer, writes on p. 305, that the "bayonet attack of Howard's [Steinwehr's] troops, leading up a steep and difficult hill (height of 200 feet) by which the enemy was completely thrown out of its barricades, was one of the most splendid pieces of bravery of the Northern army in the entire Civil War." This was Steinwehr's best deed as a leader of troops. He had worked as a staff officer. Schurz's division had particularly good luck in this night battle. As a result of the noise of battle, their mules became alarmed and ran, several hundred compacted animals in a blind rush, directly into the ranks of the approaching enemy, who thought they were dealing with a cavalry attack. In his report on this encounter, General Hooker severely reprimanded brigade commander Friedrich Hecker because he remained in place rather than advancing. Hecker led a brigade in Schurz's division. This criticism of Hecker was actually aimed at Schurz. Hooker wanted to irritate Schurz because

Schurz had so severely criticized Hooker's negligence on 2 May in Chancellorsville. But Schurz took Hecker's part, noting that Hecker did not advance as a result of a special command of the commanding general. Schurz and Hecker were totally justified and Hooker was wrong. Schurz was also able to give proof to the court martial that Hooker was not very precise with the truth when he was tripping up a comrade. In his later attempt to excuse himself using false information (after the Battle of Kennesaw Mountain in Georgia), Hooker fell into similar trouble with Sherman. Sherman, however, had the power not only to unmask Hooker, but also to punish him. Hooker was then dismissed by Sherman in the summer of 1864.

{39} Pollard, the historian of the Confederacy, asserts that this plan came from Davis alone, and that the Confederate generals tried to dissuade him. Pollard portrays President Davis on this occasion as a bungler in military matters. Davis destroyed several of the best plans of his generals. Davis always suffered from a lust for glory, and he feared that history would not name him in the first place if the Confederacy triumphed.

{40} The troops suffered dreadfully as a result of the cold nights, following daytime rain. The roads were in awful shape, food was poor, and the hungry soldiers could not forage because most of the residents of the area were pro-Union.

{41} During this fighting Schurz's division of the XI Corps stood as a reserve behind the attacking Wood's division. Schurz himself tells us that even a free spirit such as his own could be possessed by premonitions. On the morning of 23 November Schurz had the unshakable feeling that he would fall on this day. It was only with difficulty that he overcame the need to write letters of farewell to his wife and children. In the afternoon his division stood at Orchard Nob awaiting orders. There they were bombarded by a hidden enemy battery. A shell landed under Schurz's horse, and the horse of an adjutant standing behind Schurz had its thigh shattered. But the shot rolled farther and then exploded ineffectually about twenty yards behind. It was only in this instant that Schurz's premonitions of death ceased.

{42} On Osterhaus, General W. T. Sherman said, "I left one of my best divisions, that of Osterhaus, to act with Hooker, and I know it has served the country well and reflected honor to the Army of the Tennessee."

{43} A German officer, Major Hipp of the 37th Ohio Regiment, made it possible for Sherman's corps to cross the raging Tennessee River. He brought about a hundred barges which had been gathered in Chickamauga Creek, into the Tennessee and sent these vessels down the main stream in the dark of night. He sought a landing place on the opposite, enemy shore, overcame the Confederate posts located there, and took them prisoner. Then he crossed the river and tried to report to Sherman. It was totally dark. Hipp cried out, "Where in the h— is General Sherman?" Sherman came by, took off his hat to Hipp and thanked him. Hipp improvised a pontoon bridge with the barges, and Sherman's corps took its position over this. Hipp's deed was combined with great perils, for he had only a few men with him and had to advance rather deeply behind enemy lines. (From the *Geschichte des 37. Ohio-Regiments.*)

{44} Sheridan tells the same story about his division as Willich reports on the situation of his own brigade. It is quite possible that both are right, and that both recognized at the same instant that they could not hesitate even if the command demanded that they stand still. Sheridan and Willich were not just brave chargers but also capable military men who quickly saw the advantages of their new situation and knew how to act on their own.

{45} Sheridan tells in his memoirs how the German Colonel Conrad saved his life during that attack. Sheridan was not one of the generals who climbed down from his horse in attacks and followed his men on foot. He rode up close to the enemy breastwork at the top of the mountain. In this instant Conrad lept on him and demanded that Sheridan get down from his horse and not expose himself further. Sheridan obeyed, but then Conrad fell severely wounded at his side.

{46} Of the German officers who particularly distinguished themselves in these battles, besides those already mentioned, there are others to be mentioned: Colonel Arnold Sauermeister, who led an artillery brigade in which the German batteries of Zickerick, Schulz, Fröhlich, Landgräber and Grosskopf fought; infantry Colonel Deimling, who led the 2nd Brigade of Smith's division after Raum's wounding; von Blessing of the 37th Ohio and Kämmerling of the 9th Ohio (both purely German regiments); Dickermann of the 103rd Illinois; Neumann of the 3rd Missouri (Sigel's first German regiment); Cramer of the German 17th Missouri (Turner) Regiment; Seidel of the 3rd Ohio; Lochner of the 79th Pennsylvania; Cimber of the 109th Pennsylvania; von Hammerstein of the 78th New York; von Baumbach of the 24th Wisconsin; Beck of the 2nd Missouri; Krüger of the 7th Ohio; and Yager of the 121st Ohio. The German brigade commander, Matthies of Iowa, was severely wounded.

{47} To be sure, Sheridan pressed after the fleeing enemy immediately after the taking of Missionary Ridge, and he wanted to destroy the railroad bridge over the Chickamauga. He asked for the support of his current corps commander, Granger. But this gentleman belonged to the people who are always satisfied with one success. Granger believed that his soldiers were too tired, and although Sheridan pressed on past midnight and asked repeatedly for support, Granger did not stir himself. Sheridan's completely exhausted soldiers could not take the gamble alone, and the greater part of Bragg's beaten army escaped over that bridge.

{48} Captain Kircher lay severely wounded on the field. His true friend Captain Kessler from Belleville (Wangelin's adjutant) rushed up to drag his friend out of the firing line. There Kessler was shot dead. Besides his shattered arm, Kircher also lost a leg.

{49} A letter by Grant to General Sherman, dated 14 April 1864, reads as follows: "From the expedition of the Department of West Virginia (Sigel) I do not calculate on very great results, but it is the only way I can take troops from there. With the long leg of railroad Sigel has to protect, he can spare no troops except to move directly to his front. In this way he must get through to inflict great damage to the enemy, or the enemy must detach himself from one of his armies a large force to prevent it. In other words, if Sigel himself can't skin he can hold a leg while some one else skins."

{50} The 28th Ohio Regiment was purely German. It originated in Cincinnati and had been organized by Colonel Moor. It was being led on 15 May by Colonel Gottfried Becker. The 116th Ohio also had a very strong German flavor. Both regiments were war-tested and had taken an honorable part in many battles.

{51} Imboden also reports that a part of the Northern cavalry later made an attack on McLaughlin's Confederate battery, which attack was thrown back with canister shot. Sigel does not say a word about the participation of the cavalry.

{52} It is remarkable that Imboden does not mention that Sigel's infantry behind the battery (the 18th Connecticut and 123rd Ohio Regiments) participated in the defense of the guns.

{53} One would think from Imboden's portrayal that all six of von Kleyser's guns were captured, but Sigel says that only two of these cannons fell into enemy hands.

{54} That is at least to be hoped, but neither Imboden nor Sigel says anything about it. Sigel praises only his troops in Thoburn's brigade, and he says nothing about Moor's two regiments, which stood on the left wing.

{55} That is Sigel's only remark about the defeat of his left wing.

{56} Incidentally, General Grant himself later regretted having fought this battle.

{57} Von Freitag-Loringhofen, major in the German Great General Staff, certainly not a partisan judge, values the services of General Sherman much higher than those of Grant. He says of the latter, "General Grant had at his disposal almost unlimited personnel and materiel, and he applied them more with brutal force than with intelligence. Given a mission similar to that of Lee, Grant would undoubtedly have failed, and all attempts to present Grant as a great commander appear inadequate." (*Studien über Kriegführung*, III, Berlin: Mittler & Sohn, 1903).

{58} Once the secessionists destroyed a railroad tunnel along Sherman's line of march, but it was back in use on the very next day. Johnston, who could observe the work of the enemy engineers, is supposed to have shouted, "I believe this devil of a fellow Sherman carries his own tunnels in his supply train!"

{59} It is in the moves of Thomas's and Schofield's corps separated from Sherman's main army that we properly see the enormous scale of Sherman's operations. Sherman sent his two subordinate generals to central Tennessee, more than 250 miles to the northwest, in order to defeat their opponent Hood, who had reappeared there. After Thomas had accomplished that, Schofield made a 1000-mile journey to the east in the spring of 1865 to bring reinforcements of 30,000 men at Goldsboro in distant North Carolina, where Sherman was marching! Here at last is a grandiose control of war, which is able to overcome all difficulties and move parts of armies separated by distances of up to a thousand miles as if they were chess pieces and arranging their successful reunification.

{60} [This is an old hostile rumor, based on his arrest in a traveling cloak. –Ed.]

Appendix I, pp. 256–337

{1} [He was actually enlisted with Heinrich Börnstein's 2nd Missouri Regiment, soon becoming major commanding the rifle battalion.]

{2} The German-American historical researcher Emil Mannhart says that the enemy gave Osterhaus the nickname, "The American Bayard." Certainly this is both an honorable and a proper title, for indeed Osterhaus was a "knight without fear and without reproach."

{3} [Ringgold is in Georgia. –Ed.]

{4} Sigel had almost no role in this entire matter. He was much more manipulated than he was the manipulator. This dreamer never understood practical politics and its demands. Incidentally, Sigel owed his his naming both as a brigadier general and as major general essentially to the Forty-Eighters.

{5} Despite that, Halleck caused trouble enough in the West as well.

{6} To prove this assertion, there is the three-quarter-hour heroic struggle of Buschbeck on that day. Now imagine the entire XI Corps positioned behind ditches on the open area of Hawkin's Farm, where artillery could be used, that is, according to the plan proposed by Schurz. No one would say that Sigel would have ignored the advantages of such a plan. Only an ignoramus such as the West Pointer Howard could have turned Schurz away when he revealed this plan of defense. Incidentally, von Steinwehr also approved this plan and carried it out as well as he could, for the trenches in which Buschbeck fought had been made by Steinwehr.

{7} Sigel remained a bad-luck bird all his life. Good fortune smiled on him several times in later years, but there always followed a great mountain of misfortune. We recall his later political career in New York. How envied was he for the profitable offices that fell to him! And what did this profit the regrettable Sigel? Others would have earned a fortune from them. Sigel, however, suffered more than he ever had on the Potomac. He returned to private life almost impoverished and broken in body and soul. The details do not need to be mentioned here, they are well known to many. Sigel remained through all of this the man of honor he had always been. The fact that he was not suited for these offices lay in his peculiar predispositions, as well as his education.

{8} To say nothing of the many other political generals!

{9} Information to the author by the adjutant in question, Dr. J. Max Müller. Müller was adjutant on the staff of von Steinwehr's division.

{10} The Army of the Potomac always looked on itself as a sort of elite guard, and many of the officers serving in this army looked down on the Western army as a sort of organized mob. This view is derived from the fact that the goal of the Army of the Potomac was always the conquest of the rebel capital, Richmond, as well as the fact that the Army of the Potomac always fought the most significant opposition leaders, Lee and Jackson, and the best troops of the South.

{11} The strongest argument against Sigel was that he arrived in Springfield, in flight from Wilson's Creek, before his beaten troops. The fact that this derived from a particular accident was not known. The facts made a very poor impression. It was asserted that Sigel had left his troops in the lurch and had fled by himself. See the chapter on Wilson's Creek.

{12} To be sure Sigel left himself open to complaint at Carthage, as well as on his retreat to Rolla. In those actions he sought to combine his German idealism with his military duties. When he should have been holding together every man of his little brigade at Carthage to be able to deal with three enemy units approaching him, he detached Conrad's company to Neosho to protect the few Union loyalists of that little town. That was almost a tenth of his entire manpower. Conrad was captured by McCulloch on the same day in which Sigel encountered the Confederates under Jackson near Carthage. Detaching Conrad was certainly wrong by military standards. It was almost very rash on the part of Sigel to take along several hundred refugees together with their wagons, household items, cattle, women, children and dependents on his great retreat from Springfield to Rolla. This considerably delayed the march. The line was considerably extended, and the troops were in no position to provide adequate defense if they had been attacked by the enemy's numerous cavalry on this 129 mile-long retreat over mountains and poor roads. Fortunately this did not happen, but from a military standpoint bringing along those dependents could not be defended. In carrying out military missions, the good-heartedness of the leader should not play a role. The West Pointers only judged Sigel's efforts in these actions according to such principles. They had no idea how to deal with a dreamer and an idealist. And it must be admitted that emotion is a poor adviser to a soldier.

{13} Certainly these are externalites, but such things often play a large role in the military.

{14} After Sigel's second defeat at New Market, Virginia, Lexow wrote the following in the *New Yorker Kriminalzeitung,* 27 May 1864: "Earlier it was his [Sigel's] friends who brought his military career to an untimely end through their tactlessness, but now it is his enemies who bring him down." Incidentally, Lexow was one of Sigel's most overzealous friends, and if these friends committed any acts of tactlessness, then Lexow in particular was part of it.

{15} These disputes quickly subsided into good will.

{16} See Appendix II, pp. 344–5, "Sigel, Schurz, Stahel and Lincoln."

{17} Willich was a friend and zealous supporter of Karl Marx. Marx later made fun of him. He called Willich a "temperamental communist" and the "knight of the noble conscience."

{18} The war cry still played a great role in the Civil War, the last great fight with the old weapons. The firearms did not reach far, and the fighters were often very close to one another. The secessionists used a shrill, high, penetrating cry on attack ("the rebel yell"). The Union army shouted "Hurra."

{19} [Actually, Flusser was killed but his boat and crew survived by flight. –Ed.]

{20} [Hecker died in Summerfield, Illinois, a farming community several miles from Belleville.]

 • {21} Chandler recommended Wilder's immediate replacement and the naming of a new commandant, "who would unite energy with healthy judgment as well as concern for the welfare and the comfort of the mass of unfortunates entrusted to him, so far as that may be brought into harmony with measures to secure the prisoners" Chandler told Wilder that far better sanitary measures could be used, to which Wilder responded with a terrifying brutality. "It would be better that half the prisoners died so that one did not have to care for them." That is repeated in the official report of a Confederate official to the Confederate commandant of prisons!

{22} There were many brutal or degenerate fellows among the prisoners. A band of murderers and thieves had formed which robbed their own comrades and murdered a number of them. A court was set up by the prisoners themselves, with Wirz's approval, and raised an accusation against 200 comrades. This court found six of those accused guilty of murder in the first degree. and they were hanged in prison by their comrades. About fifty others had to run the gauntlet through the prisoners with whipping rods.

{23} On the treatment of prisoners, see Appendix II, pp. 345–6.

Appendix II, pp. 337–346

{1} The lower house of Congress passed a law in 1910 to increase the war pensions from about $160 million to more than $200 million. On 31 October 1910, 555,481 Civil War veterans were eligible for pensions. The pension is paid to every veteran, whether he needs it or not.

{2} [Regarding Lederer, see Don Heinrich Tolzmann, ed., *The First Germans in America, With A Biographical Directory of New York Germans.* Bowie, MD: Heritage Books, Inc., 1992.–Ed.].

{3} [For references to the Germans in Kentucky, see Don Heinrich Tolzmann, *Catalog of the German-Americana Collection, University of Cincinnati.* Muenchen: K.G. Saur, 1990–Ed.].

{4} [It is not widely known that the first protest against slavery was issued at Germantown, Pennsylvania in 1688, which was well more than a century and a half before the Civil War.–Ed.]

{5} [For references to these pre-1683 Germans, see Don Heinrich Tolzmann, ed., *Germany and America, 1450-1700: Julius Friedrich Sachse's History of the German Role in the Discovery, Exploration, and Settlement of the New World.* Bowie, MD: Heritage Books, Inc., 1991.–Ed.]

{6} [An historical marker was erected in 1997 at Jamestown, Virginia, in honor of the arrival of the first German settlers in America in 1608.–Ed.]

{7} [See Don Heinrich Tolzmann, ed., *The First Description of Ohio and other Ohio Settlements: The Travel Report of Johann Heckewelder, 1792.* Lanham, MD: University Press of America, 1988.–Ed.]

{8} [For a general introduction to the Pennsylvania Germans, see Don Heinrich Tolzmann, ed., *The Pennsylvania Germans: Jesse Leonard Rosenberger's Sketch of Their History and Life.* Bowie, MD: Heritage Books, Inc., 1998.–Ed.]

{9} [The history of the Virginia Germans can be found in Don Heinrich Tolzmann, ed., *The German Element in Virginia: Herrmann Schuricht's History.* Bowie, MD: Heritage Books, Inc., 1993.–Ed.]

{10} [It should be noted that the first attack on New Ulm took place on 19 August 1862, and that the second battle was on the 24th.–Ed.]

{11} [For further information, see Don Heinrich Tolzmann, ed., *The Sioux Uprising in Minnesota, 1862: Jacob Nix's Eyewitness History.* Indianapolis: Max Kade German-American Center, Indiana University-Purdue University, 1994.–Ed.]

{12} [For a work considered the "classic" biography of Custer, see Don Heinrich Tolzmann, ed., *Custer: Frederick Whittaker's Complete Life of General George A. Custer, Major General of Volunteers, Brevet Major U.S. Army and Lieutenant-Colonel Seventh U.S. Cavalry.* Bowie, MD: Heritage Books, Inc., 1993.–Ed.]

{13} [See Don Heinrich Tolzmann, ed., *New Ulm in Word and Picture: J.H. Strasser's History of a German-American Settlement, 1892.* Indianapolis: Max Kade German-American Center, Indiana University-Purdue University, 1997.–Ed.]

{14} [For a history of this regiment, see Frederic Trautmann, ed., *We Were the Ninth: A History of the Ninth Regiment, Ohio Volunteer Infantry, April 17, 1861, to June 7, 1864, by Constantin Grebner.* Kent: Kent State University Press, 1987.–Ed.]

{15} [Regarding Sigel, see Don Heinrich Tolzmann, ed., *German Achievements in America: Rudolf Cronau's Survey History.* Bowie, MD: Heritage Books, Inc., 1995.–Ed.]

Index

Galveston, Texas, 333
Gaines Mill, 178
Garfield, Pres. James, 228
Garibaldi Regiment, *39th New York*, 97, 104, 172, 173, 362n2
Geary, John White, 203, 211, 232–4
Geiger, Col. W. F., 221
Gellmann, Col. Frederick, 97, 104, 290
von Gerber, Gustav, 107, 161, 290
Gerhard, Col., *46th NY Regt.*, 104
Gerhardt, Joseph, 197, 290–1
German Revolution, *1848–9*, 63, 68
Gerson, Capt., Otto, 291
Gerster, Capt., *German pioneer unit*, 364n13
Gettysburg, *battle of*, 213–20, *maps* 214, 217, 220; 242, 277, 279, 281, 282, 285, 286, 288, 290, 291, 293, 294, 295, 297, 298, 299, 304, 306, 308, 309, 311, 312, 313, 314, 317, 319, 321, 323, 326, 329, 330, 331, 342, 374n12
Gibbon, John, 189
Giesler, Capt. Julius, 291
Gilbert, Charles Champion, 164
von Gilsa, Leopold, 97, 104, 173, 180, 199, 203, 205, 206, 207, 211, 216, *map* 217; 218, 268, 284, 291–2, 375n20
Glanz, Col. Charles, 292
Gnadenhütten, 341
Göbel, Gert, 111, 114, 365n17
Goebel, Lt. Col. F., 292
Gollmer, Hugo, 292
Gölzer, Lt. Col. August, 292
Gordon, William E., 292
Gould, Dr. A. B., *statistics quoted*, 70–6; 82, 104, 357n17
Grant, Ulysses S., 48, 52, 110, 115, 148, 153, 154, 155, 156, *quoted* 157, 159, 162, 197, 221, 222, 223, 224, 225, 228, 229, 230, 232, 233, 234, 235, 236, 242, 243, *campaign of 1864 map* 244; 245–9, 253, 254, 255, 258, 259, 267, 273, 286, 293, 301, 306, 324, 332
grays, 63
Grebe, Capt. Wilhelm, 292
Grebner, Konstantin, 292
Greusel, Col. Nikolas, 107, 166, 292
Grimm, Franz, 292
Grimm, Lt. Joseph, 282
Grose, William, 232, 233
Grosskopf, Edward, 293, 379n46
Grover's Division, 186
Groveton, *battle of*, 184, 186
Grumbach, Nikolaus, 293
Grünhut, Capt. Joseph B., 293
Gülich, Theodor, 293
Gumbart, Battery Chief, *2nd Illinois Artillery Regt.*, 107

von Haake, Count, 293
Haas, Capt. Max A. F., 293
Hahn, Michael, *wartime gov. of Louisiana, 1864*, 293
Halleck, Henry, 41, 48, 99, 117, 122, 137, 144, *Sigel and Halleck* 145–8; 153, 155, 162, 163, 164, 179, 195, 215, 224, 225, 228, 243, 262, 263, 264, 265, 266, 307, 317
Hambach, *uprising of 1830s in Germany*, 63

Hamlin, Augustin, *quoted* 198; 199, 206, 208, 271, 284, 373n7
Hammer, Dr. Adam, 293
von Hammerstein, Maj, in McClellan's staff, 99, 294, 379n46
Hampton, *led Ohio battery*, 180
Hancock, Winfield Scott, 206, 229, 245, 247, 288, 297
Harhaus, Col. Otto, 294
Harney, Gen. William A., 113, 116
Harper's Weekly, 300, 312
Harpers Ferry, 45, 190, 191, 192, 215, 247, 327
Harrington, *led brigade and killed*, 166
Hartmann, Lt. Col., *in Steinwehr's 29th Regt.*, 294
Hartmann, Dr. Karl A., 282
Hartmann, Lt. Col. L., 282, 294
von Hartung, Adolf, 294
Haring, Dr. Theodor, 294
Hassaurek, Fritz, 308
Hassendeubel, Franz, 77, 99, 222, 275, 294–5
Haupt, Hermann, 77, 295
von Hausen, Dr. Julius, 295
Hauschield, Lt., *75th Pennsylvania Regt.*, 295
Hecker, Friedrich, 107, 111, 119, 208, 231, 249, 288, 293, 295, 317, 319, 329
Heckermann, *led artillery battery*, 199
Heckmann, *led artillery battery*, 180
Hedterich, Col. C. B., 295–6
Heg, Col. Hans C., 296
Heiland, Dr. *surgeon of 20th NY (Turner) Regt.*, 296
Heiler, Lt. D., 282
Heine, Wilhelm, 104, 286, 296
Heintz, Capt. Karl, 296
Heintzelmann, Samuel Peter, 182, 190, 274 182, 190, 274
Helmreich, *of Missouri 4th Cavalry Regt.*, 106
von Hellmerich, Col., *of Missouri Cavalry Regt.*, 296
von Hencke, Theodor W., 296
Henkel, William, 180, 296
Henning von Minden, Maj. *in Minnesota cavalry unit*, 296
Henninghausen, L. P., 287, 296–7
Henningsen, Karl Friedrich, CSA, 333
Henry, Fort, 153, *map Forts Henry and Donelson* 154; 155
Hertzberg, Dr., *editor San Antonio Deuthsche Zeitung* 297
Hertzberg, *Battery Chief 2nd Wisconsin Artillery Regt.*, 297
Heth, Henry, CSA, 215
Heusinger, Otto, 297, 320
Hexamer, William, 99, 105, 297
Hickenlooper Battery, 162
Hildebrand, *brigade leader at Shiloh*, 161
Hildebrandt, Maj., *39th NY Regt.*, 284, 297
Hilgard, Theodore and Edward, 77, 278
Hilgard, Heinrich (*see Villard*), 278, 324
Hill, A. P., CSA, 192, 194
Hill, D. H., CSA, 190, 192, 372n36
Hillgartner, Dr. Georg, 297
Hindman, Gen. Thomas, CSA, 149
Hipp, Maj. Karl, 297, 378–9n43

388
INDEX

Takashi Nakamura† and Ken-ichi Oohara‡
†Yukawa Institute for Theoretical Physics, Kyoto University, Kyoto 606, Japan; and ‡National Laboratory for High Energy Physics, Oko, Tsukuba-shi, Ibaraki-ken 305, Japan

Coalescing Binary Neutron Stars

1. INTRODUCTION

There are several motivations for the study of coalescing binary neutron stars. One is the real existence of binary neutron stars. In particular, PSR 1913+16 has been observed precisely and it is believed to consist of two neutron stars of mass $1.445 M_\odot$ and $1.384 M_\odot$. [1] Very recently two more binary neutron stars, PSR 2127+11C and PSR 1534+12, have been discovered. Orbital parameters of these binary neutron stars are very similar to those of PSR 1913+16. Moreover the total masses are almost the same in these three systems, $\sim 2.8 M_\odot$. It seems that the six neutron stars in these three binaries have almost the same mass, $\sim 1.4 M_\odot$. Therefore the two neutron stars in each of the systems PSR 1913+16, PSR 2127+11C, and PSR 1534+12 will coalesce in $\sim 10^8$yr because of the emission of gravitational waves. Using these new data we can follow the argument by Clarke, van den Heuvel, and W. Sutantyo [2] to estimate the event rate of binary coalescence. Because the time before coalescence is much smaller than the age of the universe, we can reasonably assume the steady state between the formation and coalescence of the binary neutron stars. Depending on the Type II supernova rate, the frequency of coalescence of binary neutron stars is estimated as 6–60 events/yr $(d/100 \text{ Mpc})^3$ within the distance d Mpc. If we can observe coalescence events by gravitational waves and electromagnetic wave such as

γ-rays, we may have important information on the equation of state, the structure of neutron stars, and physics in strong gravity, including black hole physics.

Another kind of coalescence of neutron stars is theoretically expected to occur.[3] If the core of the progenitor of a Type II supernova has a large angular momentum, the centrifugal force will be important in some stage of the collapse into a final neutron star. The core radius where the centrifugal force is comparable to the gravitational force is proportional to the square of the angular momentum. When the size of the core decreases to this radius, the core contracts principally along the rotational axis, and a thin disk is formed. Such a thin disk is known to be gravitationally unstable irrespective of the equation of state [4] and fragments into several pieces in a free fall time scale. Each fragment looks like a neutron star and is called a proto–neutron star. Proto–neutron stars will coalesce again to form a single neutron star owing to the emission of gravitational waves. If the number of fragments is two, the system is essentially the same as a binary neutron star like PSR 1913+16 in the final coalescence stage. If this scenario applies to a large fraction of Type II supernovae, the frequency of events of burst emission of gravitational waves within 10 Mpc increases to $\sim$30 events/yr.

The third possibility is the accretion-induced collapse (AIC) of white dwarfs leading to the formation of neutron stars. AIC has been considered as the possible formation mechanism of neutron stars in low mass X-ray binaries as well as millisecond pulsars in globular clusters. If this occurs, the collapsing white dwarfs should have the angular momentum of the accreting matter. This situation is different from that in Type II supernovae. In Type II supernovae the collapse may be spherically symmetric. However, in AIC the collapse should be more or less nonspherical due to the angular momentum of the accreted matter. In reality depending on the strength of the magnetic field of the white dwarf and the accretion rate, the angular momentum of AIC can be so large that the scenario discussed in the previous paragraph may occur.

To know the final destiny of the coalescing binary neutron stars we must use a fully general relativistic 3D numerical code including the evolution of matter and metric. However, such a code does not exist at present. We therefore use a Newtonian 3D hydrodynamics code to asseses the final destiny of coalescing binary neutron sta as well as the wave pattern and the amplitude of the gravitational waves.

Since all the results in this paper are based on four of our previous papers,[5-8] one can refer to the original papers for details.

2. BASIC EQUATIONS AND NUMERICAL METHODS

In the early version of our simulations we used a Burke and Thorne type radiation reaction potential expressed by the fifth time derivative of the quadrupole moment.[5] However, here we use a radiation reaction potential proposed by Blanchet, Damour,

and Schäfer[5] in which only the third time derivative of the quadrupole moment is used. The basic equations are

$$\frac{\partial \rho}{\partial t} + \frac{\partial \rho v^j}{\partial x^j} = 0, \tag{2.1}$$

$$\frac{\partial \rho w^i}{\partial t} + \frac{\partial \rho w^i v^j}{\partial x^j} = -\frac{\partial P}{\partial x^i} - \rho \frac{\partial(\psi + \psi_{react})}{\partial x^i}, \tag{2.2}$$

$$\frac{\partial \rho \varepsilon}{\partial t} + \frac{\partial \rho \varepsilon v^j}{\partial x^j} = -P \frac{\partial v^j}{\partial x^j}, \tag{2.3}$$

$$P = (\gamma - 1)\rho \varepsilon \tag{2.4}$$

$$\Delta \psi = 4\pi G \rho, \tag{2.5}$$

$$\Delta R = 4\pi G \left(\frac{d^3}{dt^3} D_{ij} \right) x^i \frac{\partial \rho}{\partial x^j}, \tag{2.6}$$

$$v^i = w^i + 0.8 \frac{G}{c^5} \left(\frac{d^3}{dt^3} D_{ij} \right) w^j, \tag{2.7}$$

$$\psi_{react} = 0.4G \left[-R + \left(\frac{d^3}{dt^3} D_{ij} \right) x^i \frac{\partial \psi}{\partial x^j} \right], \tag{2.8}$$

and

$$D_{ij} = \int \rho \left(x^i x^j - \frac{1}{3} \delta_{ij} r^2 \right) dV,$$

where all the variables except w^i have the usual meanings. In the original formalism by Blanchet, Damour, and Schäfer,[9] 1PN and 2.5PN quantities should be evaluated. However, for this we must solve nine Poisson equations, which is numerically highly time-consuming. Therefore in this paper we evaluate only terms which are directly connected with radiation reaction. In this case we need to solve only three Poisson equations.

We take the units of

$$M = M_\odot, \quad L = \frac{GM_\odot}{c^2} = 1.5 \text{ km}, \quad T = \frac{GM_\odot}{c^3} = 5 \times 10^{-6} \text{ s.} \tag{2.9}$$

To express a hard equation of state, we use a polytropic equation of state with $\gamma = 2$. Then the pressure is expressed by

$$P = K\rho^2, \tag{2.10}$$

where K is a constant which is related to the radius of the spherical star as

$$K = \frac{2r_0^2 G}{\pi}. \tag{2.11}$$

We assume that each neutron is rigidly rotating around the z-axis with the angular velocity Ω. Then the equilibrium is determined by

$$\nabla \left[\psi + h - 0.5(x^2 + y^2)\Omega^2\right] = 0, \tag{2.12}$$

and

$$\triangle \psi = 4\pi G\rho, \tag{2.13}$$

where

$$h = 2K\rho.$$

The integral of Eq. (2.12) becomes

$$\psi + h - 0.5(x^2 + y^2)\Omega^2 = C. \tag{2.14}$$

The solution to the above equation can be obtained by the iteration shown in Ref. 7.

We will estimate the amount of gravitational radiation emitted using the quadrupole formula. Details of how to evaluate the third time derivative of the quadrupole moment without using the numerical time difference are given in Ref. 6.

A numerical scheme for hydrodynamics equations is given in Ref. 5. We solve three Poisson equations as Eqs. (2.5) and (2.6) by an ICCG method described in Oohara and Nakamura[6] under appropriate boundary conditions.

3. RESULTS

We take a $141 \times 141 \times 130$ grid under the assumption of the reflection symmetry about $z = 0$ plane. The grids cover $[-21, 21]$ in x and y directions and $[0, 16.9]$ in the z direction. We have performed eight simulations so far. In the conference we showed the results in a video. However, it is hard to present them in the proceedings. Here we show two typical ones called model EQ8 and TIDAL2. A typical CPU time needed to perform one model is ~ 240 hours with $\sim 90,000$ time steps. Thus a typical CPU time per 1 step is about 10 seconds by HITAC S820/80 with 3 GFLOPS peak speed. We performed the numerical calculation for each model until $t = 600$–1000 in our units.

In the case of two point-mass binaries of mass m_1 and m_2 with separation r in a circular orbit, r decreases at a rate given by

$$\dot{r} = -\frac{64 m_1 m_2 (m_1 + m_2)}{5 r^3}. \tag{3.1}$$

Inserting $r = 2r_0$, $m_1 = m_2 = 1.49$, we have $\dot{r} = -0.086$. In the model EQ8, we put the approaching velocity of each neutron star at $t = 0$. Namely for $x \geq 0$, $w_x = -0.08$ and for $x \leq 0$, $w_x = 0.08$. We show the evolution of the density contours for EQ8 in Fig. 1A–P. In EQ8 the coalescence is initiated not only by the radiation

reaction but also by the approaching velocity 0.08 at $t = 0$ since $\tau_{loss} \sim 100$ is comparable to r_0/w_x, where τ_{loss} is the time scale for 10% loss of the total angular momentum. Therefore the luminosity is not constant even at $t \leq 100$. Spiral arms can be seen (Fig. 1C–H). Two neutron stars appear again after the coalescence (Fig. 1F–H). The reason is as follows: When the coalescence proceeds and the core shrinks, the centrifugal force increases against the gravity. Then the core expands up to the reappearance of the original two neutron stars. However, in EQ8 after appearance of the two neutron stars, we have a quasi-steady binary-like system in the central part (Fig. 1I and J). Due to the angular momentum loss, the binaries coalesce very slowly in Fig. 1K. Finally the central binary becomes the ring-like system seen in Fig. 1L. This ring evolves to a disk in the final stage (Fig. 1M–P). In the final stage of the evolution the system becomes almost axisymmetric with the very low luminosity $\sim 3 \times 10^{-6}$; it is $\sim 2 \times 10^{-4}$ at $t = 0$. We show the wave form observed on the z-axis at 10 Mpc in Fig. 2. The maximum amplitude of the gravitational waves is $\sim 5 \times 10^{-21}$. Since the proposed sensitivity of large laser interferometric detectors of gravitational waves such as LIGO is $h \sim 10^{-21}$, we may observe the coalescence event up to 50 Mpc. Then the event rate will be more than 1 event/yr from the argument in the Introduction. In Fig. 3A–J we show the density contour for TIDAL2. In this case $m_1 = 1.83$ and $m_2 = 0.97$ with initial separation of 21 km. One can see the tidal disruption of the smaller-mass neutron star. The details of TIDAL2 are given in Ref. 8.

REFERENCES

1. J. H. Taylor, in *General Relativity and Gravitation 11*, ed. M. A. H. MacCallum (Cambridge University Press, Cambridge, 1987), p. 209.
2. J. P. A. Clarke, E. P. J. van den Heuvel, and W. Sutantyo, *Astron. Astrophys.* **72** (1978),120.
3. T. Nakamura and M. Fukugita, *Astrophys. J.* **337** (1989), 466.
4. P. Goldreich and D. Lynden-Bell, *Mon. Not. R. Astron. Soc.* **130** (1965), 97.
5. K. Oohara and T. Nakamura, *Prog. Theor. Phys.* **82** (1989) 535 (Paper I).
6. T. Nakamura and K. Oohara, *Prog. Theor. Phys.* **82** (1989) 1066 (Paper II).
7. K. Oohara and T. Nakamura *Prog. Theor. Phys.* **83**(1990) 906. (Paper III).
8. T. Nakamura and K. Oohara, *Prog. Theor. Phys.* to be submitted. (Paper IV).
9. L. Blanchet, T. Damour, and G. Schäfer, *Mon. Not. R. Astron. Soc.* **241** (1990), 289.
10. K. Oohara and T. Nakamura, *Prog. Theor. Phys.* **81** (1989), 360; K. Oohara and T. Nakamura, in *Frontiers of Numerical Relativity*, ed. D. Hobill, C. Evans, and S. Finn (Cambridge University Press, Cambridge, 1989), p. 74.

S. Nishizaki and T. Takatsuka
College of Humanities and Social Sciences, Iwate University, Ueda 3-18-34, Morioka 020, Japan

Proton Mixing in Hot and Dense Neutron Star Matter

The effective interactions, in which basic nucleon-correlations in nuclear matter are already incorporated, have been applied widely to the studies of finite nuclei and found to be successful. In a similar sense, it is desirable to have such effective interactions for the various phases in neutron stars, because there we are concerned with the nucleon system where the composition and/or the state are very different from neutron matter in the normal state.

Up to now, however, only the effective interactions for symmetric nuclear matter are available; that is, we do not even have those for neutron matter much less for neutron star matter with an admixture of protons. We have derived the effective interaction $\tilde{V}$ based on results from the G-matrix calculation with the Reid soft core potential. The form of $\tilde{V}$ has been chosen to be the same as that of the G0-force derived by Sprung and Banerjee[1] for symmetric nuclear matter. Our effective interaction depends on the asymmetry parameter $\alpha \equiv (N-Z)/A$ as well as nuclear matter density ρ. Furthermore $\tilde{V}$ also depends on interacting pairs, that is, neutron-neutron $(n\text{-}n)$, neutron-proton $(n\text{-}p)$, and proton-proton $(p\text{-}p)$. Force parameters have been determined to reproduce diagonal matrix elements of S-, P-, and D-waves and those contributions to energy at a fixed α. The α-dependence of force parameters has been fitted by a polynomial of α.

1. PROTON MIXING IN COLD NEUTRON STAR MATTER

We study the abundance of protons in cold neutron star matter by using the α- and ρ-dependent effective interaction. The mixing ratio of protons, $Y_p \equiv \rho_p/\rho = (1 - \alpha)/2$, in neutron star matter at the temperature $T = 0$ MeV is determined by minimizing the energy of the total system composed of n, p, and e^-. Full results with our effective interaction are shown by the solid line with e in Fig. 1. The proton mixing ratio is about 5% at $\rho > 2\rho_0$ ($\rho_0 \simeq 2.8 \times 10^{14}$ g/cc: normal nuclear matter density). Due to the small admixture of protons the approximations; $\tilde{V}_{nn} = \tilde{V}_{nn}(\alpha = 1)$, $\tilde{V}_{np} = \tilde{V}_{np}(\alpha = 0)$, and $\tilde{V}_{pp} = 0$ have been used by several authors.[2,3] Results with this approximation are plotted with the short-dashed line in Fig. 1. Comparing with full results, the conventional approximation is not a good approximation at higher density due to the omission of the α-dependence of $\tilde{V}_{nn}$ and $\tilde{V}_{np}$. The dash-dotted line in Fig. 1 denotes results with the parabolic approximation of the potential energy $< \tilde{V}(Y_p) >= V_0(\rho) + \alpha^2 V_1(\rho)$. This approximation reproduces full results well up to the higher density and is better than the conventional approximation. If the Fermi energy of electrons exceeds the muon mass, muons start to appear through the reaction $n \longleftrightarrow p + \mu^-$. The proton mixing ratio including muons is shown by the solid line with $e + \mu$ in Fig. 1. Muons appear at a density higher than the normal nuclear matter density ρ_0 and enhance the proton mixing ratio by about 25% at $\rho \geq 2\rho_0$.

2. PROTON MIXING IN HOT NEUTRON STAR MATTER

In hot neutron star matter under β-equilibrium, the proton mixing ratio is determined by minimizing the free energy $F = E - TS$ at a fixed temperature T. The free energy F is calculated after solving a set of equations[4] composed of the finite-temperature Hartree-Fock equations, baryon number conservation, charge neutrality, and chemical equilibrium. In this work, we calculate the nucleon free energy F_N at $\alpha = 0$ and 1 for several values of ρ and T, and then we use the approximation $F_N(\rho, T, \alpha) = F_N(\rho, T, \alpha = 0) + \alpha^2\{F_N(\rho, T, \alpha = 1) - F_N(\rho, T, \alpha = 0)\}$, based on the above results. Protons and electrons appear in neutron star matter as the temperature increases because the effect of entropy S, which is enhanced according to T and Y_p, plays a significant role in lowering F at a given ρ. This enhancement of the proton mixing ratio is prominent at the lower density, for example, $Y_p = 7.1(2.8)\%$ for $T = 30(0)$ MeV at $\rho = \rho_0$ and $Y_p = 6.1(4.2)\%$ for $T = 30(0)$ MeV at $\rho = 3\rho_0$.

We have also investigated proton mixing in hot neutron star matter under degenerate neutrinos relevant to supernova matter. For a fixed lepton fraction, $Y_l = 30\%$ or 40%, we have calculated the proton mixing ratio using the same approximation. The neutrino fraction Y_ν changes slightly according to T and ρ, because a change of the neutrino free energy $\Delta F_\nu = F_\nu(Y_\nu) - F_\nu(Y_\nu = 0)$ is canceled by those of the electron free energy ΔF_e and ΔF_N. This fraction is about 4.5% (8%) for the case of $Y_l = 30\%$ (40%), and then the proton mixing ratio is about 25.5% (32%) at $\rho = 1-5\rho_0$ and $T = 0-50$ MeV.

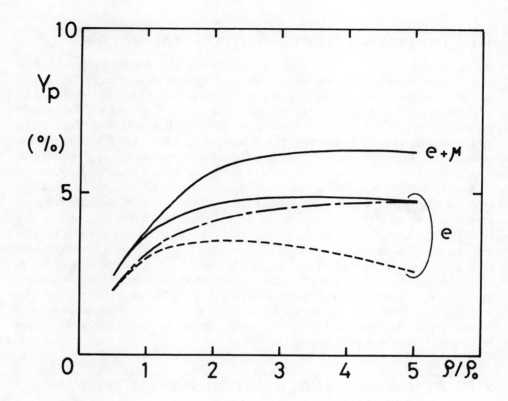

FIGURE 1 The proton mixing ratio Y_p in cold neutron star matter. The solid line with e shows full results with our α- and ρ-dependent effective interaction; short-dashed line, those with the conventional approximation; and dash-dotted line, those with the parabolic approximation. The proton mixing including muons is denoted by $e + \mu$.

REFERENCES

1. D. W. L. Sprung and P. K. Banerjee, *Nucl. Phys.* **A168**, 273 (1971).
2. J. Nemeth and D. W. L. Sprung, *Phys. Rev.* **176**, 1496 (1968).
3. T. Takatsuka, *Prog. Theor. Phys.* **72**, 252 (1984).
4. T. Takatsuka and J. Hiura, *Prog. Theor. Phys.* **79**, 268 (1988).

Magnetic and Thermal Evolution

M. Ruderman
Physics Department and Columbia Astrophysics Laboratory, Columbia University, New York, NY 10027, USA; and Center for Astrophysics and Space Sciences, University of San Diego, La Jolla, CA 92093, USA

Neutron Star Crust Breaking and Magnetic Field Evolution

Spinning-down (or up) neutron star crusts may be stressed beyond their yield strengths by crust neutron superfluid vortex line pinning and/or pull from moving crust anchored quantized magnetic flux tubes of the stellar core. Such stresses would then move crustal plates and the magnetic field imbedded in them. Consequences can include magnetic moment decrease toward $B \sim 10^{11}$ G in dead pulsars. Subsequent spin-up (e.g., by accretion from a companion) can lead to a variety of final spin periods and further reduction in magnetic dipole moments depending upon the initial pulsar magnetic field configuration. If the crust stress is relaxed by large scale cracking events, these would cause pulsar timing glitches with magnitude and recurrence rates near those observed. In old or dead radio pulsars the sudden releases of stored elastic energy should give bursts of X-rays and gamma-rays whose number, energy, and rise time suggest those of the so far unidentified Gamma-Ray Burst sources. The surface magnetic field of a spinning-down crust cracking neutron star breaks up into large surface patches (platelets) which move apart from each other. Each platelet retains its original crust matter and surface magnetic field while the expanding new interplatelet crust regions have no field. Pulsar spin-down torque observations would reflect the decrease in average surface dipole field while the field strength inferred from a cyclotron resonance spectral feature in emission above a platelet would remain high and independent of stellar age.

1. INTRODUCTION

During the spin-up or spin-down of a rapidly rotating neutron star the neutron star's crust can become strongly stressed. One cause of possible large crust stress is pinning of vortices of the neutron superfluid pervading the lower crust by nuclei of the crustal lattice embedded in it.[1,2,3,4] This can cause the angular velocity of the crust superfluid to lag that of a spinning-down or spinning-up crust and core. This velocity difference will grow and exert an increasing force on the pinning crust nuclei until limited by any of three mechanisms:

1. Unpinning (and repinning) of pinned vortex lines. This is the basic assumption in the extensive analyses of Alpar et al.[2] on the "vortex creep" response of a neutron star crust to sudden spin-up events (glitches).
2. Breaking of the crust when such pinning forces cause the crust to become stressed beyond its yield strength.[4,5]
3. Movement into the pinned vortex region of vortex lines with oppositely directed vorticity (e.g., vortex lines with S-like bends). These could relieve lattice stress without any unpinning or crust breaking[6] (cf. Appendix B of Ref. 6). Such possible vortex motion has not yet been studied enough to assess its significance. If it turns out to be important, mechanisms 1 and 2 and their proposed consequences may be irrelevant in pulsars.

A second possible cause of growing crustal stress is pull on the crust by the superconducting core's moving magnetic flux tubes. Srinivasan et al.[7] have argued that the core flux tubes should move with the core's neutron superfluid vortex lines as the paraxial array of core vortices expands (contracts) with core spin-down (spin-up). These flux tubes terminate at the base of the highly conducting crust where the magnetic field lines in them spread out to fill the crust which they traverse. Key questions which remain to be answered definitively are how strongly would the core superfluid vortex array push on the large flux tube complex which it threads before pushing through it and how core electrons and protons get around or through a moving layer of flux tubes.

Insofar as crustal stress exceeds the crust's yield strength, whether the origin of that stress is vortex pinning or core flux tube pull, the long time average motion of the crust would be the same. Because of the very high electrical conductivity of the lower crust, crust motion determines that of the pulsar's external magnetic field. This evolution of the surface magnetic field of the star is just that expected at the core surface in the model of Srinivasan et al. If the total crust breaking stress falls below the crust's yield strength this close correlation ceases. In this paper we shall summarize causes and some consequences of neutron star crustal plate motion which follow from the assumption that crusts can indeed be strained beyond their yield strength.

2. STRENGTH OF A NEUTRON STAR'S CRUST

In the deep crust region where neutron vortex line pinning is strongest ($\rho \sim 5 \times 10^{13}$ g cm^{-3}) the melting temperature of the "Coulomb lattice" $T_m \sim 4 \times 10^9$ K, and the lattice shear modulus $\mu \sim 2 \times 10^{29}$ dynes cm^{-2}. In this region the neutron superfluid transition temperature $T_c \sim 10^{10}$ K $\sim T_m$, much greater than the deep crust temperature of neutron stars more than a few decades old.

In the lower crust lattice quantum effects are unimportant and the dimensionless strain θ in the lattice ($\theta \equiv$ change in length per unit length under tension or compression) can depend upon stress (σ) only in the form

$$\sigma = \mu \theta f(\theta, \ T/T_m, \ \delta), \tag{1}$$

where δ is a dimensionless measure of the filling factor and form of a crystal's complex of dislocations. Stress experiments on near Coulomb metallic microcrystals such as Li or Mg at ordinary densities may be extrapolated by Eq. (1) to the superdense crystalline matter of a neutron star crust to yield the following features for neutron star crust microcrystals:

a) $\sigma = 3\theta\mu$ until an elastic strain limit θ_{max} is reached;
b) $\theta_{max} \sim 5 \times 10^{-3}$ at $T \sim 10^{-1}T_m$;
c) $\theta_{max} \sim 10^{-2}$ for $T \ll T_m$;
d) $\theta_{max} \ll 10^{-2}$ for $10^{-1}T_m \ll T < T_m$;
e) a transition from continuous strain to a brittle response to stress over a small temperature range (of order $10^{-2}T_m$) near $T \sim 10^{-1}T_m$.

When $\theta > \theta_{max}$, σ remains near $3\theta_{max}\mu$: the crystal lattice grains yield and continue to deform without much further increase in stress. When $T \lesssim 10^{-1}T_m$ a crystal grain yields discontinuously: it continually but erratically "breaks" on a scale $\Delta\theta < \theta_{max}$.

The crucial and unresolved problem is not so much the extrapolation through more than 13 orders of magnitude from the density of small laboratory crystals to that within the deep crust of a neutron star, but rather extrapolating from the behavior of very small single crystals or grains to that of an entire crust which extends over 10^{17} lattice constants. How does a possibly brittle neutron star crust break when stress grows slowly to that at which crust matter must yield? Does a crust develop faults along which it repeatedly slips at much lower stresses than $3\theta_{max}/\mu$? What happens at the discontinuities in atomic number and lattice spacing which exist in the layered crust? Does the crust yield only by very many microscopic breaks so that its large-scale response still resembles the plastic flow of a hot crust or does it yield by rarer large scale cracking? For the crust as a whole an effective θ_{max} as small as 10^{-4} may be plausible.

3. STRESSES IN A NEUTRON STAR CRUST

The neutron superfluid which fills the space between lattice nuclei mimics uniform rotation through a quasi-parallel array of quantized vortex lines. In most of the crust, where ρ is between 10^{13} and 10^{14} g cm^{-3}, these vortex lines are expected to be pinned to crust nuclei.[2,1,4] When the crust spin rate and crustal neutron superfluid rotation rate are equal there is no shear stress on the lattice to which the vortex lines are pinned. Otherwise there is a force density on the lattice within the pinning region of the crust,[5]

$$\mathcal{E} = 2\,\underset{\sim}{\omega} \times (\underset{\sim}{\Omega}_n \times \underset{\sim}{r})\rho_n, \tag{2}$$

for a lattice superfluid rotation velocity difference

$$\underset{\sim}{\omega} \equiv \underset{\sim}{\Omega}_n - \underset{\sim}{\Omega}. \tag{3}$$

Here ρ_n is the internuclear superfluid neutron density, $\underset{\sim}{\Omega}_n$ is its average angular velocity, $\underset{\sim}{\Omega}$ is the angular velocity of the lattice and of the neutron superfluid vortices pinned to them, and r is the distance from the spin axis. Only part of this lattice body force can be balanced by pressure from the deformed lattice and its degenerate electrons together with the gravitational force. The rest must be balanced by lattice shear strength. The lattice elastic yield strength will be exceeded when (Ref. 5, Eq. [18b]) ω exceeds the crust breaking limit

$$\omega_B \sim 10^{-1} \left(\frac{P}{10^{-3}\text{ s}} \right) \left(\frac{\theta_{\max}}{10^{-2}} \right) \text{ s}^{-1}. \tag{4}$$

If ω reaches ω_B the lattice yields to plastic flow, crumbling or cracking, and will not support any significant further increase in stress. Possible vortex unpinning from the crustal lattice nuclei could, in principle, keep ω from reaching ω_B.

From various estimates of the magnitudes of pinning forces we conclude the following.[6]

1. Even if $\theta_{\max}$ for the large scale structure of the crust is 10^{-2} and the crustal lattice is always randomly aligned at a vortex core, lattice yield strengths are exceeded before unpinning when $P \lesssim 10$ ms.
2. Arguments for microcrystal alignment at vortex cores suggest extending the lattice breaking before unpinning regime to periods $P \lesssim 10^2$ ms.
3. If the lattice has large-scale "fault planes" it can be much weaker than the microcrystals of which it is formed, and the above range of pulsar spin periods may be greatly underestimated. An effective $\theta_{\max} \sim 10^{-4}$ gives a range of spin periods $P < 10$ s for lattice breaking spin-down. (An argument for around this value for $\theta_{\max}$ is given after Eq. [9] and in Ref. 6.)

A second kind of stress on the crust is possible pull by stellar core magnetic field which passes through it. In the absence of core magnetic field microstructure

this shearing stress at the base of the crust is probably much smaller than the maximum shear stress there which the thin crust could bear before yielding ($\hat{\sigma}_{max}$) for crust thickness $\ell(\sim 10^5 \text{cm})$ and stellar radius $R(\sim 10^6 \text{cm})$:

$$\hat{\sigma}_{max} \sim \frac{\ell}{R}\mu\theta_{max} \sim 3 \cdot 10^{26}\left(\frac{\theta_{max}}{10^{-2}}\right) \text{ dynes cm}^{-2}. \tag{5}$$

However, the neutron star's core protons are superconducting. This superconducting core component will organize any magnetic field which threads it into structures such that the average $\langle B^2 \rangle \gg \langle B \rangle^2$. If, as expected, the stellar core protons form a type II superconductor, the core magnetic field is organized into an array of quantized magnetic flux tubes which terminate near the base of the crust. There they open out and traverse the crust as normal magnetic field (slightly perturbed by the diamagnetic nuclei). Each quantized magnetic flux tube in the stellar core contains an average magnetic field $B_c \gtrsim 10^{15}$ G. It is partly because neutron vortex cores imbedded in a proton superconductor are comparably magnetized[8,9] that single flux tubes and neutron vortex cores do not pass easily through each other. The core flux tubes may then be moved by the expanding (contracting) array of core neutron superfluid vortex lines as a neutron star spins down (up). The suggested evolution of a core magnetic field flux tube in a spinning-down neutron star by Srinivasan et al. is indicated in Fig. 1. As core vortex lines move out away from the spin axis the magnetic flux tubes around them are forced to move with them. The exit and entry points of the flux tubes on the surface of the core then move down (or up) toward the equator as the core spins down. (For a spinning-up stellar core the motion of flux tube exit and entry points is toward the pole of the hemisphere in which they are located.) If the crust were to remain rigid and immobile while such magnetic flux tube motion continued, the shear stress on the base of the highly conducting crust could grow to reach

$$\hat{\sigma}(B) \sim \frac{BB_c}{8\pi} \sim \left(\frac{B}{3 \times 10^{12} \text{ G}}\right) 10^{26} \text{ dynes cm}^{-2}, \tag{6}$$

where B is the average magnetic field through the crust. This estimate ignores the crucial question of whether the quasi-parallel array of core neutron vortex lines would cut through the huge ($\sim 10^{14}$ flux tubes per vortex line) flux tube complex long before the maximum crust pull of Eq. (6) is achieved (and also whether huge bundles of flux tubes can move as single isolated flux tubes do). (Such cutting through may well be the case if the core protons were to form a type I superconductor and might also occur when flux tubes are pressed together so that their collective field resembles that of the strongly but continuously magnetized normal regions in type I superconductors.)

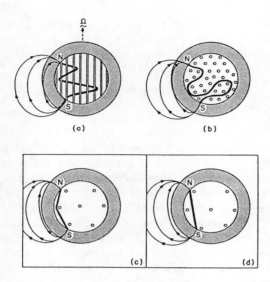

FIGURE 1 Motion of a core magnetic flux tube in a spinning-down neutron star. (a) Side view of initial flux tube path (*thicker line*). In the crust and beyond, the magnetic field is not constrained. Neutron superfluid vortex lines are indicated as hollow tubes. Because the core field would be expected to have had toroidal as well as poloidal components before the superconducting transition, the flux tube path is probably quite tortured while the vortex array is quasi-uniform. (b) Top view of (a) (along spin axis direction). (c) Top view of flux tube in the equatorial zone after long spin-down when the conducting crust moves with the neutron vortex array caps. (The crust motion may be forced by the crust's own pinned vortex lines or because the crust yields to the pull of core flux tubes.) If core neutron vortex motion also moves the entrained flux the flux tube is pushed up into the crust core boundary. (d) If not it would take a somewhat different, usually straighter, path between the points where it is anchored in the crust. The meridional motion of these two points is just that shown in Fig. 2.

4. CRUST MOTION AND MAGNETIC FIELD EVOLUTION

In a spinning down (or up) neutron star, vortex pinning stresses and magnetic field pull from core vortex moved flux tubes reinforce each other in straining the solid crust. No matter which dominates, if crust yield strength is exceeded, crustal plates should move exactly as they would from pinning stresses alone. The strongly

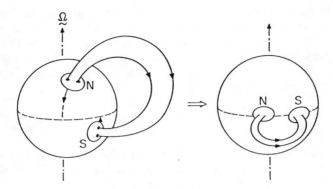

FIGURE 2 Evolution of the surface magnetic field of a short-period spinning-down neutron star when equatorial zone magnetic field line reconnection is ignored[5]

conducting metallic crust of a spinning-down neutron star would then continually move away from the spin axis toward the equator at an average tangential speed[5]

$$v_t = \frac{\dot{\Omega} R r_\perp}{2\Omega (R^2 - r_\perp^2)^{1/2}}, \tag{7}$$

with $r_\perp$ the radial distance of a crust region from the stellar spin axis. The crust motion of Eq. (7) must cease when spin-down induced stresses can no longer exceed the crust's yield strength. In Ref. 6 Eq. (18), this is shown to happen when the spin period (P) exceeds $\hat{P}$, given by

$$\hat{P} \sim 10 \left(\frac{10^{-4}}{\theta_{\max}} \right)^{1/2} \text{ s.} \tag{8}$$

Imbedded magnetic field should move with the crust as shown in Fig. 2. Magnetic pole strength would then accumulate in the equatorial zone. Even if the crust were rigid the internal pull from the core's outward-pushed flux tubes could cause the magnetic polar caps of spinning down radiopulsars to move toward the spin equator. If this was the end state of their evolution, then radiopulsars older than one or two spin-down times would be expected to have much larger angles between their spin axes and dipole moments than younger ones. Such an evolution toward orthogonal rotators is not observed in canonical radio pulsars. If surface magnetic poles do not accumulate in the equatorial zone they must find partners there and recombine with them. Because of the high conductivity of the lower crust the recombination is not achieved through ohmic decay. Rather, non-rigid azimuthal crust

motion must bring opposite poles together. The needed azimuthal stress would not come from crust-pinned vorticity or from magnetic flux expulsion from the stellar core. However, opposite poles which reach the equatorial zone on different meridians are still very strongly coupled to each other through flux tubes in the core below them as sketched in Figs. 1c and 1d. This attraction will cause the crust to yield and allow recombination as long as[6]

$$B \gtrsim 3 \times 10^{10} \left(\frac{\theta_{max}}{10^{-4}} \right). \tag{9}$$

The lack of evidence for increasing orthogonality between magnetic moment and spin in older canonical radio pulsars suggests that Eq. (9) holds for B down to at least 10^{11}G. Then Eq. (16) implies $\theta_{max} \lesssim 3 \times 10^{-4}$.

The predicted spin-down driven evolution of average B in canonical solitary radio pulsars with $\theta_{max} = 10^{-4}$ is shown in Fig. 3, where $\hat{P} = P_3 = 10$ s. Neutron stars born in binary systems may spin down and then be spun up in the same binary system. In a globular cluster, solitary pulsars evolving initially as indicated in Fig. 3 may consequently be captured to form a binary. Further evolution of the binary or of the companion star can lead to accretion powered spin-up of the neutron star.

The evolution of the neutron star's surface magnetic field during such a spin-up phase depends upon the initial field distribution when the spin-up begins. Crustal plate motion should now be away from the spin equator toward the spin poles. Three possible initial configurations and the evolution which results are shown in Figs. 4–6 and Fig. 3. In Fig. 4, with N and S magnetic polar caps in opposite hemispheres, the dipole moment becomes aligned by spin-up. It also increases very modestly. In Fig. 5, the "sunspot configuration" with both magnetic polar caps in the same hemisphere, these two polar caps are pressed together at the same spin axis pole by spin-up crust motion. If large-scale crust cracking does not occur, the configuration formed after a long spin-down from period P_0 to P_3 (cf. Fig. 3) may consist of a near uniform N-pole distribution over the hemisphere with S-poles at the equator which have not yet recombined because of the absence of N-pole partners there. In a subsequent spin-up, field evolution from crust movement still leads to the same final state as that indicated in Fig. 5. As this sort of sunspot configuration star is spun-up from P_3 to P, the plate motion causes the stellar magnetic dipole to be diminished by a factor $(P/P_3)^{1/2}$. However, the evolved field would be very inhomogeneously distributed over the star's surface, very strong at the small polar cap (if $P/P_3 \ll 1$) and almost zero elsewhere. When the magnitude of the neutron star *average* dipole field $\langle B \rangle$ is measured by observing the pulsar spin-down rate after accretion has ceased, this average would be reduced from the initial average $\langle B_3 \rangle$ when $P = P_3$ according to

$$\langle B \rangle \sim \langle B_3 \rangle \left(\frac{P}{P_3} \right)^{1/2}. \tag{10}$$

If $P/P_3 \ll 1$ all poles and moments of B would be pressed into a small (radius $\sim R \langle B \rangle / \langle B_3 \rangle$) and thus nearly plane dipolar cap at the spin axis. In the absence of

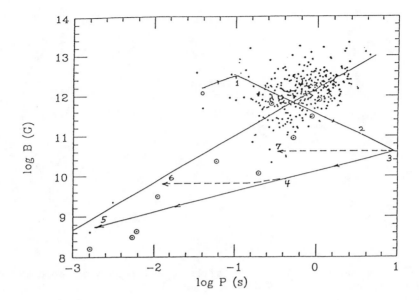

FIGURE 3 Evolution of dipole magnetic fields for a weak crust with $\theta_{max} = 10^{-4}$. Solitary radio pulsar spin-down would reach 2. Some further spin-down to 3 is assumed after capture into an accreting binary. Spin-down below 3 would not be effective in reducing B, because the crust would no longer be stressed above its yield strength. Subsequent spin-up would return the neutron star to 3, after which its evolution depends upon the magnetic field configuration. If there were no further spin-down beyond the point 2, point 3 would coincide with 2 and the subsequent evolutionary paths would be raised to those for a stronger crust neutron star. Segment $\overline{01}$: see Ref. 6. Segment $\overline{12}$: $B \propto \Omega$ as crust plates move toward the equator where pole combination takes place. The solid line $\overline{345}$ and the dashed lines $\overline{346}$ and $\overline{37}$ describe further field evolution in a pulsar spun up by accretion from the period P_3 with magnetic field $B(P_2) = 10^{11}$ G. The evolution of $\langle B \rangle$ from further accretion-driven spin-up depends upon the magnetic field configuration. Segment $\overline{45}$ (*solid line*) is that for the sunspot-like configuration of Fig. 5 and Eq. (11). Segment $\overline{37}$ (*dashed line*) is that for the configuration of Fig. 4 and Eq. (13). Fig. 6 and Eq. (12) would give $\overline{346}$, intermediate between those two. The dots are for radiopulsars; the circled dots are radiopulsars in binaries.

a specially symmetric initial configuration (e.g., axial symmetry) the star's evolving magnetic dipole should become orthogonal to its spin as $\langle B \rangle$ diminishes, according to Eq. (10). In Fig. 6 we have an intermediate initial configuration with some of the flux from the north polar cap (N) reentering the stellar surface in the same (upper) hemisphere from which it was emitted (S_1), while the rest reenters in the opposite

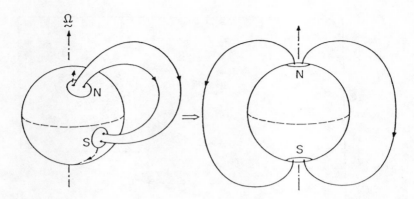

FIGURE 4 Evolution of the surface magnetic field of a spinning-up short-period neutron star when flux lines initially connect the two spin hemispheres.

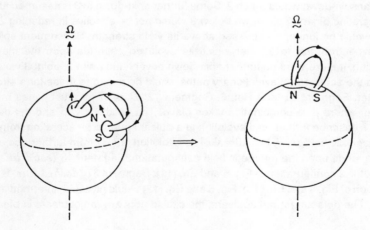

FIGURE 5 Evolution of the magnetic field of a spinning-up short-period neutron star when all flux leaving a hemisphere reenters the same hemisphere (sunspot configuration)

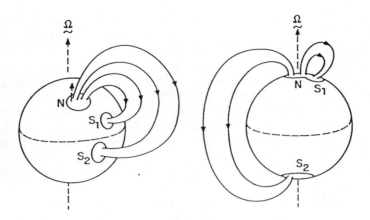

FIGURE 6 Evolution of the magnetic field of a spinning-up short-period neutron star with an initial flux configuration which is intermediate between that of Figs. 5 and 6

(lower) hemisphere (S_2). Here spin-up would lead to a dipole whose orientation and magnitude depend upon the relative fluxes into $S_1(\Phi_{S_1})$ and $S_2(\Phi_{S_2})$. If

$$\Phi_{S_2} \ll \left(\frac{P}{P_3}\right)^{1/2} \Phi_{S_1}, \tag{11}$$

the spun-up star's dipole becomes essentially that of Fig. 5, an orthogonal dipole much smaller than its original size. If

$$\Phi_{S_2} \gg \left(\frac{P}{P_3}\right)^{1/2} \Phi_{S_1}, \tag{12}$$

the spun-up star's field evolves as in Fig. 4 into a somewhat larger aligned dipole. If

$$\Phi_{S_2} \sim \left(\frac{P}{P_3}\right)^{1/2} \Phi_{S_1}, \tag{13}$$

the spun-up star's dipole is reduced in magnitude with no special final orientation relative to the stellar spin. Figure 3 shows possible evolutionary paths with a weak $(\theta_{\max} = 10^{-4})$ crust. The spin-down segment $\overline{0123}$ is discussed in Ref. 6.

The possible spin-up evolution of the average (dipole) field shown in Fig. 3 for various field configurations for spin-up of a weak crust star begins at the period $P_3 = 10$ ms. A pure sunspot-like initial configuration leads to the $\overline{345}$ path and the dipole becomes increasingly more orthogonal as $\langle B \rangle$ decreases. The path $\overline{37}$ is

followed for the geometry of Fig. 4 and the dipole moment becomes more aligned as spin-up continues. The intermediate path $\overline{346}$ is followed when the initial period P_3 is such that Eq. (11) is satisfied. However, at $P \sim P_4$ Eq. (13) becomes appropriate. Further large spin-down of $\langle B \rangle$ no longer occurs as accretion-driven spin-up brings P toward the accretion spin-up equilibrium line. In this case the magnetic dipole moment is mainly orthogonal as point 4 is approached along the path $\overline{34}$, but becomes aligned during further spin-up along $\overline{46}$. If spin-up stops along $\overline{46}$, or if the pulsar spins down to lie along that segment after reaching the accretion spin-up equilibrium line, the dipole may be oriented anywhere between alignment and orthogonality, with alignment favored nearest the spin-up line. When the point 4 occurs at $P < 10$ ms, even the lowest $\langle B \rangle$ shortest P pulsar could have non-orthogonal dipole moments.

These stars are assumed to become resurrected (i.e., spun-up) radiopulsars when accretion ceases. The region of smallest P and $\langle B \rangle$ is reached only by those pulsars for which the initial field geometries of Fig. 5 or Eq. (11) are appropriate and the accretion lasts long enough for P to reach a value near the canonical "spin-up line." About half the total dipole moment reduction is accomplished by equatorial zone magnetic pole recombination during the spin-down phase; half is accomplished by the compression to the polar cap of the remaining flux during subsequent spin-up. The special initial field geometry for the maximally spun-up class of Fig. 5 and path $\overline{45}$ of Fig. 3 also leads to nearly orthogonal dipole moments. Comparisons of these neutron star period and magnetic field evolutions with observations are given in Ref. 6.

5. CRUST CRACKING AND PERIOD GLITCHES

In none of the above considerations were details of exactly how a crust yields to a stress which exceeds its strength, whether by lattice crumbling or plastic flow or sudden slipping along faults, important. We shall turn now to some of the special phenomena and structures which result when the crust is assumed to yield to growing global stress with large scale "cracking"; parts of the crust are assumed to slip suddenly to relieve some significant fraction of an otherwise growing crustal stress.[10,4] For warm crusts such large cracking would probably not occur, because warm crusts' microcrystal yield strengths are much smaller than those in cold ones and the yielding is more likely to be by plastic flow. It was noted above that a transition from plastic flow to a more brittle response might be expected near the same ratio of transition temperature (T_t) to crystal melting temperature (T_m) as that measured in the laboratory for (near) Coulomb crystals such as Li or Mg; then $T_t/T_m \sim 10^{-1}$. The transition regime is over a very small fraction of T_m. For neutron star crusts relevant T_m are several $\times 10^9$ K and the transition may be expected to occur at around the Crab pulsar inner crust temperature. It almost certainly has already occurred in the older Vela pulsar crust where the temperature

at the base has been estimated[11] to be $T = 1.3 \times 10^8$ K so that $T/T_m \sim 3 \times 10^{-3}$. However, it should be emphasized that the crust might well everywhere limit stress entirely by microscopic crumbling even when each grain responds rather brittlely. The assumption of relatively large-scale crust cracking is a hypothesis which must still be supported mainly by comparisons of its consequences with neutron star observations. A significant fraction of the growing strain from forced crust motion is assumed below to be relieved in such sudden cracking which relieves the maximally strained crust ($\theta \sim \theta_{max}$) by $\Delta\theta$.

Because the spin-down induced crustal stresses are directed away from the spin axis poles, the sudden $\Delta\theta$ motions of stressed crust generally also move crust outward (except in the equatorial zone). A sudden outward motion of part of the crustal lattice also carries outward those crustal neutron superfluid vortices which are pinned to the moving lattice's nuclei. In this way crustal neutron superfluid which was prevented from spinning down with the crust because its vortices could not move outward, suddenly reduces the angular frequency lag ω between its rotation speed Ω_n and the rotation speed of the crustal lattice Ω. The decrease in Ω_n from an outward displacement of vortices by $R\Delta\theta/2$ is

$$\Delta\Omega_n = -\Delta\theta\Omega_n. \tag{14}$$

The crust must, of course, recoil by spinning-up, a motion which is quickly communicated to and shared with the rest of the star. Then the final shared crust spin-up is

$$\Delta\Omega = \frac{\Delta\theta\Omega_n I_n}{I - I_n}, \tag{15}$$

with I the moment of inertia of the whole neutron star and I_n that of the suddenly spun-down crustal neutron superfluid. If we identify $\Delta\Omega$ with the observed spin-up glitches of Vela-like radiopulsars, put $\Omega \sim \Omega_n$, and use a canonical estimate

$$I_n \sim 10^{-2}I, \tag{16}$$

then

$$\frac{\Delta\Omega}{\Omega} \sim 10^{-2}\Delta\theta. \tag{17}$$

For Vela glitches $\Delta\Omega/\Omega \sim 10^{-6}$. This gives

$$\Delta\theta \sim 10^{-4} \tag{18}$$

for Vela's crust. The interval between glitches (τ_g) should be the length of time needed for further spin-down to rebuild the strain $\Delta\theta$ relaxed by the crust cracking:

$$\tau_g \sim \frac{\Delta\theta}{\Omega}. \tag{19}$$

The combination $(\Delta\Omega/\Omega)(1/\tau_g)$, called the "glitch activity" rate by McKenna and Lyne,[12] is independent of $\Delta\theta$ and θ_{max}:

$$\frac{\Delta\Omega}{\Omega}\frac{1}{\tau_g} = \frac{\dot{\Omega}}{\Omega}\frac{I_n}{I} \sim \frac{10^{-5}\text{ yr}}{(\text{age}/10^3\text{ yr})}. \tag{20}$$

(The heuristic argument leading to Eq. [20] is inconsistent in its treatment of the elastic response of the lattice to growing stress between glitches and in other details. A more careful consideration which leads to Eq. [20] for spinning-down pulsars with $\Omega \lesssim 10^2\text{ s}^{-1}$ and to corrections for faster pulsars is given in Ref. 10, Appendix A.) The model result of Eq. (20) is compared with observed glitch activity rates of young pulsars in Table 1. Agreement is quite reasonable for the Vela-like family of 10^4 yr old pulsars. We would attribute the very low glitch activity in the younger Crab family solely to the fact that their lower crusts are warmer and respond to growing stress mainly by plastic flow.[4,12] A recent estimate[11] for the internal Crab pulsar temperature gives $T \sim 4 \times 10^8\text{ K} \sim 10^{-1}T_m$. It would appear from Table 1 that the transition from crust plastic flow to a more brittle response takes place after about 1700 yr, the estimated age of PSR 0540. From laboratory results shown in Ref. 10, transition would be expected during a relatively small interior temperature drop $\Delta T \sim 10^{-1}T \sim$ several times 10^7 K. The radiopulsars much older than Vela should continue to have glitches, but with much longer inter-glitch intervals τ_g, so that few have been observed so far. The observed glitch repetition rates give an effective $\Delta\theta \sim 2 \times 10^{-4}$ for Vela and 4×10^{-5} for PSR 1737.

TABLE 1 Glitch Activity in Young Radio Pulsars

Pulsar	Age (10^3 yr)	Glitch activity ($10^{-7}yr^{-1}$)	
		Observed	Eq. (11)
0531	1.2	0.1	80
1509	1.5	~ 0	70
0540	1.7	10*	60
0833	11	8	9
1800	16	?	6
1737	20	4	5
1823	21	5	5

* The estimated glitch activity of PSR 0540 is based upon the reported $\Delta\Omega/\Omega \sim 10^{-5}$ for the only glitch observed in the decade since its discovery.[13] All other data entries are taken from McKenna and Lyne.[14] [Note in proof: the report of glitch for P9R 0540 has been withdrawn.]

6. EVOLVING MAGNETIC FIELD STRUCTURE IN SPINNING-DOWN NEUTRON STARS

If a post-Crab pulsar crust relaxes with large scale cracking, the crust breaks up into "platelets."[5,10] New matter flows into the cracks between platelets which differs in important ways from the old crust matter of a platelet. First, it does not have much magnetic field. The original crust magnetic flux remains frozen in the platelets. Continued spin-down induced cracking would be expected to take place at platelet boundaries (and beyond) in the interplatelet crustal matter. The platelets themselves should then retain their integrity and their original magnetic fields during spin-down. The evolution of the surface magnetic field of a spinning-down pulsar crust is indicated in Fig. 7. When the crust is so warm that it stretches plastically without large cracking (i.e., Crab-like or younger) the original crust is stretched (and thus thinned) by the motion toward the equator of Eq. (7). As a young pulsar spins down from its initial spin period and cools, the polar cap field spreads with the highly conducting crust in which it is imbedded to fill much of its hemisphere. At $P = P_c$ cracking begins; thereafter, platelets move apart until the spin-down period reaches the $\hat{P}$ of Eq. (8). Each platelet has frozen into it the field $B(P_c)$ which it had when cracking first began. This field should be quite uniform over a platelet surface since it came from the initial stretching of the field of a relatively small polar cap. Then in the spin-down regime $P_c < P < \hat{P}$ while the *average* surface dipole field $\langle B(P) \rangle$ decreases inversely with P,[7,6]

$$\langle B(P) \rangle = \langle B(P_c) \rangle P_c / P, \tag{21}$$

the rather uniform platelet fields (B_p) remain frozen at

$$B_p = \langle B(P_c) \rangle \sim B(\text{Vela}) \sim 3 \times 10^{12} \text{G}. \tag{22}$$

Therefore measurements of B in older spun-down neutron stars should give conflicting results. Those based upon the magnitude of the magnetic dipole moment (spin-down in radiopulsars, accretion torques in X-ray pulsars) should give smaller values of B than those inferred from surface cyclotron resonance features in the X-ray spectra of X-ray pulsars and Gamma-Ray Burst sources if these are old solitary neutron stars). The predicted extreme uniformity of a platelet field could also make a cyclotron resonance feature much narrower than would be expected otherwise.

7. GAMMA-RAY BURSTS

If radiopulsar glitches are a manifestation of crust cracking, they are associated with sudden releases of stored elastic strain energy in the deep crust. The total rate of such events from the neutron star population of the Galaxy, the amount of

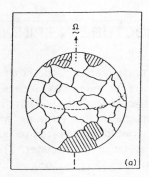
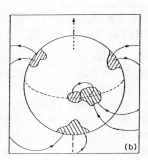

FIGURE 7 Evolution of surface platelets and magnetic field after crust cracking begins. (a) An initial configuration of cracks; the magnetic field is continuously distributed through the surface. (b) Separation of original platelets (*hatched*) after further spin-down and equatorial zone subduction. At the original platelets B maintains the value it had in (a). $B = 0$ from new interplatelet crust.

energy released per glitch, and the initial time scale for that release are all near what seem to be required for the sources of observed gamma-ray bursts (GRBs).

Because efficient generation of gamma-rays from this elastic energy release may be high only in the older longer-period neutron stars which have relatively charge-starved magnetospheres,[14] observed burst sources may be limited to dead radiopulsars which no longer have steady copious sources of $e^{\pm}$ pairs in their magnetospheres. This is an old neutron star population which should, therefore, be distributed broadly, a kiloparsec or more above and below the Galactic disk, since the younger, active radio pulsars typically have very high velocities (~ 150 km s^{-1}). Because the so-far-observed (Oct. 1990) GRB sources seem to be isotropically distributed about us, only those neutron stars nearer than about a kiloparsec should be in the candidate source population. These could number 10^7, aboutOC 10^{-2} of all Galactic neutron stars. Since GRBs are observed at a rate of about 10^2 yr^{-1}, each candidate source must give 10^2 yr$^{-1} \times 10^{10}$ yr $\times 10^{-7} = 10^5$ GRBs.

The total number of glitches expected during the spin-down of a pulsar from P_c (the spin period at which crust cracking begins) to $\hat{P}$ (the spin period of Eq. [8], at which crust cracking ceases) is

$$N_g = \frac{1}{\Delta\theta} \ln\left(\frac{\hat{P}}{P_c}\right) \sim 10^5. \tag{23}$$

The numerical value assumes $P_c = 5 \times 10^{-2}$ s (midway between Crab and Vela periods), $\hat{P} = 10$ s (Eq. [8] with $\theta_{max} = 10^{-4}$), and $\Delta\theta = 5 \times 10^{-5}$ (for PSR 1737).

The glitches will continue after radio pulsar turnoff. Each sudden release of elastic strain energy from the (lower) crust in a glitch is

$$\mathcal{E}_g \sim \ell R^2 \mu \theta_{\max} \Delta\theta \sim 10^{39} \left(\frac{\theta_{\max}}{10^{-3}}\right) \left(\frac{\Delta\theta}{10^{-4}}\right) \ell_5 \text{ ergs}, \sim 10^{38} \text{ ergs.} \quad (24)$$

An equivalent energy release comes from the sudden slowdown of crust neutron superfluid rotation.

Models for the response of a pulsar magnetosphere to a sudden onset of large-amplitude kilohertz vibrations of surface magnetic field suggest that particle depletion is a necessary condition for high efficiency extreme relativistic particle acceleration. Large GRBs may accompany glitches only in magnetospheres starved of charge because there is no longer the steady $e^{\pm}$ production of canonical radiopulsars which have not yet reached the canonical "death line." This would restrict strong GRB sources to slowly rotating extinct radiopulsars, as already suggested by Blaes et al.[14] If the needed large GRB source population consists mainly of dead radio pulsars, P_c in Eq. (23) should be replaced by the radio pulsar extinction period of about 2 s. With $\theta_m \sim 10^{-4}$, the smallest value compatible with the limit $\theta_m > \Delta\theta$, Eq. (23) then gives $N_g = 5 \times 10^4$, quite near (but perhaps disturbingly less than) the above estimate of 10^5 GRBs per neutron star.

The elastic energy released in each glitch-GRB is given by Eq. (24) as $\mathcal{E}_g \sim 10^{38}$ ergs. If most of this energy is ultimately converted into energetic radiation from the neutron star's suddenly disturbed magnetosphere, the observed GRB fluence would be $\mathcal{E}_g/4\pi/(1 \text{ kpc})^2 \sim 10^{-6}$ ergs cm^{-2}, typical of that from a GRB. The time scale for initiating this energy release (Δt) is that for a crack (which moves with the deep crust shear wave velocity $v_s \sim 2 \times 10^8$ cm s^{-1}) to propagate through the lower crust thickness (ℓ). The rise time

$$\Delta t \sim \frac{\ell}{v_s} \sim 5 \times 10^{-4} \text{ s} \quad (25)$$

is consistent with GRB observations. The time structure of the whole GRB depends upon unknown details of how a crack network develops within the crust. After the crack, the released elastic energy is initially in the form of crust shear vibrations with frequencies ($\sim v_s/\ell$) in the kilohertz regime. Blaes et al.[14] have shown how such high-frequency elastic vibrations reach the stellar surface as Alfvén waves with amplitudes greatly amplified from those of the initial deep-crust oscillations. In the GRB model of Blaes et al., elastic energy release by a mid-crust mechanical instability is replenished by stress from continued cold mass accretion onto the star surface rather than spin-down as suggested here. Spin-down powered crust cracking is deeper and thus can involve greater elastic energy storage and release. Many details of the Blaes et al. model can, however, be carried over.

No GRBs were observed during the Vela radio pulsar's glitches, implying not much more than 10^{38} ergs s^{-1} into any glitch-associated GRB from this pulsar. The model's $E_g \sim 10^{38}$ ergs might have escaped detection. Moreover, even if the

plasma density in Vela's magnetosphere were only the minimum Goldreich-Julian charge density needed to keep the near magnetosphere electric field in the star's corotating reference frame near zero, potential GRB emission from this pulsar could be suppressed by inductive effects from moving ambient magnetosphere charge.[10]

ACKNOWLEDGMENTS

It is a pleasure to thank P. Jones for very many enlightening discussions about neutron star crusts and superfluids. I am also grateful for conversations with A. Alpar, B. Bhattacharya, R. Blandford, E. van den Heuvel, G. Taylor, R. Epstein, F. Lamb, D. Pines, J. Rankin, V. Radharishnan, and J. Sauls and for the hospitality of S. Tsuruta, R. Tamagaki, N. Shibazaki, R. Dalitz, and the Department of Theoretical Physics of the University of Oxford. This research has been supported in part by NSF-89-01681 and is contribution number 459 of the Columbia Astrophysics Laboratory.

REFERENCES

1. P. Anderson and N. Itoh, *Nature,* **256**, 25 (1975).
2. A. Alpar, P. Anderson, D. Pines, and J. Shaham, *Ap. J.,* **282**, 791 (1984).
3. R. Parker, *Phys. Rev. Letters,* **28**, 1080 (1972).
4. M. Ruderman, *Ap. J.,* **203**, 213 (1976).
5. M. Ruderman, *Ap. J.,* **382**, 261 (1991).
6. M. Ruderman, *Ap. J.,* **382**, 576 (1991).
7. G. Srinivasan, B. Bhattacharya, A. Muslimov, and A. Tsygan, *Current Science,* **59**, 31 (1990).
8. A. Alpar, S. Langer, and J. Sauls, *Ap. J.,* **282**, 533 (1985).
9. J. Sauls, *Timing Neutron Stars,* H. Ögelman and E. P. J. van den Heubel (eds.) (J. Kluwer Academic Publishers, Dordrecht, 1989).
10. M. Ruderman, *Ap. J.,* **382**, 587 (1991).
11. A. Alpar, K.-S. Cheng, and D. Pines, University of Illinois preprint (1990).
12. J. McKenna and A. Lyne, *Nature,* **343**, 349 (1990).
13. H. Ögelman, G. Hasinger, and J. Trümper, IAU Circ. 5162 (1991).
14. O. Blaes, R. Blandford, P. Goldrechi, and P. Madav, *Ap. J.,* **343**, 839 (1989).

Sachiko Tsuruta
Department of Physics, Montana State University, Bozeman, MT 59717, USA

Thermal Evolution of Neutron Stars—Cooling and Heating

In this report we shall introduce the recent major developments in the area of neutron star cooling and heating. As one of the still remaining, possibly important problems in connection with the standard cooling, we discuss the effect of temperature modulations over the stellar surface due to the anisotropic heat conduction under quantized, strong magnetic fields. We present the results of the most recent calculations for cooling involving pions, quarks, kaons, and new particles yet to be discovered, cooling with the direct URCA process, and the vortex creep heating. By comparing these results with observations it may be suggested that there are two classes of these objects: hotter, less massive stars without cores of "exotic" particles such as pions and cooler, more massive ones with cores of such fast-cooling agents. A brief outline of the current work in progress follows, on systematic, generalized studies of neutron star heating. The recent work on the detectability of a neutron star in SN 1987A is summarized. The importance of these studies is emphasized in the last section.

1. INTRODUCTION

Cooling determines the thermal history of isolated neutron stars during the earlier period, of less than about 10^4 years, except during the earliest stages immediately after formation. Therefore, since the launch of the Einstein Observatory, which for the first time gave a realistic possibility of testing neutron star cooling theories, various authors explored cooling of isolated neutron stars (see, e.g., reviews by Tsuruta[1,2]). These studies have contributed significantly to the understanding of these and related problems. In the "standard" cooling scenario a neutron star cools mainly through neutrinos escaping directly from the star and photon radiation from the surface.[1,3] However, a neutron star could cool much faster through various other means, such as processes involving pions, kaons, and quarks. The latter possibilities are, for convenience, called the "nonstandard" cooling.

In the past years there has been some isolated work on neutron star heating. For instance, Greenstein[4] and Ruderman and Sutherland[5] suggested frictional heating based on the two-component model of neutron star structure. Various pulsar groups considered polar cap heating of radio pulsars.[6] Tsuruta and Rees[7] studied heating of accreting X-ray pulsars. These and other earlier studies were reviewed by Tsuruta[8] and Helfand, Chanan, and Novick.[6] These papers also included crude estimates on heating of isolated neutron stars by accretion of interstellar medium and discussed other minor heat sources such as starquakes, which may explain timing "noise," plastic flows, etc. Hanawa and Fujimoto[9] and Nomoto and Tsuruta[10] calculated heating of cold older neutron stars in binary systems by thermonuclear burning caused by accretion. More recently Shibazaki and Lamb[11] and Tsuruta[2] carried out the first crude calculations of vortex creep heating. Through these studies, it was predicted that heating may play a crucial role for neutron stars older than about ten thousand years, although its role is minor for younger neutron stars except immediately after birth.

In this report, we shall introduce recent and current major developments in the area of neutron star cooling and heating. Due to the limitation of space, our major emphasis will be on the work conducted since the last review was given in the Chicago Texas Symposium.[2] In the next sections we shall first discuss some of the still remaining important problems related to the standard cooling, followed by a review of the recent and current work on the nonstandard cooling. After introducing our recent work on vortex creep heating, we shall briefly outline the work in progress on systematic, generalized studies of neutron star heating. We shall then discuss the detectability of a neutron star in SN 1987A. Concluding remarks will be given in the last section.

2. STANDARD COOLING OF NEUTRON STARS

The standard cooling calculations were carried out by Nomoto and Tsuruta[3] by solving the fully general relativistic equations with the best available physical input. In these calculations the "exact" method was adopted in the sense that the basic stellar structure-evolution equations are solved simultaneously without the isothermal approximation. The results were compared with the temperature upper limits obtained by the *Einstein Observatory*.[1,2,12] Some interesting points are summarized. The observed temperature upper limit for the Vela neutron star is below the standard cooling curves, while it is above the nonstandard curves with both charged-pion and quark cores* The data points for the Crab, RCW 103, and 3C 58 are all consistent with the standard cooling theory. Therefore, if some of these points (e.g. RCW 103) are shown to be the actual temperature measurements, at least in these stars there should be no exotic particles such as charged-pion condensates and quarks. It was emphasized[1,13] that this apparent discrepancy is naturally accounted for if the Vela neutron star is more massive than the other three stars mentioned above.* These conclusions are valid if the effects of magnetic fields on neutron star evolution are negligible. Until relatively recently in the studies of neutron star cooling, one of the most uncertain factors was the effect of magnetic fields, which enters the problem mainly via the anisotropy of opacities. In earlier calculations this effect was found to be important, but in these calculations the work of Canuto and Chiu[14] was generally adopted to estimate the electron conduction under strong magnetic fields. Hernquist[15] and Yakovlev[16] showed that the results of Canuto and Chiu[14] are unrealistic and developed realistic methods to attack this problem. Using these methods, it has been shown that the effect of magnetic fields on neutron star cooling itself is negligible.[15,17,18]

There are still a few magnetic-field-related problems involving neutron star cooling which are yet to be solved properly. Among these, the most important appears to be the effect of possible modulation of temperatures over the surface due to strongly quantized magnetic fields. In the earlier crude studies,[19,20] this effect was found to be important. However, in these studies a "zero-temperature" approximation was adopted, and only the radiative transport was considered. Recently it was shown that for the radiative transport the effect of anisotropy is not significant when the temperature is finite.[21] Recently Schaaf[22] reported that due to the anisotropic

---

*Recent studies[44] have shown that the *Einstein* data point (most likely a temperature measurement) for PSR 0656+14, which is slightly older than the Vela pulsar, is lower than the Vela point. We have found that both the Vela and PSR 0656+14 points lie on the same superfluid pion cooling curve[45] (the contribution by Umeda et al. in this volume). This outcome may be considered strong support for our tentative interpretation that the younger stars such as RCW 103 and the Crab pulsar (with higher observation points) are a different class of objects from the slightly older pulsars Vela and PSR 0656+14 (with lower points). Namely, the former are less massive neutron stars with no cores of such exotic particles as pions, while the latter are more massive stars with cores of such fast-cooling agents.

electron conduction under strong magnetic fields a significant difference arises between the polar and equatorial temperatures. However, the effect of consequent heat flows from the hotter polar regions to the cooler equatorial regions was not properly treated. It is important to solve this problem properly, because if the effect of this temperature modulation is indeed significant, the observed temperature will depend on the inclination of the polar axis to the line of sight, and therefore without answering this question it would be impossible to make any definitive statement about the implications of the current and future observational results on neutron star cooling theories.[1,2,12,13] For instance, if this effect is significant, we may not need to invoke nonstandard cooling to explain the Vela observation point. Therefore, we are currently exploring this problem carefully, adopting a two-dimensional approach.[23]

3. NONSTANDARD COOLING

3.1 COOLING OF COMPACT STARS WITH FAST COOLING AGENTS

3.1.1 COOLING IN THE PRESENCE OF PION CONDENSATES According to the recent work by Muto and Tatsumi[24] it is reasonable to assume that the pion phase appears at $\geq \sim 2\rho_N$ (where ρ_N is the nuclear density). Therefore, we have performed the "exact" cooling calculations for stars with pion cores within this range, using the pion emissivity recently derived by Muto and Tatsumi.[24,25] The results are summarized in Umeda et al. in this volume. The more detailed report is found in Ref. 25. The pion condensation is characterized by the Landau-Migdal (LM) parameter $\tilde{g}'$, which describes the baryon-baryon short-range correlations. Our results are shown for two representative cases, with $\tilde{g}' = 0.5$ and 0.6.[24]

Some of the interesting results are summarized below. (a) The star cools much faster in the presence of pion condensates than in their absence. (b) If the observation points of sources such as the Crab, RCW 103, 3C 58, Vela, and PSR 0656+14 refer to the stellar surface temperatures, pion stars would cool too fast to be consistent with observation. If the core particles are in the superfluid state, cooling is still too fast for the Crab, RCW 103, and 3C 58, but it can be consistent with the Vela and PSR 0656+14 observation points if appropriate superfluid gap energy is chosen. (c) A sudden drop in temperature, from $\sim 3 \times 10^6$K, is expected starting at $\sim$30–100 years after birth. This drop can be as large as a factor of nearly 10 within $\sim$30 years. This sharp drop in surface temperature may be detected from SN 1987A by future X-ray satellites. (d) The use of the "exact" evolutionary method is critical in order to obtain realistic results for pion cooling calculations, because the earlier calculations with the same microphysical input but conducted with the isothermal evolutionary method[2] indicate that the cooling is far less drastic, and furthermore there should be no sudden drop of luminosity during $\sim$1–100 years. For instance, when the isothermal method is used, even with no superfluidity some

pion stars can be hot enough to be comparable with the observation points of Vela and PSR 0656+14.

The above results are obtained for the FP equation of state with medium stiffness and stellar mass $M_A = 1.4 M_\odot$, as a representative model. (M_A is the baryon mass.) The effects of magnetic fields are neglected.

The effect of stellar mass is important. For instance, with reasonably stiff equations of state the central density of stars with mass smaller than about $1.3 M_\odot$ can be lower than the critical pion density, and hence these stars possess no pion core. This may mean that stars such as 3C 58, the Crab, and RCW 103 are slightly less massive, with $M_A \lesssim 1.3 M_\odot$ while the Vela and PSR 0656+14 pulsars are more massive, with $\geq 1.4\ M_\odot$.[2,13]. The effect of the equation of state is very important. For instance, for a typical star with ~ 1–$1.4 M_\odot$, the effect of pion cooling would be negligible for sufficiently stiff equations of state such as the PS model. This is because in these cases the pion critical density would be higher than the central density of the star. On the other hand, it is important for softer equations of state. For instance, with very soft equations of state the sudden drop of temperature can happen as early as ~ 10 years after birth.

3.1.2 COOLING OF QUARK AND KAON STARS

We have carried out similar calculations for quark stars using the same input physics and method as for pion stars except that the quark emissivity is used.[26] Both the emissivities derived by Iwamoto[27] and Kiguchi and Sato[28] are adopted. Qualitatively the general behavior is similar to the pion case. In the absence of superfluidity the star again cools too fast if the observation points refer to the stellar surface temperatures. When the superfluid effect is taken into account with an appropriate energy gap, quark cooling is found to be comparable with the Vela and PSR 0656+14 points.

Recently, Page and Baron[29] and Umeda, Tsuruta, and Nomoto[30] carried out cooling calculations in the presence of kaon condensates. The method of calculations and microphysical input are similar to those of Nomoto and Tsuruta,[3] although Page and Baron[29] used somewhat different equations of state and chose the kaon critical density $\rho_{crit}^k = 2$, 3, and 4 ρ_N. Umeda, Tsuruta, and Nomoto[30] assumed that $\rho_{crit}^k = 4\rho_N$. Qualitatively the conclusion reached is similar to our pion case. Adopting $\rho_{crit}^k = 4\rho_N$, Page and Baron[29] compared their superfluid cooling curves with different masses and concluded that stars with $1.2 M_\odot$ have no kaons and are consistent with the observation points for 3C 58, the Crab, and RCW 103, while a larger mass star with 1.4–$1.8 M_\odot$ with a kaon core is consistent with the Vela point.

One must remember that the above results on quark and kaon cooling should be taken with some caution, because neither quark nor kaon theories are yet sufficiently developed to give realistic estimates of the critical density at which these particles should appear. Using the parcoration theory Kiguchi and Sato[28] suggested that the quark critical density ρ_{crit}^q could be as low as the nuclear density, while other authors argue for higher values.[27] In our quark calculations we used $\rho_{crit}^q = 2\rho_N$. However, our results were relatively insensitive to the exact value of ρ_{crit}^q as it was varied from 2 to 4.

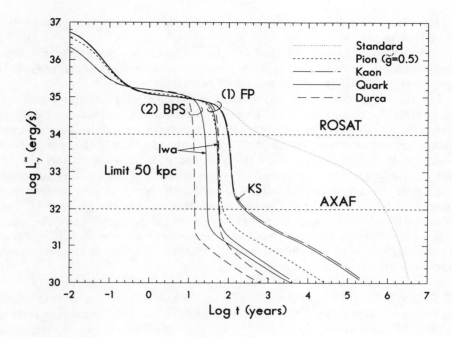

FIGURE 1 The standard and various non-standard cooling curves are compared.

3.1.3 COMPARISON AMONG DIFFERENT FAST COOLING SCENARIOS

Cooling calculations are carried out for various cases using the corresponding emissivities but otherwise adopting the same physical input. The results are compared in Figure 1. The various cases shown are the nonstandard cooling with pions with $\tilde{g}' = 0.5$ (*dashed*), quarks (*solid*), and kaons (*dot-dashed*), and the standard cooling with the modified URCA process (*dotted*). The FP model is adopted for curves marked (1), while the curves marked (2) refer to the BPS model. The Iwamoto emissivity is adopted for the fastest two quark curves, while the Kiguchi-Sato quark emissivity is used for the other curve. The effect of superfluidity is neglected. For all cases the mass is set to be $M_A = 1.4 M_\odot$. The two horizontal dashed lines refer to the observation limits of $ROSAT$ and $AXAF$ for a neutron star in SN 1987A at 50 kpc.

Qualitatively the nonstandard models with pions, quarks, and kaons exhibit similar behavior: Their cooling is much faster than the standard cooling; the effect of superfluidity is required for the models to be consistent with the Vela and PSR 0656+14 observation points (if they refer to the actual surface temperatures); and a sudden drop of surface temperature is expected within ~100 years after birth. We note that this sudden decline is most drastic for the very soft BPS model, with

luminosity declining sharply from $\sim 10^{35}$ ergs s^{-1} by a factor of more than 1000 within ~ 20 years. This sudden drop of luminosity from over 10^{35} ergs s^{-1} down to below the limit of detectability may be observed by *AXAF*. Should such a drop be detected, this may suggest that the equation of state has to be very soft.

Recently it was pointed out that a neutron star would cool much faster even without the fast-cooling exotic particles if the direct Urca process, which we shall refer to as the Durca process, is in operation. This occurs if proton concentration exceeds a certain critical value.[31] This was shown to be the case for a certain class of equations of state. Once the Durca process takes place the emissivity is estimated to be 10–1000 times higher than other existing fast-cooling scenarios (pion, kaon cooling, etc.). Therefore, we explored what would happen to our BPS and FP curves if the Durca process is indeed in operation. The results are shown in Figure 1 as the long-dashed curves. With the FP model, cooling is very similar to the pion case (when photon luminosity is $\geq \sim 10^{32}$ ergs s^{-1}). However, a significant effect is noted with the BPS model, in the sense that for the Durca cooling the sudden drop in temperature takes place ~ 20 years earlier.

Theoretical work conducted so far on quark and kaon matter has been less realistic than the work on pions. However, the most reliable currently existing estimates seem to suggest that the critical density at which pions should start appearing is significantly lower than both kaon and quark critical densities.[26,30] Then, if it is shown by some other means that a compact star has to be moderately stiff, the effects of kaons and quarks may become negligible. This is because for the typical range of $M_A \sim 1$–$1.6 M_\odot$ the central densities of these models may be below the critical densities where kaons and quarks should appear, but they may be above the pion critical density. If so, pions may become the most important of the fast-cooling agents. As to the Durca cooling, whether this process should be in operation or not depends on the fractional density of protons. In the investigation conducted so far, with some realistic equations of state such as that of Wiringa et al.,[31] the proton concentration is not sufficient for the Durca process to take place. If this trend is shown to apply to all realistic equations of state, this cooling scenario also may remain a subject of somewhat academic interest.

3.2 COOLING OF NEUTRON STARS WITH NEW PARTICLES

Among various possibilities for the nonstandard cooling scenarios is the emission of as yet undiscovered new particles. As a natural extension of axion-cooling calculations[32] (Iwamoto's contribution to this volume), we are exploring, in a systematic way, the maximum allowed strength with which new particles can interact with neutron star matter while leaving the conventional neutrino-cooling scenario unaffected.[33] Through these studies and comparison of neutron star cooling theories with the existing and future observational data, we may be able to place, quantitatively, important limits on the properties of these new particles.

We started with a standard neutrino-cooling scenario. An extra energy loss rate was then added to see how this modifies the original cooling curve. This extra emissivity due to the new particle interactions, $\in^N$, was estimated by examining the general behavior of neutrino emission processes involving nucleons, electrons, pion condensates, and quarks as well as the axion emission processes involving nucleons and electrons. The conclusion is that the emissivities for interactions involving these new particles which take place in the stellar core and the crust, $\in_{core}^N$ and $\in_{crust}^N$ (in ergs cm^{-3} s^{-1}), can be expressed as

$$\in_{core}^N = B \ 10^3 \ \left(\frac{\in_\pi}{T^6}\right) \left(\frac{T}{10^9}\right)^n , \tag{1}$$

$$\in_{crust}^N = C \ 10^{25} \ \left(\frac{Z^2}{A}\right) \left(\frac{\rho^s}{10^{13}}\right) \left(\frac{T}{10^9}\right)^n , \tag{2}$$

where we may choose as representative values $n = 4$, 6, and 8, and $s = 1/3$, 1/2, 2/3, and 1. The constants B and C are to be determined from comparison with observation. Z and A are the atomic and mass numbers of the dominant species, and $\in_\pi$ is the pion emissivity (in ergs cm^{-3} s^{-1}). In reality either the core or the crust emissivity will be dominant. Further details are found in Ref. 33. Here our preliminary results are summarized for typical cases.

Figure 2a shows cooling curves for the core emission case involving new particles, with $n = 4$ and $B = 10^3$ (*dotted*), 10 (*dashed*), and 0.1 (*long-dashed*). For comparison, pion cooling with $\tilde{g}' = 0.5$ is shown (*solid curve*). Also shown are the *Einstein* observation points. The conclusion is that if some of the observation points (e.g., RCW 103) are the temperature measurements the value for the constant B for this particular choice of n should be less than ~ 0.1. Similarly, Figure 2b shows cooling curves for the crust emission case involving new particles, when $n = 4$ and $s = 1$. The results correspond to $C = 10^5$, 10^3, 10, and 0.1, respectively, for the long-dashed, dashed, dotted, and dot-dashed curves. For comparison, the standard cooling with no new particles is shown as the solid curve. Again the *Einstein* observation points are shown. Comparing with the observation points, we may conclude that with this particular choice of the crust parameters, the constant C should be less than ~ 0.1. The implication of these results is discussed in Ref. 33.

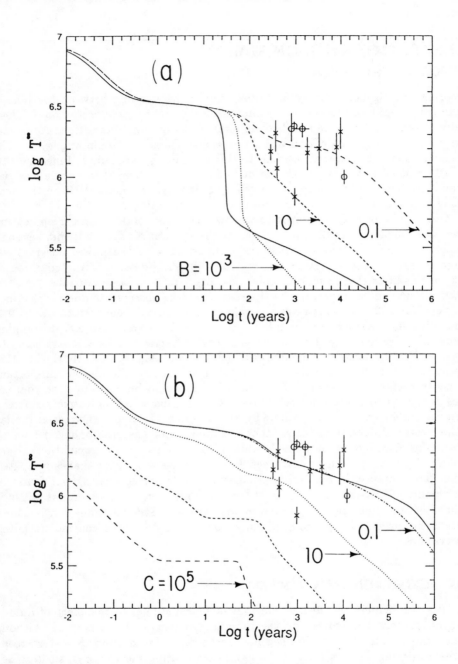

FIGURE 2 Cooling curves in the presence of new particles with (a) core and (b) crust emissions

4. HEATING OF NEUTRON STARS

4.1 VORTEX CREEP HEATING

According to a general theory of vortex creep[34] the coupling between the pinned crustal superfluid and the crust is achieved by thermal creep of vortex lines. Thermally activated vortex creep leads to an internal dissipation of the stored rotational energy. Such energy dissipation will act as a heat source in the pinning layers. The details are found in the contributions to this volume, by for example Pines and Alpar. We carried out heating calculations for the vortex creep[35] using the analytic formula for the dissipation rates derived by Shibazaki and Lamb.[11] Here the heat source was added to the standard evolutionary calculations.

Our results may be summarized as follows. The effect of the vortex creep heating is relatively small unless the equation of state is very stiff. In fact, it is small enough for the medium FP model so that the comparison with the pulsar observations cannot constrain the theory in one way or another. However, if the equation of state is as stiff as the PS model, which contains relatively large crustal layers, the effect is found to be important, in the sense that the observed temperature upper limit of PSR 1929+10 constrains the value of the critical frequency ω_{cr} to ≤ 0.1, supporting superweak-pinning models. (Here ω_{cr} refers to a measure of the pinning strength.[34]) We may note that the recent glitch observations also constrain ω_{cr} to ≤ 0.1 and the pinning to be superweak (Pines' and Alpar's contribution to this volume). The conclusion is that the vortex creep heating may become important for neutron stars older than $\sim 10^6$ years, but it would be negligible for younger stars, including the Vela and Crab pulsars. Our conclusion is qualitatively different from the earlier results, for example by Shibazaki and Lamb.[11] The reason is that in these earlier calculations the reduction of the internal energies (or specific heats) due to superfluidity was neglected, while it is included in our calculations. Here we find the effect of the vortex creep heating to be much less than anticipated earlier. For instance, in the earlier calculations vortex creep heating was found to start being effective at as early as 10^4 years, while here we find that it will not be effective until nearly 10^6 years even with the very stiff PS model. In reaching our conclusion, relatively strong pinning was excluded since it contradicts glitch observations.

4.2 OTHER HEATING MECHANISMS

Recently Van Riper[36] conducted phenomenological studies of the effect of an additional constant heat source on the thermal evolution of neutron stars, without taking into account the specific heating mechanisms. In addition to vortex creep, we are exploring various potentially significant heating mechanisms, such as accretion and polar cap heating. Detailed comparison of the theoretical models with observation may importantly constrain theories of these heating mechanisms. Both isolated and binary stars are considered, and both weak and strong field cases are

included. These studies will be important, because due to the reduction of specific heats in the presence of superfluidity at lower temperatures vortex creep heating may not be able to keep very old stars as hot as implied by observation.

5. DETECTABILITY OF A NEUTRON STAR IN SN 1987A

Nomoto and Tsuruta calculated cooling of a neutron star during the first 100 years after the explosion, without using the isothermal approximation.[37] The aim was to explore the detectability of thermal radiation directly from a neutron star in SN 1987A. The conclusion is that the star will cool so fast that after the first few to 20 days it will be impossible to observe it with the X-ray satellite *Ginga*, unless significant heating is in operation due, for example, to accretion of the falling-back ejecta. On the other hand, after the initial fast cooling the surface temperature decrease will slow down significantly. After the first month or so, this decrease will be so slow that the direct thermal radiation from a neutron star in SN 1987A should be easily detectable for more than 100 years by space satellites such as *ROSAT* and *AXAF*, if the effect of the circumstellar expanding envelope can be neglected.

In more realistic calculations the effect of the expanding envelope has been included.[38] The Monte Carlo simulation method was used to calculate the reprocessing taking place within a homogeneous circumstellar envelope. Included as the input radiation are nonthermal power-law emission from a Crab-like pulsar and thermal radiation from a hot neutron star accreting at the Eddington limit. Very recently the *Hubble Space Telescope* (*HST*) photographed an optical dust ring around SN 1987A, and due to the interaction between the supernova shock fronts and this dust ring it is estimated that the X-rays directly from the stellar surface will be hidden even after 50 years.[39] Therefore, the chance for directly observing the central neutron star may be slim for a while, unless our line of sight is cleared because the circumstellar material is very inhomogeneously distributed.

6. CONCLUDING REMARKS

We have summarized the recent major developments in the area of neutron star cooling and heating. This area will remain important for various reasons. For instance, heating theories could be tested by the observation of older neutron stars through the space missions already in operation, such as *ROSAT*, and those planned for the immediate future, such as *ASTRO-D* and *AXAF*. Also, SN 1987A may offer a timely laboratory to test evolution theories of very young neutron stars, through observations by *HST*, *ROSAT*, *ASTRO-D*, *AXAF*, and various ground based telescopes in a wide range of frequencies. Moreover, the satellite programs such as *ROSAT*, *AXAF*, and *XMM* could potentially determine actual temperature measurements

(not just upper limits) for sources such as RCW 103[40], significantly reduce the error bars, and detect more new sources like RCW 103. The current upper limits definitely would be lowered by a substantial degree. These observational improvements are expected to lead to more definitive conclusions than currently possible[1,2] when carefully compared with theories. Neutron star thermal evolution theories, in this sense, may have already reached a stage where quantitative theoretical work is critical. In addition, knowledge of the stellar temperature is essential for the understanding of many problems of neutron stars including dynamical problems such as their stability and viscosity,[41] the magnetic field decays,[42] the vortex creep,[34] and properties of transient and burst sources.[43] Also, neutron star temperatures could be estimated independently by some other means, such as the vortex creep theory.[34] Careful comparison of temperatures estimated by these different means could lead to important outcomes.

Our work on the new particles also will be important, because even with the accelerators already available and those expected in the near future, the laboratory experiments can offer only limited information about the properties of the particles whose interaction with matter is very weak.

ACKNOWLEDGEMENTS

We acknowledge with thanks useful discussions with many of our colleagues, especially H. Umeda, N. Iwamoto, K. Nomoto, T. Muto, R. Tamagaki, T. Tatsumi, and T. Ögelman. This work was supported, in part, by the NASA grant NAGW-2208 and the NSF grant RII-8921978.

REFERENCES

1. S. Tsuruta, *Comments on Astrophys.* **11**, 151 (1986).
2. S. Tsuruta, *13th Texas Symp. on Rel. Ap.*, M. P. Ulmer (ed.) (World Sci.), 499 (1987).
3. K. Nomoto and S. Tsuruta, *Ap. J.* **312**, 711 (1987).
4. G. Greenstein, *Ap. J.* **208**, 836 (1976).
5. M. A. Ruderman and P. G. Sutherland, *Nature Phys. Sci.* **246**, 93 (1973).
6. D. J. Helfand, G. A. Chanan, and R. Novick, *Nature* **283**, 337 (1980).
7. S. Tsuruta and M. J. Rees, *Mem. Soc. Astr. Italy* **3-4**, 903 (1975).
8. S. Tsuruta, *Physics Reports* **56**, 237 (1979).
9. T. Hanawa and M. Y. Fujimoto, *Publ. Astron. Soc. Japan,* **38**, 13 (1986); also see M. Y. Fujimoto, T. Hanawa, I. Iben, Jr., and M. B. Richardson, *Ap. J.* **315**, 198 (1987), etc.

10. K. Nomoto and S. Tsuruta, *Accreting Neutron Stars*, W. Brinkmann and J. Trümper (eds.), 275 (1982).

11. N. Shibazaki and F. K. Lamb, *Ap. J.* **346**, 808 (1988).

12. K. Nomoto and S. Tsuruta, *Ap. J. Lett.* **250**, L19 (1981); and K. Nomoto and S. Tsuruta, *Ap. J. Lett.* **305**, L19 (1986).

13. T. Takatsuka and R. Tamagaki, *Prog. Theor. Phys.* **79**, 274 (1988).

14. V. Canuto and H.-Y. Chiu, *Phys. Rev.* **188**, 2446 (1969).

15. L. Hernquist, *Ap. J. Suppl.* **56**, 325 (1984); and L. Hernquist, *M. N. R. A. S.*, **213**, 313 (1985).

16. D. G. Yakovlev, *Astron. Zh.* **59**, 683 (1982).

17. S. Tsuruta, B. Tritz, and B. Lapinsky, in preparation (1991).

18. K. Van Riper, *Ap. J.* **329**, 339 (1988).

19. G. Greenstein and G. J. Hartke, *Ap. J.* **271**, 283 (1983).

20. T. Daishido, *Pub. Astr. Soc. Japan* **27**, 181 (1975).

21. N. A. Silant'ev and D. G. Yakovlev, *Ap. Sp. Sci.* **71**, 45 (1980).

22. M. E. Schaaf, preprint (1990).

23. H. Umeda and S. Tsuruta, in preparation (1991).

24. T. Muto and T. Tatsumi, *Prog. Theor. Phys.* **79**, 461 (1988).

25. H. Umeda, K. Nomoto, S. Tsuruta, T. Muto, and T. Tatsumi, to be submitted to *Ap. J.* (1991).

26. H. Umeda, S. Tsuruta, and K. Nomoto, in preparation (1991).

27. N. Iwamoto, *Phys. Rev. Lett.* **44**, 1637 (1980).

28. M. Kiguchi and K. Sato, *Prog. Theor. Phys.* **66**, 725 (1981).

29. D. Page and E. Baron, *Ap. J. Lett.* **354**, L17 (1990).

30. H. Umeda, S. Tsuruta, and K. Nomoto, in preparation (1991).

31. J. M. Lattimer, C. J. Pethick, M. Prakash, and P. Haensel, *Phys. Rev. Lett.* **66**, 2701 (1991).

32. S. Tsuruta, and K. Nomoto, *Observational Cosmology*, Hewitt et al. (eds.) (Reidel Publ. Co.), 713 (1987).

33. H. Umeda, N. Iwamoto, S. Tsuruta, and K. Nomoto, in preparation (1991).

34. D. Pines and M. A. Alpar, *Nature* **316**, 27 (1985); M. A. Aplar, K. S. Cheng, and D. Pines, *Ap. J.* **346**, 823 (1989).

35. H. Umeda, N. Shibazaki, K. Nomoto, and S. Tsuruta, in preparation (1991).

36. Van Riper, preprint (1990).

37. S. Tsuruta and K. Nomoto, *Ap. Lett. and Communications* **27**, 241 (1988).

38. S. Kumagai, T. Shigeyama, K. Nomoto, M. Itoh, J. Nishimura, and S. Tsuruta, *Ap. J.* **345**, 412 (1989).

39. K. Nomoto, *Frontiers of X-Ray Astronomy*, Y. Tanaka and K. Koyama (eds.) (Universal Academy Press), in press (1991).

40. I. R. Tuohy, R. N. Garmire, R. N. Manchester, and M. A. Dopita, *Ap. J.* **268**, 778 (1983).

41. L. Lindblom, *Ap. J.* **317**, 325 (1987), etc.

42. Y. Sang, G. Chanmugam, and S. Tsuruta, *NATO ASI Series* (Dordrecht) (1989).

43. W. Lewin and P. Joss, *Space Sci. Rev.* **28**, 3 (1981).

44. R. J. Thompson, Jr., F. A. Cordova, R. M. Hjellming, and E. B. Fomalont, *Ap. J.* **366**, L83 (1991).

45. S. Tsuruta, H. Umeda, K. Nomoto, T. Muto, and T. Tatsumi, *Frontiers of X-Ray Astronomy*, Y. Tanaka and K. Koyama (eds.) (Universal Academy Press), in press (1991).

Naoki Iwamoto
Department of Physics and Astronomy, University of Toledo, Toledo, OH 43606, USA

Elementary Processes in Neutron-Star Cooling

Theoretical study of neutron-star cooling combined with either X-ray observation of thermal radiation from neutron stars inside historical supernova remnants or neutrino observations of supernova explosions provides competitive and often much better information about some of the new particles predicted in particle theories. Some of the elementary processes that are important in energy loss of neutron stars are discussed. The observability of neutron stars that contain exotic matter in the core using the next generation of X-ray satellites is also discussed.

1. PHYSICS OF NEUTRON-STAR COOLING: INTRODUCTION

Neutron stars are unique in that their interior temperatures and densities, during their formation and the subsequent period, are among the highest found in any stage of stellar evolution. The interior of neutron stars is thus an environment where thermal production of light particles can take place effectively, the energy loss of these stars being due mostly to particles other than photons. Comparisons between theoretical predictions on how they should cool and the observational data on how they actually cool provide valuable information about the nature of such particles

(existing or hypothetical) and about the neutron stars themselves. One may list the following essential topics in the physics of neutron-star cooling: (1) cooling agents, (2) equations of state, (3) other effects, and (4) observations.

Any neutral particle of mass < keV with a sufficiently strong coupling to neutron-star matter can play a role as a cooling agent when it is produced thermally and then escapes the star carrying off energy. Neutrinos and photons are two major (confirmed) agents. Other possible agents include the axion, majoron, familon, and light supersymmetric particles. When only neutrinos and photons are considered as cooling agents, the rate at which stellar energy is lost depends sensitively on the content of the neutron-star matter through the microscopic processes in which they are produced.[1] In other words, the cooling behavior depends critically on whether the core of the "neutron" star is composed of ordinary neutron-star matter (with a stiff, medium, or soft equation of state), meson condensates (charged- or neutral-pion[2] or kaon[3] condensates), or quark matter[4] (with[5] or without strangeness content). The composition of the neutron-star matter affects critically the kinematics of the neutrino production processes, allowing some processes and suppressing others as efficient energy-loss mechanisms. For a given cooling agent and an equation of state, there are other effects which can influence the cooling behavior significantly. Many-body effects change the effective masses of nucleons and the energy gap (when the nucleons become superfluid). Effective mass changes influence the energy loss by altering the density of states and thus the available phase space. Nucleon superfluidity has two effects on the cooling of neutron stars. First, due to the presence of an energy gap in the single-particle energy spectrum of the superfluid nucleons, the efficiency of the energy loss in these processes that involve superfluid nucleons is strongly reduced. Second, the specific heat of the nucleons which are in the superfluid state is also reduced exponentially at temperatures below the transition temperature. These two competing effects result in slower cooling right after the onset of superfluidity and more rapid cooling thereafter. While the effects of magnetic fields on the heat transport are considered to be less important, magnetic fields are expected to modify the structure of neutron-star surfaces, so that the deviation of the photon spectrum from its blackbody form could be observationally important. Internal heating is also possible. Its effect, however, is thought to be more pronounced in old neutron stars.

2. CONSTRAINTS ON NEW PARTICLES: AXIONS ET CETERA

The cooling behavior is strongly influenced by the nature of the coupling between the cooling agent and the neutron-star matter. One can utilize the observational data to place limits on the properties of hypothetical particles. Recently, axions have been considered in extensive studies of this sort,[6-12] which have constrained the coupling of axions to matter far better than those from laboratory experiments. The axion is a pseudoscalar particle introduced to solve the strong CP problem.[13]

Currently, the axion comes in two models, the Kim-Shifman-Vainshtein-Zakharov (KSVZ or hadronic) and Dine-Fischler-Srednicki-Zhitnitskii (DFSZ) models. Both types of axions couple to nucleons, and the most important process for the energy loss of neutron stars occurs via the nucleon-nucleon axion bremsstrahlung:[14-17] $nn \rightarrow nna$, $pp \rightarrow ppa$, and $np \rightarrow npa$. The neutrino observations of SN 1987A with the Kamiokande II and Irvine-Michigan-Brookhaven (IMB) detectors[18] have confirmed our current picture of stellar collapse—most of the gravitational binding energy of the progenitor is carried away by neutrinos. In order to be consistent with the observed data (the energy-loss rate,[7,10] the duration of the neutrino signal,[6,8,9,11] the total number of events, including the possible axion-induced events, in the Kamioka detector,[12] etc.) one can place a limit on the coupling between the matter and the light particles which could have been produced in the supernova. When such particles can freely escape from the star (the weak-coupling regime) an upper limit on the coupling constant is obtained, and when the coupling becomes so strong that such particles are reabsorbed in the collapsing matter (the strong-coupling regime), a lower limit results. The results of such studies for the axion by a number of authors are listed in Table 1.

Also listed are the limits from neutron-star cooling,[14,16,19] which are not too far from those from SN 1987A. The advantage of the neutron-star limits is that axion reabsorption never occurs (because of lower temperatures than those encountered in the supernova). This eliminates the alternative limits in the strong coupling regime of the supernova case. In addition, the results from a direct telescopic search for the photons from decaying axions ($a \rightarrow 2\gamma$) in rich clusters of galaxies[20] as well as a typical limit from accelerator experiments,[13] such as those on the decay of J/Ψ, are listed. It is noteworthy that the supernova limits are better than the laboratory limits by as much as seven orders of magnitude.[21] In fact, these coupling strengths from SN 1987A and neutron-stars, translated into the energy scale (the Peccei-Quinn symmetry-breaking scale),[13] correspond to on the order of 10^{10} GeV. The neutron-star (at its birth and in the subsequent cooling stage) is indeed an excellent high-energy physics laboratory.

Finally, let me remark on some other developments which occurred within the past year or so: The spectroscopic measurements of the decay width of Z^0 at the Stanford Linear Collider (SLC) and CERN's Large Electron-Positron Collider (LEP) have firmly established the number of light (lighter than half of the mass of Z^0) neutrinos to be three.[22] At the same time, these experimental data may be used to eliminate the sneutrino[23] as a potential cooling agent for neutron-stars.[24,25] On the other hand, there still remain other particles, such as the light photino[26] and the higgsino[25-27] (to a lesser extent), which could contribute to the cooling.[28] The simplest way of obtaining the constraints on the coupling of a new particle to matter is to use the neutrino energy-loss rate as a reference. In order to make more realistic and quantitative estimates, a comprehensive study is under way with the use of a generic form of the energy-loss rate (by allowing for different temperature and density dependences and by examining how sensitively the results depend on the uncertainties mentioned in section 1) in the neutron-star evolutionary code.[29]

TABLE 1 The Limits on the Axion-Nucleon Coupling Constants from SN 1987A. Whenever possible, the axion-neutron coupling (g_{ann}) and the axion-proton coupling (g_{app}) are taken to be equal ($\equiv g_{aNN}$) in order to make the comparison on an equal footing. The criteria, the degree of approximations in calculating the energy-loss rates (the treatment of unknown parameters in the axion models, matrix elements, etc.), and the parameters of neutron-star matter (collapse model, temperature, density, composition, etc.) differ significantly among these authors. Thus the comparison is for illustrative purposes only. When limits are listed in both the weak- and strong-coupling regimes, they are alternative limits, i.e., either of them is consistent with the criterion used. The superscripts in the last column indicate reference numbers.

Method	Weak coupling		Strong coupling	Author(year)
SN 1987A	$g_{aNN} < (2-3) \times 10^{-11}$		—	RS(1988)[6]
SN 1987A	$g_{aNN} < 6 \times 10^{-11}$	or	$g_{aNN} > 2 \times 10^{-7}$	T(1988)[7]
SN 1987A	$g_{aNN} < 8 \times 10^{-11}$	or	$g_{aNN} > 2 \times 10^{-7}$	BTB(1989)[8]
SN 1987A	$g_{app} < (3-11) \times 10^{-11}$	or	$g_{app} > 1 \times 10^{-8}$	MWEOSS(1989)[9]
SN 1987A	$g_{aNN} < 5 \times 10^{-11}$	or	$g_{aNN} > 3 \times 10^{-9}$	IY(1990)[10]
SN 1987A	—		$g_{aNN} > 2 \times 10^{-7}$	BRT(1990)[11]
SN 1987A	$g_{aNN} < 9 \times 10^{-7}$	or	$g_{aNN} > 10^{-3}$	ESH(1990)[12]
Galaxies	$g_{aNN} < 2 \times 10^{-7}$	or	$g_{aNN} > 6 \times 10^{-7}$	BRT(1991)[20]
Neutron stars	$g_{aNN} < (2-4) \times 10^{-10}$		—	I(1984,91)[14,16]
Neutron stars	$g_{aNN} < 10^{-10}$		—	TN(1987)[19]
Experiments	$g_{aNN} < 10^{-3}$		—	K(1987)[13]

3. HIGH-SENSITIVITY OBSERVATIONS WITH THE ADVANCED X-RAY ASTROPHYSICS FACILITY: EXPLORATION OF EXOTIC STATES OF MATTER INSIDE NEUTRON-STARS

Let us now turn our attention to the observational prospects in the near future. The Advanced X-Ray Astrophysics Facility (AXAF) is planned for launch in the late 1990s as one of the Great Observatories in the X-ray wavelengths.[30] The sensitivity of the detectors on AXAF has been designed to be significantly higher than those on the Einstein Observatory. For those point sources detected by Einstein inside supernova remnants (such as 3C 58, Crab, RCW 103, Vela, etc.) the spectrometers on AXAF will determine whether the radiation is thermal or not. In addition, the better statistics from the increased sensitivity may eventually allow one to distinguish different neutron star matter equations of state. On the other hand, for those historical supernova remnants where Einstein did not find point sources, one may ask an intriguing question: Can one detect the neutron-stars with exotic-matter cores (which are expected to have cooled rapidly beyond the detection limit of Einstein) with AXAF? The following are the results of a preliminary study of this question.[31]

The expected photon count rates from the neutron-stars (if they exist) inside historical supernova remnants, such as SN 1680 (Cas A), SN 1572 (Tycho), and SN 1006, have been estimated. The basic ingredients are as follows. (1) A blackbody source spectrum is assumed with the neutron-star surface temperatures that are predicted by nonstandard cooling scenarios with pion condensates or quark matter cores.[32] (2) The AXAF High Resolution Camera (HRC) effective area[30] is used. (3) For interstellar absorption, the effective photoabsorption cross section due to Brown and Gould[33] is used together with the estimated hydrogen column densities for individual sources. The results are shown in Table 2.

Although preliminary, this study already brings out the following interesting points: (1) Interstellar absorption is the most important factor that determines whether a particular source can be detected or not. The relatively low surface temperatures that result from enhanced cooling due to the presence of exotic matter,[1] in comparison with ordinary neutron-star matter, shift the peak of the photon flux to lower energies. On the other hand, at lower energies (in the EUV region) the effective photoabsorption cross section increases roughly as E^{-3}. Therefore, detection becomes exceedingly difficult with hydrogen column densities $n_H > 10^{22}$ cm^{-2} and low surface temperatures $T < 0.5 \times 10^6$ K. (2) For a neutron-star with pion cooling, SN 1006 is the most and possibly only promising candidate for detection. The estimated photon flux is well within the capability of the AXAF/HRC for detection with a reasonable observing time. For this source, the X-ray and non-X-ray background count rates with a $1'' \times 1''$ search cell are estimated to be less

TABLE 2 Photon Count Rates with AXAF High Resolution Camera for Neutron-Stars Inside Historical Supernova Remnants. The surface temperatures of neutron stars are based
on those predicted by the nonstandard cooling scenarios in the presence of either pion
condensates or quark matter cores.

Source	Distance (kpc)	Hydrogen column density $(10^{22}\ cm^{-2})$	Cooling mode	Surface temperature $(10^6\ K)$	Photon count rate (s^{-1})
SN 1006	1.0	0.10	Pion	0.49	0.53×10^{-3}
SN 1006	1.0	0.10	Quark	0.27	1.00×10^{-6}
Tycho	3.3	0.75	Pion	0.56	0.75×10^{-6}
Tycho	3.3	0.75	Quark	0.30	0.12×10^{-9}
Cas A	2.8	1.0	Pion	0.60	0.52×10^{-6}
Cas A	2.8	1.0	Quark	0.31	0.50×10^{-10}

than those from a neutron star. One obtains a similar result for the AXAF CCD Imager.[30] (3) The neutrino energy-loss rate of kaon condensates has been found to be between those of neutron-star matter with and without pion condensation,[3] so that the detection of a neutron-star with kaon condensation should be within the capability of AXAF as well. (4) Because of the low interstellar-hydrogen column density $n_H = 6 \times 10^{21}$ cm^{-2}, the neutron-star inside SN 1987A is also a promising candidate for detection with the standard or nonstandard cooling scenarios, once the supernova ejecta thin out.

ACKNOWLEDGMENTS

I wish to thank the participants of this seminar for stimulating discussions. I would also like to thank the College of Arts and Sciences at the University of Toledo for travel support through the Faculty Development Fund, which made my participation in this seminar possible, and the U.S. Consulate General, Osaka, for generous issuance of the U.S. entry visa, which enabled me to return to work. This work is supported in part by the U.S. National Science Foundation under Grant No. PHY90-08475.

REFERENCES

1. G. Baym and C. Pethick, *Annu. Rev. Nucl. Part. Sci.* **25**, 27 (1975); idem, *Annu. Rev. Astron. Astrophys.* **17**, 415 (1979); S. Tsuruta, *Phys. Rep.* **56**, 237 (1979); idem, *Comments Astrophys.* **11**, 151 (1986); S. L. Shapiro and S. A. Teukolsky, *Black Holes, White Dwarfs, and Neutron Stars* (Wiley, New York, 1983).
2. O. Maxwell, G. E. Brown, D. K. Campbell, R. F. Dashen, and J. T. Manassah, *Astrophys. J.* **216**, 77 (1977); T. Tatsumi, *Prog. Theor. Phys.* **69**, 1137 (1983).
3. D. B. Kaplan and A. E. Nelson, *Phys. Lett.* B **175**, 57 (1986); G. E. Brown, K. Kubodera, and M. Rho, *Phys. Lett.* B **192**, 273 (1987); G. E. Brown, K. Kubodera, D. Page, and P. Pizzochero, Phys. Rev. D **37**, 2042 (1988); T. Tatsumi, *Prog. Theor. Phys.* **80**, 22 (1988); D. Page and E. Baron, *Astrophys. J. Lett.* **354**, 17 (1990).
4. N. Iwamoto, *Phys. Rev. Lett.* **44**, 1637 (1980); idem, Ann. Phys. (N.Y.) **141**, 1 (1982); idem, *Phys. Rev.* D **28**, 2353 (1983); R. C. Duncan, S. L. Shapiro, and I. Wasserman, *Astrophys. J.* **267**, 358 (1983).
5. C. Alcock, E. Farhi, and A. Olinto, *Astrophys. J.* **310**, 261 (1986); *Annu. Rev. Nucl. Part. Sci.* **38**, 161 (1988); S. Datta, S. Raha, and B. Sinha, *Mod. Phys. Lett.* A **3**, 1385, (1988); A. Goyal and J. D. Anand, *Phys. Rev.* D. **42**, 992 (1990).
6. G. Raffelt and D. Seckel, *Phys. Rev. Lett.* **60**, 1793 (1988).
7. M. S. Turner, *Phys. Rev. Lett.* **60**, 1797 (1988).
8. A. Burrows, M. S. Turner, and R. P. Brinkmann, *Phys. Rev.* D **39**, 1020 (1989).
9. R. Mayle, J. R. Wilson, J. Ellis, K. Olive, D. N. Schramm, and G. Steigman, *Phys. Lett.* B **203**, 188 (1988); ibid., **219**, 515 (1989).
10. N. Ishizuka and M. Yoshimura, *Prog. Theor. Phys.* **84**, 233 (1990).
11. A. Burrows, M. T. Ressell, and M. S. Turner, *Phys. Rev.* D **42**, 3297 (1990).
12. J. Engel, D. Seckel, and A. C. Hayes, *Phys. Rev. Lett.* **65**, 960 (1990).
13. For reviews, see, e.g., J. E. Kim, *Phys. Rep.* **150**, 1 (1987); H.-Y. Cheng, *Phys. Rep.* **158**, 1 (1988); R. D. Peccei, in *CP Violation*, edited by C. Jarlskog (World Scientific, Singapore, 1989), p. 503; P. Sikivie, in *Dark Matter in the Universe*, edited by H. Sato and H. Kodama (Springer, Berlin, 1990), p. 94; M. S. Turner, *Phys. Rep.* **197**, 67 (1990); G. G. Raffelt, ibid., **198**, 1 (1990).
14. N. Iwamoto, *Phys. Rev. Lett.* **53**, 1198 (1984); idem, *Phys. Rev.* D **39**, 2120 (1989).
15. R. P. Brinkmann and M. S. Turner, *Phys. Rev.* D **38**, 2338 (1988).
16. N. Iwamoto, to be published.
17. For many-body effects in this process, which could be substantial, see T. E. O. Ericson and J.-F. Mathiot, *Phys. Lett.* B **219**, 507 (1989). According to

18. G. Raffelt and D. Seckel [*Phys. Rev. Lett.* **67**, 2605 (1991)], the nucleon-nucleon collision frequency is high in supernova matter, such that nucleon-nucleon bremsstrahlung rates of neutrinos and axions are suppressed up to an order of magnitude (the Landau–Pomeranchuk effect). Accordingly, the axion bound from Supernova 1087A is relaxed to some extent. Since the collision frequency is sufficiently low for highly degenerate matter, this effect does not modify the emission rates of neutrinos and axions that are relevant to the long-term cooling of neutron stars. For axion emission from a QCD (quark-gluon) plasma, see T. Altherr, *Z. Phys.* C **47**, 559 (1990); idem, T. Altherr, *Ann. Phys.* (N.Y.) **207**, 374 (1991). For the axion and photino flux from strange quark matter, see J. D. Anand, A. Goyal, and R. N. Jha, *Phys. Rev.* D **42**, 996, (1990).

19. K. Hirata et al., *Phys. Rev. Lett.* **58**, 149 (1987); R. M. Bionta et al., ibid., **58**, 1494 (1987).

20. S. Tsuruta and K. Nomoto, in *Proceedings of the IAU Symposium No. 124: Observational Cosmology*, edited by A. Hewitt, G. Burbidge, and L. Z. Fang (Reidel, Dordrecht, 1987), p. 713.

21. M. A. Bershady, M. T. Ressell, and M. S. Turner, *Phys. Rev. Lett.* **66**, 1398 (1991).

22. See Ref. 13 for other astrophysical limits (including those on the coupling to electrons and photons) and *Cosmic Axions*, edited by C. Jones and A. Melissinos (World Scientific, Singapore, 1990), for the recent experimental efforts to detect axions of cosmic and artificial origins in the laboratory.

23. G. S. Abrams et al. (Mark II Collaboration), *Phys. Rev. Lett.* **63**, 2173 (1989); D. Decamp et al. (ALEPH Collaboration), *Phys. Lett.* B **235**, 399 (1990); M. Z. Akrawy et al. (OPAL Collaboration), *Phys. Lett.* B **240**, 497 (1990); P. Abreu et al. (DELPHI Collaboration), *Phys. Lett.* B **241**, 493 (1990); B. Adeva et al. (L3 Collaboration), *Phys. Lett.* B **249**, 341 (1990). For a review, see D. J. Miller, *Nature* **349**, 379 (1991).

24. L. E. Ibáñez, *Phys. Lett.* B **137**, 160 (1984); J. S. Hagelin, G. L. Kane, and S. Raby, Nucl. Phys. B **241**, 638 (1984); J. A. Grifols, M. Martínez, and J. Sola, Nucl. Phys. B **268**, 151 (1986).

25. L. M. Krauss, *Phys. Rev. Lett.* **64**, 999 (1990); Yale University Report No. YCTP-P9-90, 1990.

26. N. Iwamoto, in *Proceedings of the IUPAP Conference on Primordial Nucleosynthesis and Evolution of the Early Universe*, edited by K. Sato et al. (Kluwer Academic, Dordrecht, 1991), (in press).

27. J. Ellis, K. A. Olive, S. Sarkar, and D. W. Sciama, *Phys. Lett.* B **215**, 404 (1988).

28. H. E. Haber, Stanford University Report No. SLAC-PUB-3834, 1985.

29. In this seminar it was pointed out by Dr. C. J. Pethick that some of the neutron-star matter equations of state may give a sufficiently high proton fraction so that the neutron beta decay process ($n \rightarrow pe^-\bar{\nu}_e$, $pe^- \rightarrow n\nu_e$) is kinematically allowed. J. M. Lattimer, C. J. Pethick, M. Prakash, and P. Haensel (*Phys. Rev. Lett.* **66**, 2701 [1991]) have in fact found that such a

kinematical condition is satisfied for many realistic combinations of the density dependence of the nuclear symmetry energy and the incompressibility

30. parameter; and that the energy-loss rate from this process is much larger than that from the modified URCA process ($nn \rightarrow npe^-\bar{\nu}_e$, $npe^- \rightarrow nn\nu_e$). The importance of this *direct URCA process* depends on the size of the core where the density exceeds the threshold value. See also S. Tsuruta in these proceedings.

31. H. Umeda, N. Iwamoto, S. Tsuruta, and K. Nomoto, work in progress. See also S. Tsuruta in these proceedings.

32. M. C. Weisskopf, *Space Sci. Rev.* **47**, 47 (1988).

33. N. Iwamoto, to be published.

34. K. Nomoto and S. Tsuruta, *Astrophys. J. Lett.* **305**, 19 (1986); idem, *Astrophys. J.* **312**, 711 (1987).

35. R. L. Brown and R. J. Gould, *Phys. Rev.* D **1**, 2252 (1970).

N. Shibazaki† and F. K. Lamb‡
†Department of Physics, Rikkyo University, Nishi-Ikebukuro, Tokyo 171, Japan; and
‡Department of Physics, University of Illinois, Urbana, IL 61801, USA

Neutron Star Evolution with Internal Friction

In current models of neutron stars, only the neutron superfluid in the inner crust is weakly coupled to the crust. In rotation-powered pulsars, this component is expected to be rotating faster than the rest of the star. Frictional interaction of the superfluid with the crust dissipates the free energy of superfluid differential rotation, heating the star. Conversely, the internal temperature of the star affects the amount of differential rotation. We study the effect of superfluid-crust interaction on neutron star evolution. We find that even quite small heating rates can greatly increase the temperature of the star in the photon cooling era, producing a thermal evolution quite different from the evolution predicted by models without internal heating and previous models with heating. We also find via linear analysis that the superfluid-crust interaction, predicted by some current models, may give rise to thermal and rotational instabilities in old neutron stars. The thermal flux enhanced by the internal heating and possibly some evidence for the instabilities may be observed from nearby old pulsars with future instruments.

1. INTRODUCTION

An understanding of the rotational, thermal, and magnetic field evolution of neutron stars is necessary in order to interpret observations of rotation- and accretion-powered pulsars and other neutron stars correctly. Conversely, studies of the spin rates, surface temperatures, and magnetic fields of such objects provide information about the internal structure of neutron stars and their electrical, thermal, and dynamical properties.

Although most studies have treated them separately, the magnetic, rotational, and thermal properties of neutron stars are not independent. Instead, these properties all affect one another. For example, friction between differentially rotating components in the stellar interior heats the star, thereby changing its thermal evolution. Conversely, the internal temperature of the star affects the amount of differential rotation. Both are influenced by evolution of the stellar magnetic field through its effect on the coupling of the neutron star interior to the crust and the coupling of the crust to the environment. The evolution of the stellar magnetic field is in turn influenced by the thermal evolution of the star.

Various mechanisms have been proposed for the interaction of the superfluids with the normal matter in the interiors of neutron stars. Here we report the results of a study of the implications of current superfluid-crust interaction models for the thermal and rotational evolution of neutron stars. In section 2 we describe the physical model of neutron stars which we adopt in the present study. In section 3 we discuss the effects of internal heating on the thermal evolution of neutron stars. In section 4 we examine the stability of the frictionally interacting superfluid-crust system. In the last section the implications of this study for future observations are summarized.

2. PHYSICAL PICTURE AND ASSUMPTIONS

Neutron stars are expected to have a layered structure consisting of several distinct regions:[1] (1) a surface, which may be solid or liquid; (2) an outer crust, which contains a solid array of nuclei and relativistic degenerate electrons; (3) an inner crust, which contains $^1S_0$ superfluid neutrons together with a solid lattice of neutron rich nuclei and relativistic electrons; (4) a fluid core, which contains mainly $^3P_2$ superfluid neutrons with an admixture of a few percent of superconducting protons and normal electrons; (5) possibly, in heavier stars, a distinct inner core, which might contain condensed pions or matter in some other exotic state.

The external braking torque acts on the charged components, which include the solid lattice of nuclei, electrons, and protons, and decelerates their rotation first. The superfluid components which weakly couple to the charged components respond to the external braking torque with some time delay. In consequence, in rotation-powered neutron stars the superfluid components rotate faster than the

charged components. Heat is generated by friction between these differentially rotating components.

The neutron superfluids in a rotating neutron star are expected to form vortices. The $^3P_2$ superfluid vortices in the core are strongly magnetized due to the dragging of superfluid protons by the superfluid neutrons circulating around each neutron vortex.[2] Consequently, the superfluid in the core couples strongly to the electrons there and hence to the other charged components, corotating with them on the time scales of interest here.

The $^1S_0$ superfluid vortex lines in the inner crust are pinned to the lattice nuclei, to the spaces between nuclei, or to lattice defects.[3] The ratio of the moment of inertia of the pinned superfluids to the total moment of inertia of the star depends on the neutron star model and is in the range 2×10^{-3}–10^{-1}.[4] Some of these vortex lines migrate as the result of thermal activation against the pinning energy barrier.[5] Alternatively, the crustal lattice may crack due to the stress exerted on it by the pinned vortex lines.[6] Then, the vortex lines move outward due to their frictional interaction with other components. The outward motion of vortex lines leads to deceleration of the superfluid rotation, dissipation of the differential rotational energy of the superfluid, and heating of the neutron star interior.[5]

In the present study we assume that all the matter in the star other than the neutron superfluid in the inner crust has a constant moment of inertia I_c and rotates uniformly with angular velocity Ω_c. Hereafter, the stellar material except for the inner crust superfluid is referred to as the crust. We assume that the inner crust superfluid can be treated as a sequence of components with constant moment of inertia I_i and time-varying angular velocities Ω_i. We further assume that the interior of the star is isothermal, which is a good approximation especially for older neutron stars.[7]

3. ROTATIONAL EVOLUTION

The change of angular momentum of a star is described by

$$I_c\dot{\Omega}_c + \sum_i I_i\dot{\Omega}_i = N_{\text{ext}} \quad , \tag{1}$$

where N_{ext} is the braking torque exerted on the star.

If the superfluid components and the crust are in rotational equilibrium, they decelerate at the same rate, that is,

$$\dot{\Omega}_c = \dot{\Omega}_i \quad , \tag{2}$$

and hence the angular velocity difference between the crust and the superfluid components, $\omega_i = \Omega_i - \Omega_c$, remains constant. It is expected that the equilibrium value of the angular velocity difference for each layer of superfluid is close to a

critical value ω_{cr} which, if exceeded, leads to outward motion of vortices in the layer. Alpar et al.[5] have discussed values of $\omega_{cr} \ll 0.1, \sim 0.1\text{--}1$, and $\gg 1$ rad s^{-1}, which they call superweak, weak, and strong pinning, respectively.

If we adopt a braking law of the form $N_{\text{ext}} = -K_0 e^{-t/\tau_d} \Omega_c^{\ k}$ with τ_d being the torque decay time constant, then from Eqs. (1) and (2), the crust angular velocity as a function of time is

$$\Omega_c(t) = \frac{\Omega_{c1}}{\left[1 + (\tau_d/\tau_{s1})(1 - e^{-(t-t_1)/\tau_d})\right]^{1/(k-1)}} \quad , \tag{3}$$

where Ω_{c1} is the angular velocity of the crust and τ_{s1} is the spin-down time, $\tau_s = \Omega_c/(k-1)|\dot{\Omega}_c|$, at time t_1.

4. THERMAL EVOLUTION

The thermal evolution of a star with an isothermal interior can be described approximately by the equation

$$C_V \dot{T} = H - \Lambda = H - \Lambda_\nu - \Lambda_\gamma \quad , \tag{4}$$

where C_V is the heat capacity of the star, T is the internal temperature, H is the internal heating rate, Λ is the cooling rate, and Λ_ν and Λ_γ are the neutrino and photon luminosities, respectively. The heat capacity of the star resides in the degenerate normal matter and can therefore be expressed as $C_V = aT$, where the coefficient a depends on the stellar model. The rate of internal heating caused by dissipation of the rotational energy of the neutron superfluid is given by

$$H = -\sum_i I_i \omega_i \dot{\Omega}_i \quad . \tag{5}$$

In rotational equilibrium Eq. (5) reduces to

$$H = -J\dot{\Omega}_i \quad , \tag{6}$$

where $J = \sum_i I_i \omega_i$.

The dominant neutrino process depends on the internal temperature and the neutron star model. The dominant process in stiff stars at the evolutionary times of interest to us is neutrino bremsstrahlung in the crust, while in soft stars with a pion condensate the dominant process is pion-mediated neutrino emission from the core. Choosing an appropriate constant value λ_ν, the rates of both processes may be expressed as $\Lambda_\nu = \lambda_\nu T^6$.

The photon luminosity is given approximately by blackbody radiation from the stellar surface. If we adopt the relation between the effective surface temperature and the internal temperature found by Gudmundsson, Pethick, and Epstein,[8] the

photon luminosity can be expressed as $\Lambda_\gamma = 1.4 \times 10^{15}(M/M_\odot)T^{2.2}$ ergs s^{-1}, where M is the mass of the star.

We have calculated the thermal evolution of neutron stars with and without internal heating predicted by current models of the superfluid-crust interaction.[9] Table 1 lists the parameters of two models representative of the standard and nonstandard cooling models considered by previous authors. Model 1 was constructed using a stiff equation of state, assuming no pion condensate in the core, and adopting neutrino bremsstrahlung in the crust as the dominant neutrino process, while model 2 was constructed using a relatively soft equation of state, assuming a pion condensate in the core, and adopting the pion-mediated neutrino process in the core as the dominant neutrino emission process (see Ref. 9 for the references concerning the model parameters).

TABLE 1 Neutron Star Models

Stellar parameter	Model 1 (standard cooling)	Model 2 (nonstandard cooling)
M ($M_\odot$)	1.4	1.4
R (km)	15.8	7.4
I (g cm^2)	2.18×10^{45}	6.51×10^{44}
I_s (g cm^2)	3×10^{44}	1.7×10^{42}
a (ergs K^{-2})	2.0×10^{29}	2.9×10^{29}
λ_ν (ergs s^{-1}K^{-6})	4.3×10^{-17}	3×10^{-9}
μ (G cm^3)	5×10^{30}	3×10^{30}

Fig. 1 illustrates the cooling curves obtained by integrating Eq. (4) for models 1 and 2, assuming rotational equilibrium, $k = 3$ (magnetic dipole braking), no torque evolution (constant magnetic dipole moment μ), and constant J. The evolutions were started at $t_1 = 100$ yr with $T_1 = 10^9$ K, $\Omega_{c1} = 374$ rad s^{-1}, $\tau_{s1} = 400$ yr and $T_1 = 10^{7.7}$ K, $\Omega_{c1} = 340$ rad s^{-1}, and $\tau_{s1} = 400$ yr for models 1 and 2, respectively. The curves labeled 0 show the thermal histories in the absence of internal energy dissipation. The other curves show the thermal histories produced by various rates of internal heating due to friction between the neutron superfluid and the crust. In the terminology of Alpar et al.,[5] the curves in Fig. 1a with $J_{44} \ll 0.31, \sim 0.31 - 3.1$, and $\gg 3.1$ correspond to superweak, weak, and strong pinning. The curves in Fig. 1b with $J_{42} \ll 0.17, \sim 0.17 - 1.7$, and $\gg 1.7$ correspond to these same pinning regimes. The evolutionary tracks both with and without internal heating display two distinct eras. The early, relatively flat parts of the cooling curves correspond to the neutrino cooling era, whereas the later, more steeply falling parts of the curves correspond to the photon cooling era.

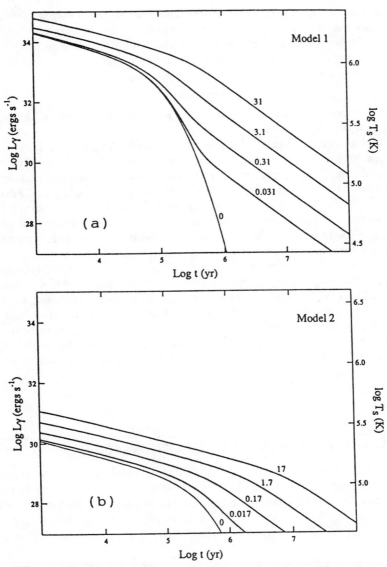

FIGURE 1 Evolutionary tracks illustrating the behavior of cooling models with and without internal heating. Models 1 and 2 correspond to standard and nonstandard cooling models, respectively. L_γ, T_s, and t are the photon luminosity, surface temperature, and age of the star. The curves labeled 0 show the thermal histories in the absence of internal heating, while the other curves show the thermal histories in the presence of internal heating. The labels of tracks in model 1 are the assumed values of J_{44}, the values of J in units of 10^{44} g cm^2 rad s^{-1}, while the labels in model 2 are the assumed values of J_{42}, the values of J in units of 10^{42} g cm^2 rad s^{-1}.

While the thermal inertia term dominates the internal heating term, the evolution of the star depends on its thermal history. Once the internal heating term dominates, however, the star quickly approaches thermal equilibrium, in which the internal heating rate H and the cooling rate Λ due to the neutrino and photon emissions are in balance,

$$H = \Lambda \quad . \tag{7}$$

Then, the temperature and luminosity of the star are determined by its deceleration rate, regardless of its history.

Internal heating increases the photon luminosity of model 1 in the neutrino cooling era by less than a factor of 3, even if J has the largest value currently thought possible. This is due to both the temperature sensitivity of the neutrino emission and the contribution of the initial heat content during this era. For model 2, however, the initial heat content is lost more rapidly and internal heating is therefore more important. Figure 1b shows that the largest internal heating rate considered increases the photon luminosity of model 2 by about an order of magnitude during the neutrino cooling era.

The internal heating predicted by current models of the superfluid-crust interaction completely changes the conventional picture of neutron star evolution in the photon cooling era. Without internal heating, the photon luminosity falls steeply, as indicated by the lines labeled 0 in Fig. 1. With internal heating, the star cools much more slowly and hence the cooling curve is much flatter, as indicated by the other lines in the figure. At ages greater than $\sim 10^6$ yr, even the models with very small values of J have photon luminosities more than an order of magnitude greater than the corresponding models without internal heating.

5. THERMAL AND ROTATIONAL INSTABILITIES

In the preceding section we have calculated the thermal evolution of neutron stars with internal heating, assuming that the superfluid and the crust are in rotational equilibrium. If the rotational equilibrium state is unstable, however, the thermal histories shown in Fig. 1 may be altered significantly. Hence, it is necessary to examine the stability of the system of superfluid and crust coupled through a frictional interaction.

In the course of neutron star evolution, several characteristic stages are encountered, involving thermal and rotational equilibria or disequilibria, as shown in Fig. 2a. If all the stages shown in Fig. 2a are realized in the course of its evolution, then the simplest scenario for the neutron star would be the one indicated by the solid line. The neutron star is born in thermal and rotational disequilibrium. Since the coupling time between the superfluid and the crust is very short at high temperatures, the neutron star settles into rotational equilibrium (stage B) immediately. Cooling due to the neutrino emission dominates frictional heating at high temperatures. Hence, the star is not in thermal equilibrium. The neutron star

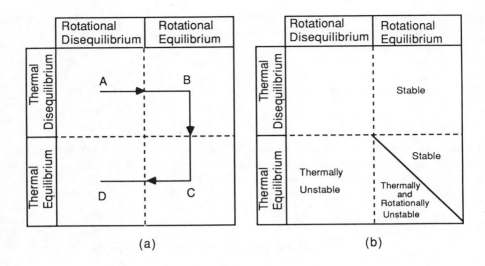

FIGURE 2 Characteristic neutron star evolutionary stages and their stability. The solid line indicates a possible evolutionary path if all the stages are realized. Stage C is thermally and rotationally unstable below a critical temperature.

stays at stage B as long as cooling dominates heating. As its temperature decreases, frictional heating increases relative to cooling and the neutron star eventually attains thermal equilibrium in addition to rotational equilibrium (stage C). As the temperature falls further, in some superfluid-crust interaction models the coupling time becomes comparable to the spin-down time. At this time the crust decouples from the superfluid and the neutron star enters stage D.

Depending on the initial condition, the neutron star model, and the interaction mechanism, however, the simple evolutionary track just described will be modified. Furthermore, the evolutionary track shown in Fig. 2a is also influenced by the stability of each stage. If a certain stage is unstable, that stage may not persist and the subsequent stages may never be reached. Hence, it is important to examine the stability of the characteristic evolutionary stages mentioned above in order to understand the neutron star evolution correctly. In what follows we summarize the stability analysis we have conducted for these characteristic stages. The details will be published elsewhere.

We begin by describing the further assumptions and the superfluid-crust interaction models that we adopt. We assume that the inner crust superfluid can be treated as a whole, with total moment of inertia I_s, average angular velocity Ω_s, and other average physical quantities. Since we are interested in time-varying

behavior with a time scale much shorter than the spin-down time, we ignore the external torque and assume angular momentum conservation, that is,

$$I_c\Omega_c + I_s\Omega_s = \text{constant} \quad . \tag{8}$$

The equation of motion of the superfluid is

$$I_s\dot{\Omega}_s = N_{\text{int}} \quad , \tag{9}$$

where N_{int} is the internal torque arising from the superfluid-crust interaction. The internal torque formulae derived from most current superfluid-crust interaction models can be represented by the following two types:

$$N_{\text{int}} = \begin{cases} -\dfrac{I_sI_c}{I}\dfrac{\Omega_s - \Omega_c}{\tau_c} & \text{(type 1)} \\[2ex] -\dfrac{2V_0}{r_p}I_s\Omega_s \exp\left[-\dfrac{E_p}{k_BT}\left(1 - \dfrac{\omega}{\omega_{cr}}\right)\right] & \text{(type 2)} \end{cases} \tag{10}$$

where $I = I_s + I_c$, τ_c is the superfluid-crust coupling time, r_p is the radial distance of the pinning site, V_0 is the velocity of the microscopic motion of the vortex line ($V_0 \sim 10^7\,\text{cm}\,\text{s}^{-1}$), E_p is the pinning energy ($E_p \sim 1\,\text{MeV}$), and k_B is the Boltzmann constant. The superfluid-crust coupling time in the type 1 torque formula can be expressed in a general form as

$$\tau_c = \frac{A}{T^m\Omega_s}\exp\left(\frac{T_a}{T}\right) \quad , \tag{11}$$

where T_a is the activation temperature and A is the coupling constant. The type 1 torque formula describes superfluid-crust interaction mechanisms such as electron-vortex scattering[10] and vortex-lattice scattering,[11] while the type 2 torque formula describes some models of superfluid vortex creep motion[5,12] (but see Ref. 12). The internal heating rate in the energy equation (4) may be expressed as $H = -I_s\omega\dot{\Omega}_s$. We adopt a general form, $\Lambda = \lambda_0 T^n$, for the energy loss rate due to the dominant cooling process.

We introduce an infinitesimal perturbation into each characteristic equilibrium state and examine its time development. If the perturbation diminishes with time, we judge that the equilibrium state is stable, whereas if it grows, we judge that it is unstable. We find no unstable mode when the superfluid-crust interaction depends on the temperature weakly or not at all. On the other hand, we find two unstable modes, which are thermal and rotational in nature, when the superfluid-crust interaction depends strongly on the temperature, as in the above models.

The results of the linear stability analysis for superfluid-crust interactions that have a strong temperature dependence (such as exponential) are shown in Fig. 2b. Stage B, where the star is in rotational equilibrium, is stable for all of the superfluid-crust interactions considered here. However, in stage C, where the star is in rotational and thermal equilibrium, there are two unstable modes. These are thermal

and rotational in nature, respectively. The thermal equilibrium state of stage D is also unstable.

The physical cause of the thermal instability may be explained as follows. First, consider a perturbation which produces a slight temperature increase. The temperature increase makes the friction between the superfluid and the crust larger. Superfluid rotational energy is therefore dissipated into heat more rapidly, which causes a further temperature increase. Now, consider a perturbation which produces a slight decrease of the differential rotation. The decrease in differential rotation accompanies the dissipation of rotational energy into heat. Thus, the temperature increases and the friction becomes larger, which leads to a further decrease of the differential rotation. This is the rotational instability.

The thermal and rotational instabilities occur in stage C when the internal temperature of the star falls below a critical temperature. The growth times of the thermal and rotational modes are, respectively,

$$
\tau_{th} \approx \frac{\tau_{cool}}{\xi} = \begin{cases} \dfrac{\tau_{cool}}{\left(\dfrac{T_a}{T} + m - n\right)} & \text{(type 1)} \\[4mm] \dfrac{\tau_{cool}}{\dfrac{E_p}{k_B T}\left(1 - \dfrac{\omega}{\omega_{cr}}\right)} & \text{(type 2)} \end{cases} \tag{12}
$$

$$
\tau_{ro} \approx \begin{cases} \tau_c & \text{(type 1)} \\[3mm] \dfrac{\xi}{n}\tau_{rr} = \dfrac{\xi}{n}\dfrac{k_B T}{E_p}\dfrac{\omega_{cr}}{|\dot{\Omega}_0|} & \text{(type 2)} \end{cases} \tag{13}
$$

where τ_{cool} is the cooling time, defined as $\tau_{cool} = C_V T/\Lambda$, and τ_{rr} is the rotational relaxation time, defined as $k_B T \omega_{cr}/E_p|\dot{\Omega}_0|$. The critical temperature T_c for the instabilities is determined from the condition that in the unstable regime $\tau_{th} < \tau_c$ or $\tau_{th} < \tau_{rr}$.

In the superfluid vortex creep case, the critical temperature is given approximately by

$$
T_c \approx 1.7 \times 10^5 \left(\frac{\xi}{40}\right) \left(\frac{E_p}{1\ \text{MeV}}\right)^{-1} \left(\frac{I_s}{10^{43}\ \text{g cm}^2}\right)\ \omega_{cr}^2 \quad \text{K.} \tag{14}
$$

For stellar model 1 and weak pinning, this critical temperature is $\sim 5 \times 10^6$ K. The star reaches this critical phase after $\sim 10^7$ yr. If we adopt the type 1 torque formula with $A = 5 \times 10^{12}$ rad K and $T_a = 10^8$ K for the frictional torque, which is suggested by the electron-vortex excitation scattering model, the critical temperature is $\sim 7 \times 10^6$ K for model 1. The age of the star at this temperature is $\sim 10^6$ yr. Hence, the thermal and rotational instabilities found here are expected to occur in old neutron stars. In order to know the ultimate fate of these instabilities, it is necessary to follow their nonlinear evolution, using numerical methods.

6. CONCLUDING REMARKS

We have shown that the internal heating predicted by current models of superfluid-crust interaction greatly increases the temperature of the star in the photon cooling era, dramatically changing the thermal evolution. Heat generation rates near the maximum expected in current models predict that neutron stars as old as 10^6 yr may have surface temperatures as high as 6×10^5 K and may therefore be detectable in soft X-rays with $AXAF$.[13] The thermal flux from nearby old pulsars may also be observable in the extreme UV using future instruments. For example, even a very low dissipation rate of the superfluid rotational energy will heat a star with standard cooling to a surface temperature $\sim 10^5$ K at 10^6 yr, producing a photon luminosity $\sim 10^{30}$ ergs s^{-1}. Observations of such pulsars would provide important information about the internal structure of neutron stars and the electrical, thermal, and dynamical properties of neutron star matter.

We have found via linear analysis that the superfluid-crust interaction predicted by most current models may lead to thermal and rotational instabilities in old neutron stars. These instabilities may affect neutron star evolution, especially in the photon cooling era. Numerical calculations of the fully nonlinear equations need to be conducted in order to see how these instabilities grow and affect the subsequent evolution of the neutron star.

REFERENCES

1. F. K. Lamb, *Galactic and Extragalactic Compact X-Ray Sources*, Y. Tanaka and W. H. G. Lewin (eds.) (Institute of Space and Astronautical Science, Tokyo, 1985), p. 19.
2. M. A. Alpar, S. A. Langer, and J. A. Sauls, Ap. J. **282**, 533 (1984).
3. P. W. Anderson and N. Itoh, *Nature* **256**, 25 (1975); M. A. Alpar, *Ap. J.* **213**, 527 (1977); R. I. Epstein and G. Baym, *Ap. J.* **328**, 680 (1988); J. A. Sauls, *Timing Neutron Stars*, H. Ögelman and E. P. J. van den Heuvel (eds.) (Kluwer, Dordrecht, 1989), p. 457.
4. R. Nandkumar, unpublished (1985).
5. M. A. Alpar, P. W. Anderson, D. Pines, and J. Shaham, *Ap. J.* **276**, 325 (1984); ibid., **278**, 791 (1984).
6. M. A. Ruderman, *Ap. J.* **203**, 213 (1976); ibid., **366**, 261 (1991).
7. K. Nomoto and S. Tsuruta, *Ap. J.* **312**, 711 (1987); Van Riper, *Ap. J. Suppl.* **75**, 449 (1991).
8. E. H. Gudmundsson, C. J. Pethick, and R. I. Epstein, *Ap. J.* **272**, 286 (1983).
9. N. Shibazaki and F. K. Lamb, *Ap. J.* **346**, 808 (1989).
10. P. J. Feibelman, *Phys. Rev. D* **4**, 1589 (1971); L. Bildsten and R. I. Epstein, *Ap. J.* **342**, 951 (1989).

11. D. Harding, R. A. Guyer, and G. Greenstein, *Ap. J.* **222**, 991 (1978); P. B. Jones, *M. N. R. A. S.* **243**, 257 (1990); ibid., **244**, 675 (1990).
12. B. K. Link and R. I. Epstein, *Ap. J.* **373**, 592 (1991).
13. A. S. Wilson, *Ap. Letters Comm.* **26**, 99 (1987).

Hideyuki Umeda,* Ken'ichi Nomoto,† Sachiko Tsuruta,* Takumi Muto,‡ and Toshitaka Tatsumi§

*Department of Physics, Montana State University, Bozeman, MT 59717, USA; †Department of Astronomy, University of Tokyo, Tokyo 113, Japan; ‡Yukawa Institute for Theoretical Physics, Kyoto University, Kyoto 606, Japan; and §Department of Physics, Kyoto University, Kyoto 606, Japan

Neutron Star Cooling and Pion Condensation

Thermal evolution of neutron stars in the presence of pion condensates is calculated without using the isothermal approximation.[1] The "standard" cooling calculations carried out by Nomoto and Tsuruta[1] show that the cooling curves are consistent with the observational upper limits of the Crab, 3 C58 and RCW 103, but those for the Vela pulsar and PSR 0656+14 lie below the standard curves. This may suggest that a "nonstandard" cooling scenario is required for these pulsars. As the nonstandard cooling agents, the pion and kaon condensates and quark matter have been proposed. Among these the pion condensates may turn out to be the most important (see the contribution by Tsuruta in this volume).[2] In the pion condensation theory the Landau-Migdal parameter, $\tilde{g}\prime$, is introduced, with $\tilde{g}\prime = 0.5$ and 0.6 as representative values.[3] In the nonstandard cooling, the effect of superfluidity is more pronounced than in the standard case. This is because the suppression of the neutrino URCA process due to the presence of superfluidity is more important for the nonstandard case. There are still large uncertainties in superfluid theories, especially in the presence of pion condensates. Therefore, here we use various models to explore the effects of superfluidity on cooling, including the modified versions of those proposed by Takatsuka and Tamagaki[4] and by Höffberg et al.,[5] which is denoted the HGRR model.

Figure 1 summarizes our results. The baryon mass of the star M_A is set to $1.4M_\odot$, and the FP equation of state is adopted. The dotted curves correspond to

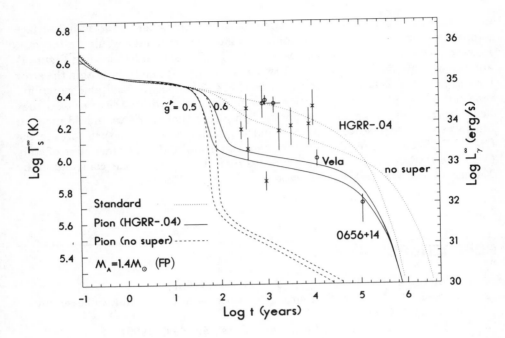

FIGURE 1 The surface temperature and luminosity to be observed at infinity are shown as a function of age

the standard cooling with and without superfluidity. The curve without superfluidity is denoted "no super." The solid and dashed curves show pion cooling with and without superfluidity. In the superfluid curves shown we adopt a modified version of the HGRR model where the original density-dependent superfluid gap energies by Höffberg et al.[5] are reduced by log 0.04 (K) at all densities. The two sets of curves of the same kind refer to the two representative pion cases, with $\tilde{g}\prime = 0.5$ and 0.6, respectively. The crosses are the upper limits to the temperatures of various supernova remnants if neutron stars are present. These are the true upper limits, in the sense that there were no detections. The circles represent detections. Since these detections may include emissions other than the direct surface radiation, strictly speaking these points also should be considered the upper limits. However, there is a very good chance that at least some of these points refer to the temperature measurement.

We note that if the three circles near $t = 1000$ years, which correspond to the Crab, 3C 58, and RCW 103, refer to the actual surface temperature measurements, the standard cooling is consistent with observation. The points for the Vela pulsar and PSR 0656+14 are below the standard curves. They are above the pion curves

in the absence of superfluidity. Therefore, if these points refer to the actual surface temperature measurements, pion cooling without superfluidity would be too fast. However, when suitable gap energies (e.g., the HGRR-.04 model shown in Figure 1) are chosen, superfluid pion curves (shown as solid curves) indeed lie within the error bars of both the Vela pulsar and PSR 0656+14. The fact that suitable superfluid pion curves indeed go through both points (not just one), within the error bars, may be interpreted as strong support for the hypothesis that there are indeed pion (or other "exotic" particle) cores in these pulsars, while there are no such cores in the Crab, 3C 58, and RCW 103. This can happen naturally if the former class of stars (Vela and PSR 0656+14) are more massive than the latter (see the contribution by Tsuruta in this volume). Further details are found in Ref. 2.

REFERENCES

1. K. Nomoto and S. Tsuruta, *Ap. J.*, **312**, 711, (1987).
2. H. Umeda, K. Nomoto, S. Tsuruta, T. Muto, and T. Tatsumi, to be submitted to Ap. J. (1991).
3. T. Muto and T. Tatsumi, *Prog. Ther. Phys.*, **83**, 499, (1990).
4. T. Takatsuka and R. Tamagaki, *Prog. Theor. Phys.*, **67**, 1649, (1982).
5. M. Höffberg, A. E. Glassgold, R. W. Richardson, and M. Ruderman, *Phys. Rev. Let.*, **24**, 775 (1970).

Shigeto Wakatsuki, Naohiro Sato, and Naoki Itoh
Department of Physics, Sophia University, Tokyo, Japan

Simulation of Pulsar Evolution

We have simulated the evolution of pulsars by tracing the motion of the pulsars in the Galaxy and assuming various decay models for the magnetic field. Then we have searched the best-fit parameters for the initial value of period, magnetic field, and their standard deviations by comparing the result of the simulation with observed pulsar data. Selection effects are accurately taken into account.

1. DECAY MODELS

We have tested the validity of three magnetic field decay models: the exponential decay model, and the power-law decay models $m \propto t^{-1/4}$ and $m \propto t^{-1}$. The fundamental conditions are given as follows.

Exponential decay model:

$$m = \exp\left(-\frac{t}{t_D}\right) m_0 \qquad t_D : \quad \text{folding time} \quad (5 \ M \ \text{yr})$$

Power-law decay model $m \propto t^{-1/4}$:

$$m = m_0 \frac{\Omega}{\Omega_0} = m_0 \left(1 + \frac{8m_0^2 \Omega_0^4}{3c^3 I \Omega_0^2} t \right)^{-1/4}$$

Power-law decay model $m \propto t^{-1}$

$$m = m_0 \left(1 + \frac{t}{t_b} \right)^{-1} \qquad t_b : \quad \text{decay time} \quad (30.2\ M\ \text{yr})$$

P_0 is the initial period, I is the moment of inertia, c is the speed of light, and m_0 is the component of the initial magnetic dipole moment perpendicular to the rotation axis.

2. METHOD

In our simulation we generate and select pulsars as follows.

The initial magnetic moment m_0 and the initial period P_0 are given according to the Gaussian distribution. For the initial location of pulsars we use a standard cylindrical coordinate (ρ, ϕ, Z). ρ is given according to the Gaussian distribution. Z is given according to the exponential distribution. ϕ is given at random. The initial velocity of pulsars is given according to Maxwellian distribution. Finally we need to give the luminosity to the pulsars, so we use the luminosity relation through a certain statistical treatment.

This is all for generating the pulsars. Next we have to select generated pulsars by several selection effects.

First we take into account the beaming effect and the death line. Second we define that a pulsar is detectable if it could be detected by at least one of the following major surveys: the Jodrell Bank Survey, the UMass-Arecibo Survey, the Second Molongro Survey, the UMass-NRAO Survey, the Princeton-NRAO Survey (Phase I, Phase II), or the Princeton-Arecibo Survey.

3. RESULTS

We have analyzed the results by comparing them with the observed data with respect to P–$\dot{P}$ plane and $|Z|$-distribution. Fig. 1 shows the P–$\dot{P}$ diagrams of the observed data and the power-law decay model $m \propto t^{-1/4}$.

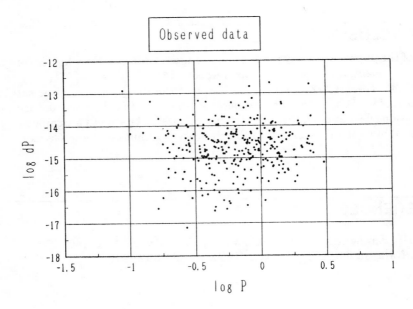

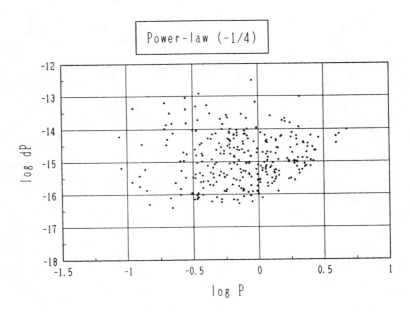

FIGURE 1 $P-\dot{P}$

4. CONCLUSIONS

Both of the power-law decay models can produce goodness of fit which is comparable to the exponential decay model with respect to the P–$\dot{P}$ result.

With respect to $|Z|$-distribution, none of the decay models gives satisfactory goodness of fit. But we think this is because we do not take into account the galactic gravitation effect and because the distance of observed data has a significant amount of error due to the uncertainty of the electron distribution in the Galaxy.

REFERENCES

1. R. T. Emmering and R. A. Chevalier, 1989, *Ap. J.*, **304**, 140.
2. R. Narayan and J. P. Ostriker, 1990, *Ap. J.*, **352**, 931.

Perspectives

Minoru Oda

Institute of Physical and Chemical Research (RIKEN), Hirosawa 2-1, Wako-shi, Saitama, 351-01, Japan

Banquet Lecture: A Cartoonist's View of the Neutron Star

In response to a request by Professor Tamagaki, I would like to present a cartoon version of the history of our study of the neutron star. I have classified the history into three eras.

First, as indicated in Fig. 1, the 1940s to the mid-1960s was the era of the prophet. Since Baade and Zwicky, we can identify several prophets, including those who are present at this banquet: Hayakawa, Tsuruta, Pines, Ruderman, and others. They predicted that the neutron star would have a strong bearing on nuclear physics, condensed matter physics, and gravitation.

The second is the era of believers and discoverers, indicated in Fig. 2. Needless to say, the discovery of pulsars provided a challenging hypothesis on the real existence of the neutron star. Then discovery of X-ray stars, X-ray bursts and X-ray pulsars confirmed that the neutron star is its major source. The Crab Nebula has been an excellent target of observation to study the neutron star itself and the interaction between the neutron star and its surrounding plasma.

Since the 1980s, as indicated in Fig. 3, the neutron star has been the place to study various disciplines of physics. There have been so many symposia and meetings on the neutron star that I can't count them. I recall that in 1983 Professors Hoshi, Nakajima, and myself organized a symposium as part of the activities of the Institute of Solid State Physics, in which Professor Tamagaki played an important role. But then our understanding of the neutron star was still immature.

415

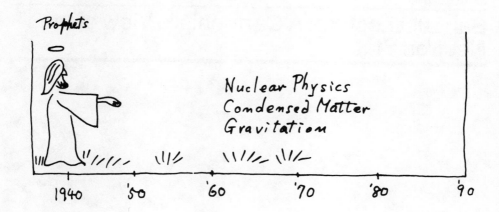

FIGURE 1 The first era.

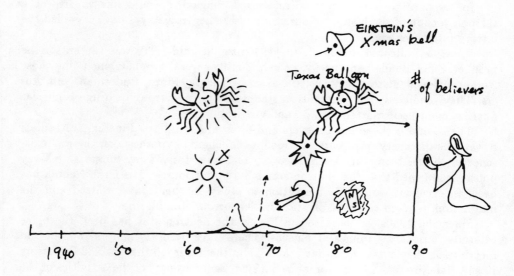

FIGURE 2 The second era.

FIGURE 3 The third era.

I am glad that now the National Science Foundation and the Japan Society for the Promotion of Science accepted the proposal of this symposium as the first priority of a US-Japan Joint Seminar. I hope this symposium will be a milestone in neutron star physics.

M. Ruderman
Physics Department and Columbia Astrophysics Laboratory, Columbia University, New York, NY 10027, USA; and Center for Astrophysics and Space Sciences, University of San Diego, La Jolla, CA 92093, USA

NON-SENS 1990

There is an apocryphal story that in 1932, on the evening of the day the news of Chadwick's discovery of the neutron was telephoned to Copenhagen, Landau suggested that the central cores of some stars might consist wholly of neutrons. If true this would have been one of the brief moments in the history of neutron star astrophysics when theory was clearly ahead of observation. This lead was soon lost. By 1940 Baade and Zwicky had correctly identified the central star of the Crab SNR as a neutron star. Twenty-three years ago Bell and Hewish discovered the first radiopulsar. Over 500 have been identified since then. We have heard at this conference the suggestion that the present birthrate for neutron stars in our Galaxy may be as high as 10^{-1} yr^{-1}. Observers have been overwhelming theorists with unpredicted neutron star populations and phenomena.

In the SENS 1990 conference this imbalance has been partly mitigated by inviting an order of magnitude fewer presentations by observers than by theorists. This dominance of theory in the conference agenda may give a distorted picture of successes by theorists in understanding neutron stars. Where nothing is understood, when no progress has been made, there is no speaker. Therefore, rather than summarize presented papers, which has been done by the authors in their abstracts far better than I could, I will try to indicate a sample of some of what has not been spoken, talks not given which I would like to have heard.

Unexplained periodicities in neutron stars

A considerable number of "observed" neutron star periodicities (apart from pulsar spin periods) have been mentioned by speakers in this conference:

a) $P_a \sim 20$ months for a large-amplitude oscillation in pulse phase (but not shape) of the Crab radiopulsar;

b) $P_b \sim 35$ days for the large-amplitude modulation of X-ray intensity from the Her X-1 binary.

c) $P_c \sim 10$ days in the radio pulses of the Vela radiopulsar after its recent "Christmas glitch."

d) $P_d \sim 23$ ms in the famous, strong March 5, 1979, gamma-ray burst whose source seems to be a neutron star with an 8-s spin period.

e) Other very long period oscillations in radiopulsar emission which were mentioned privately and may soon be presented publicly.

If the periodicities are confirmed as neutron star crust or magnetosphere motions there would seem to be a very considerable gap in our understanding of the dynamics of neutron stars. The most commonly mentioned origin for P_a and P_c is a Tykachenko oscillation of the array of superfluid neutron vortices in the crust and/or core of the neutron star. The period P_b is frequently assumed to be that for neutron star free precession. However, as more is understood about neutron stars such explanations appear to be in trouble. Tykachenko oscillations seem to have far too small a maximum amplitude to explain P_a and P_c and probably too small a maximum period for P_a. In free precession the star's crust must move through the fixed spin angular momentum vector of the star, most of which is controlled by the array of quantized superfluid neutron vortex lines. Insofar as these are pinned by crust nuclei, large-amplitude, slow free precession is not maintainable. Recently it has been argued that the quantized magnetic flux tubes of the stellar core do not pass easily through the core's neutron vortices. Because of strong core-crust coupling this would make a free precession P_b even more difficult to achieve. The problem of reconciling claimed observations of neutron star periodicity (or quasi-periodicity) with present stellar models has not yet been resolved. Even the question of what periods and amplitudes are not possible has not been answered.

Magnetic fields in white dwarfs

The magnetic field fluxes of white dwarfs resemble those of neutron stars. Both come in two families, one with strong fluxes of around 10^{25} gauss-cm^2 and a much more weakly magnetized one, smaller by a factor of 10^3 or more. Several models have now been offered for the evolution of neutron star fields and, especially recently, for how the weak-field family may evolve from the strong-field one. As far as I know, none of these scenarios would work for the genesis of the two white dwarf families. How

indeed do white dwarfs achieve their magnetic fields? Perhaps we should not put this question aside while struggling with that for neutron stars, especially since the white dwarf families resemble the stellar cores that are the neutron stars' immediate ancestors.

I'm sure each has his or her own list of favorite nonspeakers. Perhaps at the next SENS conference we could improve the balance by having a day devoted to speakers who discuss only important questions to which they certainly don't have the answers. (Perhaps we already have had that.) We should, on the other hand, be happy to have left untouched some important areas. These are our best guarantee for a U.S.-Japan SENS 2000, a meeting to which all of us who attended SENS 1990 in Kyoto would look forward with intense pleasure.

Program and List of Participants

Program of SENS '90

November 6

Opening Address　Chair: H. Sato (Kyoto University)
　R. Tamagaki (Kyoto University)

Session 1　Chair: H.Sato (Kyoto University)
　D. Pines (University of Illinois)
　　Neutron Star Superfluidity: Theory and Observation

Session 2　Chair: R. Hoshi (Rikkyo University)
　R. N. Manchester (Australia Telescope National Facility)
　　Radio Pulsar Timing
　C. J. Pethick (NORDITA)
　　Topics in the Physics of High Magnetic Fields

Session 3　Chair: G. Baym (University of Illinois)
　R. Tamagaki (Kyoto University)
　　Various Phases of Hadronic Matter in Neutron Stars and Their
　　Relevance to Pulsar Glitches
　M. A. Alpar (Middle East Technical University, Turkey)
　　Dynamics of the Neutron Star Interior

Session 4　Chair: C. J. Pethick (NORDITA)
　J. W. Clark (Washington University)
　　Microscopic Calculations of Superfluid Gaps
　R. Epstein (Los Alamos)
　　Superfluid Dynamics in the Inner Crust of Neutron Stars
　T. Tatsumi (Kyoto University)
　　Static and Dynamical Properties of Pion-Condensed Neutron Stars

November 7

Session 5   Chair: S. L. Shapiro (Cornell University)
    H. Inoue (ISAS)
        Study of Neutron Stars in X-rays
    J. M. Lattimer (Stony Brook)
        The Equation of State in Neutron Star Matter

Session 6   Chair: S. Tsuruta (Montana State University)
    R. Blandford (Caltech)
        Neutron Starquakes and Gamma-Ray Bursts
    L. Lindblom (Montana State University)
        Instabilities in Neutron Stars

Session 7   Chair: K. Sato (University of Tokyo)
    S. L. Shapiro (Cornell University)
        Compact Stars on a Supercomputer I.
    S. Teukolsky (Cornell University)
        Compact Stars on a Supercomputer II.
    T. Nakamura (YITP)
        Coalescing of Binary Neutron Stars

Session 8 — Poster Presentation — (Room 102)

November 8

Session 9   Chair: T. Nakamura (YITP)
    K. Sato (University of Tokyo)
        Explosion Mechanism of Supernovae and the Neutrino Burst
    S. E. Woosley (Santa Cruz)
        Making Neutron Stars

Session 10   Chair: K. Nomoto (University of Tokyo)
    H. Sato (Kyoto University)
        Pulsar Cavity
    F.-K. Thielemann (Harvard-Smithsonian Center for Astrophysics)
        Neutron Star Masses from Supernova Explosions

Session 11   Chair: S. E. Woosley (Santa Cruz)
    H. Suzuki (KEK)
        Cooling of Protoneutron Star and Neutrino Burst
    D. Q. Lamb (University of Chicago)
        Implications of the Neutrinos from SN1987A for Supernova Theory
        and the Mass of $\bar{\nu}$
    T. Shigeyama (University of Tokyo)
        How Will the Pulsar in SN1987A Emerge?

Session 12   Chair: R. Tamagaki (Kyoto University)
   T. Takatsuka (Iwate University)
      Equation of State of Dense Supernova Matter and Hot Neutron Stars
      Just Born
   M. Takahara (Doshisha University)
      Supernova Explosions and the Soft Equation of State

— *Banquet* —
      Speech: M. Oda (RIKEN)

November 9

Session 13   Chair: R. Blandford (Caltech)
   M. Ruderman (Columbia University)
      Evolution of Magnetic Fields
   K. Makishima (University of Tokyo)
      Magnetic Field Strengths of Neutron Stars

Session 14   Chair: D. Pines (University of Illinois)
   S. Tsuruta (Montana State University)
      Thermal Evolution of Neutron Stars
   N. Iwamoto (University of Toledo)
      Elementary Processes in Neutron Star Cooling
   N. Shibazaki (Rikkyo University)
      Neutron Star Evolution with Internal Heating

Session 15   Chair: K. Makishima (University of Tokyo)
   K. Nomoto (University of Tokyo)
      On the Origin of Low Mass Binary Pulsars
   K. Koyama (Nagoya University)
      X-ray Observations of Supernova Remnants: Birth of Neutron Stars
      and Their Evolution

Session 16   Chair: J. M. Lattimer (Stony Brook)
   F. Nagase (ISAS)
      Properties of Neutron Stars from X-ray Pulsar Observations
   R. Hoshi (Rikkyo University)
      Mass Radius Relations of Pulsating X-ray Sources

November 10

Session 17   Chair: R. N. Manchester (Australia Telescope National Facility)
   H. Ögelman (Max-Planck Institute)
      Some Early ROSAT Observations of Neutron Stars
   Y. Tanaka (ISAS)
      Prospects of Future Observations

Session 18   Chair: S. Hayakawa (Nagoya University)
    G. Baym (University of Illinois)
        Ultrarelativistic Heavy Ion Experiments and Neutron Stars
    M. Ruderman (Columbia University)
        Concluding Remarks

Participants

A. M. Abrahams	Cornell University	USA
M. A. Alpar	Middle East Technical University	Turkey
Y. Araki		Japan
G. Baym	University of Illinois	USA
R. Blandford	California Institute of Technology	USA
J. W. Clark	Washington University	USA
R. Epstein	Los Alamos National Laboratory	USA
L. S. Finn	Cornell University	USA
M. Fujimoto	Niigata University	Japan
I. Fushiki	Lick Observatory, University of California	USA
T. Hanawa	Nagoya University	Japan
S. Hayakawa	Nagoya University	Japan
R. Hoshi	Rikkyo University	Japan
H. Inoue	ISAS	Japan
M. Ishii		Japan
N. Itoh	Sophia University	Japan
M. Iwamoto	University of Toledo	USA
K. Iwasawa	Nagoya University	Japan
K. Koyama	Nagoya University	Japan
T. Kunihiro	Ryukoku University	Japan
F. K. Lamb	University of Illinois	USA
D. Q. Lamb	University of Chicago	USA
J. M. Lattimer	State University of New York at Stony Brook	USA
L. Lindblom	Montana State University	USA
B. K. Link	Los Alamos National Laboratory	USA
K. Makashima	University of Tokyo	Japan
R. M. Manchester	Australia Telescope National Facility	Australia
G. Mendell		USA
T. Murakami	ISAS	Japan
T. Muto	Yitp, Kyoto University	Japan
F. Nagase	ISAS	Japan
T. Nakamura	Yitp, Kyoto University	Japan
S. Nishizaki	Iwate University	Japan
K. Nomoro	University of Tokyo	Japan

M. Oda	RIKEN	Japan
H. Ögelman	Max-Planck Institute	FRG
K. Oohara	KEK	Japan
C. J. Pethick	NORDITA	Denmark
D. Pines	University of Illinois	USA
M. A. Ruderman	Columbia University	USA
H. Sato	Kyoto University	Japan
K. Sato	University of Tokyo	Japan
S. L. Shapiro	Cornell University	USA
S. Shibata	Yamagata University	Japan
N. Shibazaki	Rikkyo University	Japan
T. Shigeyama	University of Tokyo	Japan
H. Suganuma		Japan
H. Suzuki	KEK	Japan
Y. Suzuki		Japan
M. Takahara	Doshisha University	Japan
T. Takatsuka	Iwate University	Japan
R. Tamagaki	Kyoto University	Japan
Y. Tanaka	ISAS	Japan
T. Tatsumi	Kyoto University	Japan
S. Teukolsky	Cornell University	USA
F.-K. Thielemann	Harvard-Smithsonian Center for Astrophysics	USA
Y. Tsue		Japan
S. Tsuruta	Montana State University	USA
H. Umeda	Montana State University	USA
S. E. Woosley	Lick Observatory, University of California	USA
S. Yamauchi	Nagoya University	Japan